D1346789
horus
THE BAZAAR QUARTER
SERAGLIO POINT
SULTANAHMET
Sea of Marmara
The Black Sea
Pages 264–279
inop
0 kilometres 100
0 miles 50
Hopa
Samsun
Ordu
Trabzon
Amasya
THE BLACK SEA
Gümüshane
Erzurum
Erzincan
Sivas
CIA &
ATOLIA
EASTERN ANATOLIA
Elazığ
Kayseri
Van
Malatya
Diyarbakır
Adana
Gaziantep
Antakya
Mediterranean Turkey
Pages 208–239
Cappadocia and Central Anatolia
Pages 280–303
Eastern Anatolia
Pages 304–323

Tower Hamlets Libraries	
91000008001602	
Askews & Holts	
915.61	
THISCH	TH16000107/0080

London Borough of Tower Hamlets
91000008001602

TURKEY

Library Learning Information

To renew this item call:
0333 370 4700
(Local rate call)
or visit
www.ideastore.co.uk

TOWER HAMLETS
Created and managed by Tower Hamlets Council

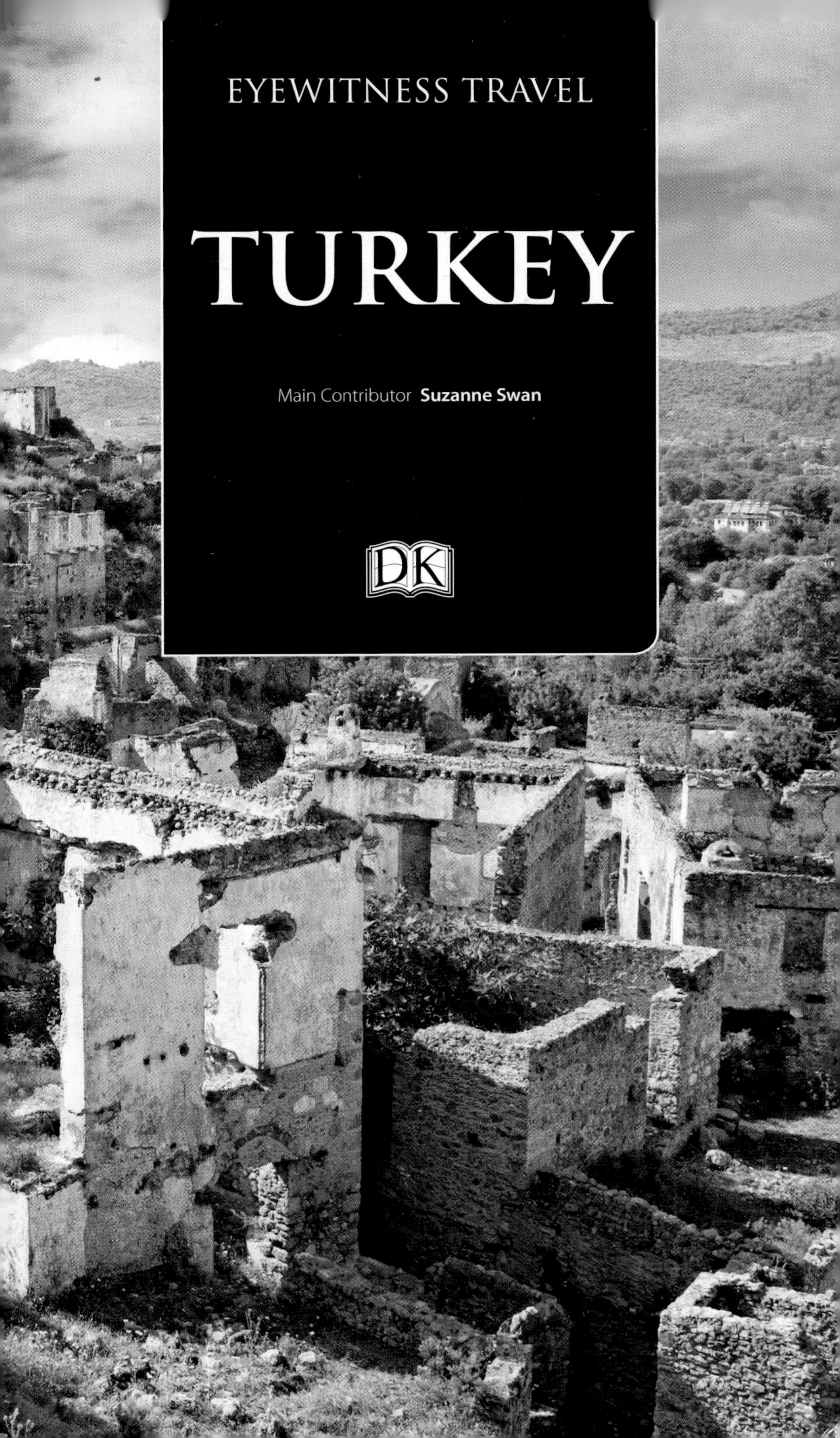

EYEWITNESS TRAVEL

TURKEY

Main Contributor **Suzanne Swan**

DK

Produced by
Struik New Holland Publishing (Pty) Ltd, Cape Town, South Africa

Managing Editors Alfred Lemaitre, Laura Milton
Managing Art Editor Steven Felmore
Editors Amichai Kapilevich, Anna Tanneberger
Editorial Assistant Christie Meyer
Designer Peter Bosman
Map Co-ordinator John Loubser
Cartographer Carl Germishuys
Picture Researchers Sandra Adomeit, Karla Kik
DTP Check Damian Gibbs
Production Manager Myrna Collins

Main Contributor
Suzanne Swan

Other Contributors
Rosie Ayliffe, Rose Baring, Barnaby Rogerson, Canan Sılay, Dominic Whiting

Photographers
Kate Clow, Terry Richardson, Anthony Souter, Dominic Whiting, Linda Whitwam, Francesca Yorke

Illustrators
Richard Bonson, Stephen Conlin, Gary Cross, Bruno De Robillard, Richard Draper, Steven Felmore, Paul Guest, Ian Lusted, Maltings Partnership, Chris Orr & Associates, David Pulvermacher, Paul Weston, John Woodcock

Printed and Bound In Malaysia

First published in the UK in 2003
By Dorling Kindersley Limited
80 Strand, London, WC2R 0RL

16 17 18 19 10 9 8 7 6 5 4 3 2 1

Reprinted with Revisions 2006, 2008, 2010, 2012, 2014, 2016

Copyright 2003, 2016 © Dorling Kindersley Limited, London
A Penguin Random House Company

All rights reserved. No part of this publication may be reproduced, stored in a retrieval system, or transmitted in any form or by any means, electronic, mechanical, photocopying, recording or otherwise, without the prior written permission of the copyright owner.

A CIP catalogue record is available from the British Library.

ISBN 978-0-24120-821-2

Floors are referred to throughout in accordance with European usage; i.e, the "First Floor" is the floor above Ground Level.

MIX
Paper from responsible sources
FSC™ C018179

The information in this DK Eyewitness Travel Guide is checked regularly.
Every effort has been made to ensure that this book is as up-to-date as possible at the time of going to press. Some details, however, such as telephone numbers, opening hours, prices, gallery hanging arrangements and travel information are liable to change. The publishers cannot accept responsibility for any consequences arising from the use of this book, nor for any material on third party websites, and cannot guarantee that any website address in this book will be a suitable source of travel information. We value the views and suggestions of our readers very highly. Please write to: Publisher, DK Eyewitness Travel Guides, Dorling Kindersley, 80 Strand, London, WC2R 0RL, UK, or email: travelguides@dk.com.

Front cover main image: El Nazar, a rock-cut church in the Görome Valley, Cappadocia

Contents

How to Use this Guide **6**

Introducing Turkey

Discovering Turkey **10**

Putting Turkey on the Map **16**

A Portrait of Turkey **18**

Turkey Through the Year **38**

The History of Turkey **44**

Commagene stone head on Mount Nemrut (Nemrut Daği)

◀ Kayaköy, an abandoned Greek village in Mediterranean Turkey that is now a UNESCO World Heritage Site

The village of Üçağız, on the Mediterranean coast

Istanbul Area by Area

Istanbul at a Glance **66**

Seraglio Point **68**

Sultanahmet **82**

The Bazaar Quarter **98**

Beyoğlu **110**

Further Afield **116**

Istanbul Street Finder **138**

Turkey Region by Region

Turkey at a Glance **152**

Thrace and the Sea of Marmara **154**

The Aegean **174**

Mediterranean Turkey **208**

Ankara and Western Anatolia **240**

The Black Sea **264**

Cappadocia and Central Anatolia **280**

Eastern Anatolia **304**

Vendor selling *boza,* a drink made from lightly fermented grain

Emblems of Istanbul, the Haghia Sophia and Blue Mosque

Travellers' Needs

Where to Stay **326**

Where to Eat and Drink **340**

Shopping in Turkey **362**

Entertainment in Turkey **368**

Outdoor Activities **372**

Survival Guide

Practical Information **380**

Travel Information **388**

General Index **400**

Phrase Book **419**

Sumela Monastery *(see p276)*

HOW TO USE THIS GUIDE

This guide helps you to get the most from your stay in Turkey. It provides expert recommendations and detailed practical advice. *Introducing Turkey* locates the country geographically, and sets it in context. *Istanbul Area by Area* and *Turkey Region by Region* are the main sightseeing sections, giving information on major sights, with photographs, maps and illustrations. Suggestions for restaurants, hotels, entertainment and shopping are found in *Travellers' Needs*, while the *Survival Guide* contains useful advice on everything from changing money to travelling by bus.

Istanbul Area by Area

Turkey's largest city has been divided into four sightseeing areas. Each has its own chapter opening with a list of the sights that are described. The *Further Afield* section covers many peripheral places of interest. All sights are numbered and plotted on an *Area Map*. Information on the sights is easy to locate as it follows the numerical order used on the map.

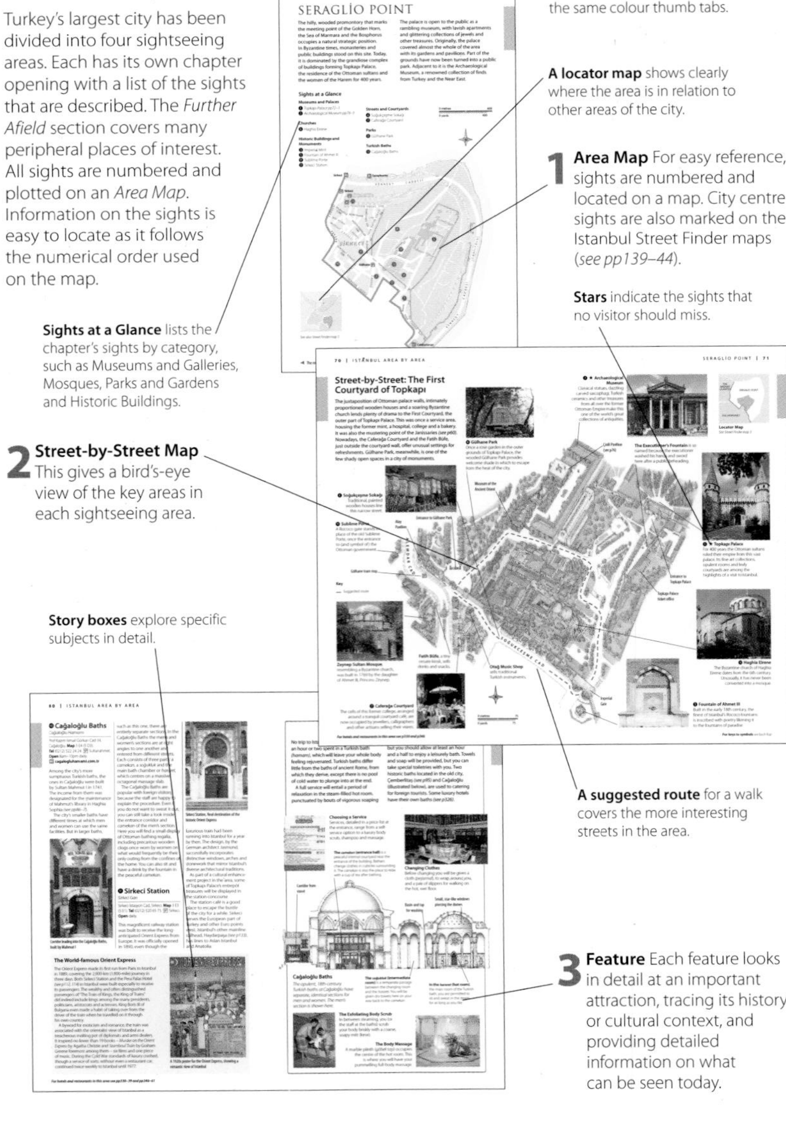

All pages relating to Istanbul have the same colour thumb tabs.

A locator map shows clearly where the area is in relation to other areas of the city.

Sights at a Glance lists the chapter's sights by category, such as Museums and Galleries, Mosques, Parks and Gardens and Historic Buildings.

1 Area Map For easy reference, sights are numbered and located on a map. City centre sights are also marked on the Istanbul Street Finder maps (*see pp139–44*).

Stars indicate the sights that no visitor should miss.

2 Street-by-Street Map This gives a bird's-eye view of the key areas in each sightseeing area.

A suggested route for a walk covers the more interesting streets in the area.

Story boxes explore specific subjects in detail.

3 Feature Each feature looks in detail at an important attraction, tracing its history or cultural context, and providing detailed information on what can be seen today.

Turkey Region by Region

Apart from Istanbul, the rest of the country is divided into seven regions, each with a separate chapter. The most interesting towns and sights to visit are numbered on a *Regional Map* at the beginning of each chapter.

1 Introduction
A general account of the landscape, history and character of each region is given here, explaining both how the area has developed over the centuries and what attractions it has to offer visitors today.

Each area of Turkey can be easily identified by its colour coding, shown on the inside front cover.

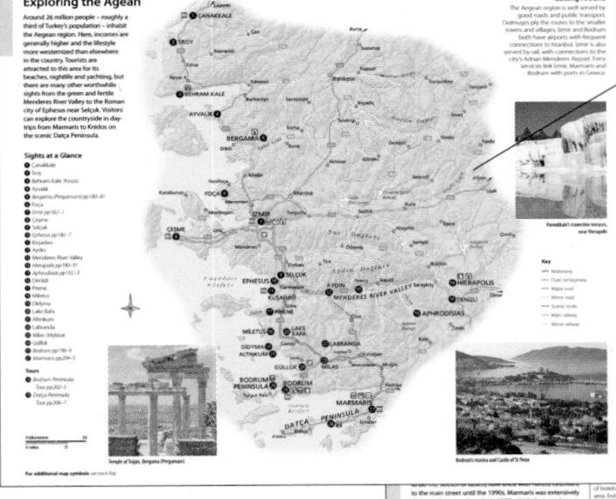

2 Regional Map This shows the main road network and gives an illustrated overview of the whole region. All interesting places to visit are numbered and there are also useful tips on getting to, and around, the region.

A town map shows the locations of all the sights described in the text.

3 Detailed Information
All the important towns and other places to visit are described individually. They are listed in order, following the numbering on the *Regional Map*. Within each entry, there is further detailed information on important buildings and other sights.

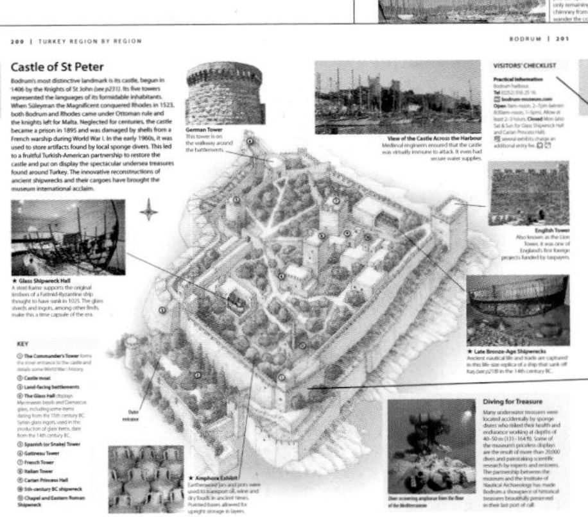

For all the top sights, a Visitors' Checklist provides the practical information you will need to plan your visit.

4 Turkey's Top Sights
Historic buildings are dissected to reveal their interiors; important archaeological sites have maps showing key sights and facilities. The most interesting towns or city centres have maps, with sights picked out and described.

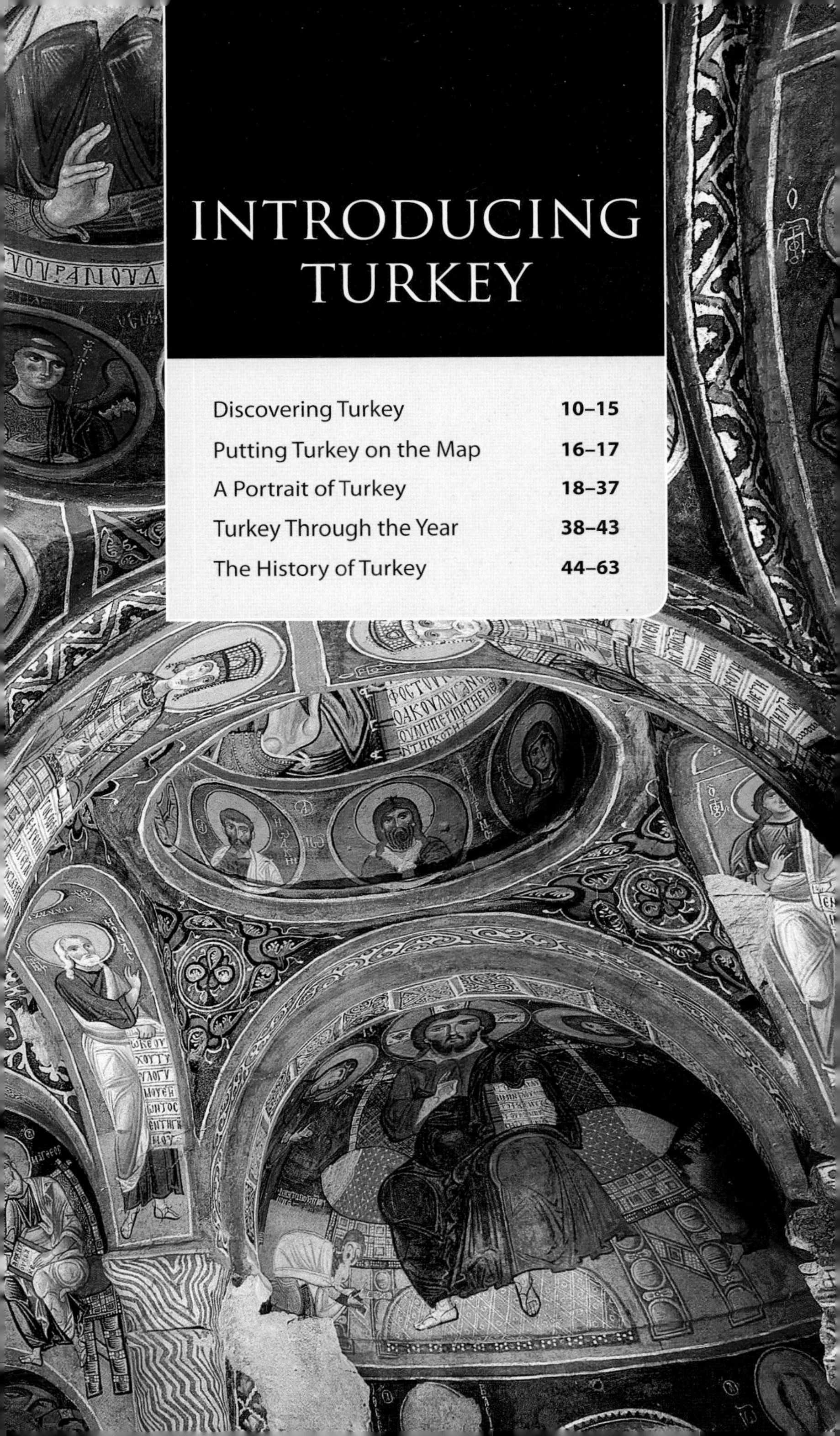

INTRODUCING TURKEY

Discovering Turkey 10–15

Putting Turkey on the Map 16–17

A Portrait of Turkey 18–37

Turkey Through the Year 38–43

The History of Turkey 44–63

DISCOVERING TURKEY

Turkey is vast – the size of France and Germany put together – so attempting to visit the entire country in one trip would be a mammoth (though hugely rewarding) task. Consequently, the following tours concentrate on the most-visited western half of this beguiling land. To start with there is a two-day tour of one of the world's truly great cities, continent-straddling Istanbul, with its rich Byzantine Christian and Muslim Turkish history. Next up are three week-long itineraries, which can be connected to form a three-week trip, taking visitors from the ancient Greek and Roman ruins of the Aegean to the sun-blessed beaches of the Mediterranean and, finally, inland across the rolling steppes of the Anatolian plateau to the geological wonderland of Cappadocia.

A Week on the Aegean Coast

- At legendary **Troy** and the World War I conflict zone of **Gallipoli**, bloody battles were fought in beautiful locations.
- The pretty traditional village of **Behram Kale** and hilltop site of ancient **Assos** make for a memorable outing.
- Ascend the craggy acropolis of ancient **Bergama** to see its stone theatre and temples.
- The extensive ruins of ancient **Ephesus** are a truly world-class ancient site.
- Discover the captivating ancient sites of **Priene, Didyma** and **Miletus**.
- Tranquil **Lake Bafa** has plenty of birdlife and remote Byzantine settlements.
- Bohemian **Bodrum** has buzzing nightlife, a Crusader castle and lots of beaches.

Key
Turquoise coast
Aegean coast
Mediterranean and Anatolian Turkey

Gallipoli Peninsula
Çanakkale
Troy
Balıkesir
Behram Kale
Bergama and Pergamum
Uşak
TURKEY
Dinar
Hierapolis
Selçuk
Ephesus
Kuşadası
Denizli
Priene
Miletus
Lake Bafa
Didyma
Euromos
Bodrum
Lake Koyceğiz
Kaunos
Dalyan
Fethiye
Tlos
Kayaköy
Saklıkent Gorge
Olympos
Phaselis
Patara
Finike
Kalkan
Kaş
Üçağız and Simena

A Week on the Turquoise Coast

- Explore the turtle-nesting beach at **Iztuzu** from charming **Dalyan**.
- The haunting remains of the Greek ghost village of **Kayaköy** stand sentinel near **Fethiye**.
- One of the longest beaches in the Mediterranean, sandy **Patara**, is delightfully uncrowded.
- Venture into the cool depths of **Saklıkent Gorge** and explore the fascinating ruins of ancient Lycian **Tlos**.
- Mellow **Çıralı** has a long shingle beach, ancient riverside ruins and eternal flames burning deep in the pine forest.
- Ancient port **Phaselis** makes for an ideal combination of romantic ruins to visit and beaches to relax on.

Bodrum harbour, overlooked by the Castle of St Peter

◄ Early 12th century Byzantine frescos in Karanlik Kilise, Göreme Open-Air Museum, Cappadocia

Saklıkent Gorge
Located around 40 minutes' drive from Fethiye, Saklıkent is Turkey's longest and deepest gorge. From April to September, energetic visitors can walk the 4 km (2 miles) along the bottom of the gorge.

A Week in Mediterranean and Anatolian Turkey

- Explore **Antalya's** quaint old walled quarter of **Kaleiçi** and swim from the attractive town beach of **Mermerli**.
- The Roman theatre at **Aspendos** is one of the best preserved in the world; a visit to the Roman ruins at **Side** can be combined with a swim at the nearby beach.
- **Eğirdir**, set high in Turkey's unspoiled Lake District, is a great town in which to relax and admire the scenery.
- Conservative **Konya** is famed for its **Mevlâna Museum**, once home to the whirling dervishes.
- The central Anatolian volcanic landscape of **Cappadocia** is bizarrely beautiful – all curiously capped rock pinnacles, rippling canyons and soaring table-top outcrops.
- Backed by the symmetrical cone of Mount Hasan, the dramatic **Ihlara Valley** with its rock-cut churches is a perfect location for hiking.

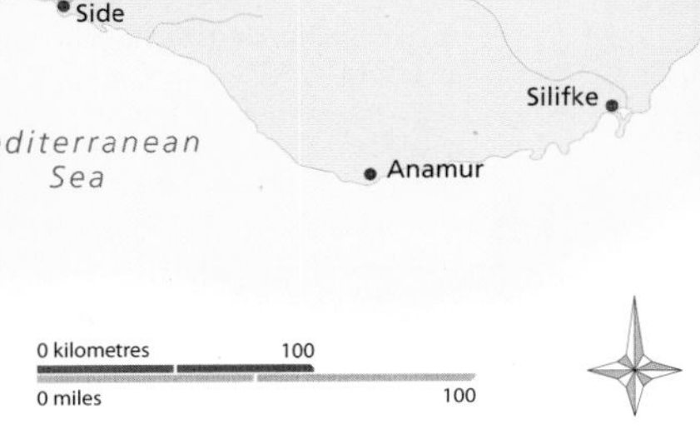

The Temples of Apollo and Athena, Side
Dating from the 2nd century BC, these partially reconstructed temples in Side frame stunning views of the Gulf of Antalya. The evening makes a particularly atmospheric time to visit the ruins.

For map symbols *see back flap*

2 Days in Istanbul

Vibrant Istanbul, standing astride Europe and Asia, boasts a wealth of remains from its time as fulcrum of both the Byzantine and Ottoman Turkish worlds. It also has a lively arts and nightlife scene.

- **Arriving** Istanbul has two major airports. Atatürk Airport on the city's European side is linked to the centre by metro, buses and taxis. Sabiha Gökçen Airport on the Asian side has buses to Taksim Square.
- **Moving on** Flights from both airports link Istanbul with many provincial cities, while ferries ply the Sea of Marmara. Buses and trains also offer good transport links.

The Blue Mosque with the Sea of Marmara in the background

Day 1

Morning Most of Istanbul's major attractions are clustered at the end of the peninsula on which the original city was founded in the 7th century BC. An obvious place to begin is the **Archaeological Museum** *(pp76–7)*, which has an excellent exhibition detailing the origins and development of the city. Delve into the Byzantine past in the eerie yet compellingly beautiful **Basilica Cistern** *(p90)* before heading to the spiritual heart of the Byzantine Christian world, the **Haghia Sophia** *(pp86–9)*, a monumental church rightly famed for its mighty dome and glittering mosaics.

Afternoon Mirroring the Haghia Sophia from the far side of a small park is the 16th-century **Blue Mosque** *(pp92–3)*. Inside is the carapace of over 20,000 superb, predominantly blue İznik tiles that give the mosque its name. Just west of the Blue Mosque, a long, paved square represents what is left of a chariot racing stadium, the **Hippodrome** *(p94)*, notable today for its hieroglyphic-carved Egyptian Obelisk and bronze Serpentine Column, originally from Delphi in Greece. For a change of scene either hop on the tram or walk to the vast **Grand Bazaar** *(pp108–9)* for some retail therapy in the 4,000 plus shops. A soak, scrub and massage in the nearby Ottoman-era **Çemberlitaş Baths** *(p95)* makes for a relaxing end to a busy day.

View over Istanbul and to the Princes' Islands beyond, as seen from the Galata Tower

Day 2

Morning An early start at the splendid **Topkapı Palace** complex *(pp72–5)* should help beat the queues. Once the nerve centre of the Ottoman Turks, it is composed of a series of pavilions set amongst attractive courtyard gardens overlooking the Bosphorus. Highpoints include the exotic women's quarters, the Harem, the Divan council room, the Pavilion of the Holy Mantle, which contains many sacred Islamic treasures, and the Treasury, which holds the famous, jewel-encrusted Topkapı dagger.

Afternoon Catch the tram out to the line of the 5th-century **Theodosian Walls** *(pp120–21)* and follow them north to the exquisite **Church of St Saviour in Chora** *(pp122–3)*. Here a dazzling collection of figurative mosaics tell biblical tales, and frescoes rival those of the Renaissance. From the terminus of the Theodosian Walls at Ayvansaray, catch a ferry down the historic **Golden Horn** *(p103)* to the people-thronged environs of Eminönü waterfront and the Galata Bridge. Walk across the angler-lined bridge and uphill to the Genoese-era **Galata Tower** *(p114)*, which affords fabulous views of the old city's skyline of domes and minarets, before grabbing a beer or glass of wine in one of buzzing Beyoğlu's many bars.

A Week on the Aegean Coast

- **Getting There** From Istanbul's Yenikapı terminal, take the fast car ferry or sea bus across the Sea of Marmara to Bandırma, then an inter-city coach to Çanakkale. The journey time is about 5 hours. Alternatively, take a coach from Istanbul's Esenler bus station (10 km/6 miles northwest of the city) or fly.
- **Transport** Inter-city coaches connect several of the major towns on this itinerary, including Çanakkale and Selçuk in around 6 hours. A hire car is a better option, however, as some sights are tricky and time-consuming to reach by public transport.

Day 1: Çanakkale
Enjoy views overlooking the narrow Dardanelles strait in **Çanakkale** *(p178)*, then head onwards to Gallipoli. Preserved as a national park, the battlefields of the **Gallipoli Peninsula** *(pp172–3)*, scene of one of the bloodiest campaigns of World War I, are hauntingly beautiful. South lays Homer's legendary **Troy** *(p178)*, a brilliantly interpreted ancient site where many millennia of human history have been uncovered and excavations are ongoing.

Day 2: Assos and Behram Kale
Enjoy breathtaking views across a deep-blue sea to the Greek island of Lesbos from the atmospheric hilltop ruins of the Temple of Athena, the high point of ancient **Assos** *(p179)*. The attractive village of **Behram Kale** *(p179)*, home to legions of traditionally garbed women proffering handicrafts and Aegean herbs, guards the approach to Assos. Overnight in **Bergama** *(pp180–81)*, whose old Greek quarter clings to the base of the acropolis.

Day 3: Pergamum and Selçuk
Built on a series of terraces wrought from a towering outcrop above Bergama, the remains of ancient **Pergamum** *(pp180–81)* are remarkable. The Temple of Trajan dominates the hilltop; even more impressive is the spectacularly steep theatre. Stay in relaxed **Selçuk** *(p184)*, where storks nest on the columns of a Byzantine aqueduct. Must-sees are the massive 6th century Basilica of St John and the Temple of Artemis – a remnant of one of the Seven Wonders of the Ancient World.

To extend your trip...
Head inland to Pamukkale, where glistening white travertine formations have been deposited on a steep hillside beneath the ruins of the Roman spa town of **Hierapolis** *(pp190–91)*.

Day 4: Ephesus
Perhaps the best-restored classical ruins in the Mediterranean world lie a couple of kilometres from Selçuk in **Ephesus** *(pp186–7)*; allow half a day or more to see the elegant Library of Celsus, the Colonnaded Street, monumental theatre, baths and much more, including intimate terraced houses. Spend the afternoon people watching, exploring the 14th-century Genoese castle, or swimming in the pretty port of **Kuşadası** *(p185)*. Stay overnight in either Selçuk or Kuşadası.

Day 5: Priene, Miletus and Didyma
South of Selçuk are three ancient sites worth visiting for their beautiful settings alone – **Priene**, **Miletus** and **Didyma** *(pp194–5)*. Priene's cobbled streets nestle beneath pines above the Meander river valley, dwarfed by a rocky spur behind. The oracular shrine at Didyma, reached by crossing the Meander river, is a vast Aegean Greek temple ruin. Miletus, marooned in marshland, sprawls around a magnificent stone theatre. Stay in either Selçuk or Kuşadası.

Day 6: Lake Bafa
Brackish yet beautiful, **Lake Bafa** *(p196)* is backed by Mount Latmos' distinctive five peaks. On its remote eastern shores, the little-visited ancient site of Heracleia-under-Latmos awaits, while Byzantine monasteries lay hidden in the mountains. There is an abundance of birdlife too, including the endangered crested pelican. En route to Bodrum, the incredibly well-preserved temple at **Euromos** *(p196)* is a must.

Day 7: Bodrum
Lively seafront **Bodrum** *(pp198–9)* is noted for its open-air Halikarnas disco. More sedate attractions include harbour-front strolls, and the impressive Castle of St Peter, complete with Bronze Age shipwrecks.

The stunning white travertine terraced pools at Pamukkale

The ancient ruins of Kaunos on the western bank of the Dalyan River

A Week on the Turquoise Coast

- **Arriving** Arrive at Dalaman Airport and depart from Antalya Airport.
- **Transport** Minibuses and midi-buses link the towns, villages and resorts along this beautiful coast, but they can be time-consuming and frustrating to use. Hiring a car allows you to travel at your leisure, head up remote mountain roads to isolated sights, and stop for a quick dip at a sandy cove.

Day 1: Dalyan
Strung out along the attractively reed-fringed banks of a lazy river backed by a cliff riddled with mock-temple rock-cut tombs, **Dalyan** *(pp214–15)* makes a refreshing change from the standard resort town. Swim in the river or take a boat down to the fine sand of beautiful Iztuzu beach, home to nesting loggerhead turtles, and explore the ruins of ancient **Kaunos** *(p214)* across the river.

To extend your trip...
Take the boat trip from Dalyan to the warm-water **mudbaths** at Ilıca *(p215)* and onto the lake at **Köyceğiz** *(p214)*.

Day 2: Kayaköy
On the way to the abandoned Greek village of Kayaköy is the market town and yacht harbour of **Fethiye** *(p216)*, with abundant eating places, rock-cut Lycian tombs, a fine archaeological museum and a lively Friday farmers' market. Made famous by Louis de Bernières' epic *Birds Without Wings*, **Kayaköy** *(p216)* is set in an idyllic valley, but is a haunting reminder of the 1923 population exchanges *(see p62)*. Hotels and rental homes are available in the valley.

To extend your trip...
Follow the marked coastal walk from Kayaköy to swim in the blue lagoon at **Ölü Deniz** *(pp216–17)*.

Day 3: Patara
En route to the well-known resort of Kalkan, stop to visit **Patara** *(p218)*, an ancient city which combines a stunning turtle-nesting beach (one of the longest in the Mediterranean) with the romantic, dune-engulfed ruins of Roman Patara. Stay in either the close-by, low-key village of Gelemiş or **Kalkan** *(p218)*.

The beautiful lagoon and restaurant-fringed beach at Ölü Deniz

Day 4: Saklıkent Gorge and Tlos
Visit the hinterland of a region known in ancient times as Lycia by exploring **Saklıkent Gorge** *(p217)*, formed by waters tumbling down from Mount Akdağ. Enjoy a trout lunch at its entrance before heading to **Tlos**, *(p217)* a well-preserved Lycian site. Finish with a dip off Patara beach before overnighting again in Gelemiş or Kalkan.

Day 5: Üçağız and Kale
Explore the lively resort of **Kaş** *(p218)*, formerly a tranquil Greek fishing village. To the southwest, on a magnificent stretch of heavily indented, islet-dotted coast, sits the village of **Üçağız** *(p220)*. Nearby, picturesque Kale (ancient **Simena**, *p220*) huddles beneath the ruins of Simena castle and is reachable only by boat or on foot. Simple accommodation is available in both places.

To extend your trip...
Head back to **Kaş** *(p218)* for a day's scuba diving, canyoning or paragliding. Alternatively, kayak or take a boat trip around **Kale** or **Kekova Island** *(p220)*.

Day 6: Cıralı
Follow the beautiful coastal road from Üçağız to **Çıralı** *(p221)*. Swamped in citrus groves fronting a shingle beach and backed by high, forested peaks, this low-rise, low-key resort is the ideal place to relax. In the evening visit the eternal flames issuing from vents in a pine-clad mountainside.

Day 7: Phaselis
A short drive brings you to the beachside ruins of ancient **Phaselis** *(p221)*, where a skeletal Roman aqueduct rises above pines. Beyond it, the rest of the ruins adjoin three beaches, and the middle one slopes gently into a lagoon. Behind Phaselis, a cable car takes visitors to the summit for superb views of Mount Olympos. Stay overnight in Cıralı or **Antalya** *(pp222–3)*.

A Week in Mediterranean and Anatolian Turkey

- **Airports** Arrive at Antalya Airport; depart from either Nevşehir or Kayseri airports.
- **Transport** This itinerary is best done by a combination of public transport, hire car and/or organized excursions. A direct inter-city coach between Antalya and Cappadocia has a journey time of around 11 hours.

Day 1: Antalya
Perched on cliffs overlooking the Gulf of Antalya and Lycian mountains, **Antalya** *(pp222–3)* is a lively city. Its heart is the walled old quarter (Kaleiçi), a maze of narrow alleys lined with Ottoman-era houses. There are plenty of restaurants and nightlife, but spare a half day either for the **Archaeological Museum** *(p222)*, a drive northwest to clamber over the mountaintop ruins of **Termessos** *(p224)*, or a swim from Mermerli Beach.

Day 2: The Pamphylian Plain
The fertile plain east of Antalya, known in antiquity as Pamphylia, was home to several powerful cities, whose ruins are now a major draw. Join a tour or hire a car to explore **Perge** *(p224)* and **Aspendos** *(p225)*, the latter famed for its superb Roman theatre. Alternatively, head east to **Side** *(pp228–9)* for a day exploring its attractive old town, Roman ruins and stunning sandy beaches.

Day 3: Lake Eğirdir
Turkey's second largest freshwater lake, **Eğirdir** *(p258)* sits at an altitude of 900 m (2,952 ft). Ringed by high peaks, it is best reached by inter-city coach from Antalya. Accommodation is either on a rocky peninsula or a tiny island linked to the mainland by a causeway. Look around the old Greek houses, church and castle, or swim from one of the small beaches.

> **To extend your trip...**
> Hire a car to tour around the lake, taking in **Antiocheia-in-Pisidia** *(p258)*.

Day 4: Konya
Trundle across the steppe lands of the Anatolian plateau on an inter-city coach to **Konya** *(pp254–5)*. The former capital of the Selçuk Turks is best known as the home of Mevlâna, founder of a mystic Islamic sect whose followers are known as "Whirling Dervishes". An afternoon at **Mevlâna Museum** *(pp256–7)* is time well spent.

> **To extend your trip...**
> For anyone with an interest in the prehistoric, the "world's first city" at **Çatalhöyük** *(p258)* is a must.

Day 5: Konya and Cappadocia
Konya, set on and around Alaeddin's Hill, has some fascinating medieval Islamic monuments left by the Selçuk Turks, including the **Alaeddin Mosque** *(p255)* and the **Karatay Museum** *(p255)*. The coach journey onto **Cappadocia** *(pp282–3)* takes in *kervansarays* that once serviced camel trains on the Silk Route. In Cappadocia, aim for a sunset view over the eerie valleys and rock formations from **Uçhisar** *(p284)*. Overnight in **Göreme** *(p287)*, **Ürgüp** or Uçhisar.

Day 6: Cappadocia
Göreme Open-Air Museum *(pp288–9)*, with its weirdly eroded rock pinnacles carved from the soft volcanic rock, requires several hours to explore. Some of the best rock formations are in nearby Zelve *(p286)*. Then head to **Avanos** *(p287)*, which is known for its pottery workshops.

Day 7: Cappadocia
The landscape of southern Cappadocia is quite different, so either hire a car or join a tour to the **Ihlara Valley** *(p296)*. Walk its beautiful gorge and explore its pretty rock-cut churches. En route visit the labyrinthine underground city of **Derinkuyu** *(p286)*.

> **To extend your trip...**
> Explore this region further on a mountain bike, horse, on foot with a guide, or even in a hot-air balloon.

Hot-air balloons glide over the spectacularly eroded landscape of the Cappadocia region

Putting Turkey on the Map

Lying between Europe, Asia and the Middle East, Turkey is located midway between the equator and the North Pole. It covers an area of 814,578 sq km (314,533 sq miles). A small area (3 per cent) called Thrace forms part of the European continent, while the larger section, Anatolia, forms part of Asia. The city of Istanbul is situated at the meeting point of Europe and Asia and is divided by the Bosphorus, the strait linking the Black Sea and the Sea of Marmara. Countries bordering Turkey are Greece and Bulgaria on the European side, and Georgia, Armenia, Iran, Iraq, Syria and Nakhichevan to the east and southeast.

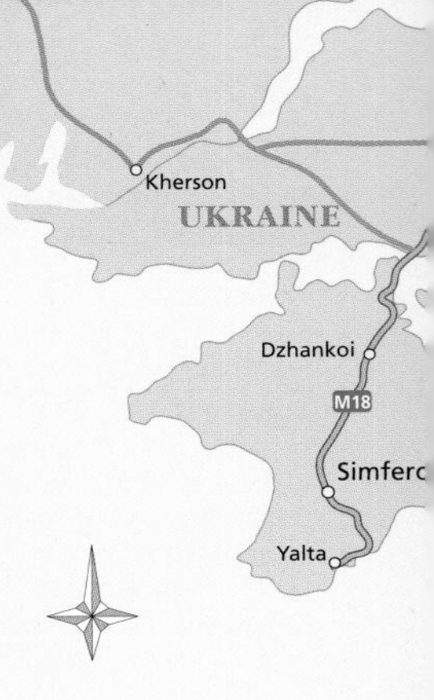

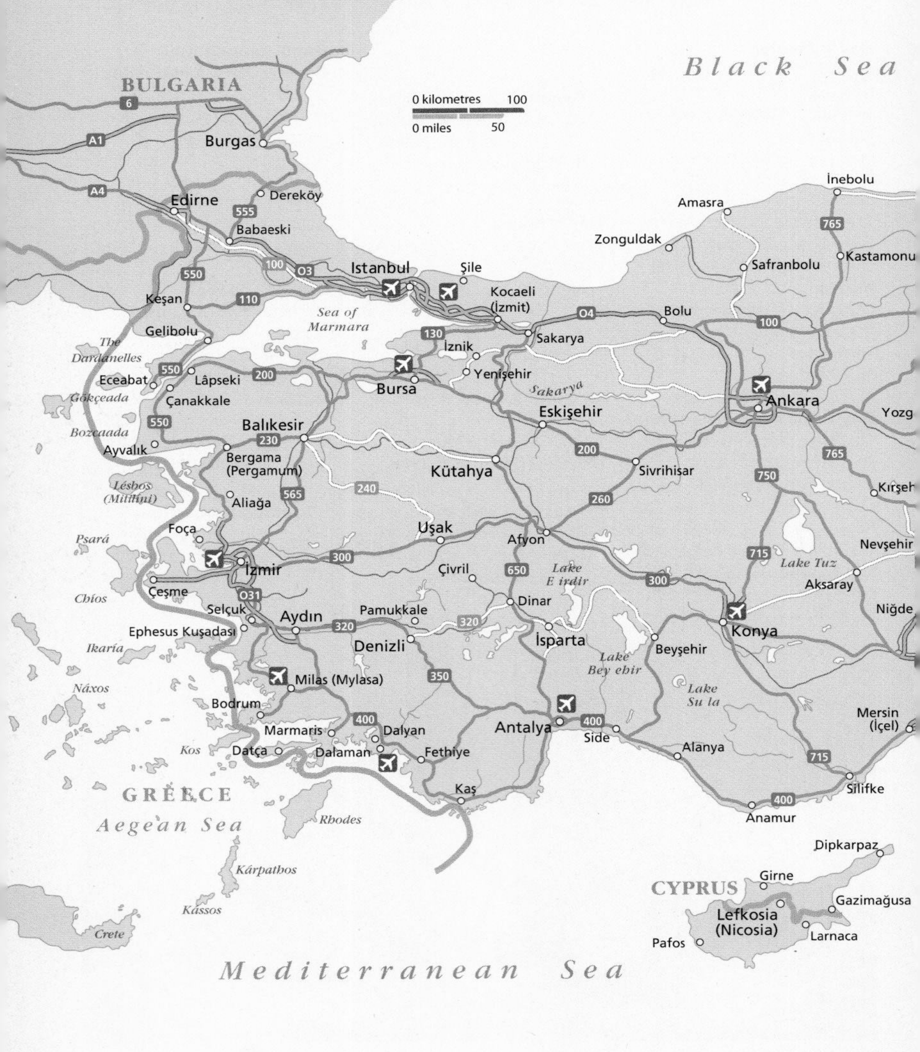

Kherson
UKRAINE
Dzhankoi
M18
Simferc
Yalta
Black Sea
BULGARIA
0 kilometres 100
0 miles 50
6
A1
Burgas
A4
Edirne
Dereköy
555
Babaeski
550
100
O3
Istanbul
Şile
Kocaeli (İzmit)
110
Keşan
Gelibolu
The Dardanelles
Sea of Marmara
130
İznik
Yenişehir
Sakarya
O4
Bolu
100
Zonguldak
Amasra
İnebolu
765
Kastamonu
Safranbolu
Ankara
Yozg
Eceabat
550
Lâpseki
200
Bursa
Sakarya
Eskişehir
Gökçeada
Çanakkale
550
Bozcaada
Balıkesir
230
Ayvalık
Bergama (Pergamum)
Kütahya
200
Sivrihisar
765
750
Kırşeh
Lésbos (Mitilíni)
Aliağa
565
240
260
Foça
Uşak
Afyon
Nevşehir
Psará
İzmir
300
Çivril
650
Lake E irdir
300
715
Lake Tuz
Aksaray
Chíos
Çeşme
O31
Dinar
Niğde
Selçuk
Pamukkale
Ephesus
Kuşadası
Aydın
320
320
İsparta
Konya
Ikaría
Denizli
Lake Bey ehir
Beyşehir
Náxos
Milas (Mylasa)
350
Lake Su la
Bodrum
400
Antalya
400
Mersin (İçel)
Marmaris
Dalyan
Side
Kos
Datça
Dalaman
Fethiye
Alanya
715
GREECE
Kaş
Silifke
Aegean Sea
Rhodes
400
Anamur
Dipkarpaz
Kárpathos
Girne
CYPRUS
Gazimağusa
Kássos
Lefkosia (Nicosia)
Crete
Pafos
Larnaca
Mediterranean Sea

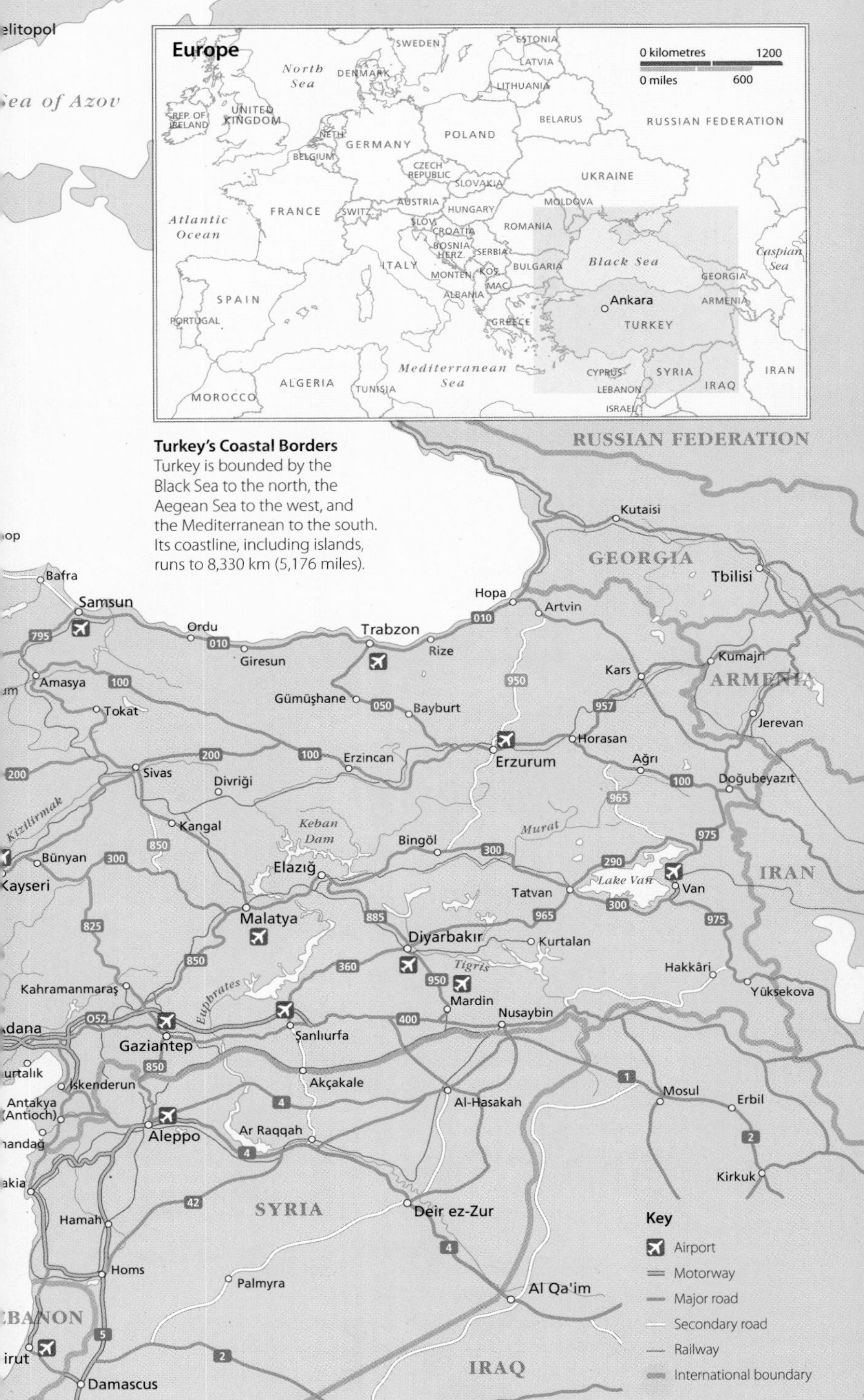

Turkey's Coastal Borders
Turkey is bounded by the Black Sea to the north, the Aegean Sea to the west, and the Mediterranean to the south. Its coastline, including islands, runs to 8,330 km (5,176 miles).

A PORTRAIT OF TURKEY

The popular image many visitors have of Turkey is one of idyllic Mediterranean beaches lapped by an azure sea. Sun and sand, however, barely hint at the riches this country has to offer. A bridge between Asia and Europe, Turkey is one of the great cradles of civilization – a proud country whose cultural and historic treasures will delight and inspire even seasoned travellers.

Contrasts between old and new add greatly to the fascination that overwhelms visitors to Turkey. Istanbul, the metropolis of this fast-changing nation, displays all the hustle and bustle of a great world city, while only a few hours away rural people congregate around communal water supplies and collect wood to light their fires.

The superb scenery and landscapes reflect a remarkable geographical diversity. Beguiling seascapes, soft beaches and brooding mountains along the Mediterranean coast yield to the tranquillity of Turkey's Lake District, while the deep forests and cool *yayla* (summer pastures) of the Black Sea region leave visitors unprepared for the vast empty steppes of the eastern provinces. Pictures can only hint at the enchantment that awaits travellers in Cappadocia. Here, centuries of underground activity have resulted in entire cities carved deep into the porous tuff, while aeons of erosion have carved the landscape into fantastic fairy-tale mushroom formations.

Many of Turkey's national parks and wetland sanctuaries are a last refuge for species that are almost extinct elsewhere in Europe, and for botanists there is an amazing display of flora.

Add to this countless ancient ruins, and the friendliness and hospitality of the Turkish nation, and you are guaranteed an unforgettable holiday.

Looking out over the Bosphorus from Sultanahmet

◀ Turks gather to break their first day of fasting during Ramadan, İstiklal Cad, Istanbul

The Library at Ephesus *(see pp186–7)*, one of the most famous Roman sites in Turkey

Historical Framework

Anatolia has seen the rise and fall of sophisticated civilizations, including that of the great Assyrians, Hittites, Phrygians and Urartians. Over the centuries, this land was populated almost continuously. The Hellenistic period produced some of the finest sites. Near Çanakkale, on the Aegean coast, lie the remains of ancient Troy *(see p178)*, and in the mountainous south-west are the ruined settlements of Lycia *(see p219)*, whose inhabitants left behind an assortment of unusual rock tombs.

In the early Christian era, St Paul travelled through Asia Minor, then part of the Roman empire, to preach the Gospel. Between the 3rd and 7th centuries, Christianity was a central force in the development of Anatolia. This was the period when the Byzantine Empire attained the pinnacle of its glory. The Romans and Byzantines endowed Turkey with glorious architectural masterpieces, which can still be seen at places like Ephesus *(see pp186–7)*, Aphrodisias *(see pp192–3)*, and in Istanbul, where the former church of Haghia Sophia has stood for more than 14 centuries *(see pp86–9)*.

Ottoman tilework at the Topkapı Palace, Istanbul

The Seljuk Turks added their superb architectural legacy, as did the Ottomans, whose empire at one point stretched from Hungary to Arabia. Many other peoples, among them Jews, Russians, Armenians and Greeks, have played an important part in Turkey's complex history. The fruits of this diversity can be seen in superb mosaics and frescoes, colourful tilework, underground cities, interesting historic and biblical sights, city walls and fortresses.

Turks are proud of the modern nation Atatürk *(see p62)* forged out of the ruined Ottoman empire. *"Ne Mutlu Türküm Diyene"* is a common Turkish phrase that means "happy is the person who can say he is a Turk."

Religion

Most of Turkey's population of 76 million people follow

the Sunni branch of Islam, but around 20 per cent of the population are Alevis, and some belong to other Muslim sects.

Although the Turkish Republic is founded on firmly secular principles, Islam has seen a major resurgence in the country since 2002. The devout attend prayer times in the mosque five times daily as laid down by the Koran, but some Turkish Muslims do not go to mosque at all.

A department of religious affairs exists and carries out the function of exercising control over family morals and to safeguard the principles of Islam. Mosque and state are not separated by statute, and so the boundaries between them can be unclear at times. Invariably, Atatürk's principles are invoked as sacred when religion appears to steer too close to politics. The issue of Islamic dress is emotionally charged and a subject of debate.

Approximately 130,000 non-Muslims, including Greek and Armenian Orthodox, are found in larger cities, and members are allowed to worship freely within their own communities.

Byzantine mosaic, Haghia Sophia

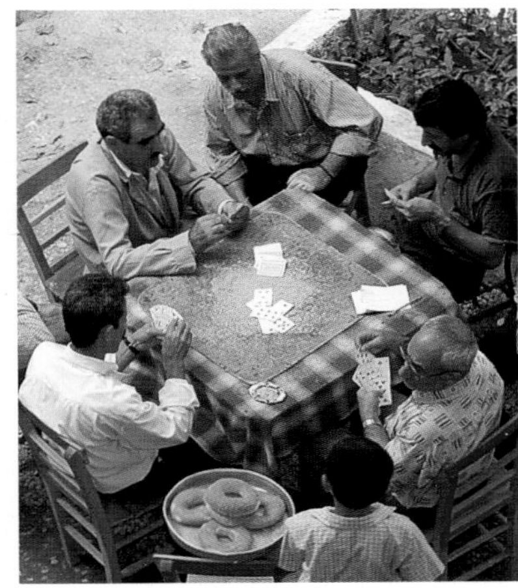

A card game interrupted for a tray of *simit*

Society

The Turkish language is of Central Asian origin but uses the Latin alphabet. It has a natural vowel harmony that makes it sound melodic and soft. Turkish terms such as *divan* and *ottoman* have entered the English vocabulary, while Turkish borrows words like *tren* and *randevu* from English and French.

Turks have an uninhibited body language that is as emphatic as speech. They are unrestrained about enjoying themselves, but traditional segregation of the sexes means that groups of men sitting around smoking, drinking endless cups of *çay* (tea) and playing dominoes, cards or *tavla* (backgammon) are a common sight. A pronounced family ethos cements the generations, and festivals unite the extended family. It is all bound together by hospitality, an age-old Turkish tradition, in which food and drink play a central role.

Children are regarded as national treasures, but many families blame the advent of television and the Internet for eroding the discipline and respect for elders that were once sacred.

The Blue Mosque *(see pp92–3)* in Istanbul

Turkey's gradual transition to a modern, Western society received a major boost in 1952, when it became a member of the North Atlantic Treaty Organization (NATO). This brought advances in communications, transport and its defence policy. New roads, highways and projects to improve the tourism infrastructure changed the face of the country.

Traditional juice vendor

Modernization is, more than ever, the hallmark of Turkish society. Today, remote villages can boast of high-speed, fibre-optic telephone connections, but may lack adequate water or reliable electricity supplies. The Internet and mobile phones have become essential accessories, and new housing projects are quickly festooned with satellite TV dishes.

Modern Turkey

For most Turks, the modern version of their ancient country dates from the founding of the Turkish Republic in 1923. Its architect was Mustafa Kemal – better known as Atatürk – a decorated former army officer who became Turkey's first President.

Atatürk set Turkey on the road to becoming a modern state. His reforms, strictly enacted, steered Turkey towards becoming European rather than Asian, and his status in the eyes of the Turkish nation has scarcely dimmed since his death. His picture is everywhere and his statue adorns almost every village square. Few statesmen have matched his integrity and style, and the soldier-turned-politician model still appeals strongly to Turks.

Turkey began experimenting with multi-party democracy in 1950, but coups in 1960, 1971 and 1980 showed that the military were the true guardians of Atatürk's legacy. In 2002 an overtly Islamist party, the AKP (Truth and Justice Party), were voted into office, and won the next two general elections. Buoyed by this unprecedented mandate to rule, they curbed the role of the military and moved the nation towards a presidential system of government.

In Ottoman times, the state provided an all-encompassing social service to

Soldiers mounting guard at the Atatürk Mausoleum *(see p248)*, Ankara

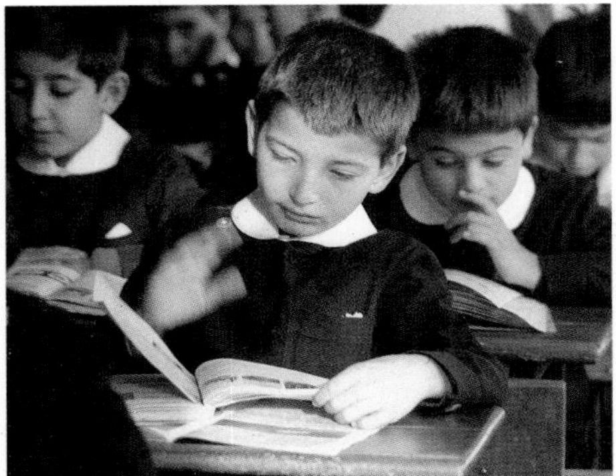

Children hard at work in school

its citizens, who willingly complied with its ordered governance. Today, the role of the state is being redefined. Officials are elected and democracy is the goal of society. Many state-owned joint-stock companies and monopolies that put Turkey on its feet have been privatized.

Since 2002, the country has encouraged inward investment, particularly from the oil-rich Gulf States. The Turkish stock market (Borsa Istanbul) has flourished, as has tourism. Inflation, running at 100 per cent in 2001, has been brought down to single digits, although unemployment still hovers around 10 per cent. The state has become less centralised and the power of the military has been curbed, but with trouble at Turkey's borders, particularly with Syria and Iraq, military spending still dwarfs that of other government departments. Many Turks consider themselves Europeans, despite income gaps and social inequalities.

Folk dancers from the Black Sea

Population Movement

In the 1960s, many Turks left for Germany to work under a government scheme offering remittances in foreign currency – an important source of export income. Many settled there, and 2.2 million Turks now call Germany their home. There are large Turkish communities in other EU states, too.

Within Turkey, the trend has been for rural people to leave the land and seek a more stable life in urban areas. Few plan to return, even if city life is not what they hoped for. Some of Turkey's best-known films, such as *Sürü* (The Herd), and *Eşkıya* (The Bandit), highlight the common themes of identity, lifestyle and poverty. Turkey's indomitable spirit and vitality are best seen and appreciated in its proud people. Journeys invariably result in friendships. If a Turk says they are your *arkadaş* (friend), they will be a steadfast soulmate long after your holiday memories have faded.

Fish sold on the quayside along Istanbul's Golden Horn *(see p103)*

Landscape and Geology

Mountain ranges are Turkey's most distinctive geographic feature, with the Taurus and Pontic ranges enclosing the high Anatolian Plateau. The mountains are geologically young, and the many faulting and folding areas indicate that mountain building is still active. In fact, 80 per cent of the country lies in an extremely active tectonic zone, and earthquakes are frequent. Turkey has eight main drainage basins but the most important ones are the Euphrates (Fırat) and the Tigris (Dicle). About one quarter of Turkey is covered with forest, with stands of pine, spruce and cedar, as well as deciduous trees. About 13 per cent of this area is productive; erosion, logging and fires have all depleted forested areas.

Saklıkent Gorge is typical of the Mediterranean coastal region, where steep valleys and gorges bisect elongated mountain ridges.

İzmit, east of Istanbul, was the epicentre of the 1999 earthquake that measured 7.4 on the Richter scale and claimed the lives of at least 25,000 people.

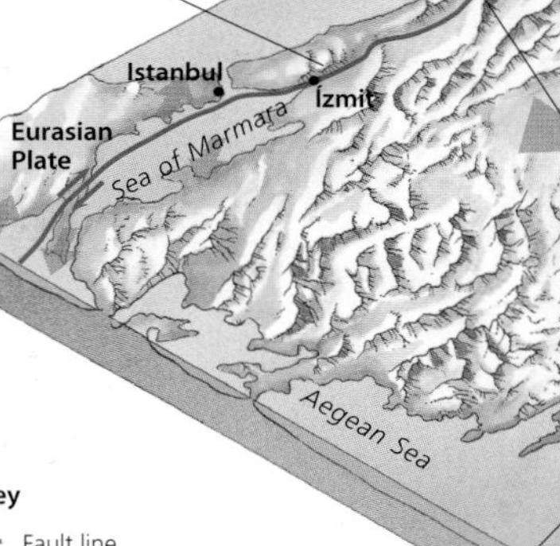

Key

- Fault line
- Direction of plate movement

Plate Movements

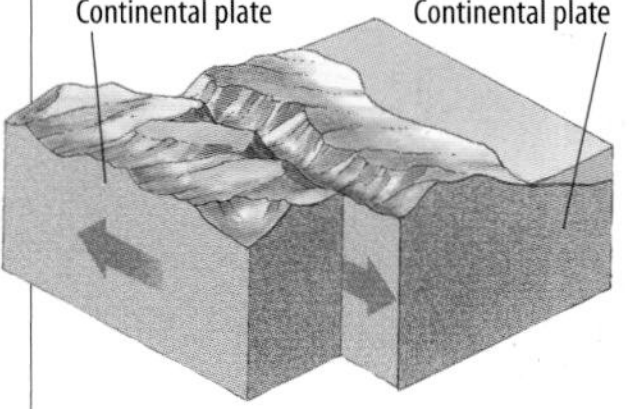

Strike-slip faulting is found along the North Anatolian Fault. When rocks suddenly shift or move along such fault lines, the tension is released as an earthquake.

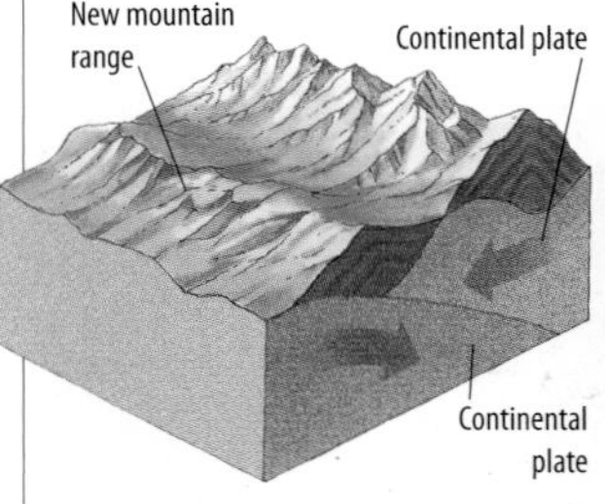

Collisions between two continental plates result in crust being pushed upwards to form mountain ranges.

The Mediterranean and Aegean coasts are characterized by mountain soils which are clay-based and red, brown and grey in colour. Plains around Adana and Antalya support extensive food, crop and horticultural production.

Lake Van lies in a crater-like depression that became landlocked when lava flows from the adjacent Pleistocene-era volcano blocked the flow of water. Today, drainage from feeder streams fills the lake and only evaporation sustains a constant water level. It has a surface area of 3,713 sq km (1,440 sq miles) and a very high level of sodium carbonate.

Pontic Mountains
Black Sea
Erzurum
Lake Van
Erzincan
Arabian Plate
Adana
Antakya
Taurus Mountains

Geology and Earthquakes

Turkey lies between three converging continental plates – the Anatolian, Eurasian and Arabian plates. As the Arabian plate moves northward into the Eurasian plate, it pushes the Anatolian plate westward, causing earthquakes along the North Anatolian Fault. Further west, the African plate pushes beneath the Anatolian plate, stretching the crust under the Aegean Sea. Tectonic activity is prevalent throughout Turkey.

East of Adıyaman, the alluvial Mesopotamian plain lies between the Tigris and Euphrates rivers. This fertile area produces much of Turkey's wheat and cotton.

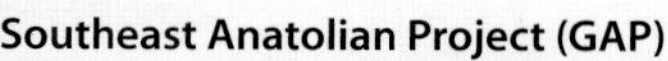

Isolated Mediterranean bays were, for centuries, havens for pirates. The Taurus Mountains made sections of the coast inaccessible, allowing peoples like the Lycians (1st and 2nd century BC) to resist Roman rule and retain their own language and culture. As harbours silted up, such civilizations declined.

Southeast Anatolian Project (GAP)

Begun in 1974, the colossal GAP project was conceived to produce hydroelectric power by harnessing the flow of the Tigris and Euphrates rivers. It resulted in the world's fourth-largest dam and a series of smaller dams. The benefits of this project have included turning infertile land into arable land that produces crops such as cotton and pistachio, and supplying electricity to cities. Critics say the project displaces local people, contributes to climate change and damages unique archaeological sites.

The massive Atatürk Dam

Flora and Fauna of Turkey

Turkey offers much for the naturalist, with rich marine ecosystems, abundant birdlife and elusive larger mammals. The rugged eastern provinces still harbour large mammals, including bears, jackals and wolves. The country is also floristically rich, with more than 11,000 plant species recorded. The tulip is perhaps the most famous of these. The great diversity of plants stems from the variety of habitats – from arid plains to mountains and temperate woodland – but also from Turkey's position as a "biological watershed" at the crossroads of Europe and Asia. There are huge tracts of unspoiled countryside, some of which have been set aside as national parks.

The Anatolian lynx can still be found in upland areas, although its habitat is under threat.

The Mediterranean Coast

Large areas of the Mediterranean and Aegean coast are dominated by evergreen scrub, with Jerusalem sage, kermes oak, broom and sun roses among the common species. More open scrub areas contain orchids, bulbs and annuals. Tucked under bushes are hellebores and Comper's orchid, with its distinctive trailing tassels. Arum lilies exude a fetid odour to entice pollinators. Late summer brings the spires of sea squill and sea daffodil. The carob tree sheds its pods in autumn while colchicum and sternbergias unfold.

Common sternbergia

Wetlands

Here, dragonflies hover over flowering rush, waterlilies and irises, while water meadows fill with buttercups, bellevalia, marsh orchids and pale blue asyneumas. Despite international recognition of their diversity, Turkish wetlands are under threat from dams, drainage, pollution and climatic change. Surviving examples are Sultansazlığı near Niğde *(see p293)*, Bird Paradise National Park near Bursa *(see p163)* and the Göksu Delta *(see p232)*.

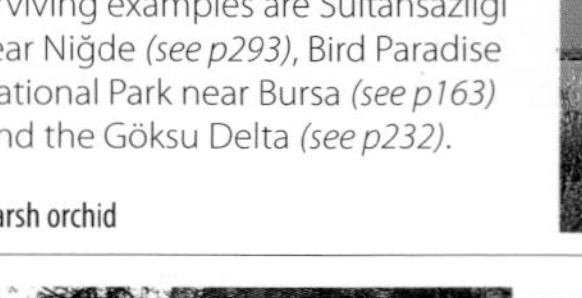

Marsh orchid

Woodlands

Coniferous forests harbour stands of peonies, orchids, foxgloves, fritillaries and golden peas. The western Taurus range has an endemic subspecies of cedar of Lebanon, and in the north are forests of Oriental beech and fir, with rhododendron, ferns, lilies, primulas and campanulas. In autumn cyclamen and edible mushrooms appear. There are giant cedar at Dokuz Göl near Elmalı, endemic oak species at Kasnak near Eğirdir *(see p258)*, and ancient mixed woodland, now threatened by a dam, in the Fırtına valley.

Peony

Steppe

Despite their sparse appearance, the broad expanses of the Anatolian Plateau support many flowering plants. Highlights include stately asphodelines, which reach 1.8 m (6 ft) in height, purple gladioli, flax in yellow, pink or blue, and the colourful parasite *Phelypaea coccinea*. On the eastern steppe are found the lovely white, purple or blue oncocyclus iris. Göreme National Park in Cappadocia and Nemrut Dağı National Park *(see p310)* are good places to see this flora. Deforestation and erosion have greatly altered the steppe, and intensive farming practices have accelerated this process.

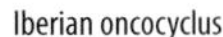

Iberian oncocyclus

Mountains

Snowdrop

In spring, subalpine meadows are carpeted with buttercups. Above the treeline, snowdrops, winter aconite and crocus crowd together near the snowmelt. These are followed by star-of-Bethlehem, grape hyacinth, fritillaries, foxtail lilies, asphodelines and bright red tulips. Scree and rocky slopes are dotted with colourful alpine flowers like iris, rock jasmine and aubretia. Important mountain reserves include Kaçkar Mountains National Park near the Black Sea coast, Aladağlar National Park, Beyşehir Gölü National Park near Eğirdir *(see p258)* and the ski centres at Uludağ *(see p163)* and Erciyes *(see p292)*.

Birds of Anatolia

More than 440 species of bird have been recorded in Turkey, which offers a range of habitats from woodlands and mountains to wetlands and steppe. The country's position on the migratory flyways makes its a paradise for bird-watchers. Autumn offers the spectacle of vast flocks of migrating storks and raptors over the Bosphorus. In winter, lakes and wetlands hold thousands of wintering wildfowl.

Alpine chough can be seen in the mountains, where they nest on ledges, nooks and crevices. They store food in cracks, which they cover with stones.

Chukar partridge is one of many game birds in Turkey, where hunting is a popular pastime.

Serin live in woodlands and vineyards. Local populations are augmented by migratory birds in autumn.

Adult golden eagles are resident, but the young of northern Europe migrate south in winter to the mountainous areas of the Mediterranean.

Hans and Kervansarays

Dotted across Anatolia are many *hans* (storage depots) and *kervansarays* (hostelries) built in Seljuk and Ottoman times to protect merchants travelling the caravan routes that crossed Anatolia along the Roman-Byzantine road system. From the 13th century, the Seljuks built more than 100 *hans* to encourage trade. It was under the Ottomans, though, that *hans* and *kervansarays* became a part of the state-sponsored social welfare system and played a key role in expanding Ottoman territory and influence. Several of these facilities can be visited today, and some have been turned into hotels or restaurants.

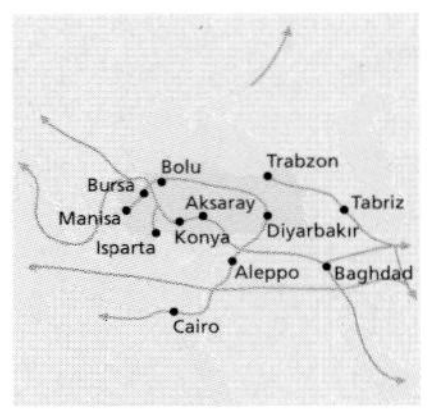

Locator Map

Major trade routes

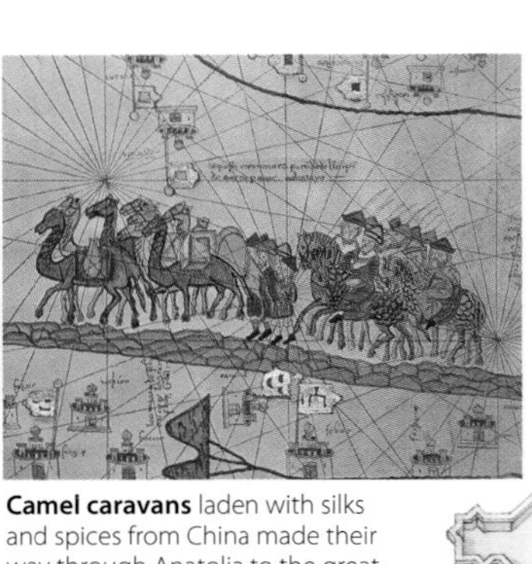

Camel caravans laden with silks and spices from China made their way through Anatolia to the great commercial centre of Bursa *(see pp166–71)*. Slaves from the Black Sea hinterland were another important trading commodity.

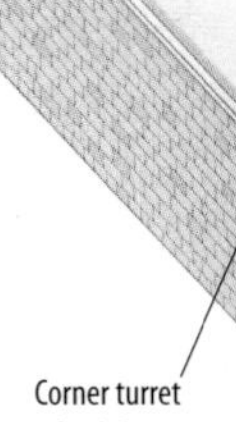

Portal of the storage hall

A small mosque raised on arches stands in the centre of the courtyard.

A thick curtain wall surrounded the *kervansaray.*

The central gate provided the only entry to the fortified structure.

The central courtyard, surrounded by arcades, provided shelter from the hot sun and contained apartments and a *hamam* (Turkish bath) to revive weary travellers.

Corner turret for defence

The stone bridge over the Köprü River near Antalya was built by the Seljuks near the site of a Roman bridge. The structure has been restored.

A *kervansaray* at Mylasa, a bustling commercial centre in western Anatolia, is shown in this 19th-century oil painting by the English artist Richard Dadd.

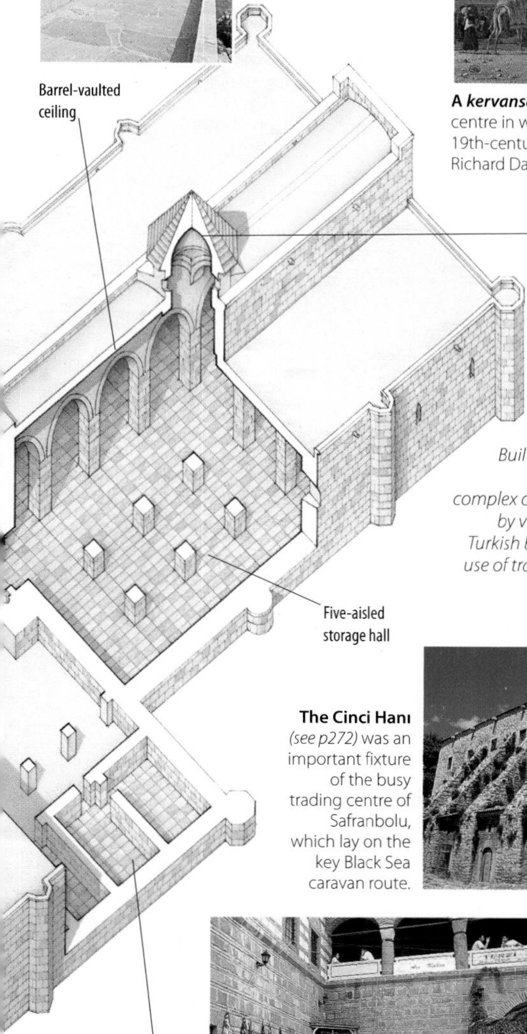

Barrel-vaulted ceiling

The octagonal lantern tower let light into the interior.

The Sultanhanı

The Sultanhanı, near the central Anatolian city of Aksaray (see pp296–7), *is one of the best-preserved Seljuk kervansarays. Built between 1226 and 1229 for Sultan Alaeddin Keykubad* (see p254), *the complex consisted of a courtyard surrounded by various amenities – stables, mosque, Turkish bath and accommodation – for the use of travellers, and a covered hall in which trade goods could be safely stored.*

Five-aisled storage hall

The Cinci Hanı *(see p272)* was an important fixture of the busy trading centre of Safranbolu, which lay on the key Black Sea caravan route.

The Kızlarağası Hanı in İzmir *(see p182)* is an Ottoman *han* dating from 1744. *Hans* had the same amenities found at a *kervansaray*, together with storerooms, offices and rows of cell-like workshops, all grouped around a central courtyard. The restored Kızlarağası Hanı houses a variety of cafés, shops and craft workshops.

Accommodation for travellers was provided in two tiers of rooms.

Customs and Traditions

Turkish customs have been passed down from generation to generation and are integrated into contemporary life. Climate, geography and ethnic background play a significant role, but many customs have their origins in Islam and have changed little over the years. An enduring faith is attached to the blue bead, or *mavi boncuk*, an amulet that protects the wearer from the evil eye. It may be seen dangling wherever good luck is needed.

Religious and social mores dictate separate lives for many men and women, so customs bring them together for celebrations such as weddings, births and rites of passage. Family life is pivotal to Turkish culture, and communities are strengthened by the social and economic ties of the extended family.

In Karagöz shadow puppet theatre, a cast of stock characters enact satiric themes. The puppets are three-dimensional cut-outs made from camel skin.

Circumcision

For the celebration of his *sünnet*, or circumcision ritual, a boy is dressed in the satin uniform of a sergeant major, and his parents throw as lavish a celebration as they can afford. Relatives and friends proffer money as gifts for the young man, and the whole event is often photographed for the family album.

Gold coins attached to ribbons

Offerings pinned to a pillow symbolize the gifts the young man will take into manhood.

In line with Islamic tradition, Turkish boys are circumcised between the ages of seven and ten. A lavish uniform is worn for this special occasion.

Village Weddings

Celebrations such as weddings may last for several days and involve a number of individual rituals. In the rural areas, families often approve and sanction wedding partners. The bride always has a *çeyiz* (trousseau) comprising lovely, handcrafted articles she and her mother have made for the new home.

Making flatbread for the marriage feast is the responsibility of the women of the family. The tradition of making *katmer* or *gözleme* (crepes) is being revived in some parts of Turkey.

Headscarves are worn by many rural women.

Village square (*meydan*)

Wedding festivities in the picturesque village of Midyat, near the Syrian border, bring a large and appreciative crowd out to watch dancers performing.

Handicrafts

Craft skills were handed down from the Ottoman guild system, and Turkey has many skilled craftspeople. One example is *oya*, or needle lace, which is noted for its intricate floral designs crocheted in silk. These were originally crafted for a bride's trousseau. As late as the 1920s, wives crocheted them as part of their husband's headdress. Quilt-making, on the other hand, was traditionally passed down from the father.

Weaving is a rural tradition and done mainly by women. Designs of carpets and *kilims* *(see pp366–7)* are handed down from one generation to the next.

Copper and brass ware, worked by hand, is an integral part of the Turkish household.

Local markets are the best places to look for traditional crafts. Shown here are handmade linens in Kalkan.

Hand-printed textiles, known as *yazma*, are a proud and venerable craft tradition in central Anatolian towns such as Tokat.

Woodworking skills were handed down from the Ottomans. Unique wooden walking sticks are made in Devrek, near the Black Sea. These wooden bowls were produced near Adana.

Traditional Dress

Traditionally, Turkish women wove their clothing according to individual designs, and dyed them using plant extracts. Today, each region has its own styles of *şalvar* (trousers worn by women) and head coverings such as *başörtüsü* (scarves).

A group of folk dancers wears the traditional costume of the Van region. Folk dancing is hugely popular, with regional costumes as much a part of the show as music and laughter.

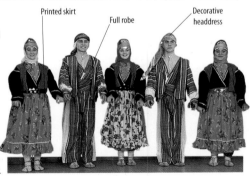

National Service

All men over the age of 20 must serve compulsory military service of varying duration, and Turkish society still considers this to be a fundamental rite of passage to manhood. For rural youths, this may be their first time away from home, and *askerlik* (military service) fulfils a social role as a bridge to adulthood. The departing conscript may be required to visit friends and relatives to ask forgiveness for any wrongdoings and be presented with gifts and money before he reports for duty.

Young soldiers of the Turkish Army on duty

Islamic Art in Turkey

In Islamic art, the highest place is held by calligraphy, or the art of beautiful writing. This is because a calligrapher's prime task is writing the Holy Koran, believed by Muslims to be the word of God. In the purest forms of Islam, the use of animal forms in works of art is regarded as detracting from pious thoughts. Thus, artists and craftsmen turned their talents to designs featuring geometric motifs and intricate foliage designs known as arabesques. As well as calligraphy, these highly disciplined forms included miniature paintings, jewellery, metal, tiles and ceramics, stone-carving and textiles. Under the Ottomans, the finest creations came from the Nakkaşhane, or sultan's design studio. Here, an apprentice system that lasted up to 10 years maintained the imperial traditions of excellence and innovation.

Floral decorations

Ornamental loops

The sultan's *tuğra* was his personal monogram, used in place of his signature. It would be drawn by a calligrapher or engraved on a wooden block as a stamp. This example shows the *tuğra* of Abdül Hamit I (1774–89).

Floral tile motif

Koranic texts provided templates for woodcarvers, metalworkers, weavers and ceramic painters. Although highly decorative, Islamic art is filled with meaning: the tulip *(lâle)*, a much-used motif, is an anagram for Allah.

Inscription in metal

Ceramic tile panels contain messages taken from the Koran, executed in Arabic or Kufic script.

Calligraphic inscription in embossed metal

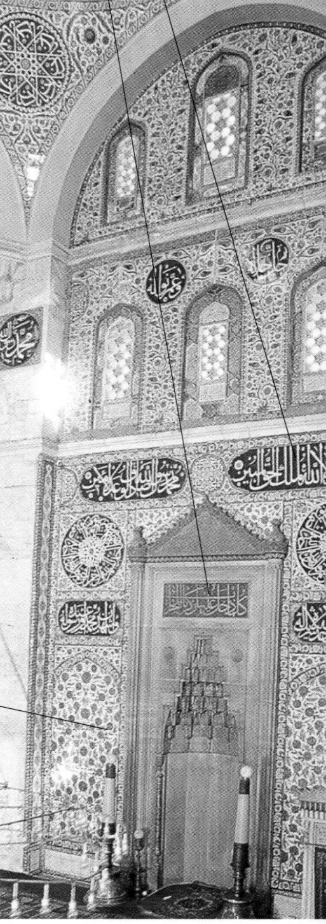

Tile panel featuring plant motifs

Sokollu Mehmet Paşa Mosque In Kadırga, Istanbul

Designed by Sinan (1577–8) for a distinguished grand vizier, the prayer hall features a beautiful qibla *(wall of the mosque at right angles to the direction of Mecca). The calligraphic decoration includes exquisite tilework and stone-carving.*

Tilework on squinches supporting the dome

The minaret of the Green Mosque (Yeşil Camii) in İznik *(see p164)* features complex patterns of coloured tiles. The mosque, which was completed in 1378, takes its name from the richly decorated minaret.

This tile panel is set into the stone wall.

The conical roof of the *minbar (see p36)* features polychrome tiling.

Stained-glass windows

An Arabic inscription winds around a gravestone in the grounds of the Alanya Museum *(see p230)*.

A tile panel over the entrance to the Mausoleum of Selim II, in the precincts of Haghia Sophia in Istanbul, shows a masterful integration of calligraphy and organic motifs.

The Art of the Ottoman Miniature

Ottoman miniature painting was primarily a courtly art form, which reached a peak of development in the late 16th century during the rule of Süleyman the Magnificent *(see p59)*. Miniature painting was influenced by Persian art, with many of the finest Persian minaturists being brought to work at the court workshops of Topkapı Palace *(see pp72–5)*. As well as illustrations for manuscripts of Koranic texts and Persian epics – Persian was the language of the Ottoman court – a unique style was developed to record the history of the dynasty. This included battle scenes, palace rituals, major festivals and topographical scenes. By the 17th century, miniature painters had mastered three-dimensional representation, while the 18th century heralded a more naturalistic style and a broadening of subjects to include landscapes, still lifes and portraits. Although there were a number of celebrated miniature artists, these exquisite works were, for the most part, neither signed nor dated.

Early 17th-century miniature showing Hasan, grandson of Mohammed, on his deathbed

Ottoman Architecture

From Albania to Tripoli, and from Baghdad to Bosnia, the Ottomans left superb examples of their architectural skills. Nowhere is this more apparent than in Istanbul, where the sultans built beautiful mosques, palaces and *külliyes* (Islamic charitable institutions).

Ottoman architecture is marked by a strict hierarchy of forms, scales and materials, reflecting the rank of a building's patron. Mosques commissioned by members of the Ottoman family, for example, were the only ones entitled to two or more minarets. Another distinguishing feature is the influence of Byzantine architecture. Many architects, among them Mimar Sinan *(see p105)*, were of Greek or Armenian origin.

Ornamental fountains *(çeşme)* were built in busy central squares or markets. This example is in the bazaar in Kayseri *(see pp294–5)*.

The Early Ottoman Mosque

The earliest form of the Ottoman mosque consisted of a single large prayer hall covered by a hemispheric dome, with a covered porch and minaret outside. The Junior Hacı Özbek Mosque (1333) in İznik is considered the earliest example of this form. It was modified by adding bays (often covered by small domes) around the central dome, and by the addition of a covered portico and arcaded courtyard.

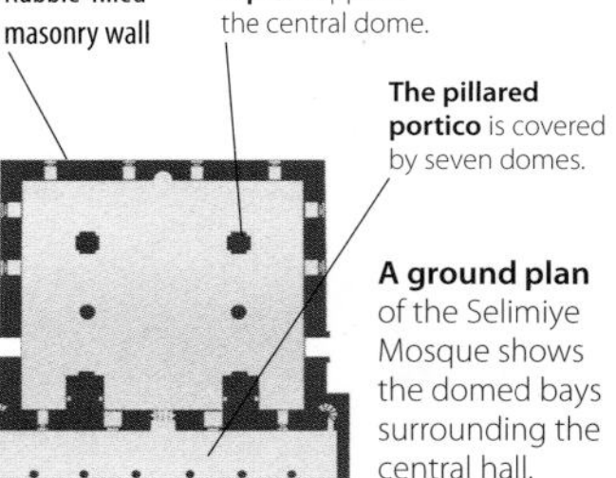

Rubble-filled masonry wall

A pier supports the central dome.

The pillared portico is covered by seven domes.

A ground plan of the Selimiye Mosque shows the domed bays surrounding the central hall.

The Selimiye Mosque, in Konya *(see pp254–5)*, was started in 1558 by Sultan Selim II when he was governor of Konya. It was finished in 1587. Clearly visible is the bulk of the central prayer hall, which is topped by a hemispheric dome. The mosque adjoins the Mevlâna Museum.

The Later Ottoman Mosque

The form of the Ottoman mosque underwent a dramatic evolution in the years following the conquest of Constantinople. The Ottomans frequently converted Orthodox churches, notably Haghia Sophia *(see pp86–9)*, into mosques. Under the influence of such models, architects began to create higher, single-domed mosques, and to greatly open up the interior space.

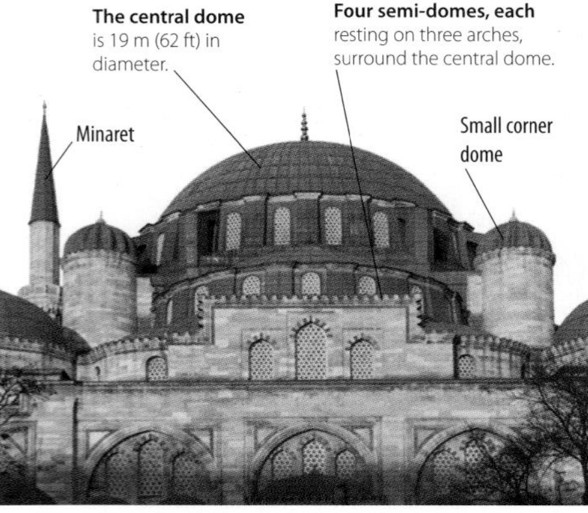

The central dome is 19 m (62 ft) in diameter.

Four semi-domes, each resting on three arches, surround the central dome.

Minaret

Small corner dome

The Şehzade Mosque (also called the Prince's Mosque) in Istanbul was the first imperial mosque built by the architect Mimar Sinan *(see p105)*. It was commissioned in 1543 by Süleyman the Magnificent.

Fountains (Şadırvan)

Based on the Koranic principle that water is the source of life, the provision of public water supplies was a civic duty. Every town had its *çeşme* (public fountain), and *külliyes* offered *sebil* (free distribution of water). The *şadırvan* was placed in a mosque courtyard for the performance of ritual ablutions.

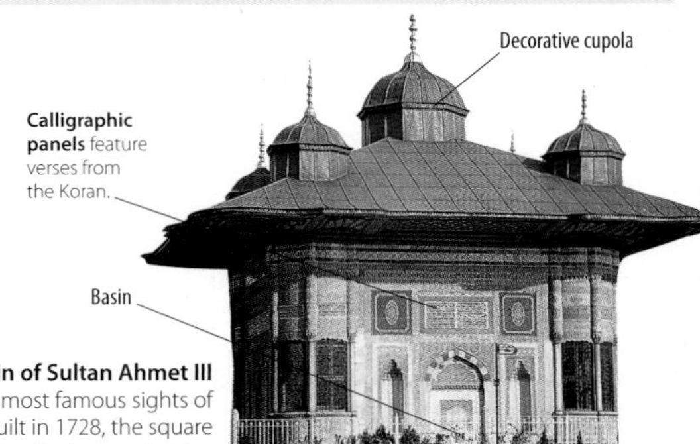
Decorative cupola
Calligraphic panels feature verses from the Koran.
Basin

The Fountain of Sultan Ahmet III is one of the most famous sights of Istanbul. Built in 1728, the square structure has basins on all sides.

The Konak

Like many other Ottoman buildings, the *konak* (mansion house) consisted of a wooden structure built on a foundation of stone and brick to withstand the cold Anatolian winter. The ground floor contained granaries, stables and storage areas. The kitchens and public rooms were on the first floor, with the private quarters on the top floor.

Living areas had *sofas* (upholstered benches) along the walls. The nook shown here is in a *konak* that has been turned into a hotel in Safranbolu *(see pp272–3)*.

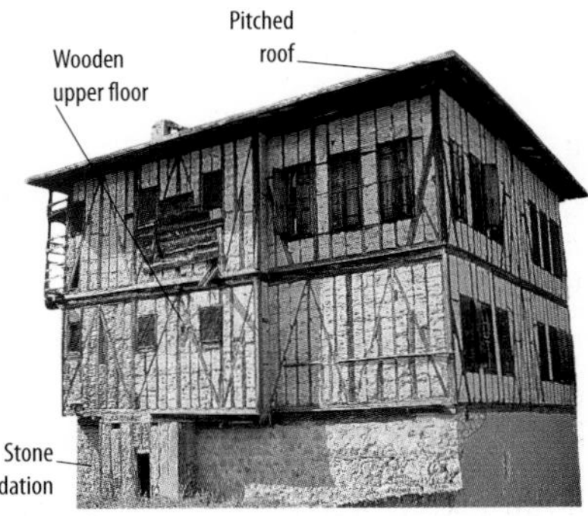
Pitched roof
Wooden upper floor
Stone foundation

A rural konak in northern Turkey shows the typical three-storey form. Some had separate entrances for the *harem* (women's quarters) and *selamlık* (men's quarters).

Yalı

The *yalı* (waterfront villa) is found along the Bosphorus. Most *yalıs* were built during the 18th and 19th centuries as grand summer residences for wealthy citizens of Ottoman Istanbul. Sited to make maximum use of the waterside location, they also incorporated boathouses or moorings.

Wood was the main building material.
Decorative pilasters
The water-side location provided easy access and maximum visibility.

Yalıs were built in a variety of forms and architectural styles, from simple wooden structures to this lavish Russian-style mansion.

Building Types

Bedesten Covered stone market

Çeşme Public water fountain

Daruşşifa Hospital

Hamam Bathhouse *(see p81)*

İmaret Soup kitchen

Külliye Educational/charitable complex surrounding a major mosque *(see pp36–7)*

Medrese Theological college *(see pp36–7)*

Mescit Small prayer hall

Tekke Dervish lodge

Tımarhane Lunatic asylum

Türbe Tomb

Exploring Mosques

Five times a day throughout Istanbul a chant is broadcast over loudspeakers set high in the city's minarets to call the faithful to prayer. Over 99 per cent of the population is Muslim, though the Turkish state is officially secular. Most belong to the Sunni branch of Islam, but there is also a small population of Shiites. Both follow the teachings of the Koran, the sacred book of Islam, and the Prophet Mohammed (c.570–632), but Shiites accept, in addition, the authority of a line of 12 imams directly descended from Mohammed. Islamic mystics are known as Sufis *(see p259)*.

Overview of the impressive Süleymaniye Mosque complex

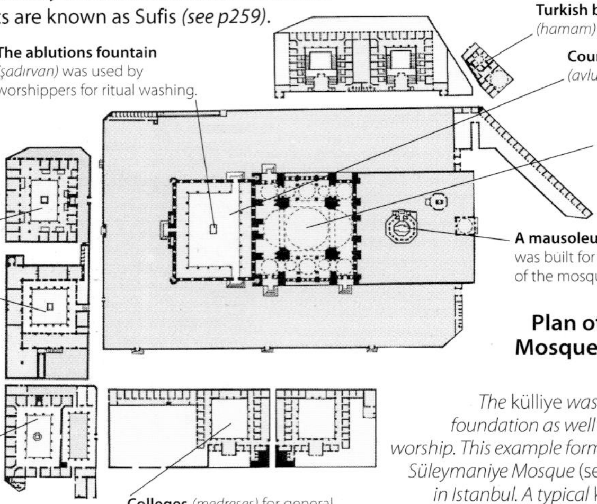

Turkish baths *(hamam)*

Courtyard *(avlu)*

The ablutions fountain *(şadırvan)* was used by worshippers for ritual washing.

Prayer hall *(cami)*

The *han* or *kervansaray* *(see pp28–9)* provided accommodation for travellers.

A mausoleum *(türbe)* was built for the founder of the mosque.

The kitchen *(imaret)* catered for mosque officials, students, the sick and the poor.

Hospital *(darüşşifa)*

Colleges *(medreses)* for general and theological education were built adjacent to the mosque. Most now serve other uses.

Plan of a typical Mosque Complex (Külliye)

The külliye *was a charitable foundation as well as a place of worship. This example forms part of the Süleymaniye Mosque* (see pp104–5) *in Istanbul. A typical* külliye *had a school, hospital, Islamic study halls,* kervansaray *(lodgings for travellers), public soup kitchen and bathhouse.*

Inside a Mosque

The prayer hall of a great mosque can offer visitors a soaring sense of space. Islam forbids images of living things (human or animal) inside a mosque, so there are never any statues or figurative paintings, but the geometric and abstract architectural details of the interior can be exquisite. Men and women pray separately. Women often use a screened-off area or a balcony.

The *müezzin mahfili* is a platform found in large mosques. The muezzin (mosque official) stands on this when chanting responses to the prayers of the imam (head of the mosque).

The *mihrab*, a niche in the wall, marks the direction of Mecca. The prayer hall is laid out so that most people can see the mihrab.

The *minbar* is a lofty pulpit to the right of the mihrab. This is used by the imam when he delivers the Friday sermon (*khutba*).

Muslim Beliefs and Practices

Muslims believe in God (Allah), and the Koran shares many prophets and stories with the Bible. However, whereas for Christians Jesus is the son of God, Muslims hold that he was just one in a line of prophets – the last being Mohammed, who brought the final revelation of God's truth to mankind. Muslims believe that Allah communicated the sacred texts of the Koran to Mohammed through the archangel Gabriel.

Muslims have five basic duties. The first of these is the profession of faith: "There is no God but Allah, and Mohammed is his Prophet". Muslims are also enjoined to pray five times a day, give alms to the poor and fast during the month of Ramazan *(see p40)*. Once during their lifetime, if they can afford it, they should make the pilgrimage *(haj)* to Mecca (in Saudi Arabia), the site of the Kaaba, a sacred shrine built by Abraham, and also the birthplace of the Prophet.

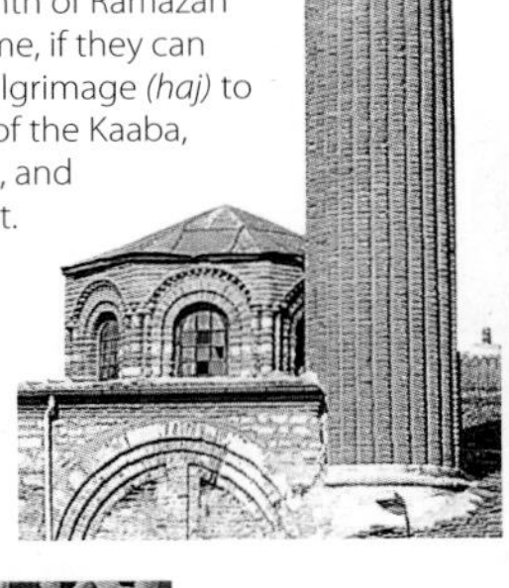

The call to prayer used to be given by the *muezzin* from the balcony of the minaret. Nowadays loudspeakers broadcast the call. Only imperial mosques have more than one minaret.

Prayer Times

The five daily prayer times are calculated according to the times of sunrise and sunset, and thus change throughout the year. Exact times are posted on boards outside large mosques. Those given here are a guide.

Prayer	Summer	Winter
Sabah	5am	7am
Öğle	1pm	1pm
İkindi	6pm	4pm
Akşam	8pm	6pm
Yatsi	9:30pm	8pm

When praying, Muslims face the Kaaba in Mecca, even if they are not in a mosque, where the *mihrab* indicates the right direction. Kneeling and lowering the head to the ground are gestures of humility and respect for Allah.

Ritual ablutions must be undertaken before prayer. Worshippers wash their head, hands and feet either at the fountain in the courtyard or at taps set in a wall of the mosque.

Visiting a Mosque

Visitors are welcome at any mosque in Turkey, but non-Muslims should avoid visiting at prayer times, especially the main weekly congregation and sermon on Fridays. Take off your shoes before entering the prayer hall. Shoulders and knees should be covered. In remote areas women should cover their head with a scarf, but main tourist mosques insist less on this. Do not eat, take photographs with a flash or stand very close to worshippers. A contribution to a donation box or mosque official is courteous.

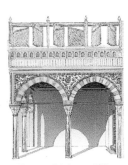

The *loge* *(hünkar mahfili)* provided the sultan with a screened-off balcony where he could pray, safe from would-be assassins.

The *kürsü*, seen in some mosques, is a throne used by the imam while he reads extracts from the Koran.

Board outside a mosque giving times of prayers

TURKEY THROUGH THE YEAR

Turkey's national and regional holidays fall into three categories: religious feasts celebrated throughout the Islamic world, festivities associated with events or people in Turkish history, and traditional festivals, usually with a seasonal theme. The joyful spirit is tangible on public holidays and religious feast days, when old and young, rich and poor unite and extended families gather. Regional events celebrate Turkey's diverse origins in terms of music, folklore, sport and the performing arts. Urban centres like İzmir and Istanbul host well-publicized festivals, but smaller towns also stage lively celebrations. *Luna park* (fun fairs) are popular. The passage of the seasons is important, as many venues are outdoors. In the eastern provinces, harsh winters restrict the types of events that can be staged.

Spring

This is the best season for visiting Turkey. Temperatures are comfortable and the days longer and warmer. Many places are spruced up after winter and restaurants arrange their tables outdoors. This is also the time to see Turkey's wild flower displays. Most tourist attractions, such as the historic sights, are far less crowded and thus more peaceful at this time of year.

March

International Film Festival *(late Mar–mid-Apr)*, Istanbul. Various cinemas in the city screen a selection of Turkish and foreign films.

April

Tulip Festival *(Apr–May)*, Emirgan, Istanbul. This two-week-long festival sees over 15 million bulbs planted across the city. The best places to admire the blooms include Emirgan Park and Gülhane Park.

Tulips in Emirgan Park, part of the Tulip Festival in spring

Turkish children paying their respects to the memory of Atatürk

National Sovereignty and Children's Day *(23 Apr)*. Anniversary of the first Grand National Assembly that convened in Ankara in 1920. Children from all around Turkey commemorate the life of the revered Atatürk.

ANZAC Day *(24–25 Apr)*, Çanakkale and Gallipoli Peninsula *(see pp172–3)*. Representatives from Australia, New Zealand and Turkey commemorate the courage in battle displayed by both sides in World War I.

May

Yunus Emre Culture and Art Week *(6–10 May)*, Eskişehir *(see p261)*. A weeklong commemoration of the life and devotional love poetry of the 13th-century mystic, Yunus Emre.

Marmaris International Yachting Festival *(2nd week in May)*, at Marmaris *(see pp204–5)*. Mainly a convention for yacht owners, brokers and buyers, this event fills the marina with all kinds of vessels and is sure to appeal to anyone interested in yachting.

Memorial at Gallipoli

National Youth and Sports Day *(19 May)*. Celebrated all over the country, this event marks Atatürk's birthdate in 1881 and the anniversary of his arrival in the town of Samsun *(see p269)* in 1919 to plan the War of Independence.

Conquest of Istanbul *(29 May)*, Istanbul. The anniversary of Constantinople's capture by Sultan Mehmet the Conqueror in 1453.

Cirit Games *(May–Sep; see September p40)*.

Turkey's beaches, popular with locals and visitors in summer

Summer

Turks take their holidays seriously, and summer sees coastal areas of the Aegean and Mediterranean, in particular, crowded with university students and families on the move. Those city dwellers lucky enough to own a summer house usually move to the coast to escape the oppressive heat when the school holidays begin in June.

Turkey's beaches offer opportunities for all kinds of activities, and resorts such as Bodrum and Marmaris are renowned for their active nightlife. Be on the lookout for impromptu festivals involving grease-wrestling or folk dancing, for example. Although local tourist offices have information on events in their area, these may not be well publicized and full details may be unavailable until just prior to the event.

June

Kaş-Lycia Culture and Art Festival *(first week Jun)*, Kaş. Three days of contemporary dance and theatre held at various venues in the town. There is also an international swimming race to the nearby Greek island of Meis.

Kafkasör Culture and Arts Festival *(second week Jun)*, Artvin *(see p279)*. A festival in an alpine meadow that offers country handicrafts, folk dancing and singing, as well as bull wrestling.

Istanbul Music Festival *(mid-Jun–mid-Jul)*, venues around the city. A prestigious event for opera, theatre and ballet performances. Both Turkish and Western classical music are featured and the highlight is a one-night performance of Mozart's *Abduction from the Seraglio*, which is authentically staged at the Topkapı Palace.

Grease-wrestling tournament

Kırkpınar Festival and Grease Wrestling Championship *(last week Jun)*, Edirne *(see pp158–9)*. A popular event with men, in which the contenders, in *kıspet* (leather breeches) and smeared with olive oil, compete for the coveted honour in this traditional national sport.

International Opera and Ballet Festival poster, Aspendos

International Opera and Ballet Festival *(Jun–mid-Sep)*, Aspendos *(see p225)*. The Roman amphitheatre is the venue for thrilling, open-air performances of opera, ballet and orchestral music. Visitors can also enjoy a picnic at the site before performances.

July

Navy Day *(1 Jul)*. This holiday has some symbolism for Turks as it commemorates the anniversary of the end of the capitulations, or trade concessions, granted by the Ottoman sultans to a number of European powers from the mid-16th century onwards.

International Hittite Festival *(first week Jul)*, Çorum *(see pp298–9)*. Students of Hittite art and culture and enthusiasts from around the globe gather for this annual event to attend lectures, debates and related outings.

Istanbul Jazz Festival *(first two weeks Jul)*, Istanbul. An eclectic programme of jazz, world music, soul and R&B performances takes place at venues across the city.

August

Troy Festival *(10–15 Aug)*, Çanakkale *(see p178)*. Dance, theatre and art events that attract foreign performers.

Hacı Bektaş Commemorative Ceremony *(mid-Aug)*, Avanos *(see p287)*. Annual ceremony held in remembrance of Hacı Bektaş Veli, the mystic and philosopher who founded an Islamic sect based on the principles of unity and human tolerance.

International İzmir Festival *(last week Aug–early Sep)*, İzmir *(see pp182–3)*. An excellent programme for connoisseurs of music, ballet and theatre. Some performances also take place at Çeşme and Ephesus.

Victory Day *(30 Aug)*. This day, known as Zafer Bayramı, is celebrated throughout Turkey. It celebrates the victory of the Turkish Republican army over the Greeks at the battle of Dumlupınar in 1922 during the War of Independence.

Racing yachts competing in Marmaris Race Week

Autumn

Autumn is an ideal time for visiting Turkey. The rural regions have grape or wine festivals and many villages celebrate their successful harvests of wheat, apricots, cotton or other crops. In coastal regions, the sea is still warm and watersports can continue well into October. Along the south coast, warm weather can last until quite late in November.

September

Cirit Games *(May–Sep)*, Erzurum *(see pp322–3)*. Cirit originated with nomads from Central Asia. It is a rough-and-tumble cross between polo and javelin-throwing in which horse and rider enjoy equal prestige. The games take place every Sunday.

Horse and rider at the Cirit Games in Erzurum

Tango Festival *(second week in Sep)*, Marmaris *(see pp204–5)*. A popular six-day event in which couples follow the lead of professional dance couples.

Watermelon cart, Diyarbakır

Watermelon Festival *(16–23 Sep)*, Diyarbakır *(see pp314–15)*. One of only a few festivals in eastern Turkey, this one focuses on the gigantic watermelons grown by the local farmers.

Cappadocia Grape Harvest Festival *(mid-Sep)*, Ürgüp *(see p287)*. Celebration of local food and wine in an area that has been called the birthplace of viticulture.

Istanbul Biennial *(mid-Sep–Nov)*, Istanbul *(see pp64–149)*. This major international arts event is held on odd years at various locations across the city. The next Biennial will be held in 2017.

October

Golden Orange Film Festival *(second week Oct)*, Antalya *(see pp222–3)*. Turkey's premier film festival, established in the 1960s, screens both domestic and international films at a number of cinemas and cultural venues across the city.

International Bodrum Cup Regatta *(third week of Oct)*, Bodrum *(see pp202–3)*. This regatta is open to several classes of wooden yachts only. Both Turkish and foreign yachtsmen compete.

Race Week *(last week Oct to first week Nov)*, Marmaris *(see pp204–5)*. Inland and offshore races held in three divisions under authority of the Turkish Sailing Federation. There is also a fancy-dress night, and cocktail and dinner parties.

Republic Day *(29 Oct)*. This important national holiday commemorates the proclamation of the Turkish Republic in 1923.

November

Atatürk Commemoration Day *(10 Nov)*. Atatürk's death in 1938 is recalled each year with a poignant one-minute silence. This show of respect is observed throughout the country at 9:05am, the exact moment the revered leader passed away in Istanbul's Dolmabahçe Palace. Everything in the country grinds to a halt – people, and even the traffic stops.

Muslim Holidays

The dates of the Muslim calendar and its holy days are governed by the phases of the moon and therefore change from year to year. In the holy month of **Ramadan**, Muslims do not eat or drink between dawn and dusk. Some restaurants are closed during the day and tourists should be discreet when eating in public. Straight after this follows the three-day **Şeker Bayramı** (Sugar Festival), when sweetmeats are prepared. Two months and 10 days later, a four-day celebration, **Kurban Bayramı** (Feast of the Sacrifice), commemorates the Koranic version of Abraham's sacrifice. This is the main annual public holiday in Turkey, and hotels, trains and roads are packed.

Whirling Dervishes at the Mevlevi Monastery in Istanbul

Winter

When the street vendors begin roasting chestnuts in Ankara and Istanbul, it is a sign that winter is near. Both cities can be damp and cold. Ankara frequently has temperatures below freezing and gets a lot of snow. This is when coastal regions have their rainy season. Winter is a good time for visitors to explore Turkey's museums, as major sights are open and uncrowded. The ski centres *(see p372)* at Palandöken *(see p323)* and Uludağ *(see p163)* have their busiest season from December to April, and offer activities both on and off the slopes.

Turks do not celebrate Christmas, but most hotel chains offer a special menu on the day. New Year's Day, however, is an official holiday throughout Turkey.

It is celebrated heartily in restaurants and at home, and a lavish meal is served. Often Christmas trees are decorated. Visitors are always welcome to join in these celebrations, but advance booking is advisable for popular places. Some establishments that close for the winter open again just for the New Year's Eve celebrations.

December

St Nicholas Symposium and Festival *(first week Dec)*, Demre *(see p220)*. Visitors who have an interest in the legend of Santa Claus will not want to miss this symposium and the discussions and ceremonies that accompany it. A host of related debates is organized, and pilgrimages are made to the 4th-century church of St Nicholas in Demre, located near Antalya, and to the birthplace of Nicholas in Patara, near Kaş.

Mevlâna Festival *(10–17 Dec)*, Konya *(see pp254–5)*. A festival that commemorates Celaleddin Rumi *(see p259)*, the mystic who founded the Mevlevi order. This is the only time that the whirling dervishes are in residence in their home city and offers one of the best performances anywhere in Turkey.

New Year's celebrations in Istanbul

January

New Year's Day *(1 Jan)*. A national holiday.

Camel Wrestling *(mid-Jan)*, Selçuk *(see p184)*. Premier championship event held in the ruined Roman theatre at Ephesus *(see pp186–7)*.

February

Camel Wrestling *(through Feb)*, Aydın, İzmir and other Aegean towns. Impromptu camel wrestling bouts *(deve güreşi)* that coincide with the mating season (Dec–Feb), after which male camels become docile again.

A champion camel, adorned with tassels and rugs

National Holidays

New Year's Day (1 Jan)

National Sovereignty and Children's Day *Ulusal Egemenlik ve Çocuk Bayramı* (23 Apr)

Labour and Solidarity Day *Emek ve Dayanışma Günü* (1 May)

National Youth and Sports Day *Gençlik ve Spor Günü* (19 May)

Navy Day *Denizcilik Günü* (1 Jul)

Victory Day *Zafer Bayramı* (30 Aug)

Republic Day *Cumhuriyet Bayramı* (29 Oct)

Atatürk Commemoration Day (10 Nov)

The Climate of Turkey

Turkey's mountainous terrain and maritime influence have created diverse climatic regions. The Aegean and Mediterranean coasts enjoy mean temperatures of 29°C (84°F) in July and 9°C (48°F) in January. Rain falls mainly in winter; Antalya receives an annual average of 991 mm (39 in). Along the Black Sea, rainfall is heavier, averaging 2,438 mm (96 in) a year. The rugged northeast has warm summers, but severe winters, with temperatures averaging −9°C (16°F). Precipitation is more evenly spread throughout the year, and snow lasts 120 days. The central plateau has hot, dry summers averaging 23°C (73°F), and cold, moist winters, when temperatures average below 0°C (32°F).

ISTANBUL

month	Apr	Jul	Oct	Jan
°C	17	29	20	9
	9	20	14	4
	6 hrs	10 hrs	5 hrs	2 hrs
	53 mm	21 mm	68 mm	83 mm

THRACE AND THE SEA OF MARMARA

month	Apr	Jul	Oct	Jan
°C	17	29	20	9
	9	20	14	4
	6 hrs	10 hrs	5 hrs	2 hrs
	53 mm	21 mm	68 mm	83 mm

THE AEGEAN

month	Apr	Jul	Oct	Jan
°C	21	33	24	12
	11	23	15	6
	7 hrs	12 hrs	7 hrs	4 hrs
	48 mm	2 mm	45 mm	119 mm

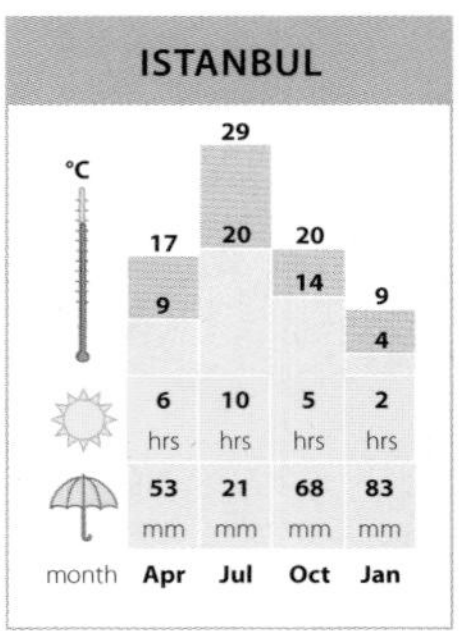

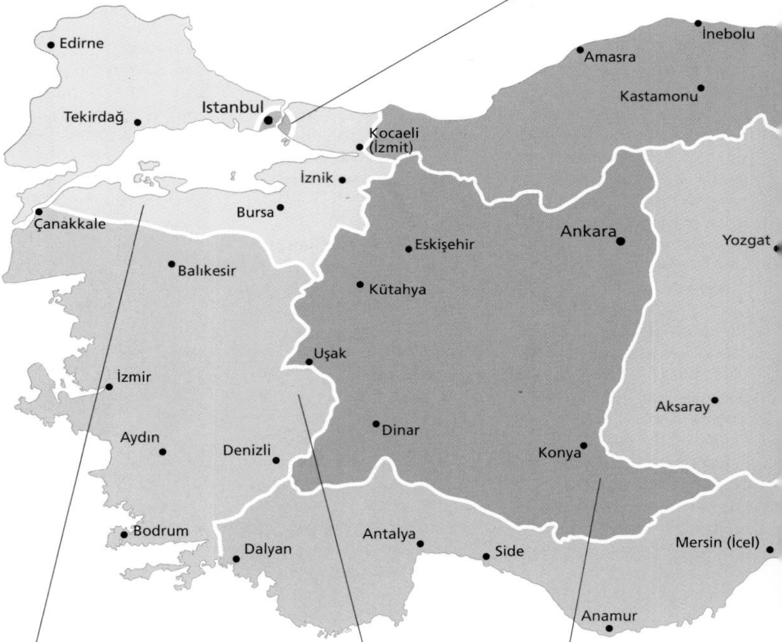

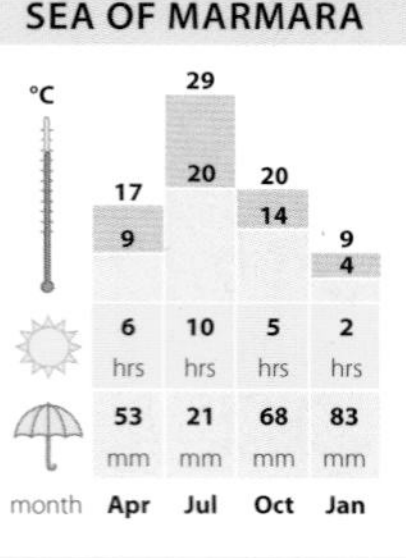

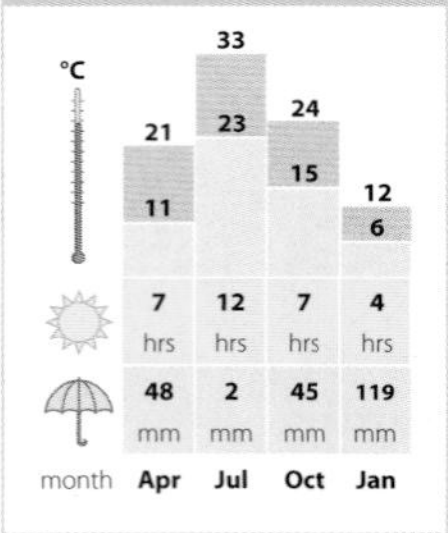

ANKARA AND WESTERN ANATOLIA

month	Apr	Jul	Oct	Jan
°C	17	30	20	4
	6	16	7	−3
	6 hrs	11 hrs	7 hrs	3 hrs
	49 mm	15 mm	30 mm	42 mm

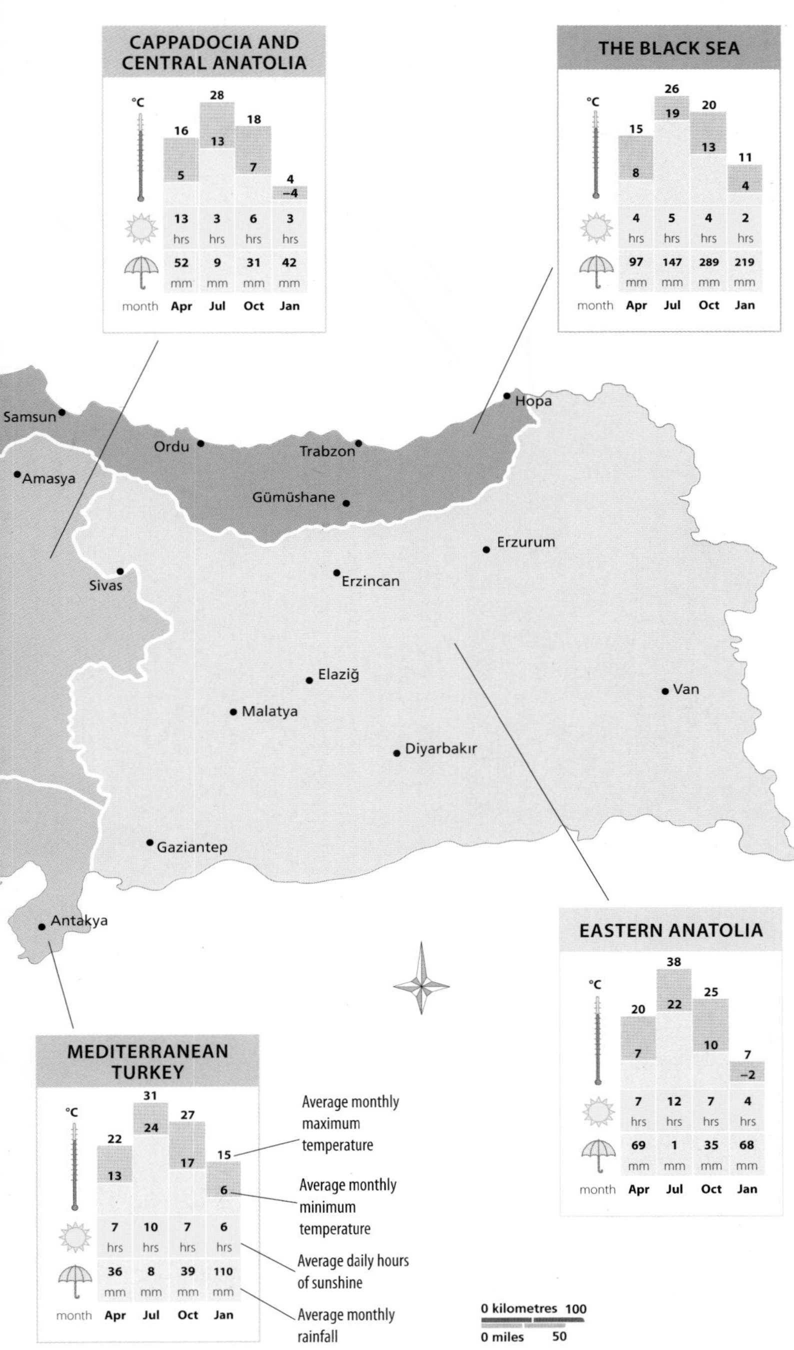
CAPPADOCIA AND CENTRAL ANATOLIA
°C
16
5
28
13
18
7
4
–4
13 hrs
3 hrs
6 hrs
3 hrs
52 mm
9 mm
31 mm
42 mm
month
Apr
Jul
Oct
Jan
THE BLACK SEA
°C
15
8
26
19
20
13
11
4
4 hrs
5 hrs
4 hrs
2 hrs
97 mm
147 mm
289 mm
219 mm
month
Apr
Jul
Oct
Jan
Samsun
Ordu
Trabzon
Hopa
Amasya
Gümüshane
Erzurum
Sivas
Erzincan
Elaziğ
Van
Malatya
Diyarbakır
Gaziantep
Antakya
EASTERN ANATOLIA
°C
20
7
38
22
25
10
7
–2
7 hrs
12 hrs
7 hrs
4 hrs
69 mm
1 mm
35 mm
68 mm
month
Apr
Jul
Oct
Jan
MEDITERRANEAN TURKEY
°C
22
13
31
24
27
17
15
6
7 hrs
10 hrs
7 hrs
6 hrs
36 mm
8 mm
39 mm
110 mm
month
Apr
Jul
Oct
Jan
Average monthly maximum temperature
Average monthly minimum temperature
Average daily hours of sunshine
Average monthly rainfall
0 kilometres 100
0 miles 50

THE HISTORY OF TURKEY

The history of Turkey is as ancient as that of humankind. Known as Anatolia and previously as Asia Minor, this land has witnessed the rise and fall of many great and advanced civilizations, from the early Hittites to the Persians, Lydians, Greeks, Romans, Byzantines and Ottomans. A singular heritage of splendid art and architecture bears the mark of an often tumultuous past.

Long before great empires such as the Persian, Roman, Byzantine and Ottoman began to exploit the strategic position of Asia Minor, important ancient civilizations flourished in the fertile river valleys, on the windswept, arid interior plains and along the southern coastline of Anatolia. The early communities were replaced by successive waves of migration that saw the rise and fall of new cultures, each of which left reminders of its dominance and glory and contributed to the astoundingly varied cultural tapestry that forms the basis of today's proud, modern republic.

Prehistoric Turkey

The Old Stone Age tools, crude artifacts, animal bones and food fossils found near Burdur, north of Antalya *(see pp222–3)*, prove that people have lived in Turkey since at least 20,000 BC. The earliest inhabitants were nomadic hunter-gatherers who migrated in response to changing weather patterns and seasons. They followed the wild animal herds they depended upon for their sustenance, clothing, tools and weapons.

The Fertile Crescent

The earliest settlers were the hunter-gatherer communities of Mesopotamia, living in the well-watered stretch of land between the Tigris and Euphrates rivers in what is now northern Syria and Iraq. One of the world's most remarkable archaeological sites, Göbekli Tepe *(see p312)*, challenged the theory that only settled farming communities were capable of monumental works of art.

By 8,000 BC the hunter-gatherers had learned to cultivate crops of wheat, barley and legumes and thus lead more settled lives. They also kept domestic animals and used dogs to protect and herd their livestock. These early farmers were the first to venture beyond the boundaries of the Fertile Crescent, establishing communities along the Mediterranean and Red Sea, as well as around the Persian Gulf. Here, the archaeological remains of Neolithic villages date back to 8000 BC, and by 7000 BC countless thriving settlements had sprung up.

It was during this period that people discovered how to smelt metal and work with it. They developed methods of extracting and casting various useful weapons and ornamental items. The earliest items cast from copper were made in Anatolia around 5000 BC.

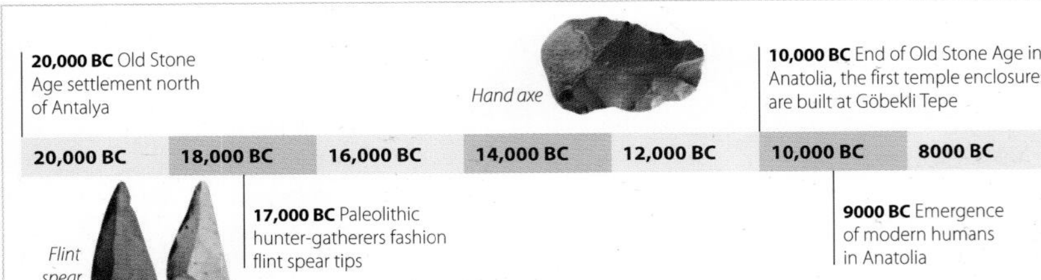
20,000 BC Old Stone Age settlement north of Antalya
Hand axe
10,000 BC End of Old Stone Age in Anatolia, the first temple enclosures are built at Göbekli Tepe
20,000 BC
18,000 BC
16,000 BC
14,000 BC
12,000 BC
10,000 BC
8000 BC
Flint spear tips
17,000 BC Paleolithic hunter-gatherers fashion flint spear tips
9000 BC Emergence of modern humans in Anatolia

◀ Constantine IX Monomachus, ruler of the Byzantine Empire from 1042 to 1055

The First Town

Together with Hacılar, Çatalhöyük *(see p258)* near Konya was possibly the world's first town. It had a population of around 5,000 people and is thought to have been the largest settlement at the time. Most of its inhabitants were farmers, but there was also brisk trade in obsidian (volcanic glass), brought into workshops from nearby volcanoes and used to fashion sharp cutting tools.

Archaeologists have been able to determine with certainty that Çatalhöyük's houses were sturdy structures built of brick and timber. The architectural designs also reflect the demands of an advanced culture that valued comfort. They typically feature separate living quarters and cooking areas, as well as several sheds and a number of storerooms.

Cattle seem to have played a rather important part in this ancient culture of Anatolia. This is evident from the fact that many of the rooms that were excavated at Çatalhöyük were decorated with elaborate wall paintings depicting cows, as well as clay heads with real horns moulded in relief onto the walls. Since Çatalhöyük's people had animistic beliefs, it has been suggested that the murals and bull's-head emblems could point to the practice of ritual or cult activities. Similarly, small terracotta figurines of a voluptuous female deity (the mother goddess) probably played a part in fertility rites, offerings or other religious ceremonies.

The Copper Age

By the Copper Age (from about 5500 to 3000 BC), farming had become a way of life and people were raising crops and animals for a living. The increase in agricultural activity created a growing need for tools and implements. Methods for ore extraction and smelting were refined and passed on from father to son. Copper implements were widely used. Focal points of this period were Hacılar and Canhasan, both of which also manufactured fine pottery items, using advanced techniques. Their attractive clay vessels were decorated with distinctive multicoloured backgrounds.

Flint dagger with bone handle

The Bronze Age

Between 3000–1200 BC, the Anatolian metalworkers began to experiment with various techniques and developed new skills. Their workshops produced a surplus of goods and a brisk trade began to flourish. Among these items were gold jewellery, ornaments, belts, drinking vessels and statuettes of the mother goddess.

Artist's impression of Çatalhöyük, possibly the world's first town

8000 BC Start of the Neolithic period in Anatolia

Statuette of mother goddess, Çatalhöyük

5600 BC Fertility figurines made of terracotta at Hacılar and Çatalhöyük

8000 BC | **7000 BC** | **6000 BC** | **5000 BC**

7250–7500 BC Community at Çayönü near Diyarbakır farms with sheep and goats

6800 BC Çatalhöyük develops into a farming town of 5,000 people

Terracotta jar from Canhasan

5000 BC Pottery begins to combine functionality with attractive design

The Assyrians

The empire of Assyria developed in northern Mesopotamia sometime in the 3rd millennium BC. It expanded and, by about 1900 BC, a network of Assyrian trading colonies had been established. Commerce between northern Mesopotamia and Anatolia began to take shape.

As trade goods circulated, the demand for them quickly grew and merchants found themselves catering to a rapidly expanding market.

The Assyrians grasped the importance of keeping track of their transactions, and developed a writing system using cuneiform symbols to represent words. Their trade agreements and accounts were imprinted on clay tablets, several of which have been preserved. The commercial records that were found at the Assyrian trading colony at Kanesh (modern Kültepe, *see p295*) are the earliest examples of writing to have been discovered in Anatolia.

Assyrian clay "letter" and envelope

Lively trade meant increased travel and demands on transport. Some areas saw the introduction of simple taxation systems. For the first time in history, money came to be regarded as the primary source of wealth, and envy, conflict and violence ensued as communities sought to protect territories, routes and resources from outsiders.

Not all inhabitants of the area presently occupied by Turkey gathered in central Anatolia. The city of Troy, immortalized by Homer and Virgil, stood at the strategic entrance to the Dardanelles Straits *(see p172)*. Some scholars believe that the fall of Troy, as told in Homer's *Iliad*, coincides with the end of the Bronze Age, an era that had helped to establish an artistic and civilized culture in which the next civilization, the Hittites, would thrive and flourish.

Helen of Troy

According to Greek mythology, Helen was the most beautiful woman of the ancient world. She was the daughter of King Tyndareus and Leda, who had been seduced by Zeus. In childhood, Helen was abducted by Theseus, who hoped to marry her when the time came. After having been rescued by her twin brothers Castor and Pollux, King Tyndareus decreed that Helen should marry the man of her choice. Helen chose Menelaus, king of Sparta, and lived happily at his side until she met Paris. Her elopement with the Trojan prince resulted in a heated battle between Greece and Troy as Menelaus fought to free his wife. After nine years of futile warfare Menelaus and Paris agreed to meet in single combat. Paris died as a result of his wounds; the victorious Menelaus reclaimed his Helen and returned with her to Sparta, where they lived happily to an old age.

Helen of Troy with Paris, depicted in a 1631 painting by Guido Reni

4000–3000 BC Settlement at Alacahöyük flourishes

Gold cup, Alacahöyük

4000 BC

3900 BC Cities begin to emerge and a simple form of writing develops

3000 BC Beginning of Bronze Age in Anatolia; Troy, Ephesus and Smyrna become important cities

3000 BC

2500 BC Hatti civilization establishes city kingdoms

1900–2000 BC Arrival of Hittites from the Caucasus; rise of Hittite empire

1900 BC Brisk trade by Assyrian trading colonies

2000 BC

Assyrian cylinder seal made of serpentine

The Hittites

Historians are uncertain about the origins of the Hittites and how they got to Anatolia. It is clear that they arrived some time before the second millennium BC and were established at the time of the Assyrian trading colonies. Theirs was the first powerful empire to arise in Anatolia. Its capital was at Hattuşaş, present-day Boğazkale *(see pp300–1)*.

The Hittite language, which was written in both cuneiform script and hieroglyphics, is believed to be the oldest of the Indo-European languages and was deciphered only in 1915. Large collections of Hittite writings were discovered at Hattuşaş. They contained cuneiform texts on various subjects, such as religious rituals, omens, myths and prayers, as well as royal annals, state treaties and diplomatic letters. Religion and appeasing the gods played an important role in Hittite life. They worshipped the "Thousand Gods of the Land of Hatti", an impressive pantheon of semitic deities, chief among whom were the Weather or Storm god, and his wife, the Sun goddess.

An advanced people, Hittites knew the art of forging iron, an advantage that made them a powerful military force.

Carved reliefs on the Sphinx Gate at Alacahöyük

Their cuneiform texts also revealed a complex legal system and their remarkably fair treatment of criminals and prisoners.

King Anitta conquered large parts of central Anatolia, including the Assyrian trading colony at Kanesh. His conquests increased the might of the kingdom, but also led to decentralization. The empire splintered into several city-states, until King Huzziya began to reunite the independent elements and fought to regain parts of Anatolia.

Remains of Hittite relief, Boğazkale

One of King Huzziya's successors, Labarna Hattushili I, is considered to be the founder of the Old Hittite Empire. He had his eye on wealthy Syria, then an important centre of trade, crafts and agriculture, and in an effort to annex its city-states he began to extend his campaigns into northern Syria. One of his grandsons finally managed to conquer Babylon around 1530 BC, but the constant wars made expansion difficult, and in general Hittite rulers repeatedly gained, lost and regained territories throughout the duration of their empire.

Golden Age of the Hittites

The Hittite empire reached its peak in 1259 BC, when Hattushili III and Ramses II, the ruler of Egypt, signed an agreement of peace and friendship. As a result of this treaty, Hittite culture could flourish and the city of Hattuşaş grew rapidly. The Hittite empire entered its Golden Age. Hattuşaş grew into a large city. It was surrounded by sturdy walls and had an impressive temple and palace complex. The columns of the royal palace were supported on bases in

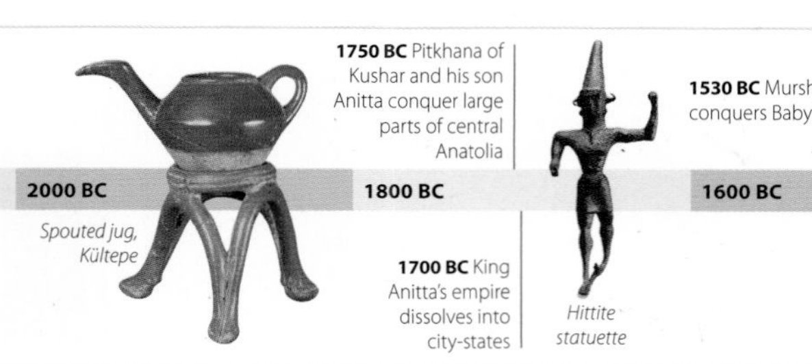

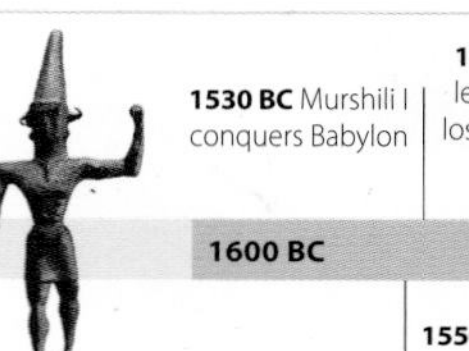

1750 BC Pitkhana of Kushar and his son Anitta conquer large parts of central Anatolia

1530 BC Murshili I conquers Babylon

1400 BC Disputes lead to temporary loss of control over northern Syria

2000 BC | **1800 BC** | **1600 BC** | **1400 BC**

Spouted jug, Kültepe

1700 BC King Anitta's empire dissolves into city-states

Hittite statuette

1550 BC Labarna Hattushili I establishes capital at Hattuşaş (present-day Boğazkale)

the shape of bulls and lions, while the city gates were decorated with elaborate relief sculptures of fantastic sphinxes and armed gods.

Relative peace and stability saw a flowering of Hittite culture. Elegant pottery items, metal figures, animal-shaped vessels and stamp seals bearing royal symbols were produced. They also collected the documents in cuneiform script that now provide valuable information about their culture for archaeologists. According to records written at the time, Hittite kingdoms flourished throughout Anatolia.

Croesus, the wealthy king of the Lydians

Decline of the Hittites

In the early 12th century BC, an indistinct group of maritime marauders knowns as the "Sea Peoples" migrated to the eastern Mediterranean, and the collapse of the Hittites is attributed to their warring tactics. Around 1205 BC, Mediterranean pirates harried the boundaries of the empire, while the empire was suffering under a terrible famine. Many people died or fled, leaving only vestiges of the former empire in Syria and southern Anatolia. The Assyrians used the sufferings of the Hittites to their advantage and incorporated many of their kingdoms. The remaining pieces of the former Hittite empire were occupied by the Phrygians, a Balkan tribe, who had invaded from the northwest.

Towards the Hellenistic Age

During the 7th century BC, Anatolia gradually became dominated by the Lydians, while the Lycian civilization flourished along the Mediterranean coastline. Their rock tombs *(see p219)* can still today be seen between Fethiye and Antalya *(see pp222–3)*.

The Lydians, a powerful Hittite-related tribe, settled in western Anatolia. Under the leadership of their king, Croesus, they conquered and annexed many Anatolian city-states around 700 BC. Renowned silversmiths, they are credited with the invention of coinage.

Lydian coin from 700 BC

In the meanwhile, the Ionian Renaissance saw a flowering of Greek culture and economy along the Aegean coast. Pioneers from Miletus *(see pp194–5)* established colonies along the shores of the Mediterranean and Black Sea. City-states such as Knidos and Halicarnassus flourished, setting the stage for the next act in Anatolia's history.

1274 BC War between Syria and Egypt

1200 BC

1259 BC War with Egypt ends with the first written peace treaty signed by Ramses II and Hittite king Hattushili III

1000 BC Urartians establish a state near Lake Van

1000 BC

Urartian gold button

Assyrian-influenced statue of King Tarhunza

800 BC

800 BC Phrygians rise to power in central and southeastern Anatolia

700 BC Remaining Hittite kingdoms annexed by Assyria

The Hellenistic Age

Eastward expansion of Greek influence, roughly between 330 BC and 132 BC, was led by Alexander the Great (356–324 BC). After the assassination of his father, Philip II of Macedon, the young Alexander first consolidated his position in Europe and then took on the might of the Persian Empire, which had absorbed most of Anatolia during the 5th century BC. He first invaded Anatolia and Phoenicia, proceeding on to Egypt and India, setting up cities and leaving garrisons behind as he went. In Anatolia, the new colonists soon became the ruling class and imposed laws to promote Hellenization.

Alexander's Empire

Alexander's campaigns

Pergamum
This artist's impression shows what the hilltop city would have looked like in 200 BC. It depicts the magnitude of Alexander's vision to create Pergamum as the perfect Greek city.

***Sarisses* (spears)** used by the Macedonian phalanx (battle formation) were 5.5 m (18 ft) long.

Alexander is on his stallion, Bucephalus.

Perge
The city of Perge, reputedly founded by two Greek seers after the Trojan War, welcomed Alexander the Great in 333 BC and gave him guides for his journey from Phaselis to Pamphylia.

The Battle at Issus

After campaigning in Asia Minor for just one year, Alexander won his first major battle. In November 333 BC, he and the Persian king, Darius III, clashed for the second time. At a mountain pass at Issus (near İskenderun), Macedonian troops managed to encircle the Persian cavalry. When Darius saw Alexander cut through his men and head straight for him, he fled the field, leaving his troops in disarray and his mother, wife and children as hostages. Victorious Alexander pressed on to Egypt and then across Persia to the Himalayas, until a mutiny by his exhausted soldiers in 324 BC forced him to turn back. He died of a sudden fever in Babylon the following year, at the age of 32.

Alexander Sarcophagus
Dating from the late 4th century BC, this sarcophagus is named after Alexander because he is depicted in the battle-scene friezes. The carvings are regarded as being among the most exquisite examples of Hellenistic art ever discovered.

Gold Octodrachma
This coin was minted by one of Alexander's successors, King Seleukos III of Syria, who ruled from 226 to 223 BC.

The Lycian Sarcophagus and Harpy Tomb at Xanthos
Xanthos was the chief city of ancient Lycia. Ravaged by the Persians around 540 BC, it was rebuilt and soon regained its former prominence. The Lycian sarcophagus and the Harpy Tomb shown here date from this period. Together with Pinara and many other Lycian cities, Xanthos surrendered to Alexander the Great in 334 BC.

Alexander and the Gordian knot

The Gordian Knot

Zeus, the father of the gods, had decreed that the people of Phrygia should choose as their king the first person to ride a wagon to his temple. The unlikely candidate, according to legend, was a peasant by the name of Gordius. Hardly able to believe his good fortune, the newly crowned king dedicated his wagon to Zeus, tying it to a pillar of the temple with an intricate knot. A subsequent oracle prophesied that the person who managed to untie it would become ruler of all Asia. That honour fell to Alexander the Great, who cheated the oracle by using his sword to cut the strands.

Rome Moves Eastward

The Roman Republic, established in central Italy around 500 BC, began a rapid expansion to the east during the 2nd century BC. After defeating their old enemies and rivals, the Carthaginians, the Roman armies defeated the Greeks at Corinth and Galatian forces in northern Anatolia. While the Romans were victorious in battle, the civilization of the Greeks in time exerted a great influence on Rome. This led the poet Horace to write *"Graecia capta ferum victorum cept"* (Greece took her fierce conqueror captive). Greek art and culture dominated the Roman way of life. The Romans even adopted Greek as lingua franca in their newly acquired territories east of the Adriatic Sea.

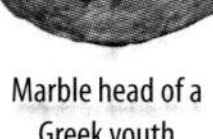
Marble head of a Greek youth

Roman rule brought the benefits of Roman civilization, such as law, better hygiene and civil engineering. As they advanced, Roman armies built impressive military roads. These were of vital importance for trade. At the height of the Roman empire, it was possible to travel from the Adriatic coast to Syria on well-constructed, wide stone roads. The Stadiusmus (guidepost) monument at Patara (near Kalkan), possibly erected by Claudius, displays an inventory of roads and distances throughout Lycia.

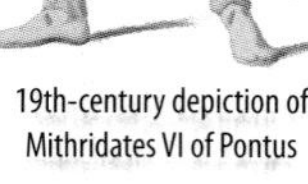
19th-century depiction of Mithridates VI of Pontus

Roman Expansion

The short-lived empire of Alexander the Great produced a number of successor states, including the Seleucid empire, which controlled much of Anatolia by the 2nd century BC. In two wars, known as the First and Second Macedonian Wars, Rome gained control of key city-states and kingdoms on the Mediterranean coast and in the Anatolian interior. Most submitted without resistance; others were simply handed over. King Attalus III of Pergamum, for example, simply left his kingdom to Rome in 133 BC when he realized that resistance was futile. Those who fought back, such as Mithridates VI of Pontus, were eventually defeated. But the wars against Mithridates marked the beginning of the turbulent Roman civil wars.

In 31 BC, Octavian, the nephew of Julius Caesar, emerged as victor of the civil wars. As a sign of its gratitude, the Roman Senate declared him emperor, and he was henceforth known as Augustus. Apart from extending the Roman territory and reorganizing the army, Octavian also established *colonia*, communal villages for retired soldiers. Examples of these can still be seen today, at Sagalassos and Antiocheia-in-Pisidia (near modern-day Eğirdir).

Roman Religion

The Romans worshipped an impressive array of gods. The greatest were Jupiter, his wife Juno, Minerva, the goddess of wisdom, and Mars, god of war. Apart from their own deities, the Romans also adopted those of the people they conquered, and allowed

Cyrus the Great

600 BC

560–546 BC King Croesus rules the Lydian empire

546 BC Sardis, captial of the Lydian Empire, is overthrown by the Persians under Cyrus the Great

400 BC

334 BC Alexander the Great claims Anatolian peninsula from the Persians

200 BC

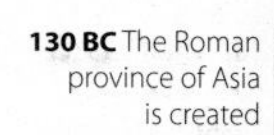
130 BC The Roman province of Asia is created

68 BC Pompey defeats the pirates

St Paul's Well in Tarsus

AD 1

AD 1 St Paul (Saul of Tarsus) born in Cilicia

Emperor Hadrian

AD 96–180 Five good emperors rule Rome

the local customs to continue. The people of Anatolia, therefore, continued to perform the fertility rites that were associated with the mother goddess, Cybele. Other, smaller sects and cults also flourished. Mithraism, originating with the Zoroastrian religion that was practised in Persia, was extremely influential, particularly among the soldiers of the Roman army. Many people, especially the poor, were drawn to the popular cult of the Egyptian god, Osiris.

Statuette of the Mother Goddess, Cybele

Five Good Emperors

By the 2nd century AD, peace and order again prevailed in Rome's outlying provinces. At home, the empire prospered under the rule of the "five good emperors" (Nerva, Trajan, Hadrian, Antonius Pius, and Marcus Aurelius with Lucius Verus). During this period of relative peace and prosperity, the Romans endowed their far-flung territories with countless sophisticated aqueducts and *nymphaea* (reservoir systems) to distribute fresh water and remove waste products. Theatres and council chambers were built, as were *stadia* and *gymnasia* to host the popular sporting events. When Emperor Hadrian (AD 117–138) toured the remote provinces, the delighted citizens of Attaleia (modern Antalya) *(see pp222–3)*, Termessos *(see p224)* and numerous other towns erected elaborate, beautiful memorial arches to honour the emperor and commemorate his visit.

Hadrian, one of the "five good emperors"

Christianity

St Paul, born Saul of Tarsus around AD 1, established the first churches in Asia Minor. Early Christian communities soon came into conflict with Roman authorities when they refused to make sacrifices to the emperor. However, all this changed in the 4th century AD, when Constantine, who ruled from AD 324 to 337, converted to Christianity. His conversion came about just before the Battle of the Milvian Bridge in AD 311, when he had a vision of a flaming cross inscribed with the words "in this sign, conquer".

In AD 324, Constantine founded the city of Constantinople (the site of modern-day Istanbul), and within six years had made it the capital and Christian centre of the empire. Massive walls enclosed its seven hills, and the emperor ordered the construction of a hippodrome, forum and public baths. Coastal cities were plundered for works of art to adorn the new capital, and new settlers were enticed by offers of bread and land. Constantine was succeeded by Theodosius, after whose death the empire was divided into two halves ruled by his sons, Arcadius and Honorius. The division sowed the seeds of Rome's eventual decline.

141 Major earthquake in southern Asia Minor

284–305 Diocletian divides the Roman Empire into east and west

311 Edict of tolerance towards Christianity

324 Constantine becomes sole ruler of the Roman Empire

330 Constantinople is founded by emperor Constantine

Constantine and his wife, Helen

Justinian

518 Dynasty of Justinian begins with the rule of Justin (518–527)

641 Constantine III, born Heraclonas in 626, becomes co-ruler at age 15

716 Treaty signed by Theodosius III and Bulgarian Khan Tervel establishes the border of Thrace

200 | 400 | 600 | 800

The Byzantine Empire

The Byzantine empire reached its height under Justinian (AD 527–65), who reconquered much of North Africa, Italy and southern Spain and initiated major building programmes, including the construction of the Haghia Sophia *(see pp86–7)*. Under his rule, Constantinople was endowed with beautiful palaces, churches and public buildings. In the 8th century, the empire became wracked by the iconoclastic dispute, which centred on the role of images in religious life, and its territory steadily shrank under pressure from Arab expansion and the influx of the Seljuk Turks.

Byzantine Empire

Extent in AD 565

Constantinople in 1200

For almost a thousand years, Constantinople was the richest city in Christendom. At its core were the church of Haghia Sophia, the Hippodrome (see p94) *and the Great Palace* (see pp96–7). *In 1204 a Crusader army sacked the city and carried off many of its treasures.*

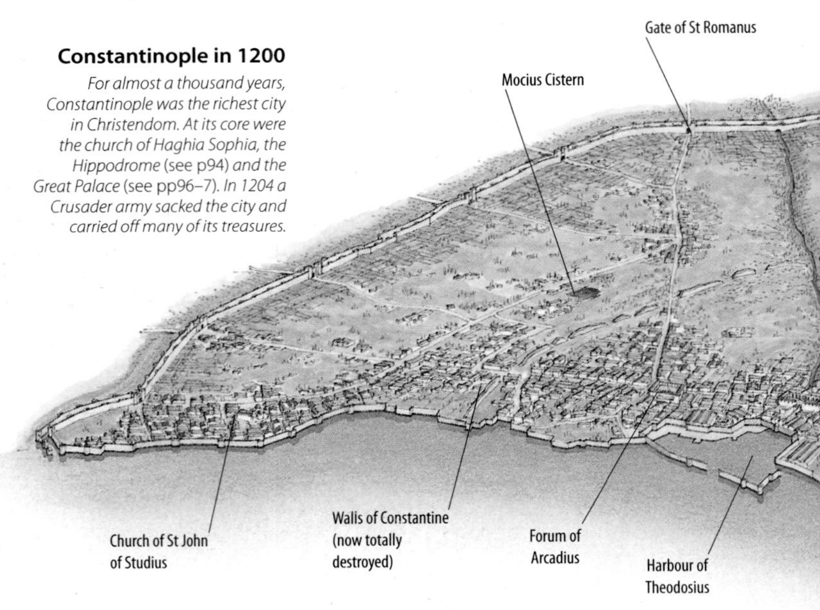
Gate of St Romanus
Mocius Cistern
Church of St John of Studius
Walls of Constantine (now totally destroyed)
Forum of Arcadius
Harbour of Theodosius

Byzantine Church Architecture

Early Byzantine churches were either basilical (such as St John of Studius, *see p120*) or built to a centralized plan (as in SS Sergius and Bacchus, *see p96*). From the 9th century, churches were built around four corner piers, or columns. Exteriors consisted mostly of unadorned brickwork, but the interiors were lavishly decorated with golden mosaics. Although the Ottoman sultans converted Constantinople's churches into mosques after their conquest of the city, many original features are still clearly discernible today.

Typical Late Byzantine Church

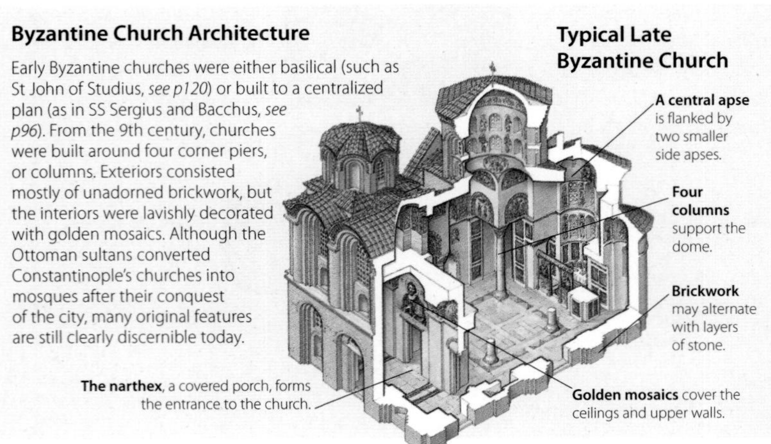
A central apse is flanked by two smaller side apses.
Four columns support the dome.
Brickwork may alternate with layers of stone.
Golden mosaics cover the ceilings and upper walls.
The narthex, a covered porch, forms the entrance to the church.

Walls of Theodosius
The land walls built by Theodosius II withstood many sieges until the Ottoman conquest in 1453.

"Greek Fire"
The Byzantines defended their shores using powerful ships called *dromons*, oared vessels from which "Greek fire" (an early form of napalm) could be directed at enemy vessels.

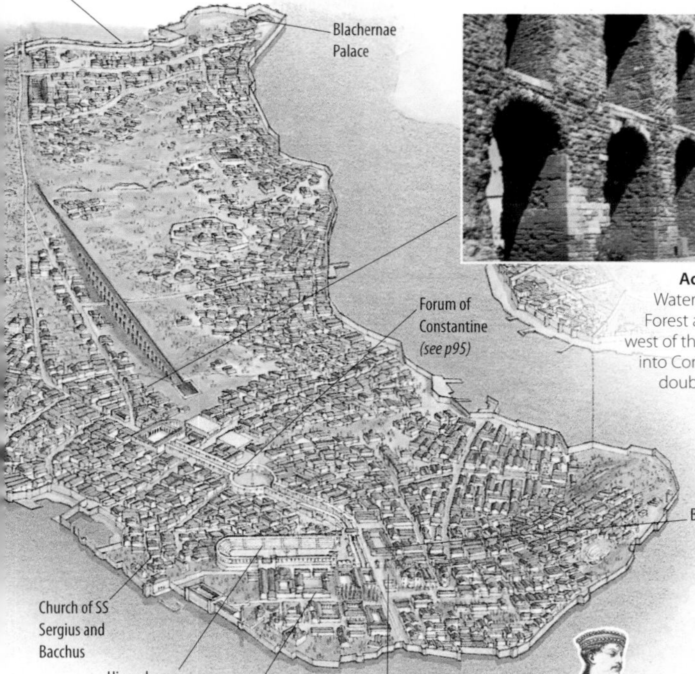

Blachernae Palace

Aqueduct of Valens
Water from the Belgrade Forest and the mountains west of the city was brought into Constaninople on this double-tiered structure.

Forum of Constantine *(see p95)*

Basilica Cistern *(see p90)*

Church of SS Sergius and Bacchus

Hippodrome *(see p94)*

Great Palace *(see pp96–7)*

Haghia Sophia
The great church *(see pp86–7)* blazed with mosaics, including this example showing Christ flanked by the Emperor Constantine IX and Empress Zoe.

Justinian and Theodora, who ruled the Byzantine Empire at its height

Origins of the Turks

The Turkish people are descended from tribes of Central Asian nomads, known as the Turkmen. In the 10th century, some of these tribes moved into Russia, China and India, while others began raiding Byzantine-ruled Anatolia. The attacks increased as the century progressed, until one group, the Seljuks, broke away and gradually began to move eastward.

Around the middle of the 11th century, the Seljuk Turks crossed the Oxus River and invaded Persia. Baghdad fell in 1055, and it was here that Seljuk leader Tuğrul Bey, was crowned caliph – ruler of the Islamic world. Tuğrul Bey established the powerful Great Seljuk Sultanate, which ruled much of the Islamic world from 1055 until 1156.

The Seljuk Rum Sultanate

Alp Arslan, nephew of Tuğrul Bey, succeeded him as sultan in 1063, and went on to occupy Syria and Armenia, and to launch various raids into Anatolia. In 1071, the Byzantines tried to defeat the Seljuks, but their army was destroyed at the Battle of Manzikert (Malazgirt) on 26 August 1071, a disaster which saw the capture of the emperor, Romanus IV Diogenes.

Romanus IV Diogenes (left), vanquished at Manzikert

Although the victorious Seljuks did not actively seek to govern Anatolia, the vacuum left by the Byzantine defeat resulted in the formation of a series of Islamic-Turkish states. The most famous of these states was the Seljuk Sultanate of Rum (1077–1308), initially based in Nicaea (modern İznik) *(seepp164–5).*

Seljuk manuscript depicting Aristotle and disciples

Other states established by the Seljuks were those of the Danışman at Sivas (1095–1175) and Saltuks (1080–1201) at Erzurum.

The period from the late 11th to late 12th century was one of turmoil in Anatolia. The arrival of the Crusaders, who seized Nicaea (modern-day İznik) in 1097, and then Antioch (modern Antakya) the following year, altered the balance of power drastically. The Crusader influence was especially pronounced in southern Anatolia, where Crusader knights established the Principality of Antioch and the County of Edessa (centred on modern-day Şanlıurfa). The Seljuks moved their capital to Konya, and the Byzantines tried once more to repel the Seljuks, only to be soundly defeated at the Battle of Myriocephalon in 1176.

Under the rule of Kılıç Arslan II (1156–92), the Seljuk Sultanate of Rum became the most powerful state in Anatolia. The capture of Antalya *(see pp222–3)* in 1207 gave access to the Mediterranean, and Seljuk Anatolia prospered. The capture of Sinop

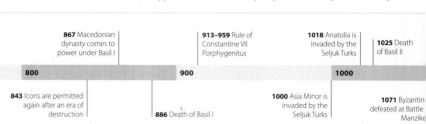

- **843** Icons are permitted again after an era of destruction
- **867** Macedonian dynasty comes to power under Basil I
- **800**
- **886** Death of Basil I
- **900**
- **913–959** Rule of Constantine VII Porphygenitus
- **1000** Asia Minor is invaded by the Seljuk Turks
- **1000**
- **1018** Anatolia is invaded by the Seljuk Turks
- **1025** Death of Basil II
- **1071** Byzantin defeated at Battle Manzike

Seljuk stone bridge near Aspendos

in 1214 secured trade across the Black Sea, and the capture of Alanya *(see p230)* in 1221 provided an additional boost to maritime trade.

Wealth and Prosperity

To consolidate their power, the Seljuks forged trade relations with other states signing agreements with Byzantium, Cyprus, Provence, Pisa, Venice, Florence and Genoa between 1207 and 1253. They constructed bridges to facilitate overland trade and built *hans* and *kervanserays* *(see pp28–9)* to provide shelter for travelling merchants and their goods.

The Seljuk empire was at its height under Sultan Malik Şah (1072–92), who generously patronized the arts and sciences. Yet the hallmark of Seljuk civilization was their architecture, which reached a peak in the 13th century. The hospital complex at Divriği *(see p323)*, harbour fortifications at Alanya, the Sultanhanı near Aksaray *(see pp28–9)* and the Karatay theological college in Konya *(see pp254–5)* were all built during this efflorescence. Under the Rum Seljuks, science and literature flourished, together with painting and sculpture. This cultural renaissance was partly caused by an influx of skilled and educated people fleeing the advance of the Mongols from the east.

Mongol Domination

In 1243 Mongol forces defeated the Seljuk army at Kösedağ, and until 1308 the Seljuk sultans were reduced to the status of vassals under the Mongols. During the 13th and 14th centuries, many Christians converted to Islam, because the Mongols offered reduced taxation for Muslims.

The Mongols ruled Anatolia until 1335, when the first Beylik states were set up by rebel Turkmen. These included the Karamanids in the Taurus highlands and the Danişmandids in central Anatolia. However, it was the small emirate of Ertuğrul, based in Eskişehir, that triumphed. Ertuğrul's son, Osman, founded a dynasty known as the Ottomans, and created one of the greatest empires the world has known.

Mongol archers attacking Seljuk cavalry

Crusader

1100–1400 Start of the Crusades, undertaken to liberate the Holy Land

1131 Sultan Mesut I establishes the Seljuk Rum sultanate with its capital at Konya

1176 Defeat of Byzantines at Myriocephalon

1200

1204 Constantinople is besieged, sacked and looted during the Fourth Crusade

1243 Mongol invasion of Anatolia

1299 Osman Bey establishes Ottoman principalities in Söğut and Domaniç

1300

1326 Ottoman armies capture Bursa; Orhan Bey is the first Ottoman ruler to call himself sultan

The Ottoman Empire

The expansion of the Ottoman lands accelerated during the late 13th century. A turning point was Mehmet II's capture of Constantinople in 1453. Constant wars advanced the imperial frontiers deep into the Balkans and the Middle East. Syria and Egypt fell in 1516–17, bringing the holy cities of Mecca and Medina under Ottoman control. By the mid-1500s the Ottoman sultan was the central figure of the (Sunni) Muslim world. The Ottoman Empire, though often associated with excessive opulence, was characterized also by its efficient administration, religious tolerance and immense military power.

Ottoman Empire

Maximum Extent (1566)

Osman I
The founder of the Ottoman dynasty ruled a small emirate on the frontiers of the declining Byzantine empire. Expansion of the Ottoman lands began under his son, Orhan.

The elite Janissaries *(see p60)* were professional soldiers.

Foot soldiers were often poorly trained auxiliaries.

Cannons were used in large numbers by the Ottoman armies.

The Fall of Constantinople
Constantinople, the last remnant of Byzantium, fell to the army of Mehmet II on 29 May 1453. This view shows the Turkish camp, and the bridge of boats built to cross the Golden Horn.

Mehmet II (The Conqueror)
The sultan safeguarded freedom of worship and successfully repopulated Constantinople.

Barbarossa
Regarded as a glorious Ottoman hero, and in 1533 admiral of the navy, to adversaries Barbarossa was a fearless corsair. Ottoman naval power was less invincible after his death.

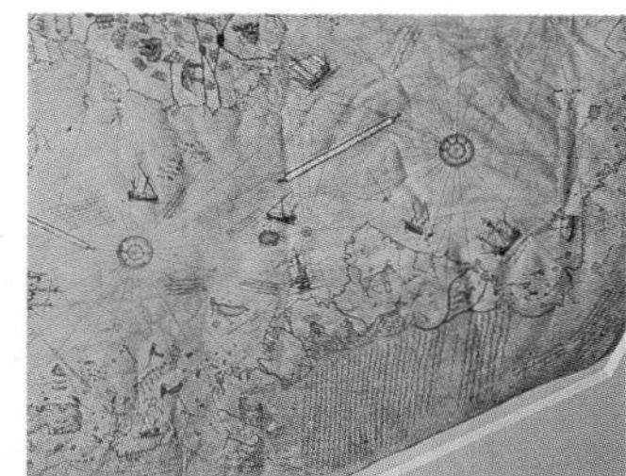

Ottoman Cartography
In 1521, the Ottoman admiral and cartographer Piri Reis drew on the accounts of Spanish and Portuguese explorers and captured sailors to compile a remarkable map of the world on gazelle hide.

Horses were held in high regard. The banner of the sultan's troops was a horsetail.

Ottoman soldiers were known for their skilful archery.

Sipahis fought on horseback.

Süleyman the Magnificent
One of the most enlightened sultans, Süleyman (1520–66) was a poet, lawmaker and patron of the arts. Art and architecture flourished during his prosperous rule.

The Battle Of Mohacs

At Mohacs, on 28 August 1526, Süleyman the Magnificent led an army of 200,000 against the forces of Louis II, the 14-year-old king of Hungary. The Hungarian forces were outmanoeuvred by the Janissaries (see p60) *and faltered under massed Ottoman artillery fire. Despite this great success, the expansion of the Ottoman empire into Europe came to an end after two unsuccessful sieges of Vienna in 1529 and 1532.*

The Battle of Lepanto, 1571
Ottoman sea power was fatally weakened after the defeat by Don John of Austria, commanding the fleet of the Holy League in the waters of the Gulf of Patros.

The Empire of Suleyman

The Ottoman Empire reached its zenith under the leadership of Sultan Süleyman the Magnificent (1520–66). It stretched from the borderlands of southern Hungary to Yemen, and from the Crimea to Morocco.

This advance was aided by well-organized administration, as well as military organization. A key practice was *devşirme*, which required rural Christian subjects to give one son to the service of the sultan. The boys converted to Islam and were educated to become civil servants or Janissaries (soldiers).

Members of the Janissary corps

Janissaries were subject to strict discipline, including celibacy, but could gain high-ranking privileges that were previously reserved for bureaucrats. An ambitious *kul* (slave) could attain powerful status. In fact, many grand viziers (prime ministers) were products of the *devşirme* system.

By the 18th century, however, the former elite corps had become a corrupt political power and a serious threat to the sultanate. Whenever the Janissaries felt that their privileges were under threat, they rioted violently and no-one dared to intervene.

Dolmabahçe Palace, a lavish display of opulence

Displays of Wealth

After Süleyman's death, the empire was ruled by a succession of mediocre sultans who concentrated on enjoying their riches rather than ruling their vast territories. Selim II (Selim the Sot) was known more for his fondness for wine than his interest in the affairs of state. Thus the empire became easy prey for the plotting and intrigue of the Janissaries, as well as the expansionist ambitions of other powers.

At the signing of the Treaty of Karlowitz in 1699, the empire lost half its European possessions. This marked the beginning of the empire's decline and opened the way for Russian advances in the Black Sea region. Long years of war followed, forcing the state to reorganize its finances.

Families that could afford to buy state land began to accumulate great personal wealth. In imitation of Sultan Ahmet III (1703–30), the elite built palaces on the Bosphorus, sported the latest European fashions and lived in luxury. Corruption and nepotism affected the entire empire, while its borders were constantly threatened. In 1730, an uprising in Istanbul overthrew Ahmet III. In short wars with Russia, Venice, Austria and Persia, the empire continued to lose territory.

Revival and Decline

A period of peace, from 1739 to 1768, produced an economic upswing and a brief artistic renaissance that saw the

1335 Beginning of the Beylik Period

1364 Sultan Orhan recaptures Edirne (Adrianople)

1397 The first Ottoman siege of Constantinople

1453 Constantinople falls to Mehmet II, the Conqueror, and is renamed Istanbul

Mehmet the Conqueror

1513 Piri Reis creates a map of the world

1533 Barbarossa becomes admiral of Ottoman fleet

1569 Great fire of Istanbul destroys much of the city

1300 | 1400 | 1500 | 1600

completion of the Nurosmaniye in 1755 – the first sultanic mosque complex built in Istanbul since that of Ahmet I in 1617. This interlude was shattered when Russian troops mobilized by Catherine the Great invaded the feeble Ottoman Empire. In two periods of war (1768–74 and 1788–91), the Russians gained access to the Black Sea and managed to annex the Crimean region. This was the first Muslim territory lost by the Ottomans and they were also forced to pay reparations to Russia.

In 1826, Mahmut II suppressed the Janissaries in a massacre known as the "Auspicious Event" and reorganized the bureaucracy in an effort to modernize the empire. Russia, meanwhile, encouraged Greece, Serbia, Moldavia and the Ottoman vassal state of Wallachia (in modern Romania) to demand self-rule. Mahmut II hoped that by passing the Tanzimat Reforms (1839 and 1856) he could ensure good government, equality for all and a stronger state. However, the edict of 1856, written under pressure from European powers after the disastrous Crimean War (1853–56) and based on Western-style, secular ideals, was greeted with indignation.

Portrait of the hero Sultan Abdül Hamit II

Russian troops fighting Turkish forces in the Caucasus in 1914

Times of War

In the 1870s, a reformist movement known as the Young Ottomans began to press for a constitutional monarchy. Sultan Abdül Hamit II enacted some liberal reforms, but dissolved the infant parliament in 1878 as the country entered a disastrous war with Russia.

During the next few years, further debilitating wars took place, gradually ensuring the independence of the Balkan provinces. In 1908, a rebellious group of officers formed the Committee of Union and Progress, dubbed the Young Turks. When Abdül Hamit II refused to accept a constitution, he was replaced by the weak Mehmet V, and the CUP took control.

In 1912 and 1913, the empire lost most of its remaining European possessions in the Balkan Wars. Greatly weakened, it slid into World War I a year later on the side of Germany and Austria-Hungary. The cost of the war in economic and human terms was immeasurable. By 1918, only the heartland of Anatolia remained of the Ottoman Empire. Foreign troops occupied Istanbul, İzmir, Antakya and Antalya. Turkish nationalists reacted by setting up an assembly in Ankara, but the ensuing war for independence set the seal on a Turkey that determined its own destiny.

648 Great arthquake f Istanbul

686 Ottomans are forced to evacuate Hungary

1699 Treaty of Karlowitz

1700

1740 Stirrings of dissent in Egypt

1807 Janissaries rebel against reforms to control their power

1800

1826 Mahmut II crushes the Janissaries in a brutal revolt

1840–55 Tanzimat reforms attempt to modernize and revive the Ottoman Empire

1881 Mustafa Kemal (later Atatürk) is born in Salonika

1900

1906 Early movement towards the Committee of Union and Progress (CUP)

Atatürk

The Treaty of Lausanne

Signatories at Lausanne, with Mussolini among them

The disastrous losses of World War I, and the subsequent occupation of parts of Turkey by powers such as Britain, France and Italy, fuelled Turkish nationalism. When Greek troops occupied İzmir on 15 May 1919 and pushed eastwards to Ankara, the seeds for war were sown. Turkish efforts met with little success until Mustafa Kemal, an army officer respected for his heroism during the Gallipoli campaign of 1915–16, assumed the leadership. At Nationalist congresses in Erzurum and Sivas in 1919, his ideas for the establishment of a Turkish republic aroused unanimous support.

Greek forces were routed by Nationalist forces in 1922 and Allied ambitions for power sharing in what remained of Ottoman territories faded. The Treaty of Lausanne (1923) recognized the borders and territories of the newly formed state, and the Turkish Republic was proclaimed the same year, with Ankara as the new capital city.

As part of the peace settlement and to underpin the framework for a cohesive Turkish state, Greece and Turkey agreed to exchange their ethnic populations. Around 1.25 million Greeks returned to Greece, and 450,000 Muslims were repatriated to Turkey. The impact of resettling such considerable numbers delayed the recovery of both countries after the war.

Ataturk's Vision

Mustafa Kemal's election as leader of the new state came as no surprise and he was, thereafter, known as Atatürk, father of the Turks. He greatly admired European lifestyles and culture and his forward-thinking ideas envisaged a modern, secular Turkish state. His aim was to establish a multi-party democracy with an opposition party. He instituted radical reforms and borrowed legal and social codes from other European countries. Ottoman scripts were replaced by the Latin alphabet and the new Turkish language. Dress codes changed and surnames were adopted. Schools and courts based on religious laws were abolished and, in 1928, a secular state underwritten by a civil constitution was recognized. Most Turks embraced democratic reform but some minorities, notably Kurds, who had been guaranteed land by Allied countries in

Atatürk demonstrating the Latin alphabet

1900 | **1910** | **1920** | **1930** | **1940** | **1950**

Turkish flag

1915–16 Gallipoli campaign

1923 First Constitution implemented with the formation of the Republic

1924 Caliphate abolished

1925–38 Atatürk introduces reforms destined to modernize Turkey

Atatürk memorial

1938 Atatürk dies

1950 Call to prayer returned to Arabic after 27 years in Turkish

1952 Turkey becomes a member of NATO

1960 First military coup

1961 Second Constitution of the Republic

World War I under the Treaty of Sèvres (1920), saw İslam and a chance for autonomy slipping away.

Building the State

Atatürk's founding doctrines gave Turks a distinct identity and set the seal on the indivisibility of the Turkish state. When Atatürk died in 1938, Turkey had an impressive infrastructure and state-run enterprises which satisfied basic needs. During World War II, Turkey pursued peaceful and friendly policies and remained neutral. The Truman Doctrine and Marshall Plan strengthened foreign policy and ties with the West. Turkey became a NATO member in 1952 and 5,500 Turkish troops fought in the Korean War (1950–54).

Veteran political leader Bülent Ecevit

Growing Pains

Turkey's military services, defenders of secularism and Atatürk's principles, intervened in 1960, 1971 and 1980 to restore law and order, with remote regions of Turkey remaining under martial law until the mid-1990s. During this period, civilian leaders such as Bülent Ecevit grappled with the challenges of political instability and economic modernization. The invasion of Cyprus by Turkey in 1974 left the island partitioned into Turkish and Greek sides. A Kurdish challenge for more self-expression slid into armed conflict, which continues despite the capture of the Kurdish Workers' Party leader Abdullah Öcalan in 1999.

Balancing political stability and the demands of a modern economic state often undermined democratic goals. However, when Turgut Özal became Prime Minister in 1983, he encouraged private enterprise, sought reconciliation with the Kurds and opened the country for investment and tourism.

Economic Miracle

In 2002, the pro-Islamic AKP (Justice and Development Party) was elected with a substantial majority. Their success in dealing with the economy ensured that they were re-elected in 2007, and then in 2011 for a record-breaking third term. Although many secular Turks are suspicious of the AKP's long-term Islamic goals, a major factor in the Gezi Park protests of 2013, their future seems stable given the country's healthy economy and divided political opposition. In 2014, Turkey was ranked a creditable 18th in the world in terms of GDP. Foreign investment continues to flood into the country, Istanbul has become a major financial centre and the country received around 38 million tourists in 2014. However, this growth is threatened by the crises unfolding in neighbouring Iraq and Syria. Trouble at Turkey's borders has the potential to deter both tourists and foreign investment in the country.

Folklore dancers in traditional dress

1970 | 1980 | 1990 | 2000 | 2010 | 2020

1971 Military coup

1978 Kurdish Workers' Party formed

1980 Military coup; third Constitution (1982)

NATO emblem

1991 As NATO partner, Turkey provides support for the US during the Gulf War

1996 Turkey enters European customs union, bringing potential trade advantages

1999 Earthquake shatters İzmit

2006 The new Turkish Lira (₺) becomes the country's official currency

2009 Arrests made over the Ergenekon plot to bring down the government

2010 A referendum aims to bring Turkish constitution in line with European Union standards

2011 Earthquake shakes Ercis and Van in eastern Turkey

2013 Gezi Park Protests

INTRODUCING ISTANBUL

Istanbul at a Glance	**66–67**
Seraglio Point	**68–81**
Sultanahmet	**82–97**
The Bazaar Quarter	**98–109**
Beyoğlu	**110–115**
Further Afield	**116–133**
Shopping in Istanbul	**134–135**
Entertainment in Istanbul	**136–137**
Istanbul Street Finder	**138–149**

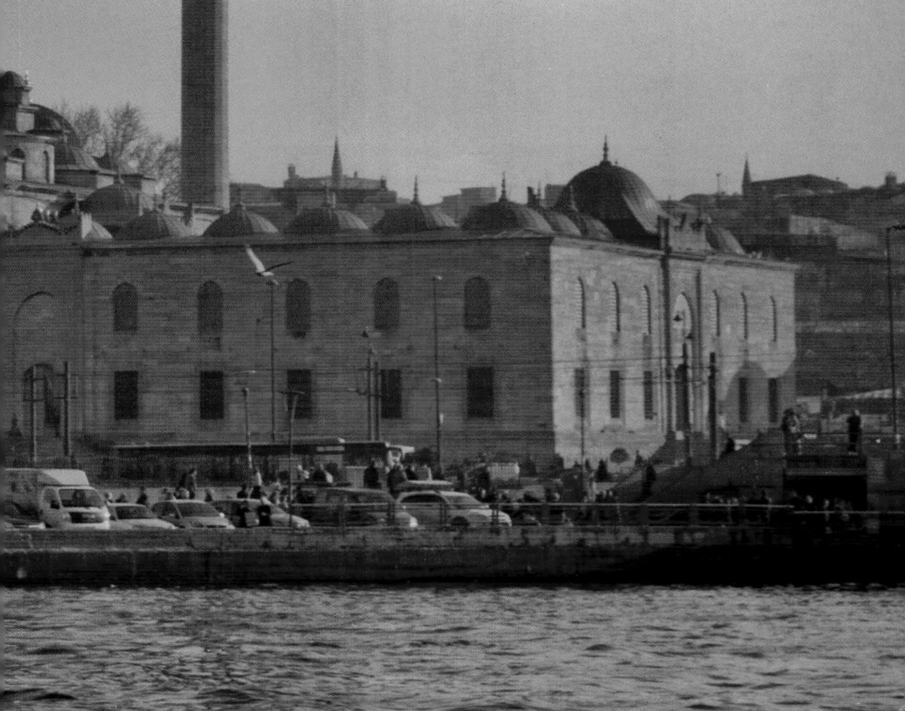

Istanbul at a Glance

Numerous interesting places to visit in Istanbul are described in the *Area by Area* section of this book, which covers the sights of central Istanbul as well as those a short way out of the city centre. They range from mosques, churches, palaces and museums to bazaars, Turkish baths and parks. For a breathtaking view across the city, climb Galata Tower *(see p114)* or take a ferry ride *(see p399)* to the city's Asian shore. If you are short of time, you will probably want to concentrate on only the most famous monuments, namely Topkapı Palace, Haghia Sophia and the Blue Mosque, which are located conveniently close to each other.

Istanbul

The Mevlevi Lodge *(see p114)* houses an interesting museum dedicated to classical Ottoman poetry. The Whirling Dervishes also perform here on the last Sunday of every month.

A boat trip along the Bosphorus *(see pp130–31)* is a wonderful way to view sights such as the 14th-century Genoese Castle (above the village of Anadolu Kavağı).

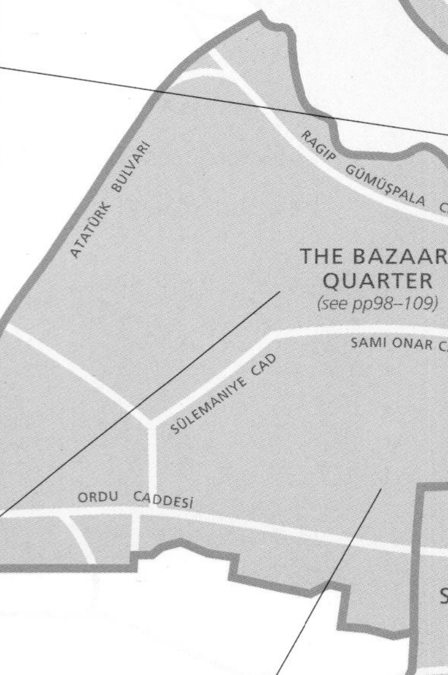

Süleymaniye Mosque *(see pp104–5)* was built by the great architect, Sinan, in honour of his patron, Süleyman the Magnificent *(see p59)*.

The Grand Bazaar *(see pp108–9)* is a maze of shops under an intricately painted, vaulted roof. Shopkeepers are relentless, and bargaining *(see p134)* is a must.

◀ The New Mosque at sunset, Istanbul

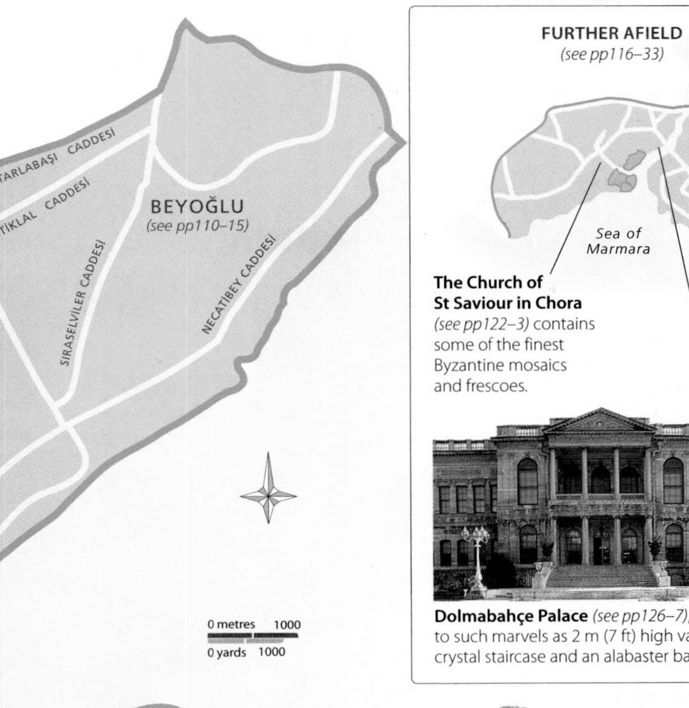

The Church of St Saviour in Chora *(see pp122–3)* contains some of the finest Byzantine mosaics and frescoes.

Dolmabahçe Palace *(see pp126–7)*, is home to such marvels as 2 m (7 ft) high vases, a crystal staircase and an alabaster bathroom.

SERAGLİO POINT
(see pp68–81)

KENNEDY CADDESİ

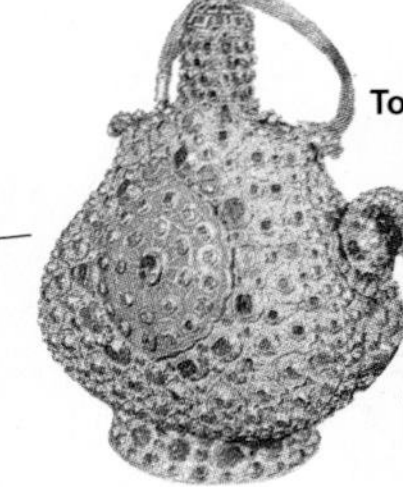

Topkapı Palace *(see pp72–3)* was the official residence of the sultans for more than 400 years. Its treasury contains many precious objects, such as jewel-encrusted thrones and this ornate ceremonial canteen.

Haghia Sophia *(see pp86–7)*, built in AD 537, remains one of the world's great buildings. The calligraphic roundels were added during the 19th century.

The Blue Mosque *(see pp92–3)* was built by some of the same stonemasons who helped to build the Taj Mahal.

SERAGLİO POINT

The hilly, wooded promontory that marks the meeting point of the Golden Horn, the Sea of Marmara and the Bosphorus occupies a natural strategic position. In Byzantine times, monasteries and public buildings stood on this site. Today, it is dominated by the grandiose complex of buildings forming Topkapı Palace, the residence of the Ottoman sultans and the women of the Harem for 400 years. The palace is open to the public as a rambling museum, with lavish apartments and glittering collections of jewels and other treasures. Originally, the palace covered almost the whole of the area with its gardens and pavilions. Part of the grounds have now been turned into a public park. Adjacent to it is the Archaeological Museum, showcasing a renowned collection of finds from Turkey and the Near East.

Sights at a Glance

Museums and Palaces

1 *Topkapı Palace pp72–3*
2 *Archaeological Museum pp76–7*

Churches

4 Haghia Eirene

Historic Buildings and Monuments

3 Museum of the History of Science and Technology in Islam
5 Fountain of Ahmet III
9 Sublime Porte
11 Sirkeci Station

Streets and Courtyards

6 Soğukçeşme Sokağı
7 Caferağa Courtyard

Parks

8 Gülhane Park

Turkish Baths

10 Cağaloğlu Baths

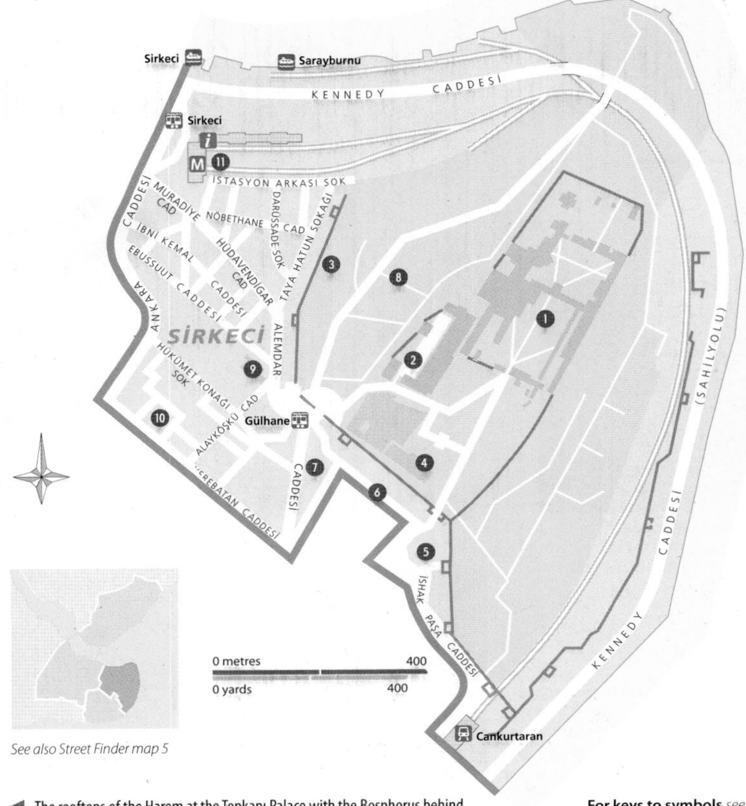

See also Street Finder map 5

◀ The rooftops of the Harem at the Topkapı Palace with the Bosphorus behind

For keys to symbols *see back flap*

Street-by-Street: The First Courtyard of Topkapı

The juxtaposition of Ottoman palace walls, intimately proportioned wooden houses and a soaring Byzantine church lends plenty of drama to the First Courtyard, the outer part of Topkapı Palace. This was once a service area, housing the former mint, a hospital, college and a bakery. It was also the mustering point of the Janissaries *(see p60)*. Nowadays, the Caferağa Courtyard and the Fatih Büfe, just outside the courtyard wall, offer unusual settings for refreshments. Gülhane Park, meanwhile, is one of the few shady open spaces in a city of monuments.

8 Gülhane Park
Once a rose garden in the outer grounds of Topkapı Palace, the wooded Gülhane Park provides welcome shade in which to escape from the heat of the city.

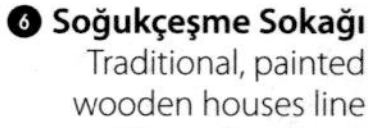

6 Soğukçeşme Sokağı
Traditional, painted wooden houses line this narrow street.

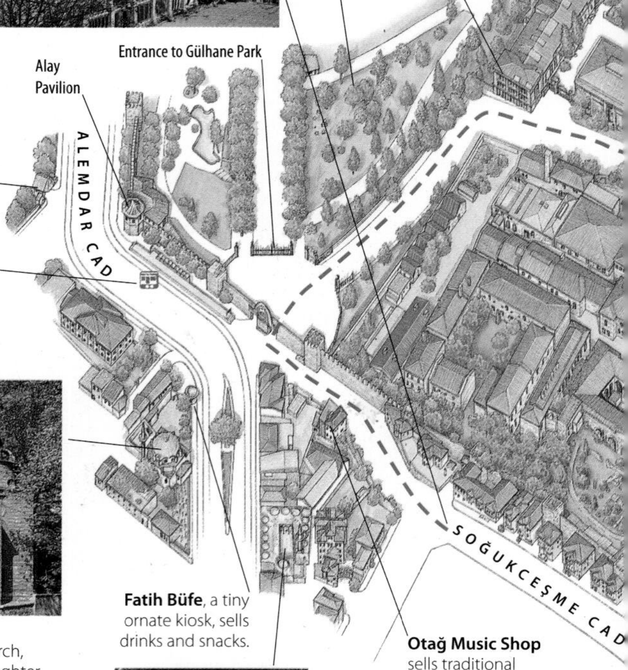

Museum of the Ancient Orient

Entrance to Gülhane Park

Alay Pavilion

ALEMDAR CAD

9 Sublime Porte
A Rococo gate stands in place of the old Sublime Porte, once the entrance to (and symbol of) the Ottoman government.

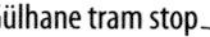

Gülhane tram stop

Key

— Suggested route

Zeynep Sultan Mosque, resembling a Byzantine church, was built in 1769 by the daughter of Ahmet III, Princess Zeynep.

Fatih Büfe, a tiny ornate kiosk, sells drinks and snacks.

SOĞUKCEŞME CAD

Otağ Music Shop sells traditional Turkish instruments.

7 Caferağa Courtyard
The cells of this former college, arranged around a tranquil courtyard café, are now occupied by jewellers, calligraphers and other artisans selling their wares.

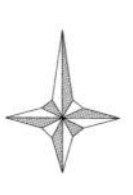

0 metres 75

0 yards 75

For hotels and restaurants in this area see p330 and p346

❷ ★ Archaeological Museum
Classical statues, dazzling carved sarcophagi, Turkish ceramics and other treasures from all over the former Ottoman Empire make this one of the world's great collections of antiquities.

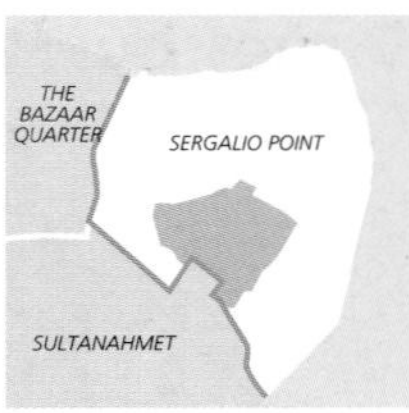

Locator Map
See Street Finder map 5

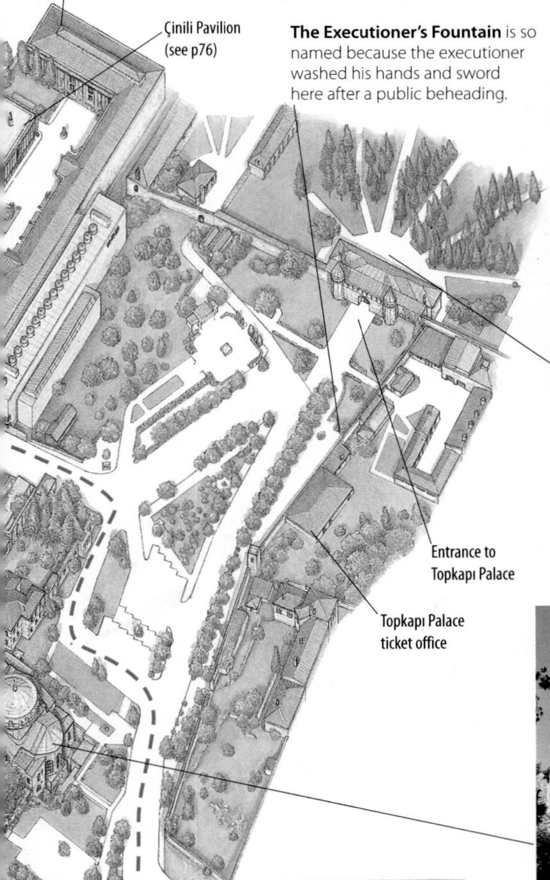

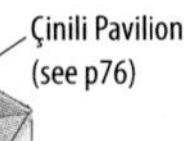

The Executioner's Fountain is so named because the executioner washed his hands and sword here after a public beheading.

❶ ★ Topkapı Palace
For 400 years the Ottoman sultans ruled their empire from this vast palace. Its fine art collections, opulent rooms and leafy courtyards are among the highlights of a visit to Istanbul.

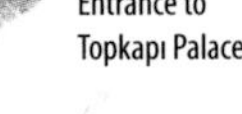

Topkapı Palace ticket office

❹ Haghia Eirene
The Byzantine church of Haghia Eirene dates from the 6th century. Unusually, it has never been converted into a mosque.

Imperial Gate

❺ Fountain of Ahmet III
Built in the early 18th century, the finest of Istanbul's Rococo fountains is inscribed with poetry likening it to the fountains of paradise.

For keys to symbols *see back flap*

❶ Topkapı Palace

Topkapı Sarayı

Between 1459 and 1465, shortly after his conquest of Constantinople *(see p58)*, Mehmet II built Topkapı Palace as his principal residence. Rather than a single building, it was conceived as a series of pavilions contained by four enormous courtyards, a stone version of the tented encampments from which the nomadic Ottomans had emerged. Initially, the palace served as the seat of government and contained a school in which civil servants and soldiers were trained. In the 16th century, however, the government was moved to the Sublime Porte *(see p79)*. Sultan Abdül Mecit I abandoned Topkapı in 1853 in favour of Dolmabahçe Palace *(see pp126–7)*. In 1924 it was opened to the public as a museum.

★ Harem
The labyrinth of exquisite rooms where the sultan's wives and concubines lived can be visited on a guided tour *(see p75)*.

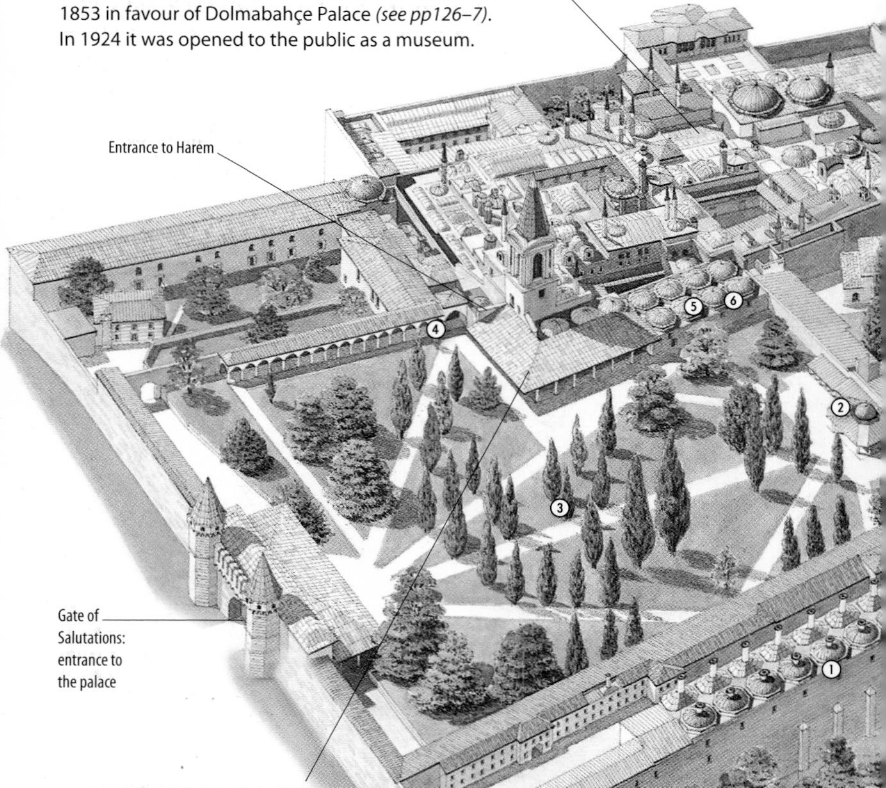

Entrance to Harem

Gate of Salutations: entrance to the palace

Divan
The viziers of the imperial council met in this chamber, sometimes watched covertly by the sultan.

İftariye Pavilion
Standing between the Baghdad and Circumcision pavilions, this canopied balcony provides views down to the Golden Horn.

VISITORS' CHECKLIST

Practical Information
Babıhümayun Cad. **Map** 5 F3. **Tel** (0212) 512 04 80. **W** **topkapisarayi.gov.tr**. **Open** Apr–Oct: 9am–7pm daily; Nov–Mar: 9am–5pm daily. Harem: **Open** 10am–4pm Wed–Mon.

Transport
Sultanahmet.

Baghdad Pavilion
In 1639 Murat IV built this pavilion to celebrate his capture of Baghdad. It has exquisite blue-and-white tilework.

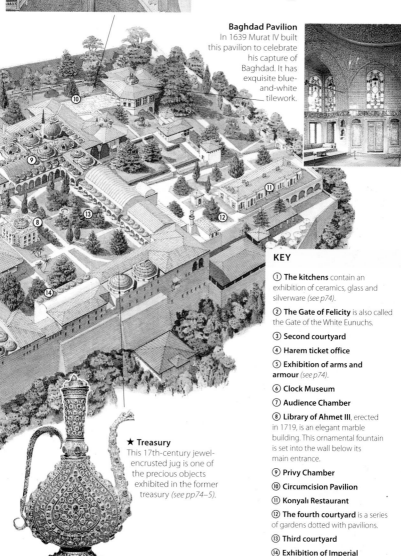

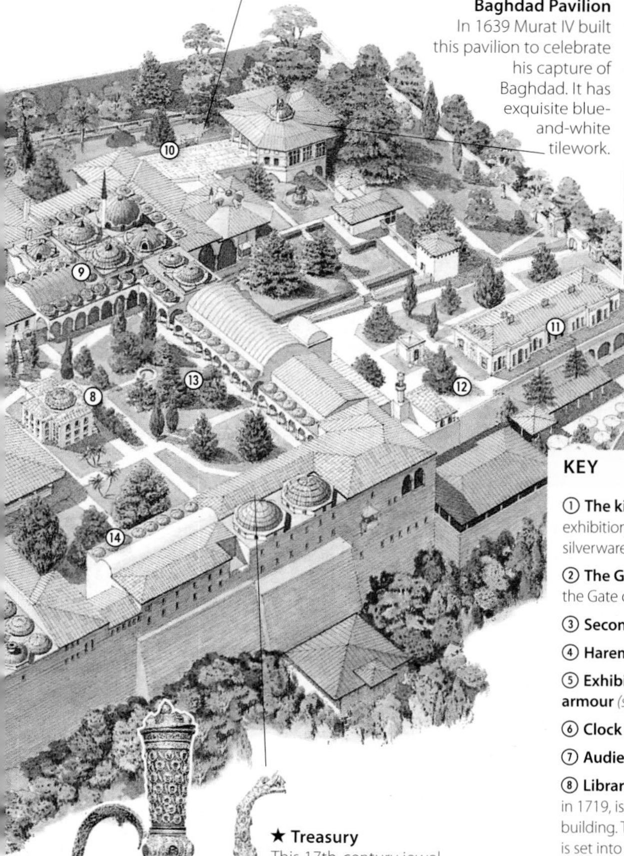

KEY

① **The kitchens** contain an exhibition of ceramics, glass and silverware *(see p74)*.

② **The Gate of Felicity** is also called the Gate of the White Eunuchs.

③ **Second courtyard**

④ **Harem ticket office**

⑤ **Exhibition of arms and armour** *(see p74)*.

⑥ **Clock Museum**

⑦ **Audience Chamber**

⑧ **Library of Ahmet III**, erected in 1719, is an elegant marble building. This ornamental fountain is set into the wall below its main entrance.

⑨ **Privy Chamber**

⑩ **Circumcision Pavilion**

⑪ **Konyalı Restaurant**

⑫ **The fourth courtyard** is a series of gardens dotted with pavilions.

⑬ **Third courtyard**

⑭ **Exhibition of Imperial costumes** *(see p74)*.

★ Treasury
This 17th-century jewel-encrusted jug is one of the precious objects exhibited in the former treasury *(see pp74–5)*.

Exploring the Palace's Collections

During their 470-year reign, the Ottoman sultans amassed a glittering collection of treasures. After the foundation of the Turkish Republic in 1923 *(see p62)*, this was nationalized and the bulk of it put on display in Topkapı Palace. As well as diplomatic gifts and articles commissioned from the craftsmen of the palace workshops, many of the items in the collection were the booty from successful military campaigns. Many date from the massive expansion of the Ottoman Empire during the reign of Selim the Grim (1512–20), when Syria, Arabia and Egypt were conquered.

Ceramics, Glass and Silverware

The kitchens contain the palace's ceramics, glass and silverware collections. Turkish and European pieces are massively overshadowed by the vast display of Chinese (as well as Japanese) porcelain. This was brought to Turkey along the Silk Route, the overland trading link between the Far East and Europe. Topkapı's collection of Chinese porcelain is the world's second best, after China.

Japanese porcelain plate

The Chinese porcelain on display spans four dynasties: the Sung (10–13th centuries), followed by the Yüan (13–14th centuries), the Ming (14–17th centuries) and the Ching (17–20th centuries). Celadon, the earliest form of Chinese porcelain collected by the sultans, was made to look like jade, a stone believed by the Chinese to be lucky. The Ottomans prized it because it was said to neutralize poison in food. More delicate than these are a number of exquisite blue-and-white pieces, mostly of the Ming era.

Chinese aesthetics were an important influence on Ottoman craftsmen, particularly in the creation of designs for their fledgling ceramics industry at İznik *(see p165)*. Although there are no İznik pieces in the Topkapı collection, many of the tiles on the palace walls originated there. These clearly show the influence of designs used for Chinese blue-and-white porcelain, such as stylized flowers and cloud scrolls. Much of the later porcelain, particularly the Japanese Imari ware, was made for the export market. The most obvious examples of this are some plates decorated with quotations from the Koran.

A part of the kitchens, the old confectioners' pantry, has been preserved as it would have been when in use. On display are huge cauldrons and other utensils wielded by the palace's chefs as they prepared to feed its 12,000 residents and guests.

Arms and Armour

Taxes and tributes from all over the empire were once stored in this chamber, which was known as the Inner Treasury. Straight ahead as you enter are a series of horsetail standards. Carried in processions or displayed outside tents, these proclaimed the rank of their owners. Viziers *(see p60)*, for example, merited three, and the grand vizier five, while the sultan's banner would flaunt nine.

The weaponry includes ornately embellished swords and several bows made by sultans themselves (Beyazıt II was a particularly fine craftsman). Seen next to these exquisite items, the huge iron swords used by European crusaders look crude by comparison. Also on view are pieces of 15th-century Ottoman chainmail and colourful shields. The shields have metal centres surrounded by closely woven straw that has been painted with flowers.

Imperial Costumes

A collection of imperial costumes is displayed in the Hall of the Campaign Pages, whose task was to look after the royal wardrobe. It was a palace tradition that on the death of a sultan his clothes were carefully folded and placed in sealed bags. As a result, it is possible to see a perfectly preserved kaftan once worn by Mehmet the Conqueror *(see p58)*. The reforms of Sultan Mahmut II included a revolution in the dress code. The end of an era came as plain grey serge replaced the earlier luxurious silken textiles.

Sumptuous silk kaftan once worn by Mehmet the Conqueror

Treasury

Of all the exhibitions in the palace, the Treasury's collection is the easiest to appreciate, glittering as it does with thousands of precious and semi-precious stones. Possibly the only surprise is that there are so few women's jewels here. Whereas the treasures of the sultans and viziers were owned by the state, reverting to the palace on their deaths, those belonging to the women of the court did not.

In the first hall stands a diamond-encrusted suit of chainmail, designed for Mustafa III (1757–74) for ceremonial use. Diplomatic gifts include a fine pearl statuette of a prince seated beneath a canopy, which was sent to Sultan Abdül Aziz (1861–76) from India. The greatest pieces are to be seen in the second hall. Foremost among these is the Topkapı dagger (1741). This splendid object was commissioned by the sultan from his own jewellers. It was intended as a present for the Shah of Persia, but he died before it reached him. Among the exhibits are a selection of bejewelled *aigrettes* (plumes), which were used to add splendour to imperial turbans.

The Topkapı dagger

In the third hall is the 86-carat Spoonmaker's diamond, said to have been discovered in a rubbish heap in Istanbul in the 17th century, and bought from a scrap merchant for three spoons. The gold-plated Bayram throne was given to Murat III by the Governor of Egypt in 1574 and used for state ceremonies.

The throne in the fourth hall, a gift from the Shah of Persia, was acknowledged by the equally magnificent gift of the Topkapı dagger. In a cabinet near the throne is an unusual relic: a case containing bones said to be from the hand of St John the Baptist.

The Divan

In many ways the Divan was not only the heart of the Topkapı Palace, but of the Ottoman Empire itself. Here, four days a week, the sultan's viziers (top state officials) would meet, and their gatherings were presided over by the grand vizier. Important issues and matters of state were discussed and decisions were made – though these had first to be ratified by the sultan. The domed chamber is named after the low benches (divans) running around three of its walls.

Clocks

European clocks given as diplomatic gifts to, or bought by, various sultans form the majority of this collection, despite the fact that there were makers of clocks and watches in Istanbul from the 17th century. The clocks museum is located next to the armoury. There are some 380 clocks on display, ranging from simple, weight-driven 16th-century examples to an exquisite 18th-century English mechanism encased in mother-of-pearl and featuring a German organ which played tunes every hour, on the hour. The only male European eyewitness accounts of life in the Harem were written by mechanics who serviced the clocks.

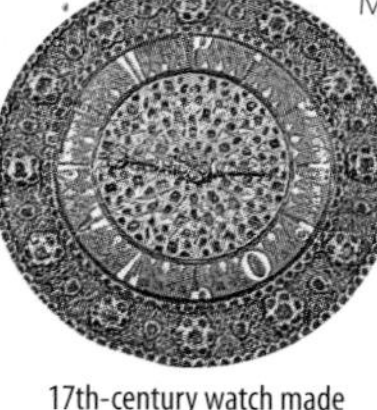

17th-century watch made of gold, enamel and precious stones

Pavilion of the Holy Mantle

Some of the holiest relics of Islam are displayed in the Pavilion of the Holy Mantle, five domed rooms that are a place of pilgrimage for Muslims. Most of the relics found their way to Istanbul as a result of the conquest by Sultan Selim the Grim of Egypt and Arabia, and his assumption of the caliphate (the leadership of Islam) in 1517.

The most sacred treasure is the mantle once worn by the Prophet Mohammed. Visitors cannot actually enter the room in which it is stored; instead they look into it from an antechamber through an open doorway. Night and day, holy men chant passages from the Koran over the gold chest in which the mantle is stored. A stand in front of the chest holds two of Mohammed's swords. Behind a glass cabinet in the anteroom are hairs from the beard of the Prophet, a tooth, a letter written by him and an impression of his footprint.

In other rooms are some of the ornate locks and keys for the Kaaba (Muslim shrine in Mecca), which were sent to Mecca by successive sultans.

Life in the Harem

Apart from the sultan's mother, the most powerful woman in the Harem, and the sultan's daughters, the women of the Harem were slaves, gathered from the furthest corners of the Ottoman Empire and beyond. Their dream was to become a favourite of the sultan and bear him a son, which, on some occasions, led to marriage. Competition was stiff, however, for at its height the Harem contained over 1,000 concubines, many of whom never rose beyond the service of their fellow captives. The last women eventually left the Harem in 1909.

A Western view of life in the Harem, from a 19th-century engraving

❷ Archaeological Museum

Arkeoloji Müzesi

Although this collection of antiquities was begun only in the mid-19th century, provincial governors were soon sending in objects from the length and breadth of the Ottoman Empire. Today the museum has one of the world's richest collections of classical artifacts, and also includes treasures from the pre-classical world. The main building was erected under the directorship of Osman Hamdi Bey (1881–1910), to house his finds. This archaeologist, painter and polymath discovered the exquisite sarcophagi in the royal necropolis at Sidon in present-day Lebanon.

★ Alexander Sarcophagus
This fabulously carved marble tomb from the late 4th century BC is thought to have been built for King Abdalonymos of Sidon. It is called the Alexander Sarcophagus because Alexander the Great is depicted on it winning a victory over the Persians.

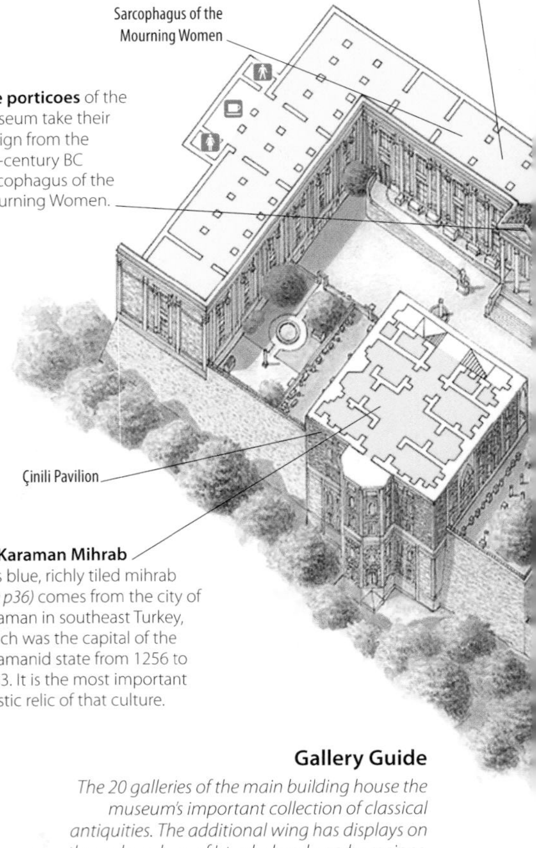

Key

- Classical Archaeology
- Thracian, Bithynian and Byzantine Collections
- Istanbul Through the Ages
- Anatolia and Troy
- Anatolia's Neighbouring Cultures
- Turkish Tiles and Ceramics
- Museum of the Ancient Orient
- Non-exhibition space

The porticoes of the museum take their design from the 4th-century BC Sarcophagus of the Mourning Women.

★ Karaman Mihrab
This blue, richly tiled mihrab *(see p36)* comes from the city of Karaman in southeast Turkey, which was the capital of the Karamanid state from 1256 to 1483. It is the most important artistic relic of that culture.

Gallery Guide

The 20 galleries of the main building house the museum's important collection of classical antiquities. The additional wing has displays on the archaeology of Istanbul and nearby regions. There are two other buildings within the grounds: the Çinili Pavilion, which houses Turkish tiles and ceramics, and the Museum of the Ancient Orient.

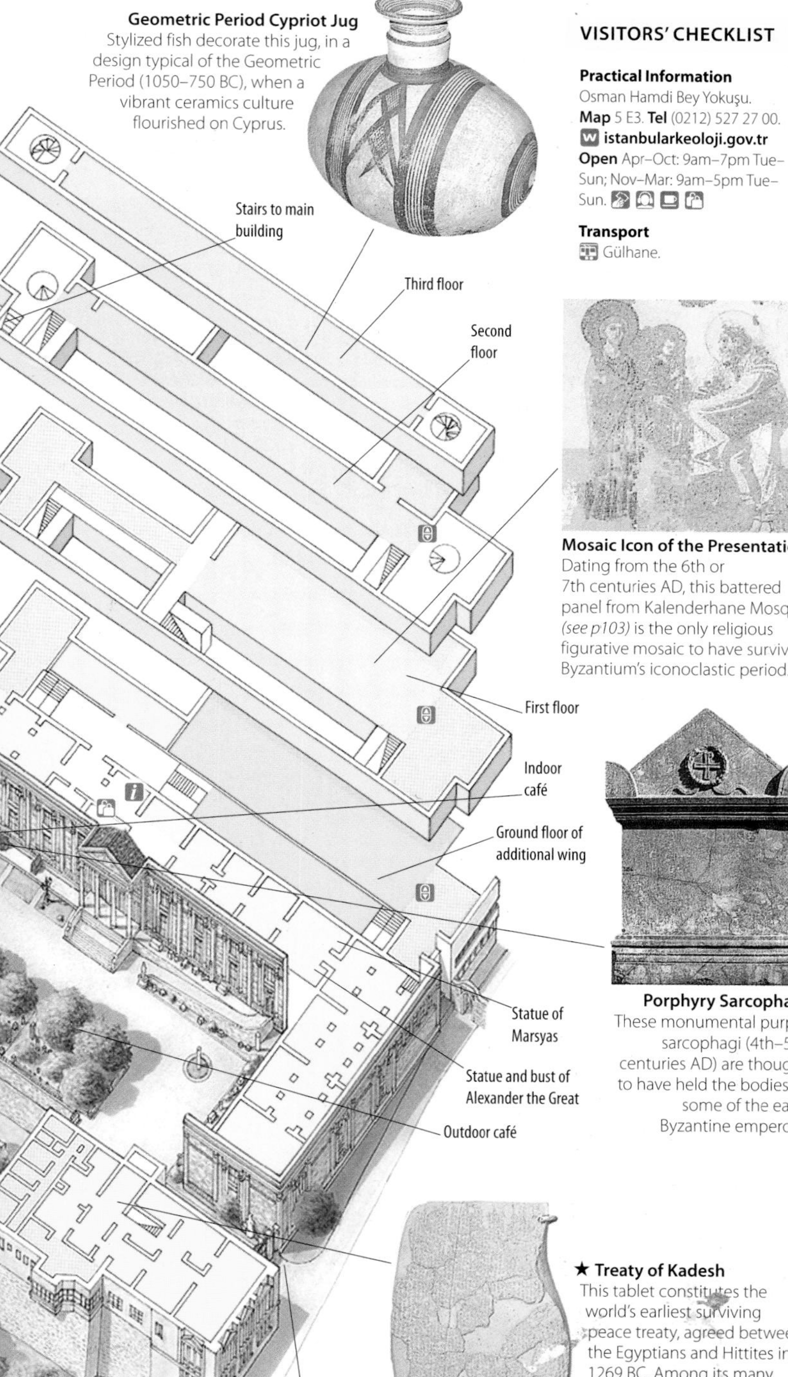

Geometric Period Cypriot Jug
Stylized fish decorate this jug, in a design typical of the Geometric Period (1050–750 BC), when a vibrant ceramics culture flourished on Cyprus.

VISITORS' CHECKLIST

Practical Information
Osman Hamdi Bey Yokuşu.
Map 5 E3. **Tel** (0212) 527 27 00.
istanbularkeoloji.gov.tr
Open Apr–Oct: 9am–7pm Tue–Sun; Nov–Mar: 9am–5pm Tue–Sun.

Transport
Gülhane.

Mosaic Icon of the Presentation
Dating from the 6th or 7th centuries AD, this battered panel from Kalenderhane Mosque *(see p103)* is the only religious figurative mosaic to have survived Byzantium's iconoclastic period.

Porphyry Sarcophagi
These monumental purple sarcophagi (4th–5th centuries AD) are thought to have held the bodies of some of the early Byzantine emperors.

★ Treaty of Kadesh
This tablet constitutes the world's earliest surviving peace treaty, agreed between the Egyptians and Hittites in 1269 BC. Among its many clauses are provisions for the return of political refugees.

❸ Museum of the History of Science and Technology in Islam

MuseumIstanbul Islam Bilim ve Teknoloji Tarihi Müzesi

Has Ahırlar Binaları, Sirkeci. **Map** 5 E3. **Tel** (0212) 528 80 65. Gülhane. **Open** 9am–5pm Wed–Mon. **ibttm.org**

This museum showcases inventions made by Muslim scientists between the 8th and 16th centuries, revealing that many Islamic advances in science and technology paved the way for later discoveries in Europe. Housed in the old stables of the Topkapı Palace, exhibits include astrolabes, a model planetarium and a water clock. Most of the scientific instruments on display are replicas that have been carefully constructed from drawings and descriptions in contemporary texts. All the models were made at the behest of the Johann Wolfgang Goethe University in Frankfurt.

One of the four elaborately decorated sides of the Fountain of Ahmet III

❹ Haghia Eirene

Aya İrini Kilisesi

First courtyard of Topkapı Palace. **Map** 5 E4. **Tel** (0212) 522 17 50. Gülhane or Sultanahmet. **Open** 9am–4pm Wed–Mon.

Though the present church dates only from the 6th century, it is at least the third building to be erected on what is thought to be the oldest site of Christian worship in Istanbul. Within a decade of the Muslim conquest of the city in 1453 *(see p58)* it had been incorporated within the Topkapı Palace complex and pressed into use as an arsenal. Today the building, which has good acoustics, is the setting for concerts during the Istanbul Music Festival *(see p39)*.

Inside are three fascinating features that have not survived in any other Byzantine church in the city. The *synthronon*, the five rows of built-in seats hugging the apse, were occupied by clergy officiating during services. Above this looms a simple black mosaic cross on a gold background, which dates from the iconoclastic period in the 8th century, when figurative images were forbidden. At the back of the church is a cloister-like courtyard where deceased Byzantine emperors once lay in their porphyry sarcophagi. Most have been moved to the Archaeological Museum.

The apse of Haghia Eirene, with its imposing black-on-gold cross

❺ Fountain of Ahmet III

III Ahmet Çeşmesi

Junction of İshak Paşa Cad & Babıhümayun Cad. **Map** 5 E4. Gülhane or Sultanahmet.

Built in 1729, the most beautiful of Istanbul's countless fountains survived the violent deposition of Sultan Ahmet III two years later. Many other monuments constructed by the sultan during his reign, which has become known as the Tulip Period, were destroyed. The fountain is in the delicate Turkish Rococo style, with five small domes, mihrab-shaped niches and dizzying floral reliefs.

Ottoman "fountains" do not spout jets of water, but are more like ornate public taps. They sometimes incorporated a counter, or *sebil*, from which refreshments would be served.

In this case, each of the fountain's four walls is equipped with a tap, or *çeşme*, above a carved marble basin. Over each tap is an elaborate calligraphic inscription by the 18th-century poet Seyit Vehbi Efendi. The inscription, in gold on a blue-green background, is in honour of the fountain and its founder. At each of the four corners there is a *sebil* backed

For hotels and restaurants in this area see p330 and p346

by three windows covered by ornate marble grilles. Instead of the customary iced water, passers-by at this fountain would have been offered sherbets and flavoured waters in silver goblets.

❻ Soğukçeşme Sokağı

Map 5 E4. Gülhane.

Charming old wooden houses line this narrow, sloping cobbled lane ("the street of the cold fountain"), which squeezes between the outer walls of Topkapı Palace and the towering minarets of Haghia Sophia. Traditional houses like these were built in the city from the late 18th century onwards.

The buildings in the lane were renovated by the Turkish Touring and Automobile Club (TTOK, *see p395*) in the 1980s. Of these, nine buildings now form the Ayasofya Pansiyonları, a series of attractive pastel-painted guesthouses popular with tourists. Another building has been converted by the TTOK into a library of historical writings on Istanbul, and archive of engravings and photographs of the city.

Traditional calligraphy on sale in Caferağa Courtyard

❼ Caferağa Courtyard

Caferağa Medresesi

Caferiye Sok. **Map** 5 E3. Gülhane. **Open** 8:30am–8pm daily.

This peaceful courtyard at the end of an alley was built in 1559 by the architect Sinan (*see p105*) for the chief black eunuch as a *medrese* (theological college, *see p36*). Sinan's bust presides over the café tables in the courtyard. The former students' lodgings are now used to display a variety of craft goods typically including jewellery, silk prints, ceramics and calligraphy.

Restored Ottoman house on Soğukçeşme Sokağı

Ottoman Houses

The typical, smart town house of 19th-century Istanbul had a stone ground floor above which were one or two wooden storeys. The building invariably sported a *çıkma*, a section projecting out over the street. This developed from the traditional Turkish balcony, which was enclosed in the northern part of the country because of the colder climate. Wooden lattice covers, or *kafesler*, over the windows on the upper storeys ensured that the women of the house were able to watch life on the street below without being seen themselves. Few wooden houses have survived. Those that remain usually owe their existence to tourism and many have been restored as hotels. While the law forbids their demolition, it is very expensive to obtain insurance for them in a city that has experienced so many fires.

❽ Gülhane Park

Gülhane Parkı

Alemdar Cad. **Map** 5 E4. Gülhane. **Open** daily.

Gülhane Park occupies what were the lower grounds of Topkapı Palace. Today it is a green and pleasant outdoor place with several interesting landmarks and museums.

The Archaeological Museum (*see pp76–77*) is within the park, to the left of the Topkapı Palace.

At the far end of the park is the Goths' Column, a well-preserved 3rd-century victory monument, surrounded by a cluster of clapboard teahouses. Its name comes from the Latin inscription on it which reads: "Fortune is restored to us because of victory over the Goths".

Across Kennedy Caddesi, the main road running along the northeast side of the park, there is a viewpoint over the busy waters where the Golden Horn meets the Bosphorus.

❾ Sublime Porte

Bab-ı Ali

Alemdar Cad. **Map** 5 E3. Gülhane.

Foreign ambassadors to Ottoman Turkey were known as Ambassadors to the Sublime Porte, after this monumental gateway which once led into the offices and palace of the grand vizier. The institution of the Sublime Porte filled an important role in Ottoman society because it could often provide an effective counterbalance to the whims of sultans.

The Rococo gateway that stands here today was built in the 1840s. Its guarded entrance now shields the offices of Istanbul's provincial government.

Rococo decoration on the roof of the Sublime Porte

⑩ Cağaloğlu Baths

Cağaloğlu Hamamı

Prof Kazım İsmail Gürkan Cad 34, Cağaloğlu. **Map** 5 E4. **Tel** (0212) 522 24 24. Sultanahmet. **Open** 8am–10pm daily. **cagalogluhamami.com.tr**

Among the city's more sumptuous Turkish baths, the ones in Cağaloğlu were built by Sultan Mahmut I in 1741. The income from them was designated for the maintenance of Mahmut's library in Haghia Sophia *(see pp86–7)*.

The city's smaller baths have different times at which men and women can use the same facilities. But in larger baths, such as this one, there are entirely separate sections. In the Cağaloğlu Baths the men's and women's sections are at right angles to one another and entered from different streets. Each consists of three parts: a *camekan*, a *soğukluk* and the main bath chamber or *hararet*, which centres on a massive octagonal massage slab.

Corridor leading into the Cağaloğlu Baths, built by Mahmut I

The Cağaloğlu Baths are popular with foreign visitors because the staff are happy to explain the procedure. Even if you do not want to sweat it out, you can still take a look inside the entrance corridor and *camekan* of the men's section. Here you will find a small display of Ottoman bathing regalia, including precarious wooden clogs once worn by women on what would frequently be their only outing from the confines of the home. You can also sit and have a drink by the fountain in the peaceful *camekan*.

⑪ Sirkeci Station

Sirkeci Garı

Sirkeci İstasyon Cad, Sirkeci. **Map** 5 E3. **Tel** (0212) 520 65 75. Sirkeci. **Open** daily.

This magnificent railway station was built to receive the long-anticipated Orient Express from Europe. It was officially opened in 1890,

Steps leading to the entrance of Sirkeci Station

even though the luxurious train had been running into Istanbul for a year by then. The design, by the German architect August Jasmund, incorporates distinctive windows, arches and stonework that mirror Istanbul's diverse history and architectural traditions.

The Orient Express stopped its service to Istanbul in 1977. In 2013, the station became a stop on the Marmaray metro rail, which runs under the Bosphorus and connects the European and Asian halves of the city.

The station also has a good restaurant – historically a popular haunt for writers and journalists – and a small museum devoted to railway memorabilia.

The World-Famous Orient Express

The Orient Express made its first run from Paris to Istanbul in 1889, covering the 2,900 km (1,800 mile) journey in three days. Both Sirkeci Station and the Pera Palas Hotel *(see p112, 114)* in Istanbul were built especially to receive its passengers. The wealthy and often distinguished passengers of "The Train of Kings, the King of Trains" did indeed include kings among the many presidents, politicians, aristocrats and actresses. King Boris III of Bulgaria even made a habit of taking over from the driver of the train when he travelled on it through his own country.

A byword for exoticism and romance, the train was associated with the orientalist view of Istanbul as a treacherous melting pot of diplomats and arms dealers. It inspired no fewer than 19 books – *Murder on the Orient Express* by Agatha Christie and *Stamboul Train* by Graham Greene foremost among them – six films and one piece of music. During the Cold War, standards of luxury crashed, though a service of sorts, without even a restaurant car, continued twice weekly to Istanbul until 1977.

A 1920s poster for the Orient Express, showing a romantic view of Istanbul

For hotels and restaurants in this area see p330 and p346

Turkish Baths

No trip to Istanbul is complete without an hour or two spent in a Turkish bath *(hamam)*, which will leave your whole body feeling rejuvenated. Turkish baths differ little from the baths of ancient Rome, from which they derive, except there is no pool of cold water to plunge into at the end.

A full service will entail a period of relaxation in the steam-filled hot room, punctuated by bouts of vigorous soaping and massaging. There is no time limit, but you should allow at least an hour and a half to enjoy a leisurely bath. Towels and soap will be provided, but you can take special toiletries with you. Two historic baths located in the old city, Çemberlitaş *(see p95)* and Cağaloğlu (illustrated below), are used to catering for foreign tourists. Some luxury hotels have their own baths *(see p326)*.

Choosing a Service
Services, detailed in a price list at the entrance, range from a self-service option to a luxury body scrub, shampoo and massage.

Changing Clothes
Before changing you will be given a cloth *(peştemal)*, to wrap around you, and a pair of slippers for walking on the hot, wet floor.

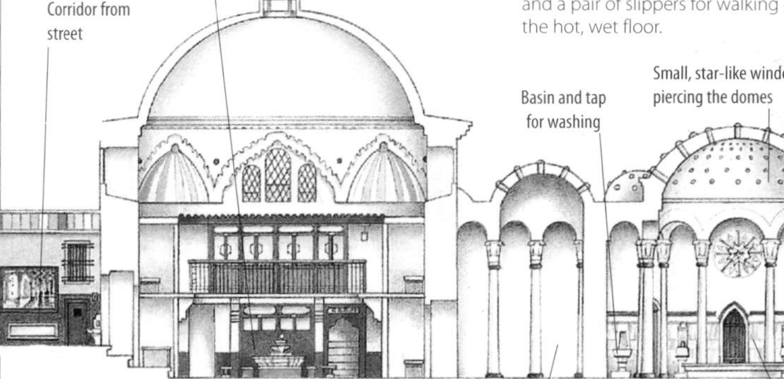

The *camekan* (entrance hall) is a peaceful internal courtyard near the entrance of the building. Bathers change clothes in cubicles surrounding it. The *camekan* is also the place to relax with a cup of tea after bathing.

The *soğukluk* (intermediate room) is a temperate passage between the changing room and the *hararet*. You will be given dry towels here on your way back to the *camekan*.

In the *hararet* (hot room), the main room of the Turkish bath, you are permitted to sit and sweat in the steam for as long as you like.

Cağaloğlu Baths

The opulent, 18th-century Turkish baths at Cağaloğlu have separate, identical sections for men and women. The men's section is shown here.

The Exfoliating Body Scrub
In between steaming, you (or the staff at the baths) scrub your body briskly with a coarse, soapy mitt (*kese*).

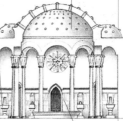

The Body Massage
A marble plinth (*göbek taşı*) occupies the centre of the hot room. This is where you will have your pummelling full-body massage.

SULTANAHMET

Two of the city's most significant monuments face each other across gardens, known as Sultanahmet Square. The Blue Mosque was built by Sultan Ahmet I, from whom this part of the city gets its name. Opposite is Haghia Sophia, an outstanding example of early Byzantine architecture. It is still regarded as one of the world's most remarkable churches, although it served as a mosque for several centuries and is now a museum. A square next to the Blue Mosque marks the site of the Hippodrome, a chariot-racing stadium built by the Romans in about AD 200. On the other side of the Blue Mosque, the city slopes down to the Sea of Marmara in a jumble of alleyways. Traditional-style Ottoman houses have been built over the remains of the Great Palace of the Byzantine emperors.

Sights at a Glance

Mosques and Churches

1 *Haghia Sophia pp86–7*
7 *Blue Mosque pp92–3*
14 Sokollu Mehmet Paşa Mosque
15 Church of SS Sergius and Bacchus

Museums

4 Carpet Museum
6 Mosaic Museum
8 Museum of Turkish and Islamic Arts
10 Marmara University Museum of the Republic

Squares and Courtyards

3 Istanbul Crafts Centre
9 Hippodrome

Historic Buildings and Monuments

2 Basilica Cistern
5 Baths of Roxelana
11 Cistern of 1,001 Columns
12 Tomb of Sultan Mahmut II
13 Constantine's Column
16 Bucoleon Palace

See also Street Finder map 5

0 metres 250
0 yards 250

For keys to symbols *see back flap*

Street-by-Street: Sultanahmet Square

Two of Istanbul's most venerable monuments, the Blue Mosque and Haghia Sophia, face each other across a leafy square, informally known as Sultanahmet Square (Sultanahmet Meydanı), next to the Hippodrome of Byzantium. Also in this fascinating historic quarter are a handful of museums, including the Mosaic Museum, built over part of the old Byzantine Great Palace *(see pp96–7)*, and the Museum of Turkish and Islamic Arts. Look out for street vendors pushing smart red handcarts, and hawking boiled sweet corn and roast chestnuts.

Tomb of Sultan Ahmet I
Stunning 17th-century İznik tiles *(see p165)* adorn the inside of this tomb, which is part of the outer complex of the Blue Mosque.

7 ★ Blue Mosque
Towering above Sultanahmet Square are the six beautiful minarets of this world-famous mosque. It was built in the early 17th century for Ahmet I.

Sultanahmet tram stop

Firuz Ağa Mosque

Fountain of Kaiser Wilhelm II

Egyptian Obelisk

8 Museum of Turkish and Islamic Arts
Tents and rugs used by Turkey's nomadic peoples are included in this impressive collection.

ATMEYDANI SOK

ATMEYDANI SOK

TAVUKHANE SOK

TORUN SOK

Key

— Suggested route

Serpentine Column

Brazen Column

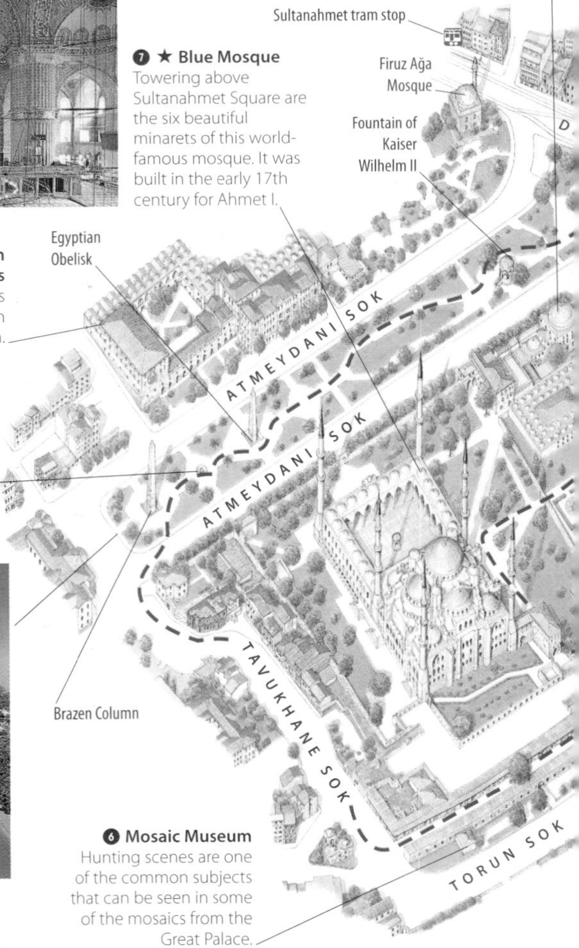

9 Hippodrome
This stadium was the city's focus for more than 1,000 years before it fell into ruin. Only a few sections, such as the central line of monuments, remain.

6 Mosaic Museum
Hunting scenes are one of the common subjects that can be seen in some of the mosaics from the Great Palace.

For hotels and restaurants in this area see pp330–31 and p346

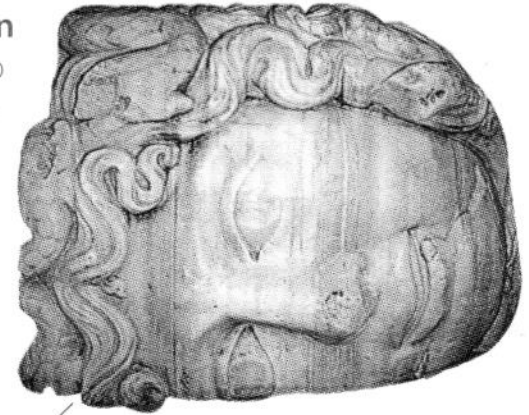

2 ★ Basilica Cistern
This marble Medusa head is one of two classical column bases found in the Basilica Cistern. The cavernous cistern dates from the reign of Justinian I *(see p53)* in the 6th century.

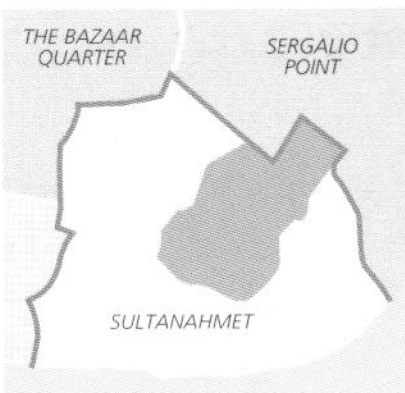

Locator Map
See Street Finder map 5

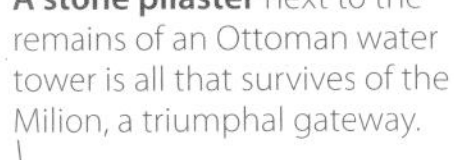

A stone pilaster next to the remains of an Ottoman water tower is all that survives of the Milion, a triumphal gateway.

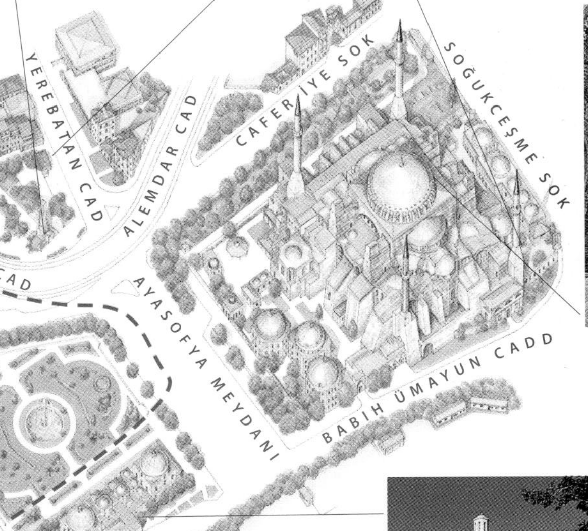

1 ★ Haghia Sophia
The supreme church of Byzantium is over 1,400 years old but has survived in a remarkably good state. Inside it are several glorious figurative mosaics.

5 Baths of Roxelana
Sinan *(see p105)* designed these beautiful baths in the mid-16th century. After housing a carpet shop for several years, the building reopened as a public bathhouse in 2011.

3 Istanbul Crafts Centre
Visitors have a rare opportunity here to observe Turkish craftsmen practising a range of skills.

Cavalry Bazaar
Eager salesmen will call you over to peruse their wares – mainly carpets and handicrafts – in this bazaar. With two long rows of shops on either side of a lane, the bazaar was once a stable yard.

0 metres 75
0 yards 75

❶ Haghia Sophia

Ayasofya

The "church of holy wisdom", Haghia Sophia is among the world's greatest architectural achievements. More than 1,400 years old, it stands as a testament to the sophistication of the 6th-century Byzantine capital and had a great influence on architecture in the following centuries. The vast edifice was built over two earlier churches and inaugurated by Emperor Justinian in 537. In the 15th century the Ottomans converted it into a mosque: the minarets, tombs and fountains date from this period. To help support the structure's great weight, the exterior has been buttressed on numerous occasions, which has partly obscured its original shape.

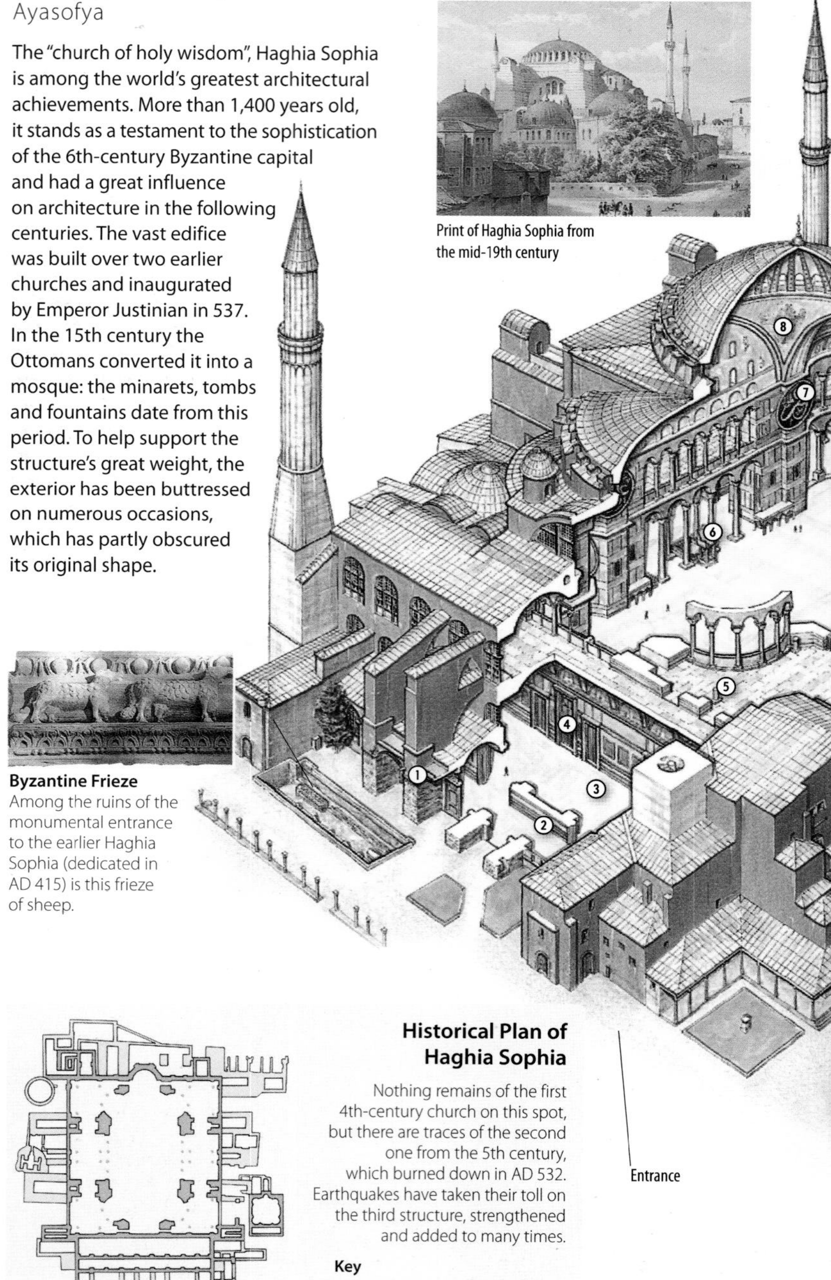

Print of Haghia Sophia from the mid-19th century

Byzantine Frieze
Among the ruins of the monumental entrance to the earlier Haghia Sophia (dedicated in AD 415) is this frieze of sheep.

Historical Plan of Haghia Sophia

Nothing remains of the first 4th-century church on this spot, but there are traces of the second one from the 5th century, which burned down in AD 532. Earthquakes have taken their toll on the third structure, strengthened and added to many times.

Key

- 5th-century church
- 6th-century church
- Ottoman additions

For hotels and restaurants in this area see pp330–31 and p346

★ **Nave**
Visitors cannot fail to be staggered by this vast space, which is covered by a huge dome reaching to a height of 56 m (184 ft).

VISITORS' CHECKLIST

Practical Information
Ayasofya Sultanahmet Meydanı 1. **Map** 5 E4. **Tel** (0212) 522 17 50. **Open** Apr–Oct: 9am–7pm; Nov–Mar: 9am–5pm Tue–Sun. ground floor only.

Transport
Sultanahmet.

★ **The Mosaics**
The church's splendid Byzantine mosaics include this one at the end of the south gallery. It depicts Christ flanked by Emperor Constantine IX and his wife, the Empress Zoe.

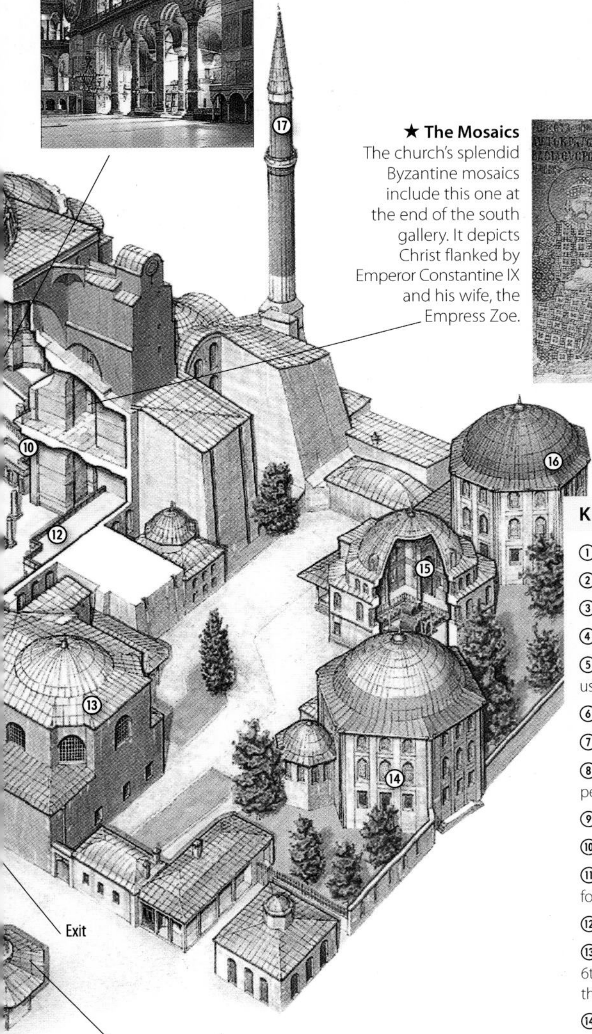

Exit

KEY

① **Buttress**

② **Outer narthex**

③ **Inner narthex**

④ **Imperial Gate**

⑤ **The galleries** were originally used by women during services.

⑥ **Kürsü** *(see p37)*.

⑦ **Calligraphic roundel**

⑧ **Seraphims** adorn the pendentives at the base of the dome.

⑨ **Sultan's loge**

⑩ **Müezzin mahfili** *(see p36)*.

⑪ **The Coronation Square** served for the crowning of emperors.

⑫ **Library of Sultan Mahmut I**

⑬ **The Baptistry**, part of the 6th-century church, now serves as the tomb of two sultans.

⑭ **The mausoleum of Murat III** was used for his burial in 1599. Murat had by that time sired 103 children.

⑮ **Mausoleum of Selim II**, the oldest of the three mausoleums, was completed in 1577 to the plans of Sinan *(see p105)*. Its interior is entirely decorated with İznik tiles *(see p165)*.

⑯ **Mausoleum of Mehmet III**

⑰ **Brick minaret**

★ **Ablutions Fountain**
Built around 1740, this fountain is an exquisite example of Turkish Rococo style. Its projecting roof is painted with floral reliefs.

Exploring Haghia Sophia

Designed as an earthly mirror of the heavens, the interior of Haghia Sophia succeeds in imparting a truly celestial feel. The artistic highlights are a number of glistening figurative mosaics – remains of the decoration that once covered the upper walls but which has otherwise mostly disappeared. The remarkable works of Byzantine art date from the 9th century or later, after the iconoclastic era. Some of the patterned mosaic ceilings, however, particularly those adorning the narthex and the neighbouring Vestibule of the Warriors, are part of the cathedral's original 6th-century decoration.

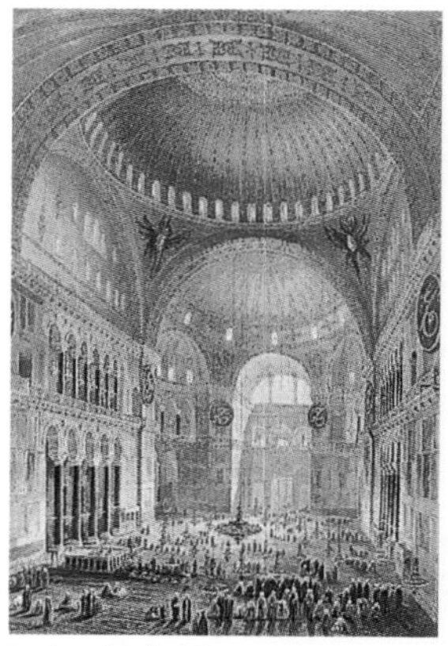

Interior as it looked after restoration in the 19th century

Ground Floor

The first of the surviving Byzantine mosaics can be seen over the Imperial Gate. This is now the public entrance into the church, although previously only the emperor and his entourage were allowed to pass through it. The mosaic shows **Christ on a throne with an emperor kneeling beside him** ① and has been dated to between 886 and 912. The emperor is thought to be Leo VI, the Wise.

The most conspicuous features at ground level in the nave are those added by the Ottoman sultans after the conquest of Istanbul in 1453, when the church was converted into a mosque.

The **mihrab** ②, the niche indicating the direction of Mecca, was installed in the apse of the church directly opposite the entrance. The **sultan's loge** ③, on the left of the mihrab as you face it, was built by the Fossati brothers. These Italian-Swiss architects undertook a major restoration of Haghia Sophia for Sultan Abdül Mecit in 1847–9.

To the right of the mihrab is the ***minbar*** ④, or pulpit, which was installed by Murat III (1574–95). He also erected four ***müezzin mahfilis*** ⑤, marble platforms for readers of the Koran *(see p36)*. The largest of these is adjacent to the *minbar*. The patterned marble **coronation square** ⑥ next to it marks the supposed site of the Byzantine emperor's throne, or omphalos (centre of the world). Nearby, in the south aisle, is the **library of Mahmut I** ⑦, which was built in 1739 and is entered by a decorative bronze door.

Across the nave, between two columns, is the 17th-century marble **preacher's throne** ⑧, the contribution of Murat IV (1623–40). Behind it is one of several **maqsuras** ⑨. These low, fenced platforms were placed beside walls and pillars to provide places for elders to sit, listen and read the Koran.

In the northwestern and western corners of the church are two **marble urns** ⑩, thought to date from the Hellenistic or early Byzantine period. A rectangular pillar behind one of the urns, the **pillar of St Gregory the Miracle-Worker** ⑪, is believed to have healing powers. As you leave the church you pass through the Vestibule of the Warriors, so called because the emperor's bodyguards would wait here for him when he came to worship. Look behind you as you enter it at the wonderful mosaic of the **Virgin with Constantine and Justinian** ⑫ above the door. It shows Mary seated on a throne holding the infant

Floorplan of Haghia Sophia

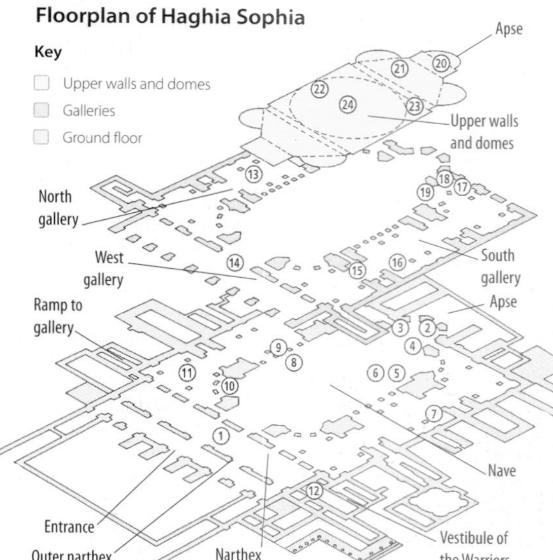

Jesus and flanked by two of the greatest emperors of the city. Constantine, on her right, presents her with the city of Constantinople, while Justinian offers her Haghia Sophia. This was made long after either of these two emperors lived, probably in the 10th century, during the reign of Basil II *(see p56)*. Visitors exit the church by the door that was once reserved for the emperor, due to its proximity to the Great Palace *(see pp96–7)*.

Figure of Christ, detail from the Deësis Mosaic in the south gallery

Galleries

A ramp leads from the ground floor to the north gallery. Here, on the eastern side of the great northwest pier, you will find the 10th-century mosaic of **Emperor Alexander holding a skull** ⑬. On the west face of the same pier is a medieval drawing of a galleon in full sail. The only point of interest in the west gallery is a green marble disk marking the location of the Byzantine **Empress's throne** ⑭.

There is much more to see in the south gallery. You begin by passing through the so-called **Gates of Heaven and Hell** ⑮, a marble doorway of which little is known except that it predates the Ottoman conquest.

Around the corner to the right after passing through this doorway is the **Deësis Mosaic** ⑯ showing the Virgin Mary and John the Baptist with Christ Pantocrator (the All-Powerful). Set into the floor opposite it is the tomb of Enrico Dandalo, the Doge of Venice responsible for the sacking of Constantinople in 1204 *(see p57)*.

In the last bay of the south gallery there are two more mosaics. The right-hand one of these is of the **Virgin holding Christ, flanked by Emperor John II Comnenus and Empress Irene** ⑰. The other shows **Christ with Emperor Constantine IX Monomachus and Empress Zoe** ⑱. The faces of the emperor and empress have been altered.

Eight **wooden plaques** ⑲ bearing calligraphic inscriptions hang over the nave at the level of the gallery. An addition of the Fossati brothers, they bear the names of Allah, the Prophet Mohammed, the first four caliphs and Hasan and Hussein, two of the Prophet's grandsons who are revered as martyrs.

Mosaic depicting the archangel Gabriel, adorning the lower wall of the apse

Upper Walls and Domes

The apse is dominated by a large and striking mosaic showing the **Virgin with the infant Jesus on her lap** ⑳. Two other mosaics in the apse depict the archangels **Gabriel** ㉑ and, opposite him, Michael, but only fragments of the latter now remain. The unveiling of these mosaics on Easter Sunday 867 was a triumphal event celebrating victory over the iconoclasts.

Three mosaic portraits of **saints** ㉒ adorn niches in the north tympanum and are visible from the south gallery and the nave. From left to right they depict: St Ignatius the Younger, St John Chrysostom and St Ignatius Theophorus.

In the four pendentives (the triangular, concave areas at the base of the dome) are mosaics of six-winged **seraphim** ㉓. The ones in the east pendentives date from 1346 to 1355, but may be copies of much older ones. Those on the west side are 19th-century imitations that were added by the Fossati brothers.

The great **dome** ㉔ itself is decorated with Koranic inscriptions. It was once covered in golden mosaic and the tinkling sound of pieces dropping to the ground was familiar to visitors until the building's 19th-century restoration.

Mosaic of the Virgin with Emperor John II Comnenus and Empress Irene

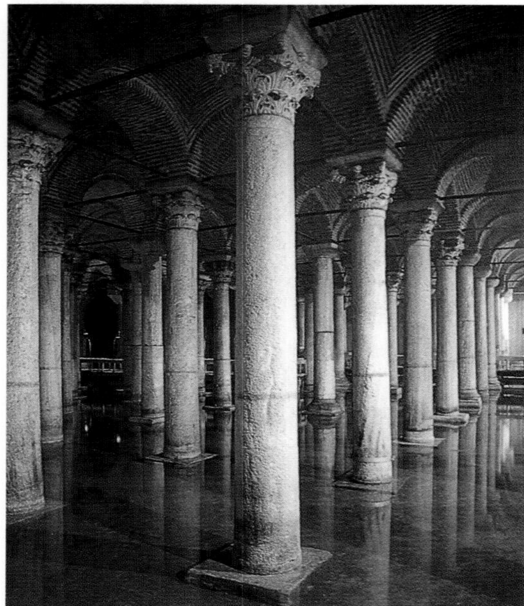

The cavernous interior of the Byzantine Basilica Cistern

❷ Basilica Cistern

Yerebatan Sarnıcı

13 Yerebatan Cad, Sultanahmet.
Map 5 E4. **Tel** (0212) 522 12 59. Sultanahmet. **Open** 9am–7pm daily.
yerebatan.com

This vast underground water cistern, a beautiful piece of Byzantine engineering, is the most unusual tourist attraction in the city. Although there may have been an earlier, smaller cistern here, this cavernous vault was laid out under Justinian in 532, mainly to satisfy the growing demands of the Great Palace *(see pp96–7)* on the other side of the Hippodrome *(see p94)*. For a century after the conquest *(see p58)*, the Ottomans did not know of the cistern's existence. It was rediscovered after people were found to be collecting water, and even fish, by lowering buckets through holes in their basements.

Visitors tread walkways to the mixed sounds of classical music and dripping water. The cistern's roof is held up by 336 columns, each over 8 m (26 ft) high. Only about two-thirds of the original structure is visible today, the rest having been bricked up in the 19th century.

In the far left-hand corner two columns rest on Medusa head bases. These bases are evidence of plundering by the Byzantines from earlier monuments. They are thought to mark a *nymphaeum*, a shrine to the water nymphs.

❸ Istanbul Crafts Centre

Istanbul El Sanatları Çarşısı

Kabasakal Cad 5, Sultanahmet.
Map 5 E4. **Tel** (0212) 517 67 84.
Adliye. **Open** 9am–5pm daily.

If you are interested in Turkish craftwork, this former Koranic college is worth a visit. You can watch skilled artisans at work: they may be binding a book, executing an elegant piece of calligraphy or painting glaze onto ceramics. All the pieces that are produced here are for sale. Other good buys include exquisite dolls, meerschaum pipes and jewellery based on Ottoman designs.

Next door is the Yeşil Ev Hotel *(see p330)*, a restored Ottoman building with a pleasant café in its courtyard.

❹ Carpet Museum

Halı Müzesi

Bab-ı-Hümayan Caddesi.
Map 5 E4. **Tel** (0212) 512 69 93.
Gülhane ort Sultanahmet.
Open 9am–noon, 1–5pm Mon–Fri.
halimuzesi.com

One of Turkey's finest collections of carpets and flat-weave rugs is housed in the İmaret building, the mosque's former soup kitchens. The collection includes pieces weaved throughout Anatolia between 14th and 20th centuries.

Roxelana

Süleyman the Magnificent's power-hungry wife Roxelana (1500–58, Haseki Hürrem in Turkish), rose from being a concubine in the imperial harem to become his chief wife, or first *kadın (see p75)*. Thought to be of Russian origin, she was also the first consort permitted to reside within the walls of Topkapı Palace *(see pp72–5)*. Roxelana would stop at nothing to get her own way. When Süleyman's grand vizier and friend from youth, İbrahim Paşa, became a threat to her position, she persuaded the sultan to have him strangled. Much later, Roxelana performed her *coup de grâce*. In 1553 she persuaded Süleyman to have his handsome and popular heir, Mustafa, murdered by deaf mutes to clear the way for her own son, Selim, to inherit the throne.

The exterior of the 16th-century Baths of Roxelana

The first gallery is dedicated to carpets from the Seljuk Empire, the second gallery displays carpets produced during the height of the Ottoman Empire, and the third gallery shows more recent carpets and prayer rugs from Uşak.

❺ Baths of Roxelana

Haseki Hürrem Hamamı

Ayasofya Meydanı, Sultanahmet. **Map** 5 E4. **Tel** (0212) 638 00 35. Sultanahmet. **Open** 8:30am–5:30pm daily (to 6:30pm summer). **ayasofyahamami.com**

These baths, also known as Ayasofya Hürrem Sultan Hamam, were built in 1556 for Süleyman the Magnificent *(see p59)* by Sinan *(see p105)*, and are named after Roxelana, the sultan's wife. They were designated for the use of the congregation of Haghia Sophia *(see pp86–7)* when it was used as a mosque. With the women's entrance at one end of the building and the men's at the other, their absolute symmetry makes them perhaps the most handsome baths in the city.

Each end of the baths starts with a *camekan*, a massive domed hall that would originally have been centred on a fountain. Next is a small *soğukluk*, or intermediate room, which opens into a *hararet*, or steam room. The hexagonal massage slab in each *hararet*, the *göbek taşı*, is inlaid with coloured marbles, indicating that the baths are of imperial origin.

The Baths of Roxelana functioned as a public bathhouse for more than 350 years, until 1910. After their closure, they continued to be used for various purposes, including as a coal and fuel store and as a government-run carpet shop. Following a programme of renovation to restore the baths to their original function, the building was reopened to the public as a bathhouse.

❻ Mosaic Museum

Mozaik Müzesi

Arasta Çarşısı, Sultanahmet. **Map** 5 E5. **Tel** (0212) 518 12 05. Sultanahmet. **Open** Apr–Oct: 9am–7pm; Nov–Mar: 9am–5pm Tue–Sun.

Located near Arasta Bazaar, among a warren of small shops, this museum was created simply by roofing over a part of the Great Palace of the Byzantine Emperors *(see pp96–7)*, which was discovered in the 1930s. In its heyday the palace boasted hundreds of rooms, many of them glittering with gold mosaics.

The surviving mosaic has a surface area of 1,872 sq m (1,969 sq ft), making it one of the largest preserved mosaics in Europe. It is thought to have been created by an imperial workshop that employed the best craftsmen from across the Empire under the guidance of a master artist. In terms of imagery, the mosaic is particularly diverse, with many different landscapes depicted, including domestic and pastoral episodes, such as herdsmen with their grazing animals, as well as hunting and fighting scenes.

The mosaic is thought to have adorned the colonnade leading from the royal apartments to the imperial enclosure beside the Hippodrome, and dates from the late 5th century AD.

❼ Blue Mosque

See pp92–3.

❽ Museum of Turkish and Islamic Arts

Türk ve İslam Eserleri Müzesi

Atmeydanı Sok, Sultanahmet. **Map** 5 D4. **Tel** (0212) 518 18 05 or 518 18 06. Sultanahmet. **Open** Apr–Oct: 9am–7pm; Nov–Mar: 9am–5pm Tue–Sun.

Over 40,000 items are on display in the former palace of İbrahim Paşa (c.1493–1536), the most gifted of Süleyman's many grand viziers. Paşa married Süleyman's sister when the sultan came to the throne. The collection was begun in the 19th century and ranges from the earliest period of Islam, under the Omayyad caliphate (661–750), through to modern times.

Each room concentrates on a different chronological period or geographical area of the Islamic world, with detailed explanations in both Turkish and English. The museum is particularly renowned for its collection of rugs. These range from 13th-century Seljuk fragments to the palatial Persian silks that cover the walls from floor to ceiling in the palace's great hall.

On the ground floor, an ethnographic section focuses on the lifestyles of different Turkish peoples, particularly the nomads of central and eastern Anatolia. The exhibits include recreations of a round felt *yurt* (Turkic nomadic tent) and a traditional brown tent.

Recreated *yurt* interior, Museum of Turkish and Islamic Arts

❼ Blue Mosque

Sultan Ahmet Camii

The Blue Mosque, which takes its name from the mainly blue İznik tilework *(see p165)* decorating its interior, is one of the most famous religious buildings in the world. Serene at any time, its minarets circled by keening seagulls, it is at its most magical when floodlit at night. Sultan Ahmet I commissioned the mosque during a period of declining Ottoman fortunes, and it was built between 1609 and 1616 by Mehmet Ağa, the imperial architect. The splendour of the plans provoked great hostility at the time, because a mosque with six minarets was considered a sacrilegious attempt to rival the architecture of Mecca.

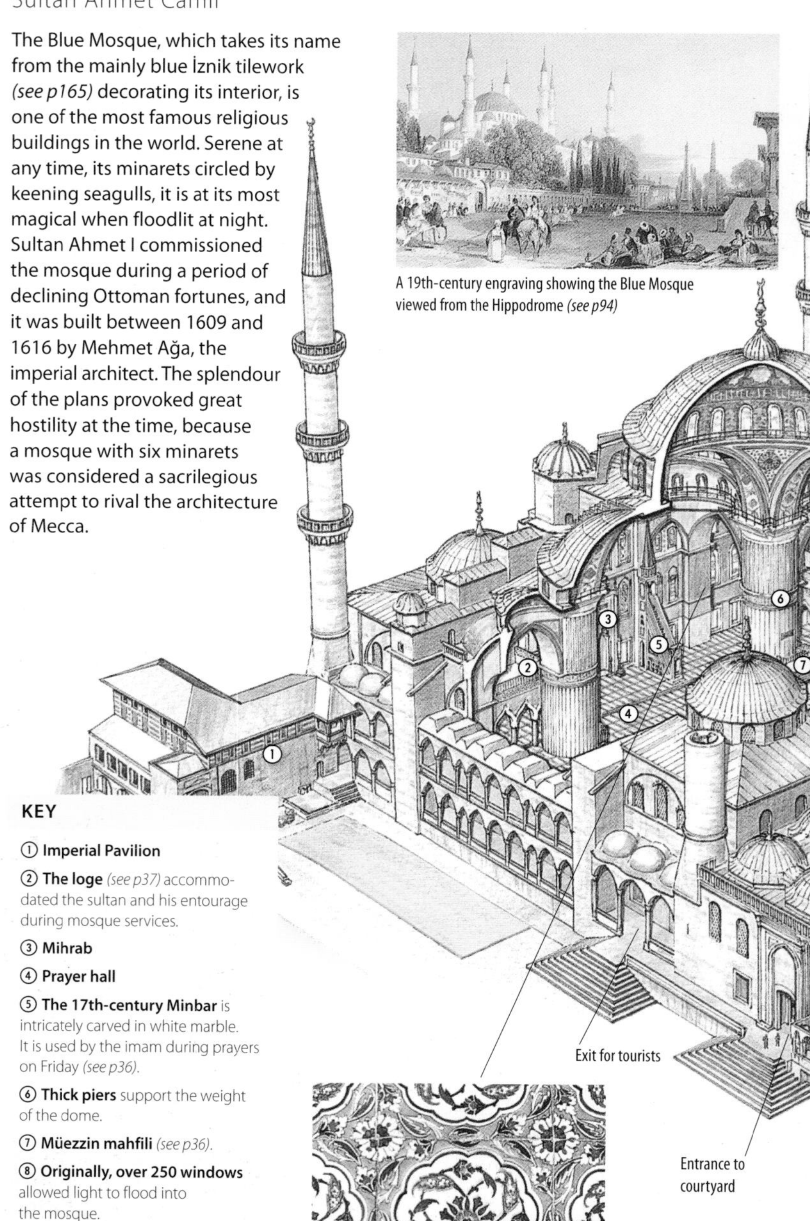

A 19th-century engraving showing the Blue Mosque viewed from the Hippodrome *(see p94)*

KEY

① **Imperial Pavilion**

② **The loge** *(see p37)* accommodated the sultan and his entourage during mosque services.

③ **Mihrab**

④ **Prayer hall**

⑤ **The 17th-century Minbar** is intricately carved in white marble. It is used by the imam during prayers on Friday *(see p36)*.

⑥ **Thick piers** support the weight of the dome.

⑦ **Müezzin mahfili** *(see p36)*.

⑧ **Originally, over 250 windows** allowed light to flood into the mosque.

⑨ **The courtyard** covers an area the same size as the prayer hall, balancing the whole building.

⑩ **Each minaret** has two or three balconies.

★ İznik Tiles

No cost was spared in the decoration. The tiles were made at the peak of tile production in İznik *(see p165)*.

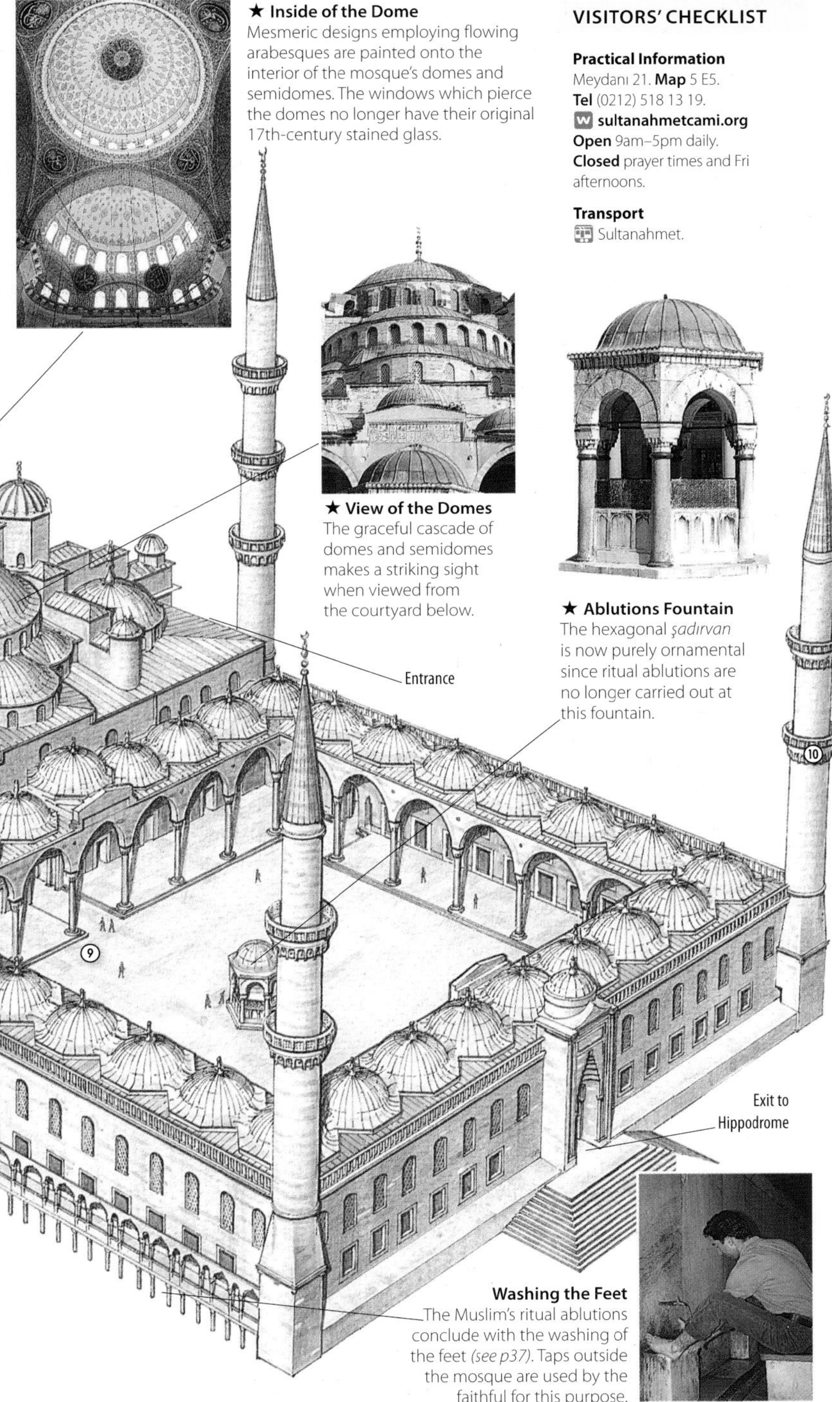

★ **Inside of the Dome**
Mesmeric designs employing flowing arabesques are painted onto the interior of the mosque's domes and semidomes. The windows which pierce the domes no longer have their original 17th-century stained glass.

★ **View of the Domes**
The graceful cascade of domes and semidomes makes a striking sight when viewed from the courtyard below.

★ **Ablutions Fountain**
The hexagonal *şadırvan* is now purely ornamental since ritual ablutions are no longer carried out at this fountain.

Washing the Feet
The Muslim's ritual ablutions conclude with the washing of the feet *(see p37)*. Taps outside the mosque are used by the faithful for this purpose.

VISITORS' CHECKLIST

Practical Information
Meydanı 21. **Map** 5 E5.
Tel (0212) 518 13 19.
W **sultanahmetcami.org**
Open 9am–5pm daily.
Closed prayer times and Fri afternoons.

Transport
Sultanahmet.

Egyptian Obelisk and the Column of Constantine Porphyrogenitus

❾ Hippodrome

At Meydanı

Sultanahmet. **Map** 5 E4.
Sultanahmet.

Little is left of the gigantic stadium which once stood at the heart of the Byzantine city of Constantinople *(see pp54–5)*. It was originally laid out by Emperor Septimus Severus during his rebuilding of the city in the 3rd century AD. Emperor Constantine I *(see p53)* enlarged the Hippodrome and connected its *kathisma*, or royal box, to the nearby Great Palace *(see pp96–7)*. It is thought that the stadium held up to 100,000 people. The site is now an elongated public garden, At Meydanı, the Square of the Horses. There are, however, enough remains of the Hippodrome to get a sense of its scale and importance.

The road running around the square almost directly follows the line of the chariot racing track. You can also make out some of the arches of the *sphendone* (the curved end of the Hippodrome) by walking a few steps down İbret Sokağı. Constantine adorned the *spina*, the central line of the stadium, with obelisks and columns from Ancient Egypt and Greece. Conspicuous by its absence is the column, which once stood on the spot where the tourist information office is located. This was topped by four bronze horses which were pillaged during the Fourth Crusade *(see p56)* and taken to St Mark's in Venice. Three ancient monuments remain, however. The **Egyptian Obelisk**, which was built in 1500 BC, stood outside Luxor until Constantine had it brought to his city. This carved monument is probably only one third of its original height.

Relief carved on the base of the Egyptian Obelisk

Next to it is the **Serpentine Column**, believed to date from 479 BC, which was shipped here from Delphi.

Another obelisk still standing, but of unknown date, is usually referred to as the **Column of Constantine Porphyrogenitus**, after the emperor who restored it in the 10th century AD. Its dilapidated state owes much to the fact that young Janissaries *(see p60)* would routinely scale it as a test of their bravery.

The only other structure in the Hippodrome is a domed fountain, which commemorates the visit of Kaiser Wilhelm II to Istanbul in 1898.

The Hippodrome was the scene of one of the bloodiest events in Istanbul's history. In 532 a brawl between rival chariot-racing teams developed into the Nika Revolt, during which much of the city was destroyed. The end of the revolt came when an army of mercenaries, under the command of Justinian's general Belisarius, massacred an estimated 30,000 people trapped in the Hippodrome.

❿ Marmara University Museum of the Republic

Cumhuriyet Müzesi

Atmeydanı Sok 1, Sultanahmet.
Map 5 D5. **Tel** (0212) 518 16 00.
Sultanahmet. **Open** 10am–6pm Tue–Sun.

This fine art collection run by Marmara University includes works by more than 85 artists from Turkey and around the world. The museum started in 1973 as an etching exhibition held to celebrate 50 years of Turkey as a republic. Today, print, painting, calligraphy and other traditional Turkish art forms are part of the collection.

⓫ Cistern of 1,001 Columns

Binbirdirek Sarnıcı

Klodfarer Cad, Sultanahmet.
Map 5 D4. Çemberlitaş.

This cistern dates back to around the 4th century AD, and was second in size only to the nearby Basilica Cistern *(see p90)*. It was also known as the Cistern of Philoxenus and measured

Ceremonies in the Hippodrome

Beginning with the inauguration of Constantinople on 11 May 330 *(see p53)*, the Hippodrome formed the stage for the city's greatest public events for the next 1,300 years. The Byzantines' most popular pastime was watching chariot racing in the stadium. Even after the Hippodrome fell into ruins following the Ottoman conquest of Istanbul *(see pp58–9)*, it continued to be used for great public occasions. This 16th-century illustration depicts Murat III watching the 52-day-long festivities staged for the circumcision of his son Mehmet. All the guilds of Istanbul paraded before the Sultan displaying their crafts.

Sultan Murat III

Palace of İbrahim Paşa (Museum of Turkish and Islamic Arts, *see p167*)

Column of Constantine Porphyrogenitus

Serpentine Column

Egyptian Obelisk

64 m (210 ft) by 56 m (184 ft). It could hold enough water to supply a population of 360,000 for about 10 days.

The herringbone brick roof vaults are supported by 264 marble columns – the 1,001 columns of its name is poetic exaggeration. Interestingly, due to its dampness, the cistern building proved to provide the ideal atmosphere for the silk weaving process and, for many decades, it was used by Istanbul's silk weavers as a workplace.

⓬ Tomb of Sultan Mahmut II

Mahmut II Türbesi

Divanyolu Cad, Çemberlitaş.
Map 5 D4. Çemberlitaş. **Open** 9:30am–4:30pm daily.

This large octagonal mausoleum is in the Empire style (modelled on Roman architecture), made popular by Napoleon. It was built in 1838, the year before Sultan Mahmut II's death and is shared by sultans Mahmut II, Abdül Aziz and Abdül Hamit II *(see p61)*. Within, Corinthian pilasters divide up walls which groan with symbols of prosperity and victory. The huge tomb dominates a cemetery that has beautiful headstones, a fountain and, at the far end, a good café.

⓭ Constantine's Column

Çemberlitaş

Yeniçeriler Cad, Çemberlitaş.
Map 5 D4. Çemberlitaş.
Çemberlitaş Baths: Vezirhanı Cad 8.
Tel (0212) 522 79 74.
Open 6am–midnight daily.
W **cemberlitas**hamami.com

This 35 m- (115 ft-) high column was constructed in AD 330 as part of the celebrations to inaugurate the new Byzantine capital *(see p53)*. It once dominated the magnificent Forum of Constantine.

Made of porphyry brought from Heliopolis in Egypt, it was originally surmounted by a Corinthian capital bearing a statue of Emperor Constantine dressed as Apollo. This was brought down in a storm in 1106. Although what is left is relatively unimpressive, it has been carefully preserved. In the year 416 the 10 stone drums making up the column were reinforced with metal rings. These were renewed in 1701 by Sultan Mustafa III, and consequently the column is known as Çemberlitaş (the Hooped Column) in Turkish. In English it is sometimes referred to as the Burned Column because it was damaged by several fires, especially one in 1779 which decimated the Grand Bazaar *(see pp108–9)*.

Constantine's Column

A variety of fantastical holy relics were supposedly entombed in the base of the column, which has since been encased in stone to strengthen it. These included the axe which Noah used to build the ark, Mary Magdalene's flask of anointing oil, and remains of the loaves of bread with which Christ fed the multitude. Next to Constantine's Column, on the corner of Divanyolu Caddesi, stand the Çemberlitaş Baths. This splendid *hamam* complex *(see p81)* was commissioned by Nur Banu, wife of Sultan Selim II, and built in 1584 to a plan by the great Sinan *(see p105)*.

The original women's section no longer survives, but the baths still have separate facilities for men and women. The staff are used to foreign visitors, so this is a good place for your first experience of a Turkish bath.

⓮ Sokollu Mehmet Paşa Mosque

Sokollu Mehmet Paşa Camii

Şehit Çeşmesi Sok, Sultanahmet. **Map** 5 D5. **Tel** (0212) 518 16 33. Çemberlitaş or Sultanahmet. **Open** daily. **Closed** prayer times. donation.

Built by the architect Sinan *(see p105)* in 1571–2, this mosque was commissioned by Sokollu Mehmet Paşa, grand vizier to Selim II. The simplicity of Sinan's design solution for the mosque's sloping site has been widely admired. A steep entrance stairway leads up to the mosque courtyard from the street, passing beneath the teaching hall of its *medrese (see p36)*. Only the tiled lunettes above the windows in the portico give a hint of the jewelled mosque interior to come.

Inside, the far wall around the carved mihrab is entirely covered in İznik tiles *(see p165)* of a sumptuous green-blue hue. This tile panel, designed specifically for the space, is complemented by six stained-glass windows. The "hat" of the *minbar* is covered with the same tiles. Most of the mosque's other walls are of plain stone, but they are enlivened by a few more tile panels. Set into the wall over the entrance there is a small piece of greenish stone, which is supposedly from the Kaaba, the holy stone at the centre of Mecca.

Interior of the 16th-century Sokollu Mehmet Paşa Mosque

The Byzantine Church of SS Sergius and Bacchus, now a mosque

⓯ Church of SS Sergius and Bacchus

Küçük Ayasofya Camii

Küçük Ayasofya Cad. **Map** 5 D5. Çemberlitaş or Sultanahmet. **Open** daily. **Closed** prayer times.

Commonly referred to as "Little Haghia Sophia", this church was built in 527, a few years before its namesake *(see pp86–7)*. It too was founded by Emperor Justinian *(see pp54–5)*, together with his empress, Theodora, at the beginning of his long reign. Ingenious and highly decorative, the church gives a somewhat higgledy-piggledy impression both inside and out and is one of the most charming of all the city's architectural treasures.

Inside, an irregular octagon of columns on two floors supports a broad central dome composed of 16 vaults. The mosaic decoration, which once

Reconstruction of the Great Palace

In Byzantine times, present-day Sultanahmet was the site of the Great Palace, which, in its heyday, had no equal in Europe and dazzled medieval visitors with its opulence. This great complex of buildings – including royal apartments, state rooms, churches, courtyards and gardens – extended over a sloping, terraced site from the Hippodrome to the imperial harbour on the shore of the Sea of Marmara. The palace was built in stages, beginning under Constantine in the 4th century. It was enlarged by Justinian following the fire caused by the Nika Revolt in 532. Later emperors, especially the 9th-century Basil I, extended it further. After several hundred years of occupation, it was finally abandoned in the second half of the 13th century in favour of Blachernae Palace.

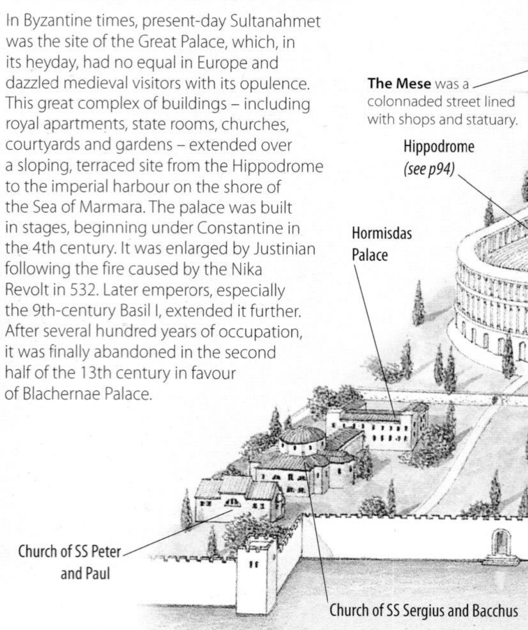

adorned some of the walls, has long since crumbled away. However, the green and red marble columns, the delicate tracery of the capitals and the carved frieze above the columns are original features of the church.

The inscription on this frieze, in boldly carved Greek script, mentions the founders of the church and St Sergius, but not St Bacchus. The two saints were Roman centurions who converted to Christianity and were martyred. Justinian credited them with saving his life when, as a young man, he was implicated in a plot to kill his uncle, Justin I. The saints supposedly appeared to Justin in a dream and told him to release his nephew.

The Church of SS Sergius and Bacchus was built between two important edifices to which it was connected, the Palace of Hormisdas and the Church of SS Peter and Paul, but has outlived them both. After the conquest of Istanbul in 1453 *(see p58)*, it was converted into a mosque.

⑯ Bucoleon Palace

Bukoleon Sarayı

Kennedy Cad, Sultanahmet.
Map 5 E5. Sultanahmet.

Finding the site of what remains of the Great Palace of the Byzantine emperors requires precision. It is not advisable to visit the ruins alone as they are sometimes frequented by tramps.

Take the path under the railway from the Church of SS Sergius and Bacchus, turn left and walk beside Kennedy Caddesi, the main road along the shore of the Sea of Marmara, for about 400 m (440 yards). This will bring you to a stretch of the ancient sea walls, constructed to protect the city from a naval assault. Within these walls you will find a creeper-clad section of stonework pierced by three vast windows framed in marble. This is all that now survives of the Bucoleon Palace, a maritime residence that formed part of the sprawling Great Palace. The waters of a small private harbour lapped right up to the palace and a private flight of steps led down into the water, allowing the emperor to board imperial *caïques*. The ruined tower just east of the palace was a lighthouse, called the Pharos, in Byzantine times.

Wall of Bucoleon Palace, the only part of the Byzantine Great Palace still standing

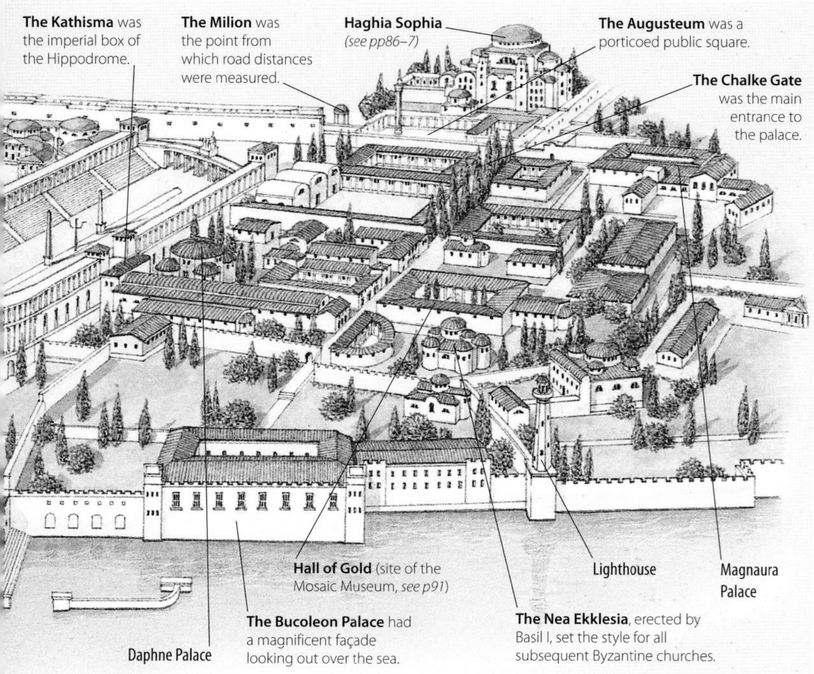

The Kathisma was the imperial box of the Hippodrome.

The Milion was the point from which road distances were measured.

Haghia Sophia *(see pp86–7)*

The Augusteum was a porticoed public square.

The Chalke Gate was the main entrance to the palace.

Hall of Gold (site of the Mosaic Museum, *see p91*)

Lighthouse

Magnaura Palace

The Nea Ekklesia, erected by Basil I, set the style for all subsequent Byzantine churches.

The Bucoleon Palace had a magnificent façade looking out over the sea.

Daphne Palace

10.000.000
ÜRÜN ADI
ERAN
ZERDEÇAL
TL
10.000.000

THE BAZAAR QUARTER

Trade has always been important in a city straddling the continents of Asia and Europe. Nowhere is this more evident than in the warren of streets lying between the Grand Bazaar and Galata Bridge. Everywhere, goods tumble out of shops onto the pavement. Look through any of the archways in between shops and you will discover courtyards or *hans (see pp28–9)* containing feverishly industrious workshops. With its seemingly limitless range of goods, the labyrinthine Grand Bazaar is at the centre of all this commercial activity. The Egyptian Bazaar is equally colourful but smaller and more manageable.

Up on the hill, next to the university, is Süleymaniye Mosque, a glorious expression of 16th-century Ottoman culture. It is just one of numerous beautiful mosques in this area.

Sights at a Glance

Mosques and Churches

1 New Mosque
3 Rüstem Paşa Mosque
5 *Sülemaniye Mosque pp104–5*
6 Prince's Mosque
7 Kalenderhane Mosque
8 Tulip Mosque

Bazaars, Hans and Shops

2 Egyptian Bazaar
11 Book Bazaar
12 Valide Han
13 *Grand Bazaar pp108–9*

Museums and Monuments

9 Forum of Theodosius

Squares and Courtyards

10 Beyazıt Square
14 Çorlulu Ali Paşa Courtyard

Waterways

4 Golden Horn

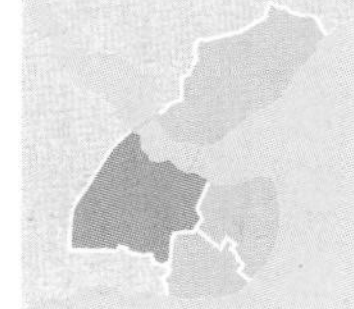

See also Street Finder maps 4 and 5

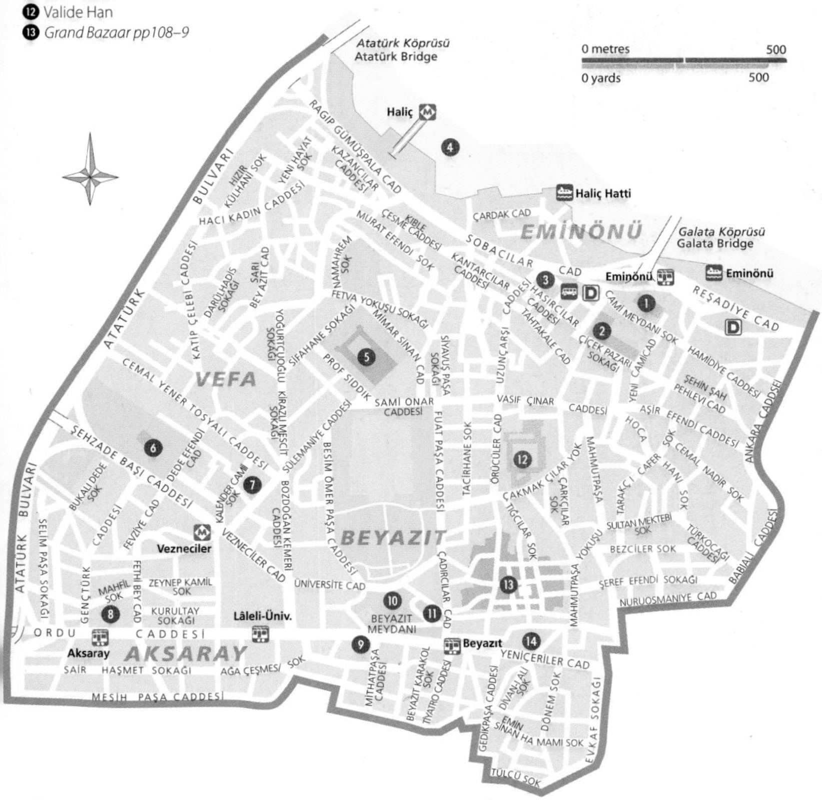

◀ Colourful spices arranged on a stall at the Egyptian Bazaar

For keys to symbols *see back flap*

Street-by-Street: Around the Egyptian Bazaar

The narrow streets around the Egyptian Bazaar encapsulate the spirit of old Istanbul. From here, buses, taxis and trams head off across the Galata Bridge and into the interior of the city. The blast of ships' horns signals the departure of ferries from Eminönü to Asian Istanbul. It is the quarter's shops and markets, though, that are the focus of attention for the eager shoppers who crowd the Egyptian Bazaar and the streets around it, sometimes breaking for a leisurely tea beneath the trees in its courtyard. Across the way, and entirely aloof from the bustle, rise the domes of the New Mosque. On one of the commercial alleyways that radiate out from the mosque, an inconspicuous doorway leads up stairs to the terrace of the serene, tile-covered Rüstem Paşa Mosque.

3 ★ Rüstem Paşa Mosque
The interior of this secluded mosque is a brilliant pattern-book made of İznik tiles *(see p165)* of the finest quality.

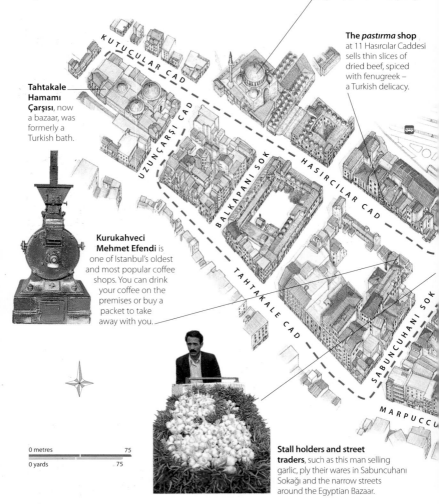

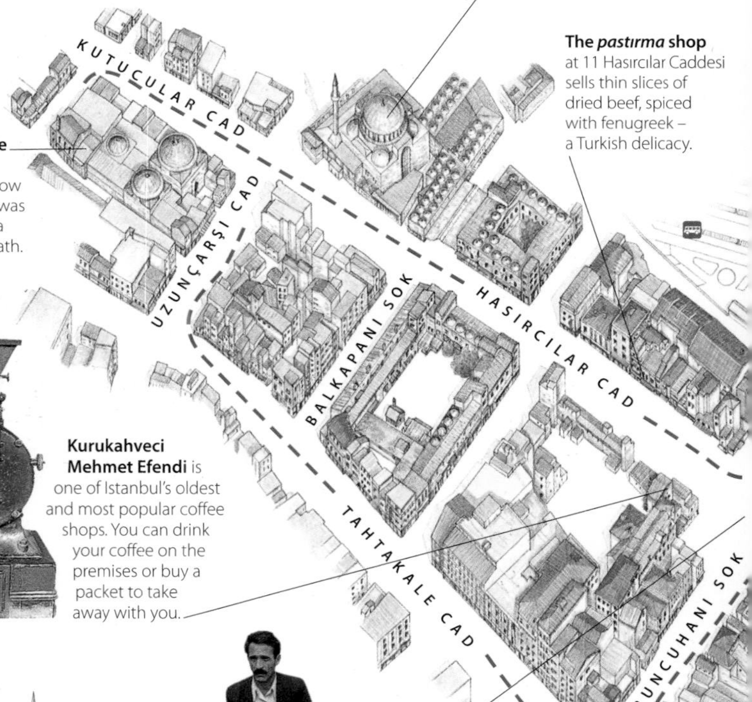

The *pastırma* shop at 11 Hasırcılar Caddesi sells thin slices of dried beef, spiced with fenugreek – a Turkish delicacy.

Tahtakale Hamamı Çarşısı, now a bazaar, was formerly a Turkish bath.

KUTUCULAR CAD
UZUNÇARŞI CAD
BALKAPANI SOK
HASIRCILAR CAD
TAHTAKALE CAD
SABUNCUHANI SOK
MARPUCCU

Kurukahveci Mehmet Efendi is one of Istanbul's oldest and most popular coffee shops. You can drink your coffee on the premises or buy a packet to take away with you.

0 metres 75
0 yards 75

Stall holders and street traders, such as this man selling garlic, ply their wares in Sabuncuhanı Sokağı and the narrow streets around the Egyptian Bazaar.

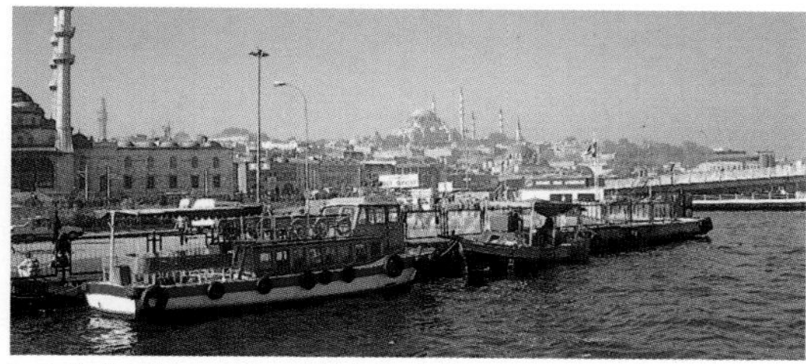

Eminönü is the port from which ferries depart to many destinations and also for trips along the Bosphorus (*see pp130–31*). It bustles with activity as traders compete to sell drinks and snacks.

Golden Horn
THE BAZAAR QUARTER
SULTANAHMET

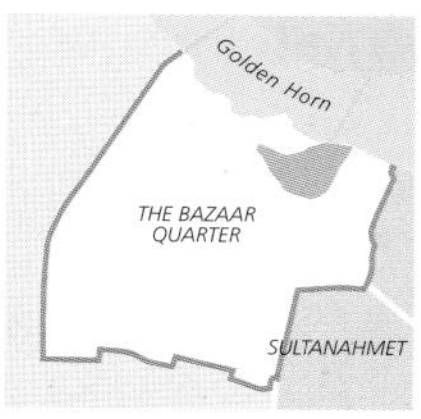

Locator Map

See Street Finder maps 4 and 5

The Royal Pavilion, a suite of beautifully tiled private rooms, is linked by a passage to the sultan's loge inside the New Mosque.

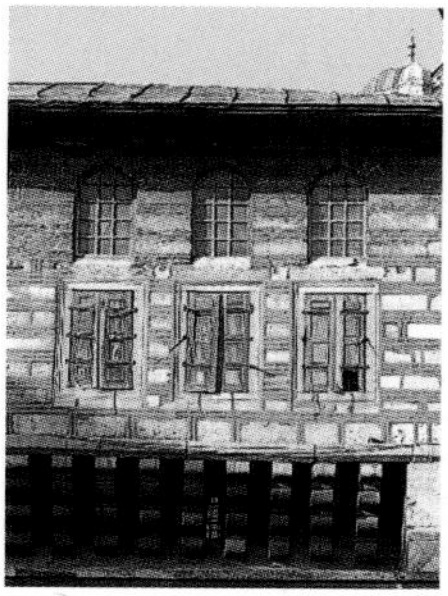

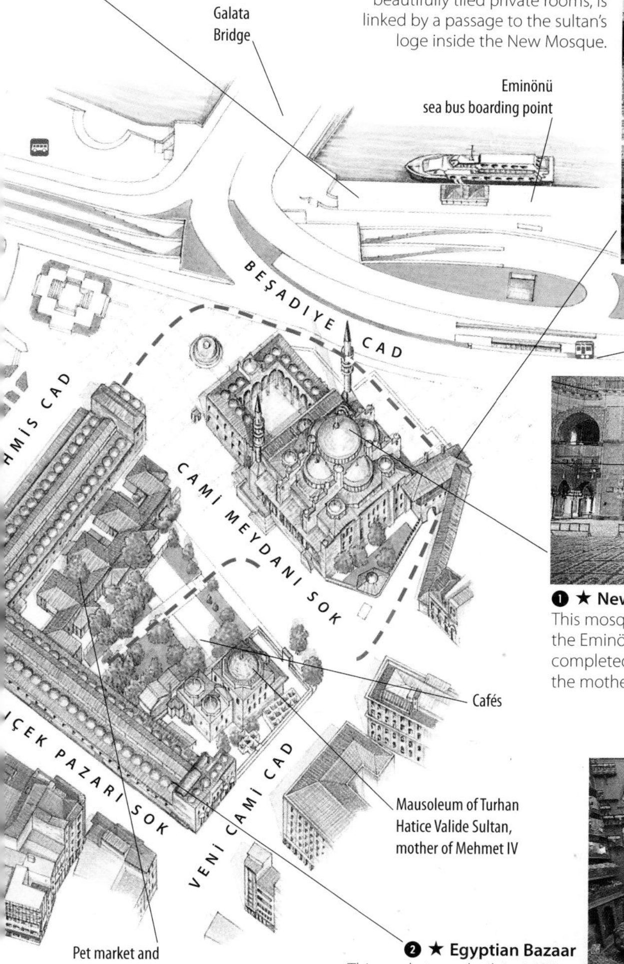

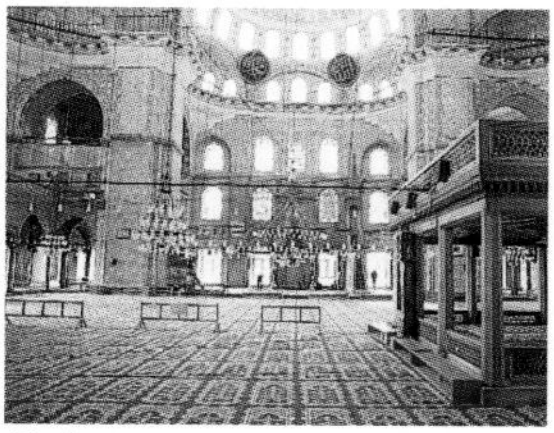

Galata Bridge
Eminönü sea bus boarding point
BEŞADIYE CAD
Eminönü tram stop
HMİS CAD
CAMİ MEYDANI SOK
Cafés
ÇEK PAZARI SOK
YENİ CAMİ CAD
Mausoleum of Turhan Hatice Valide Sultan, mother of Mehmet IV
Pet market and garden centre

❶ ★ New Mosque

This mosque, which dominates the Eminönü waterfront, was completed in the 17th century by the mother of Sultan Mehmet IV.

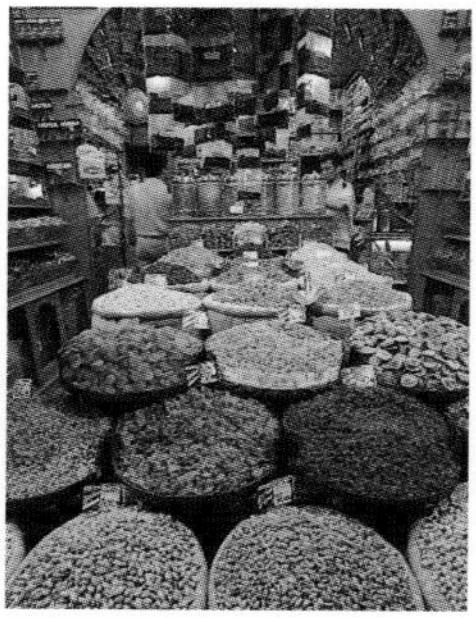

❷ ★ Egyptian Bazaar

This market was built in 1660 as part of the New Mosque complex, and it has always been associated with the sale of spices, though today there is much more on offer.

Key

— Suggested route

❶ New Mosque

Yeni Cami

Yeni Cami Meydanı, Eminönü. **Map** 5 D2. 🚋 Eminönü. **Open** daily. **Closed** prayer times.

Situated at the southern end of Galata Bridge, the New Mosque is one of the most prominent mosques in the city. It dates from the time when a few women from the harem became powerful enough to dictate the policies of the Ottoman sultans.

The mosque was started in 1597 by Safiye, mother of Mehmet III, but building was suspended on the sultan's death as his mother then lost her position. It was not completed until 1663, after Turhan Hatice, mother of Mehmet IV, had taken up the project.

Though the mosque was built after the classical period of Ottoman architecture, it shares many traits with earlier imperial foundations, including a monumental courtyard. The mosque once had a hospital, school and public baths.

The turquoise, blue and white floral tiles decorating the interior are from İznik *(see p165)* and date from the mid-17th century, though by this time the quality of the tiles produced there was already in decline. More striking are the tiled lunettes and bold Koranic frieze decorating the porch between the courtyard and the prayer hall.

At the far left-hand corner of the upper gallery is the sultan's loge *(see p37)*, which is linked to his personal suite of rooms.

A selection of nuts and seeds for sale in the Egyptian Bazaar

❷ Egyptian Bazaar

Mısır Çarşısı

Cami Meydanı Sok. **Map** 5 D2. 🚋 Eminönü. **Open** 8am–7pm daily.

This cavernous, L-shaped market was built in the early 17th century as an extension of the New Mosque complex. Its revenues once helped maintain the mosque's philanthropic institutions.

In Turkish the market is named the Mısır Çarşısı – the Egyptian Bazaar – because it was built with money paid as duty on Egyptian imports. In English it is also known as the Spice Bazaar. From medieval times spices were a vital and expensive part of cooking and they became the market's main produce. The bazaar came to specialize in spices from the Orient, taking advantage of Istanbul's site on the trade route between the East (where most spices were grown) and Europe.

Stalls in the bazaar stock spices, herbs and other foods such as honey, nuts, sweetmeats and *pastırma* (dried beef). Today's expensive Eastern commodity, caviar, is also available, the best variety being Iranian. Nowadays an eclectic range of items can be found in the Egyptian Bazaar, from household goods, toys and clothes to exotic aphrodisiacs. The square between the two arms of the bazaar is full of commercial activity, with cafés, and stalls selling plants and pets.

Floral İznik tiles adorning the interior of Rüstem Paşa Mosque

❸ Rüstem Paşa Mosque

Rüstem Paşa Camii

Hasırcılar Cad, Eminönü. **Map** 5 D2. 🚋 Eminönü. **Open** daily. **Closed** prayer times.

Raised above the busy shops and warehouses around the Egyptian Bazaar, this mosque was built in 1561 by the great architect Sinan *(see p105)* for Rüstem Paşa, son-in-law of and grand vizier to Süleyman I *(see p59)*.

The staggering wealth of its decoration says something about the amount of money that the corrupt Rüstem managed to salt away. Most of the interior is covered in İznik tiles of the highest quality. The four piers are adorned with tiles of one design, but the rest of the prayer hall is a riot of different patterns, from abstract to floral. Some of the finest tiles can be found on the galleries, making it the most magnificently tiled mosque in the city.

The New Mosque, a prominent feature on the Eminönü waterfront

❹ Golden Horn

Haliç

Map 4 C1. Eminönü.
55T, 99A.

Often described as the world's greatest natural harbour, the Golden Horn is a flooded river valley that flows southwest into the Bosphorus. The estuary attracted settlers to its shores in the 7th century BC and later enabled Constantinople to become a rich and powerful port. According to legend, the Byzantines threw so many valuables into it during the Ottoman conquest *(see p58)* that the waters glistened with gold. Today, numerous small boats can be seen plying the upper reaches of the estuary.

Spanning the mouth of the Horn is the Galata Bridge, which joins Eminönü to Galata. The bridge, built in 1992, opens in the middle to allow access for tall ships. It is a good place from which to appreciate the complex geography of the city and admire the minaret-filled skyline. Fishermen's boats selling mackerel sandwiches are usually moored at each end.

The present Galata Bridge replaced a pontoon bridge with a lower level of restaurants. The Old Galata Bridge has been reconstructed further up the Golden Horn, just south of the Rahmi Koç Museum.

❺ Süleymaniye Mosque

See pp104–5.

❻ Prince's Mosque

Şehzade Camii

70 Şehzade Başı Cad, Saraçhane.
Map 4 B3. Laleli. Vezneciler.
Open daily. Tombs: **Open** 9am–5pm Tue–Sun.

This mosque complex was erected by Süleyman the Magnificent *(see p59)* in memory of his eldest son by Roxelana, Şehzade (Prince) Mehmet, who died of smallpox at the age of 21. The building was Sinan's *(see p105)* first major imperial commission and was completed in 1548. The architect used a delightful decorative style in this mosque before abandoning it in favour of the classical austerity of his later work. The mosque is approached through an elegant porticoed inner courtyard, while the other institutions making up the mosque complex, including a *medrese (see p36)*, are enclosed within an outer courtyard. The mosque's interior is unusual and was something of an experiment: symmetrical, it has a half-dome on all four sides.

Dome of the Prince's Mosque, Sinan's first imperial mosque

The three tombs to the rear of the mosque, belonging to Şehzade Mehmet himself and grand viziers İbrahim Paşa and Rüstem Paşa, are the finest in the city. Each has beautiful İznik tiles *(see p165)* and original stained glass. That of Şehzade Mehmet also boasts the finest painted dome in Istanbul.

On Fridays you may notice a crowd of women flocking to another tomb within the complex, that of Helvacı Baba. This has been done traditionally for over 400 years. Helvacı Baba is said to miraculously cure crippled children, solve any fertility problems and find husbands or accommodation for those who beseech him.

❼ Kalenderhane Mosque

Kalenderhane Camii

16 Mart Şehitleri Cad, Saraçhane.
Map 4 B3. Üniversite.
Vezneciler. **Open** prayer times only.

Sitting in the lee of the Valens Aqueduct, on the site where a Roman bath once stood, is this Byzantine church with a chequered history. Built and rebuilt several times between the 6th and 12th centuries, it was converted into a mosque shortly after the conquest in 1453 *(see p58)*. The mosque is named after the Kalender brotherhood of dervishes, which used the church as its headquarters for some years after the conquest.

The building has the cruciform layout characteristic of Byzantine churches of the period. Some of the decoration remaining from its last incarnation, as the Church of Theotokos Kyriotissa (her Ladyship Mary, Mother of God), also survives in the prayer hall with its marble panelling and in the fragments of fresco in the narthex (entrance hall).

A shaft of light illuminates the interior of Kalenderhane Mosque

❺ Süleymaniye Mosque

Süleymaniye Camii

Istanbul's most important mosque is both a tribute to its architect, the great Sinan, and a fitting memorial to its founder, Süleyman the Magnificent *(see p59)*. It was built above the Golden Horn in the grounds of the old palace, Eski Saray, between 1550 and 1557. Like the city's other imperial mosques, the Süleymaniye Mosque was not only a place of worship, but also a charitable foundation, or *külliye* *(see p36)*. The mosque is surrounded by its former hospital, soup kitchen, schools, *kervanseray* and bathhouse. This complex provided a welfare system which fed over 1,000 of the city's poor – Muslims, Christians and Jews alike – every day.

Courtyard
The ancient columns that surround the courtyard are said to have come originally from the *kathisma*, the Byzantine royal box in the Hippodrome *(see p94)*.

Muvakkithane Gateway
The main courtyard entrance (now closed) contained the rooms of the mosque astronomer, who determined prayer times.

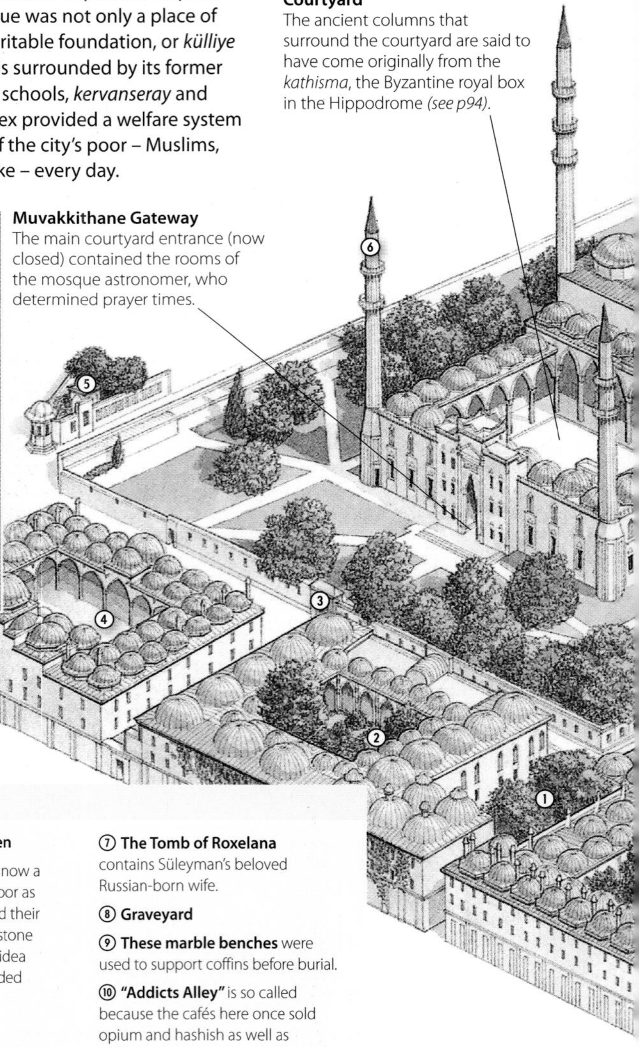

KEY

① **Café in a sunken garden**

② **The İmaret (kitchen)** – now a restaurant – fed the city's poor as well as the mosque staff and their families. The size of the millstone in its courtyard gives some idea of the amount of grain needed to feed everyone.

③ **İmaret Gate**

④ **The *kervansaray*** provided lodging and food for travellers and their animals.

⑤ **Tomb of Sinan**

⑥ **Minaret**

⑦ **The Tomb of Roxelana** contains Süleyman's beloved Russian-born wife.

⑧ **Graveyard**

⑨ **These marble benches** were used to support coffins before burial.

⑩ **"Addicts Alley"** is so called because the cafés here once sold opium and hashish as well as coffee and tea.

⑪ **The medreses** to the south of the mosque house a library containing 110,000 manuscripts.

⑫ **Former hospital and asylum**

For hotels and restaurants in this area see p331 and pp346–7

★ Mosque Interior
A sense of soaring space and calm strikes you as you enter the mosque. The effect is enhanced by the fact that the height of the dome from the floor is exactly double its diameter, which is 26 m (85 ft).

VISITORS' CHECKLIST

Practical Information
Prof Sıddık Sami Onar Cad, Faith.
Map 4 C3.
Tel (0212) 522 02 98.
Open daily. **Closed** prayer times. Seek permission for photos/ access to minarets.

Transport
Beyazıt or Eminönü.

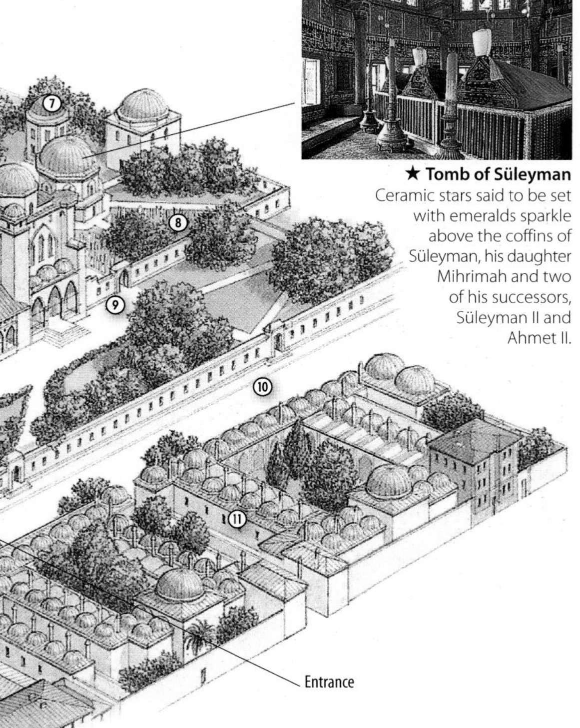

★ Tomb of Süleyman
Ceramic stars said to be set with emeralds sparkle above the coffins of Süleyman, his daughter Mihrimah and two of his successors, Süleyman II and Ahmet II.

Sinan, the Imperial Architect

Like many of his eminent contemporaries, Koca Mimar Sinan (c.1491–1588) was brought from Anatolia to Istanbul in the *devşirme*, the annual roundup of talented Christian youths, and educated at one of the elite palace schools. He became a military engineer but won the eye of Süleyman I, who made him chief imperial architect in 1538. With the far-sighted patronage of the sultan, Sinan – the closest Turkey gets to a Renaissance architect – created masterpieces which demonstrated his master's status as the most magnificent of monarchs. Sinan died aged 97, having built 131 mosques and 200 other buildings.

Bust of the great architect Sinan

❽ Tulip Mosque

Laleli Camii

Ordu Cad, Laleli. **Map** 4 B4. Laleli. Vezneciler. **Open** prayer times only.

Built in 1759–63, this mosque complex is the city's best example of the Baroque style, of which its architect, Mehmet Tahir Ağa, was the greatest exponent. A variety of gaudy, coloured marble covers all of its surfaces. Underneath the body of the mosque is a great hall, supported on eight piers with a fountain in the middle, used as a market and packed with Eastern Europeans and Central Asians haggling over clothing.

The nearby Büyük Taş Hanı, or Big Stone Han, probably part of the mosque's original complex *(see pp36–7)*, now houses shops and a restaurant. To get to it, turn left outside the mosque into Fethi Bey Caddesi, and take the second left into Çukur Çeşme Sokağı. The main courtyard of the han is at the end of a long passage off this lane.

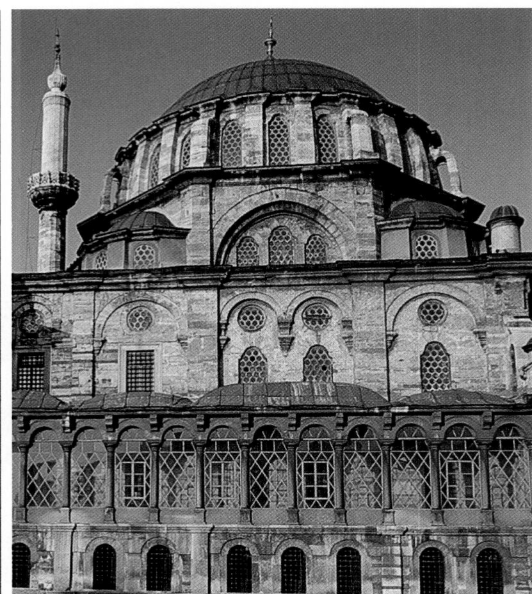

The Baroque Tulip Mosque, housing a marketplace in its basement

❾ Forum of Theodosius

Ordu Cad, Beyazıt. **Map** 4 C4. Üniversite or Beyazıt.

The city of Constantinople *(see pp54–5)* was built around large public squares or forums, the largest of which stood on the site of Beyazıt Square. It was once known as the Forum Tauri (Forum of the Bull) because of the huge bronze bull in which sacrificial animals, and sometimes criminals, were roasted. The huge columns, decorated with a motif reminiscent of a peacock's tail, are particularly striking. When the forum became derelict these columns were reused in the city, some in the Basilica Cistern *(see p90)*, and fragments from the forum were built into Beyazıt Hamamı, a Turkish bath *(see p81)* further west down Ordu Caddesi, now a bazaar.

Peacock feather design on a column at the Forum of Theodosius

❿ Beyazıt Square

Beyazıt Meydanı

Ordu Cad, Beyazıt. **Map** 4 C4. Beyazıt.

Always filled with crowds of people and huge flocks of pigeons, Beyazıt Square is the most vibrant space in the old part of the city. During the week the square hosts a flea market, with carpets *(see pp366–7)*, silks and general bric-a-brac on sale and many cafés located beneath shady plane trees.

On the northern side of the square is the Moorish-style gateway leading into Istanbul University. Within the wooded grounds rises **Beyazıt Tower**, a fire lookout point built in 1828. Two original timber towers were destroyed by fire. At one time you could climb to the top of the tower, but it has been closed to the public since 1972.

On the square's eastern side is **Beyazıt Mosque**. Completed in 1506, it is the oldest surviving imperial mosque in the city. Behind the impressive outer portal is a harmonious courtyard with an elegant domed fountain at its centre. The layout of its interior is heavily inspired by the design of Haghia Sophia *(see pp86–7)*.

Beyazıt Tower, within the wooded grounds of Istanbul University

⓫ Book Bazaar

Sahaflar Çarşısı

Sahaflar Çarşısı Sok, Beyazıt. **Map** 4 C4. Üniversite. **Open** 8am–8pm daily.

This charming booksellers' courtyard, on the site of the Byzantine book and paper market, can be entered either from Beyazıt Square or from inside the Grand Bazaar *(see pp108–9)*. Early in the Ottoman period *(see pp58–9)*, printed books were seen as a corrupting influence and were banned in Turkey, so the bazaar sold only manuscripts. On 31 January 1729 İbrahim Müteferrika (1674–1745) produced the first printed Turkish book, an Arabic dictionary, and today his bust stands in the centre of the market. Book prices are fixed and cannot be haggled over.

Customers browsing in the Book Bazaar (Sahaflar Çarşisi)

⓬ Valide Han

Valide Hanı

Junction of Çakmakçılar Yokuşu & Tarakçılar Sok, Beyazıt. **Map** 4 C3. Beyazıt, then 10 mins' walk. **Open** 9:30am–5pm Mon–Sat.

If the Grand Bazaar *(see pp108–9)* seems large, it is sobering to realize that it is only the covered part of a huge area of seething commercial activity which reaches all the way to the Golden Horn. Most of the manufacturing and trade takes place in *hans (see pp28–9)* hidden away from the street behind shaded gateways.

The largest *han* in Istanbul is Valide Han, built in 1651 by Kösem, the mother of Sultan Mehmet IV. You enter it from Çakmakçılar Yokuşu through a massive portal, pass through an irregularly shaped forecourt, and come out into a large courtyard centring on a Shiite mosque. This was built when the *han* became the centre of Persian trade in the city. The *han* now throbs to the rhythm of hundreds of weaving looms.

A short walk further down Çakmakçılar Yokuşu is Büyük Yeni Han, hidden behind another impressive doorway. This 1764 Baroque *han* has three arcaded levels. In the labyrinth of streets around the *hans*, artisans are grouped according to their wares.

⓭ Grand Bazaar

See pp108–9.

⓮ Çorlulu Ali Paşa Courtyard

Çorlulu Ali Paşa Külliyesi

Yeniçeriler Cad, Beyazıt. **Map** 4 C4. Beyazıt. **Open** daily.

Like many others in the city, the *medrese (see p36)* of this mosque complex outside the Grand Bazaar has become the setting for a tranquil outdoor café. It was built for Çorlulu Ali Paşa, son-in-law of Mustafa II, the grand vizier under Ahmet III.

The complex is entered from Yeniçeriler Caddesi by two alleyways. Several carpet shops now inhabit the *medrese* and rugs are spread all around for prospective buyers. The carpet shops share the *medrese* with a *kahve*, a traditional café, which is popular with locals and university students. It advertises itself irresistibly as the "Traditional Mystic Water Pipe and Erenler Tea Garden", where you can sit, drink tea and perhaps smoke a *nargile* (water pipe), while deciding which carpet to buy *(see pp366–7)*.

Situated across Bıleycıler Sokak, an alleyway off Çorlulu Ali Paşa Courtyard, is the Koca Sinan Paşa tomb complex, the courtyard of which is another tea garden. The charming *medrese*, mausoleum and *sebil* (a fountain where water was handed out to passers-by) were built in 1593 by Davut Ağa, who succeeded Sinan *(see p105)* as chief architect of the empire. The tomb of Koca Sinan Paşa, grand vizier under Murat III and Mehmet III, is a striking 16-sided structure.

Just off the other side of Yeniçeriler Caddesi is Gedik Paşa Hamamı, probably the city's oldest working Turkish baths *(see p81)*, built around 1475 for Gedik Ahmet Paşa, grand vizier under Mehmet the Conqueror *(see p58)*.

Carpet shops in Çorlulu Ali Paşa Courtyard

⓭ The Grand Bazaar

Kapalı Çarşı

Nothing can prepare you for the Grand Bazaar. This labyrinth of streets covered by painted vaults is lined with thousands of booth-like shops, whose wares spill out to tempt you and whose shopkeepers are relentless in their quest for a sale. The bazaar was established by Mehmet II shortly after his conquest of the city in 1453 *(see p58)*. It can be entered by several gateways, two of the most useful being Çarşıkapı Gate (from Beyazıt tram stop) and Nuruosmaniye Gate (from Nuruosmaniye Mosque). It is easy to get lost in the bazaar in spite of the signposting. Many of the bazaar's goods are made behind the scenes in secluded ateliers.

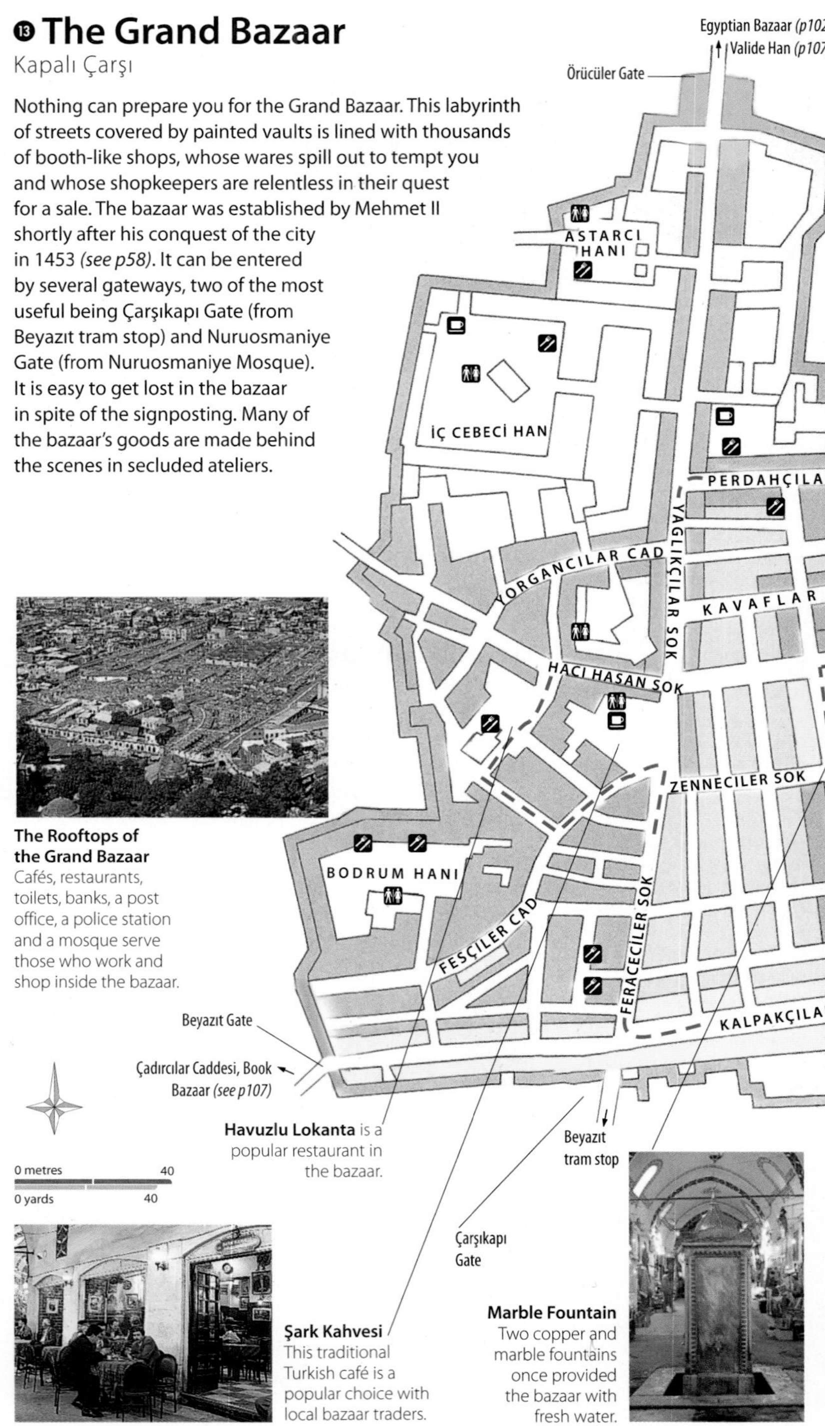

The Rooftops of the Grand Bazaar
Cafés, restaurants, toilets, banks, a post office, a police station and a mosque serve those who work and shop inside the bazaar.

Havuzlu Lokanta is a popular restaurant in the bazaar.

Şark Kahvesi
This traditional Turkish café is a popular choice with local bazaar traders.

Marble Fountain
Two copper and marble fountains once provided the bazaar with fresh water.

For additional map symbols *see back flap*

Zincirli Han
This is one of the prettiest *hans* in the bazaar. Here a piece of jewellery can be made to your own choice of design.

VISITORS' CHECKLIST

Practical Information
Çarşıkapı Cad, Beyazıt. **Map** 4 C4.
Tel (0212) 522 31 73.
Open 9am–7pm Mon–Sat.

Transport
Çemberlitaş (for Nuruosmaniye Gate), Beyazıt (for Çarşıkapı Gate). 61B.

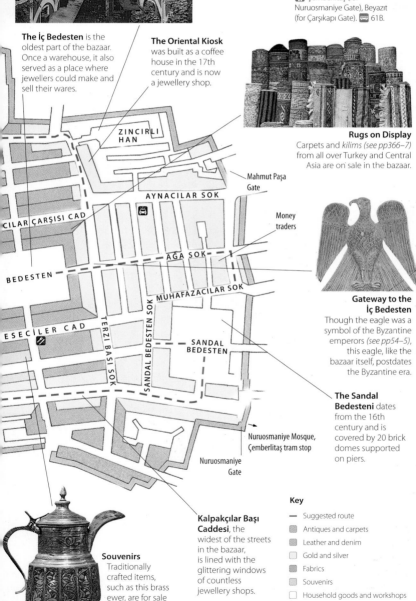

The İç Bedesten is the oldest part of the bazaar. Once a warehouse, it also served as a place where jewellers could make and sell their wares.

The Oriental Kiosk was built as a coffee house in the 17th century and is now a jewellery shop.

Rugs on Display
Carpets and *kilims (see pp366–7)* from all over Turkey and Central Asia are on sale in the bazaar.

ZINCIRLI HAN
Mahmut Paşa Gate
AYNACILAR SOK
CILAR ÇARŞISI CAD
Money traders
AĞA SOK
BEDESTEN
MUHAFAZACILAR SOK
ESECİLER CAD
TERZI BAŞI SOK
SANDAL BEDESTEN SOK
SANDAL BEDESTEN
Nuruosmaniye Mosque, Çemberlitaş tram stop
Nuruosmaniye Gate

Gateway to the İç Bedesten
Though the eagle was a symbol of the Byzantine emperors *(see pp54–5)*, this eagle, like the bazaar itself, postdates the Byzantine era.

The Sandal Bedesteni dates from the 16th century and is covered by 20 brick domes supported on piers.

Kalpakçılar Başı Caddesi, the widest of the streets in the bazaar, is lined with the glittering windows of countless jewellery shops.

Souvenirs
Traditionally crafted items, such as this brass ewer, are for sale in the bazaar.

Key
- Suggested route
- Antiques and carpets
- Leather and denim
- Gold and silver
- Fabrics
- Souvenirs
- Household goods and workshops
- Boundary of the bazaar

For hotels and restaurants in this area see p331 and pp346–7

TURKCELL
TURKCELL
TURKCELL
1
TAKSIM–TÜNEL
47
47

BEYOĞLU

For centuries Beyoğlu, a steep hill north of the Golden Horn, was home to the city's foreign residents. First to arrive here were the Genoese. As a reward for aiding the reconquest of the city from the crusader-backed Latin Empire in 1261, they were given the Galata area, which is now dominated by the Galata Tower. During the Ottoman period, Jews from Spain, Arabs, Greeks and Armenians settled in communities here. From the 16th century, the European powers established embassies in the area to further their interests within the lucrative territories of the Ottoman Empire. The district has not changed much in character over the centuries and is still a thriving commercial quarter today.

Sights at a Glance

Historic Buildings and Monuments

1. Pera Palace Hotel
3. Mevlevi Lodge
4. Galata Tower

Museums

2. Pera Museum
5. Ottoman Bank Museum
7. Istanbul Museum of Modern Art
8. Museum of Innocence

Mosques and Churches

6. Nusretiye Mosque

Quarters

9. Taksim

See also Street Finder maps 1 and 5

◀ A vintage tram on İstiklâl Caddesi in Taksim

For keys to symbols *see back flap*

Street-by-Street: İstiklâl Caddesi

The pedestrianized İstiklâl Caddesi is Beyoğlu's main street. Once known as the Grande Rue de Pera, it is lined by late 19th-century apartment blocks and European embassy buildings whose grandiose gates and façades belie their use as mere consulates since Ankara became the Turkish capital in 1923 *(see p62)*. Hidden from view stand the churches, which used to serve the foreign communities of Pera (as this area was formerly called), some still buzzing with worshippers, others just quiet echoes of a bygone era. Today, the once seedy backstreets of Beyoğlu, off İstiklâl Caddesi, have taken on a new lease of life, with trendy bars and clubs opening and shops selling hand-crafted jewellery, furniture and the like. Crowds are also drawn by the area's cinemas and numerous stylish restaurants.

1 ★ Pera Palace Hotel
This hotel is an atmospheric period piece. Many famous guests, like Agatha Christie, have stayed here since it opened in 1892. The hotel has been extensively restored to its original splendour.

St Mary Draperis is a Franciscan church dating from 1789. This small statue of the Virgin stands above the entrance from the street. The vaulted interior of the church is colourfully decorated. An icon of the Virgin, said to perform miracles, hangs over the altar.

3 ★ Mevlevi Lodge
A peaceful garden surrounds this small museum of the Mevlevi Sufi sect *(see p259)*. On the last Sunday of every month visitors can see dervishes perform their famous swirling dance.

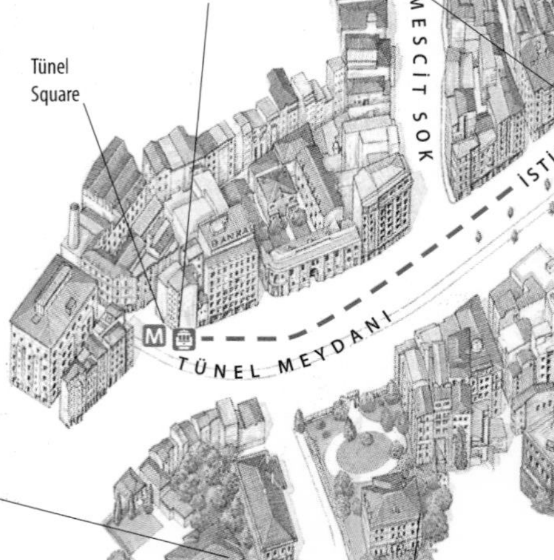

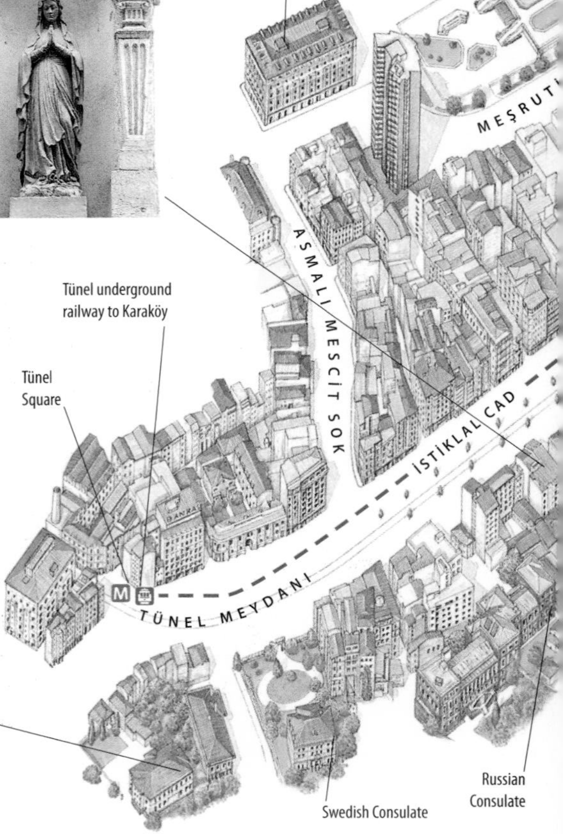

Key

— Suggested route

For additional map symbols *see back flap*

Galatasaray Fish Market (Balık Pazarı) mainly sells fresh fish, but inside you will also find delicatessens offering everything from meats and cheeses to sweetmeats and pickles.

Locator Map
See Street Finder map 1

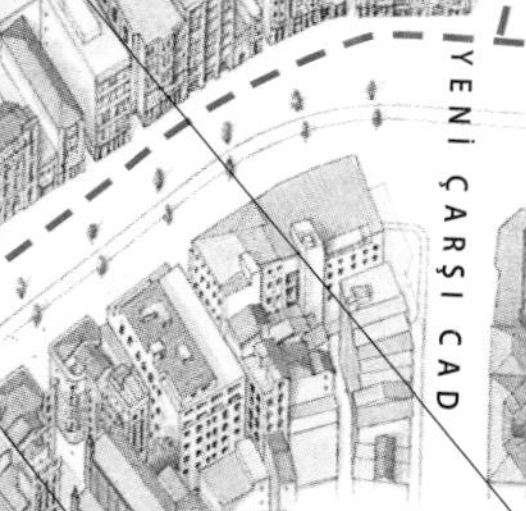

Çiçek Pasajı was originally a flower market. Its stalls have been replaced by bars and restaurants, which are particularly lively in the evenings.

❷ Pera Museum Oriental paintings, Anatolian weights and measures and Kütahya tiles and ceramics are part of the collection.

The Church of the Panaghia serves the now much-reduced Greek Orthodox population of Beyoğlu. Dedicated to the Virgin Mary, it contains this beautiful classical iconostasis.

0 metres 75
0 yards 75

The peaceful courtyard of the Mevlevi Lodge

❶ Pera Palace Hotel

Pera Palace Oteli

52 Meşrutiyet Cad, Tepebaşı. **Map** 1 A5. **Tel** (0212) 251 40 00. Tünel. by arrangement. **perapalace.com**

Throughout the world there are hotels that have attained a legendary status. One such hotel is the Pera Palace, which opened in 1892 to cater for travellers on the Orient Express *(see p80)*.

After an extensive renovation, it still evokes images of uniformed porters and exotic destinations such as Baghdad. The Grand Orient bar serves cocktails beneath its original chandeliers, while the patisserie offers irresistible cakes and a genteel ambience. A room used by the thriller writer Agatha Christie can be visited on request.

❷ Pera Museum

Pera Müzesi

Merutiyet Cad 141, Tepebaı. **Map** 1 A4. **Tel** (0212) 334 99 00. Tünel. From Taksim Square down Tarlabaşı. **Open** 10am–7pm Tue–Thu & Sat; 10am–10pm Fri; noon–6pm Sun. **Closed** 1 Jan, first day of Religious Holidays. (disabled visitors enter free). **peramuzesi.org.tr**

The Pera Museum was opened in 2005 by the Suna and İnan Kıraç Foundation.

Formerly the Hotel Bristol, it has been transformed into a fully equipped modern museum. Notable collections include Ottoman weights and measures, over 400 examples of 18th-century Kütahya tiles and ceramics, and the Suna and İnan Kıraç Foundation's exhibition of Orientalist art. This collection brings together works by European artists inspired by the Ottoman world from the 17th century to the early 19th century and also covers the last two centuries of the Ottoman Empire. There are also regular temporary exhibitions featuring works by artists such as Warhol and Miro.

❸ Mevlevi Lodge

Mevlevi Tekkesi

15 Galip Dede Cad, Beyoğlu. **Map** 1 D3. **Tel** (0212) 245 41 41. Tünel. **Open** 9:30am–5pm Wed–Mon.

Although Sufism was banned by Atatürk in 1925, this Dervish lodge has survived as the Divan Edebiyatı Müzesi, a museum of *divan* literature (classical Ottoman poetry). The lodge belonged to the most famous Sufi sect, known as the Whirling Dervishes *(see p259)*. The original dervishes were disciples of the mystical poet and Sufi master Celaleddin Rumi, known as "Mevlâna" (Our Leader).

Tucked away off Galip Dede, the focus of the 18th-century lodge is a beautiful octagonal wooden dance floor where the *sema* (ritual dance) is usually performed every Sunday in May and September, and twice monthly between October and April. Tickets are available from the lodge on the day of the performance.

❹ Galata Tower

Galata Kulesi

Büyük Hendek Sok, Şişhane. **Map** 5 D1. **Tel** (0212) 293 81 80. Tünel. **Open** 9am–8pm daily. Restaurant & Show **Open** 8pm–midnight daily. **galatatower.net**

The most recognizable feature on the Golden Horn, the Galata Tower, is 60 m (196 ft) high and topped by a conical tower. Its origins date from the 6th century when it was used to monitor shipping. After the conquest of Istanbul in 1453, the Ottomans turned it into a prison and naval depot. Aviation pioneer, Hezarfen Ahmet Çelebi attached wings to his arms and "flew" from the tower to Üsküdar in the 1700s. The building was subsequently used as a fire watchtower.

It has been refurbished to blend with local improvement schemes and, in the evenings, the 9th floor is a restaurant with authentic Turkish entertainment. The unmissable view from the top encompasses the Istanbul skyline and beyond to Princes' Islands *(see p162)*.

The distinctive Galata Tower, as seen from across the Golden Horn

For hotels and restaurants in this area see pp331–2 and p347

5 Ottoman Bank Museum

Osmanlı Bankası Müzesi

Bankalar Cad 35–37, Karaköy. **Map** 5 D1. **Tel** (0212) 292 76 05. Tünel. 25E, 56. **Open** 10am–6pm daily.

The Ottoman Bank Museum has the most interesting collection of state archives in Turkey. From the official Ottoman state bank in 1856 to its incorporation into Garanti Bank in 2001, no other records mirror Turkey's recent social, political and economic events so authentically. Exhibits include Ottoman banknotes, promissory notes, photos of the Empire's ornately crafted bank branches and outstanding photos of employees throughout the bank's history.

Nusretiye Mosque

6 Nusretiye Mosque

Nusretiye Camii

Necatibey Cad, Tophane. **Map** 1 B5. 25E, 56. **Open** daily.

The Baroque "Mosque of Victory" was built in the 1820s by Kirkor Balian. A very ornate building, it is in fact more like a large palace pavilion than a typical mosque. It was commissioned by Mahmut II to commemorate his abolition of the Janissary corps in 1826 *(see p61)*. The marble panel of calligraphy around the interior of the mosque is particularly fine.

Colourful display at the museum shop, Istanbul Museum of Modern Art

7 Istanbul Museum of Modern Art

İstanbul Modern Sanat Müzesi

Meclis-i Mebusan Cad, Liman İşletmeleri Sahası, Antrepo 4, Karaköy. **Map** 2 A5. **Tel** (0212) 334 73 00. Tophane. 56. **Open** 10am–6pm Tue–Sun (to 8pm Thu). free on Thu. **istanbulmodern.org**

Perched on the Golden Horn, this is the most upbeat and thoroughly European museum in Turkey. It houses both permanent collections and temporary exhibitions, providing a showcase for many of the eccentric and talented personalities who have shaped modern art in Turkey, and reflecting the main trends and themes of Turkish art from the early 20th century to the present day. Many of the paintings and drawings are from the private collection of the Ecacıbaşı family, who founded the museum.

The collection includes abstract art, landscapes, watercolours and the plastic arts as well as a sculpture garden and a stunning exhibition of black-and-white photography. Exhibitions by contemporary artists from abroad are held regularly, as the museum embraces "Modern Experiences".

8 Museum of Innocence

Masumiyet Müzesi

Cukurcuma Cad, Dalgıç Çıkmaz. **Map** 1 B5. **Tel** (0212) 252 97 38. **Open** 10am–6pm Tue–Sun (to 9pm Fri). **masumiyetmuzesi.org** Taksim.

Located in the trendy district of Cukurcuma, this museum is the pet project of Turkey's best-known Nobel-prize winning author, Orhan Pamuk. A real-life incarnation of the fictional museum in his eponymous novel, the museum chronicles the lives of the central characters through a collection of everyday objects dating from 1976–84. These were collected by the author whilst writing the novel.

9 Taksim

Map 1 E3. Taksim. Taksim Art Gallery: **Tel** (0212) 245 20 68. **Open** 11am–7pm Mon–Sat.

Centring on the vast, open Taksim Square (Taksim Meydanı), the Taksim area is the hub of activity in modern Beyoğlu. Taksim means "water distribution centre", and from the early 18th century it was from this site that water from the Belgrade Forest was distributed throughout the modern city. The original stone reservoir, built in 1732 by Mahmut I, still stands at the top of İstiklal Caddesi.

On Cumhuriyet Caddesi is the modern building of the **Taksim Art Gallery**, which shows temporary exhibitions as well as permanent displays of Istanbul landscapes by some of Turkey's most important 20th-century painters.

An extensive redevelopment project of Taksim Square was halted by the Gezı Park protests of 2013, but may resume and cause disruptions to public transport and traffic.

FURTHER AFIELD

Away from Istanbul's city centre there are numerous sights worth visiting. Stretching from the Golden Horn to the Sea of Marmara, the Theodosian Walls are one of the city's most impressive monuments. Along the walls stand several ancient palaces and churches: particularly interesting is the Church of St Saviour in Chora, with its stunning Byzantine mosaics. If you follow the Bosphorus northwards, it will bring you to Dolmabahçe Palace, an opulent fantasy not to be missed. Beyond it is peaceful Yıldız Park, with yet more beautiful palaces and pavilions.

Not all visitors have time to see the Asian side of the city, but it is worth spending half a day here. Attractions include splendid mosques, an ornate railway station and a museum dedicated to Florence Nightingale.

Sights at a Glance

Mosques and Churches

1 Ahrida Synagogue
2 Church of St Stephen of the Bulgars
3 Church of the Pammakaristos
4 Greek Orthodox Patriarchate
5 Mosque of Selim I
6 Fatih Mosque
7 Zeyrek Mosque
8 Church of St John of Studius
13 Gazi Ahmet Paşa Mosque
15 *Church of St Saviour in Chora pp122–3*
16 Eyüp Sultan Mosque
25 Şemsi Paşa Mosque
26 İskele Mosque
27 Atik Valide Mosque

Historic Sights

9 Fortress of Seven Towers
10 Theodosian Walls
11 Shrine of Zoodochus Pege
12 Panorama 1453 Museum
18 Pierre Loti Café
19 Rahmi Koç Industrial Museum
20 Military Museum
21 Naval Museum
23 Yıldız Park
24 Leander's Tower
28 Selimiye Barracks
29 Haydarpaşa Station
30 Ortaköy
31 Bosphorus Bridge
33 Fortress of Asia
34 Sakıp Sabancı Museum
35 Fortress of Europe

Palaces

14 Palace of the Porphyrogenitus
17 Complex of Valide Sultan Mihrişah
22 *Dolmabahçe Palace pp126–7*
32 Beylerbeyi Palace

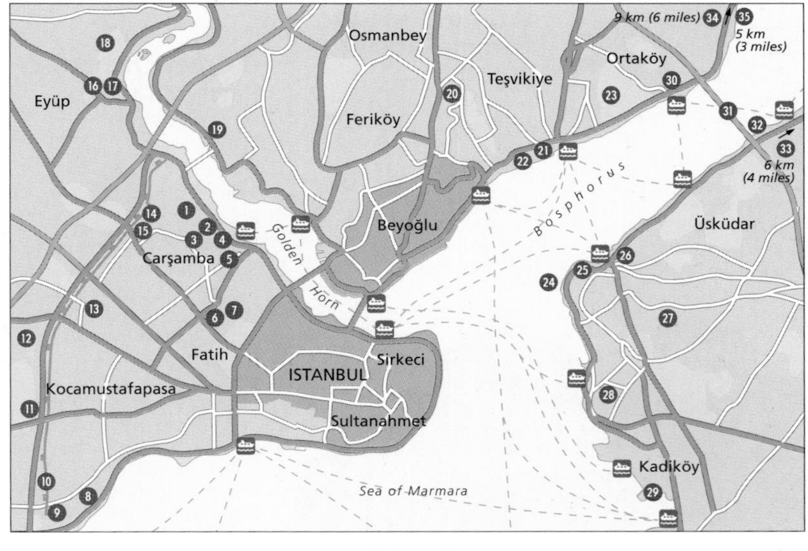

Key

Central Istanbul

Greater Istanbul

Motorway

Main road

Other road

0 kilometres 1

0 miles 1

◀ The spectacular ceiling of the Ceremonial Hall at Dolmabahçe Palace

For additional map symbols *see back flap*

❶ Ahrida Synagogue

Ahrida Sinagogu

Gevgili Sok, Balat. 55T, 99A.
Open by appointment only.
Tel Karavan Travel, (0212) 523 47 29.

The name of the oldest and most beautiful synagogue in Istanbul is a corruption of Ohrid, the name of a town in the former Yugoslavia from which its congregation came.

Founded before the Muslim conquest of Istanbul in 1453, it has been in constant use ever since. The painted walls and ceilings, dating from the late 17th century, have been restored to their Baroque glory. Pride of place is the central Holy Ark, which is covered in rich tapestries.

Visits are possible by prior arrangement with specialist tour operators, such as Karavan Travel. Alternatively, contact the Chief rabbinate well in advance.

❷ Church of St Stephen of the Bulgars

Bulgar Kilisesi

85 Mürsel Paşa Cad, Balat. 55T, 99A. Ayvansaray. **Open** 9am–4pm daily.

Astonishingly, this entire church was cast in iron, even the internal columns and galleries. It was created in Vienna in 1871, shipped all the way to the Golden Horn *(see p103)* and assembled on its shore.

The Church of St Stephen of the Bulgars, wholly made of cast iron

The church was needed for the Bulgarian community who had broken away from the authority of the Greek Orthodox Patriarchate just up the hill. Today, it is still used by this community, who keep the marble tombs of the first Bulgarian patriarchs permanently decorated with flowers. The church stands in a pretty little park dotted with trees, and which runs down to the edge of the Golden Horn.

❸ Church of the Pammakaristos

Fethiye Camii

Fethiye Cad, Çarşamba-Fatih. 90, 90B. **Open** prayer times only. Museum: **Open** 9am–4:30pm Tue–Thu. for museum.

This Byzantine church is one of the hidden secrets of Istanbul. It is rarely visited despite the important role it has played in the history of the city, and its breathtaking series of mosaics. For over 100 years after the Ottoman conquest, it housed the Greek Orthodox Patriarchate, but was converted into a mosque in the late 16th century by Sultan Murat III.

The charming exterior is obviously Byzantine, with its alternating stone and brick courses and finely carved marble details. The main body of the building is the working mosque, while the extraordinary mosaics and frescoes are in a side chapel. This now operates as a museum.

Dating from the 14th century, the great Byzantine renaissance, the mosaics show holy figures isolated in a sea of gold, a reflection of the heavens. On either side are portraits of the Virgin Mary and John the Baptist beseeching Christ. They are overlooked by the four archangels, while the side apses are filled with other saintly figures. In the centre of the main dome are images of Christ Pantocrator ("the All-Powerful") and the Old Testament prophets.

Byzantine façade of the Church of the Pammakaristos

❹ Greek Orthodox Patriarchate

Ortodoks Patrikhanesi

35 Sadrazam Ali Paşa Cad, Fener.
Tel (0212) 521 19 21. 55T, 99A.
Open 9am–5pm daily.

This walled complex has been the seat of the patriarch of the Greek Orthodox Church since the early 17th century. Though nominally head of the whole church, the patriarch is now shepherd to a diminishing Istanbul flock.

The main door to the Patriarchate has been welded shut in memory of Patriarch Gregory V, hanged here for treason in 1821 after encouraging the Greeks to throw off Ottoman rule at the start of the Greek War of Independence (1821–32). Turkish–Greek antagonism worsened with the Greek occupation of parts of Turkey in the 1920s *(see p62)*, anti-Greek riots in 1955, and the expulsion of Greek residents in the

The ornate, gilded interior of the Church of St George in the Greek Orthodox Patriarchate

mid-1960s. Today the clergy at the Patriarchate is protected by a metal detector at the entrance.

The Patriarchate centres on the basilica-style Church of St George, dating back to 1720, yet the church contains much older relics and furniture. The patriarch's throne is thought to be Byzantine, while the pulpit is adorned with fine wooden inlay and icons.

❺ Mosque of Selim I

Yavuz Selim Camii

Yavuz Selim Cad, Fener. 🚌 55T, 90, 90B, 99A. **Open** daily.

This much-admired mosque is also known locally as Yavuz Sultan Mosque: Yavuz, "the Grim", being the nickname the infamous Selim acquired. It is idyllic in a rather offbeat way, which does seem at odds with Selim's barbaric reputation.

The mosque, built between 1522 and 1529, sits alone on a hill beside what is now a vast sunken park area, once the Byzantine Cistern of Aspar. Beautifully restored, it is one of the most attractive mosques in Istanbul, with a shallow dome covering an austere prayer hall.

The windows set into the porticoes in the courtyard are capped by early İznik tiles *(see p165)* made by the *cuerda seca* technique, whereby each colour is separated during the firing process, affording the patterns greater definition. Similar tiles lend decorative effect to the simple prayer hall, with its fine mosque furniture *(see pp36–7)* and original, carefully painted woodwork.

İznik tile panel in the Mosque of Selim I

❻ Fatih Mosque

Fatih Camii

Macar Kardeşler Cad, Fatih. **Map** 4 A2. 🚌 28, 87, 90, 91. **Open** daily.

A spacious outer courtyard surrounds this vast Baroque mosque, the third major structure on this site. The first was the Church of the Holy Apostles, the burial place of most of the Byzantine emperors. Most of what you see today was the work of Mehmet Tahir Ağa, the chief imperial architect under Mustafa III. Many of the buildings he constructed around the prayer hall, including eight Koranic colleges *(medreses)* and a hospice, still stand. The only surviving parts of Mehmet the Conqueror's mosque are the three porticoes of the courtyard, the ablutions fountain, the main gate into the prayer hall and, inside, the mihrab. Two exquisite forms of 15th-century decoration can be seen over the windows in the porticoes: İznik tiles and lunettes adorned with calligraphic marble inlay. Stencilled patterns decorate the domes of the prayer hall, and parts of the walls are covered with beautiful tiles.

The tomb of Mehmet the Conqueror stands behind the prayer hall, near that of his consort, Gülbahar. His sarcophagus and the turban decorating it are both appropriately large. It is a place of enormous gravity, always busy with supplicants.

If you pay a visit to the mosque on a Wednesday, you will also see the weekly market, which turns the streets around it into a circus of commerce. From tables piled high with fruit and vegetables to trucks loaded with unspun wool, this is a real spectacle.

Church of the Pantocrator, built by Empress Irene in the 12th century

❼ Zeyrek Mosque

Zeyrek Camii

İbadethane Sok, Küçükpazar. **Map** 4 B2. 🚌 28, 61B, 87. **Open** prayer times daily. ♿

This building was a church in the Byzantine period, founded by Empress Irene, the wife of John II Comnenus, and was known as the Church of the Pantocrator ("Christ the Almighty") during the 12th century. It was once the centrepiece of one of Istanbul's most important religious foundations, the Monastery of the Pantocrator. The complex included an asylum, a hospice and a hospital. Converted into a mosque after the Ottoman conquest, it boasts a magnificent figurative marble floor and is composed of three interlinked chapels. Closed for restoration for many years, the mosque reopened in late 2014.

❽ Church of St John of Studius

İmrahor Camii

İmam Aşir Sok, Yedikule. 80, 80T. Yedikule.

Istanbul's oldest surviving church, St John of Studius, is now merely a shell consisting of its outer walls.

The church was completed in AD 463 by Studius, a Roman patrician who served as consul during the reign of Emperor Marcian (450–57). Originally connected to the most powerful monastery in the Byzantine Empire and populated with ascetic monks, in the late 8th century it was a spiritual and intellectual centre under the rule of Abbot Theodore, who is now highly venerated in the Greek Orthodox Church as St Theodore.

In the 15th century the church was converted into a mosque. The building was abandoned in 1894 after it was damaged by an earthquake. The church is still in ruins, but visitors can admire the impressive exterior of the basilica, with a single apse at the east end, preceded by a narthex and a courtyard. There are plans to restore the building and convert it into a mosque.

Ruins of the Church of St John of Studius

❾ Fortress of Seven Towers

Yedikule

Kale Meydanı 4, Yedikule İmrahor Mahallesi. **Tel** (0212) 585 89 33. 31, 80, 93T. Kazlıçeşme. **Open** 8:30am–6:30pm daily.

Yedikule, the "Fortress of Seven Towers", was built in 1455 against the southern section of the Theodosian Walls. It displays both Byzantine and Ottoman features, being built in stages over a long period. Its seven towers are joined by thick walls to make a five-sided fortification. The two square marble towers built into the great land walls once flanked the Golden Gate (now blocked), which consisted of three magnificent golden portals. The gate was built by Emperor Theodosius I in AD 390 as the triumphal entrance into the thriving medieval city of Byzantium.

In the 15th century, Sultan Mehmet II (the Conqueror) completed Yedikule by adding three round towers and connecting curtain walls. After viewing the castle from the outside, you can enter through a doorway in the northeastern wall. The tower to your left as you enter is the *yazılı kule*, "the tower with inscriptions". It was used as a prison for foreign envoys and others who fell out of favour with the sultan. Its name is derived from the names and epitaphs which many of these doomed individuals carved into the walls. Some of these morbid inscriptions are still visible.

There are two towers flanking the Golden Gate. The north tower was a place of execution. Among those who met their end here was the 17-year-old Sultan Osman II, who was dragged off to Yedikule by his own Janissaries in 1622, after four years of misrule. The walkway around the ramparts is accessible via a steep flight of stone steps and offers good views of the land walls, the southern marble tower and market garden allotments.

Battlements at Yedikule, an Ottoman addition to the fortress

❿ Theodosian Walls

Teodos II Surları

From Yedikule to Ayvansaray. Kazlıçeşme, Ulubatlı. Pazarteke. Ayvansaray.

With its 11 fortified gates and 192 towers, this great chain of double walls sealed Constantinople's landward side against invasion for more than a thousand years. Extending for a distance of 6.5 km (4 miles) from the Sea of Marmara to the Golden Horn, the walls are built in layers of red tile alternating with limestone blocks. They can be reached by metro, tram or train, but to see their whole length you will need to take a taxi or *dolmuş* *(see p396)* along the main road that runs outside them.

The walls were built by Theodosius II in AD 412–22. They endured many sieges, and were only breached by Mehmet the Conqueror in May 1453 *(see p58)*, when the Ottomans took Constantinople. Successive Ottoman sultans continued to maintain the walls until the end of the 17th century.

Many parts of the walls have been rebuilt, and the new sections give an idea of how the walls used to look. Some of the gateways are still in good repair, but a section of walls was demolished in the 1950s to make way for a road. The Charsius Gate (now called Edirnekapı), Silivrikapı, Yeni Mevlanakapı and other original gates still give access to the city.

⓫ Shrine of Zoodochus Pege

Balıklı Kilise

3 Seyit Nizam Cad, Silivrikapı. **Tel** (0212) 582 30 81. Seyitnizam. 93T. **Open** 8:30am–4pm daily.

The fountain of Zoodochus Pege ("Life-Giving Spring") is built over Istanbul's most famous sacred spring, which is believed to have miraculous powers. The fish in it are said to have arrived by miracle shortly before the fall of Constantinople *(see p58)*. They are believed to have leapt into the water from a monk's frying pan on hearing him declare that a Turkish invasion of the fortified town was as likely as fish coming back to life. The spring was probably the site of an ancient sanctuary of Artemis.

⓬ Panorama 1453 Museum

Panoramik Müzesi

Topkapı Kültür Parkı. **Tel** (0212) 415 14 53. Topkapı. **Open** 9am–6:30pm daily. **panoramikmuze.com**

The inside of the dome of this modern building has been decorated with a brilliant panoramic painting depicting the 1453 siege of Constantinople by the Ottoman Turks *(see p58)*. The museum is located right

Silivrikapı, one of the gateways through the Theodosian Walls

opposite the section of the Theodosian Walls where Mehmet the conquerer, positioned his best troops and mightiest cannon. The magnificence of the painting, with over ten thousand figures, is heightened by sound effects inspired by the conquest. An informative audio guide is available in Turkish.

⓭ Gazi Ahmet Paşa Mosque

Gazi Ahmet Paşa Camii

Undeğirmeni Sok, Fatma Sultan. **Open** Prayer times only. Ulubatlı. Topkapı. 93T.

One of the most worthwhile detours along the city walls is the Gazi Ahmet Paşa Mosque. This lovely building, with its peaceful leafy courtyard and graceful proportions, is one of the imperial architect Sinan's *(see p105)* lesser-known achievements, which he built in 1554 for Kara Ahmet Paşa, a grand vizier of Süleyman the Magnificent *(see p59)*. The courtyard is surrounded by the cells of a *medrese* and a *dershane*, or main classroom. Attractive apple-green and yellow İznik tiles *(see p165)* dating from the mid-1500s grace the porch, with blue-and-white tiles on the east wall of the prayer hall.

⓮ Palace of the Porphyrogenitus

Tekfur Sarayı

Şişehane Cad, Edirnekapı. **Tel** (0212) 522 175. 87, 90, 126. Ayvansaray then 20 minutes' walk **Open** daily.

The Palace of the Porphyrogenitus was a shadow of its former grandeur until 2012, when a major restoration programme was undertaken. This is likely to see the palace converted into a convention centre on its completion. The former palace has an attractive three-storey façade in typically Byzantine style. It was most likely built in the late Byzantine era as an annexe of the Blachernae Palace. These palaces became the principal residences of the imperial sovereigns during the last two centuries before the fall of Constantinople to the Ottomans in 1453.

During the reign of Ahmet III (1703–30), the last remaining İznik potters *(see p165)* moved to the palace and it became a centre for tile production. Cezri Kasım Paşa Mosque in Eyüp has some very fine examples of these tiles.

Tilework over *medrese* doorway at Gazi Ahmet Paşa Mosque

⓯ Church of St Saviour in Chora

Kariye Camii

Some of the very finest Byzantine mosaics and frescoes can be found in the Church of St Saviour in Chora. Little is known of the early history of the church, although its name "in Chora", which means "in the country", suggests that the church originally stood in a rural setting. The present church dates from the 11th century. From 1315 to 1321 it was remodelled, and the mosaics and frescoes were added by Theodore Metochites, a theologian, philosopher and one of the elite Byzantine officials of his day.

View of St Saviour in Chora

The Genealogy of Christ

Theodore Metochites, who restored St Saviour, wrote that his mission was to relate how "the Lord himself became a mortal on our behalf". He takes the *Genealogy of Christ* as his starting point: the mosaics in the two domes of the inner narthex portray 66 of Christ's forebears.

The crown of the southern dome is occupied by a figure of Christ. In the dome's flutes are two rows of his ancestors: Adam to Jacob ranged above the 12 sons of Jacob. In the northern dome, there is a central image of the Virgin and Child with the kings of the House of David in the upper row and lesser ancestors of Christ in the lower row.

Mosaic showing Christ and his ancestors, in the southern dome of the inner narthex

The Life of the Virgin

All but one of the 20 mosaics in the inner narthex depicting the *Life of the Virgin* are well preserved. This cycle is based mainly on the apocryphal Gospel of St James, written in the 2nd century, which gives an account of the Virgin's life. This was popular in the Middle Ages and was a rich source of material for ecclesiastical artists.

Among the events shown are the first seven steps of the Virgin, the Virgin entrusted to Joseph and the Virgin receiving bread from an angel.

The Infancy of Christ

Scenes from the *Infancy of Christ*, based largely on the New Testament, occupy the semi-circular panels of the outer narthex. They begin on the north wall of the outer narthex

Guide to the Mosaics and Frescoes

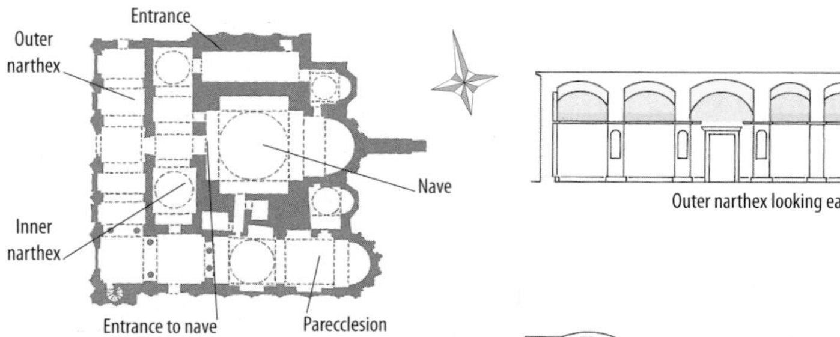

Key

- The Genealogy of Christ
- The Life of the Virgin
- The Infancy of Christ
- Christ's Ministry
- Other Mosaics
- The Frescoes

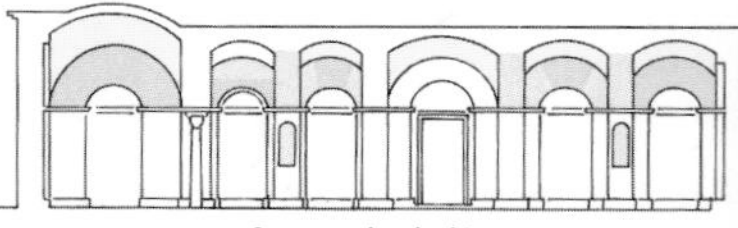

Outer narthex looking west

with a scene of Joseph being visited by an angel in a dream. Subsequent panels include Mary and Joseph's *Journey to Bethlehem for Taxation*, the *Nativity of Christ* and, finally, Herod ordering the *Massacre of the Innocents*.

The *Enrolment for Taxation*

Christ's Ministry

While many of the mosaics in this series are badly damaged, some beautiful panels remain. The cycle occupies the vaults of the seven bays of the outer narthex and some of the south bay of the inner narthex. The most striking mosaic is the portrayal of Christ's temptation in the wilderness, in the second bay of the outer narthex.

Theodore Metochites presents St Saviour in Chora to Christ

Other Mosaics

There are three panels in the nave of the church, one of which, above the main door from the inner narthex, illustrates the *Dormition of the Virgin*. This mosaic, protected by a marble frame, is the best preserved in the church. The Virgin is depicted laid out on a bier, watched over by the Apostles, with Christ seated behind. Other devotional panels in the two narthexes include one, on the east wall of the south bay of the inner narthex, of the *Deësis*, depicting Christ with the Virgin Mary and, unusually, without St John. Another, in the inner narthex over the door into the nave, is of Theodore Metochites himself, shown wearing a large turban, and humbly presenting the restored church as an offering to Christ.

The Frescoes

The frescoes in the parecclesion are thought to have been painted just after the mosaics were completed, probably in around 1320. The most engaging of the frescoes – which reflect the purpose of the parecclesion as a place of burial – is the *Anastasis*, in the semidome above the apse. In it, the central figure of Christ, the vanquisher of death, is shown dragging Adam and Eve out of their tombs. Under Christ's feet are the gates of hell, while Satan lies before him. The fresco in the vault overhead depicts *The Last Judgment*, with the souls of the saved on the right and those of the damned to the left.

VISITORS' CHECKLIST

Practical Information
Kariye Camii Sok, Edirnekapı.
Tel (0212) 631 92 41.
Open 9am–4:30pm Thu–Tue.

Transport
28, 86 or 90 then 5 minutes' walk.

Figure of Christ from the *Anastasis* fresco in the parecclesion

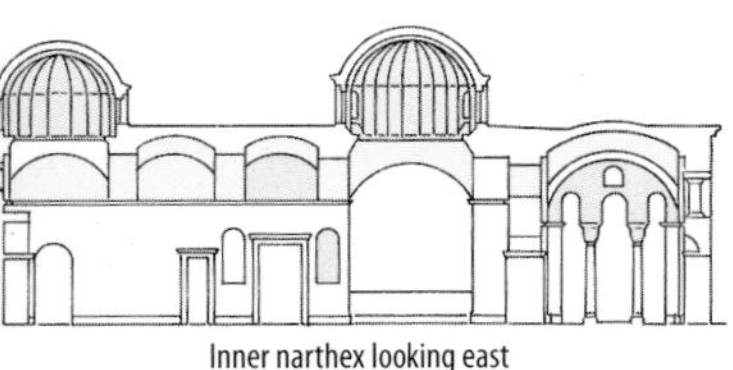

Inner narthex looking east

Parecclesion and outer narthex looking south

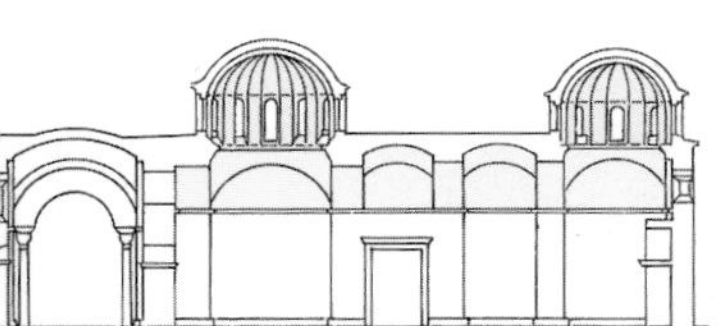

Inner narthex looking west

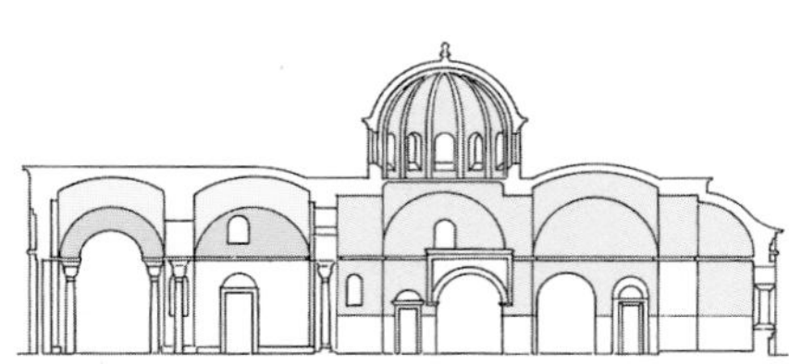

Parecclesion and outer narthex looking north

Visitors at the tomb of Eyüp Ensari, Mohammed's standard bearer

⓰ Eyüp Sultan Mosque

Eyüp Sultan Camii

Cami-i Kebir Sok. **Tel** (0212) 564 73 68. 39, 55T, 99A. Eyüp. **Open** daily.

Mehmet the Conqueror built the original mosque on this site in 1458, five years after his conquest of Istanbul, in honour of Eyüp Ensari. That building fell into ruins and the present mosque was completed in 1800, by Selim III.

The mosque's delightful inner courtyard features two huge plane trees on a platform. This was the setting for the Girding of the Sword of Osman, part of a sultan's inauguration in the days of Mehmet the Conqueror.

Opposite the mosque is the tomb of Eyüp Ensari himself, said to have been killed during the first Arab siege of Constantinople in the 7th century. The tomb dates from the same period as the mosque and its decoration is in the Ottoman Baroque style.

⓱ Complex of Valide Sultan Mihrişah

Mihrişah Valide Sultan Külliyesi

Seyit Reşat Cad. 39, 55T, 99A. **Open** 9:30am–4:30pm Tue–Sun.

Most of the northern side of the street leading from Eyüp Mosque's northern gate is occupied by the largest Baroque *külliye (see p36)* in Istanbul, although unusually it is not centred on a mosque. Built for Mihrişah, mother of Selim III, the *külliye* was completed in 1791.

The complex includes the ornate marble tomb of Mihrişah and a soup kitchen, which is still in use today.

⓲ Pierre Loti Café

Piyer Loti Kahvehanesi

Gümüşsuyu Cad, Balmumku Sok 5, Eyüp. **Tel** (0212) 616 23 44. 39, 55T, 99A. Eyüp. **Open** 8am–midnight daily.

This famous café stands at the top of the hill in Eyüp Cemetery, a 20-minute walk up Karyağdı Sokağı from Eyüp Mosque. It is named after the French novelist, Julien Viaud, a French naval officer, popularly known as Pierre Loti, who frequented the café during his stay here in 1876. Loti defiantly fell in love with a married Turkish woman and wrote an auto-biographical novel, *Aziyade*, about their affair. The café is prettily decked out with 19th-century furniture and the waiters wear period outfits.

⓳ Rahmi Koç Industrial Museum

Hasköy Cad 27, Eyüp. **Tel** (0212) 369 66 00. **Open** 10am–5pm Tue–Fri, 10am–6pm Sat & Sun (to 8pm Apr–Sep.

This is Turkey's best industrial museum, which was formerly a factory producing anchors, chains and other similar goods for the shipping industry. Well located on the banks of the Golden Horn, the museum can be easily reached by ferry from Eminönü. The exhibits here range from amphicars to penny farthings. Visitors will also find Royal Enfield motorcycles, Trabants, old steam ships, a Douglas DC-3 Dakota, a working railway and a submarine. For those weary after exploring the extensive collection, the museum also has three good on-site restaurants.

⓴ Military Museum

Askeri Müze

Vali Konağı Cad, Harbiye. **Map** 1 C1. **Tel** (0212) 233 27 20. 46H. **Open** 9am–5pm Wed–Sun. Mehter Band performances: 3–4pm Wed–Sun.

One of Istanbul's most impressive museums, the Military Museum traces the history of the country's conflicts from the conquest of Constantinople in 1453 *(see p58)* through to modern warfare. The building used to be the military academy where Atatürk studied from 1899 to 1905.

The museum is also the main location for performances by the Mehter Band *(see p371)*, formed in the 14th century during the reign of Osman I *(see p58)*. Until the 19th century the musicians were Janissaries, who accompanied the sultan into battle and performed songs about hero-ancestors and battle victories. The band had a wide

Period interior of the Pierre Loti Café

influence and is thought to have provided some inspiration for Mozart and Beethoven.

Some of the most striking weapons on display on the ground floor are the curved daggers *(cembiyes)* carried at the waist by foot soldiers in the 15th century. These are ornamented with plant, flower and geometric motifs in relief and silver filigree. Other exhibits include 17th-century copper head armour for horses and Ottoman shields made from cane and willow covered in silk thread.

A moving portrayal of trench warfare is included in the section concerned with the ANZAC landings of 1915 at Chunuk Bair on the Gallipoli peninsula *(see pp172–3)*, and upstairs is a spectacular exhibit of the tents used by sultans on their campaigns.

From the nearby station on Taşkışla Caddesi you can take the cable car across Maçka Park to Abdi İpekçi Caddesi in Teşvikiye. Some of the best designer clothes, jewellery, furniture and art shops in the city are here *(see pp134–5)*.

㉑ Naval Museum

Deniz Müzesi

Barbaraos Hayrettin, Paşa İskele Sok. **Map** 2 B3. 🚌 22, 22/RE, 25/E. **Open** 9am–5pm Tue–Sun.

The Naval Museum opened in 2013 after several years of restoration. Housed in a state-of-the-art complex on the seafront, it offers superb views of the Bosphorus Strait. The exhibits at the museum include a beautifully renovated series of imperial *caïques*. These were long, narrow rowboats that once took the sultans and their entourages up and down the waterways around the city. The museum also has a good café and play area for children.

㉒ Dolmabahçe Palace

See pp126–7.

㉓ Yıldız Park

Çırağan Cad, Beşiktaş. **Map** 3 D2. 🚌 25E, 40. **Open** dawn to dusk daily. for vehicles.

Yildiz Park was originally laid out as the garden of the first Çırağan Palace. It later formed the grounds of **Yıldız Palace**, an assortment of buildings from different eras now enclosed behind a wall and entered separately from Ihlamur-Yıldız Caddesi. The palace is a collection of pavilions and villas built in the 19th and 20th centuries. Many of them are the work of the eccentric Sultan Abdül Hamit II (1876–1909, *see p61*), who made it his principal residence as he feared a seaborne attack on Dolmabahçe Palace *(see pp126–7)*. The main building in the entrance courtyard is the State Apartments (Büyük Mabeyn), dating from the reign of Sultan Selim III (1789–1807). Around the corner, the **City Museum** (Şehir Müzesi) has a display of Yıldız porcelain. The Italianate building opposite is the former armoury, or Silahhane. Next door to the City Museum is the **Yıldız Palace Museum**, housed in what was the Marangozhane (Abdül Hamit's carpentry workshop), and containing a changing collection of the palace's art and objects.

Further on is Yıldız Palace Theatre (completed in 1889 by Abdül Hamit), now a museum. The theatre's restored interior is mainly blue and gold, and the stars on the domed ceiling refer to the palace's name: yıldız means "star" in Turkish. Backstage, the former dressing rooms contain theatre displays, including original costumes and playbills.

The lake in the grounds is shaped like Abdül Hamit's *tuğra* *(see p32)*. A menagerie was once kept on the lake's islands, where some 30 keepers tended tigers, lions, giraffes and zebras.

Several other little pavilions dot Yıldız Park. Şale Köşkü is one of the most impressive in the park and built by Abdül Hamit. Although its façade appears as a whole, it was in fact built in three stages.

The Malta and Çadır pavilions were built during the reign of Abdül Aziz who ruled from 1861 to 1876. Both of them formerly served as prisons but are open as cafés. Malta Pavilion, also a restaurant, is a favoured haunt of locals on Sundays.

Mitat Paşa, reformist and architect of the constitution, was among those imprisoned in Çadır Pavilion, for instigating the murder of Abdül Aziz. Meanwhile, Murat V and his mother were locked away in Malta Pavilion for 27 years after a brief incarceration in the Çırağan Palace.

In 1895 the Imperial Porcelain Factory began production here, to satisfy the demand of the upper classes for chic European-style ceramics. The unusual building was designed to look like a stylized medieval castle of Europe, complete with several turrets and portcullis windows.

City Museum
Tel (0212) 258 53 44.

Yıldız Palace Museum
Tel (0212) 258 30 80 (ext 280).

A bridge in the grounds of Yıldız Palace

㉒ Dolmabahçe Palace

Dolmabahçe Sarayı

Sultan Abdülmecit built Dolmabahçe Palace in 1856. As its designers he employed Karabet Balyan and his son Nikoğos, members of the great family of Armenian architects who lined the Bosphorus *(see pp130–31)* with many of their creations during the 19th century. The extravagant opulence of the Dolmabahçe belies the fact that it was built at a time when the Ottoman Empire was in decline. The palace can be visited only on a guided tour, of which two are on offer. The best tour takes you through the Selamlık (or Mabeyn-i Hümayun), the part of the palace that was reserved for men and which contains the state rooms and the enormous Ceremonial Hall. The other tour goes through the Harem, the living quarters of the sultan and his entourage. If you want to go only on one tour, visit the Selamlık.

★ Crystal Staircase
The apparent fragility of this glass staircase stunned observers when it was built. In the shape of a double horseshoe, it is made from English crystal and brass, and has a polished mahogany rail.

Imperial Gate of the Palace
Once used only by the sultan and his ministers, this gate is now the main entrance to the palace. The Mehter, or Janissary, Band *(see pp371, 124)* performs in front of the gate every Tuesday afternoon throughout the summer.

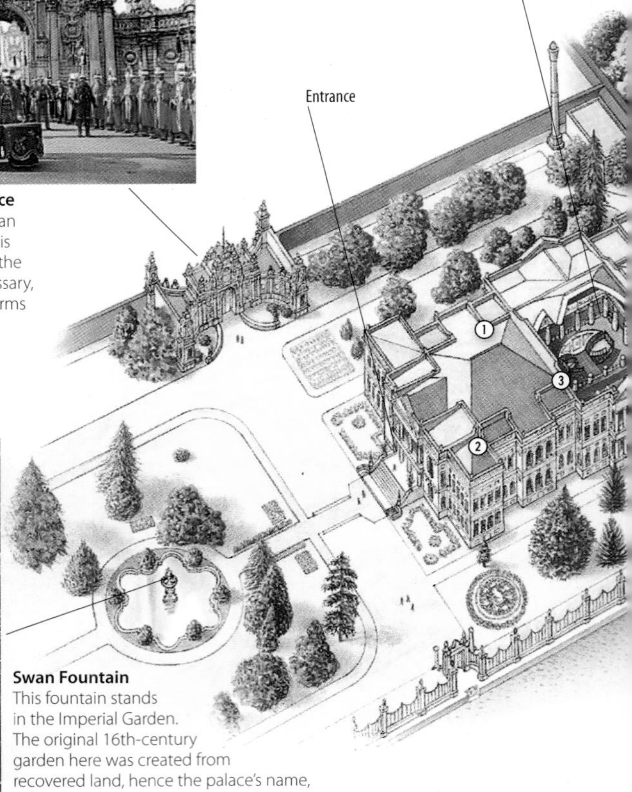

Entrance

Swan Fountain
This fountain stands in the Imperial Garden. The original 16th-century garden here was created from recovered land, hence the palace's name, Dolmabahçe, meaning "Filled-in Garden".

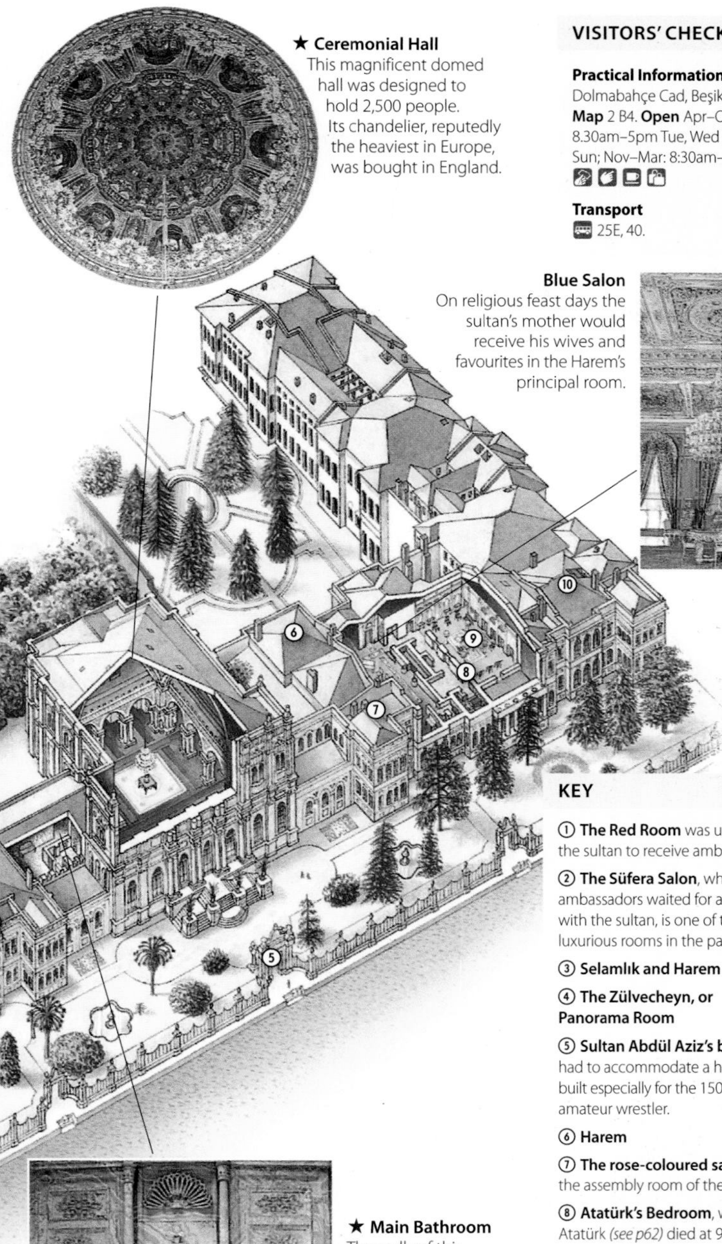

★ Ceremonial Hall
This magnificent domed hall was designed to hold 2,500 people. Its chandelier, reputedly the heaviest in Europe, was bought in England.

Blue Salon
On religious feast days the sultan's mother would receive his wives and favourites in the Harem's principal room.

★ Main Bathroom
The walls of this bathroom are revetted in finest Egyptian alabaster, while the taps are solid silver. The brass-framed bathroom windows afford stunning views across the Bosphorus.

VISITORS' CHECKLIST

Practical Information
Dolmabahçe Cad, Beşiktaş.
Map 2 B4. **Open** Apr–Oct: 8.30am–5pm Tue, Wed & Fri–Sun; Nov–Mar: 8:30am–4pm.

Transport
25E, 40.

KEY

① **The Red Room** was used by the sultan to receive ambassadors.

② **The Süfera Salon**, where ambassadors waited for an audience with the sultan, is one of the most luxurious rooms in the palace.

③ **Selamlık and Harem**

④ **The Zülvecheyn, or Panorama Room**

⑤ **Sultan Abdül Aziz's bedroom** had to accommodate a huge bed built especially for the 150 kg (330 lb) amateur wrestler.

⑥ **Harem**

⑦ **The rose-coloured salon** was the assembly room of the Harem.

⑧ **Atatürk's Bedroom**, where Atatürk *(see p62)* died at 9:05am on 10 November 1938. Some of the clocks in the palace, such as the one near the crystal staircase, are stopped at this time.

⑨ **Reception room of the sultan's mother**

⑩ **Main shore gate**

Leander's Tower, on its own small island in the Bosphorus

㉔ Leander's Tower

Kız Kulesi

Üsküdar. **Map** 6 A3. Üsküdar. Üsküdar. **Tel** (0216) 342 47 47. **kizkulesi.com.tr**

Located on an islet offshore from Üsküdar, the tiny, white Leander's Tower is a well-known Bosphorus landmark, dating from the 18th century. The tower once served as a quarantine centre during a cholera outbreak, as a lighthouse, a customs control point and a maritime toll gate. The tower is now used as a restaurant and pricey offshore nightclub.

In Turkish the tower is known as the "Maiden's Tower" after a legendary princess, confined here after a prophet foretold that she would die of a snake-bite. The tower's English name derives from the Greek myth of Leander, who swam the Hellespont (the modern-day Dardanelles, *see pp172–3*) to see his lover, priestess Hero.

㉕ Şemsi Paşa Mosque

Şemsi Paşa Camii

Sahil Yolu, Üsküdar. **Map** 6 A2. Üsküdar. **Open** daily.

This is one of the smallest mosques to be commissioned by a grand vizier (Ottoman prime minister). Its miniature dimensions combined with its picturesque waterfront location make it one of the most attractive little mosques in the city. It was built in 1580 by the architect Sinan *(see p105)*, at the request of Şemsi Ahmet Paşa, who succeeded Sokollu Mehmet Paşa.

The mosque's garden, overlooking the Bosphorus, is surrounded on two sides by the theological college or *medrese (see p36)*, with the small mosque on the third side and the seawall on the fourth. The mosque itself is also quite unusual in that the tomb of Şemsi Ahmet Paşa is joined to the main building, divided from the interior by a grille.

Dome in the entrance to Atik Valide Mosque

㉖ İskele Mosque

İskele Camii

Hakimiyeti Milliye Cad, Üsküdar. **Map** 6 B2. Üsküdar. **Open** daily.

One of Uskūdar's most prominent landmarks, the İskele Mosque (also known as Mihrimah Sultan Mosque), takes its name from the ferry landing where it stands. A massive structure on a raised platform, it was built by Sinan between 1547 and 1548 for Mihriman Sultan, favourite daughter of Süleyman the Magnificent. Without space to build a courtyard, Sinan constructed a large protruding roof which extends to cover the *şadırvan* (ablutions fountain) in front of the mosque.

Fountain set into the platform below the İskele Mosque

㉗ Atik Valide Mosque

Atik Valide Camii

Çinili Camii Sok, Üsküdar. **Map** 6 C3. 12C (from Üsküdar). **Open** prayer times only.

The Atik Valide mosque, set on the hill above Üsküdar, was one of the most extensive mosque complexes in the whole of Istanbul. The name translates as "Old Mosque of the Sultan's Mother", as the mosque was built for Nur Banu, the wife of Selim II ("the Sot") and the mother of Murat III. She was the first of the sultans' mothers to rule the Ottoman Empire from the Harem *(see p75)*. Sinan completed the mosque, which was his last major work, in 1583. It has a wide shallow dome which rests on five semidomes, with a flat arch over the entrance portal.

The interior is surrounded on three sides by galleries, the undersides of which retain the rich stencilling typical of the period. The mihrab apse is almost completely covered with panels of fine İznik tiles *(see p165)*, while the mihrab itself and the *minbar* are both made of sculpted marble. Side aisles were added in the 17th century, while the grilles and architectural trompe l'oeil paintings on the royal loge in the western gallery date from the 18th century.

Outside, a door in the north wall of the courtyard leads down a flight of stairs to the *medrese* (theological college), where the *dershane* (classroom) projects out over the street below, supported by an arch. The *şifahane* (hospital), built around a central courtyard just east of the mosque, is also worth a visit.

㉘ Selimiye Barracks

Selimiye Kışlası

Çeşmei Kebir Cad, Selimiye. **Map** 6 B5. Harem. 12.

The Selimiye Barracks were originally made of wood and completed in 1799 under Selim III, who was sultan from 1789 to 1807. They were built to house the "New Army" that formed part of Selim's plan for reforming the Imperial command structure and replacing the powerful Janissaries *(see pp60–61)*. The plan backfired and Selim was deposed but the barracks were, nevertheless, a striking symbol of Constantinople's military might, perhaps becoming even more so when they were rebuilt in stone in 1829 by Mahmut II. The building still houses Istanbul's First Army Division and is off limits to the public.

The Florence Nightingale Museum is found within the Selimiye Barracks. It still contains some of the original furniture and the famous lamp which gave her the epitaph "Lady of the Lamp". Visits must be arranged in advance by faxing the Army Headquarters on (0216) 333 10 09.

Nearby are two other sites worth seeing – the Selimiye Mosque and the British War Cemetery (also known as the Crimean Memorial Cemetery). The mosque was built in 1804 and is set in a lovely courtyard. The Cemetery, south on Burhan Felek Caddesi, contains the graves of men who died in the Crimean War, World War I battles at Gallipoli *(see pp172–3)* and during World War II in the Middle East.

Haydarpaşa Station, former terminus for trains arriving from Anatolia

Florence Nightingale

The British nurse Florence Nightingale (1820–1910) was a tireless campaigner for hospital, military and social reform. During the Crimean War, in which Britain and France fought on the Ottoman side against the Russian Empire, she organized a party of 38 British nurses. They took charge of medical services at the Selimiye Barracks in Scutari (Üsküdar) in 1854. By the time she returned to Britain in 1856, at the end of the war, the mortality rate in the barracks had decreased from 20 to 2 per cent, and the fundamental principles of modern nursing had been established. On her return home, Florence Nightingale opened a training school for nurses.

A 19th-century painting of Florence Nightingale in Selimiye Barracks

㉙ Haydarpaşa Station

Haydarpaşa Garı

Haydarpaşa İstasyon Cad. **Tel** (0216) 348 80 20. Haydarpaşa or Kadıköy.

A fire in 2010 did not diminish the grandeur of Haydarpaşa Station, which, with its tiled jetty, was once the most impressive point of arrival or departure in Istanbul. Built on land reclaimed from the sea, the station is surrounded by water on three sides – a unique feature.

The first Anatolian railway line, which was built in 1873, ran from here to İznik *(see p164)*. The extension of this railway was a major part of Abdül Hamit II's drive to modernize the Ottoman Empire. Lacking sufficient funds, he applied for help to his German ally, Kaiser Wilhelm II. The Deutsche Bank agreed to invest in the construction and operation of the railway. In 1898 German engineers were contracted to build the new railway lines running across Anatolia and beyond into the far reaches of the Ottoman Empire.

Construction on Haydarpaşa, the grandest of these, started in 1906. Its two German architects, Otto Ritter and Helmut Conu, chose to build on a grand scale, using a Neo-Classic German style. Work was completed in 1908.

The station ceased operations following the fire of 2010. Its future remains unclear, but there are plans to use the station as the terminal of a new high-speed rail line between Istanbul and Ankara.

The Bosphorus Trip

One of the great pleasures of a visit to Istanbul is a cruise up the Bosphorus. It is relaxing and offers a great vantage point from which to view the city's famous landmarks. You can go on a prearranged guided tour or take one of the small boats that tout for passengers at Eminönü. But the best way to travel is on the official trip run by Istanbul Şehir Hatları *(SH, see p399)*. The SH ferry makes a round-trip to the upper Bosphorus once or twice daily, stopping at six piers along the way, including a leisurely stop at Anadolu Kavağı for lunch. You can return to Eminönü on the same boat or make your way back to the city by bus, *dolmuş* or taxi. The route shown here is the full Bosphorus Cruise.

Black Sea
Bosphorus
ISTANBUL

Locator Map

Sadberk Hanım Museum
Housed in two *yalıs (see p35)*, this private museum contains ethnographic displays and a private archaeology collection.

Fortress of Europe
Situated at the narrowest point on the Bosphorus, this fortress was built by Mehmet II in 1452 as a prelude to his invasion of Constantinople.

Dolmabahçe Palace
This opulent 19th-century Baroque palace is a symbol of Ottoman grandeur.

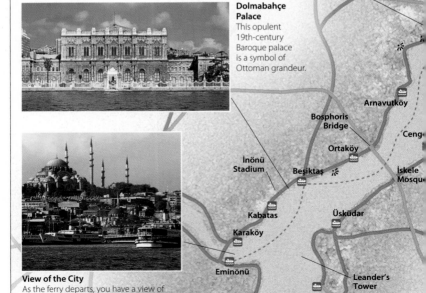

View of the City
As the ferry departs, you have a view of many of the old monuments of Istanbul, including Süleymaniye Mosque.

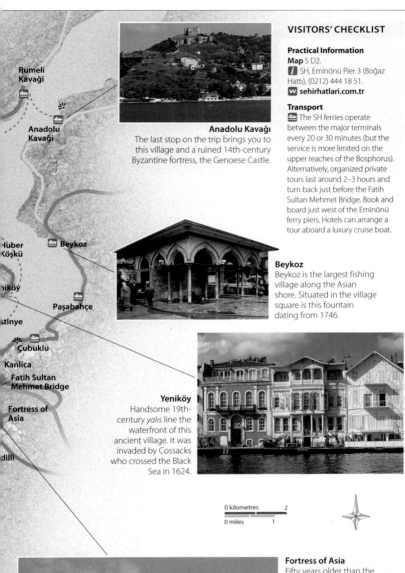

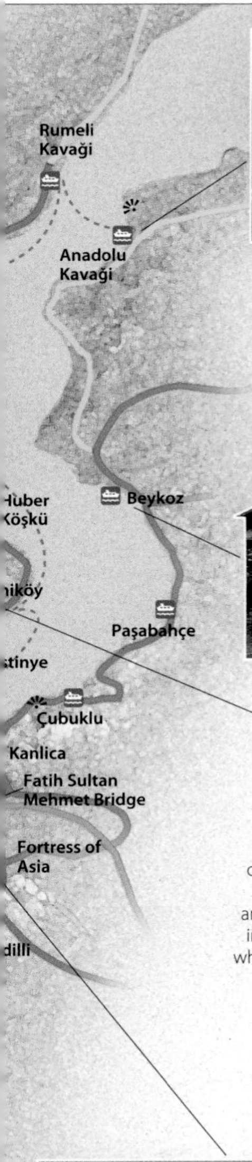

Rumeli Kavaği

Anadolu Kavaği

uber
öşkü

Beykoz

iköy

Paşabahçe

stinye

Çubuklu

Kanlica

Fatih Sultan Mehmet Bridge

Fortress of Asia

dilli

Anadolu Kavağı
The last stop on the trip brings you to this village and a ruined 14th-century Byzantine fortress, the Genoese Castle.

VISITORS' CHECKLIST

Practical Information
Map 5 D2.
SH, Eminönü Pier 3 (Boğaz Hattı), (0212) 444 18 51.
sehirhatlari.com.tr

Transport
The SH ferries operate between the major terminals every 20 or 30 minutes (but the service is more limited on the upper reaches of the Bosphorus). Alternatively, organized private tours last around 2–3 hours and turn back just before the Fatih Sultan Mehmet Bridge. Book and board just west of the Eminönü ferry piers. Hotels can arrange a tour aboard a luxury cruise boat.

Beykoz
Beykoz is the largest fishing village along the Asian shore. Situated in the village square is this fountain dating from 1746.

Yeniköy
Handsome 19th-century *yalıs* line the waterfront of this ancient village. It was invaded by Cossacks who crossed the Black Sea in 1624.

0 kilometres 2
0 miles 1

Fortress of Asia
Fifty years older than the Fortress of Europe, this fortress was built by Sultan Beyazıt I just before the failed Ottoman siege of Constantinople in 1396–7.

Key
Motorway
Main road
Other road

For additional map symbols *see back flap*

The Bosphorus suspension bridge between Ortaköy and Beylerbeyi

㉚ Ortaköy

Map 3 F2. 25E, 40, 41.

Crouched at the foot of the Bosphorus Bridge, the suburb of Ortaköy has retained a village feel. Life centres on İskele Meydanı, the quayside square, which was once busy with fishermen unloading the day's catch. Nowadays, though, Ortaköy is better known for its lively Sunday market, which crowds out the square and surrounding streets, and its shops selling the varied wares of local artisans. It is also the location for a thriving bar and café scene, which in the summer is the hub of Istanbul's nightlife *(see pp136–7)*.

Mecidiye Mosque (better known as Ortaköy Cami), Ortaköy's most impressive landmark, sits on the waterfront. It was built in 1853 by Nikoğos Balyan, who was also responsible for Dolmabahçe Palace *(see pp126–7)*.

Ortaköy's fashionable waterfront square and ferry landing

㉛ Bosphorus Bridge

Boğaziçi Köprüsü

Ortaköy and Beylerbeyi. **Map** 3 F2. 22, 22/RE, 25/E.

Spanning the Bosphorus between the districts of Ortaköy and Beylerbeyi, this was the first bridge to be built across the straits that divide Istanbul. Construction began in 1970, and the bridge was inaugurated on 29 October 1973, to coincide with the 50th anniversary of the founding of the Turkish Republic *(see p62)*. It is 1,074 m (3,524 ft) long, and is the world's ninth-longest suspension bridge. It reaches 64 m (210 ft) above the water.

The Bosphorus is especially popular in summer, when cool breezes waft off the water.

㉜ Beylerbeyi Palace

Beylerbeyi Sarayı

Abdullah Ağa Cad, Beylerbeyi Mahallesi, Asian side. **Tel** (0216) 321 93 20. 15, 15B (from Üsküdar), 10 (from Beşiktaş). D from Üsküdar. **Open** 8:30am–5pm Tue–Wed & Fri–Sun.

Designed in the Baroque style of the late Ottoman period, Beylerbeyi Palace was built between 1861 and 1865 by members of the Balyan family under the orders of Sultan Abdül Aziz. A previous palace had stood here, and the gardens were already laid out by Murat IV in 1639. As the Ottoman empire withered, palaces proliferated in a flourish of grandeur and showmanship. Abdül Aziz had Beylerbeyi built as a pleasure palace to entertain dignitaries and royalty. The Empress Eugénie of France (wife of Napoleon III) was a guest at the palace in 1869 on her way to the opening of the Suez Canal. The Duke and Duchess of Windsor also visited Beylerbeyi. The fountains, baths and colonnades were meant to impress, as were the lovely frescoes of Ottoman warships.

To keep himself distracted, Aziz also had a zoo built on the site and, apparently, delighted in the flocks of ostriches and several Bengal tigers. The zoo is no longer there, but parts of the palace have been refurbished and restored to some of their former elegance.

Third-but-last of the line of sultans, the autocratic Abdül Hamit II spent six years as a prisoner in an anteroom of the palace and died there, virtually forgotten, after being deposed in 1909.

There are superb views of the palace from the Bosphorus, from where the two prominent bathing pavilions – one for the Harem and the other for the *selamlık* (the men's quarters), can best be seen.

The most attractive room is the reception hall, which has a pool and fountain.

Ornate landing at the top of the stairs in Beylerbeyi Palace

㉝ Fortress of Asia

Anadolu Hisarı

Riyaziyeci Sokak (on the harbourfront), Asian side. **Tel** (0212) 263 53 05.

The Fortress of Asia was built around 1398 by Mehmet II's grandfather, Sultan Yildirim

The Fortress of Europe, built by Mehmet the Conqueror to enable him to capture Constantinople

Beyazıt I (1389–1402). It was the Sultan's trump card in his attempt to defend Constantinople from the haughty Venetians, who walked a tightrope between consolidating their territorial ambitions and trying to avoid conflicts that might threaten the riches of their lucrative Ottoman trade. In spite of the fortress as a deterrent, a low-level war took place, lasting from 1463 to 1497.

The Fortress of Asia is closed to the public, but the neighbourhood is one of Istanbul's most charming and least affected by modern life.

34 Sakıp Sabancı Museum

Sakıp Sabancı Müzesi

İstinye Cad 22, Emirgan 34467. **Tel** (0212) 277 22 00. 40, 41 from Taksim Sq; 22, 22/RE, 25/E (from Kabataş). **Open** 10am–6pm Tue, Thu, Fri, Sun; 10am–10pm Wed, Sat.
muze.sabanciuniv.edu

With a superb view over the Bosphorus, the Sakıp Sabancı Museum is also known as the Horse Mansion (Altı Köşk). Exhibitions comprise over 400 years of Ottoman calligraphy and other Koranic and secular art treasures. The collection of paintings is exquisite, with works by Ottoman court painters and European artists enthralled with Turkey. A Picasso exhibition in 2005 made this museum the first in Turkey to host a major solo exhibition of a Western artist. The museum continues to host must-see exhibitions.

35 Fortress of Europe

Rumeli Hisarı

Yahya Kemal Cad 42, European side. **Tel** (0212) 263 53 05. 40 and 41 (from Taksim Square); 22, 22/RE, 25/E (from Kabataş). **Open** 9am–5pm Thu–Tue.

This fortress was built by Mehmet the Conqueror in 1452 as his first step in the conquest of Constantinople *(see p58)*. Situated at the narrowest point of the Bosphorus, the fortress controlled a major Byzantine supply route. Across the straits is Anadolu Hisarı, the Fortress of Asia, which was built in the 14th century by Beyazıt I.

The Fortress of Europe's layout was planned by Mehmet himself. While his grand vizier *(see pp60–61)* and two other viziers were each responsible for the building of one of the three great towers, the sultan took charge of the walls. Local buildings were torn down to provide the stones and other building materials. One thousand masons laboured on the walls alone. It was completed in four months – a considerable feat, given the steep terrain.

The new fortress was garrisoned by a force of Janissaries *(see pp60–61)*, whose troops trained their cannons on the straits to prevent the passage of foreign ships. After they had sunk a Venetian vessel, this approach to Constantinople was cut off. Following the conquest of the city, the fortress lost its importance as a military base and was used as a prison, particularly for out-of-favour foreign envoys and prisoners of war. The structure was restored only in 1953.

Today it is in excellent condition and is a pleasant place for an afternoon outing. Some open-air theatre performances are staged here during the Istanbul Festival of Arts and Culture *(see p39)*.

Birds of the Bosphorus

In September and October, thousands of white storks and birds of prey fly over the Bosphorus on their way from their breeding grounds in Eastern Europe to wintering regions in Africa. Large birds usually prefer to cross narrow straits like the Bosphorus rather than fly over an expanse of open water such as the Mediterranean. Among birds of prey on this route you can see the lesser-spotted eagle and the honey buzzard. The birds also cross the straits in spring on their way to Europe but, before the breeding season, they are fewer in number.

The white stork, which migrates over the straits

SHOPPING IN ISTANBUL

Istanbul's shops and markets, crowded and noisy at most times of the day and year, sell a colourful mixture of goods from all over the world. The city's most famous shopping centre is the massive Grand Bazaar. Turkey is a centre of textile production, and Istanbul has a wealth of carpet and fashion shops. If you prefer to do all your shopping under one roof, head for one of the city's modern shopping malls. Wherever you shop, be wary of imitations of famous brand products – even if they appear to be of a high standard and the salesman maintains that they are authentic. Be prepared to bargain where required: it is an important part of a shopping trip.

General Information

Most shops trade from 9am to 8pm Monday to Saturday, and markets open at 8am. Large shops and department stores open later in the morning. The Grand Bazaar and Spice Bazaar are open from 8:30am to 8pm. Malls are open from 10am to 10pm seven days a week. Details on payment, VAT exemption, buying antiques and sending purchases home appear on pp362–3.

Carpets and Kilims

In the Grand Bazaar *(see pp108–9)*, **Şişko Osman** has a good range of carpets, and **Galeri Şirvan** sells Anatolian tribal *kilims* (rugs).

Award-winning **Bereket Halıcılık** is the most reliable seller of antique carpets. **Hazal Halı**, in Ortaköy, stocks a fine collection of kilims.

Fabrics

In addition to carpets and kilims, colourful fabrics in traditional designs from all over Turkey and Central Asia are widely sold. **Sivaslı Yazmacısı** sells village textiles, headscarves and embroidered cloths.

Leather

Turkish leatherwear, while not always of the best quality hides, is durable, of good craftsmanship and reasonably priced.

The Grand Bazaar is full of shops selling leather goods. **Meb Deri**, for example, offers a good range of fashion handbags and accessories, and **Desa** has an extensive range of both classic and fashionable designs.

Jewellery

The Grand Bazaar is the best place to find gold jewellery – it is sold by weight, with only a modest sum added for craftsmanship. The daily price of gold is displayed in the shop windows. Other shops in the same area sell silver jewellery, and pieces inlaid with precious stones. **Urart** stocks collections of unique gold and silver jewellery inspired by the designs of ancient civilizations. **Antikart** specializes in restored antique silver jewellery.

Pottery, Metal and Glassware

Shops in the Grand Bazaar are stocked with traditional ceramics, including pieces decorated with exquisite

Brightly decorated candle lanterns in the Grand Bazaar

How to Bargain

In up-market shops in Istanbul, bargaining is rare. However, in the Grand Bazaar and the shops located in or around the old city (Sultanahmet and Beyazıt) haggling is a must, otherwise you may be cheated. Bazaar shopkeepers, known for their abrasive insistence, expect you to bargain. Take your time and decide where to buy after visiting a few shops selling similar goods. The procedure is as follows:

- You will often be invited inside and offered a cup of tea. Feel free to accept, as this is the customary introduction to any kind of exchange and will not oblige you to buy.
- Do not feel pressurized if the shopkeeper turns the shop upside down to show you his stock – this is normal practice and most salesmen are proud of their goods.
- If you are seriously interested in any item, be brave enough to offer half the price you are asked.
- Take no notice if the shopkeeper looks offended and refuses, but raise the price slightly, aiming to pay about 70–75 per cent of the original offer. If that price is really unacceptable to the owner, he will stop bargaining over the item and turn your attention to other merchandise in the shop.

Haggling over the price of a carpet

blue-and-white İznik designs *(see p165)*. Other types of pottery come from Kütahya, which makes use of a free style of decoration, and Çanakkale, which features more modern designs. For a modern piece of Kütahya ware, visit **Iznik Classics**, which sells handmade ceramics sourced from traditional artisans. Most museum shops also sell a good range of pottery.

The Grand Bazaar and the Cavalry Bazaar are centres of the copper and brass trade and offer a huge selection.

For glassware, **Paşabahçe**, the largest glass manufacturer in Turkey, offers the best range, and some exquisite, delicate pieces with gilded decoration.

Handicrafts

Ideal gifts and souvenirs include embroidered hats, waistcoats and slippers, inlaid jewellery boxes, meerschaum pipes, prayer beads, alabaster ornaments, blue-eye charms to ward off the evil eye and *nargiles* (bubble pipes). At the Istanbul Crafts Centre you can see calligraphers at work. **Rölyef** in Beyoğlu, the Book Bazaar and **Sofa** sell antique and reproduction calligraphy, as well as *ebru* (marbled paintings) and reproductions of Ottoman miniatures.

Bookshops

Books written in English on architecture, history, religion and travel, as well as popular and classic fiction, can be found at **Galeri Kayseri** in the heart of Sultanahmet and at **Homer Kitapevi** in Beyoğlu.

Food, Drink, Herbs and Spices

The Egyptian Bazaar *(see p102)*, also known as the Spice Bazaar, is the place to buy nuts, dried fruits, herbs and spices, jams, various herbal teas, and even exotic delicacies such as caviar. The Galatasaray Fish Market is excellent.

International names alongside Turkish shops in Akmerkez

Shopping Malls

Istanbul's modern shopping malls contain cinemas, "food courts", cafés and hundreds of shops. The most popular are **Akmerkez** in Etiler, **Demirören**, located in İstiklâl Caddesi, and **Kanyon**, which features 160 local and global brands. Seasonal sales take place mainly in clothes shops, but also in department stores and some speciality shops.

DIRECTORY

Carpets and Kilims

Bereket Halıcılık
Peykhane Cad, Sultanahmet.
Map 5 D4.
Tel (0212) 517 46 77.

Galeri Şirvan
52–54 Halıcılar Cad, Grand Bazaar.
Map 4 C4.
Tel (0212) 520 62 24.

Hazal Halı
27–9 Mecidiye Köprüsü Sok, Ortaköy.
Map 3 F3.
Tel (0212) 261 72 33.

Şişko Osman
49 Halıcılar Cad, Grand Bazaar.
Map 4 C4.
Tel (0212) 528 35 48.

Fabrics

Sivaslı Yazmacısı
57 Yağlıkçılar Sok, Grand Bazaar.
Map 4 C4.
Tel (0212) 526 77 48.

Leather

Desa
140 İstiklâl Cad, Beyoğlu.
Map 1 A4.
Tel (0212) 243 37 86.

Meb Deri
14/2 Abdi İspekci Cad, Nişantası.
Map 1 C1.
Tel (0212) 576 26 10.

Jewellery

Antikart
209 İstiklâl Cad, 32 Atlas Kuyumcular Çarşısı, Beyoğlu.
Map 1 A4.
Tel (0212) 252 44 82.

Urart
18 Abdi İpekçi Cad, Nişantaşı. **Map** 1 C1.
Tel (0212) 246 71 94.

Pottery, Metal and Glassware

Iznik Classics
Arasta Çarşısı 67, Sultanahmet. **Map** 5 E5.
Tel (0212) 517 17 05.

Paşabahçe
314 İstiklâl Cad, Beyoğlu. **Map** 1 A5.
Tel (0212) 244 05 44.

Handicrafts

Rölyef
16 Emir Nevruz Sok, Beyoğlu. **Map** 1 A4.
Tel (0212) 244 04 94.

Sofa
85 Nuruosmaniye Cad, Cağaloğlu. **Map** 5 D4.
Tel (0212) 520 28 50.

Bookshops

Galeri Kayseri
58 Divanyolu Cad, Sultanahmet. **Map** 5 D4.
Tel (0212) 512 04 56.

Homer Kitapevi
Yeni Çarşı Cad 28, Beyoğlu. **Map** 1 A4.
Tel (0212) 249 59 02.

Food, Drink, Herbs and Spices

Antre Gourmet
40A Akarsu Cad, Cihangir. **Map** 5 D1.
Tel (0212) 292 89 72.

Kurukahveci Mehmet Efendi
66 Tahmis Cad, Eminönü.
Map 5 D1.
Tel (0212) 511 42 62.

Şekerci Hacı Bekir
83 Hamidiye Cad, Eminönü. **Map** 5 D3.
Tel (0212) 522 06 66.

Shopping Malls

Akmerkez
Nispetiye Cad, Etiler.
Tel (0212) 282 01 70.

Demirören
54 İstiklâl Cad, Beyoğlu.
Map 1 A5. **Tel** (0212) 249 99 99.

Kanyon
185 Büyükdere Cad, Levent.
Tel (0212) 353 53 00.

ENTERTAINMENT IN ISTANBUL

Istanbul offers a great variety of leisure pursuits, ranging from arts festivals and folk music to belly dancing and nightclubs. The most important cultural event is the series of festivals organized by the Istanbul Foundation for Culture and the Arts between March and November. Throughout the year, traditional Turkish music, opera, ballet, Western classical music and plays are performed at Cemal Reşit Rey Concert Hall (CRR) and some other venues around the city. Beyoğlu is the main centre for entertainment of all kinds. This area also has the highest concentration of cinemas in the city, and numerous lively bars and cafés. Though Konya *(see pp254–5)* is the home of the religious dervish order, productions of the mystical whirling dervish dance are staged at the Mevlevi Monastery in Beyoğlu once a month. Ortaköy, on the European shore of the Bosphorus, is another very popular venue for dining, music and dancing. For a trip to the beach on a hot day, the Princes' Islands *(see p162)* are best.

Entertainment Guides

A bimonthly magazine in English, *The Guide* lists cultural events and activities in the city, as does *Time Out Istanbul*. Entertainment information and contact numbers are available in the English *Hürriyet Daily News*, as well as Turkish Airlines' in-flight magazine.

Entertainment guides available in Istanbul

Festivals

Five major annual festivals (theatre, film, music and dance, jazz, and a biennial fine arts exposition) are organized by the Istanbul Foundation for Culture and the Arts. All tickets can be obtained via telephone from the **Istanbul Festival Committee** or at the individual venues themselves.

Istanbul also hosts the Yapı Kredi Arts, Akbank Jazz and Efes Pilsen Blues festivals in autumn each year.

During festivals a special bus service runs between show venues and the city centre.

Western Classical Music and Dance

The **Cemal Reşit Rey Concert Hall (CRR)** stages Western classical music concerts and hosts music and dance groups. Concerts are also held at smaller venues across the city. Contact the Sultanahmet Tourist Office *(see p83)* for details.

Laser disc screenings of opera, ballet and classical music performances are held most days at 2pm and 6pm at the **Aksanat Cultural and Arts Centre**. It also sometimes stages live plays and music recitals.

Booking Tickets

Most concert, theatre, arts and sports tickets can be booked by phone through Biletix (tel: 0216 556 98 00). You can also go to the website at www.biletix.com for more information about ticket availability; the website also shows point of sale outlets.

Rock and Jazz

Many of Istanbul's clubs and bars plays good live music. **Hayal Kahvesi** is a bar dedicated to jazz, rock and blues and has an outdoor summer venue in Çubuklu. **Nardis Jazz Club** is an atmospheric venue for domestic and international acts, located just down the road from the Galata Tower. **Babylon** is arguably the best venue in Istanbul for world, rock and dance music, while **Peyote** is great for afficionados of alternative rock.

Traditional Turkish Music and Dance

Traditional Turkish music performed at the CRR includes Ottoman classical, mystical Sufi and Turkish folk music.

Fasıl is a popular form of traditional music that is best enjoyed live in *meyhanes* (taverns) such as **Kallavi**. It is performed on the *kanun* (zither), as well as *tambur* and *ud* (both similar to the lute). For the traditional folk sounds of Anatolia, try *halk* or *Türkü* music. At venues such as **Munzur**, soulful melodies are played on long-necked lute-like instruments known as *saz* or *bağlama*. **Galata Tower** restaurant is an alternative

Folk dancing at the Kervansaray venue

venue for Turkish folk music and dance, while belly dancing is a nightclub attraction in Beyoğlu.

Other places featuring top performers of traditional art are **Kervansaray, Orient House** and **Manzara**.

Nightclubs

A glitzy nightclub is the **Sortie Bar Restaurant**, a bar-restaurant complex popular with celebrities and located in the centre of town. Its large outdoor space is a must for hot summer nights. Its nearby neighbour **Reina** provides more of the same. For something more youth-orientated, try the pulsing sounds of **Indigo**, or the more sophisticated **Mini Muzikhol**.

Cinemas and Theatre

The latest foreign films are on circuit at the same time as in the rest of Europe, albeit with

Classical concert in the church of Haghia Eirene *(see p78)*

Turkish subtitles. **Atlas** and **Beyoğlu** show mainly art-house films. The first show is half-price. Many cinemas offer half-price tickets on Wednesdays, and students with a valid student card are entitled to discounts.

Theatres stage local and international plays, but only in Turkish. The theatre season runs from September to June.

Sports

Main five-star hotels have good swimming pools and welcome non-residents for a fee. Turks are fanatical about football: **Beşiktaş, Fenerbahçe** and **Galatasaray** are the league players.

Horse races take place at the **Veli Efendi Hipodromu** on weekends and Wednesdays.

Children

Yildiz Park *(see p125)* has much to offer children, as does **Miniatürk**, with over 100 miniature replicas of Turkey's famous cultural landmarks.

Late-Night Transport

The metro closes around midnight, which is also when the last buses and *dolmuşes* run, but taxis are available all night. For more information see pp396–9.

DIRECTORY

Istanbul Festival Committee

Tel (0216) 454 15 55.
W **iksv.org**

Western Classical Music and Dance

Aksanat Cultural and Arts Centre
İstiklal Cad 16, Taksim. **Map** 1 B4.
Tel (0212) 252 35 00.

CRR
Gümüş Sok, Harbiye.
Map 1 C1.
Tel (0212) 232 98 30.

Rock and Jazz

Babylon
Sehbender Sok 3, Asmalimescit, Tünel, Beyoğlu.
Tel (0212) 292 73 68.

Hayal Kahvesi (Beyoğlu)
Büyükparmak Kapı Sok 19, Beyoğlu. **Map** 1 B4.
Tel (0212) 244 25 28.

Nardis Jazz Club
Kuledibi Sok, Galata.
Map 5 D1.
Tel (0212) 244 63 27.

Peyote
Kameriye Sok 4, Balık Pazarı, Beyoğlu.
Tel (0212) 251 43 98.

Traditional Turkish Music and Dance

Galata Tower
Büyükhendek Cad, Galata. **Map** 1 A1.
Tel (0212) 213 81 80.

Kallavi
Kallavi Sok 20, Beyoğlu. **Map** 1 A4.
Tel (0212) 251 10 10.

Kervansaray
Cumhuriyet Cad 30, Harbiye. **Map** 1 C2.
Tel (0212) 247 16 30.

Manzara
Conrad Hotel, Yıldız Cad, Beşiktaş.
Map 2 C3.
Tel (0212) 227 30 00.

Munzur
Hasnun Galip Sok, Beyoğlu. **Map** 1 B4
Tel (0212) 245 46 69.

Orient House
Tiyatro Cad 27, Beyazıt.
Map 4 C4.
Tel (0212) 517 61 63.

Nightclubs

Indigo
Akarsu Sok 1/2, İstiklal Cad, Beyoğlu. **Map** 1 A4.
Tel (0212) 244 85 67.

Mini Muzikhol
Soğancı Sok, Sıraselviler Cad, Beyoğlu. **Map** 1 B4.
Tel (0212) 245 19 96.

Sortie Bar Restaurant
Muallim Naci Cad 54, Ortaköy. **Map** 3 F3.
Tel (0212) 327 85 85.

Cinemas

Atlas
İstiklal Cad, Atlas Pasajı.
Map 1 B4.
Tel (0212) 252 85 76.

Beyoğlu
İstiklal Cad 140, Halep-Pasajı, Beyoğlu.
Map 1 B4.
Tel (0212) 251 32 40.

Sports

Beşiktaş FC
Spor Cad 92, Beşiktaş.
Map 2 A4.
Tel (0212) 227 87 80.

Fenerbahçe FC
Kızıltoprak, Kadıköy.
Tel (0216) 345 09 40.

Galatasaray FC
Türk Telekom Arena, Şişli.
Map 1 C2.
Tel (0212) 305 19 01.

Veli Efendi Hipodromu
Osmaniye, Bakırköy.
Tel (0212) 444 08 55.

Children

Miniatürk
Imrahar Cad, Sütlüce.
Tel (0212) 222 28 82.

STREET FINDER

The map references that are given throughout this section refer to the maps on the following pages. Some small streets with references may not be named on the map. References are also given for hotels *(see pp330–32)*, restaurants *(see pp346–9)*, shops *(see pp134–5)* and entertainment venues *(see pp136–7)*.

The map provided below shows the area covered by the six maps, and the key lists the symbols that are used. The first figure of the reference tells you which map page to turn to; the letter and number indicate the grid reference. The map on the inside back cover shows public transport routes.

Key to Street Finder

- Major sight
- Place of interest
- Other building
- Ferry boarding point
- Sea bus boarding point
- Railway station
- Metro station
- Tram stop
- Cable car station
- Main bus terminus
- Funicular/*Tünel* station
- *Dolmuş* terminus
- Tourist information
- Hospital
- Police station
- Turkish baths
- Mosque
- Synagogue
- Church
- Railway line
- Tram line
- Motorway
- Pedestrian-only street
- City wall

Scale of Maps 1–6

0 metres 250

0 yards 250

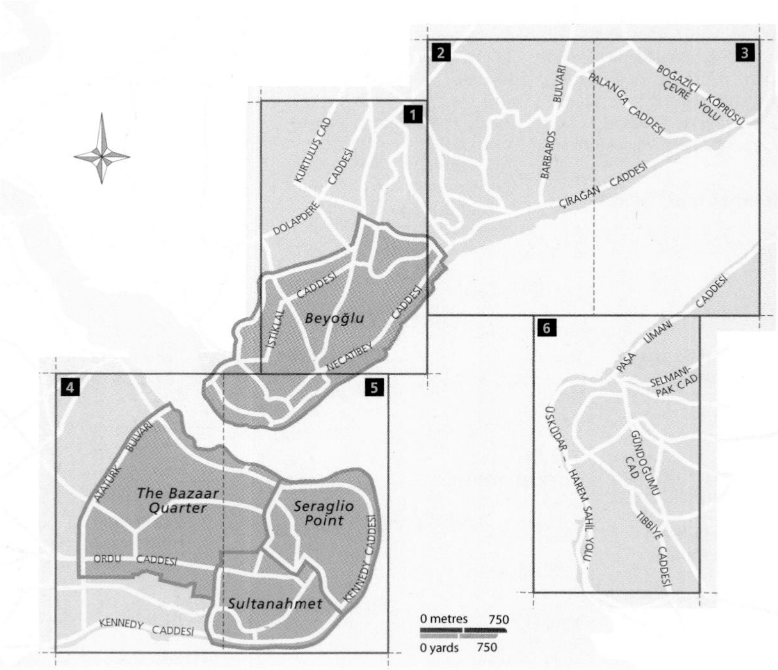

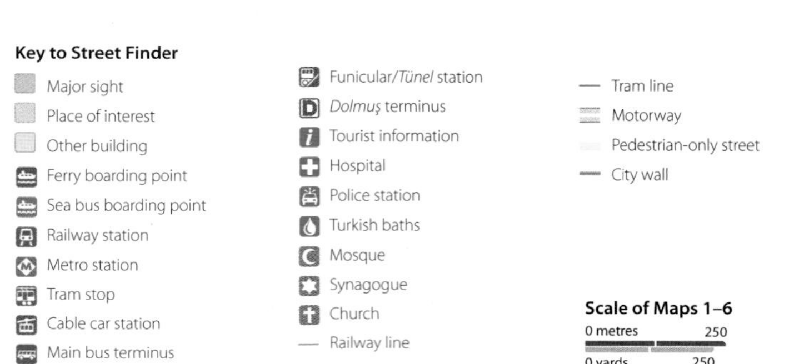

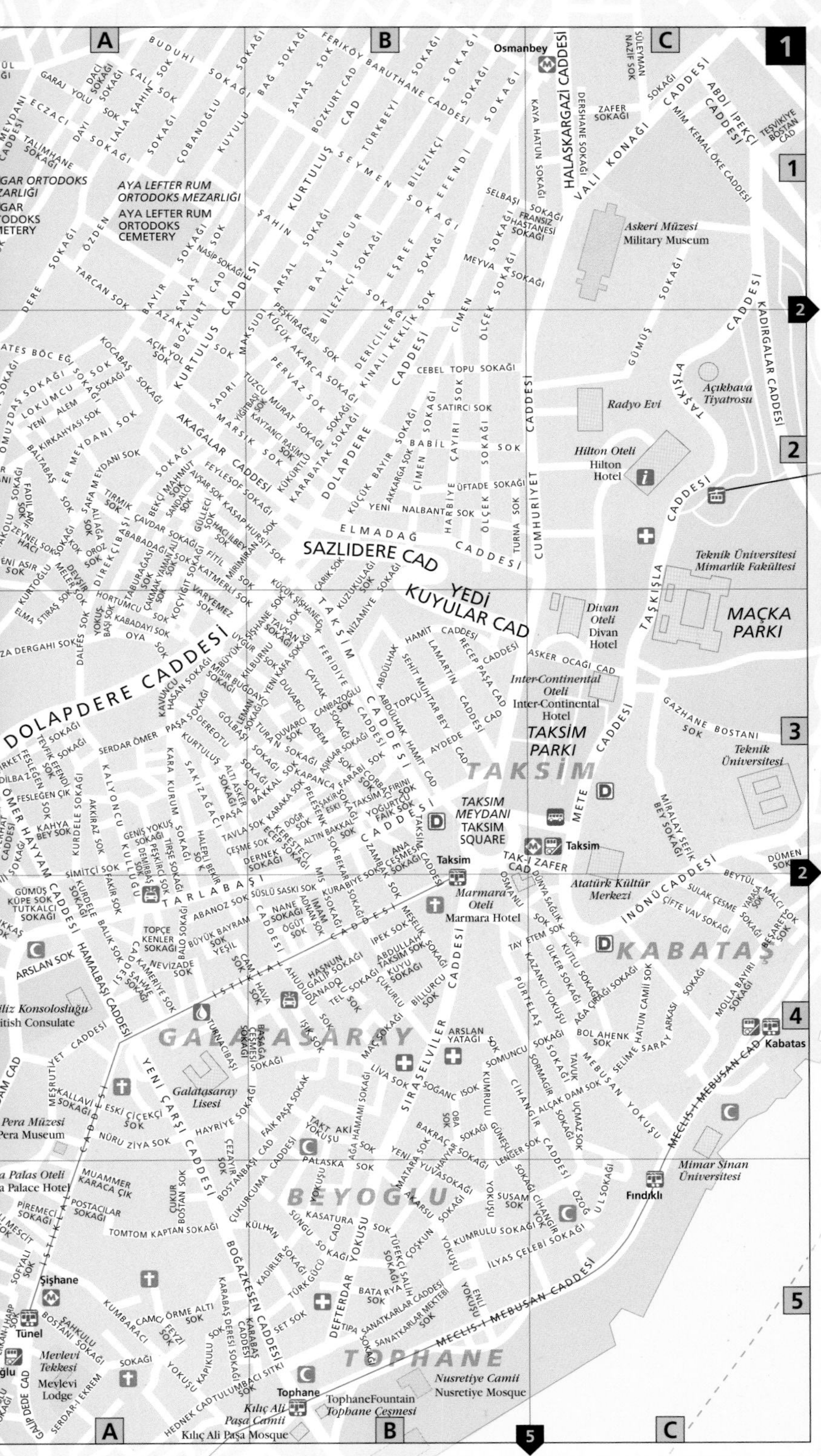

A
B
C
1
Osmanbey
HALASKARGAZİ CADDESİ
VALİ KONAĞI CADDESİ
ABDİ İPEKÇİ CADDESİ
AYA LEFTER RUM ORTODOKS MEZARLIĞI
AYA LEFTER RUM ORTODOKS CEMETERY
KURTULUŞ CADDESİ
Askeri Müzesi
Military Museum
TAŞKIŞLA CADDESİ
KADIRGALAR CADDESİ
Açıkhava Tiyatrosu
Radyo Evi
Hilton Oteli
Hilton Hotel
2
CUMHURİYET CADDESİ
ELMADAĞ CADDESİ
SAZLIDERE CAD
YEDİ KUYULAR CAD
AKAĞALAR CADDESİ
DOLAPDERE CADDESİ
Teknik Üniversitesi Mimarlik Fakültesi
MAÇKA PARKI
Divan Oteli
Divan Hotel
Inter-Continental Oteli
Inter-Continental Hotel
TAKSİM PARKI
TAKSİM
TAKSIM MEYDANI
TAKSIM SQUARE
Taksim
3
Teknik Üniversitesi
Atatürk Kültür Merkezi
İNÖNÜ CADDESİ
KABATAŞ
Marmara Oteli
Marmara Hotel
TARLABAŞI
İSTİKLAL CADDESİ
GALATASARAY
Galatasaray Lisesi
SIRASELVİLER CADDESİ
4
Kabataş
MECLİS-İ MEBUSAN CAD
Pera Müzesi
Pera Museum
BEYOĞLU
Mimar Sinan Üniversitesi
Fındıklı
Şişhane
Tünel
Mevlevi Tekkesi
Mevlevi Lodge
BOĞAZKESEN CADDESİ
5
TOPHANE
Nusretiye Camii
Nusretiye Mosque
Tophane
TophaneFountain
Tophane Çeşmesi
Kılıç Ali Paşa Camii
Kılıç Ali Paşa Mosque

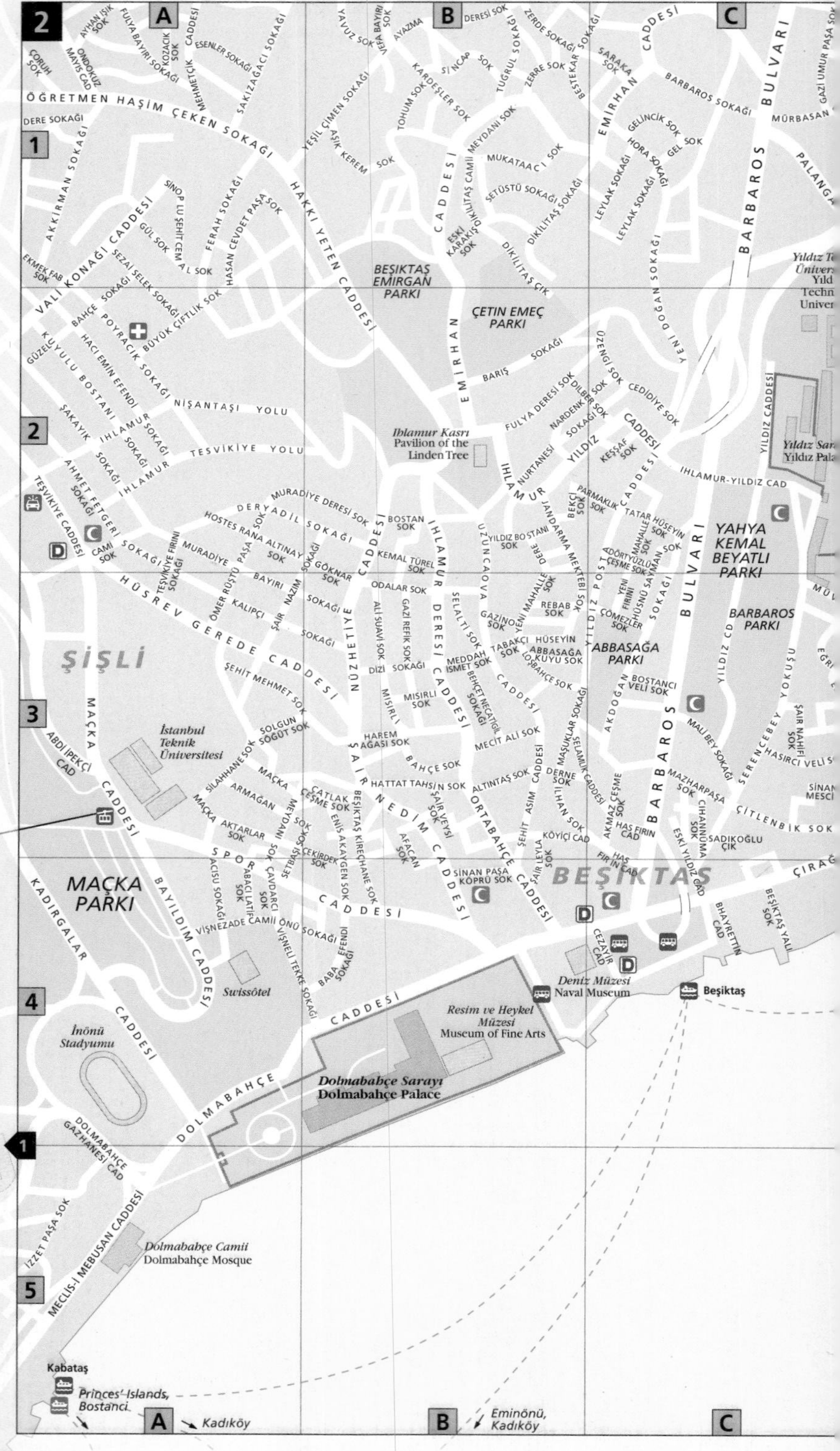

2
A
B
C
1
2
3
4
5
ÖĞRETMEN HAŞİM ÇEKEN SOKAĞI
HAKKI YETEN CADDESİ
EMİRHAN CADDESİ
BARBAROS BULVARI
YILDIZ CADDESİ
VALİ KONAĞI CADDESİ
NİŞANTAŞI YOLU
TEŞVİKİYE YOLU
IHLAMUR SOKAĞI
HÜSREV GEREDE CADDESİ
NÜZHETİYE CADDESİ
IHLAMUR DERESİ CADDESİ
ŞAİR NEDİM CADDESİ
ORTABAHÇE CADDESİ
SPOR CADDESİ
MAÇKA CADDESİ
BAYILDIM CADDESİ
KADIRGALAR CADDESİ
DOLMABAHÇE CADDESİ
MECLİS-İ MEBUSAN CADDESİ
IHLAMUR-YILDIZ CAD
ÇIRAĞAN
BEŞİKTAŞ EMİRGAN PARKI
ÇETİN EMEÇ PARKI
YAHYA KEMAL BEYATLI PARKI
BARBAROS PARKI
ABBASAĞA PARKI
ŞİŞLİ
BEŞİKTAŞ
MAÇKA PARKI
Iblamur Kasrı
Pavilion of the Linden Tree
İstanbul Teknik Üniversitesi
Yıldız Sarayı
Swissôtel
İnönü Stadyumu
Deniz Müzesi
Naval Museum
Resim ve Heykel Müzesi
Museum of Fine Arts
Dolmabahçe Sarayı
Dolmabahçe Palace
Dolmabahçe Camii
Dolmabahçe Mosque
Beşiktaş
Kabataş
Princes' Islands, Bostancı
Kadıköy
Eminönü, Kadıköy

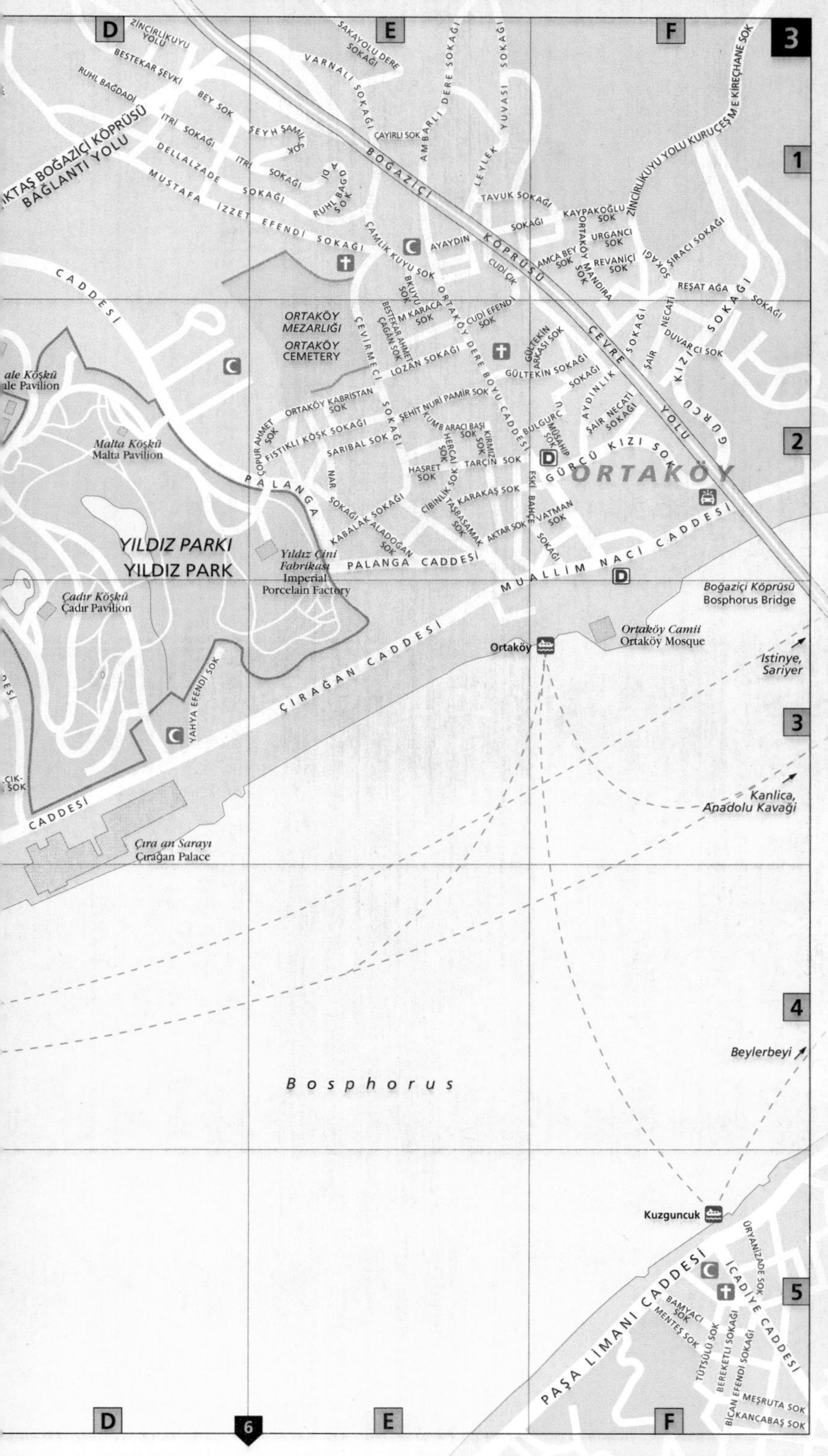

3
D
E
F
1
2
3
4
5
ZİNCİRLİKUYU YOLU
BESTEKAR ŞEVKİ BEY SOK
RUHİ BAĞDADİ
İTRİ SOKAĞI
ŞEYH ŞAMİL SOK
DELLALZADE SOKAĞI
MUSTAFA İZZET EFENDİ SOKAĞI
RUHİ BAĞDADİ SOK
BEŞİKTAŞ BOĞAZİÇİ KÖPRÜSÜ BAĞLANTI YOLU
SAKAYOLU DERE SOKAĞI
VARNALI SOKAĞI
ÇAYIRLI SOK
AMBARLI DERE SOKAĞI
YUVASI SOKAĞI
LEYLEK
BOĞAZİÇİ KÖPRÜSÜ ÇEVRE YOLU
ZİNCİRLİKUYU YOLU KURUÇEŞME KİREÇHANE SOK
TAVUK SOKAĞI
KAYPAKOĞLU SOK
URGANCI SOK
AMCA BEY SOK
ORTAKÖY MANDIRA SOK
REVANİÇİ SOK
ŞIRACI SOKAĞI
REŞAT AĞA SOKAĞI
AYAYDIN
ÇAMLIK KUYU SOK
CUDİ ÇIK
CUDİ EFENDİ SOK
CADDESİ
ORTAKÖY MEZARLIĞI
ORTAKÖY CEMETERY
BESTEKAR AHMET ÇAĞAN SOK
M KARACA SOK
ÇEVİRMECİ SOKAĞI
LOZAN SOKAĞI
ORTAKÖY DERE BOYU CADDESİ
GÜLTEKİN ARKASI SOK
GÜLTEKİN SOKAĞI
NECATİ SOKAĞI
ŞAİR
KIZI SOKAĞI
DUVARCI SOK
GÜRCÜ
ale Köşkü
ale Pavilion
ORTAKÖY KABRİSTAN SOK
ŞEHİT NURİ PAMİR SOK
AYDINLIK SOKAĞI
ŞAİR NECATİ SOKAĞI
ÇOPUR AHMET SOK
FISTIKLI KÖŞK SOKAĞI
KUMBARACI BAŞI SOK
BULGURCU SOK
MÜSAHİP SOK
Malta Köşkü
Malta Pavilion
SARIBAL SOK
HERCAİ SOK
KIRMIZI SOK
GÜRCÜ KIZI SOK
ORTAKÖY
HASRET SOK
TARÇIN SOK
PALANGA
NAR SOKAĞI
CİBİNLİK SOK
KARAKAŞ SOK
ESKİ BAHÇE SOKAĞI
VATMAN SOK
KABALAK SOKAĞI
TAŞBASAMAK SOK
AKTAR SOK
ALADOĞAN SOK
YILDIZ PARKI
YILDIZ PARK
Yıldız Çini Fabrikası
Imperial Porcelain Factory
PALANGA CADDESİ
MUALLİM NACİ CADDESİ
Boğaziçi Köprüsü
Bosphorus Bridge
Çadır Köşkü
Çadır Pavilion
Ortaköy Camii
Ortaköy Mosque
Ortaköy
Istinye, Sariyer
ÇIRAĞAN CADDESİ
YAHYA EFENDİ SOK
Kanlica, Anadolu Kavağı
Çıra an Sarayı
Çırağan Palace
Bosphorus
Beylerbeyi
Kuzguncuk
ÜRYANİZADE SOK
İCADİYE CADDESİ
PAŞA LİMANI CADDESİ
BAMYACI SOK
MENTEŞ SOK
TÜTSÜLÜ SOK
BEREKETLİ SOKAĞI
BİCAN EFENDİ SOKAĞI
MEŞRUTA SOK
KANCABAŞ SOK
D
6
E
F

4
A
B
C
1
2
3
4
5
Eyüp
Azap Kapı Camii
Azap Kapı Mosque
Atatürk Köprüsü
Atatürk Bridge
Golden Horn
Haliç
UNKAPANI
ABDÜLEZEL PAŞA CADDESİ
ATATÜRK BULVARI
RAGIP GÜMÜŞPALA CAD
KÜÇÜKPAZAR
HACI KADIN CADDESİ
Fatih Camii
Fatih Mosque
Zeyrek Camii
Church of the Pantocrator
Kilise Camii
Church of St Theodore
Süleymaniye Camii
Süleymaniye Mosque
VEFA
Bozdoğan Kemeri
Valens Aqueduct
SARAÇHANE
Kız Taşı
Column of Marcian
Şehzade Camii
Prince's Mosque
Belediye Sarayı
ŞEHZADE BAŞI CADDESİ
MACAR KARDEŞLER CAD
Kalenderhane Camii
Kalenderhane Mosque
Istanbul Üniversitesi
Beyazıt Kulesi
Beyazıt Tower
BEYAZIT
BEYAZIT MEYDANI
BEYAZIT SQUARE
Vezneciler
VEZNECİLER CAD
Kapalı Çarşı
Grand Bazaar
Laleli Camii
Tulip Mosque
ORDU CADDESİ
Aksaray
Laleli-Univ.
Beyazıt Camii
Beyazıt Mosque
Beyazıt
YENİÇERİLER
AKSARAY
ATATÜRK BULVARI
MUSTAFA KEMAL CADDESİ
Bodrum Camii
Bodrum Mosque
ÇARŞIKAPI
KUMKAPI
TÜRKELİ CADDESİ
TÜCCARI CADDESİ
NAMIK KEMAL CADDESİ
Yenikapı
KENNEDY CADDESİ
Sea of Marmara
Marmara, Bandirma, Bursa
Yalova, Cinarcik, Gemlik
Kadiköy, Bostanci

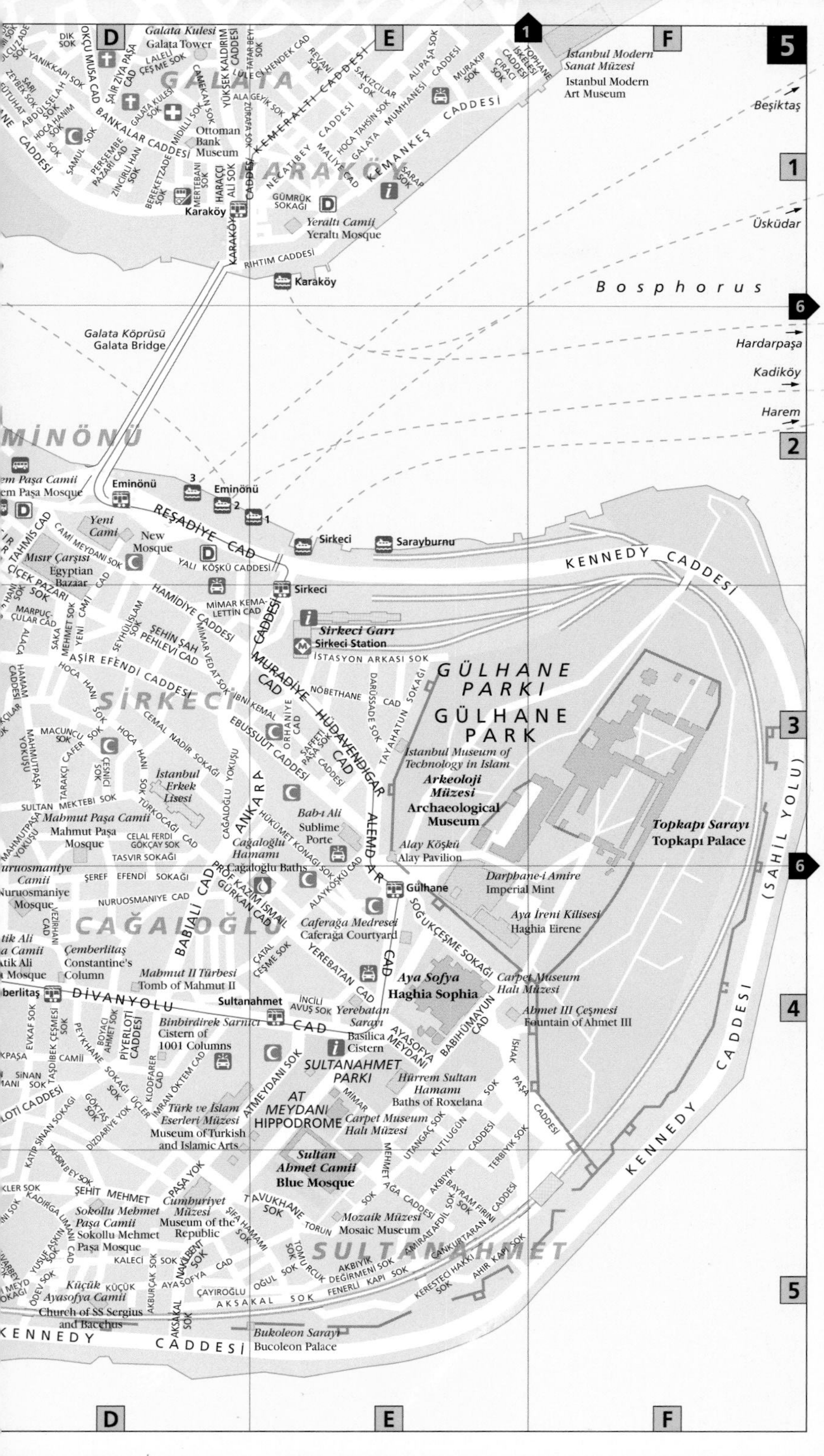

5
Galata Kulesi
Galata Tower
GALATA
KARAKÖY
Ottoman Bank Museum
Yeraltı Camii
Yeraltı Mosque
Karaköy
İstanbul Modern Sanat Müzesi
Istanbul Modern Art Museum
Beşiktaş
Üsküdar
Bosphorus
Galata Köprüsü
Galata Bridge
Hardarpaşa
Kadiköy
Harem
EMİNÖNÜ
Eminönü
Sirkeci
Sarayburnu
Yeni Cami
New Mosque
Mısır Çarşısı
Egyptian Bazaar
KENNEDY CADDESİ
Sirkeci Garı
Sirkeci Station
GÜLHANE PARKI
GÜLHANE PARK
SİRKECİ
İstanbul Museum of Technology in Islam
Arkeoloji Müzesi
Archaeological Museum
İstanbul Erkek Lisesi
Bab-ı Ali
Sublime Porte
Mahmut Paşa Camii
Mahmut Paşa Mosque
Topkapı Sarayı
Topkapı Palace
Alay Köşkü
Alay Pavilion
Cağaloğlu Hamamı
Cağaloğlu Baths
Darphane-i Amire
Imperial Mint
Nuruosmaniye Camii
Nuruosmaniye Mosque
Gülhane
Aya İreni Kilisesi
Haghia Eirene
CAĞALOĞLU
Caferağa Medresei
Caferağa Courtyard
Çemberlitaş
Constantine's Column
Mahmut II Türbesi
Tomb of Mahmut II
Aya Sofya
Haghia Sophia
Carpet Museum
Halı Müzesi
Sultanahmet
Ahmet III Çeşmesi
Fountain of Ahmet III
Binbirdirek Sarnıcı
Cistern of 1001 Columns
Yerebatan Sarayı
Basilica Cistern
SULTANAHMET PARKI
Hürrem Sultan Hamamı
Baths of Roxelana
AT MEYDANI
HIPPODROME
Türk ve İslam Eserleri Müzesi
Museum of Turkish and Islamic Arts
Sultan Ahmet Camii
Blue Mosque
Sokollu Mehmet Paşa Camii
Sokollu Mehmet Paşa Mosque
Cumhuriyet Müzesi
Museum of the Republic
Mozaik Müzesi
Mosaic Museum
SULTANAHMET
Küçük Ayasofya Camii
Church of SS Sergius and Bacchus
Bukoleon Sarayı
Bucoleon Palace
(SAHİL YOLU)
D
E
F

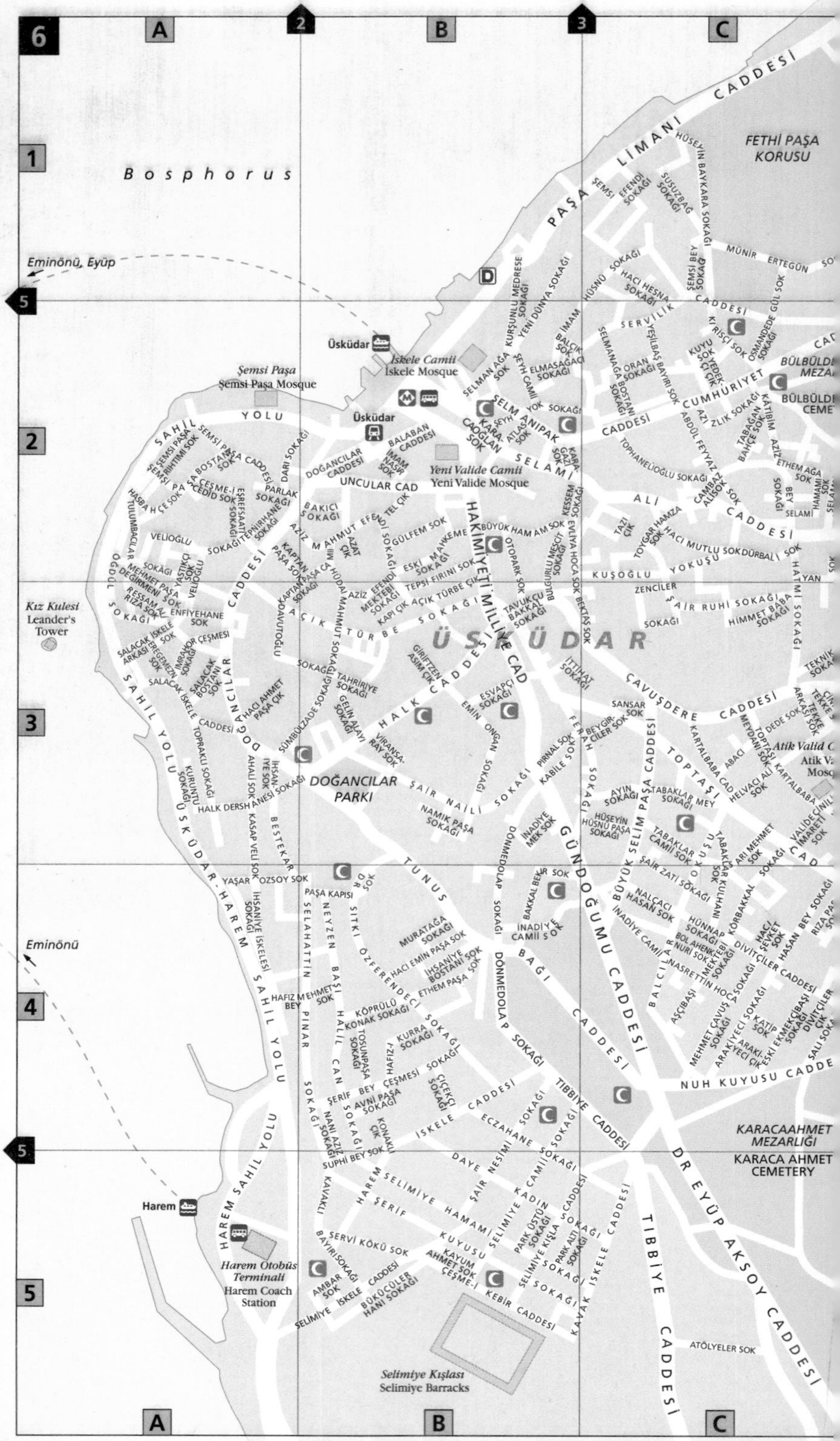
6
A
B
C
1
2
3
4
5
Bosphorus
Eminönü, Eyüp
Eminönü
Üsküdar
İskele Camii
İskele Mosque
Şemsi Paşa
Şemsi Paşa Mosque
Yeni Valide Camii
Yeni Valide Mosque
Kız Kulesi
Leander's Tower
FETHİ PAŞA KORUSU
PAŞA LİMANI CADDESİ
SAHİL YOLU
HAKİMİYETİ MİLLİYE CAD
SELAMİ ALİ CADDESİ
CUMHURİYET CADDESİ
UNCULAR CAD
DOĞANCILAR CADDESİ
HALK CADDESİ
ÜSKÜDAR
DOĞANCILAR PARKI
ÇAVUŞDERE CADDESİ
TOPTAŞI
BÜYÜK SELİM PAŞA CADDESİ
GÜNDOĞUMU CADDESİ
BAĞI CADDESİ
DÖNMEDOLAP SOKAĞI
TUNUS BAĞI
KUŞOĞLU YOKUŞU
NUH KUYUSU CADDESİ
TIBBİYE CADDESİ
DR EYÜP AKSOY CADDESİ
KARACAAHMET MEZARLIĞI
KARACA AHMET CEMETERY
Atik Valide
Harem
Harem Otobüs Terminali
Harem Coach Station
HAREM SAHİL YOLU
ÜSKÜDAR-HAREM SAHİL YOLU
Selimiye Kışlası
Selimiye Barracks
SELİMİYE İSKELE CADDESİ
ÇEŞME-İ KEBİR CADDESİ
KAVAK İSKELE CADDESİ
ATÖLYELER SOK

Street Finder Index

In Turkish, Ç, Ğ, İ, Ö, Ş and Ü are listed as separate letters in the alphabet, coming after C, G, I, O, S and U, respectively. In this book, however, Ç is treated as C for the purposes of alphabetization and so on with the other letters. Hence Çiçek follows Cibinlik as if both names began with C. Following standard Turkish practice we have abbreviated Sokak to Sok, Caddesi to Cad and Çıkmazı to Çık.

A

Abacı Dede Sok 6 C3
Abacı Latif Sok 2 A4
Abanoz Sok 1 A4
Abbasaşa Kuyu Sok 2 B3
Abdi İpekçi Cad 2 A3
Abdi Ipekçi Cad 1 C1
Abdül Feyyaz Sok 6 C2
Abdülezel Paşa Cad 4 B1
Abdülhak Hamit Cad 1 B3
Abdullah Taksim Sok 1 B4
Abdülselah Sok 5 D1
Açık Tübbe Sok 6 B3
Açık Türbe Çık 6 B3
Açık Yol Sok 1 A2
Açıklar Sok 4 A3
Acısu Sok 2 A4
Adliye Sok 5 E4
Afacan Sok 2 B3
Ağa Çeşmesi Sok 4 B4
Ağa Çırağı Sok 1 C4
Ağa Hamamı Sok 1 B4
Ağa Yokuşu Sok 4 A3
Ağızlıkçı Sok 4 C3
Ahalı Sok 6 A3
Ahır Kapı Sok 5 E5
Ahmet Fetgeri Sok 2 A2
Ahmet Şuayip Sok 4 B4
Ahududu Sok 1 B4
Akarsu Yokuşu 1 B5
Akbıyık Cad 5 E5
Akbıyık Değirmeni Sok 5 E5
Akburçak Sok 5 D5
Akdoğan Sok 2 C3
Akif Paşa Sok 4 B3
Akkarga Sok 1 B2
Akkavak Sok 2 A2
Akkiraz Sok 1 A3
Akkirman Sok 2 A1
Akmaz Çeşme Sok 2 C3
Aksakal Sok 5 D5
Aksaray Cad 4 A4
Aksaray Hamamı Sok 4 A4
Aktar Sok 3 E2
Al Boyacılar Sok 4 A5
Ala Geyik Cad 5 E1
Alaca Camii Sok 4 A4
Alaca Hamam Cad 5 D3
Aladoğan Sok 3 E2
Alayköşkü Cad 5 E4
Albay Sadi Alantar Sok 2 A1
Alçak Dam Sok 1 C4
Alemdar Cad 5 E3
Ali Ağa Sok 1 A2
Ali Hoca Sok 1 A5
Ali Paşa Sok 5 E1
Ali Suavi Sok 2 B3
Alişan Sok 4 B5
Altı Asker Sok 1 A3
Altı Poğaça Sok 4 A1
Altın Bakkal Sok 1 B3
Altıntaş Sok 2 B3
Ambar Sok 6 B5
Ambarlı Dere Sok 3 E1
Amca Bey Sok 3 F1
Amiral Tafdil Sok 5 E5
Ana Çeşmesi Sok 1 B3
Anadolu Sok 1 B4
Ankara Cad 5 D3
Arakiyeci Çık 6 C4
Arakiyeci Sok 6 C4
Arapzade Ahmet Sok 4 C5
Arasta Çarşısı 5 E5
Arayıcı Sok 4 C5
Armağan Sok 2 A3
Arslan Sok 1 A4
Arslan Yatağı Sok 1 B4
Asama Kandil Sok 4 C4
Aşir Efendi Cad 5 D3
Asker Ocağı Cad 1 C3
Asker Sok 4 B4
Asmalı Han Sok 4 C5
Asmalı Mescit Sok 1 A5
Asmalı Sok 6 A2
Aşçıbası Mektebi Sok 6 C4
Aşık Kerem Sok 2 B1
Aşık Paşa Sok 4 A1
Aşıklar Sok 1 B3
Astar Sok 4 A1
Asya Sok 4 B5
Atatürk Bulvarı 4 B2
Ates Böceği Sok 1 A2
Atlamatası Cad 4 B2
Atlas Çik 6 B2
Atlas Sok 6 B2
Atmeydanı Sok 5 D4
Atölyeler Sok 6 C5
Atpazarı Sok 4 A2
Avni Paşa Sok 6 B4
Avşar Sok 1 A2
Ayasofya Meydanı 5 E4
Ayaydın Sok 3 E1
Ayazma Deresi Sok 2 B1
Aydede Cad 1 B3
Aydın Bey Sok 4 A1
Aydınlık Sok 3 F2
Ayhan Işık Sok 2 A1
Ayın Sok 6 C3
Aynacılar Sok 4 C3
Ayşe Kadın Hamamı Sok 4 B3
Azak Sok 1 A2
Azap Çeşmesi Sok 4 B2
Azat Çık 6 B2
Azat Yok 6 B2
Azep Askeri Sok 4 B2
Azimkar Sok 4 A4
Aziz Efendi Mektebi Sok 6 B3
Aziz Mahmut Efendi Sok 6 B2
Azizlik Sok 6 C2

B

B Kuyu Sok 3 E1
Baba Efendi Sok 2 B4
Baba Hasan Sok 4 A3
Babadağı Sok 1 A2
Babayiğit Sok 4 C5
Babıali Cad 5 D4
Babıhümayun Cad 5 E4
Babil Sok 1 B2
Bakıcı Sok 6 B2
Bakırcılar Cad 4 C3
Bakkal Bekir Sok 6 B4
Bakraç Sok 1 B4
Balaban Cad 6 B2
Balçık Sok 6 B2
Balcılar Yok 6 C4
Bali Paşa Yokuşu 4 C4
Balık Sok 1 A4
Balo Sok 1 A4
Baltabaş Sok 1 A2
Balyoz Sok 1 A5
Barbaros Bulvarı 2 C3
Barbaros Sok 2 C1
Barış Sok 2 B2
Basak Sok 4 B3
Baş Musahip Sok 5 D4
Başağa Çeşmesi Sok 1 B4
Batarya Sok 1 B5
Batumlu Sok 4 B5
Bayır Sok 1 A1
Baylıdım Cad 2 A4
Bayram Fırını Sok 5 E5
Baysungur Sok 1 B1
Behçet Necatigil Sok 2 B3
Behran Çavuş Sok 4 C5
Bekçi Mahmut Sok 1 A2
Bekçi Sok 2 B2
Bektaş Sok 6 C3
Bereketzade Sok 5 D1
Beşaret Sok 1 C4
Beşiktaş Boğaziçi Köprüsü Baglantı Yolu 3 D1
Beşiktaş Cad 2 B4
Beşiktaş Kireçhane Sok 2 B3
Beşiktas Yalı Sok 2 C4
Besim Ömer Paşa Cad 4 B3
B Hayrettin Cad 2 C4
Bestekar Ahmet Çagan Sok 3 E2
Bestekar Selahattin Pınar Sok 6 B4
Bestekar Şevki Bey Sok 3 D1
Bestekar Sok 2 B1
Beyazıt Karakol Sok 4 C4
Beyazıt Külhanı Sok 4 B4
Beygirciler Sok 6 C3
Beytül Malcı Sok 1 C4
Bezciler Sok 5 D3
Bıçakçı Çeşmesi Sok 4 B2
Bilezikçi Sok 1 B1
Billurcu Sok 1 B4
Boğaziçi Köprüsü Çevre Yolu 3 E1
Boğazkesen Cad 1 B5
Bol Ahenk Nuri Sok 6 C4
Bol Ahenk Sok 1 C4
Börekçi Ali Sok 4 B4
Bostan Hamamı Sok 4 B1
Bostan Sok 2 B2
Bostanbaşı Cad 1 A5
Bostancı Veli Sok 2 C3
Bostanı Sok 1 A2
Boyacı Ahmet Sok 5 D4
Bozdoğan Kemeri Cad 4 B3
Bozkurt Cad 1 B1
Buduhi Sok 1 A1
Bukalı Dede Sok 4 A3
Bükücüler Hanı Sok 6 B5
Bulgurcu Sok 3 F2
Bulgurlu Mescit Sok 6 B2
Büyük Bayram Sok 1 A4
Büyük Çiftlik Sok 2 A2
Büyük Hamam Sok 6 B2
Büyük Haydar Efendi Sok 4 B4
Büyük Karaman Cad 4 A2
Büyük Reşit Paşa Cad 4 B4
Büyük Selim Paşa Cad 6 C3
Büyük Şişhane Sok 1 A3

C

Çadırcı Camii Sok 4 C5
Çadırcılar Cad 4 C4
Caferiye Sok 5 E4
Cağaloğlu Yokuşu 5 D3
Çakmak Sok 1 A3
Çakmakçılar Sok 4 C3
Çakmaktaşı Sok 4 C5
Çalı Sok 1 A1
Cambaz Ali Sok 6 C2
Camcıfeyzi Sok 1 A5
Camekan Sok 5 D1
Cami Meydanı Sok 5 D2
Cami Sok 2 A2
Camii Sok 5 D4
Çamlik Kuyu Sok 3 E1
Canbazoğlu Sok 1 B3
Cankurtaran Cad 5 E5
Çapari Sok 4 C5
Çardak Cad 4 C2
Çarık Sok 1 B2
Çarkçılar Sok 5 D3
Çarşı Sok 4 C3
Çarşıkapı Cad 4 C4
Çatal Çeşme Sok 5 D4
Çatıkkaş Sok 1 A4
Çatlak Çeşme Sok 2 B3
Çavdar Sok 1 A2
Çavdarcı Sok 2 A4
Çavuşdere Cad 6 C3
Çayırlı Sok 3 E1
Çayıroğlu Oğul Sok 5 D5
Çaylak Sok 1 B3
Cebel Topu Sok 1 B2
Cedidiye Sok 2 C2
Çekirdek Sok 2 B3
Celal Ferdi Gökçay Sok 5 D3
Cemal Nadir Sok 5 D3
Cemal Yener Tosyalı Cad 4 B3
Cemre Sok 4 C5
Çesnici Sok 5 D3
Çeşme-I Cedid Sok 6 A2
Çeşme-i Kebir Cad 6 B5

Çevirmeci Sok 3 E2
Cezayir Cad 2 C4
Cezmi Sok 4 A4
Cibali Cad 4 B1
Cibinlik Sok 3 E2
Çiçek Pazarı 5 D2
Çiçekçi Sok 6 B4
Çifte Gelinler Cad 4 C5
Çifte Vav Sok 1 C4
Cihangir Cad 1 B4
Cihangir Yokuşu 1 C5
Cıhannüma Sok 2 C3
Çılavcı Sok 4 C5
Çimen Sok 1 B2
Cinci Meyd Sok 5 D5
Çıngıraklı Bostan Sok 4 A3
Çinili Camii Sok 6 C3
Çinili Tekke Sok 6 C3
Çıracı Sok 5 E1
Çırağan Cad 3 D3
Çırakçı Çeşmeşı Sok 4 A1
Çırçır Cad 4 A2
Çitlenbik Sok 2 C3
Çobanoğlu Sok 1 A1
Cömertler Sok 4 C5
Çömezler Sok 2 C3
Çopur Ahmet Sok 3 E2
Corbaçı Sok 1 B3
Çorbacıbaşı Sok 4 A5
Çoruh Sok 2 A1
Çoşkun Sok 1 B5
Cüce Çeşmesi Sok 4 B3
Cudi Çık 3 E1
Cudi Efendi Sok 3 E2
Çuhacıoğlu Sok 4 A5
Çukur Bostan Sok 1 A5
Çukur Çeşme Sok 4 A4
Çukurcuma Cad 1 B5
Cumhuriyet Cad 1 C2
Cumhuriyet Cad 6 C2

D

Daci Sok 1 A1
Dağarcık Sok 4 A4
Dalbastı Sok 5 E5
Dalfes Sok 1 A3
Daltaban Yok Sok 4 B4
Darı Sok 6 A2
Darülelhan Sok 4 B3
Darülhadis Sok 4 B2
Darüssade Sok 5 E3
Davutoğlu Sok 6 A3
Daye Kadın Sok 6 B5
Dayı Sok 1 A1
Dede Efendi Cad 4 B3
Defterdar Yokuşu 1 B5
Dellalzade Sok 3 D1
Demirbaş Sok 1 A3
Den Sok 1 A1
Dere Sok 2 A1
Dereotu Sok 1 A3
Dericiler Sok 1 B2
Derin Kuyu Sok 4 B4
Derne Sok 2 B3
Dernek Sok 1 B3
Ders Vekili Sok 4 A2
Dershane Sok 1 C1
Dervişler Sok 5 E3
Deryadil Sok 2 A2
Devirhan Çeşmesi Sok 4 B2
Devşir Meler Sok 1 A2
Dibek Sok 1 A5
Dık Sok 5 D1
Dikilitaş Camii Meydanı Sok 2 B1
Dikilitaş Çık 2 B1
Dikilitaş Sok 2 B1
Dilbaz Sok 1 A3
Dilber Sok 2 B2
Dinibütün Sok 4 A1
Direkçibaşı Sok 1 A2
Direkli Camii Sok 4 C4
Divan-ı Ali Sok 4 C4
Divanyolu Cad 5 D4
Divitçiler Cad 6 C4
Divitçiler Çık 6 C4
Dizdariye Medresesı Sok 5 D4
Dizdariye Yok 5 D4
Dizi Sok 2 B3
Doğancılar Cad 6 A3
Doğancılar Cad 6 B2
Doğr Şakir Sok 1 B3
Dökmeciler Hamamı Sok 4 C2
Dökmeciler Sok 4 C3
Dolambaç Sok 6 B4
Dolap Cad 4 A3
Dolapdere Cad 1 A3
Dolmabahçe Cad 2 A4
Dolmabahçe Gazhanesi Cad 2 A4
Dönmedolap Sok 6 B4
Dörtyüzlü Çeşme Sok 2 C2
Dr Eyüp Aksoy Cad 6 C5
Dr Sıtkı Özferendeci Sok 6 B4
Dümen Sok 1 C3
Dünya Sağlık Sok 1 C4
Dürbali Sok 6 C2
Duvarcı Adem Sok 1 B3
Duvarcı Sok 1 B3
Duvarcı Sok 3 F2

E

Ebürrıza Dergahı Sok 1 A3
Ebussuut Cad 5 E3
Eczacı Sok 1 A1
Eczahane Sok 6 B4
Eğri Eski Konak Sok 2 C3
Ekmek Fab Sok 2 A1
Elmadağ Cad 1 B2
Elmasağacı Sok 6 B2
Elmastıraş Sok 1 A3
Elvanizade Camii Sok 4 B1
Elvanlar Sok 4 B1
Emin Ongan Sok 6 B3
Emin Sinan 4 C4
Emirhan Cad 2 C1
Emirname Sok 5 D3
Enfiyehane Sok 6 A3
Enis Akaygen Sok 2 B3
Enli Yokuşu 1 B5
Er Meydanı Sok 1 A2
Erdoğan Sok 5 E3
Eregemen Sok 6 A3
Erkan-ı Harp Sok 1 A5
Esenler Sok 2 A1
Eski Bahçe Sok 3 F2
Eski Belediye Önü Sok 6 B3
Eski Çeşme Sok 1 B3
Eski Çiçekçi Sok 1 A4
Eski Ekmekçibaşı Sok 6 C4
Eski Karakış Sok 2 B1
Eski Kerestecıler Sok 6 B2
Eski Mahkeme Sok 6 B2
Eski Mutaflar Sok 4 A2
Eski Yıldız Cad 2 C3
Esrar Dede Sok 4 A1
Eşref Efendi Sok 1 B1
Eşrefsaati Sok 6 A2
Esvapçı Sok 6 B3
Ethem Ağa Sok 6 C2
Ethem Paşa Sok 6 B4
Evkaf Sok 5 D4

F

Fadıl Arif Sok 1 A2
Faik Paşa Yok 1 B4
Fakir Sok 1 A4
Farabi Sok 1 B3
Fatih Türbesi Sok 4 A2
Fazilet Sok 4 A2
Fenerli Kapı Sok 5 E5
Ferah Sok 2 A1
Ferah Sok 6 C3
Ferhat Ağa Sok 4 A2
Feridiye Cad 1 B3
Feriköy Baruthane Cad 1 B1
Fesleğen Çık 1 A3
Fesleğen Sok 1 A3
Fethi Bey Cad 4 B4
Fetva Yokuşu Sok 4 C2
Fevziye Cad 4 B3
Fil Yokuşu Sok 4 B2
Fincancılar Sok 5 D3
Fındık Kıran Sok 4 B5
Fındıkçılar Sok 5 D2
Fıstıklı Köşk Sok 3 E2
Fitil Sok 1 A2
Fransız Hastanesi Sok 1 C1
Fuat Paşa Cad 4 C3
Fulya Bayırı Sok 2 A1
Fulya Deresi Sok 2 B2
Fütuhat Sok 5 D1

G

Galata Kulesi Sok 5 D1
Galata Mumhanesi Cad 5 E1
Galip Dede Cad 1 A5
Garaj Yolu Sok 1 A1
Gazhane Bostanı Sok 1 C3
Gazi Refik Sok 2 B3
Gazi Sinan Paşa Sok 5 D4
Gazi Umur Paşa Sok 2 C1
Gazino Sok 2 B3
Gedikpaşa Cad 4 C4
Gedikpaşa Fırını Sok 4 C4
Gel Sok 2 C1
Gelenbevı Müftü Sok 4 A1
Gelin Alayı Sok 6 B3
Gelinicik Sok 2 C1
Gençtürk Cad 4 A3
Genis Yokuş Sok 1 A3
Gerdanlık Sok 4 C5
Giriftzen Asım Çık 6 B3
Göknar Sok 2 B2
Göktaş Sok 5 D4
Gül Sok 2 A1
Gül Sok 6 C1
Gülfem Sok 6 B2
Gülleci Sok 1 A2
Gültekin Arkası Sok 3 F2
Gültekin Sok 3 E2
Gümrük Emini Sok 4 A4
Gümrük Sok 5 E1
Gümüş Küpe Sok 1 A4
Gümüş Sok 1 C2
Gündoğumu Cad 6 B3
Güneşli Sok 1 B4
Gürcü Kızı Sok 3 F2
Güvenlik Cad 4 A4
Güzel Bahçe Sok 2 A2

H

Hacı Ahmet Paşa Çık 6 A3
Hacı Emin Efendi Sok 2 A2
Hacı Emın Paşa Sok 6 B4
Hacı Hasan Sok 4 A2
Hacı Hesna Sok 6 C1
Hacı İlbey Sok 1 A2
Hacı Kadın Bastanı Sok 4 B2
Hacı Kadın Cad 4 B2
Hacı Mutlu Sok 6 C2
Hacı Ömer Paşa Sok 4 A2
Hacı Şevket Sok 6 C4
Hacı Zeynel Sok 1 A2
Hadımodaları Sok 4 A5
Hafız Ali Paşa Çık 6 A3
Hafız-ı Kurra Sok 6 B4
Hafız Mehmet Bey Sok 6 A4
Hakimiyeti Milliye Cad 6 B2
Halaskargazi Cad 1 C1
Halepli Bekir Sok 1 A3
Haliç Cad 4 A1
Halıcılar Sok 4 C4
Halk Cad 6 B3
Halk Dershanesi Sok 6 A3
Hamalbaşı Cad 1 A4
Hamamı Sok 4 A1
Hamanı Sok 5 D4
Hamidiye Cad 5 D3
Hanedan Sok 4 A1
Hanımeli Sok 5 D3
Haraççı Ali Sok 5 D1
Harbiye Çayırı Sok 1 B2
Harem Ağası Sok 2 B3
Harem Sahil Yolu 6 A5
Harem Selimiye Hamamı Sok 6 B5
Harikzedeler Sok 4 B4
Has Fırın Cad 2 C3
Has Odalar Çık 6 C4
Hasan Baba Sok 4 A2
Hasan Bey Sok 6 C4
Hasan Cevdet Paşa Sok 2 A1
Hasbahçe Sok 6 A2
Hasırcı Veli Sok 2 C3
Hasret Sok 3 E2
Haşnun Galip Sok 1 B4
Hatmi Sok 6 C3
Hattat İzzet Sok 4 A1
Hattat Nazif Sok 4 A2
Hattat Tahsin Sok 2 B3
Hava Sok 1 B4
Havancı Sok 4 C3
Havyar Sok 1 B5
Haydar Bey Sok 4 A2

Haydar Cad 4 A2
Haydar Hamamı Sok 4 B1
Hayrı Efendi Cad 5 D2
Hayrıef Cad 5 D3
Hayriye Hanım
Kepenekçi Sok 4 C2
Hayriye Sok 1 A4
Hednek Cad 1 A5
Helvacı Ali Sok 6 C3
Hemsire Sok 4 B5
Hemşehri Sok 4 B5
Hercai Sok 3 E2
Himmet Baba Sok 6 C3
Himmet Sok 4 B3
Hisar Altı Sok 4 B1
Hızır Külhani Sok 4 B2
Hoca Hanı Sok 5 D3
Hoca Hanım Sok 5 D1
Hoca Tahsin Sok 5 E1
Hora Sok 2 C1
Horhor Cad 4 A3
Hortumcu Sok 1 A3
Hostes Rana Altınay Sok 2 A2
Hüdai Mahmut Sok 6 B3
Hükümet Konağl Sok 5 E3
Hünnap Sok 6 C4
Hüsam Bey Sok 4 A2
Hüseyin Baykara Sok 6 C1
Hüseyin Hüsnü Paşa Sok 6 C3
Hüseyin Remzi Bey Sok 4 A1
Hüsnü Sayman Sok 2 C3
Hüsrev Gerede Cad 2 A3

I

İbadethane Sok 4 A2
İbni Kemal Cad 5 E3
İbrahim Paşa Yokuşu 4 C4
Ihlamur Nişantaşı Yolu 2 A2
Ihlamur Teşvikiye Yolu 2 A2
Ihlamur Yıdır Cad 2 B2
Ihlamur-Yildar Cad 2 B2
İhsaniye İskelesi Sok 6 A4
İhsaniye Bostanı Sok 6 B4
İhsanıye Sok 6 A3
İhtıyatlı Sok 4 A2
İlhan Sok 2 B3
İlyas Çelebi Sok 1 C5
Ihlamur Deresi Cad 2 B3
İmam Adnan Sok 1 B4
İmam Hüsnü Sok 6 C1
İmam Murat Sok 4 A4
İmam Nasır Sok 6 B2
Imam Niyazi Sok 4 A2
Imaret Sabunhanesi Sok 4 B2
Imrahor Çeşmesı Sok 6 A3
İmran Öktem Cad 5 D4
İnadiye Cami Sok 6 B4
İnadiye Camii Nasrettin
Hoca Sok 6 C4
İnadiye Mek Sok 6 B3
İncili Çavuş Sok 5 E4
İnklılap Cad 4 A4
İnönü Cad 1 C4
İpek Sok 1 B4
İrfan Ahmet Sok 4 A1
İshak Paşa Cad 5 E4
Isık Sok 4 C5
Işık Sok 1 B4
Işık Sok 5 D4
İskele Cad 6 B4
İsmail Sefa Sok 4 B5
İsmetiye Cad 4 C3
İstasyan Arkası Sok 5 E3
İstiklal Cad 1 A5
İtfaiye Cad 4 A3
İttihat Sok 6 B3
Itri Sok 3 D1
İzzet Paşa Sok 2 A5

J

Jandarma Mektebi Sok 2 B2

K

Kabadayı Sok 1 A3
Kabalak Sok 3 E2
Kabaskal Cad 5 E4
Kabile Sok 6 B3
Kadı Çeşmeşi Sok 4 A1
Kadırga Hamamı Sok 4 C5
Kadırga Limanı Cad 4 C5
Kadırga Limanı Cad 5 D5
Kadırgalar Cad 1 C2
Kadırgalar Cad 2 A4
Kadirler Yokuşu 1 B5
Kafesli Çadır Çık 4 C4
Kahya Bey Sok 1 A3
Kakmacı Sok 4 A4
Kaleci Sok 5 D5
Kalender Camii Sok 4 B3
Kalender Mektebi Sok 4 B3
Kalıpçı Sok 2 A3
Kallavi Sok 1 A4
Kalyoncu Kulluğu Cad 1 A3
Kameriye Sok 1 A4
Kamil Paşa Sok 4 A3
Kani Paşa Sok 4 B1
Kanısıcak Sok 4 A1
Kantarcılar Cad 4 C2
Kanuni Medresesi Sok 4 B3
Kapanca Sok 1 B3
Kapı Ağası Sok 5 E5
Kapı Çık Sok 6 B3
Kapıkulu Sok 1 A5
Kaptan Paşa Camii Sok 6 B2
Kaptan Paşa Sok 6 A2
Kaputçular Sok 5 D3
Kara Hasan Sok 3 D1
Kara Kurum Sok 1 A3
Kara Sarıklı Sok 4 A1
Karabaş Cad 1 B5
Karabaş Deresi Sok 1 A5
Karabatak Sok 1 B2
Karacaoğlan Sok 6 B2
Karadeniz Cad 4 A1
Karaka Sok 1 B3
Karakaş Sok 3 E2
Karaköy Cad 5 D1
Kardeşler Sok 2 B1
Kartalbaba Cad 6 C3
Kartalbaba Sok 6 C3
Kasap Hurşit Sok 1 B2
Kasap Osman Sok 5 D5
Kasap Veli Sok 6 A3
Kasatura Sok 1 B5
Kasnakçılar Cad 4 B2
Kâtibim Aziz Bey Sok 6 C2
Katip Çelebi Sok 4 B2
Katip Çeşmesi Sok 4 A5
Katip Kasım Bostanı Sok 4 A5
Katip Kasım Camii Sok 4 A4
Katip Semsettin Sok 4 B2
Katip Sok 6 C4
Katmerli Sok 1 A2
Kavak İskele Cad 6 C5
Kavaklı Bayırı Sok 6 B5
Kavaklı İskele Sok 6 B2
Kavalalı Sok 4 A3
Kavuncu Hasan Sok 1 A3
Kaya Hatun Sok 1 C1
Kaypakoğlu Sok 3 F1
Kaytancı Rasim Sok 1 B2
Kayum Ahmet Sok 6 B5
Kazancı Yokuşu 1 C4
Kazancılar Cad 4 C2
Kemal Türel Sok 2 B2
Kemalettin Camii Sok 4 C4
Kemankeş Cad 5 E1
Kemeraltı Cad 5 E1
Kenan Bey Sok 4 B5
Kendir Sok 4 A2
Kennedy Cad 4 A5
Keresteci Hakkı Sok 5 E5
Keresteci Recep Sok 1 B3
Kerpiç Sok 4 B1
Kessem Sok 6 B2
Keşşaf Sok 2 C2
Kıble Çesme Cad 4 C2
Kılburnu Sok 1 B3
Kimyager Derviş Paşa Sok 4 B4
Kınalı Keklik Sok 1 B2
Kirazlı Mescit Sok 4 B3
Kırbaççı Sok 4 A2
Kirişci Sok 6 C2
Kırkahyası Sok 1 A2
Kırma Tulumba Sok 4 A3
Kırmız Sok 3 E2
Kıyak Sok 4 A1
Kızıltaş Sok 4 B4
Kıztaşı Cad 4 A3
Klodfarer Sok 5 D4
Koca Ragıp Cad 4 B4
Kocabaş Sok 1 A2
Koçi Bey Sok 4 A4
Koçyigit Sok 1 A3
Kokoroz Sok 1 A2
Konaklı Çık 6 B4
Kopça Sok 4 A1
Köprülü Konak Sok 6 B4
Körbakkal Sok 6 C4
Koska Cad 4 B4
Kovacılar Sok 4 A2
Köyiçi Cad 2 B3
Kozacık Sok 2 A1
Küçük Akarca Sok 1 B2
Küçük Ayasofya Cad 5 D5
Küçük Bayır Sok 1 B2
Küçük Pazar Cad 4 C2
Küçük Şişhane Sok 1 B3
Küçük Langa Cad 4 A4
Küçük Sok 5 D3
Kücük Sok 5 E4
Kükürtlü Sok 1 B2
Külhan Sok 1 B5
Kum Meydanı Sok 5 E3
Kumbaracı Başi Sok 3 E2
Kumbaracı Yokuşu 1 A5
Kumkapı Hanı Sok 4 C4
Kumluk Sok 4 C5
Kumrulu Sok 1 B5
Kumrulu Yok 1 B4
Kurabiye Sok 1 B4
Kurban Sok 4 C5
Kurdele Sok 1 A3
Kurdele Sok 1 A4
Kurşunlu Medrese Sok 6 B2
Kurtuluş Cad 1 B1
Kurtuluş Sok 1 A3
Kuruçeşme Kireçhane Sok 3 F1
Kürüçübası Mekebi Sok 4 C5
Kurultay Sok 4 B4
Kuruntu Sok 6 A3
Kuşoğlu Yokuşu 6 C2
Kutlu Sok 1 C4
Kutlugün Sok 5 E4
Kutucular Cad 4 C2
Kuyu Sok 1 B4
Kuyu Sok 6 C2
Kuyulu Bostanı Sok 2 A2
Kuyumcular Cad 4 C4
Kuzukulağı Sok 1 B3

L

Lala Şahin Sok 1 A1
Lâleli Cad 4 A4
Laleli Çeşme Sok 5 D1
Lamartin Cad 1 B3
Langa Bostanları Sok 4 A4
Langa Hisarı Sok 4 A5
Langa Karakolu Sok 4 A4
Leman Sok 1 B3
Lenger Sok 1 B5
Leylak Sok 2 C1
Leylek Yuvası Sok 3 E1
Liva Sok 1 B4
Lokumcu Sok 1 A2
Loşbahçe Sok 2 B3
Lozan Sok 3 E2
Lüleci Hendek Cad 5 E1
Lütfü Efendi Sok 4 A3
Lütfullah Sok 4 C3

M

M Karaca Sok 3 E2
Maç Sok 1 B4
Macar Kardeşler Cad 4 A3
Maçka Aktarlar Sok 2 A3
Maçka Cad 2 A3
Maçka Meydanı Sok 2 A3
Macuncu Sok 5 D3
Mahfil Sok 4 A4
Mahmutpaşa Yokuşu 5 D3
Mali Bey Sok 2 C3
Maliye Cad 5 E1
Manastırlı İsmail Hakkı
Sok 6 B3
Manav Sok 4 B3
Mangalcı Paşa Camii Sok 4 C3
Marpuççular Cad 5 D3
Marsık Sok 1 A2
Maşuklar Sok 2 B3
Matara Sok 1 B5
Maybeyinçi Yok 4 B4
Mazharpaşa Sok 2 C3
Mebusan Yokuşu 1 C4
Mecit Ali Sok 2 B3

Meclis-i Mebusan Cad 2 A5
Meddah Ismet Sok 2 B3
Mehmet Çavuş Sok 6 C4
Mehmet Murat Sok 5 E3
Mehmet Paşa Değirmeni Sok 6 A2
Mehmet Paşa Yok 4 B2
Mehmetçik Cad 2 A1
Mercan Cad 4 C3
Mertebanı Sok 5 D1
Mesih Paşa Cad 4 B4
Meşelik Sok 1 B4
Meşrutiyet Cad 1 A4
Mete Cad 1 C3
Meyva Sok 1 B1
Midilli Sok 5 D1
Mıhcılar Cad 4 A2
Mim Kemal Öke Cad 1 C1
Mimar Çeşmesi Sok 4 A1
Mimar Kemalettin Cad 5 D3
Mimar Mehmet Ağa Sok 5 E4
Mimar Sinan Cad 4 C2
Mimar Vedat Sok 5 D3
Miralay Şefik Bey Sok 1 C3
Miri Kalem Sok 4 A1
Mis Sok 1 B4
Mısır Buğdaycı Sok 1 A3
Mısırlı Bahçe Sok 2 B3
Mısırlı Sok 2 B3
Mithat Paşa Cad 4 C4
Molla Bayırı Sok 1 C4
Molla Bey Sok 4 C4
Molla Fenari Sok 5 D4
Molla Hüsrev Sok 4 A3
Molla Şemsettin Camii Sok 4 B3
Mollataşı Cad 4 B5
Muallim Naci Cad 3 F2
Muammer Karaca Çık 1 A5
Mukataacı Sok 2 B1
Münir Ertegün Sok 6 C1
Muradiye Deresi Sok 2 B2
Muradiye Hüdavendigar Cad 5 E3
Murakıp Sok 5 E1
Murat Efendi Sok 4 C2
Muratağa Sok 6 B4
Mürbasan Sok 2 C1
Musa Bey Sok 4 B2
Müsahıp Sok 3 F2
Müsellım Sok 4 C4
Mustafa İzzet Efendi Sok 3 D1
Mustafa Kemal Cad 4 A4
Müstantik Sok 4 A1
Müsteşar Sok 4 C5
Müvezzi Cad 2 C3

N

Nakilbent Sok 5 D5
Nalbant Camii Sok 4 B5
Nalbant Demir Sok 4 A2
Nalçacı Hasan Sok 6 C4
Nalıncı Cemal Sok 4 B1
Namahrem Sok 4 C2
Namık Paşa Sok 6 B3
Nane Sok 1 B4
Nanı Aziz Sok 6 B4
Nar Sok 3 E2
Nardenk Sok 2 B2
Narlıbahçe Sok 5 D3
Nasip Sok 1 A1
Nasuhiye Sok 4 C3
Necatibey Cad 1 C4
Necatıbey Cad 5 E1
Necip Efendı Sok 5 D3
Nefer Sok 4 A3
Neviye Sok 4 C4
Nevizade Sok 1 A4
Nevşehirılı İbrahim Paşa Cad 4 A2
Neyzen Başı Hali Can Sok 6 B4
Nişanca Bostan Sok 4 B4
Nişanca Yok 4 B4
Nizamiye Sok 1 B3
Nöbethane Cad 5 E3
Nuh Kuyusu Cad 6 C4
Nüri Zıya Sok 1 A4
Nurtanesi Sok 2 B2
Nuruosmanıye Cad 5 D4
Nüzhetiye Cad 2 B3

O

Oba Sok 1 B4
Odalar Sok 2 B3
Ödev Sok 5 D5
Odun İskelesi Sok 4 B1
Öğdül Sok 6 A2
Öğretmen Haşim Çeken Sok 2 A1
Ögüt Sok 1 B4
Okçu Musa Cad 5 D1
Okçular Başı Cad 4 C4
Ölçek Sok 1 B2
Ömer Efendi Sok 4 A2
Ömer Hayyam Cad 1 A3
Ömer Rüştü Paşa Sok 2 A3
Ömer Yilmaz Sok 4 A3
Omuzdaş Sok 1 A2
Ondokuz Cad 2 A1
Onur Sok 4 C5
Oran Sok 6 C2
Ord Prof Cemilbilsel Cad 4 C2
Ördekli Bakkal Sok 4 C5
Orhanıye Sok 5 E3
Örme Altı Sok 1 A5
Ortabahçe Cad 2 B3
Ortakır Dere Sok 1 A1
Ortakır Sok 1 A1
Ortaköy Dere Boyu Cad 3 E2
Ortaköy Kabristan Sok 3 E2
Ortaköy Mandıra Sok 3 F1
Oruç Gazi Sok 4 A3
Oruçbozan Sok 4 A3
Örücüler Cad 4 C3
Osman Dede Sok 6 C2
Osmanlı Sok 1 B4
Otopark Sok 6 B2
Oya Sok 1 A3
Özbekler Sok 5 D5
Özoğul Sok 1 C5

P

Palanga Cad 3 E2
Palaska Sok 1 B5
Parçacı Sok 4 C2
Park Altı Sok 6 B5
Park üstü Sok 6 B5
Parlak Sok 6 A2
Parmaklık Sok 4 A2
Parmaklık Sok 2 C2
Paşa Kapısı Sok 6 B4
Paşa Limanı Cad 6 C1
Paşazade Sok 4 A4
Pelesenk Sok 1 B3
Perşembe Pazarı Cad 5 D1
Pertev Paşa Sok 5 D4
Pervaz Sok 1 B2
Peşkirağası Sok 1 B2
Peşkirci Sok 1 A3
Peylhane Sok 5 D4
Piremeci Sok 1 A5
Piri Sok 4 A2
Pırnal Sok 6 B3
Piyerloti Cad 5 D4
Postacılar Sok 1 A5
Poyracık Sok 2 A2
Prof Kazım İsmail Gürkan Cad 5 D4
Prof Sıddık Sami Onar Cad 4 C3
Pürtelaş Sok 1 C4

R

Ragıp Gümüşpala Cad 4 C2
Rahvancı Sok 5 D3
Rebab Sok 2 B3
Recep Paşa Cad 1 B3
Refah Sok 4 A2
Resadiye Cad 5 D2
Ressam Ali Sok 6 A3
Reşat Ağa Sok 3 F1
Revani Çelebi Sok 4 B3
Revani Sok 5 E1
Revaniçi Sok 3 F1
Rıhtım Cad 5 E1
Rıza Paşa Sok 6 C4
Ruhl Bağdadi Sok 3 E1

S

16 Mart Şehitleri Cad 4 B3
Sabunca Hanı Sok 5 D3
Sabunhanesi Sok 4 C2
Sadıkoğlu Çık 2 C3
Şadırvan Sok 5 E5
Sadri Maksudi Arsal Sok 1 B1
Safa Meydanı Sok 1 A2
Saffet Paşa Sok 4 B3
Saffeti Paşa Sok 5 E3
Sahaflar Çarşışı Sok 4 C4
Sahil Yolu üsküdar-Harem 6 A3
Sahil Yolu 6 A2
Şahin Sok 1 B1
Şahinde Sok 4 C3
Şahkulu Bostanı Sok 1 A5
Şahkulu Sok 1 A5
Sahne Sok 1 A4
Şair Baki Sok 4 A1
Şair Fitnat Sok 4 B4
Şair Haşmet Sok 4 B4
Şair Leyla Sok 2 B4
Şair Nabi Sok 4 A1
Şair Nahifi Sok 2 C3
Şair Naili Sok 6 B3
Şair Nazım Sok 2 A3
Şair Necati Sok 3 F2
Şair Nedim Cad 2 B3
Şair Nesimi Sok 6 B5
Şair Ruhi Sok 6 C3
Şair Sermet Sok 4 C5
Şair Veysi Sok 2 B3
Şair Zati Sok 6 C4
Şair Ziya Paşa Cad 5 D1
Sait Efendi Sok 4 A4
Saka Mehmet Sok 5 D3
Şakayık Sok 2 A2
Sakayolu Dere Sok 3 E1
Sakızağacı Cad 1 A3
Sakızağacı Sok 2 A1
Sakızcılar Sok 5 E1
Salacak Bostanı Sok 6 A3
Salacak İskele Arkası 6 A3
Salçıklar Sok 3 D3
Salı Sok 6 C4
Salih Paşa Cad 4 B1
Salım Sogüt Sok 5 E4
Samancı Ferhat Sok 1 A3
Samsa Sok 4 C5
Samul Sok 5 D1
Sanatkarlar Cad 1 B5
Sanatkarlar Mektebi Sok 1 B5
Sandalcı Sok 1 A2
Sansar Sok 6 C3
Saraç İshak Sok 4 C4
Saraçhane Sok 4 A3
Saraka Sok 2 C1
Sarap Sok 5 E1
Şarapnel Sok 4 B5
Sarayiçi Sok 4 C5
Saray Arkası Sok 1 C4
Sarı Beyazıt Cad 4 B2
Sarı Mehmet Sok 6 C3
Sarı Zeybek Sok 5 D1
Sarıbal Sok 3 E2
Satır Sok 5 D4
Satırcı Sok 1 B2
Savaş Sok 1 A1
Sazlıdere Sok 1 B2
Şebnem Sok 4 A1
Şehin Şah Pehlerı Cad 5 D3
Şehit Asım Cad 2 B3
Şehit Mehmet Paşa Yok 5 D5
Şehit Mehmet Sok 2 A3
Şehit Muhtar Bey Cad 1 B3
Şehit Nuri Pamir Sok 3 E2
Şehla Sok 4 A1
Şehnamecı Sok 4 B4
Şehzade Başı Cad 4 B3
Şeker Ahmet Paşa Sok 4 C3
Şekerci Sok 4 A4
Selalti Sok 2 B3
Selami Ali Cad 6 C2
Selamlık Cad 2 B3
Selamsiz Kulhhanı Sok 6 C2
Selanikliler Sok 6 C2
Selbaşı Sok 1 B1
Selim Paşa Sok 4 A3
Selime Hatun Camii Sok 1 C4
Selimiye İskele Cad 6 B5
Selimiye Camii Sok 6 B5
Selimiye Kışla Cad 6 B5
Selman Ağa Sok 6 B2
Selmanağa Bostanı Sok 6 C2
Selmanıpak Cad 6 B2

Semaver Sok	4 C3
Şemsi Bey Sok	6 C1
Şemsi Efendi Sok	6 C1
Şemsi Paşa Bostanı Sok	6 A2
Şemsi Paşa Cad	6 A2
Şemsi Paşa Rıhtımı Sok	6 A2
Serdar Ömer Paşa Sok	1 A3
Serdar Sok	4 A2
Serdar Sok	5 E3
Serdar-ı Ekrem Sok	1 A5
Şeref Efendi Sok	5 D4
Şerefli Sok	4 B1
Serencebey Yokuşu	2 C3
Şerif Bey Çeşmesi Sok	6 B4
Şerif Kuyusu Sok	6 B5
Servi Kökü Sok	6 B5
Servilik Cad	6 C2
Set Sok	1 B5
Setüstü Sok	2 B1
Şeyh Şamil Sok	3 E1
Şeyh Yok Sok	6 B2
Şeyhülislam Sok	5 D3
Seymen Sok	1 B1
Şeysuvarbey Sok	5 D5
Seyyah Sok	4 B5
Sezai Selek Sok	2 A1
Şifa Hamanı Sok	5 D5
Şifahane Sok	4 B3
Silahhane Sok	2 A3
Silahtar Mektebi Sok	5 D5
Simitçi Sok	1 A3
Sinan Camii Sok	4 A1
Sinan Paşa Köprü Sok	2 B4
Sincap Sok	2 B1
Sinoplu Şehit Cemal Sok	2 A1
Şiracı Sok	3 F1
Sıraselviler Cad	1 B4
Şirket Sok	1 A3
Siyavuş Paşa Sok	4 C3
Sobacılar Cad	4 C2
Sofyalı Sok	1 A5
Soğan Ağa Camii Sok	4 B4
Soğancı Sok	1 B4
Soğukçeşme Sok	5 E4
Solgun Söğüt Sok	2 A3
Sormagir Sok	1 C4
Spor Cad	2 A4
Su Yolu Sok	4 A2
Sulak Çeşme Sok	1 C4
Şule Sok	4 A1
Sülemaniye Cad	4 B3
Süleyman Nazif Sok	1 C1
Süleymaniye İmareti Sok	4 B2
Sultan Mektebi Sok	5 D3
Sümbül Sinan Sok	4 B4
Sümbülzade Sok	6 A3
Sumuncu Sok	1 B4
Süngu Sok	1 B5
Suphi Bey Sok	6 B5
Susam Sok	1 B5
Süslü Saskı Sok	1 B4
Susuzbağ Sok	6 C1

T

Tabağan Bahçe Sok	6 C2
Tabakcı Hüseyin Sok	2 B3
Tabaklar Camii Sok	6 C3
Tabaklar Kulhanı Sok	6 C3
Tabaklar Mey Sok	6 C3
Tabur Sok	4 B5
Taburağası Sok	1 A2
Tacirhane Sok	4 C3
Tahmis Cad	5 D2
Tahririye Sok	6 B3
Tahsıin Bey Sok	5 D5
Tahtakale Cad	4 C2
Tak-ı Zafer Cad	1 C3
Taksim Cad	1 B3
Taksim Firini Sok	1 B3
Taktaki Yok Sok	1 B4
Talimhane Sok	1 A1
Tarakçı Cafer Sok	5 D3
Tarakçılar Cad	5 D3
Tarcan Sok	1 A1
Tarçın Sok	3 E2
Tarlabaşı Cad	1 A4
Taş Savaklar Sok	5 E4
Taş Tekneler Sok	4 B3
Taşbasamak Sok	3 E2
Taşdibek Çeşmesi Sok	5 D4
Taşkışla Cad	1 C2
Taşodaları Sok	4 B3
Tasvir Sok	5 D3
Tatar Hüseyin Sok	2 C2
Tatlı Kuyu Hamamı Sok	4 C4
Tatlı Kuyu Sok	4 C4
Tavaşi Çeşme Sok	4 B5
Tavla Sok	1 A3
Tavşan Sok	1 B3
Tavşantaşı Sok	4 B4
Tavuk Sok	3 E1
Tavukçu Bakkal Sok	6 B3
Tavukhane Sok	5 E5
Tay Etem Sok	1 C4
Taya Hatun Sok	5 E3
Tazı Çık	6 C2
Teccedut Sok	4 A4
Tekke Arkası Sok	6 C3
Teknik Sok	6 C3
Tel Çık	6 B2
Tel Sok	1 B4
Telli Odaları Sok	4 C5
Tepedelen Sok	4 B1
Tepnirhane Sok	6 A2
Tepsi Fırını Sok	6 B2
Terbıyık Sok	5 E5
Tersane Cad	5 D1
Teşvikiye Bostan Cad	1 C1
Teşvikiye Cad	2 A2
Tetimmeler Cad	4 A2
Tevfık Efendi Sok	1 A3
Tezgahçılar Sok	4 A2
Tığcılar Sok	4 C3
Tıbbiye Cad	6 C5
Tıbbiye Cad	6 B4
Ticarethane Sok	5 E4
Tiftik Sok	4 A1
Tıpa Sok	1 B5
Tırmık Sok	1 A2
Tirşe Sok	1 A3
Tiryaki Hasan Paşa Sok	4 A4
Tiyatro Cad	4 C4
Tohum Sok	2 B1
Tomruk Sok	4 C2
Tomtom Kaptan Sok	1 A5
Tomurcuk Sok	5 E5
Topçe Kenler Sok	1 A4
Topçu Cad	1 B3
Tophane İskelesi Cad	5 E1
Tophanelioğlu Sok	6 C2
Toprak Sok	4 A3
Topraklı Sok	6 A3
Toptaşı Cad	6 C3
Toptaşı Meydanı Sok	6 C3
Torun Sok	5 E5
Tosunpaşa Sok	6 B4
Toygar Hamza Sok	6 C2
Tüfekçi Salih Sok	1 B5
Tuğrul Sok	2 B1
Tüccarı Cad	4 A4
Tülcü Sok	4 C4
Tulumbacı Sıtkı Sok	1 A5
Tulumbacılar Sok	6 A2
Tunus Bağı Cad	6 B4
Turan Sok	1 B3
Turanlı Sok	4 C4
Türbedar Sok	5 D4
Türkbeyi Sok	1 B1
Türkeli Cad	4 B4
Türkgücü Cad	1 B5
Türkocağı Cad	5 D3
Turna Sok	1 B2
Turnacıbaşı Sok	1 A4
Turşucu Halil Sok	4 A2
Tutkalcı Sok	1 A4
Tuzcu Murat Sok	1 B2

U

Üçobalar Sok	2 A1
Üftade Sok	1 B2
Ülçer Sok	5 D4
Ülker Sok	1 C4
Uncular Cad	6 B2
Üniversite Cad	4 B4
Urgancı Sok	3 F1
Üskuplü Cad	4 B1
Üstad Sok	4 C5
Utangaç Sok	5 E5
Uygur Sok	1 B3
Üzengi Sok	2 C2
Uzunçarşı Cad	4 C3

V

Vali Konağı Cad	2 A1
Vali Konağı Cad	1 C1
Valide İmareti Sok	6 C3
Valide Camii Sok	4 A4
Varnalı Sok	3 E1
Varyemez Sok	1 A3
Vatman Sok	3 F2
Vefa Bayırı Sok	2 B1
Vefa Türbesi Sok	4 B2
Velioğlu Sok	6 A2
Vezir Çeşmesi Sok	4 A4
Vezirhan Cad	5 D4
Vezneciler Cad	4 B3
Vidinli Tevfik Paşa Cad	4 B3
Viransaray Sok	6 B3
Vişnezade Camii Önü Sok	2 A4
Vişneli Tekke Sok	2 A4
Voyvoda Cad	5 D1

Y

Yağlıkçılar Cad	4 C3
Yahni Kapan Sok	4 C4
Yahya Efendi Sok	3 D3
Yahya Paşa Sok	4 C4
Yakıf Hanı Sok	5 D3
Yalı Köşü Cad	5 D2
Yaman Ali Sok	1 A2
Yan Sok	6 C2
Yanıkkapı Sok	5 D1
Yarasa Sok	1 C4
Yasıf Çınar Cad	4 C3
Yaşar Ozsoy Sok	6 A4
Yastıkçı Sok	6 A2
Yavaşça Şahin Sok	4 C3
Yavuz Selim Cad	4 A1
Yavuz Sok	2 B1
Yay Meydanı Cad	1 A1
Yedi Kuyular Cad	1 B3
Yeni Alem Sok	1 A2
Yeni Cami Cad	5 D3
Yeni Çarşı Cad	1 A4
Yeni Devir Sok	4 C4
Yeni Doğan Sok	2 C2
Yeni Dünya Sok	6 B2
Yeni Hayat Sok	4 B2
Yeni Kafa Sok	1 B3
Yeni Mahalle Dere Sok	2 B3
Yeni Mahalle Fırını Sok	2 C3
Yeni Nalbant Sok	1 B2
Yeni Saraçhane Sok	5 E5
Yeni Yuva Sok	1 B5
Yenikapı Kumsal Sok	4 A5
Yerebatan Cad	5 E4
Yesarizade Cad	4 A2
Yeşil Cam Sok	1 A4
Yeşil Çimen Sok	2 B1
Yeşil Tekke Sok	4 A3
Yeşil Tulumba Sok	4 A3
Yeşilbaş Bayırı Sok	6 C2
Yiğitbaşı Sok	1 B2
Yıldız Bostanı Sok	2 B2
Yıldız Cad	2 C3
Yoğurtçu Faik Sok	1 B3
Yokuşbaşı Sok	1 A3
Yolcuzade Sok	5 D1
Yüsek Kaldırım Cad	5 D1
Yusuf Aşkin Sok	5 D5
Yüz Akı Sok	4 C5

Z

Zafer Sok	1 C1
Zambak Sok	1 B3
Zenciler Sok	6 C3
Zerde Sok	2 B1
Zerre Sok	2 B1
Zeynep Kamil Sok	4 B4
Zeyrek Cad	4 A2
Zeyrek Mehmet Paşa Sok	4 B2
Zincirlikuyu Yolu	3 D1
Zincirlikuyu Yolu	3 F1
Züraf Sok	5 D1

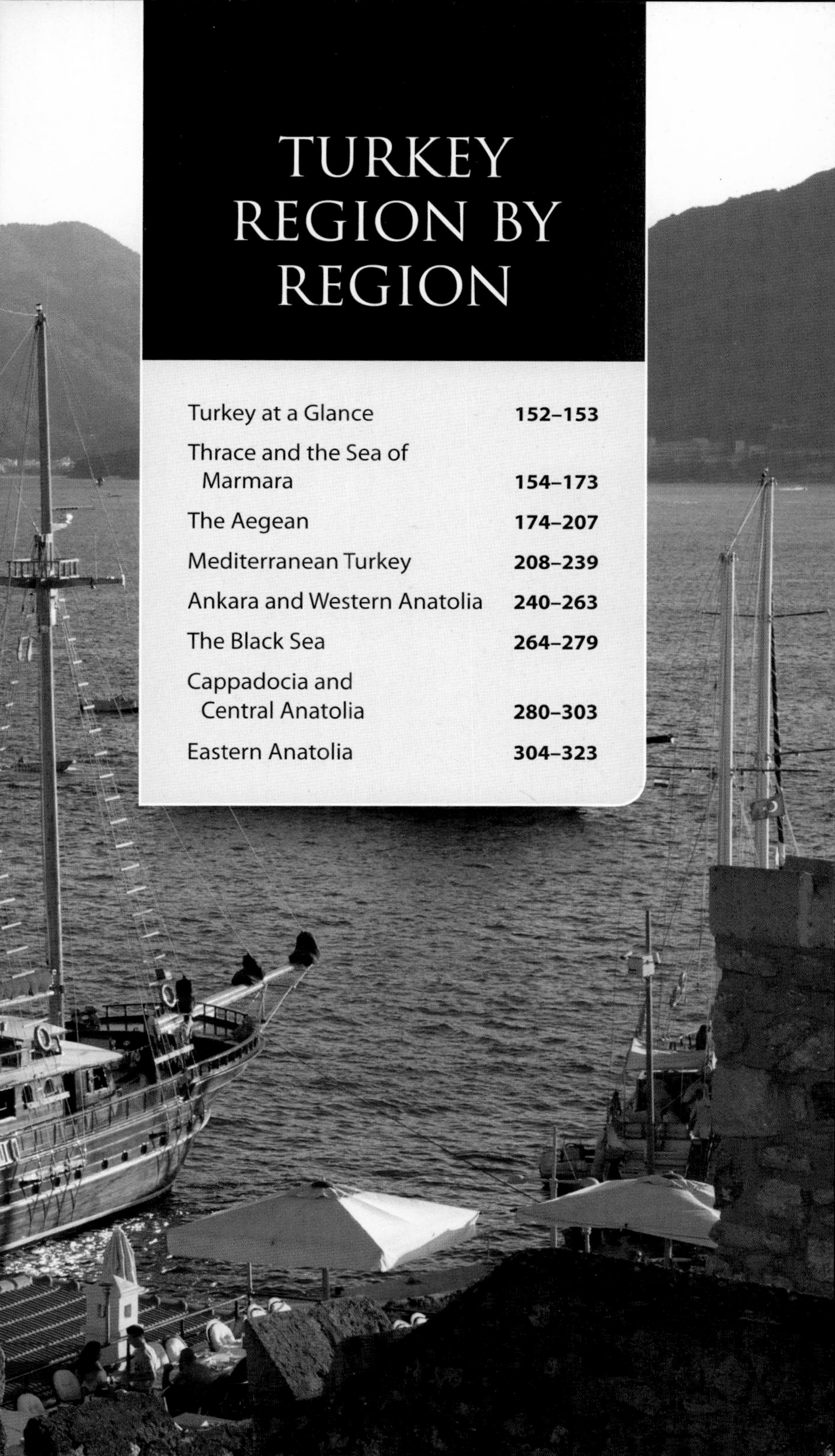

TURKEY REGION BY REGION

Turkey at a Glance 152–153

Thrace and the Sea of Marmara 154–173

The Aegean 174–207

Mediterranean Turkey 208–239

Ankara and Western Anatolia 240–263

The Black Sea 264–279

Cappadocia and Central Anatolia 280–303

Eastern Anatolia 304–323

Turkey at a Glance

Turkey occupies the rugged Anatolian Plateau, an arid upland region that is encircled by the mighty Taurus and Pontic mountain systems. The country's unrivalled wealth of historic sights includes Istanbul – the capital of three empires, as well as the ruins of classical sites such as Ephesus, Hierapolis and Aphrodisias. In the interior of the country are the unique cave cities and churches of Cappadocia. The eastern provinces of Turkey are less frequently visited, but offer such spectacular attractions as Lake Van, Armenian churches and the enigmatic stone heads at the summit of Mount Nemrut.

Istanbul's skyline is defined by the silhouettes of great mosques such as Süleymaniye Mosque *(see pp104–5)*, built by the architect Sinan in the 16th century.

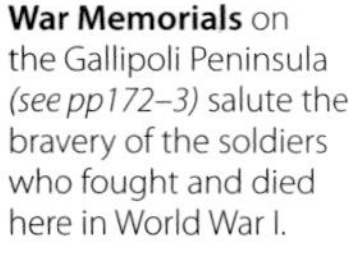

War Memorials on the Gallipoli Peninsula *(see pp172–3)* salute the bravery of the soldiers who fought and died here in World War I.

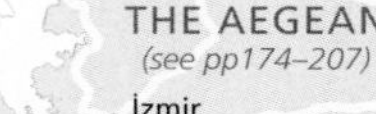

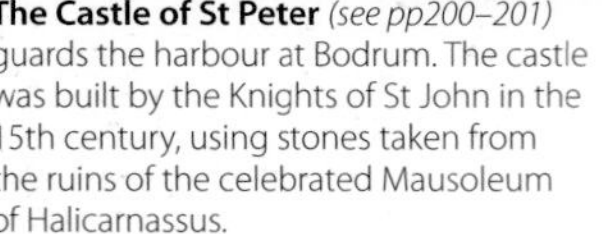

The Castle of St Peter *(see pp200–201)* guards the harbour at Bodrum. The castle was built by the Knights of St John in the 15th century, using stones taken from the ruins of the celebrated Mausoleum of Halicarnassus.

The Mevlâna Museum *(see pp256–7)* is a place of pilgrimage that contains the tombs of important Mevlevi Dervish mystics. Nearby is the Selimiye Mosque, an emblem of Konya.

◀ Marmaris Castle and harbour on the Datça Peninsula

Haghia Sophia, a Byzantine church in the historic port of Trabzon *(see pp274–5)*, was rebuilt in the mid-13th century on the site of a Roman temple. After the Ottoman conquest, the church became a mosque and was then converted into a museum. Controversially, it may soon be converted back into a mosque.

Mount Ağri (Ararat), said to be where Noah's Ark came to rest after the biblical flood, looms over the eastern Anatolian town of Doğubayazıt. İshak Paşa Sarayı *(see p319)*, an 18th-century palace, lies outside the town.

Cappadocia's many churches, cave dwellings, monasteries and underground cities *(see p285)* were carved out of hardened volcanic ash deposited many thousands of years ago.

Sabancı Central Mosque in Adana *(see p234)* is one of the largest mosques in the Islamic world. The Ottoman-era clock tower is an older landmark of this fast-growing southern city.

THRACE AND THE SEA OF MARMARA

Standing at a natural crossroads, Istanbul makes a good base for excursions into the neighbouring areas of Thrace and the Sea of Marmara. Whether you want to see great Islamic architecture, immerse yourself in a busy bazaar, relax on an island or catch a glimpse of Turkey's rich birdlife, you will find a choice of destinations within easy reach of the city.

On public holidays and at weekends, nearby resorts are crowded with Istanbul residents taking a break from the noisy city. For longer breaks, they head for the Mediterranean or Aegean, so summer is a good, quiet time to explore the Thrace and Marmara regions.

The country around Istanbul varies immensely from lush forests to open plains and, beyond them, impressive mountains. The Princes' Islands, where pine forests and monasteries can be toured by a pleasant ride in a horse-drawn carriage, are also just a short boat trip away from the city. A little further away, the lakeside town of İznik is world famous for its ceramics. This art form, which reached its zenith in the 16th and 17th centuries, is one of the wonders of Ottoman art, and original pieces are highly prized.

To the northwest, near the Greek border, is Edirne, a former Ottoman capital. It is visited today for its mosques, especially the Selimiye with its towering minarets. Edirne also stages Kırkpınar grease-wrestling matches every June, when enthusiastic crowds flock to enjoy the contest and the accompanying folk festival.

South of the Sea of Marmara is the pretty spa-town of Bursa. Originally a Greek city, it was founded in 183 BC. The first Ottoman capital, it has some fine architecture and also maintains the tradition of the Karagöz shadow puppet theatre. Near the mouth of the straits of the Dardanelles lie the ruins of the legendary city of Troy, dating from about 3600 BC. North of the Dardanelles are cemeteries commemorating the thousands of soldiers killed in the battles fought over the Gallipoli Peninsula during World War I.

Boats in Burgaz Harbour on the Princes' Islands, a short ferry ride from Istanbul

◀ The vast Selimiye Mosque, a prominent landmark in Edirne

Exploring Thrace and the Sea of Marmara

Istanbul is the jewel of the Thrace and Marmara region, but places like Edirne and Bursa – and others within a radius of about 250 km (150 miles) – each have their own history and importance, with some fine museums and mosques. Şile, located on the Black Sea coast, is a day's outing from Istanbul, as is the quaint hamlet of Polonezköy. Bird parks, the superb tiles of İznik, along with the spas and ski slopes around Bursa, give the Marmara area the edge for variety. A visit to the World War I battlefields and cemeteries of the Gallipoli Peninsula is a moving experience.

French war cemetery, Gallipoli Peninsula

Bird Paradise National Park – an area rich in protected wildlife

Sights at a Glance

1. *Edirne pp158–61*
2. Princes' Islands
3. Polonezköy
4. Şile
5. İznik
6. Uludağ National Park
7. *Bursa pp166–71*
8. Bird Paradise National Park
9. *Gallipoli Peninsula pp172–3*

Getting Around

The Trans European Motorway (TEM) system means that a six-lane superhighway bypasses the hub of Istanbul using the Fatih Sultan Mehmet Bridge over the Bosphorus. On this toll road, the Istanbul to Ankara journey takes about 3 hours. Car ferries (no reservations required) commute frequently between Gebze and Yalova. A sea bus service (advance booking essential) does the Yenikapı (central Istanbul) to Bandırma run in a few hours. From Istanbul, local and intercity trains depart from Sirkeci Station on the European side and Haydarpaşa Station on the Asian side. Ferries depart from the Eminönü ferry piers in Istanbul to four of the Princes' Islands and from Kabataş, near the Dolmabahçe Palace, to the islands on the south coast of the Sea of Marmara, as well as from Bostanci on the Asian side.

Children walking up a picturesque street in an old quarter of Bursa

BLACK SEA

Sea of Marmara

ŞİLE 4

3 POLONEZKÖY

İSTANBUL

PRINCES' ISLANDS 2

Gebze

Kocaeli (İzmit)

Ankara

Yalova

İZNİK 5

BURSA 7

6 ULUDAĞ NATIONAL PARK

Eskişehir

Balıkesir

Key

- Motorway
- Major road
- Minor road
- Scenic route
- Main railway
- Minor railway
- International border

❶ Edirne

Standing on the river Tunca near the border with Greece, Edirne is a provincial university town that is home to one of Turkey's star attractions, the Selimiye Mosque *(see pp160–61)*. As this huge monument attests, Edirne was historically of great importance. It dates back to AD 125, when the Emperor Hadrian joined two small towns to form Hadrianopolis, or Adrianople. For nearly a century, from 1361 when Murat I took the city until Constantinople was conquered in 1453 *(see p58)*, Edirne was the Ottoman capital. The town has one other claim to fame – the annual grease-wrestling championships in June.

Entrance arch, Mosque of the Three Balconies

Entrance to Beyazıt II Mosque viewed from its inner courtyard

Beyazıt II Mosque

Beyazıt II Külliyesi

Yeni Maharet Cad. **Open** daily. Health Museum: **Tel** (0284) 212 09 22. **Open** 9:30am–5:30pm daily.

Beyazıt II Mosque stands in a peaceful location on the northern bank of the Tunca River, 1.5 km (1 mile) from the city centre. It was built in 1484–8, soon after Beyazıt II succeeded Mehmet the Conqueror *(see p58)* as sultan.

The mosque and its courtyards are open to the public. Of the surrounding buildings in the complex, the old hospital, which incorporated an asylum, has been converted into the **Health Museum**. Disturbed patients were treated in this asylum – a model facility for its time – with water, music and flower therapies. The Turkish writer Evliya Çelebi (1611–84) reported that singers and instrumentalists would play soothing music here three times a week. Overuse of hashish was one of the most common afflictions. The colonnaded inner mosque courtyard, unlike most later examples, covers three times the area of the mosque itself. Inside, the weight of the impressive dome is supported on sweeping pendentives.

Mosque of the Three Balconies

Üç Şerefeli Camii

Hükümet Cad. **Open** daily.

Until the fall of Constantinople, this was the grandest building of the early Ottoman state. It was finished in 1447 and takes its name from the three balconies which adorn its southeastern minaret – at the time the tallest in existence. In an unusual touch, the other three minarets of the mosque are each of a different design and height. Unlike its predecessors in Bursa *(see pp166–7)*, the mosque has an open courtyard, a feature that set a precedent for the great imperial mosques of Istanbul. The interior plan was also innovative. With minimal obstructions, both the *mihrab* and *minbar* can be seen from almost every corner of the prayer hall.

Old Mosque

Eski Cami

Talat Paşa Asfaltı. **Open** daily.

The oldest of Edirne's major mosques, this is a smaller version of the Great Mosque in Bursa *(see p168)*. The eldest son of Beyazıt I, Süleyman, began the mosque in 1403, but it was his youngest son, Mehmet I, who completed it in 1414.

A perfect square, the mosque is divided by four massive piers into nine domed sections. On either side of the prayer hall entrance there are massive

Grease-Wrestling

The Kırkpınar Grease-Wrestling Championships take place annually in June, on the island of Sarayiçi in the Tunca River. The event is famed throughout Turkey and accompanied by a week-long carnival. Before competing, the wrestlers don knee-length leather shorts *(kıspet)* and grease themselves from head to foot in diluted olive oil. The master of ceremonies, the *cazgır*, then invites the competitors to take part in a high-stepping, arm-flinging parade across the field, accompanied by music played on a deep-toned drum *(davul)* and a single-reed oboe *(zurna)*. Wrestling bouts can last up to two hours and involve long periods of frozen, silent concentration interspersed by attempts to throw down the opponent.

Wrestlers performing a ceremonial ritual before the contest

Arabic inscriptions proclaiming "Allah" and "Mohammed".

Rüstem Paşa Caravanserai

Rüstem Paşa Kervansarayı
İki Kapılı Han Cad 57.
Tel (0284) 212 61 19.

Sinan *(see p105)* designed this *kervanseray* for Süleyman's most powerful grand vizier, Rüstem Paşa, in 1560–61. It was constructed in two distinct parts. The larger courtyard, or *han* *(see pp28–9)*, which is now the Rüstem Paşa Kervansaray Hotel, was built for the merchants of Edirne, while the smaller courtyard, now a student hostel, was an inn for other travellers.

A short walk away, on the other side of Saraçlar Caddesi, is the **Semiz Ali Paşa Bazaar**. This is also the work of Sinan, and dates from 1589. It consists of a long, narrow street of vaulted shops.

Museum of Turkish and Islamic Arts

Türk ve İslam Eserleri Müzesi
Kadir Paşa Mektep Sok.
Tel (0284) 225 11 20. **Open** 8am–6pm Tue–Sun.

Edirne's small collection of Turkish and Islamic works of art is attractively located in the *medrese (see p36)* of the Selimiye Mosque.

The museum's first room is devoted to the local sport of grease-wrestling. It includes enlarged reproductions of miniatures depicting 600 years of the sport. These show the wrestling stars resplendent in their leather shorts, their skin glistening with olive oil.

Other objects on display include the original doors of the Beyazıt II Mosque. There are also military exhibits. Among them are some beautiful 18th-century Ottoman shields, with woven silk exteriors, and paintings of military subjects.

The tranquil 15th-century Muradiye Mosque

VISITORS' CHECKLIST

Practical Information
150,000. Hürriyet Meydanı 17, (0284) 213 92 08. Mon, Wed, Sat. Grease-Wrestling (Jun). **kirkpinar.org**

Transport
Ayşekadın, (0284) 235 26 73. E5 exit at Highway Maintenance Depot, (0284) 226 00 20. in front of tourist office (Hürriyet Meydanı 17).

Muradiye Mosque

Muradiye Camii
Küçükpazar Cad. **Open** daily.

What is today a tranquil mosque was first built as a *zaviye* (dervish hospice) in 1421 by Murat II, who dreamed that the great dervish leader Celaleddin Rumi *(see pp256, 259)* asked him to build a hospice in Edirne. Only later was it converted into a mosque. Its interior is notable for its massive inscriptions, similar to those in the Old Mosque, and for some fine early 15th-century İznik tiles *(see p165)*. It may be locked outside prayer times.

Edirne City Centre

1. Beyazıt II Mosque
2. Mosque of the Three Balconies
3. Old Mosque
4. Rüstem Paşa Caravanserai
5. Selimiye Mosque
6. Museum of Turkish and Islamic Arts
7. Muradiye Mosque

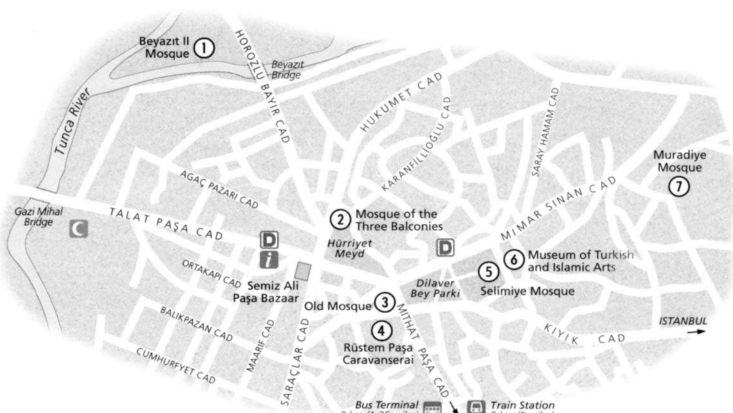

Edirne: Selimiye Mosque

Selimiye Camii

The Selimiye is the greatest of all the Ottoman mosque complexes, the apogee of an art form and the culmination of a life's ambition for its architect, Sinan *(see p105)*. Built on a slight hill, the mosque is a prominent landmark. Its complex includes a medrese *(see p36)*, housing the Museum of Turkish and Islamic Arts, a school and the Kavaflar Arasta, a covered bazaar.

Selim II commissioned the mosque. It was begun in 1569 and completed in 1575, a year after his death. The dome was Sinan's proudest achievement. In his memoirs, he wrote: "With the help of Allah and the favour of Sultan Selim Khan, I have succeeded in building a cupola six cubits wider and four cubits deeper than that of Haghia Sophia." In fact, the dome is comparable in diameter and slightly shallower than the building Sinan had so longed to surpass.

★ Minarets
The mosque's four slender minarets tower to a height of 84 m (275 ft). Each one has three balconies. The two northern minarets contain three inter-twining staircases, each one leading to a different balcony.

Ablutions Fountain
Intricate, pierced carving decorates the top of the 16-sided open *şadırvan* (ablutions fountain), which stands in the centre of the courtyard. The absence of a canopy helps to retain the uncluttered aspect.

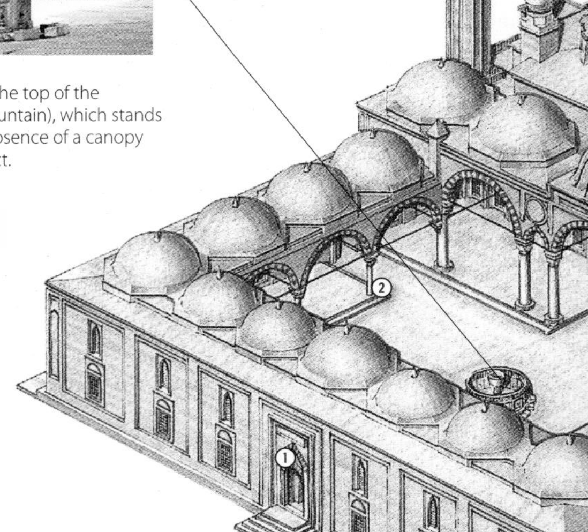

KEY

① **Above the courtyard portals** are striking arches that were built using alternating red and honey-coloured slabs of stone. This echoes the decoration of the magnificent arches running around the mosque courtyard itself.

② **The columns** supporting the arches of the courtyard are made of old marble, plundered from Byzantine architecture.

③ **The *müezzin mahfili*** still retains original, intricate 16th-century paintwork on its underside. Beneath it is a small fountain.

④ **Mihrab**, cut from Marmara marble.

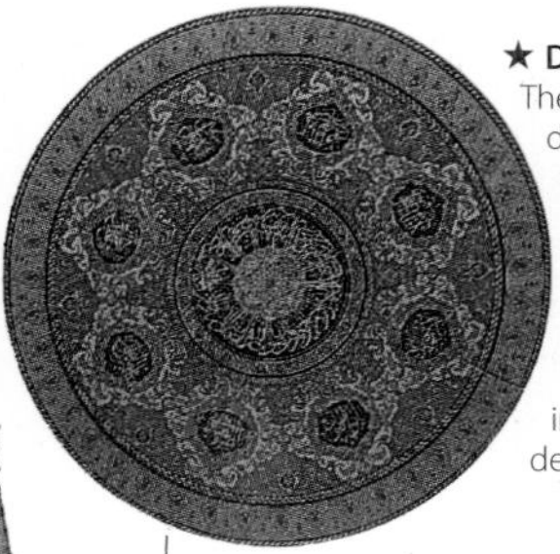

★ Dome
The 43 m (141 ft) dome dominates the interior of the mosque. Not even the florid paintwork – the original 16th-century decoration underwent restoration in the 19th century – detracts from its effect.

★ Minbar
Many experts claim that the Selimiye's *minbar*, with its conical tiled cap, is the finest in Turkey. Its lace-like side panels are exquisitely carved.

VISITORS' CHECKLIST

Practical Information
Mimar Sinan Cad, Edirne.
Tel (0284) 213 97 35.
Open daily. **Closed** prayer times.
donation.

The Interior
The mosque is the supreme achievement of Islamic architecture. Its octagonal plan allows for a reduction in the size of the buttresses supporting the dome. This permitted extra windows to be incorporated, making the interior exceptionally light.

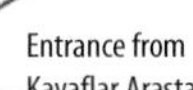

Entrance from Kavaflar Arasta

Sultan's Loge
The imperial loge is supported on green marble columns. They are connected by pointed arches, whose surrounds are adorned with floral İznik tiles *(see p165)*. Unusually, its ornately decorated mihrab contains a shuttered window, which opened on to countryside when the mosque was built.

Main entrance

Burgazada, one of the relaxed and picturesque Princes' Islands

❷ Princes' Islands

Kızıl Adalar

17,200. ferry and sea bus from Kabataş (European side), sea bus from Kadıköy (Asian side) or from Bostancı (further Asian side). Town Hall, (0216) 382 70 71 and (0216) 382 78 56.

The pine-forested Princes' Islands provide a welcome break from the bustle of the city and are just a short ferry ride southeast of Istanbul. Most ferries call in turn at the four largest of the nine islands: **Kınalıada**, **Burgazada**, **Heybeliada** and **Büyükada**.

Easily visited on a day trip, the islands take their name from a royal palace built by Justin II on Büyükada, then known as Prinkipo (Island of the Prince) in 569. In Byzantine times the islands became infamous as a place of exile for royalty, and also as the site of several monasteries.

In the latter half of the 19th century, with the inauguration of a regular steamboat service from Istanbul, many wealthy foreigners settled on the islands. One who found the tolerant attitude to foreigners and generous morality attractive was Leon Trotsky, who lived in one of Büyükada's finest mansions from 1929 to 1933. Zia Gökalp *(see p314)*, a key figure in the rise of Turkish nationalism, lived here during the waning years of the Ottoman era.

Visitors strolling along a street in the village of Büyükada

Büyükada is the largest of the Princes' Islands, and it attracts many visitors because of its beaches, outdoor summer culture and the Art Nouveau style of the wooden dwellings that have given the island much of its lingering Ottoman atmosphere. Büyükada and Heybeliada shun any form of motorized transport in favour of horse-drawn carriages or donkeys. At the top of Büyükada's wooded southern hill stands the Monastery of St George, built on Byzantine foundations.

Heybeliada, the second largest island, houses the imposing former Naval High School (Deniz Harp Okulu), built in 1942. Less touristy than Büyükada, this island offers quieter pleasures such as lovely, tiny beaches and walks in pine groves. The island's northern hill is the stunning location of the Greek Orthodox School of Theology, which was built in 1841.

The smaller islands of Kınalıada and Burgazada are less developed and therefore more peaceful. Kınalıada is home to a fine Armenian church built in 1857. At Burgazada, visitors can see the 19th-century Greek Orthodox Church of John the Baptist.

❸ Polonezköy

800. 15KC from Üsküdar to Beykoz, then take a taxi. Cherry festival (first two weeks of Jun).

Polonezköy still reflects clear signs of the Polish roots of its founders, who came here in 1842 fleeing Russian oppression. United by politics, Poles fought in Abdül Mecit I's army against Russia in the Crimean War (1853–6).

Door to the Monastery of St George, Büyükada

Exempted from taxes for their efforts in the war, they settled in their namesake village. Unlike many people who came to Istanbul principally for trade, Poles came here in search of freedom and some of them converted to Islam. Polonezköy's old-world charm and culinary traditions are still there, but it has become very popular for a day's outing or a weekend break. Turks make up most of its current population.

There are excellent walks in the surrounding countryside and, even though villas and spas have sprung up, there are still several authentic restaurants serving Polish specialities, including the wild boar for which the town was once well known.

The surrounding beech forest, which also offers pleasant walks, has become a conservation area protected from further development.

❹ Şile

5,000. from Üsküdar.

The quintessential Black Sea holiday village Şile has several fine, sandy beaches and a large, black-and-white

For hotels and restaurants in this area see p332 and pp349–50

striped lighthouse high on a clifftop. In ancient times, the village, then known as Kalpe, was a port used by ships sailing eastward from the Bosphorus. Şile's lighthouse, the largest in Turkey, was built by the French for Sultan Abdül Aziz in 1858–9. Visiting it after dusk on a warm evening makes a pleasant outing. Apart from tourism, Şile is known for producing cotton, as well as a cool, loose-weave cotton cloth, known as *şile bezi*, which is sold in local shops.

❺ İznik

See pp164–5.

❻ Uludağ National Park

Uludağ Milli Parkı

Tel (0224) 283 21 97. City bus marked "Teleferik" from Koza Park, then cable car to the lookout point at Sarıalan. to Sarıalan, then *dolmuş*. **Open** daily. only for vehicles.

One of a number of Turkish mountains to claim the title of Mount Olympus, Uludağ, at 2,540 m (8,340 ft), was believed by the Bithynians (of northwestern Asia Minor) to be the abode of the gods. In the Byzantine era, it was home to several monastic orders. After the Ottoman conquest of Bursa, Muslim dervishes *(p259)* moved into the abandoned monasteries. Nowadays, however, no traces of Uludağ's former religious communities remain.

Spring and summer are the best times for visiting Uludağ National Park, as its alpine heights remain relatively cool, offering a welcome escape from the heat of the lower areas. Visitors will find plenty of good opportunities for peaceful walking and picnicking.

The park includes about 670 sq km (258 sq miles) of woodland. As you ascend, the deciduous beech, oak and hazel gradually give way to juniper and aspen, and finally to dwarf junipers. In springtime, the slopes are blanketed with hyacinths and crocuses.

The main tourist season in Uludağ starts in November, when it becomes Turkey's most fashionable and accessible ski resort, with a reliable cable car service and a good selection of hotels.

Osman Gazi *(see p58)* is supposed to have founded seven villages for his seven sons and their brides here. **Cumalıkızık**, on the lower slopes of Uludağ, is the most perfectly preserved of the five surviving villages and it is a UNESCO World Heritage Site. Among its houses are many 750-year-old half-timbered buildings.

❼ Bursa

See pp166–71.

Uludağ National Park, a popular ski resort in winter

Spoonbill wading in the lake at Bird Paradise National Park

❽ Bird Paradise National Park

Kuşcenneti Milli Parkı

Tel (0266) 735 54 22. D no public transport, take a taxi from Bandırma. **Open** sunrise to sunset daily.

An estimated 255 species of birds visit Bird Paradise National Park at the edge of Kuş Gölü, the lake formerly known as Manyas Gölü. Located on the great migratory paths between Europe and Asia, the park is a happy combination of plant cover, reedbeds and a lake that supports at least 20 species of fish. The park will delight amateur and professional birdwatchers alike, and a good field guide and some mosquito repellent will enhance the experience.

At the entrance to the park, there is a small museum with displays about various birds. Binoculars are provided at the desk and visitors make their way to an observation tower.

Two main groups of birds visit the lake: those that come here to breed (March–July), and those that pass by during migration, either heading south (November) or north (April–May). Among the birds that breed around the lake are the endangered Dalmatian pelican, the great crested grebe, cormorants, herons, bitterns and spoonbills. Over three million birds fly across the area on their migratory routes – storks, cranes, pelicans and birds of prey like sparrowhawks and spotted eagles. April and May are the best months to enjoy this area. Close to the main park area, there is a restaurant that serves fresh trout, and it is a good spot to break for lunch.

5 İznik

42,000. Yeni Mahalle, Yakup Sok, (0224) 757 25 83. Sea bus from Istanbul to Yalova then dolmuş to İznik. Belediye Hizmet Binası, Kılıçaslan Cad 97, (0224) 757 19 33, (0224) 757 14 54. Wed. İznik Flower and Summer Festival (1st or 2nd week of May); Liberation Day (28 Nov).

Grand domed portico fronting the Archaeological Museum

A charming lakeside town, İznik gives little clue now of its former glory as a capital of the Byzantine Empire. Its most important legacy, however, dates from the 16th century, when its kilns produced the finest ceramics ever made in the Ottoman world.

The town first reached prominence in AD 325, when it was known as Nicaea. In that year Emperor Constantine *(see p53)* chose it as the location of the first Ecumenical Council of the Christian Church. The meeting produced the Nicene Creed, a statement of doctrine on the nature of Christ in relation to God.

The Seljuks *(see p56)* took Nicaea in 1081 and renamed it İznik. It was recaptured in 1097, during the First Crusade, on behalf of Emperor Alexius I Comnenus. After the Crusader capture of Constantinople in 1204 *(see p57)*, the city served as the capital of the "Empire of Nicaea" for 50 years. In 1331, Orhan Gazi captured İznik and incorporated it into the Ottoman empire. İznik still retains its original layout. Surrounded by the town walls, its two main streets are in the form of a cross, with minor streets running out from them on a grid plan. The walls still more or less delineate the town's boundaries. They were built in 300 BC by the Greek Lysimachus, then ruler of the town, but were frequently repaired by the Byzantines and, later, the Ottomans. Extending for some 3 km (2 miles), the walls are punctuated by huge gateways. The main one, Istanbul Gate (İstanbul Kapısı), marks İznik's northern limit. It is decorated with a carved relief of fighting horsemen and is flanked by Byzantine towers.

One of the town's oldest surviving monuments, the church of **Haghia Sophia**, stands at the intersection of the main streets, Atatürk Caddesi and Kılıçaslan Caddesi. The current building was erected after an earthquake in 1065. The remains of a fine mosaic floor, and also of a Deësis (a fresco depicting Christ, the Virgin and John the Baptist), are protected from damage behind glass screens. The church became a mosque after the Ottoman conquest, but was converted into a museum in the Republican era. Controversially, it was reconsecrated as a mosque in 2012. Just off the eastern end of Kılıçaslan Caddesi, the 14th-century **Green Mosque** (Yeşil Camii) is named after the tiles covering its minaret. Unfortunately, the original tiles have been replaced by modern copies of inferior quality. Opposite the mosque, the Kitchen of Lady Nilüfer (Nilüfer Hatun İmareti), one of İznik's loveliest buildings, now houses the town's **Archaeological Museum**. This *imaret* was set up in 1388 by Nilüfer Hatun, wife of Orhan Gazi, and served as a hospice for wandering dervishes. Entered through a spacious five-domed portico, the central domed area is flanked by two more domed rooms. The museum has displays of Roman antiquities and glass, as well as some examples of Seljuk and Ottoman tiles.

Istanbul Gate from within the town walls

Haghia Sophia
Atatürk Cad. **Tel** (0224) 757 10 27. **Open** daily.

Green Mosque
Müze Sok. **Open** daily (except prayer times).

Archaeological Museum
Müze Sok. **Tel** (0224) 757 10 27. **Open** 9am–noon & 1–5pm Tue–Sun.

Green Mosque, named after the green tiles adorning its minaret

İznik Ceramics

İznik was one of two major centres (the other being Kütahya) where fine, painted and glazed pottery was fashioned during the Ottoman period. Pottery vessels, plates, and flat and shaped tiles were produced at İznik from the 15th to the 17th century. The last major commission was for 21,043 tiles of some 50 different designs for the Sultanahmet Mosque in Istanbul, completed in 1616. Early İznik pottery is brilliant blue and white. The potteries reached their peak in the 16th century, when the famous "tomato red" colour was fully developed. Today visitors can see it sparkle on the superb tilework of the 1561 Rüstem Paşa Mosque *(see p102)* in Istanbul. This period of İznik greatness in ceramic art coincided with the great period of design at the Nakkaşhane design studio in the Topkapı Palace *(see pp72–5)*.

Chinese porcelain, which was imported into Turkey from the 14th century and of which there is a large collection in Topkapı Palace, often inspired the designs used for İznik pottery. During the 16th century, İznik potters produced imitations of pieces of Chinese porcelain, such as this copy of a Ming dish.

Rock and wave border pattern

Damascus ware was the name erroneously given to ceramics produced at İznik during the first half of the 16th century. They had fantastic floral designs in the new colours of turquoise, sage green and manganese. When such tiles were discovered at Damascus, the similar İznik pots were wrongly assumed to have been made there.

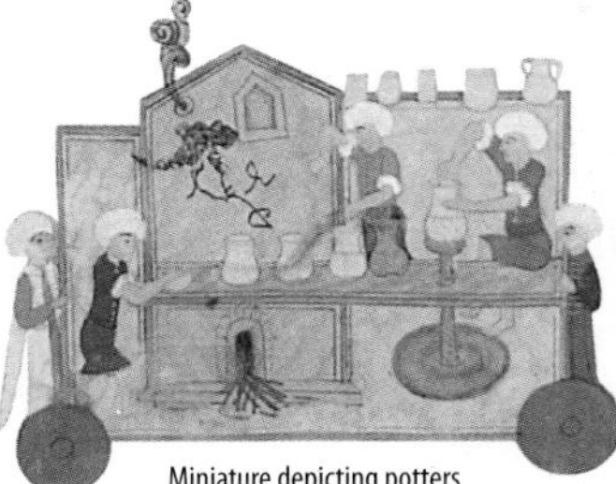

Miniature depicting potters

Cobalt blue and white was the striking combination of colours used in early İznik pottery (produced between c.1470 and 1520). The designs used were a mixture of Chinese and Arabesque, as seen on this tiled panel on the wall of the Circumcision Chamber in Topkapı Palace. Floral patterns and animal motifs were both popular at this time.

Armenian bole, an iron-rich red colour, began to be used around 1550, as seen in this 16th-century tankard. New, realistic tulip and other floral designs were also introduced, and İznik ware enjoyed its heyday, which lasted until around 1630.

Wall tiles were not made in any quantity until the reign of Süleyman the Magnificent (1520–66). Süleyman used İznik tiles to refurbish the Dome of the Rock in Jerusalem. Some of the best examples are seen in Istanbul's mosques, notably in the Süleymaniye *(see pp104–5)*, Rüstem Paşa Mosque and, here, in this example from the Blue Mosque *(pp92–3)*.

7 Bursa

View over the rooftops of the city of Bursa

The city of Bursa – known to Turks as *yeşil Bursa* ("green Bursa") – has tranquil parks and leafy suburbs set on the lower slopes of Mount Uludağ *(see p163)*. This disguises the vibrant commercial heart of the city, which is today made prosperous by automobiles, food and textiles, as it was by the silk trade in the 15th and 16th centuries. The Romans developed the potential of Bursa's mineral springs, and there are estimated to be about 3,000 thermal baths in the city today. In 1326 Bursa became the first capital of the Ottoman Empire after it succumbed to Osman *(see p58)*.

Bursa has been a provincial capital since 1841 and, despite its commercial centre, it has retained its pious dignity. No city in Turkey has more mosques and tombs. Paradoxically, it is also the home of the satirical shadow-puppet genre known as Karagöz *(see p30)*.

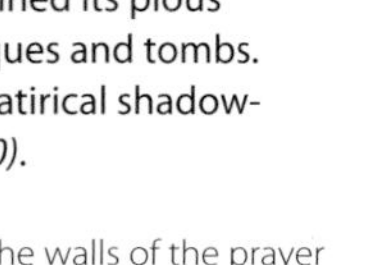

Yıldırım Beyazıt Mosque

Yıldırım Beyazıt Camii
Yıldırım Cad.
Open daily (except prayer times).

This mosque is named after Beyazıt I, whose nickname was "Yıldırım", meaning "thunderbolt". This referred to the speed with which he reacted to his enemies. Built in 1389, just after Beyazıt became sultan, the mosque at first doubled as a lodge for Sufi dervishes *(see p259)*. It has a lovely portico with five domed bays.

Inside, the prayer hall and interior court (a covered "courtyard" in Bursa mosques, which prefigures the open ones preferred by later Ottoman architects) are divided by an impressive, gravity-defying arch. This rises from two *mihrab*-like niches. The walls of the prayer hall itself are adorned with several attractive pieces of calligraphic design *(see pp32–3)*.

Green Tomb

Yeşil Türbe
Yeşil Cad. **Open** daily. donation.

The tomb of Mehmet I, which stands elevated among tall cypress trees, is one of the city's most prominent landmarks. It was built between 1414 and 1421.

The tomb is much closer to the Seljuk style of architecture than classical Ottoman. Its exterior is covered in green tiles – mainly 19th-century replacements for the original faïence. A few older tiles survive around the entrance portal. The interior, entered through a pair of superbly carved wooden doors, is simply dazzling. The space is small and the ornamentation, covering a relatively large surface area, is breathtaking in its depth of colour and detail. The *mihrab* has especially intricate tile panels, including a representation of a mosque lamp hanging from a gold chain between two candles.

The sultan's magnificent sarcophagus is covered in exquisite tiles and adorned by a long Koranic inscription. Nearby sarcophagi contain the remains of his sons, daughters and nursemaid.

The distinctive and prominent Green Tomb of Sultan Mehmet I

Green Mosque

Yeşil Camii
Yeşil Cad. **Open** daily (except prayer times).

Bursa's most famous monument was commissioned by Mehmet I in 1412, but it remained unfinished at his death in 1421 and still lacks a portico. Nevertheless, it is the finest Ottoman mosque built prior to the conquest of Constantinople *(see p58)*.

The main portal is tall and elegant, with an intricately carved canopy. It opens into the entrance hall. Beyond this is an interior court with a carved fountain at its centre. A flight of three steps leads up from here into the prayer hall. On either side of the steps are niches for worshippers to leave their shoes. Above the entrance to the court is the sultan's loge *(see p37)*, resplendent in richly patterned tiles created using the *cuerda seca* technique. They are in beautiful greens, blues and yellows, with threads

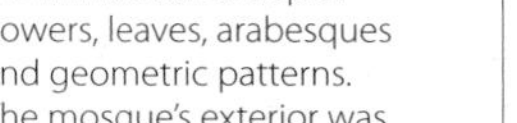

of gold that were added after firing. The tiling of the prayer hall was carried out by Ali Ibn İlyas Ali, who learned his art in Samarkand. This was the first time that tiles were used extensively in an Ottoman mosque, and it set a precedent for the later widespread use of İznik tiles *(see p165)*. The tiles covering the walls of the prayer hall, which is well lit by floor-level windows, are simple, green and hexagonal. Against this plain backdrop, the effect of the *mihrab* is especially glorious. Predominantly turquoise, deep blue and white, with touches of gold, the *mihrab*'s tiles depict flowers, leaves, arabesques and geometric patterns. The mosque's exterior was also once clad in tiles, but these have disappeared over time.

Museum of Turkish and Islamic Arts

Türk ve İslam Eserleri Müzesi
Yeşil Cad. **Tel** (0224) 327 76 79.
Open 8am–noon, 1–5pm Mon–Fri.

This interesting museum is housed in a fine Ottoman-era building, once the *medrese* *(see p36)* associated with the Green Mosque. The façade of the building is quite striking. A colonnade surrounds its courtyard on three sides. The cells leading off from this courtyard are now exhibition galleries. Exhibits date from the 12th to the 20th centuries, and include Seljuk and Ottoman ceramics, elaborately decorated Korans and beautiful ceremonial costumes.

Façade of the Museum of Turkish and Islamic Arts

VISITORS' CHECKLIST

Practical Information
2,787,000.
Ulucami Parkı, Orhangazı Altgeçidi 1 (0224) 220 18 48.
International Bursa Festival (1st week of Jun–3rd week of Jul); International Karagöz Festival (2nd–3rd weeks of Nov).

Transport
20 km (12 miles) NW of city centre. Yeni Yalova Yolu, (0224) 261 54 00. D Atatürk Cad, near the State Theatre or behind Heykel.

Bursa City Museum

Bursa Kent Müzesi
Atatürk Cad 8. **Tel** (0224) 220 26 26.
Open 9:30am–5:30pm Tue–Sun.

The former Justice courts have been restored as a lively museum that traces local life over many years. Displays show how culinary skills, handicrafts, costumes, archaeological artifacts and city planning moulded urban spirit. Bursa city fathers, Atatürk and the local *commedia dell arte* puppet genre of Karagöz *(see p30)* have first-rate exhibits.

Bursa City Centre

1. Yıldırım Beyazıt Mosque
2. Green Tomb
3. Green Mosque
4. Museum of Turkish and Islamic Arts
5. Bursa City Museum
6. Tophane Citadel
7. Tombs of Osman and Orhan Gazi
8. Alaeddin Mosque
9. Muradiye Mosque
10. Archaeological Museum

Key

Street-by-Street area *see pp168–9*

Bursa: The Market Area

Bursa's central market area is a warren of streets and Ottoman *hans* (warehouses). The area emphasizes the more colourful and traditional aspects of this busy industrial city and is a good place to experience the bustle of inner-city life. Here too you can buy the local fabrics for which the city is famous, particularly hand-made lace, towelling and silk. The silkworm was introduced to the Byzantine empire in the 6th century, and for centuries there was a brisk trade in silk cocoons in Koza Han. Today, as well as silk products, you can also find hand-made, camelskin Karagöz puppets *(see p30)*.

★ Covered Bazaar
The great bazaar, built by Mehmet I in the 15th century, consists of a long hall with domed bays, with an adjoining high, vaulted hall. The Bedesten is home to jewellers' shops.

★ Great Mosque (Ulu Cami)
A three-tiered ablutions fountain stands beneath the central dome of this monumental mosque, which was erected in 1396–9.

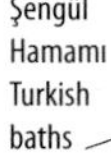

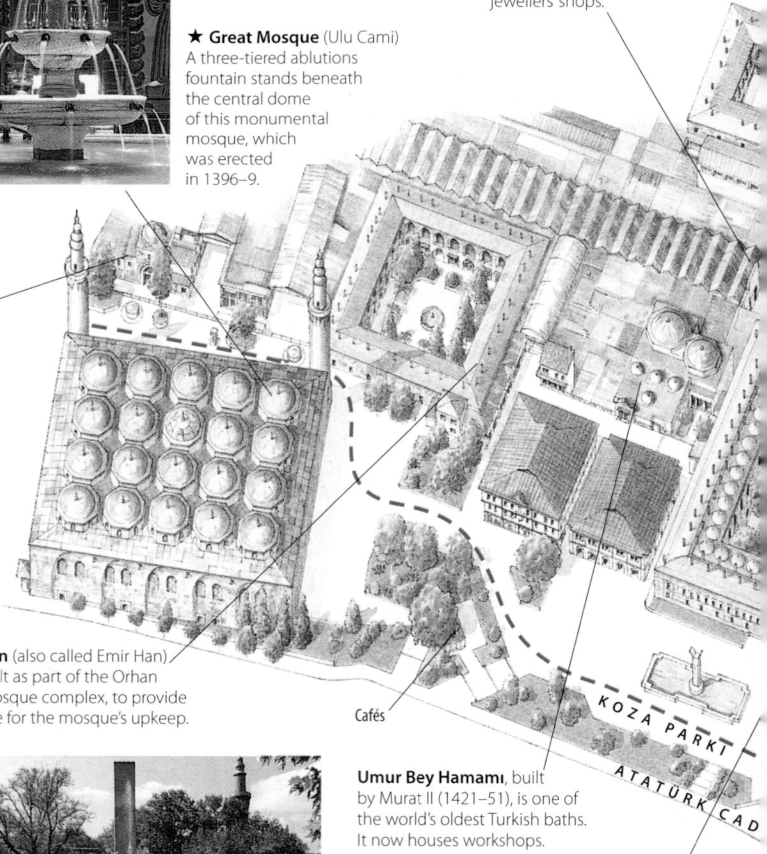

Şengül Hamamı Turkish baths

Bey Han (also called Emir Han) was built as part of the Orhan Gazi Mosque complex, to provide revenue for the mosque's upkeep.

Cafés

KOZA PARKI

ATATÜRK CAD

Umur Bey Hamamı, built by Murat II (1421–51), is one of the world's oldest Turkish baths. It now houses workshops.

Koza Park
The gardens in front of Koza Han, with their fountains, benches and shaded café tables, are a popular meeting place for locals and visitors throughout the day.

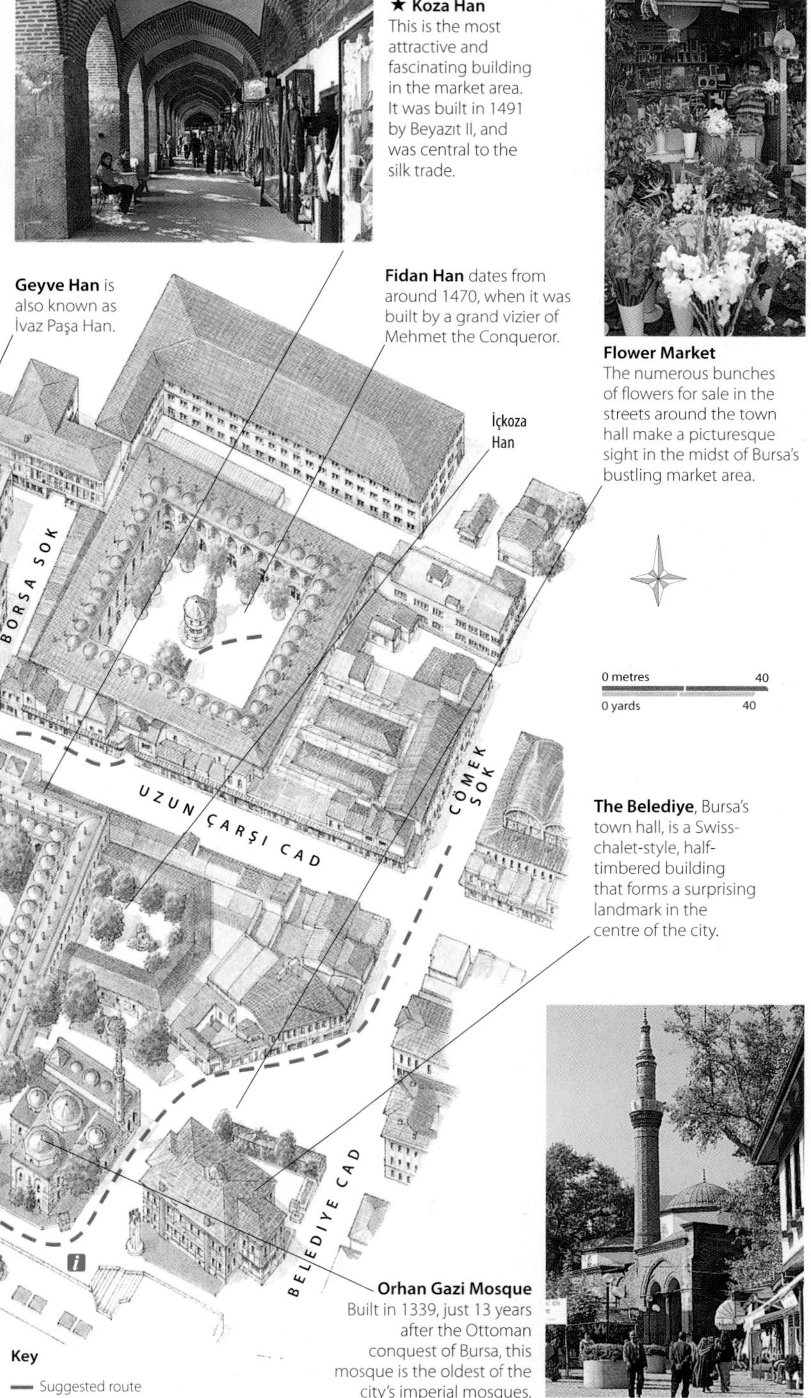

★ Koza Han
This is the most attractive and fascinating building in the market area. It was built in 1491 by Beyazıt II, and was central to the silk trade.
Geyve Han is also known as İvaz Paşa Han.
Fidan Han dates from around 1470, when it was built by a grand vizier of Mehmet the Conqueror.
İçkoza Han
Flower Market
The numerous bunches of flowers for sale in the streets around the town hall make a picturesque sight in the midst of Bursa's bustling market area.
BORSA SOK
0 metres 40
0 yards 40
UZUN ÇARŞI CAD
ÇÖMEK SOK
The Belediye, Bursa's town hall, is a Swiss-chalet-style, half-timbered building that forms a surprising landmark in the centre of the city.
BELEDIYE CAD
Orhan Gazi Mosque
Built in 1339, just 13 years after the Ottoman conquest of Bursa, this mosque is the oldest of the city's imperial mosques.
Key
Suggested route

For additional map symbols *see back flap*

Exploring Bursa

Tophane, the most ancient part of Bursa, is distinguished by its clock tower, which stands on top of a hill. This area was formerly the site of the citadel and is bounded by what remains of the original Byzantine walls. It is also known as Hisar, which means "fortress" in Turkish. If you continue westwards for 2 km (1 mile), crossing the Cılımboz River, you come to the historic district of Muradiye. Çekirge (or "cricket") is Bursa's most westerly area. The origin of this name is not known, but the cool, leafy character of this suburb gives Bursa the tag of *yeşil*, or "green", by which it is known in Turkey.

Tophane

Tophane's northern limit is marked by the best-preserved section of the citadel walls, built on an outcrop of rock. At the top is a pleasant park, filled with cafés, which also contains the imposing clock tower and the tombs of Osman and Orhan Gazi, the founders of the Ottoman dynasty.

Tophane Citadel

Hisar

Osman Gazi Cad. **Open** daily.

The Citadel walls can be viewed from a set of steps leading uphill from the intersection of Cemal Nadir Caddesi and Atatürk Caddesi. These steps end at the tea gardens above. The citadel fell into Ottoman hands when Orhan Gazi's troops broke through its walls. Later, he built a wooden palace inside the citadel and had the old Byzantine ramparts re-fortified. Until this era the walls had delineated the entire circumference of the ancient city. However, Orhan encouraged Bursa's expansion and developed the present-day commercial heart of the city further to the east.

Tombs of Osman and Orhan Gazi

Osman & Orhan Gazi Türbeleri

Ulu Cami Cad. **Open** daily. donation.

Osman Gazi began the process of Ottoman expansion in the 13th century *(see p56)* and attempted to capture Bursa. But it was his son, Orhan, who took the city just before Osman Gazi died. Orhan brought his father's body to be buried in the baptistry of a converted church and he himself was later buried in the nave. The tombs that can be seen today date from 1868.

Tomb of Osman Gazi, the first great Ottoman leader

Alaeddin Mosque

Alaeddin Camii

Alaeddin Mahallesi. **Open** daily.

The Alaeddin Mosque is the oldest in Bursa: it was built in 1335, only nine years after the city was conquered in 1326. It is in the form of a simple domed square, fronted by a portico of four Byzantine columns with capitals. The mosque was commissioned by Alaeddin Bey, brother of and vizier to Orhan Gazi.

Popular café in the park above the ancient citadel walls in Tophane

Muradiye

Muradiye is a leafy, residential district of Bursa. Close to the Muradiye Mosque, the Hüsnü Züber House is a fine example of traditional 19th-century Ottoman architecture. The interior is open to the public and contains a display of Anatolian wooden implements. To the north is a park, which is home to the Archaeological Museum.

Muradiye Mosque

Muradiye Külliyesi

Murat II Cad. **Open** daily. donation.

This mosque complex was built by Murat II, the father of Mehmet the Conqueror *(see p58)*, in 1447. The mosque itself is preceded by a graceful domed portico. Its wooden door is finely carved and the interior decorated with early İznik tiles *(see p165)*. The *medrese (see p36)*, next to the mosque, now serves as a dispensary. It is a perfectly square building, with cells surrounding a central garden courtyard. Its *dershane*, or main classroom, is richly tiled and adorned with an ornate brick façade.

The mosque garden, with its cypresses, well-tended flowerbeds and fountains, is one of Bursa's most tranquil retreats. Murat II was the last of the Ottoman sultans to be buried in Bursa and his mausoleum stands in the garden beside the mosque. The other 11 tombs in the garden are a reminder of the Ottoman code of succession, which recognized a future sultan as the strongest (or most cunning) male relative, even if not always the most

Interior of Muradiye Mosque, showing the decorative *mihrab*

suitable to rule. Competing male relatives could expect to be put to death or spend most of their lives in enforced solitary confinement, known as "the cage". This did not, however, prevent the ruling offspring from having an emotive memorial built for a deposed brother. Selim II ("the Sot"), for example, had an elaborate octagonal mausoleum built in Bursa for his older brother, Mustafa.

Archaeological Museum

Arkeoloji Müzesi

Resat Oyal, Kültür Parkı. **Tel** (0224) 234 49 18. **Open** 8am–noon & 1–5pm Tue–Sun.

Finds dating from the 3rd millennium BC up to the Ottoman conquest of Bursa in 1326 are collected in this museum. The ceremonial armour accessories are the most interesting items, with the Roman glass a close second. There are a number of Roman statues and bronzes, as well as Byzantine religious objects and coins. The labelling of objects has been improved.

Bursa Museum of Anatolian Carriages

Bursa Anadolu Arabaları Müzesi

Umurbey Mah, Kapıcı Cad, Yıldırım. **Tel** (0224) 329 39 41. **Open** 10am–5pm Tue–Sun. (the museum is mostly on one floor).

The discovery of a 2,600-year-old carriage made of iron and wood stimulated interest in the city's non-motorized transport heritage. This museum traces the wheeled history of *kupa* (war chariots), ox carts, gun mountings, hay ricks, pleasure carriages and horse-drawn railway rolling stock. Artistic motifs painted on carriages were a craftsman's early trademark.

The museum skilfully highlights carriage-making as a precision engineering trade. Bursa is modern Turkey's "motown" and a local automotive producer sponsored the research and reconstruction, applying modern spare-parts cataloguing techniques to latter-day wagons. Housed in a former silk-making factory, the museum is enhanced by beautiful gardens and mature trees. A bookshop sells mainly books and posters of the various wagons.

The art of carriage-making, Bursa Museum of Anatolian Carriages

Çekirge

The Çekirge neighbourhood offers some of the most prominent and best developed natural mineral springs *(kaplıca)* in Turkey. In the 6th century, Emperor Justinian *(see p53)* built a bathhouse here; his wife, Theodora, arrived later with a retinue of about 4,000 to take the waters.

Today, Çekirge is the city's most attractive residential area, still known for its therapeutic hot springs and having excellent spa accommodation. Located above the city, there are wonderful alpine vistas and cool breezes.

New Spa

Yeni Kaplıca-Karamustafa

Kaynarca Termal Otel and Baths, Kükürtlü Mah, Osmangazi. **Tel** (0224) 236 69 68. **Open** 7am–11pm daily (separate spas for men and women).

Contrarily, the New Spa baths have a substantial pedigree and were rebuilt in 1522 by Rüstem Paşa, grand vizier to Süleyman the Magnificent. Two steamy thermal water sources, Kaynarca and Karamustafa, feed the therapeutic pools and treatment centres, all set in expansive tropical gardens.

Karamustafa has been restored as an aqua culture residential complex. Kaynarca is only for women, with professional spa staff, private baths and social facilities. Visitors unfamiliar with Turkey's spa heritage will be warmly welcomed here.

Çelik Palas Hotel

Çelik Palas Otel Çekirge Cad 79. **Tel** (0224) 233 38 00.

This five-star hotel is a famous local icon. Built in 1933, it is the city's oldest and most prestigious spa hotel. Atatürk *(see p62)* frequented its baths, which are open to both sexes.

Old Spa

Eski Kaplıca

Kervansaray Termal Oteli, Çekirge Meydanı **Tel** (0224) 233 93 00. **Open** 7am–10:30pm daily.

The Old Spa baths were established by Sultan Murat I in the late 14th century and renovated in 1512 during the reign of Beyazıt II. Bathers can enjoy the shallow pools of the hot room while admiring the Byzantine columns supporting the domed roof.

Attractive, tranquil interior of the Old Spa baths

❾ Gallipoli Peninsula

Gelibolu Yarımadası

Washed by the Aegean Sea to the west, the Gallipoli Peninsula is bordered to the east by the Dardanelles, a strategic waterway giving access to the Sea of Marmara, the Bosphorus and the Black Sea. In ancient times, this deep channel was called the Hellespont. Today, the peninsula is an unspoiled area of farmland and pine forest, with some lovely stretches of sandy beach. However, it was also the scene of one of the bloodiest campaigns of World War I, in which more than 500,000 Allied (Australian, British, French, Indian and New Zealand) and Turkish soldiers laid down their lives. The region has three museums, and is dotted with cemeteries and monuments. In 1973, the Gallipoli National Historic Park was created in recognition of the area's great historical significance.

Suvla Bay
On 7 August 1915, British troops landed here in an attempt to break the stalemate further south.

★ Çanakkale Destanı Tanıtım Merkezi
The centre is also a museum, with exhibits of uniforms, weapons, letters, photographs, shrapnel, other memorabilia, and realistic video simulations relating to the Gallipoli campaign.

French Cemetery
A sombre obelisk and rows of striking black crosses honour the French troops who fell during the Anglo-French landing at Cape Helles on 25 April 1915.

KEY

① **The Çanakkale Şehitleri Abidesi** commemorates fallen Turkish soldiers.

② **At Y Beach**, ambiguous signals led to an unauthorized withdrawal on both sides.

For hotels and restaurants in this area see pp332 and pp349–50

Reconstructed Trenches
At some points, the Allied and Turkish trenches were no more than a few metres apart.

VISITORS' CHECKLIST

Practical Information
Gallipoli National Park.
Open 8am–5pm daily (winter); 9am–6pm daily (summer).
"Çannakale Destanı Tanıtım Merkezi": **Open** 8:30am–6pm daily. **Tel** (0286) 814 11 28.
Mehmetcik Memorial: **Open** 9am–6pm daily.
ANZAC Day (24–25 Apr).

Transport
from Çanakkale to Eceabat.
from Bursa and Istanbul.

★ Chunuk Bair
Various monuments honour the 28,000 men who died here on 6–9 August 1915.

★ Mehmetcik Memorial
This memorial was unveiled in 1985. Atatürk's eulogy unites the fallen sons of Turkey (Mehmetcik) with the Allied dead ("Johnnies").

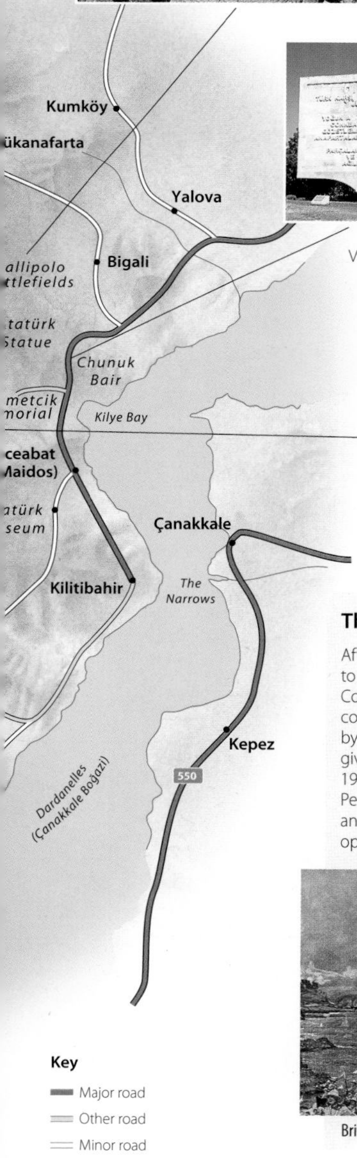

Kumköy
ükanafarta
Yalova
allipolo ttlefields
Bigali
tatürk Statue
Chunuk Bair
metcik morial
Kilye Bay
ceabat Maidos)
atürk seum
Çanakkale
Kilitibahir
The Narrows
Kepez
550
Dardanelles (Çanakkale Boğazi)

Key
Major road
Other road
Minor road

The Gallipoli Campaign 1915–16

After the start of World War I, Allied leaders developed a plan to seize the Dardanelles. This would give them control of Constantinople and diminish the threat of Russia gaining control of the strategic waterway. A naval assault was repulsed by Turkish shore batteries and minefields, so the order was given to land troops to secure the straits. At dawn on 25 April 1915, British and French troops landed at the tip of the Gallipoli Peninsula. Further north, a large force of ANZACs (Australia and New Zealand Army Corps) came ashore but met dogged opposition from the Turkish defenders. A second landing at Suvla Bay failed to win any new ground. Many soldiers died from disease, drowning or the appalling conditions of trench warfare. After nine months, the Allied force withdrew.

British troops landing under fire at Cape Helles

For additional map symbols *see back flap*

THE AEGEAN

Discovering the Aegean region of Turkey takes visitors on a panoramic, classical journey, from Çanakkale on the Dardanelles (the ancient Hellespont) to the finger of land off Marmaris known as the Datça Peninsula. Together, the coast and hinterland tell a story spanning some 5,000 years of Greek and Roman history. This is where Homer's myths and heroes come to life.

Here, it is easy to imagine the sculpture classes at Aphrodisias, the busy streets of ancient Ephesus or a medical lecture at the famous Asclepium at Pergamum (Bergama).

Most of modern-day Turkey was once part of the eastern Roman empire, known as Asia Minor. Many of the remote classical sites in the Aegean region formed part of ancient Caria, an independent kingdom whose boundaries roughly corresponded to the Turkish province of Muğla. Caria's origins are disputed, but its resistance to Hellenization is well documented. The Carians prospered under Roman rule but retained some autonomy, with their sanctuary at Labranda, and Zeus as their deity. The Carian symbol, a double-headed axe, was inscribed on many buildings as a defiant trademark. The Mausoleum at Halicarnassus (modern-day Bodrum), built as the tomb of the Carian king Mausolus, was one of the Seven Wonders of the Ancient World.

The Aegean region contains many Christian sights. The Seven Churches of the Apocalypse, mentioned in the Book of Revelation, surround İzmir; the last resting place of the Virgin Mary is just outside Ephesus; St John's Basilica is in Selçuk and the castle of the Knights of St John still guards the harbour at Bodrum.

The Aegean's original tourist resorts, such as Kuşadası, Marmaris and Bodrum, have now matured, and offer superb facilities and sophisticated nightlife. Bodrum's Halikarnas disco has an international reputation, and Kuşadası is known for its shopping.

Roman arched gateway at the ruined city of Hierapolis, near Denizli

◀ Beautiful sandy beaches and azure sea along the coastline at Ayvalık

Exploring the Aegean

Around 26 million people – roughly a third of Turkey's population – inhabit the Aegean region. Here, incomes are generally higher and the lifestyle more westernized than elsewhere in the country. Tourists are attracted to this area for its beaches, nightlife and yachting, but there are many other worthwhile sights from the green and fertile Menderes River Valley to the Roman city of Ephesus near Selçuk. Visitors can explore the countryside in day trips from Marmaris to Knidos on the scenic Datça Peninsula. The Carian trail also links many beautiful sites between Lake Bafa and the tip of Datça Peninsula.

Sights at a Glance

1. Çanakkale
2. Troy
3. Behram Kale (Assos)
4. Ayvalık
5. *Bergama (Pergamum) pp180–81*
6. Foça
7. *İzmir pp182–3*
8. Çeşme
9. Selçuk
10. *Ephesus pp186–7*
11. Kuşadası
12. Aydın
13. Menderes River Valley
14. *Hierapolis pp190–91*
15. *Aphrodisias pp192–3*
16. Denizli
17. Priene
18. Miletus
19. Didyma
20. Lake Bafa
21. Altınkum
22. Labranda
23. Milas (Mylasa)
24. Güllük
25. *Bodrum pp198–201*
27. *Marmaris pp204–5*

Tours

26. *Bodrum Peninsula Tour pp202–3*
28. *Datça Peninsula Tour pp206–7*

Temple of Trajan, Bergama (Pergamum)

For additional map symbols *see back flap*

Getting Around

The Aegean region is well served by good roads and public transport. *Dolmuşes* ply the routes to the smaller towns and villages. İzmir and Bodrum both have airports with frequent connections to Istanbul. İzmir is also served by rail, with connections to the city's Adnan Menderes Airport. Ferry services link İzmir, Marmaris and Bodrum with ports in Greece.

Pamukkale's travertine terraces, near Hierapolis

Key

- Motorway
- Dual carriageway
- Major road
- Minor road
- Scenic route
- Main railway
- Minor railway

Bodrum's marina and Castle of St Peter

Çanakkale, a historic crossing point between Asia and Europe

❶ Çanakkale

214,000. from Eceabat or Kilitbahir. Atatürk Cad. İskele Meydanı 67, (0286) 217 11 87. Fri. Navy Days (13–18 Mar), ANZAC Days (24–25 Apr), Sardine Festival (30–31 Jul – Gelibolu).

Çanakkale occupies the narrowest point of the straits called the Dardanelles, which are 1,200 m (3,937 ft) wide at this point. In 450 BC, the Persian King Xerxes built a bridge of boats here to land his troops in Thrace, and the final battles of the Peloponnesian War took place in these waters around 400 BC.

During his campaign to take Constantinople in 1453, Mehmet II (the Conqueror) built two fortresses to secure the straits: Kilitbahir (on the European side) and Çimenlik (in Çanakkale harbour). Today, ferry services link Çanakkale with Kilitbahir and Eceabat on the other side.

Çanakkale makes the most convenient base for tours of the Gallipoli battlefields *(see pp172–3)* across the straits.

The town has an attractive harbour, a naval museum and a colossal wooden horse that stands on the town's waterfront. Çanakkale means "pottery castle" and the town was once a centre for the production of high-quality kaolin for a flourishing ceramics industry. Today this type of clay is imported, but the vitreous enamel ware *(see p364)* made in Çanakkale remains one of Turkey's top export earners.

Reconstruction of the Trojan Horse

Environs

A few kilometres south of the town is the **Archaeological Museum**, which is small but should not be missed.

Archaeological Museum
Arkeoloji Müzesi
Barbaros Mahallesi, Yüzüncü Yıl Cad.
Tel (0286) 217 23 71. **Open** 8am–5pm Tue–Sun.

❷ Troy

İskele Meydanı 67, Çanakkale, (0286) 217 11 87. from Çanakkale, then taxi. Troy Festival (based in Çanakkale but includes Troy and environs, 10–18 Aug).

Few areas of Turkey have been as thoroughly excavated as Troy (Truva in Turkish). Nine different strata have yielded pieces of a history that runs from around 4000 BC until about AD 300. Troy was the pivot of Homer's *Iliad* and was where the decade-long Trojan War (13th century BC) was fought.

The site is known as **Hisarlık**, or "castle kingdom" in Turkish. The stonework and walls are impressive. Visible today are a defence wall, two sanctuaries (probably dating from the 8th century BC), houses from various periods and a Roman theatre. The site called the Pillar House at the southern gate may have been the palace of King Priam.

The site is well marked with 12 information points and some ongoing excavations. The most visible attraction is a large wooden Trojan Horse, a reconstruction of the device used by the Greeks to deceive and ultimately vanquish the Trojans, and a universal symbol of treachery today. In August each year, Turkish school-children release a white dove from the Trojan Horse to celebrate peace.

Hisarlık
5 km (3 miles) from main E87 road. from Çanakkale every 30/40 minutes.
Open Apr–Oct: 9am–7pm daily; Nov–Mar: 9am–5pm daily.

Schliemann's Search for Ancient Troy

The German-born Heinrich Schliemann – regarded by many as an unscrupulous plunderer and by others as an archaeological pioneer – nurtured a lifelong ambition to discover Homer's Troy. In 1873, three years after starting excavations at Hisarlık, he stumbled upon what he claimed to be King Priam's hoard of gold and silver jewellery. The over-eager explorer damaged the site, but his valuable find demonstrated that Greek civilization started 1,000 years earlier than previously believed. Part of the hoard, which was on display in a Berlin museum, vanished after World War II. It reappeared in the Pushkin Museum in Russia in 1996. Its return, authenticity and origins are still controversial.

Heinrich Schliemann's wife, wearing "Priam's" jewellery

Humpbacked Ottoman bridge on the outskirts of Behram Kale

❸ Behram Kale (Assos)

3,000. to Ayvacık, 19 km (12 miles) N, then dolmuş. from Edremit or Çanakkale.

Nestled on the shores of the Gulf of Edremit and sheltered by the Greek island of Lesbos, 10 km (6 miles) offshore, it is easy to see why Assos enjoyed the reputation of being the most beautiful place in Asia Minor. Ancient **Assos** reached the pinnacle of its glory when Plato's protégé, Aristotle, founded a school of philosophy here in 340 BC. In the 2nd century BC, the town included not only the present citadel, with the remaining Doric columns of the Temple of Athena (built in the 6th century BC), but also the village of Behram Kale, 238 m (781 ft) below.

St Paul is reputed to have passed through Assos on his third biblical journey, and the town is referred to in the Acts of the Apostles. After the fall of the Byzantine empire, the town's commercial fortunes declined, but today this charming and cultured retreat attracts many artists and scholars, who leave the bustle of the city and find a source of inspiration here.

As you come into the town, note the fine Ottoman bridge dating from the 14th century. There is also a mosque and a fort from this time, all built by Sultan Murat I. Residents of Assos favour houses with archways and overhanging balconies, and there is bougainvillea everywhere.

Assos
Open Apr–Oct: 9am–7:30pm daily; Nov–Mar: 8am–5pm daily.

❹ Ayvalık

64,000. 1.5 km (1 mile) N of town centre. Opposite the yacht harbour, (0266) 312 21 22. Thu.

Ayvalık takes its name from *ayva*, the Turkish word for quince, but the fruit is only available in season (January and February). Of the many villages along the Aegean coast peopled by Greeks until 1923 *(see p62)*, Ayvalık is the one that has most retained the flavour of a bygone age. There are many stone houses, and the town's mosques betray their Greek Orthodox origins. A Greek church and a few Greek-speakers remain.

Ayvalık's appeal stems from its cobbled streets and leisurely lifestyle. The beach at Sarımsaklı and peninsula of Alibey (also known by its Greek name of Cunda) are within reach by road.

❺ Bergama (Pergamum)

See pp180–81.

❻ Foça

32,000. Atatürk Bulvarı 1 (entrance to Foça), (0232) 812 55 34. from İzmir to Foça turn off on main E87. from junction of E87. Tourism & Culture Festival (Aug–Sep).

Phocaea, ancient Foça, was probably settled around 1000 BC and was part of the Ionian League *(see p194)*. Around 500 BC the Phocaeans were famed as mariners, sending vessels powered by 50 oarsmen into the Aegean, Mediterranean and Black Sea. There is a small theatre dating from antiquity at the entrance to the town. Near the centre of town, you will find a stone tomb known as **Taş Küle**. There is also a restored Genoese **fortress**. But apart from a few *hamams* (Turkish baths), this is the extent of Old Foça.

Environs
23 km (14 miles) up the coast is the town of Yenifoça (New Foça), with good campsites and beaches. The military presence in the area may have helped keep it off the tourist trail. Apart from summer weekends and holidays, it is an ideal place to escape the crowds. The area is known for its monk seal conservation programme, but they are seldom seen.

Boats, old houses and up-market cafés in Foça's harbour

❺ Bergama (Pergamum)

Perched on a hilltop above the modern town of Bergama, the great acropolis of Pergamum is one of the most dramatic sights in Turkey. Originally settled by the Aeolian Greeks in the 8th century BC, it was ruled for a time by one of Alexander the Great's generals. The city prospered under the Pergamene dynasty founded by Eumenes I, who ruled from 263 to 241 BC, when this was one of the ancient world's main centres of learning. The last ruler of this dynasty, Attalus III, bequeathed the kingdom to Rome in 133 BC, and Pergamum became capital of the Roman province of Asia. The great physician Galen was born here in AD 129, and established a famous medical centre, the Asclepieum, which is situated on a low hill around 8 km (5 miles) from the Acropolis of Pergamum.

★ Temple of Trajan
Built of white marble, it was completed during Hadrian II's reign (AD 125–138).

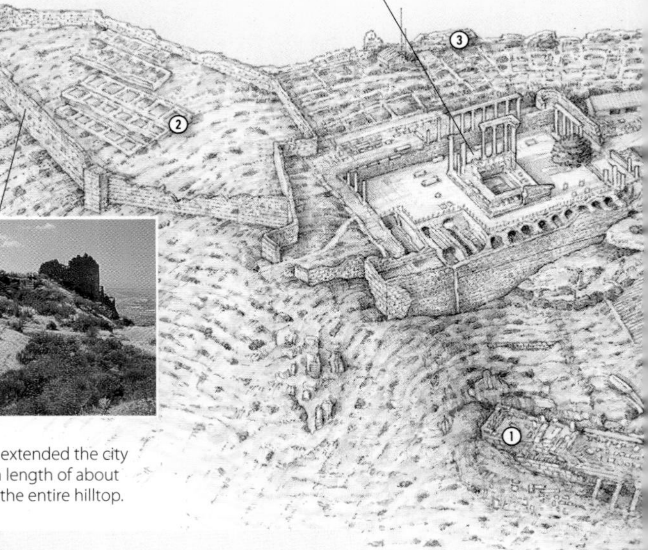

③

②

①

City Walls
Eumenes II (197–159 BC) extended the city walls until they reached a length of about 4 km (3 miles), enclosing the entire hilltop.

Plan of Pergamum

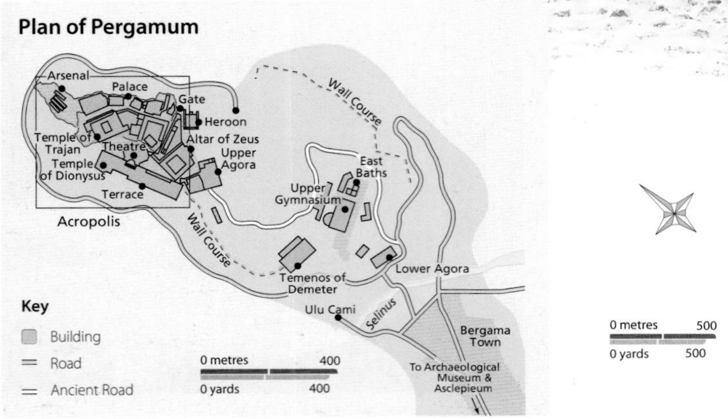

Arsenal
Palace
Gate
Heroon
Temple of Trajan
Theatre
Altar of Zeus
Upper Agora
Temple of Dionysus
Terrace
Acropolis
Wall Course
Wall Course
East Baths
Upper Gymnasium
Temenos of Demeter
Lower Agora
Ulu Cami
Selinus
Bergama Town
To Archaeological Museum & Asclepieum

Key
Building
Road
Ancient Road

0 metres 400
0 yards 400

0 metres 500
0 yards 500

For hotels and restaurants in this area see pp333–5 and pp351–4

VISITORS' CHECKLIST

Practical Information
Pergamum: **Tel** (0232) 483 51 17.
Open Apr–Oct: 8am–7pm daily (to 5pm Nov–Mar).
Asclepieum: **Tel** (0232) 483 51 17.
Open Apr–Oct: 8:30am–7pm daily; Nov–Mar: 8am–5pm daily.

Transport
from İzmir.

Library Ruins
Reputedly containing 200,000 parchment scrolls, many works from Pergamum went to its rival library in Alexandria as part of Mark Anthony's wedding gift to Cleopatra in 41 BC.

★ Altar of Zeus
One of Pergamum's largest temples, the first stone reliefs of the building were found in the 1870s. The altar was rebuilt in Berlin's Pergamum Museum.

KEY

① **Temple of Dionysus**

② **Arsenal**

③ **King's Palace**

④ **Temple of Athena**

⑤ **The Heroon** was a shrine built to honour the kings of Pergamum.

⑥ **The Upper Agora** (marketplace) lay immediately below the Altar of Zeus. From here, a ramp led up to to the main city gate.

⑦ **Theatre Terrace**

★ Theatre
Constructed in the 3rd century BC, the theatre has 80 rows of seats and an estimated capacity of 10,000. The seats were constructed of andesite, and the royal box in the lower section is made of marble.

7 İzmir

The most western-leaning of Turkish cities, İzmir's position at the head of the Gulf of İzmir (İzmir Körfezi) has given it a trading edge that has lasted from the 3rd century AD to today. For centuries, it was known as Smyrna, a name possibly derived from the myrrh trees that grow here. The city's origins are believed to date from 8500 BC, based on finds from the Teşılova Mound. Until 1922, the city had a large Christian population, including thousands of Greek Orthodox, most of whom fled during the turmoil of the War of Independence *(see p61)*. As Turkey's third largest city and the regional headquarters of NATO, İzmir has a multicultural sophistication.

The Governor's Palace, in the centre of the city

Exploring İzmir

İzmir's broad boulevards are balanced by leafy pedestrian precincts. Buses, ferries and a metro make it easy to get around. Horse-drawn carriages also offer a more traditional way to get around the city. Be sure to explore the old wharf area (İskele), now restored as a stylish shipping pier.

Archaeology Museum

Halil Paşa Cad, Bahri Baba Park İçı. **Tel** (0232) 483 51 17. **Open** Apr–Oct: 9am–7pm; Nov–Mar: 8am–5pm. with permission.

The main displays consist of artifacts from the Teşılova Mound, which was settled from about 3000 to 300 BC. The Byzantine glassware is especially eye-catching, but the highlight is the Treasury *(Hazine)*. It is kept locked and the guard may need to be summoned, but the gold jewellery dating from the 6th to the 3rd centuries BC offers ample proof of ancient artistic talent. The Roman and Byzantine imperial silver and gold coins are well displayed.

Ethnographic Museum

Next to the Archaeology Museum. **Open** 8:30am–4:30pm Tue–Sun.

Housed in a former French hospital, built in 1831, the museum highlights local crafts and skills – from quilting and felt-making to weapons and woodblock printing. Bridal costumes, glassware, an oven used to fire blue beads *(mavi boncuk)* and a replica of İzmir's first apothecary shop. The museum remains open during renovation work.

Konak Clock Tower

Saat Kulesi

Konak Square. any bus marked "Konak".

Built in 1901, the clock tower is the symbol of İzmir. It was one of 58 built in Ottoman times to encourage Turks to adopt European timekeeping habits. İzmir's is one of the finest of these monuments. Its ornate decorative style offers a strong contrast to the exquisite simplicity of the tiny Konak Mosque (Konak Camii) that nestles beside it.

The Konak mosque, adorned with ceramic tiles from Kütahya

Kızlarağası Han

Look for signs off the N end of Fevzi Paşa Cad. **Open** 8am–9pm Mon–Sat.

This typical Ottoman trading complex *(see pp28–9)* has been restored, with the courtyard turned into a café. There are craft and furniture restoration workshops on the upper floor. This is a good place to purchase handicrafts and copper.

St Polycarp Church

Necatibey Sok 2. **Tel** (0232) 484 84 36. **Open** to groups only, 9am–noon & 3–5pm daily.

The patron saint of İzmir, St Polycarp was a Christian martyr who gave us the adage, "The spirit indeed is willing, but the flesh is weak." This is the oldest Roman Catholic church in İzmir and the seat of the Catholic archbishop. Permission to build a chapel to St Polycarp was granted in 1620 by Süleyman the Magnificent *(see p60)*. To the right of the altarpiece is a self-portrait of Raymond Peré, designer of the Konak Clock Tower.

For hotels and restaurants in this area see pp333–5 and pp351–4

Corinthian columns in the Agora, the city market in Roman times

Agora

Tel (0232) 483 46 96.
Open Apr–Oct: 9am–7pm; Nov–Mar: 8am–5pm.

The present remains of the Agora, the central market of the Roman city of Smyrna, date from about the 2nd century AD, when it was rebuilt by the Emperor Marcus Aurelius following an earthquake in AD 178. There are several Corinthian columns with well-preserved capitols still standing, and enough arches, as well as part of a basilica (city hall), to give the flavour of a Roman town. It was used until the Byzantine period.

Velvet Castle

Kadifekale
from Konak Clock Tower marked "Kale", then on foot.

Also known as Mount Pagos, the Velvet Castle was built on Hellenistic foundations. Originally it had 40 towers, with numerous additions made by the Romans, Genoese and Ottomans over the centuries.

The castle is a good spot for an afternoon's outing, and offers unsurpassed vistas over İzmir Bay.

VISITORS' CHECKLIST

Practical Information
4,100,000. Akdeniz Mah 1344 Sok No 2, Pasaport İzmir, (0232) 483 51 17. Liberation Day (9 Sep), International Arts Festival (10 Jun–10 Jul).
izmirturizm.gov.tr

Transport
Alsancak. Basmane, Eyül Meydanı 9; Alsancak, Ziya Gökalp Bulvarı, (0232) 464 77 95. Adnan Menderes, 12 km (8 miles) SE of city centre, (0232) 274 26 26. 8 km (5 miles) NE of city centre, (0232) 472 10 10.

Dario Moreno Street, with the Asansör in the background

Asansör

Open 7am–late.
Tel (0232) 261 26 26 (restaurant).

The Asansör is a working 19th-century elevator in the Karataş district. From its roof-top restaurant, there are fine views over the city.

Leafy Dario Moreno Street (Dario Moreno Sokaği) lies in a restored section of İzmir's old Jewish quarter. The street is named after a 1960s singer who was fond of the city.

Sights at a Glance

1. Archaeology Museum
2. Ethnographic Museum
3. Konak Clock Tower
4. Kızlarağası Han
5. St Polycarp Church
6. Agora
7. Velvet Castle

The Velvet Castle (Kadifekale), İzmir's ancient citadel

8 Çeşme

39,000. from Chios. 1 km (0.5 mile) S of ferry dock. D for local sights. İskele Meydani 8, (0232) 712 66 53. Wed and Sun; Sat (Alaçatı). İzmir International Arts Festival (10 Jun–10 Jul).

The town's main feature is the 14th-century Genoese Castle of St Peter, a powerful symbol of Italian Renaissance mercantilism. Sultan Beyazıt II (1481–1512) fortified the castle to counter attacks by both pirates and the Knights of St John, who operated from bases on the island of Rhodes and at Bodrum *(see pp200–1)*. The castle contains a **museum** with nautical exhibits. The hotel next to the harbour was formerly a *kervansaray (see pp28–9)*.

Unlike other more popular resorts, Çeşme is dedicated to promenading, yachting and the simpler pleasures of life. There are several fine restaurants, and the cosmopolitan, tolerant atmosphere attracts world-class performers, who come here for the month-long İzmir International Arts Festival.

The long peninsula around Çeşme is serviced by a fast, six-lane highway from İzmir. However, you can still take the old road, stopping at beaches in Ilıca or spending an afternoon at Alaçatı, the kite- and windsurfing capital of Turkey, where wind energy supplies a quarter of the town's power requirements.

Museum
Çeşme Castle. **Open** 9am–noon & 1–5:30pm Tue–Sun.

Çeşme waterfront, with the Castle of St Peter above the town

9 Selçuk

35,000. from İzmir or Denizli. Atatürk Cad. Agora Çarşısı 35 (0232) 892 63 28. **selcuk.gov.tr.** Sat. Camel Wrestling (3rd and 4th week in Jan).

Visitors often bypass Selçuk on their way to Ephesus, but it deserves a stopover. The town is dominated by a 6th-century Byzantine citadel (Ayasoluk Hill) with 15 well-preserved towers. Nearby are the remains of a Byzantine church and a Seljuk mosque. You enter the citadel through a Byzantine gate. At the foot of the hill is the Basilica of St John, built by the Emperor Justinian *(see pp54–5)* in the 6th century on the site of an earlier shrine. It is believed to contain the tomb of St John the Evangelist, who spent his later years at Ephesus during the 1st century. Restoration has brought back some of the basilica's former glory, and there are some fine frescoes in the chapel.

The **Ephesus Museum** is one of Turkey's best. Marble and bronze statues and frescoes are beautifully displayed, and exhibits include a sculpture of Artemis, jewels and numerous artifacts thought to have come from the nearby Artemision, the ancient Temple of Artemis (one of the Seven Wonders of the Ancient World). Today, the waterlogged ruins of the Artemision are home to storks, who nest on the columns.

The İsa Bey Mosque, an ornate 14th-century Seljuk mosque, is located near the museum. It is not always open to visitors but the exterior calligraphy and inlaid tilework are worth a visit.

Ephesus Museum
Behind Tourism Information Office. **Tel** (0232) 892 60 10. **Open** 8:30am–noon & 12:30–5pm daily.

Environs

The former Greek village of Şirince, 8 km (5 miles) east of Selçuk, is set in verdant hills, but it can get very busy with coach tours.

At Çamlık is the **Open-Air Steam Train Exhibition**, a museum run by Turkish State Railways. There are more than 24 steam locomotives and other railway vehicles on display at the site.

Open-Air Steam Train Exhibition
Çamlık, 12 km (7 miles) S of Selçuk on the E87.

Byzantine gateway in Selçuk, at the foot of Ayasoluk Hill

10 Ephesus

See pp186–7.

⓫ Kuşadası

50,000. from Samos (Apr–Oct). from Selçuk, Söke and İzmir. 1 km (0.5 mile) S of town centre on Söke road. Liman Cad 13, (0256) 614 11 03. Wed.

Kuşadası is a frequent port of call for luxury cruise liners. It has a lively restaurant and nightlife scene in the summer months.

The town's name, meaning "bird island", is taken from an islet, known as Pigeon Island, tacked onto the mainland by a causeway. A 14th-century Genoese fort reveals the town's commercial origins.

Environs

Dilek Peninsula National Park protects the last of Turkey's wild horses and rare Anatolian cheetahs. The military presence has ensured that the area has been left undisturbed. Hike to the summit of Samsun Dağı (ancient Mount Mycale) for fine views of the peninsula.

Dilek Peninsula National Park
Dilek Yarımadası Milli Parkı 18 km (11 miles) W of Söke. from Kuşadası or Söke. **Tel** (0256) 646 10 79. **Open** 8am–6pm daily. extra for vehicles.

Camel wrestling, a popular event in Aydın

⓬ Aydın

195,000. 700 m (0.5 mile) S of town centre. from İzmir and Denizli. Adnan Menderes Mah-Denizli Bul 2, (0256) 211 28 42. Tue. Camel Wrestling (Sep–Mar), Fig Festival (1st week in Sep), Chestnut Festival (Dec).

Known in Roman times as Tralles, Aydın's tranquil appearance stems from long periods of prosperity. It was known variously as Caesarea and Güzelhisar before falling under Ottoman rule in the late 14th century. Frequent earthquakes have meant that there are few ruins to be seen, and the region is still subject to tremors.

The region is famous for its figs *(incir)*, black olives, cereals and cotton, and Aydın is a leading exporter of snails and salmon. In the 1920s, Atatürk *(see p62)* targeted the region as the focus of a new state-owned cotton industry. Today, raw cotton and ready-to-wear clothing remain Turkey's biggest export commodities.

Suffering badly in the War of Independence *(see p62)*, nowadays Aydın is more peaceful, with a **museum** and several distinctive mosques.

Museum
Next to the Forum shopping centre. **Tel** (0256) 225 22 59. **Open** 9am–noon, 1:30–5pm Tue–Sun.

⓭ Menderes River Valley

One of Turkey's main grain-growing regions, and a major producer of fruit and cotton, the Menderes Valley is made up of the Büyük Menderes (Great Meander) and Küçük Menderes (Lesser Meander) rivers, with a wide alluvial plain in between. The S-shaped bends formed by the slow-moving Büyük Menderes below Aydın have given us the word "meander".

Nysa, a Seleucid foundation dating from around 280 BC, presents a lovely sight as you approach from Sultanhisar (just to the south). There is a theatre overlooking a tributary of the Büyük Menderes, and a gymnasium, library, agora and council house. The whole city is built in and over a ravine (although the bridge is in poor condition). Its claim to fame was as a sanctuary to Pluto, god of the underworld.

At **Tire**, north of Aydın, lie the remains of a number of *kervansarays (see pp28–9)* dating from the 14th and 15th centuries. In the wake of the capture of Constantinople in 1453, Mehmet II *(see p58)* ordered the removal of the inhabitants of Tire, as part of the effort to repopulate the capital. There is a dramatic domed bazaar building here and a lively bazaar is still held each week on Tuesdays.

The yacht marina at Kuşadası, one of the largest on the Aegean coast

⑩ Ephesus

Ephesus is one of the greatest ruined cities in the Western world. A Greek city was first built here in about 1000 BC and it soon rose to fame as a centre for the worship of Cybele, the Anatolian Mother Goddess. The city we see today was founded in the 4th century BC by Alexander the Great's successor, Lysimachus. But it was under the Romans that Ephesus became the chief port on the Aegean. Most of the surviving structures date from this period. As the harbour silted up the city declined, but played an important role in the spread of Christianity. Two great Councils of the early Church were held here in AD 431 and 449. It is said that the Virgin Mary spent her last days nearby and that St John the Evangelist came from the island of Patmos to look after her.

Terraced Houses
The murals and fine interior decor of the houses opposite the Temple of Hadrian suggest the occupants were wealthy.

★ Library of Celsus
Built in AD 114–117 by Consul Gaius Julius Aquila for his father, the library was damaged first by the Goths and then by an earthquake in 1000. The statues occupying the niches in front are Sophia (wisdom), Arete (virtue), Ennoia (intellect) and Episteme (knowledge).

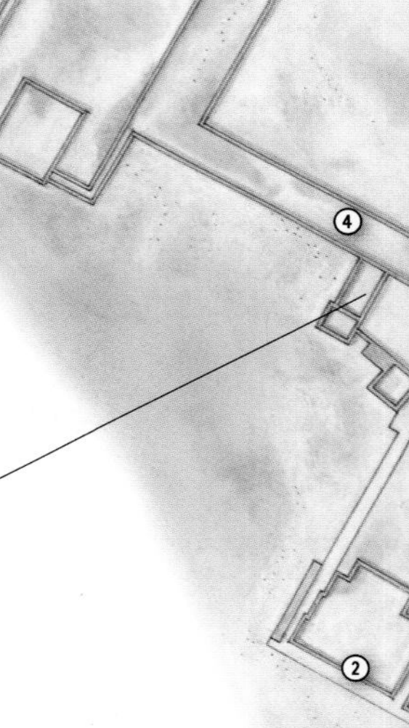

0 metres 200
0 yards 200

The House of Mary

According to the Bible, the crucified Jesus asked St John the Evangelist to look after his mother, Mary. John brought Mary with him to Ephesus in AD 37, and she spent the last years of her life here in a modest stone house. The house of the Blessed Virgin is located at Meryemana, 6 km (4 miles) from the centre of Ephesus. The shrine, known as the Meryemana Kultur Parkı, is revered by both Christians and Muslims, and pilgrims of both faiths visit the shrine, especially on 15 August every year.

The house of the Blessed Virgin

For hotels and restaurants in this area see pp333–5 and pp351–4

★ Theatre
Carved into the flank of Mount Pion during the Hellenistic period, the theatre was later renovated by the Romans.

VISITORS' CHECKLIST

Practical Information
3 km (2 miles) W of Selçuk, on Efes Müzesi Uğur Mumcu Sevgi Yolu. **Tel** (0232) 892 60 11 (museum). Selçuk tourist office, (0232) 892 69 45.
Open Apr–Oct: 8:30am–7pm; Nov–Mar: 8am–5pm.

Transport
D from Selçuk.

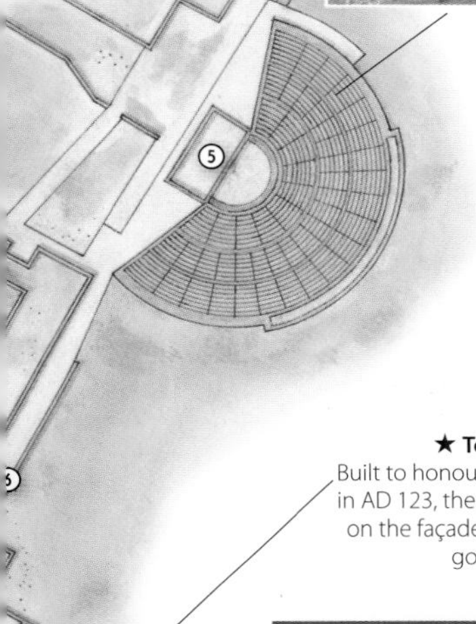

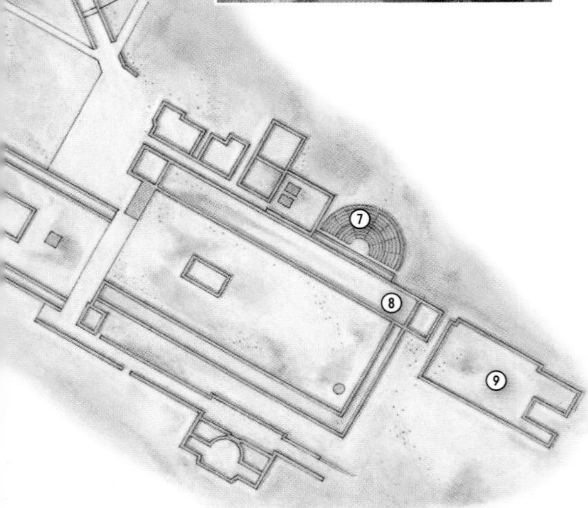

★ Temple of Hadrian
Built to honour a visit by Hadrian in AD 123, the relief marble work on the façade portrays mythical gods and goddesses.

Gate of Hercules
The gate at the entrance to Curetes Street takes its name from two reliefs showing Hercules draped in a lion skin. Originally a two-storey structure, and believed to date from the 4th century AD, it had a large central arch with winged victories on the upper corners of the archway. Curetes Street was lined by statues of civic notables.

KEY

① **Temple of Domitian**

② **Private houses** featured murals and mosaics.

③ **The brothel** was adorned with a statue of Priapus, the Greek god of fertility.

④ **The Commercial Agora** was the main marketplace of the city.

⑤ **The *skene*** (stage building) featured elaborate ornamentation.

⑥ **Marble Street** was paved with blocks of marble.

⑦ **The Odeon** (meeting hall) was built in AD 150.

⑧ **Colonnaded Street** Lined with Ionic and Corinthian columns, the street runs from the Baths of Varius to the Temple of Domitian.

⑨ **Baths of Varius**

Spectacular travertine pools at Pamukkale ▶

⓮ Hierapolis

In Hellenistic times, the thermal springs at Hierapolis made the city a popular spa. Today, the ruins of Hierapolis still draw visitors, who come to swim in its mineral-rich pools and to see the startling white travertine terraces of nearby Pamukkale. Founded by Eumenes II, king of Pergamum *(see pp180–81)*, the city was noted for its textiles, particularly wool. Hierapolis was ceded to Rome in 133 BC along with the rest of the Pergamene kingdom. The city was destroyed by an earthquake in AD 60, and was rebuilt and reached its peak in AD 196–215. Hierapolis fell into decline in the 6th century, and the site became partially submerged by water and deposits of travertine.

★ Arch of Domitian
The main thoroughfare of Hierapolis was a wide, colonnaded street called the Plateia, which ran from the Arch of Domitian to the south gate.

Ancient Pool
The popular bathing pool, littered with fragments of marble columns, may be the remains of a sacred pool associated with the Temple of Apollo.

8
7
6
5
4
3
2
1

Pamukkale

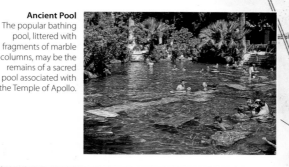

The spectacular white travertine terraces at Pamukkale, next to Hierapolis, have long been one of Turkey's most popular (and photographed) sights. The terraces form when water from the hot springs loses carbon dioxide as it flows down the slopes, leaving deposits of limestone. The layers of white calcium carbonate, built up in steps on the plateau, have earned the name of Pamukkale (cotton castle). To protect them from damage, the terraces are now off-limits to visitors.

Travertine terraces, Pamukkale

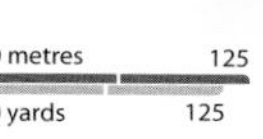

For hotels and restaurants in this area see pp333–5 and pp351–4

Necropolis
The largest ancient graveyard in Anatolia, with more than 1,200 tombs, the necropolis (one of two at Hierapolis) contains tumuli, sarcophagi and house-shaped tombs from the Roman, Hellenistic and early Christian periods.

VISITORS' CHECKLIST

Practical Information
19 km (12 miles) N of Denizli.
Tel (0258) 272 20 77.
Open Apr–Oct: 9am–7pm daily; Nov–Mar: 8am–5pm daily.
additional fee for parking.
Pamukkale Festival (music and folklore performances, late May/early Jun).
W pamukkale.gov.tr

Transport
from İzmir, get off at Denizli.
D from Denizli.

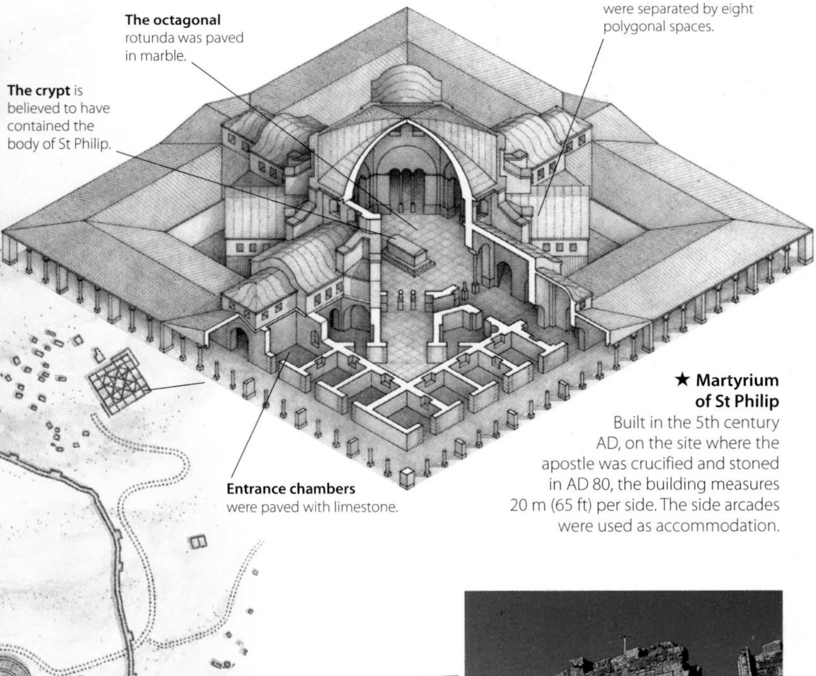

The octagonal rotunda was paved in marble.

The crypt is believed to have contained the body of St Philip.

Eight-sided chambers were separated by eight polygonal spaces.

Entrance chambers were paved with limestone.

★ Martyrium of St Philip
Built in the 5th century AD, on the site where the apostle was crucified and stoned in AD 80, the building measures 20 m (65 ft) per side. The side arcades were used as accommodation.

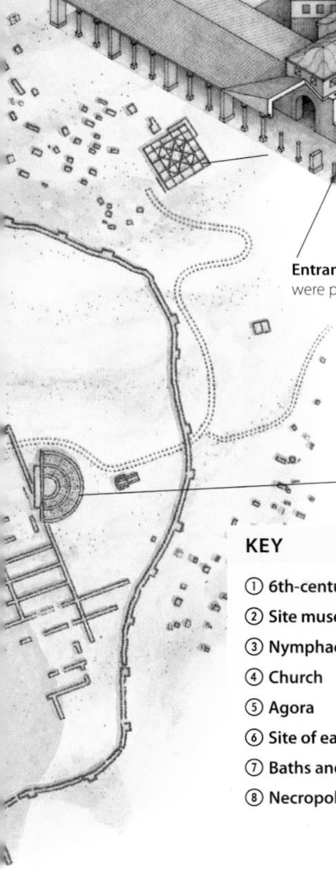

KEY

① 6th-century basilica
② Site museum in Roman baths
③ Nymphaeum
④ Church
⑤ Agora
⑥ Site of early theatre
⑦ Baths and church
⑧ Necropolis

★ Theatre
The well-preserved theatre, built in 200 BC, could seat 20,000. However only 30 rows of seats have survived. Shown here is the *skene*, or stage building.

⓯ Aphrodisias

The site of Aphrodisias was a shrine as early as 5800 BC, when Neolithic farmers came here to worship the Mother Goddess of fertility and crops. At some point, the site was dedicated to Aphrodite, goddess of love, and was given the name Aphrodisias during the 2nd century BC. For centuries it remained little more than a shrine, but when the Romans defeated the Pontic ruler Mithridates *(see p52)* in 74 BC, Aphrodisias was rewarded for its loyalty and prospered as a cultural and artistic hub known for its exquisite marble sculptures. During the Byzantine era, the Temple of Aphrodite became a Christian basilica. Gradually, the city faded into obscurity, later becoming the Turkish village of Geyre.

★ Stadium
The stadium is one of the best-preserved structures of its kind from the classical era.

★ Temple of Aphrodite
Fourteen columns of the temple have been re-erected. The lateral colonnades shown here became the nave of the Christian basilica.

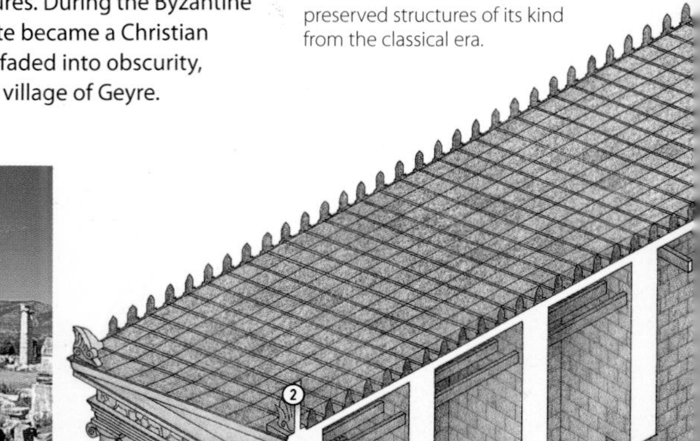

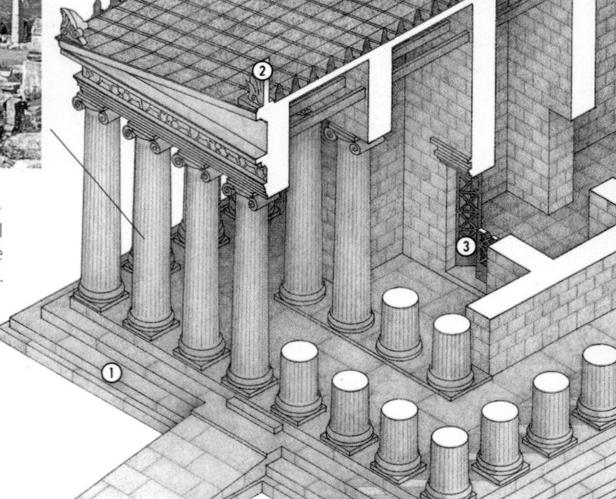

KEY

① **The stepped platform** was built on a stone foundation.

② **Gable ends** were surmounted by statues, called *akroteria*.

③ **The west cella** was used as a treasury.

④ **The cult statue** of Aphrodite stood in the cella.

⑤ **Fluted columns** were constructed from marble drums that were quarried nearby.

Theatre
Completed in 27 BC, structural changes were made in AD 200 to make it suitable for gladiatorial spectacles.

★ Tetrapylon
One of the jewels of Aphrodisias, this 2nd-century gateway was reconstructed with four groups of Corinthian columns.

VISITORS' CHECKLIST

Practical Information
Between Aydın and Denizli, 40 km (24 miles) S of E87 highway to Geyre. **Tel** (0256) 448 80 86 (museum). **Open** 8am–7pm daily (to 5pm Nov–Mar).

Sculptures
Works produced by the city's famous school of sculpture were exported as far afield as North Africa and Rome. Some are exhibited in the museum.

★ Temple of Aphrodite
Completed in the 1st century AD, the temple was the heart of Aphrodisias. It was later converted for Christian worship, with walls and colonnades dismantled and reused to enlarge and modify the building.

Plan of Aphrodisias

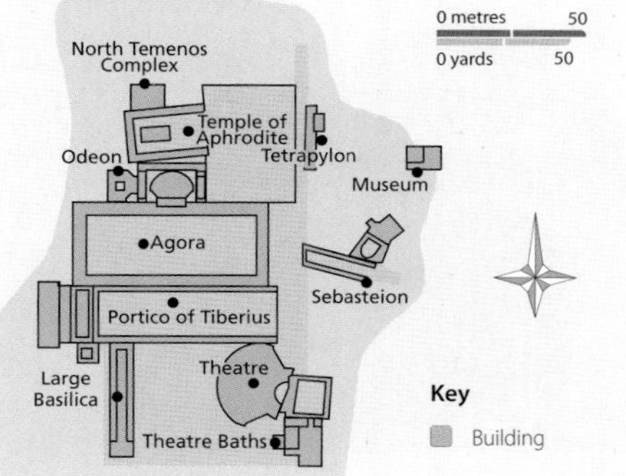

The Atatürk Ethnography Museum in Denizli

⓰ Denizli

275,000. 554/1 Sokak 5, (0258) 264 39 71.

Denizli is often thought of as a tourist backwater, but the town has little need to pander to visitors. It is a thriving agricultural centre, a centre for carpet production and one of Turkey's major textile towns, continuing a prosperous trade begun as far back as Roman times. Today, Aegean cotton fibres fetch more on world markets than many other spun cottons.

Denizli, literally translated as "with sea", takes its name from the many springs that feed the River Lycus. In pre-Roman times, another city linked with water, Hydrela, was located here. Denizli is a good base for touring the ancient sites of Hierapolis and Pamukkale *(see pp190–91)*, the latter being about 22 km (16 miles) away.

The town was conquered by the Seljuks in the 11th century and came under Ottoman rule in 1428. At some point in between, when Denizli was known as Ladik, it seems that the inhabitants of nearby Laodiceia moved here after their own city was ravaged by one of the many earthquakes that have marked this region.

The **Atatürk Ethnography Museum** has some interesting local folk art and decorative artifacts on display. Denizli's Great Mosque (Ulu Camii) is also worth a visit.

Atatürk Ethnography Museum
Kayalık Cad, Saraylar Mah 459 Sok 10. **Tel** (0258) 262 00 66. **Open** 8am–5pm Tue–Sun (to 7pm summer).

The Temple of Athena at Priene, a superb example of Ionian architecture

⑰ Priene

D from Söke or Milas to Güllübahçe. **Open** Apr–Oct: 9am–7pm daily; Nov–Mar: 8am–5pm daily.

The ancient city of Priene has a breathtaking setting between the Büyük Menderes River and Mount Mykale. Like Miletus and Ephesus *(see pp186–7)*, it was a member of the Ionian League, a group of 12 city-states believed to have been settled by Greek colonists before 1000 BC.

Laid out by the architect Hippodamos of Miletus in about 450 BC, Priene is in a good state of preservation. The Temple of Athena, built in the 4th century BC in honour of the city's patron goddess, is considered one of the great achievements of Ionian architecture. The work was supervised and financed by Alexander the Great *(see pp50–51)* when he occupied the city. Because of Priene's strong Greek ties, it was not viewed with favour by the Romans. Its importance declined and by Byzantine times it had been abandoned. This neglect has meant that Priene is one of the most intact Hellenistic settlements to be seen. The theatre, dating from the 3rd century BC, could seat 5,000 people. The *bouleuterion* (council chamber) could hold 640 delegates. There is also a stadium, complete with starting blocks for athletes, and sanctuaries to Demeter and Kore. The lower gymnasium walls are adorned with schoolboy graffiti from over 2,000 years ago.

⑱ Miletus

D from Söke or Milas. **Open** Apr–Oct: 9am–7pm daily; Nov–Mar: 8am–5pm daily. Directions: take the road that descends to Didyma, turn W at the village of Akköy, 7km (4 miles) from the main road.

Although less impressive than Priene, Miletus was more renowned for its art, politics and trade than many other Greek cities. Known as Milet today, it was once the principal port of the Ionian League, and flourished as a centre for art and industry. In Roman times it supplied wool and textile dyes to the wool trade in Ankara *(see pp244–5)*. One of its sons, the scientist and mathematician Thales – known as one of the Seven Sages of Antiquity – correctly forecast a total eclipse of the sun in 580 BC.

The Persians took control of the Ionian cities in the mid-6th century BC. Miletus led a revolt against Persian rule in 500–494 BC, but in 479 BC succumbed to the tyrannical Persian king, Darius. It was rebuilt by the Romans.

Of the surviving buildings, the finest is the 15,000-seat theatre, dating from AD 100. Over the centuries, Greeks, Romans and Byzantines all made alterations to the structure. The *bouleuterion* (council chamber) was built in 175–164 BC during the reign of the Seleucid king, Antiochus IV Ephiphanes. The well-preserved Baths of Faustina date from AD 43, and were named for the wife of Emperor Marcus Aurelius. The complex includes a *palaestra* (gymnasium), and there is a stadium nearby. The Baths of Faustina was a model for the development of the Turkish bath, or *hamam* *(see p81)*. It is also worth strolling around the

İlyas Bey Mosque, built in the 15th century at Miletus

stadium, nymphaeum (reservoir) and shrine of Apollo Delphinius (built in 500 BC).

Incongruously, a mosque reposes amid the ruins of ancient Miletus. The İlyas Bey (or Balat) Mosque was built in 1403 by İlyas Bey, emir (ruler) of the Beylik of Menteşe. It celebrated his return from exile at the court of the Mongol ruler Timur, also known as Tamerlane, after Timur's invasion of Anatolia in 1402. The mosque is built of brick and both white and coloured marble that was taken from Roman Miletus. There is splendidly detailed carving on the marble window grilles, screen and prayer niche *(mihrab)*, and the use of coloured marble on the façade is impressive. The dome measures 14 m (45 ft) in diameter and was the largest built during the Beylik period *(see p57)*. İlyas Bey died the year after the mosque was completed and is buried in the adjacent tomb (dated 1404). The mosque is a beautiful early forerunner of the Ottoman *külliye (see p36)*, a building style that flourished during the 16th century. The *külliye* combined social welfare and residential functions with facilities for Islamic worship.

The Temple of Apollo in Didyma, with its ornate carved columns

⓳ Didyma

from Söke or Milas to Yenihisar. from Bodrum twice a week in summer (check first). Kaymakamlık Binası, (0256) 811 37 25.
Open Apr–Oct: 9am–7pm daily; Nov–Mar: 8am–5pm daily.

The prime reason to visit Didyma (modern Didim) is for the Temple of Apollo, built in the 7th century BC to honour the god of prophecy and oracles. By 500 BC, the shrine at Didyma was one of the leading oracles of the Greek world. It even had a sacred spring. Branchid priests, who were reputedly connected to the great oracle at Delphi, were in charge of the shrine. Marble from nearby Lake Bafa *(see p196)* was used to build the temple. A carved relief of the head of Medusa, with its serpentine curls, has become almost synonymous with Didyma.

Head of Medusa, Didyma

The well below the Medusa head was the place where arriving pilgrims would purify themselves before approaching the oracle. It is now roped off to prevent accidents.

In its heyday, the Temple of Apollo featured 108 Ionic columns. Only three are still intact. However, the surviving stumps are still impressive.

The Temple of Apollo was destroyed by Persians in the mid-6th century BC, but was restored around 350 BC by Alexander the Great. With the coming of Christianity, the temple was converted into a church and Didyma became a bishopric. In 1493, an earthquake destroyed the temple and Didyma was abandoned. The Ottomans renamed it Yenihisar (new castle) in the 18th century.

The impressive theatre at Miletus, capable of seating 15,000 in Roman times

⑳ Lake Bafa

25 km (16 miles) W of Söke. via Söke or Milas.

Considered one of the most picturesque landscapes in Turkey, the Lake Bafa area is the setting for several classical gems, with the peaks of Mount Latmos as a backdrop. Rising to 1,500 m (4,915 ft), the mountain is aptly known as Beş Parmak (five fingers).

In ancient times, Lake Bafa was an arm of the sea. When silt eventually closed the gulf, the port of **Herakleia**, near the eastern shore of the lake, was left landlocked. The same process was responsible for the decline of Miletus and Priene *(see pp194–5)*. Lake Bafa is brackish and supports many species of fish.

Herakleia, also known as Herakleia-under-Latmos, occupies a dramatic setting at the lakeside. Its fortifications, towers and well-preserved Temple of Athena are tangible vestiges of its former status. A shrine to the shepherd-hero, Endymion, can be visited near the lake. Visitors can also hire a local guide to show them the difficult-to-reach monasteries high up the mountain and some of the prehistoric rock carvings in the area.

Herakleia
10 km (6 miles) from Camiçi (by car on track). from Lake Bafa.

Lake Bafa, an arm of the Aegean in ancient times

Environs

Euromos, located to the southeast of Lake Bafa, wholly deserves its reputation as having one of the best-preserved temples in Turkey. Euromos was, in fact, an amalgamation of several cities, including Herakleia, owing allegiance to Milas *(see p197)*. In time, rivalries emerged between them, and Euromos (meaning "strong" in Greek) turned out to be politically fickle. Like many cities of ancient Caria, it opted to ally itself with Rome and Rhodes, not Greece.

Euromos
12 km (7 miles) NW of Milas. from Selimiya to Milas. **Open** 8am–7pm (5pm in winter).

㉑ Altınkum

4 km (3 miles) S of Didyma. 2,300. via Priene and Miletus.

The protected sandy bay of Altınkum offers a relaxing spot to unwind, especially after a day spent tramping around classical ruins. Most day trips to Priene, Miletus and Didyma *(see pp194–5)* end up here. In fact, locals generally refer to the area as Didyma, or Didim (on bus schedules, for example). Like many idyllic retreats that have experienced rapid growth, Didyma's success has spilled over to nearby towns. Charter groups and tours flock to Altınkum and it can be very busy in summer. This was one of Turkey's original camping venues. As it grew, pensions opened, and Turkish families began to flock here for sun and sand. There is not much else here – for anything more, you will have to go to Yenihisar (ancient Didyma). Few people know how to enjoy themselves as much as Turks, and Altınkum finds them in full holiday mode.

The popular beach at Altınkum

㉒ Labranda

15 km (9 miles) N of Milas on unsurfaced track (by car, taxi, or on foot from Milas). **Open** 8:30am–5:30pm Wed–Mon.

Getting to Labranda is certainly worth the effort for those who persevere. This Carian sanctuary nestles high on the mountains above Milas, at an impressive elevation of 610 m (2,000 ft), giving good views of the surrounding area. From early times, it fell under the jurisdiction of Milas (Mylasa). The remains of the sacred way leading there are one of the sights to note.

Despite being damaged by several fires and earthquakes, the remains of a stadium have been uncovered by Swedish archaeologists. Baths and a fountain house (which may have been a water storage depot) date from about the 1st century BC and the area still boasts an abundant source of spring water. The most interesting buildings are three *androns* (banqueting halls), the second built by Mausolus *(see p198)*, who ruled from nearby Milas.

The chamber tombs and sarcophagi, although pillaged, are unusual and reveal much about ancient burial practices.

㉓ Milas (Mylasa)

129,000. 13 km (8 miles) SW of town, (0252) 523 01 01. Intercity buses to Bodrum. at airport, (0252) 523 00 66. Tue.

The origins of Milas are uncertain and the many theories are largely unsubstantiated. What is clear is that its most noteworthy and prosperous period was when it was capital of Caria and the administrative seat for the Persian satrap (subordinate ruler), Mausolus. Like most Carian cities, Milas was ruled in turn by the Persians, Alexander the Great, the Romans and the Byzantines before finally falling under Ottoman control in 1425.

Local carpet in Milas

The remains of the ancient city lie within the present town centre. The first thing you notice is the two-storey **Gümüşkesen** (silver money-bag) **Mausoleum**, a structure of uncertain age. The lower floor is the actual tomb, with an aperture in the roof to provide sustenance to the deceased. The town's most intact monument is the handsome Baltılı (Axe) Gate.

As an administrative seat, Milas issued regulatory decrees, notably concerning money. Inscriptions dating from the 3rd century AD list detailed regulations that ban illegal conversions from imperial (Roman) to local money and black-market money dealings.

Save some time for modern Milas, which has some charming timber houses with latticework shutters. The town is justly famed for its carpets, characterized by soft neutral and beige tones.

The Gümüşkesen Mausoleum, a Carian monument in Milas

Environs

Yatağan, site of a thermal power station and known for its environmental pollution, has little to offer, but two interesting sights are located in the area. **Stratonikeia** was founded in 295 BC. It was apparently named after the wife of Seleucas I, king of Syria. The ruins to be seen – an agora (marketplace), a rather unkempt Hellenistic theatre with seating for 10,000 and the Temple of Sarapis – are in the village of Eskihisar on the 330 road, south of the city.

The town's small museum houses mainly Roman finds but includes a Mycenaean mug from about 1000 BC.

Lagina is located northwest of Yatağan and is best known for its association with the cult of Hecate, the Greek goddess of darkness and sorcery. The gate of the temple precinct dates from between 125 and 80 BC. The Temple of Hecate would have stood here but the site has not yielded major finds.

Stratonikeia
20 km (12 miles) W of Milas. Own transport. on main Yatağan–Milas road. **Open** 8:30am–5:30pm daily.

Lagina
15 km (9 miles) N of Yatağan. Own transport essential. **Open** 8:30am–5:30pm daily.

㉔ Güllük

5,600. from Milas, 28 km (17 miles) SE of Güllük, then 8 km (5 miles) to town.

This is a lovely bay and harbour with a genuine nautical atmosphere and lots of accommodation. The real reason for coming to Güllük is to see the site of ancient **Iasus**, with its elaborate wall, 810 m (2,658 ft) long, built during the 5th century AD.

The fortunes of Iasus were tied to fishing. Bronze Age finds from here bear detailed inscriptions that have shed new light on the lifestyles of the ancients. Legends of boys frolicking with dolphins also originated here.

Almost opposite Güllük on the main 330 road is the site of Cindya. To the south is the ancient Barbylia (modern Varvil Bay), a town that grew wealthy by trading in salt.

Iasus
by boat from Güllük to Kıyıkışlacık. 18 km (11 miles) from main Milas road.

The large ruined theatre at Stratonikeia

25 Bodrum

Bodrum is the modern name for the ancient Dorian city of Halicarnassus, location of the famous Mausoleum built by Mausolus (375–353 BC), ruler of ancient Caria, who made the city his capital. The city walls, also built by Mausolus, were almost destroyed during Alexander the Great's siege in the 4th century BC. Herodotus, the father of written history, was born here in 484 BC, as was Dionysius, the great rhetoric teacher of the 1st century BC. Modern Bodrum was the first Turkish town to experience a tourist boom, its major sight being the 15th-century Castle of St Peter *(see pp200–201)*, now a museum of nautical archaeology.

The busy harbour at Bodrum, attracting cruising yachts of all sizes

Exploring Bodrum

Bodrum is subtly divided by the Castle of St Peter into a bustling, vehicle-free eastern sector with beaches and a quieter western hub which borders the yacht harbour. *Dolmuşes* make transport easy. Those marked "Şehir İçi" (inner city) stop at all major points. Boat trips to nearby beaches are also available from the harbour.

Halikarnas Club

Cumhuriyet Cad, No 178.
Open Apr–Sep. **Tel** (0252) 316 80 00.
W halikarnas.com.tr

Located at the water's edge with a view of the Castle of St Peter, open-air Halikarnas is one of the most famous clubs in Turkey and an emblem of hedonistic nightlife. With a capacity of 5,000, Halikarnas offers a spectacular laser light show and the best DJs. The open-air cabaret, revue and musical acts feature top performers. Smart dress is required.

Zeki Müren Museum

Zeki Müren Sanat Müzesi
Zeki Müren Cad 11. **Tel** (0252) 313 19 39. **Open** Apr–Oct: 9am–7pm daily; Nov–Mar: 8am–5pm daily.

Zeki Müren (1931–96) was one of Turkey's most accomplished and beloved singers and composers, with a career that spanned 45 years. He was fondly known as "The Sun of Art" and, although considered the Turkish Liberace, only the glitzy attire was comparable. Müren was a professional musician and actor, and his unpretentious home is preserved as a delightful museum. His extravagant costumes are in the limelight along with record albums, radiograms and other musical and personal memorabilia.

Rooms and furnishings seem to be anticipating his arrival, for example, the 1950s Cadillac reposing on the front lawn.

The museum is an inspiring memory to an outstanding Turkish cultural idol, who died in 1996 during a live performance. Thousands attended his funeral.

The famous open-air Halikarnas club

Bodrum Hamam

Cevat Şakir Cad, Fabrika Sok (opposite the bus station).
Open 6am–midnight daily.
Tel (0252) 313 41 29.
W bodrumhamami.com.tr.

Linked to the Çemberlitaş Baths in Istanbul, the Bodrum Hamam is housed in a lovely old stone building. Service is highly professional, emphasizing cleanliness and an authentic Turkish bath experience. Masseurs are well trained and you are bound to feel like a "new penny" when you exit. The owners claim a 500-year lineage. The *hamam* runs a shuttle that will collect and return you, suitably pampered.

Old Dockyard (Tersane) and Arsenal Point

W of the marina entrance at the end of Neyzen Tevfik Cad.
Open dawn to dusk.

The ancient dockyard on the end of Arsenal Point is part of the effort to restore Bodrum's walls. Its position, opposite the Castle of St Peter, overlooks the main harbour. The dockyard was built in the 18th century, when the Ottoman sultans made an attempt to revive the empire's naval strength. Attractions include a cistern, an Ottoman Tower on the west side of the harbour, a graveyard, fortification to protect the shipyard and a grand tomb built in 1729 to commemorate Cafer Paşa, who was a naval hero and prominent city patron.

The scant remains of the great Mausoleum

Mausoleum

Turgut Reis Cad (corner of Hamam Sok). **Open** Apr–Oct: 8am–7pm Tue–Sun; Nov–Mar: 8am–5pm Tue–Sun.

The colossal Mausoleum of Halicarnassus was one of the Seven Wonders of the Ancient World. Named for Mausolus, ruler of Caria, and intended as his tomb, work on the structure began in 355 BC and was completed by his widow, Artemisia, the only woman to rule Caria. It measured 41 m (134 ft) in height, with a podium, a colonnade of 36 columns and a pyramid, resplendently topped by a horse-drawn chariot statue.

The tomb stood for about 1,500 years but had fallen into ruin by 1402, when the Knights of St John arrived and used many of the stones to construct the Castle of St Peter.

As you enter, don't miss the authentic reconstruction models to the left.

Ancient Theatre

Kıbrıs Şehitler Cad (N of the Mausoleum). **Open** dawn to dusk.

Little remains of the ancient city of Halicarnassus, but the theatre on the south slopes of the Göktepe district is one of the more intact sites. Excavations began here in 1973 and restoration still goes on. Dating from the 4th century BC, the theatre consists of a stage building, an orchestra and rows of seating. It was probably used more for gladiatorial fights than for theatrical performances. The unusual balustrades in the orchestra may have been put there to protect spectators.

The Myndos Gate, the western portal of the city in ancient times

VISITORS' CHECKLIST

Practical Information

140,000. Barış Meydanı, (0252) 316 10 91. Tue (clothes), Thu & Fri (food & produce). Bodrum Yacht Week (3rd week in Oct); Bodrum International Ballet Festival (2nd half of Aug). **bodrum-info.org**

Transport

Milas, (0252) 536 65 65. Cevat Şakir Cad, (0252) 316 26 37.

Myndos Gate

Cafer Paşa Cad. **Open** dawn to dusk.

The Myndos Gate was the western exit from ancient Halicarnassus and originally featured two monumental towers made of andesite blocks. The gate and most of the city walls were demolished by Alexander the Great and his army in 334 BC. The structure was restored in 1998.

Bodrum City Centre

① Halikarnas Club
② Zeki Müren Museum
③ Bodrum Hamam
④ Castle of St Peter *(see pp200–1)*
⑤ Old Dockyard and Arsenal Point
⑥ Mausoleum
⑦ Ancient Theatre

0 metres 200
0 yards 200

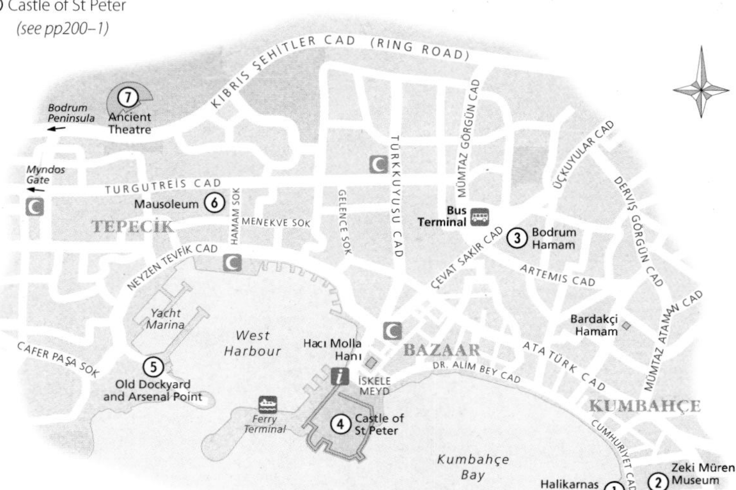

Castle of St Peter

Bodrum's most distinctive landmark is its castle, begun in 1406 by the Knights of St John *(see p231)*. Its five towers represented the languages of its formidable inhabitants. When Süleyman the Magnificent conquered Rhodes in 1523, both Bodrum and Rhodes came under Ottoman rule and the knights left for Malta. Neglected for centuries, the castle became a prison in 1895 and was damaged by shells from a French warship during World War I. In the early 1960s, it was used to store artifacts found by local sponge divers. This led to a fruitful Turkish-American partnership to restore the castle and put on display the spectacular undersea treasures found around Turkey. The innovative reconstructions of ancient shipwrecks and their cargoes have brought the museum international acclaim.

German Tower
This tower is on the walkway around the battlements.

★ Glass Shipwreck Hall
A steel frame supports the original timbers of a Fatimid-Byzantine ship thought to have sunk in 1025. The glass shards and ingots, among other finds, make this a time capsule of the era.

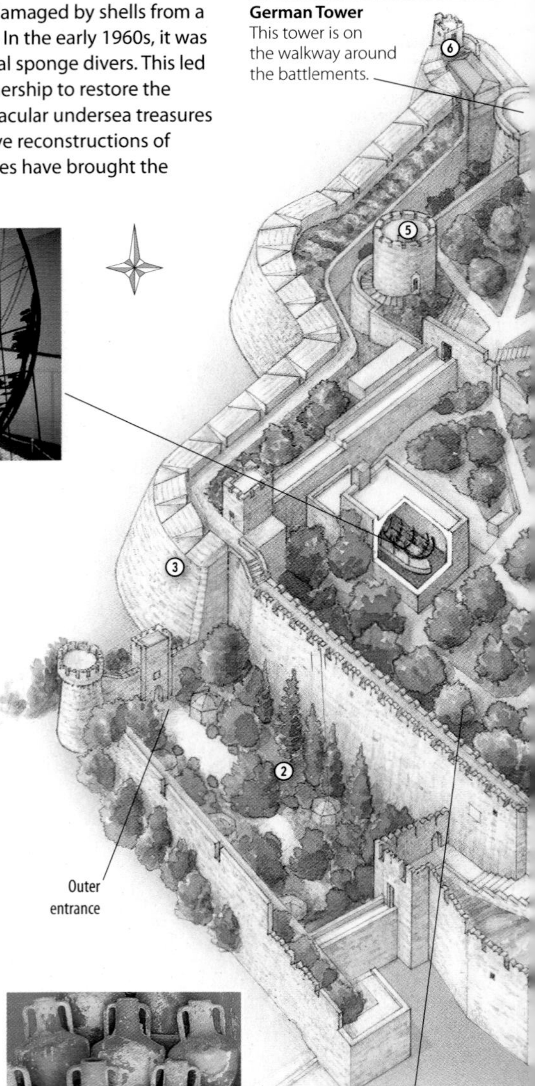

KEY

① **The Commander's Tower** forms the inner entrance to the castle and details some World War I history.

② **Castle moat**

③ **Land-facing battlements**

④ **The Glass Hall** displays Mycenaean beads and Damascus glass, including some items dating from the 15th century BC. Syrian glass ingots, used in the production of glass items, date from the 14th century BC.

⑤ **Spanish (or Snake) Tower**

⑥ **Gatineau Tower**

⑦ **French Tower**

⑧ **Italian Tower**

⑨ **Carian Princess Hall**

⑩ **5th-century BC shipwreck**

⑪ **Chapel and eastern Roman shipwreck**

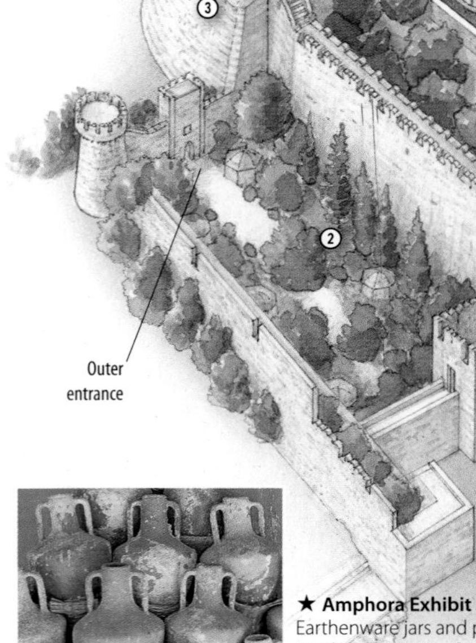

★ Amphora Exhibit
Earthenware jars and pots were used to transport oil, wine and dry foods in ancient times. Pointed bases allowed for upright storage in layers.

For hotels and restaurants in this area see pp333–5 and pp351–4

View of the Castle Across the Harbour
Medieval engineers ensured that the castle was virtually immune to attack. It even had secure water supplies.

VISITORS' CHECKLIST

Practical Information
Bodrum harbour. **Tel** (0252) 316 25 16. **W** **bodrum-museum.com**. **Open** Apr–Oct: 8am–7pm daily; Nov–Mar: 8am–5pm daily. Allow at least 2–3 hours.
Closed Mon (also Sat & Sun for Glass Shipwreck Hall and Carian Princess Hall). several exhibits charge an additional entry fee.

English Tower
Also known as the Lion Tower, it was one of England's first foreign projects funded by taxpayers.

★ Late Bronze Age Shipwrecks
Ancient nautical life and trade are captured in this life-size replica of a ship that sank off Kaş *(see p218)* in the 14th century BC.

Diving for Treasure

Diver recovering amphorae from the floor of the Mediterranean

Many underwater treasures were located accidentally by sponge divers who risked their health and endurance working at depths of 40–50 m (131–164 ft). Some of the museum's priceless displays are the result of more than 20,000 dives and painstaking scientific research by experts and restorers. The partnership between the museum and the Institute of Nautical Archaeology has made Bodrum a showpiece of historical treasures beautifully preserved in their last port of call.

㉖ Bodrum Peninsula Tour

The Bodrum Peninsula was originally peopled by the Lelegians, migrants from mainland Greece who maintained historic ties to the Carians. There were eight Lelegian cities, dating from as early as the 4th or 5th century BC. Myndos was the most prominent, but Pedasa offers the most to see.

Today, the Bodrum Peninsula is renowned as a holiday paradise. Its secluded bays are ideal for yachting, watersports and getting away from it all. The windmills to be seen on the hills were once used to grind grain. The terrain varies from lush coniferous forests to rocky cliffs and sandy coasts. The coastline claimed many ancient ships and some of their treasures are displayed in Bodrum's Castle of St Peter *(see pp200–201)*.

⑥ Yalıkavak
Formerly an important sponge-fishing port, Yalıkavak is an ideal spot for a meal. Local delicacies include sea beans and stuffed marrow flowers.

⑤ Gümüşlük (Myndos)
Gümüşlük occupies the site of ancient Myndos, founded by King Mausolus *(see pp198–9)* in about 350 BC. The remains of a sunken city lie offshore.

④ Kadıkalesi
The town takes its name from *kadı* (Arabic for "judge"), after a former resident. The old Greek church (now awaiting restoration) on the hill is the most intact Greek building in the area. Tangerine groves are a beautiful sight, either in blossom or bearing fruit, and there are superb views of the nearby islets.

③ Turgut Reis
The town is named after a famous Ottoman admiral and naval hero. The rich alluvial soil is perfect for growing figs, which abound in this area.

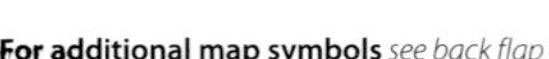

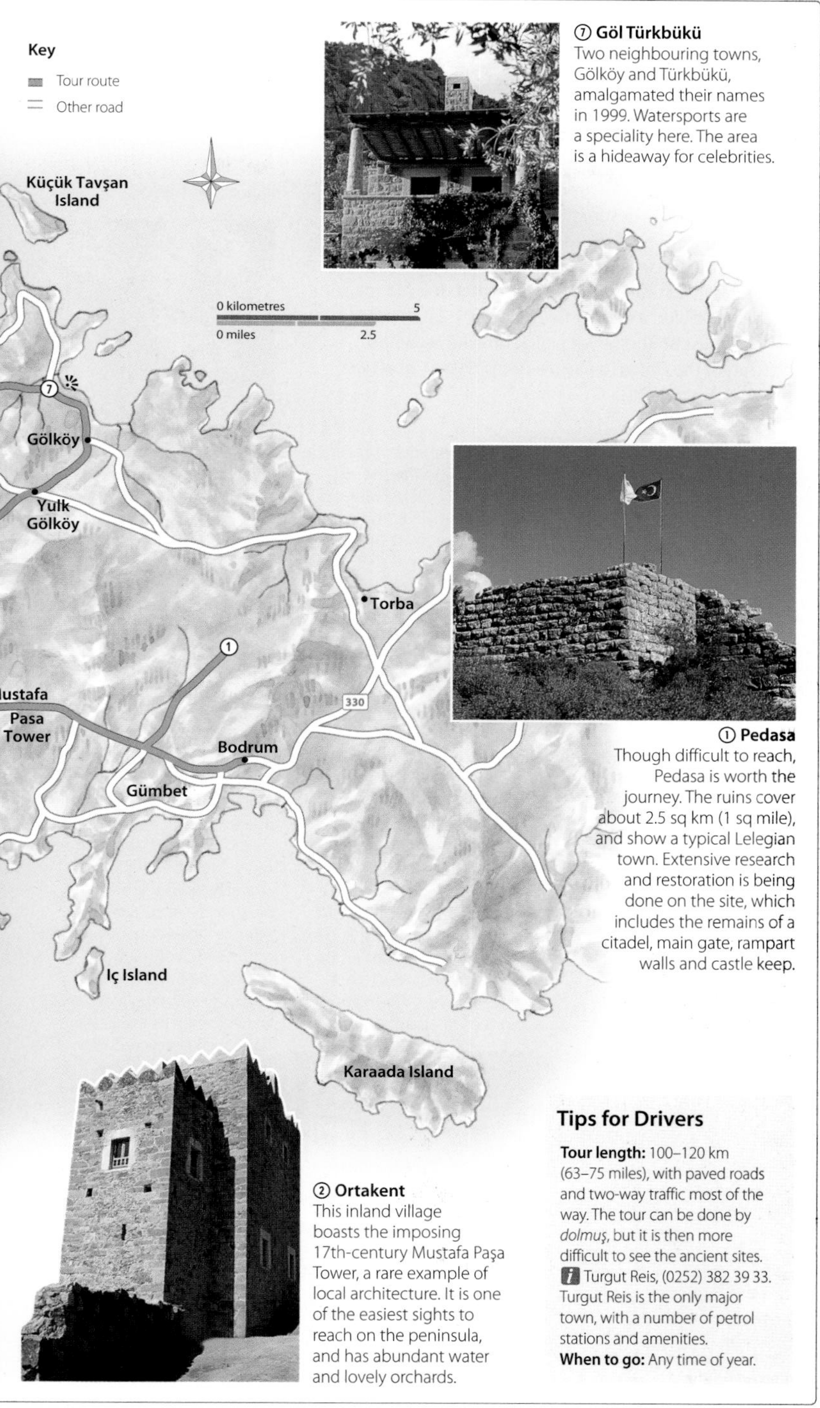

⑦ Göl Türkbükü
Two neighbouring towns, Gölköy and Türkbükü, amalgamated their names in 1999. Watersports are a speciality here. The area is a hideaway for celebrities.

① Pedasa
Though difficult to reach, Pedasa is worth the journey. The ruins cover about 2.5 sq km (1 sq mile), and show a typical Lelegian town. Extensive research and restoration is being done on the site, which includes the remains of a citadel, main gate, rampart walls and castle keep.

② Ortakent
This inland village boasts the imposing 17th-century Mustafa Paşa Tower, a rare example of local architecture. It is one of the easiest sights to reach on the peninsula, and has abundant water and lovely orchards.

Tips for Drivers

Tour length: 100–120 km (63–75 miles), with paved roads and two-way traffic most of the way. The tour can be done by *dolmuş*, but it is then more difficult to see the ancient sites.
i Turgut Reis, (0252) 382 39 33. Turgut Reis is the only major town, with a number of petrol stations and amenities.
When to go: Any time of year.

㉗ Marmaris

Like most of the resorts along the Aegean coast, it is difficult to envisage Marmaris as the quaint fishing village it used to be. The stretch of beach, now lined with hotels, extended to the main street until the 1990s. Marmaris was extensively damaged by an earthquake in 1957, which destroyed most of the old town. Today the rebuilt (and greatly expanded) town is a top holiday destination.

Ancient inscriptions indicate that Marmaris was once the Dorian city of Physcus, attached to the city of Lindos and part of the island state of Rhodes. Süleyman the Magnificent *(see p60)* assembled a mighty fleet here in 1522 to prepare for his conquest of Rhodes, at which time he regained possession of the Datça Peninsula *(see pp206–7)* and had Marmaris castle rebuilt.

Exploring Marmaris

Few places can compete with Marmaris' exclusive setting in a sheltered bay rimmed with oleanders, liquidambar trees and pine forests. All major attractions are located within a few metres of the seafront and can be reached on foot. The harbour and quay extend along a beach walkway that runs the length of the town.

Netsel Marina

Tel (0252) 412 27 08 and 412 14 39.
W netselmarina.com

Turkey's largest and most luxurious marina has it all – parking, top-class restaurants, entertainment, bars, excellent shops and plenty of service facilities such as banks, ATMs and travel agents. All major currencies and credit cards are accepted for mooring, refuelling and other marina services.

Among several yacht brokerage firms here, **Gino Marine** will arrange luxury charter cruises for a view of Marmaris from the water. There is berthing for over 750 yachts up to 40 m- (130 ft-) long.

The Netsel call sign on VHF channel 06 is "Port Marmaris". Marmaris is a safe anchorage, with no underwater currents, sandbanks or rocks, and can be approached night and day in most weather conditions.

Gino Marine

Tel (0252) 412 06 76.
W ginogroup.com

Bar Street

Hacı Mustafa Sokağı.

Most tourist towns have their bars and pubs concentrated on a couple of streets. Those in Marmaris occupy much of Hacı Mustafa Sokağı. Despite the noise, it is always worth strolling along the street and people watching. Some of the bars have been nicely done up and, decibels aside, this is not an unattractive area. There are also a number of hotels and pensions in the area, but visitors in search of rest and relaxation would do better to look elsewhere.

Netsel Marina, offering a complete service to touring yachts

Restored Greek houses in the Old Quarter near the harbour

Greek Revival Houses in Old Quarter

Tepe Mahallesi.

The Old Quarter around the Castle is by far the most charming part of Marmaris. Many houses that were either abandoned or derelict have been restored to their former glory. Most belong to professional people who seem to be accustomed to strangers peeking into a shady courtyard or admiring a handsome brass knocker. Karaca Restaurant, just outside the entrance to the Castle, has a well-preserved interior. From the top terrace of the restaurant, you will get a wonderful view of the town and its numerous delightful "barbecue" chimneys. See if you can spot the one and only remaining original Greek chimney from here. As you wander the cool and shady lanes above the bustle of the harbour, you could find yourself wishing that some of Turkey's other coastal resorts had retained the same quaint neighbourhood appeal as this corner of Marmaris.

For hotels and restaurants in this area see pp333–5 and pp351–4

The Castle, incorporating a nautical museum

VISITORS' CHECKLIST

Practical Information
85,000. iskele Meydanı (central harbour), (0252) 412 10 35. Thu. Yacht Race Week (Oct/Nov every year).

Transport
from Rhodes. Dalaman, 120 km (75 miles) E of town, (0252) 792 52 91. NE of town centre on Muğla road.

Castle and Museum

Tel (0252) 412 14 59. Open Apr–Oct: 8am–6:30pm daily; Nov–Mar: 8am–5pm daily.

The original castle was rebuilt by Süleyman the Magnificent in 1522 after his successful campaign against Rhodes. Today, the restored structure is a museum housing a small collection of nautical items. There are also inscriptions and sculptures displayed in the courtyard. More engaging for most visitors, however, will be the panoramic view of the harbour and old renovated Greek houses.

Bazaar

Entrance from Kordon Caddesi and the street beside the tourist office.

You may find a unique item among the tourist bric-a-brac offered up for sale in the bazaar, among the leather goods, jewellery, herbs, spices and teas. A delicious local speciality is Marmaris honey, which is produced along the scenic Datça Peninsula *(see pp206–7)*. Both pine *(çam)* or flower *(çiçek)* honey are fragrant, thick and dark. By the end of October the last of the honey and fresh summer produce will have been sold.

Marmaris honey

Environs
A number of large holiday villages are located in **Içmeler**, about 6 km (4 miles) around the bay from Marmaris. Transport to and from Marmaris is easy, as *dolmuşes* make the trip on a regular basis. İçmeler lacks the quaint atmosphere of an old Turkish town, as do many parts of Marmaris, but visitors (particularly families) often prefer the more up-to-date facilities and much cleaner beaches here.

Marmaris Town Centre

① Netsel Marina
② Bar Street
③ Greek Revival Houses in Old Quarter
④ Castle and Museumi
⑤ Bazaar

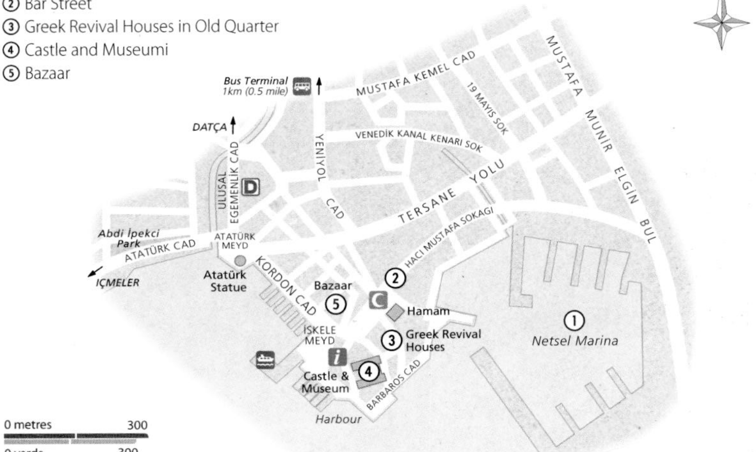

28 Datça Peninsula Tour

The narrow finger of the Datça Peninsula, pointing westward from Marmaris, lies at the place where the Mediterranean and the Aegean meet. Locals claim that the air is rich in oxygen, thanks to the prevailing wind *(meltem)* and the mixing of salinity levels and current patterns in the sea.The route along the peninsula follows narrow and twisting roads, affording glimpses of the sea through pine-clad gullies. At the western tip, about 35 km (21 miles) west of Datça, lie the ruins of Knidos, one of the most prosperous port cities of antiquity. In its heyday it was home to an eminent medical school. The Carian Trail walking route circles the peninsula and continues eastwards towards Bozburun.

⑤ Knidos
This port was the site of a shrine of Aphrodite, dating from about 360 BC. The remains of a theatre, agora, houses and a round temple are visible today.

④ Yazıköy
The western half of the peninsula consists of rugged, pine-clad mountains dotted with olive and almond groves. The village of Yazıköy, at the end of the paved portion of the road, lies deep in the olive-growing region.

③ Palamut Bükü
This bay can also be reached by boat from Datça, and offers a long, tranquil pebble beach lapped by brisk, clear water. Palamut Bükü is a good spot for lunch, with several simple but good fish restaurants.

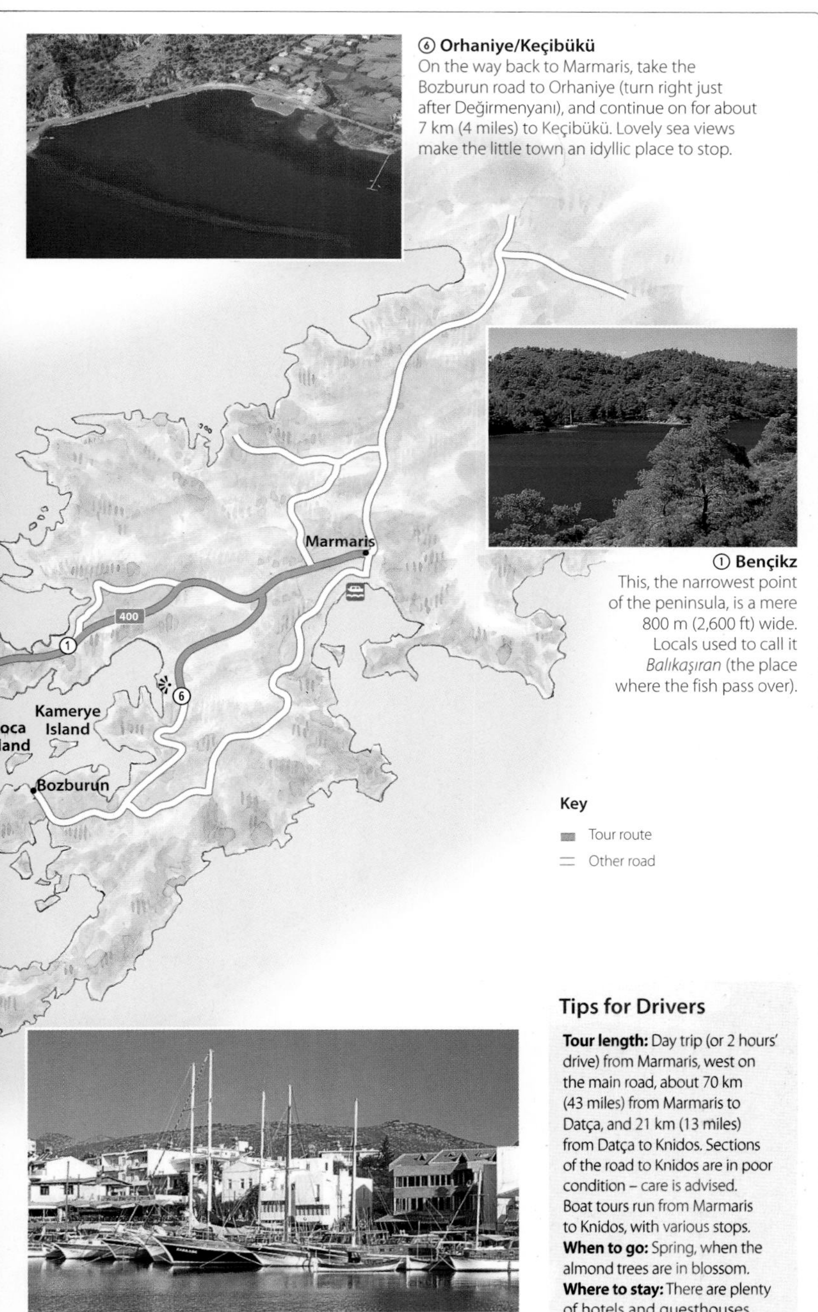

⑥ **Orhaniye/Keçibükü**

On the way back to Marmaris, take the Bozburun road to Orhaniye (turn right just after Değirmenyanı), and continue on for about 7 km (4 miles) to Keçibükü. Lovely sea views make the little town an idyllic place to stop.

① **Bençikz**

This, the narrowest point of the peninsula, is a mere 800 m (2,600 ft) wide. Locals used to call it *Balıkaşıran* (the place where the fish pass over).

② **Datça**

The small town of Datça has a busy yacht harbour, and many shops and restaurants. A few kilometres inland is the old town, Eski Datça, with many lovely stone houses.

Tips for Drivers

Tour length: Day trip (or 2 hours' drive) from Marmaris, west on the main road, about 70 km (43 miles) from Marmaris to Datça, and 21 km (13 miles) from Datça to Knidos. Sections of the road to Knidos are in poor condition – care is advised. Boat tours run from Marmaris to Knidos, with various stops.
When to go: Spring, when the almond trees are in blossom.
Where to stay: There are plenty of hotels and guesthouses available in Datça, Palamut Bükü and Eski Datça. **Open** Both sites are open May–Oct.

MEDITERRANEAN TURKEY

Turkey's Mediterranean coast is synonymous with turquoise seas, sun and blue skies, and has a wealth of ancient remains. Originally colonized by the Greeks and later ruled by the Romans, the region is littered with well-preserved classical sites. However, Hittites, Seljuks, Ottomans, Armenians and even the Crusaders have all left their distinctive imprints upon these shores.

The highlands of Lycia, between Fethiye and Antalya, were the seat of an impressive civilization whose distinctive stone tombs – both freestanding and cliff-hewn – still dot the landscape. At ruined cities such as Pınara, Myra and Xanthos, it is possible to glimpse the achievements and scale of Lycian civilization.

The city of Antalya, an important gateway to the Mediterranean region, boasts a spectacular clifftop setting and quaint walled quarter. It is also a good base for visits to the romantic mountain-top ruins of the Pisidian capital of Termessos and the monumental Roman remains at Perge and Aspendos. Bustling Side, with its temples of Apollo and Athena, is renowned for stunning sunsets.

The Cave of St Peter in Antakya and St Paul's well in Tarsus – birthplace of the Apostle – are reminders of the role of Christianity in fostering the area's cultural and religious diversity.

The short French protectorate era (1918–39) in the Hatay, in the far southeast, left a European colonial legacy in urban planning and local architecture. This corner of the Mediterranean region contains the multicultural cities of İskenderun and Antakya (ancient Antioch on the Orontes), where Arab-Syrian influence is clearly visible. Antakya is also renowned for its Roman mosaics.

An ancient Lycian tomb rising above the placid waters of a coastal inlet

◀ The beautiful lagoon at Ölü Deniz, near Fethiye, viewed from above

Exploring the Western Mediterranean Coast

Separated from the dry Anatolian plateau by the Taurus Mountains, the Mediterranean coast of Turkey is dominated by plunging cliffs and headlands interspersed with fertile alluvial floodplains, and fringed in places with fine sandy beaches. Throughout the region, the many civilizations that have shaped Turkey left their mark on cities, harbours, roads and rivers. To see many of the most beautiful and interesting parts of this section of the coast, venture along the Lycian Way from Fethiye to Antalya, which is rated as one of the world's top treks, or take the "Blue Voyage" on a traditional *gület* (wooden yacht).

Butterfly Valley, near Ölü Deniz

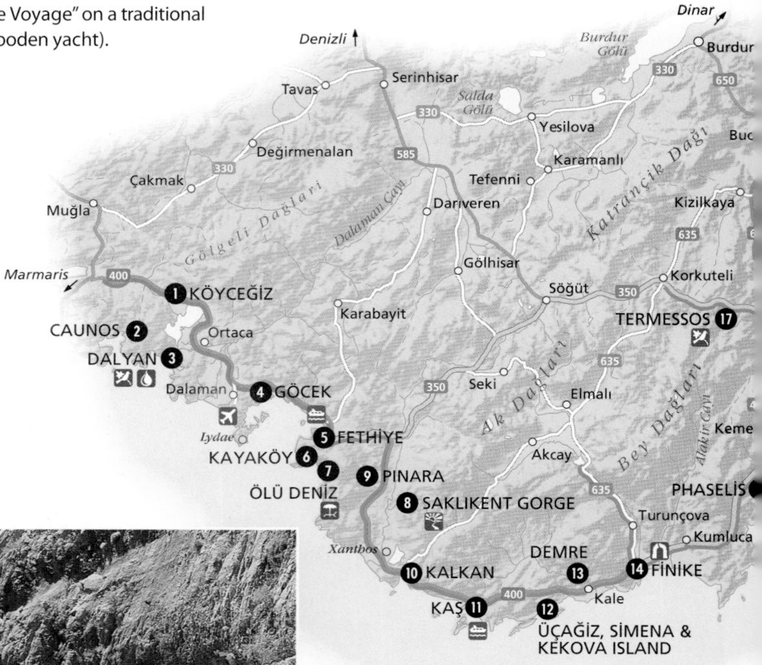

Hiking in Saklıkent Gorge

Getting Around

Antalya's Bayındır International Airport has direct access to many European destinations. From here, fast main roads run east and west, parallel to the coast. In many places, two-lane roads snake around steep, rocky gorges. Views are dramatic, but care is required. With only a few exceptions, all the main sights and attractions are easily accessible by both bus and *dolmuş*.

For additional map symbols *see back flap*

The Vespasian Monument, a Roman fountain in Side

Sights at a Glance

1. Köyceğiz
2. Kaunos
3. Dalyan
4. Göcek
5. Fethiye
6. Kayaköy
7. Ölü Deniz
8. Saklıkent Gorge
9. Pınara
10. Kalkan
11. Kaş
12. Uçağız, Simena and Kekova Island
13. Demre (Myra)
14. Finike
15. Phaselis
16. *Antalya pp222–3*
17. Termessos
18. Perge
19. Selge
20. *Aspendos p225*
21. *Side pp228–9*
22. Alanya
23. Anamur and Anemurium

Key

- Dual carriageway
- Major road
- Minor road
- Scenic route
- △ Summit

The picturesque yacht harbour in Kaleiçi, Antalya

Exploring the Eastern Mediterranean Coast

Apart from Adana and Mersin, the Mediterranean coastline east of Alanya is much less populous (and visited) than the western portion, but offers sights every bit as diverse. These include the bird-watcher's paradise of the Göksu Delta, several Armenian and Crusader castles, and the important Hittite site of Karatepe. The region also has a decidedly Middle Eastern flavour: the further east you go, the more lively and colourful the bazaars become and the foods tingle with stronger spices. This influence is most apparent in the southeast, around İskenderun and Antakya. Turkey's fourth largest city, Adana, is the main centre in the area. It has a subtropical climate, which receives rainfall mainly during the autumn and winter months.

Remnants of the Temple of Zeus, Uzuncaburç near Silifke

The sea-castle set on an island off Kızkalesi (ancient Korykos)

Key

- Motorway
- Dual carriageway
- Major road
- Minor road
- Scenic route
- Main railway
- Minor railway
- International border
- Summit

For additional map symbols *see back flap*

Sights at a Glance

- 24 Silifke
- 25 Kızkalesi
- 26 Mersin (İçel)
- 27 Tarsus
- 28 *Adana pp234–5*
- 29 *Karatepe p236*
- 30 Hierapolis (Castabala)
- 31 Yakacık
- 32 İskenderun
- 33 *Antakya pp238–9*
- 34 Samandağ

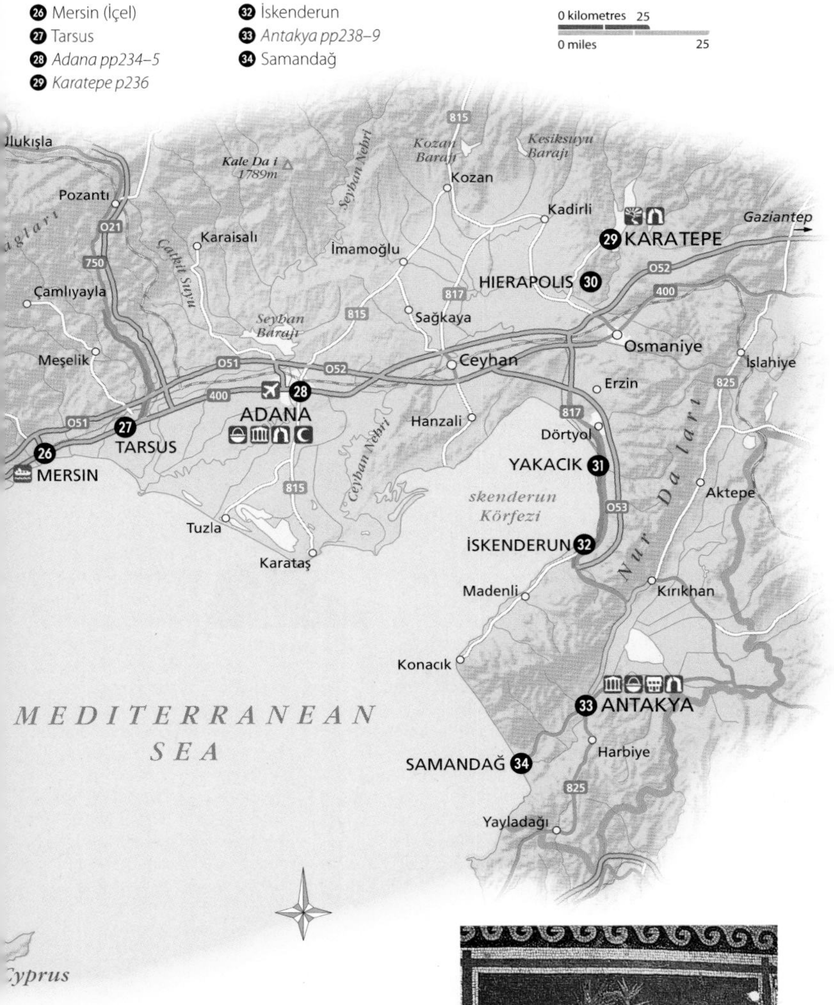

Getting Around

From Mersin to Gaziantep a motorway system is in place, with the hub at Ceyhan, but this is the only section of the Mediterranean coast that is served by fast-track highways. Venturing off the east–west axis of the coastal road, the roads are picturesque and generally passable, but winding and narrow. The Taurus mountain range runs the length of the coast; respect the mountains and remember that, in winter, minor roads may be blocked by snow and tyre chains are essential if you plan to drive over the mountain passes.

Mosaic in the Antakya Archaeological Museum

Lake Köyceğiz, a haven for waterbirds

❶ Köyceğiz

30 km (19 miles) N of Dalyan. 8,600. **Tel** (0252) 262 47 03.

Independent Menteşe clans governed this area even after the beginning of Ottoman rule in 1424. By the late 1830s, when the English archaeologist Charles Fellows visited the area, the power of the family had declined, however. The family *konak* (manor house) has been restored. Another manor, once the centre of a cotton estate belonging to the *khedive* (viceroy) of Egypt, is now the Dalaman state farm. Many people in Köyceğiz village are distant descendants of African slaves brought here to work on cotton plantations. A plantation of *liquidambar orientalis*, the tree used to produce church incense, survives as a reminder of a once-important local industry.

The reed-fringed lake of Köyceğiz, 10 m (33 ft) deep in places, is home to many waterbirds, including the rare Smyrna kingfisher.

❷ Kaunos

6 km (4 miles) from Dalyan. **Tel** (0252) 614 11 50. **Open** Apr–Oct: 8:30am–7pm; Nov–Mar: 8:30am–5pm.

The ancient city of Kaunos bordered the kingdoms of Lycia and Caria. Although a Carian foundation, its culture shared aspects of both states. The local tombs are Lycian *(see p219)* in style, but were in fact carved by the Carians. Like Xanthos, capital of Lycia, Kaunos resisted the Persian general, Harpagus, during the 6th century BC, for which many citizens of Kaunos were slaughtered in a final sally. The city was re-established and Hellenized, especially by the Carian ruler, Mausolus *(see pp198–9)*. Kaunos welcomed Alexander the Great, but after his death came under the rule of Rhodes. It won independence from Rome, but after supporting Mithridates against the Romans, the city was punished by return to Rhodian rule. Kaunos was known both for its figs and malarial mosquitoes. It was a major seaport until the harbour silted up.

At the site are defensive walls built in the 4th century BC, a theatre dating from the 2nd century BC, a temple to Apollo and a Roman bath. There is a Doric temple and an agora (marketplace) with a nymphaeum (fountain) thought to have been built to honour Emperor Vespasian.

❸ Dalyan

13 km (8 miles) from the main D400 road. 8,250. Dalaman, 25 km (16 miles) E of Dalyan, (0252) 792 52 91. Ortaca, 13 km (8 miles) NE of Dalyan. entry road to Dalyan, (0252) 284 24 58. (0252) 284 42 35. Caretta (turtle) Festival (end Aug–early Sep). Sat.

This bustling resort takes its name from the Dalyan River (Dalyan Çayı), meaning "fishing weir", which flows through the town. Although the town is a fast-growing tourist centre, fishing has long been the mainstay of the local economy. Over the years, the town replaced ancient Kaunos as a fishery when the latter's harbour became choked by silt. A weir built on the river, together with a fish-processing plant, means that you can enjoy the delicious local red roe caviar, which comes in a pot sealed with beeswax. Local fish is available at waterside eateries.

The threatened loggerhead turtle *(see p215)* has become a symbol of Dalyan, drawing increasing numbers of visitors to the area. This came about in 1986, when conservationists managed to persuade civic authorities to protect the turtles' breeding ground from development. Since then, local people have adopted the loggerhead turtle as a motif for the town. The Turtle Statue (Kaplumbağa Heykeli) on Cumhuriyet Meydanı is a

Turtle Statue in Dalyan

The resort town of Dalyan, by the tranquil Dalyan River

tangible symbol of Dalyan's passion for conservation.

On the eastern bank of the Dalyan River are two rows of tombs cut into the cliffs. Constructed for the citizens of Kaunos, the tombs are mainly of the house type and date from the 4th century BC *(see p219)*, with Ionic columns and triangular pediments. Most have a small chamber with three stone benches to accommodate the dead. The surviving inscriptions are mainly in Latin, for the tombs were reused during Roman times. They are fenced off and must be viewed from some distance away. The rock tombs can be reached by riverboat tours, which depart from the Dalyan Sea Co-operative.

Yachts moored in Göcek's harbour

Environs

A short distance upriver from Dalyan (about 10 minutes by boat) lie the **mud baths** of Ilıca. With a constant temperature of 40°C (104°F), they are reputed to be beneficial for rheumatism and gynaecological disorders, and are certainly relaxing. Beyond Ilıca, at Sultaniye Kaplıcaları, on the shores of Lake Köyceğiz, a domed building lined with marble surrounds a natural pool where water wells up at 39–41°C (102–106°F). Locals report that, after the Adana earthquake of 1998, the water at the bathhouse gave off a plume of sulphur gas and that the water changed colour and appeared gassy.

Turtle Beach (İztuzu Plajı), which partly bars the mouth of the Dalyan River, has for centuries been a refuge for breeding loggerhead turtles and is now a protected area. The beach is closed to tourists at night so that the young turtles are not attracted by the bright lights, which would lead them away from the life-giving sea.

As staying on the beach after dark is forbidden, you are unlikely to catch a glimpse of the turtles, but you may see blue crabs. The best way to get to the beach is to take one of the frequent, co-operative-run boat-taxis from the river bank near the centre of Dalyan. Alternatively, there are full-day tours to the beach that take in both Kaunos and the mud baths at Ilıca.

Mud Baths
Çamurlu Kaplıcası
Tel (0252) 284 20 35.
Open daily.

Turtle Beach
İztuzu Plajı
12 km (7.5 miles) from town centre.
from Dalyan (40 min): depart before 10:30am, return between 3pm and sunset. for car park only.

4 Göcek

23 km (14 miles) E of Dalaman.
1 km (0.5 mile) from town centre.
Club Marina *(private yacht club)*, (0252) 645 18 00; municipal yacht club, (0252) 645 19 38.

Near the pass of the same name, and just south of the main D400 road, Göcek is now a major yachting centre. Popularized by Prince Charles and former Turkish president, Turgut Özal, the town has a remarkable concentration of up-market facilities, including a luxury hotel and several striking waterside housing developments. The public marinas have berths for about 350 boats, with a further 200 berths available in a secluded private marina. Near the tip of the peninsula can be seen the ruins of the Roman town of Lydae, with two mausoleums and a fort.

Loggerhead Turtles

The loggerhead turtle *(Caretta caretta)* has become closely associated with Dalyan, where soft sand and a tranquil south-facing beach provide an ideal nesting ground.

Loggerhead turtles can mate several times in a season. Between May and September, the females arrive *en masse* to drag themselves up onto the beaches where they themselves hatched. There they laboriously dig a pit and lay their eggs above the tide line. The sand keeps the eggs at an even temperature until they are ready to hatch.

Loggerhead turtle *(Caretta caretta)*

Kayaköy, once the prosperous Greek community of Levissi but abandoned in 1923

❺ Fethiye

140,000. Dalaman, 50 km (31 miles) NW of town. 2 km (1 mile) E of town centre. from Rhodes (summer only). İskele Karşısı, No. 1, (0252) 614 15 27 and 612 19 75. Tue & Fri.

A large market town and agricultural centre, Fethiye fringes a sheltered bay with a large harbour, making it a good place for scuba diving and boating. In addition to having many upscale holiday resorts, Fethiye has a splendid farmers' market every Friday that attracts crowds of locals as well as visitors.

Modern Fethiye stands on the ruins of the Lycian city of Telmessus. Earthquakes in 1856 and 1957 levelled most of the ancient edifices, which included a temple of Apollo, but a Roman theatre near the harbour survives. Cut into the cliffs above the town's market are several Lycian temple tombs *(see p219)*, some from the 4th century BC. Charles Texier, a 19th-century French explorer, carved his initials on one of these tombs.

Fethiye Museum displays artifacts from the half-flooded ruins of Letoön *(see p218)*, including stelae, which scholars used in their efforts to decode the Lycian language.

Fethiye Museum
Fethiye Müzesi
Off Atatürk Cad. **Tel** (0252) 614 11 50.
Open 8:30am–5pm Tue–Sun.

Lycian tombs cut into the cliffs above Fethiye

❻ Kayaköy

10 km (6 miles) SW of Fethiye.
from Fethiye or Ölü Deniz.
Open Apr–Oct: 8:30am–6:30pm daily; Nov–Mar: 8:30am–5pm daily.

Derelict Kayaköy, formerly known as Karmylassos, then Levissi, was a thriving Greek town until it was abandoned in the 1923 exchange of populations *(see p62)*. About 400 roofless houses stand on the hillside overlooking a fertile plain. The Orthodox church of Panayia Pyrgiotissa has been restored and is the main focus of movement for peace and international reconciliation.

Now a UNESCO World Heritage Site, Kayaköy and its ruins have been preserved as an historic settlement. The town inspired the novel *Birds Without Wings*, which focuses on the rise of Turkish patriotism after the disintegration of the Ottoman Empire.

❼ Ölü Deniz

20 km (12 miles) S of Fethiye.
1,200. from Fethiye.
Tourism Co-operative, (0252) 617 04 38, (0252) 617 01 45.

Made famous in the 1970s by visitors from Britain, the inviting beach and lagoon at Ölü Deniz (which means "Dead Sea" – because of the calm water) now adorn many posters promoting

Turkish travel. The land behind the restaurant-fringed beach is lined with hotels, pensions and camp sites. The lagoon itself is part of a national park, open dawn to dusk, with a small entry fee. The adjoining mountain, Baba Dağı, is the jump-off point for paragliders. Ölü Deniz also marks the start of the Lycian Way, Turkey's first long-distance walking route, which ends just short of Antalya.

The beautiful lagoon and beach at Ölü Deniz

8 Saklıkent Gorge

30 km (18 miles) E of Fethiye. D from Fethiye and then on foot. summer only. Tlos: **Open** Apr–Oct: 9am–7pm daily; Nov–Mar: 8am–5pm daily.

Saklıkent Gorge cuts into the rugged flank of the 3,016-m (9,895-ft) Gömbe Akdağı, and delivers a rushing stream of pure limestone-filtered water. From the restaurants at the base of the gorge, which specialize in local trout, you can walk for a few hundred metres into the gorge on platforms built over the torrent. To walk further up the canyon, you need to join a guided walk, led by one of the guides offering their services at the entrance. Bougainville Travel of Kaş *(see p375)* organizes abseiling trips into the gorge. These involve scrambling over rocks to cross the waterfalls that tumble down the walls. If you enter by road and footpath, along the flank of Akdağı, there is quite a steep descent, but this brings you to the trout farms. At Saklıkent, 7 km (4.5 miles) from the main D400 road, consider a meal at one of the trout restaurants, which have low tables placed over the water. Enjoy the cool air before you return to sea level – when the temperature is 40°C (104°F) at the coast, Saklıkent is refreshing.

Also in the area is the ruined city of Tlos, one of the oldest and most important Lycian cities. Hittite records from the 14th century BC refer to a settlement called Tlawa, which was probably Tlos. Built on a hill, with a commanding view over the valley of the Eşen River (Eşen Çayı) – known in ancient times as the Xanthos – the main Lycian/Roman remains consist of tombs hewn from rock, as well as a stadium, gymnasium and palaestra, and baths. In Byzantine times, Tlos was a bishopric, and the churches at the site were most probably former temples. The acropolis was used until the 19th century, when it was the stronghold of a pirate known as Kanlı Ali Ağa (Bloody Ali).

Agencies in Fethiye and Kaş offer tours of both Saklıkent Gorge and Tlos.

Catwalk built over the water in Saklıkent Gorge

Butterfly Valley

From Ölü Deniz, it is a short boat ride to Butterfly Valley (Kelebek Vadisi), a flat-bottomed valley enclosed by towering cliffs. The valley was named for the migratory *Euplagia quadripunctaria*, commonly known as the Jersey Tiger, a spectacular red, black and white tiger moth that colonizes the valley by the thousand during the summer. Other species are present year-round, with some unique to the area. A 20-minute trek leads to a waterfall from the mill stream at Faralya, which cascades into the valley, providing damp conditions for the butterflies and supporting a variety of plants. No permanent buildings are allowed on or behind the beach, but a wooden bar-restaurant supplies beer and food to those wishing to camp. Alternative access is by steep path from Faralya, the village perched 600 m (1,968 ft) above, but this route is not recommended since the path is dangerous.

Euplagia quadripunctaria

Tombs cut into the rock at Pınara

❾ Pınara

50 km (31 miles) E of Fethiye.
Open 8:30am–dusk daily.

One of the most important cities of ancient Lycia, Pınara, whose name means "round", is situated on and around a huge circular plug of rock above the village of Minare, some 5 km (3 miles) west of the main D400 road. The entrance is about 3 km (2 miles) along an unpaved track that is passable by car.

The rock face is honeycombed with tombs, mainly square holes, which must have been sealed after use. The acropolis is approached by steps carved into the rock. A well-preserved theatre is cut into the hillside below, with baths nearby. The *agora* (marketplace) lies just above the ticket office.

Visitors strolling through the picturesque streets of Kalkan

❿ Kalkan

6,000. at junction with main coast road. Thu.

The village of Kalkan has been permanently inhabited only since the eradication of malaria-bearing mosquitoes in the 1950s. In earlier times, the local people avoided the pests by migrating in summer to the *yayla* (summer pasture) of Bezirgan, above the village. The core of stone, Greek-style houses built around the harbour is today surrounded by tiered ranks of modern villas on the hills. Good accommodation and a choice of restaurants make it an ideal base for the ancient Lycian cities of Xanthos, Letoön and Patara.

Xanthos (now Kınık), the ancient capital of the Lycian League *(see p219)*, is 30 minutes by bus west of Kalkan, just before the bridge spanning the Eşen River. The site is extensive and spectacular, and includes superb examples of Lycian tombs. A bilingual Greek-Lycian pillar found at the site helped researchers to decipher the Lycian language.

Letoön, site of the temples of Leto, Artemis and Apollo, was a cult centre favoured by Alexander the Great. Letoön and Xanthos are both UNESCO World Heritage Sites and reflect the way Hellenistic and Lycian cultures influenced each other.

Patara was once the major port of the Lycian League. Damaged by severe earthquakes in AD 141 and AD 240, its harbour silted up.

⓫ Kaş

8,500. Dalaman, 155 km (96 miles) NW of town, or Bayındır Intl Airport (Antalya), (0242) 330 36 00, 210 km (130 miles) NE of town. Atatürk Cad. 5 Cumhuriyet Meydanı, (0242) 836 12 38. Fri. Kaş/Lycia Festival (Sep).

Kaş was built adjoining a long, narrow peninsula, over the ancient port city of Antiphellos (port of Phellos), and was noted for its cork oaks. In 1839, it was so tiny and impoverished that the English archaeologist Charles Fellows (who excavated the nearby Lycian site of Xanthos) had to cross to the island of Castellorizo to buy chickens to eat. Today, the situation is reversed: the islanders buy their chickens at Kaş market on Fridays. The harbours are filled with scuba-diving boats and yachts making trips to the Blue Cave and the sunken city at Kekova *(see p220)*, with hotels and pensions along the waterfront. Uzun Çarşı, the shopping street, has many unusual and original handicraft and antique shops. A 5th-century-BC Lycian sarcophagus is at the top of the street.

"Hand of Fatma" door knocker, Kaş

The tourism information office in the main square can provide information on the annual Kaş/Lycia Festival, which makes good use of the tiny Hellenistic theatre located on the peninsula road just west of the town.

Fishing boats and touring yachts in the harbour at Kaş

Lycian Tombs

Ancient Lycia, a federation of 19 independent cities, lay in the mountainous area between modern Fethiye and Antalya. Burials must have had an important role in the beliefs of the Lycians, for they cut hundreds of tombs into cliff faces and crags that can be seen throughout the area. They were probably copies of domestic architecture, intended as houses for the dead. Most have carved doors, beam ends, pitched roofs and prominent lintels – typical of construction in wood. During the 4th century BC, the rulers of Xanthos (modern Kınık) produced some of the most remarkable tombs, combining Greek and Persian styles. One of the most famous of these, the Nereid Monument, is now in the British Museum in London.

The doorway of a house tomb, often featured a sliding slab.

The house tomb of one to three storeys, shown here at Tlos, was carved into solid rock. A sliding slab door opened into an inner chamber. Some tombs had exterior porticoes with carvings.

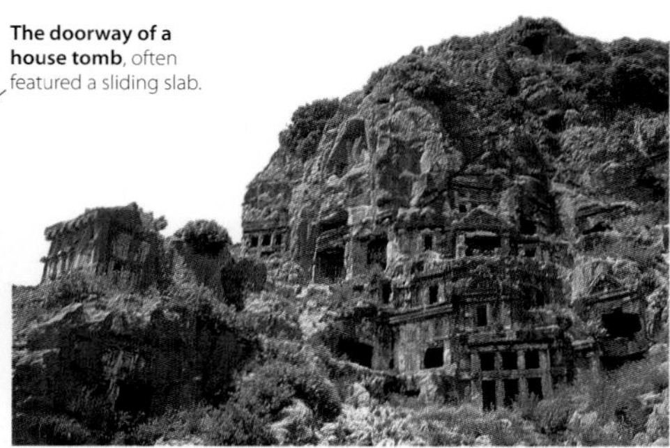

House tombs at Myra, near Demre, feature richly carved façades. The elaborate reliefs on some of the tombs still bear traces of paint applied by the original builders.

Rock cut away to make a roof space

The freestanding temple tomb had a temple façade and a portico, from which a door led to a grave chamber with benches for the dead.

Sarcophagus placed atop the pillar base

Partly hollow base topped by a stepped lid

Pillar tombs (on a stepped base or built directly on rock) are the oldest Lycian tombs. These are found only at Xanthos, the chief city of Lycia, and Apollonia. This example is from Xanthos.

"Beam ends" used to open the lid of the sarcophagus

Prominent lid ridge

Stepped base

Sarcophagus tombs had a stepped base, a lower grave chamber (called a hyposorion), a flat plate for the coffin and a lid. The pitched, rounded lid symbolized a house roof, and had a prominent ridge. From 500 BC to AD 300, elaborate "saddlebacked" sarcophagus tombs were produced.

Varnished charter vessels and quaint fishing boats share the little harbour at Üçağız

⓬ Üçağız, Simena and Kekova Island

38 km (24 miles) E of Kaş. 2,800. from Demre or Kaş.

The picturesque waterfront village of Üçağız ("Three Mouths") is a 19 km (12 mile) drive south of the D400, just east of Kaş. *Dolmuşes* will drop you at the main road, but no scheduled transport leads directly to the village.

Built on the site of (and using stones from) the Lycian town of Teimiussa, houses, restaurants and pensions front a sheltered bay with three openings to the sea. There are some signs of subsidence, probably as a result of an earthquake that took place in about AD 530. Submerged saddleback tombs *(see p219)* can be seen at the Lycian site of Aperlae and the village of Kale (ancient Simena) nearby, where a castle built in around 1440 surrounds a tiny theatre cut into the rock. A pleasant stroll along the coast via the marked Lycian Way leads to its rarely visited twin.

Above Demre, an asphalt road provides a short-cut to Üçağız. Daily boat tours call in to the pretty bay enclosed by Kekova Island (Kekova Adası).

⓭ Demre (Myra)

19,200. 100 m (100 yards) from main square.

The small market town of Demre would have little appeal to visitors were it not for its claims to be home to the original Santa Claus, St Nicholas, and the proximity of the superb ancient site of Myra. St Nicholas legends originated in Mediterranean Patara (his birthplace), but the Church of St Nicholas is the most charming reason to linger in Demre. This petite Byzantine church is spiritually and architecturally heavenly and some long-concealed frescoes are being brushed back into life.

The ancient city of Myra and the port of Andriake, 3 km (2 miles) southwest of Demre, date from around the 5th century BC, and grew rich on coastal trade, supplying incense to Egypt and Constantinople.

The most popular parts of Myra are the theatre and two cliffs carved with spectacular house tombs. When Charles Fellows visited the site in 1840, the paint on the tombs was still visible and letters of the inscriptions were picked out in red and blue. The oldest part of Myra was on the acropolis hill, with a 5th-century BC defensive wall. Myra's water supply ran in channels cut into the wall of the Demre gorge and the frigid sulphur springs at Andriake provided therapeutic baths and healing drinking waters.

The Real Santa Claus

Nicholas, the 4th-century Bishop of Myra, was famed for his unfailing generosity and piety. He was beatified, and legend established him as the patron of fishermen and children, and the town as a place of pilgrimage. (He is also the patron saint of bakers, brewers and brides.) There are two statues of St Nicholas (Noel Baba in Turkish) in Demre: one is a gift from the Russian Orthodox Church, and is mounted on a revolving pedestal.

The saint's myrrh-impregnated bones were buried on his church's premises. Although this church was destroyed by the Arabs in 809, the bones survived and were moved to Bari, Italy, in 1087. The church at Demre was rebuilt by a Russian prince in the 19th century. Demre is also the headquarters of the St Nicholas Foundation.

Statue of St Nicholas in Demre

Carved mask relief from the theatre at Myra

⓮ Finike

25,000. Halk Kütüphane, (0242) 855 39 92. off D400 highway. Sat.

Finike is a market town located at the foot of the Gülmez Dağları, a long spur of the Taurus Mountains, and on the banks of the Karasu (Black Water) River.

In ancient times, Finike was known as Phoenicus. The original harbour, once noted for its export of the timber that was used in building the Ottoman fleet, is now buried under silt, and a modern yacht harbour has replaced it. In Byzantine times, the surrounding mountains were a source of cedar of Lebanon (used in shipbuilding), but the tree is rarely found in these parts today.

Finike has since prospered through the export of citrus fruit and other produce. Its fertile orchards brim with orange and lemon trees, and the town's logo is an orange.

Not much is known about the early history of **Olympos**, although it was an influential member of the Lycian League. The site is reached by a narrow road through a gorge with a seasonally dry river bed. The ruined city occupies a charming setting adjoining a 4 km- (3 mile-) long beach. To the south is an extensive necropolis, including unique square tombs with sliding doors. A theatre, baths and landing stages also occupy the south bank. The northern side has an acropolis, more tombs, a temple dating from the time of Emperor Marcus Aurelius and a Byzantine bath-house. The whole site is starred with anemones in spring; kingfishers whirr over the stream and ducks nest in the reeds.

Fronting the same beach as Olympos, but reached from the main road by a different valley, low-key Çıralı boasts more than 100 pensions and hotels nestling in the shade of citrus orchards. Turtle-nesting beach apart, the main point of interest here is the Chimaera. Set at an altitude of 300 m (984 ft), are two outcrops of volcanic rock, where escaping natural gas is

Escaping natural gas burning near Olympos

permanently alight. The flame is known as Yanartaş (burning stone). In ancient times, the fire was guided upwards to light a beacon to warn ships of impending danger. There is also a Byzantine church here, probably once a temple of Vulcan.

According to myth, this mountain is where the hero Bellerophon, mounted on the winged horse, Pegasus, killed the three-headed Chimaera by pouring molten lead into the monster's mouth.

Olympos

11 km (7 miles) E of main D400 road. from café on D400, or taxi.
Open Apr–Oct: 9am–7pm daily; Nov–Mar: 8am–5pm daily.

⓯ Phaselis

40 km (24 miles) SW of Antalya.
Open Apr–Oct: 9am–7pm daily; Nov–Mar: 8:30am–5pm daily.

Decked with flowers in spring, the ruined city of Phaselis is a popular stopping place for cruise yachts.

The Lycian port city was sold to Greek settlers from Rhodes by a local shepherd in the 7th century BC. They built an extensive town with three harbours around an acropolis on a headland. The canny Phaselians, noted for their skill in trade and commerce, invited Alexander the Great to winter here in 333 BC, even presenting him with a golden crown in return for valuable protection. Phaselis became a pirate stronghold before it was absorbed into the Roman province of Lycia-Pamphylia in AD 43. It survived Arab raiding, only to be eclipsed by Antalya in Seljuk times.

Most of the ruins date from the Roman era. They include a theatre, two sets of baths, an agora, an aqueduct leading from Mount Olympos and a marble gateway erected in honour of Emperor Hadrian.

The north harbour at Phaselis, with Mt Olympos in the background

⑯ Antalya

Antalya's population has increased to more than one million since the tourism boom began in the late 1980s. Mountains, beaches and the seaside setting are the obvious magnets, and the city is now one of Turkey's premier resort areas. Antalya (ancient Attaleia) was founded by Attalus II, a king of Pergamum, in 159 BC. The city prospered during the Roman, Byzantine and Seljuk eras before coming under Ottoman rule in 1390. The most important remains are the Roman city walls and imposing Hadrian's Gate.

The attractive old harbour, showing remnants of the city walls

Exploring Antalya

Antalya's broad, palm-lined boulevards and interesting Old Town (Kaleiçi) make it a pleasant place to explore. The beaches, parks, excellent shops and lively cultural scene make it a focal point of the Mediterranean coast.

Antalya has one speciality not found anywhere else in Turkey – *hibeş*, a hot, spicy sesame-paste dip.

Minicity Antalya

Arapsu Mahallesi, Konyaaltı. **Tel** (0242) 229 45 45. **Open** 8am–7pm daily (Nov–Apr: from 9am).

A Mediterranean theme pervades here, with diminutive beaches and sailing boats as well as miniature replicas of many of Turkey's historic sights. Replicas of the Gallipoli graves are particularly moving.

Antalya's Beaches

For visitors staying in the Old Town of Kaleiçi, the most convenient beach is the small, pebbly Mermerli beach, located at the foot of the cliffs just south of the harbour. Owned by the Mermerli restaurant, a fee is charged to access it. Konyaaltı beach, a long shingle strip backed by cafés and hotels is easily reached from the city centre on the nostalgic tram. Get off at the last stop (Archaeological Museum) and walk down the hill. Some 10 km (6 miles) east of the city, and reached from the centre by bus, is sandy Lara Beach. Both Konyaaltı and Lara beaches have sunloungers for hire.

Antalya Archaeological Museum

Konyaaltı Cad 1, Konyaaltı.
Tel (0242) 238 56 88.
Open 8am–5:30pm Tue–Sun. with prior permission.

The museum, perched on the cliffs 2 km (1.25 miles) west of the city centre, is the true jewel of Antalya. It houses a unique collection of Roman marble sculptures dating from the 2nd century AD, many of them from nearby Perge *(see p224)*. The statues are beautifully lit and superbly displayed. Displays also include Bronze Age urn burials, silver found in Phrygian tumulus burials, relics of St Nicholas *(see p220)* and a collection of early Byzantine church silver. There is also an ethnography section. If your time in Antalya is limited, save it for this – one of the handful of Turkish museums that is truly outstanding. The Sarcophagi Hall and Gallery of the Gods are also recommended viewing. Don't miss the sarcophagus of a dog called Stephanos.

Roman marble sculpture from the Antalya Archaeological Museum

Antalya's Harbours

Limanılar

Marina (Kaleiçi): Selsuk Mah. **Tel** (0242) 248 45 30. Harbour (Port Akdeniz): Büyük Lıman Mevkii. **Tel** (0242) 259 13 80. **Open** 8am–5pm Tue–Sun.

The picturesque Old Harbour in Kaleiçi is used mainly for gulet *(see p210)* tours to Rat Island or the waterfalls at Lara. The waterfront is lined with restaurants and is a pleasant place to stroll. The harbour has won an award for its attractive setting, plan and use of resources. The city's main harbour is 10 km (6 miles) west of the centre and is used mainly by commercial and private yachts, as well as cruise ships. It is also the site of Antalya's fish market.

Fluted Minaret

Yivli Minare

A 13th-century minaret dating from the reign of Seljuk Sultan Alaeddin Keykubad *(see p254)*, this has become the symbol of Antalya. The red bricks were once decorated with turquoise tiles. The adjoining mosque is still used, and just above is the Fine Arts Gallery.

The Fluted Minaret

For hotels and restaurants in this area see pp335–6 and pp353–6

Hadrian's Gate, with the deep wheel ruts clearly visible

Kaleiçi Museum

Kokatepe Sok 25, Kaleiçi. **Tel** (0242) 243 42 74. **Open** 9am–noon & 1pm–6pm Tue–Thu.

This charming museum is housed in two beautifully restored Ottoman mansions. One contains rooms recreated as they would have been in the 19th century, with lifelike mannequins. The other is a research library. A renovated Greek Orthodox church houses a collection of Çannakale pottery.

Hadrian's Gate

Üçkapılar
Atatürk Cad.

Built to honour the visit of Emperor Hadrian in AD 130, Hadrian's Gate consists of three arched gateways fronted by four Corinthian columns. For years, the structure was encased in the Seljuk city wall and was uncovered only in the 1950s. Restoration work has been carried out and the pavement between the arches stripped back to the Roman level, showing clearly the wheel ruts cut into the stone.

Truncated Minaret

Kesik Minare
Hesapçı Sok.

The Truncated Minaret is the landmark decapitated tower next to the ruins of what has been, variously, a Greek temple, the Church of St Peter and a mosque. The tower was badly damaged by fire in 1851. Various architectural styles, especially on the capitals, give clues to its past. You cannot go inside, as railings surround the site, but the exterior is fascinating.

Karaalioğlu Park and Hıdırlık Tower

Located on the southeastern side of the harbour, the park has a variety of mature exotic trees in which wild ring-necked parakeets nest. It also has tea gardens with fabulous views over the Gulf of Antalya, Mount Tahtalı and the distant Beydağlar Mountains. The circular Hıdırlık tower dates from the 2nd century BC, and was probably a lighthouse in Roman times. Locals linger here to watch the setting sun.

VISITORS' CHECKLIST

Practical Information

1,130,000. Cumhuriyet Cad, (0242) 241 17 47.
Aspendos Festival (2nd week Jun–1st week Jul), Golden Orange Film Festival (1st or 2nd week Oct).

Transport

JCF Airport, 12 km (8 miles) E of city, (0242) 330 36 00. 4 km (2.5 miles) N of city centre, (0242) 331 12 50. from Işiklar Cad to Konyaaltı Cad. D Doğu Garajı.

Tea garden beside a reflecting pool in Karaalioğlu Park

Antalya City Centre

① Konyaaltı and Mermerli beaches
② Archaeological Museum
③ Old Harbour
④ Fluted Minaret
⑤ Kaleiçi Museum
⑥ Hadrian's Gate
⑦ Truncated Minaret
⑧ Karaalioğlu Park

For keys to symbols *see back flap*

⑰ Termessos

35 km (22 miles) NW of Antalya; 9 km (6 miles) off the main road. **Open** Apr–Oct: 9am–7pm daily; Nov–Mar: 8am–5pm daily.

Termessos was built by the Solymians in a strategic position on the shipping route to the Aegean. The Greek historian Arrian (around AD 95–180) said of the location that "the two cliffs make a sort of natural gateway so that quite a small force can, by holding the high ground, prevent an enemy from getting through". The city's formidable natural defences convinced Alexander the Great not to attempt to take the city during the 4th century BC.

The main buildings visible today are a theatre, the defensive walls below the gymnasium, the gymnasium itself, the temples of Hadrian and Zeus, an odeon (for musical performances), cisterns in the agora, the stoas (covered walks) of Attalos and Osbaras, and the temple of Artemis. A large necropolis extends upwards as far as a modern fire-watch tower on the hill. You can walk from the gymnasium down to sea level along the old road, ending in a gorge.

Termessos lies in Güllük Dağ National Park, which includes an area for breeding wild goats and deer, and may be the last refuge of the Anatolian lynx. The area is also known for its butterflies.

The remains of the Hellenistic Gate at Perge

⑱ Perge

18 km (11 miles) NE of Antalya. **Open** Apr–Oct: 9am–7pm daily; Nov–Mar: 8.30am–5.30pm daily.

Located on the Kestros River (modern-day Aksu), Perge was once a wealthy city. It declined in Byzantine times, and was abandoned in the 7th century. However, it still presents an impressive sight. The theatre is one of the most impressive remnants: its frieze of Neptune can be seen in the Archaeological Museum in Antalya *(see p222)*. The huge stadium is largely intact. Much excavation and reconstruction work has been done here, with explanatory panels near most major buildings.

A pair of Hellenistic towers marks the entry to the city. The towers front a courtyard with a fountain. On the left, baths with under-floor heating systems face a colonnaded agora. A water channel leads from a second fountain on the acropolis hill into a channel down the main street, which cooled the air in summer. Plancia Magna, the city's benefactress, was buried outside the walls; a marble statue of her is in Antalya Archaeological Museum.

⑲ Selge

92 km (57 miles) NE of Antalya. **Open** daily.

The village now occupying the site gives no idea of the former importance of Selge. Founded by Calchas of Argos (who also founded Perge) in the 5th century BC, it was the first Pisidian city to mint coins. Coins from Selge were used until the 5th century AD. The classical geographer Strabo cites olives, wine and medicinal plants as sources of revenue. Selge seldom features in classical histories, but we know from the Greek historian Polybius that, in 218 BC, when Selge was at war with the city of Pednelissos, it was able to field an army of 20,000 men. Selge was defeated in this war and had to pay tribute to its enemy. However, it regained prosperity and independence and flourished, especially in the 2nd century AD.

Visible today are a theatre, a stadium, a large temple to Zeus, a smaller one to Artemis, and a cistern. The site, with its spectacular mountain surroundings and cool air, is now part of the Köprülü Çayı National Park.

The theatre at Termessos, with seating for more than 4,000 people

⑳ Aspendos

Aspendos, located on the Eurymedon River (now the Köprülü River), was once the easternmost city of the kingdom of Pergamum *(see pp180–81)*. In Roman times it became an important trading centre. Today, its main attraction is a beautifully preserved Roman theatre, built around AD 162 by the architect Zeno. The structure is enclosed by a stage building that once had a timber canopy. The theatre hosts the annual Aspendos Opera and Ballet Festival (usually mid-June–early July). Aspendos also has a remarkable aqueduct, and numerous remains.

VISITORS' CHECKLIST

Practical Information
50 km (31 miles) E of Antalya.
Open Apr–Oct: 9am–7pm daily; Nov–Mar: 8am–5pm daily. **Closed** early closing (4pm) for festival performances (on some days in Jun–mid-Sep). in Belkis village. ground level only.

Arched Gallery
Running right round the top of the theatre, the restored gallery provided patrons with an all-weather vantage point.

★ Theatre
The theatre, which can seat 12,000, was maintained by the Seljuks, and traces of 13th-century paint still adorn the stage building.

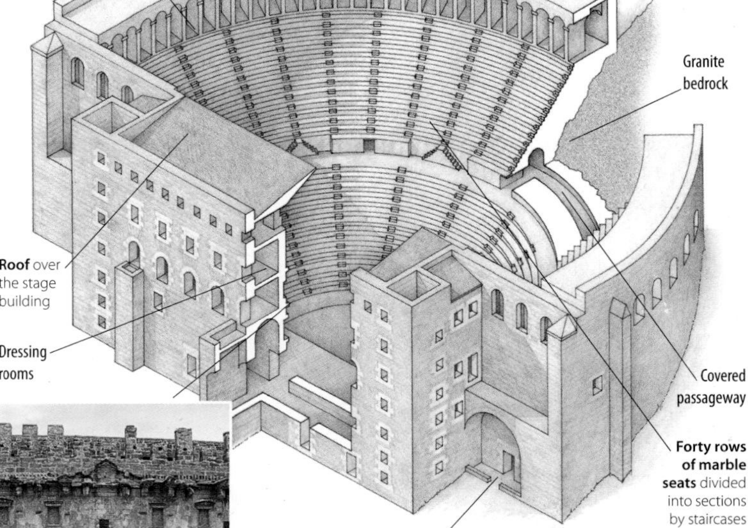

Stage Building
The stage building features carved niches intended to hold statues. Originally, the niches were separated by columns.

★ Aqueduct
The aqueduct, built in around AD 100 by the architect Tiberius Claudius Italicus, incorporated a 1 km (0.5 mile) siphon system.

21 Side

The classical geographer Strabo tells us that Side (whose name means pomegranate) was settled by Greek colonists from Aeolia, near Smyrna (modern İzmir), in the 7th century BC. In the 2nd century BC, Side became a centre for pirates, who made large profits from slave trading. Under the Romans, it remained an important slave market. Excavations have shown that the city was burned by Arab raiders in the 7th century, but it revived under the Seljuks. During the 1920s, Side was settled by Muslims expelled from Crete in the Greet–Turkish population exchange *(see p62)*.

The partially reconstructed Temple of Apollo

The tranquil harbour, cradled by the remains of ancient breakwaters

Exploring Side

The busy resort of Side is an ideal place to take in ancient ruins, beaches and shopping without venturing too far afield. It is a haven for shoppers, with its leather, jewellery and souvenir stores and many bars and eateries in summer. Pedestrianization, the small pensions and quaint, family-run facilities have enabled the town to retain its "village" charm. Its monuments lend discipline and historic value to the narrow streets.

Waterfall on the Manavgat River, upstream from the town

Harbour

Side occupies a peninsula that terminates in a small harbour. The remains of moles built in antiquity are visible in places offshore. From here, you can take a luxurious boat trip up the Manavgat River (Melas in ancient times), see a waterfall and stop for some lunch at a trout restaurant.

Temples of Apollo and Athena

At sunset, the marble columns and re-erected pediments of the temples of Apollo and Athena frame superb views of the Gulf of Antalya. Around the temples is a basilica, built later in a contrasting rough aggregate stone. The Medusa heads of the friezes date from the 2nd century AD.

Theatre

Open Apr–Oct: 9am–7pm daily; Nov–Mar: 8am–5pm daily. at theatre, grants entrance to the whole site, reduction after 5pm.

Almost entirely freestanding, Side's large theatre was built on arches over Hellenistic foundations during the 2nd century AD. The lower seats are partially supported by the hillside, but the upper seats rest entirely on huge arches.

This was the largest theatre in Pamphylia, and could hold 17,000 spectators. There are 29 rows of seats above and

Golfing in Belek

Between Side and Antalya lies the purpose-built golfing resort of Belek. Here, there are fourteen 18-hole courses, all beautifully landscaped through mature pine forests and offering considerable contrast, ranging from a links course to one set amid lakes and huge trees. The Belek courses operate in close partnership with excellent five-star hotels and have golf professionals who speak a variety of languages. The Mediterranean region's mild winter and early spring make this the most attractive time to visit. Several tournaments are held here each year.

Typical landscaped golf course

For hotels and restaurants in this area see pp335–6 and pp354–6

The large Roman theatre, built on Hellenistic foundations

29 below the main lateral aisle. Changes to the structure of the building permitted the orchestra pit to be flooded in order to enact naval dramas. The stage building had two storeys, decorated, as at Perge *(see p224)*, with friezes of the story of Dionysus. These are currently being displayed in the nearby agora or museum garden while restoration work is carried out on them.

Vespasian Monument, Arch and Colonnaded Street

The arched gateway that marks the entrance to Side from its neighbour, Manavgat, blocks most vehicular traffic. Next to the arch is a fountain adorned with carved basins, dedicated to the Emperor Vespasian. From here runs a colonnaded street lined with plain granite columns and the remains of Roman shops leading to the main street. A local tractor pulls an open bus, saving visitors the walk from the bus station.

Museum in Roman Bathhouse

Tel (0242) 753 10 06.
Open Apr–Oct: 9am–7pm daily; Nov–Mar: 8am–5pm daily.

The museum occupies a charming setting – the largest of Side's baths – and includes a number of superb marble sarcophagi, a trio of statues known as the Three Graces and another statue showing Hercules holding the golden apples of the Hesperides. There are also elegant portrait heads and tiny carvings that include a house complete with dog peering around the door. The garden features a cupola with maze decoration and many friezes.

The Vespasian Monument, with a carved pediment and inscription

VISITORS' CHECKLIST

Practical Information
23,350. Side Yolu Üzeri, Manavgat, (0242) 753 12 65. Sat.

Transport
Antalya, 70 km (43 miles) NE of Side. on main coast road in Manavgat, 2 km (1 mile) E of main entrance.

Aqueduct, Nymphaeum and City Walls

The Romans installed an impressive water-supply system. Outside the main gate was a nymphaeum (ornamental fountain), which was fed by a two-storey aqueduct running on arches for 30 km (19 miles) from the Melas (now the Manavgat) River. Clay pipes were used to distribute water to homes from the city cisterns.

Outside the massive Roman city walls are necropoli, with examples of temple tombs.

Side Town Centre

① Harbour
② Temples of Apollo and Athena
③ Theatre
④ Vespasian Monument, Arch and Colonnaded Street
⑤ Museum in Roman Bathhouse
⑥ Aqueduct, Nymphaeum and City Walls

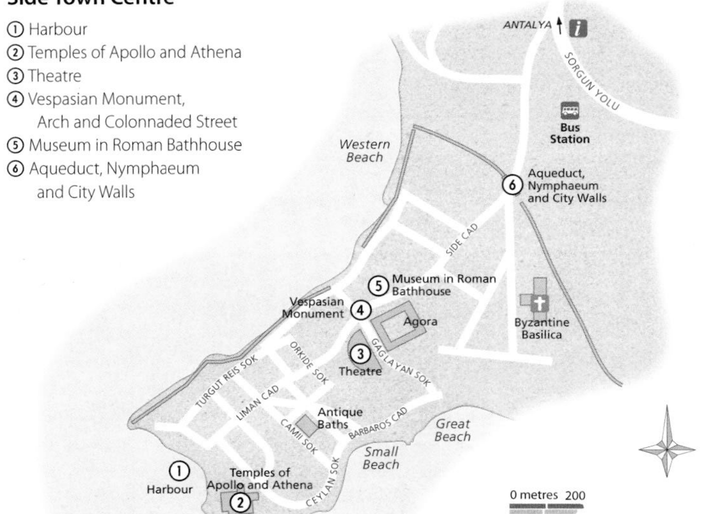

The Red Tower, dominating the harbour at Alanya

22 Alanya

110,000. 3 km (2 miles) W of city centre. Damlataş Cad 1 (near the cave), (0242) 513 12 40. Wed & Fri. International Triathlon (Sep). **sunsearch.info**

The promontory and castle of Alanya are visible for miles and offer superb views of beaches and mountains. Now a large modern resort, in Roman times Alanya was called Coracesium, and was a stronghold of the pirates who menaced the grain fleets on their passage to Rome. After the defeat of the pirates in 65 BC, Coracesium became a thriving city. The Seljuk ruler, Alaeddin I Keykubad, made Alanya his winter residence and fortified it heavily.

A double line of defensive walls mount the promontory to enclose the Citadel (Kale), inside which is a Byzantine church. Punctuated by towers and gates, the walls are still in good condition. It takes about an hour to walk to the top, but there is an hourly bus service.

The harbour is commanded by the 35 m (115 ft) Red Tower (Kızılkule), a hexagonal structure built by Alaeddin Keykubad I in 1226 and now restored. The Red Tower protected Alanya's strategic dockyard, or *tersane*, which could accommodate five ships under construction at once. In Seljuk times, the plentiful local forests provided ample timber for shipbuilding and even for export. The garden of the museum has a collection of farming tools as well as items from Pamphylian sites in the area. A Phoenician inscription from the 6th century BC shows the development of lettering from its cuneiform origins.

Atatürk visited Alanya for a few days in 1935. The owner of the house where he stayed turned it into a **museum**. The ground floor has photographs and Atatürk memorabilia, and the upper floor displays the furniture of a typical Alanya house in Republican times.

There are several caves around the base of the cliffs, including a phosphorus cave, a pirate cave and a lovers' cave. The best known is the stalactite-hung **Damlataş Cave**, said to provide relief from asthma. The internal temperature registers a steady 23°C (73°F). Access is from the western beach, behind the Damlataş restaurant.

Museum
Hilmi Balcı Cad, Damlataş Cad.
Tel (0242) 513 12 28 and 513 71 16.
Open 8:30am–noon & 1–5pm Tue–Sun.

Damlataş Cave
Damlataş Mağarası
Open 6–10am for spa patients & 10am–7pm for the public.

Environs

Near Ehmedek, a village where local women sell silk and lace handicrafts, is a *bedesten* (trading hall) converted into a hotel, with high-arched rooms around a courtyard. There is a pool, a vaulted hall and cisterns below. Nearby is the restored 16th-century Süleymaniye Mosque and a 13th-century *türbe* (tomb).

23 Anamur and Anemurium

110 km (68 miles) SE of Alanya. on the coast road. at the bus station, (0324) 814 35 29.

The town of Anamur is bisected by the D400 coastal road, with the town centre to the north and the harbour to the south. There are good beaches and important turtle nesting sites here. More nesting sites can be found west of Anamur at ancient Anemurium, located on a coastal headland – the southernmost tip of Turkey.

Anemurim ("Place of the Winds"), first noted by the classical geographer Strabo (63 BC–AD 23), was founded in the 1st century AD, and thrived under the Byzantines. It was battered by an earthquake in around 580, and after the Arabs took Cyprus in 649, the vulnerable city was abandoned. It was never resettled, so many of the old Roman and Byzantine houses and tombs remain in good condition.

Environs

On the coast road 2 km (1 mile) east of Anamur lies **Mamure Castle**. Built over a Byzantine fort, it was occupied by the Crusaders. Rebuilt by Alaeddin Keykubad I, the castle was used by the Karamanoğlu dynasty and garrisoned by the Ottomans. Today, the fortress is often used as a film set.

Anemurim
Open Apr–Oct: 9am–7pm daily; Nov–Mar: 8am–5pm daily.

Mamure Castle
Mamure Kalesi. **Open** Apr–Oct: 9am–7pm daily; Nov–Mar: 8am–5pm daily.

The large baths complex at Anemurium

For hotels and restaurants in this area see pp335–6 and pp354–6

The Crusades in Turkey

Mediterranean Turkey is closely associated with the impact of the Crusades – the military campaigns mounted from the late 11th century onwards, in order to wrest the Holy Land from Muslim control.

The crusader armies marched through Anatolia to reach the Holy Land, capturing cities such as Edessa (Şanlıurfa) and Antioch (Antakya). The period reached its nadir with the sack of Constantinople by a crusader army in 1204 *(see p54)*. The military orders – the Knights Templar, Hospitaller Knights of St John and the Teutonic Order – were active all along the coast. The most prominent symbol of their presence is the Castle of St Peter at Bodrum *(see pp200–201)*.

Coastal Fortresses

Mamure Castle, near Anamur, is one of the best-preserved crusader castles on the southern coast of Turkey. The Ottomans expanded the castle and used it until 1921.

The 36 towers are still intact.

Crenellated walls

The castle is surrounded on three sides by the sea.

Shallow moat

Great Court

Death of Friedrich I
The Holy Roman Emperor drowned near Silifke in 1190. Silifke itself was held by the Knights of St John in 1211–66.

The Siege of Antioch 1095
Captured from the Seljuks during the First Crusade after a seven-month siege, Antioch (Antakya) became the seat of the Principality of Antioch, one of the three main Crusader kingdoms. It fell to the Mamelukes in 1284.

Insignia of the Templar order

The Knights Templar
The order was active in the Amanus Mountains and around Antioch (Antakya). The knights safeguarded the route into Syria.

The Capture of Rhodes
After taking Rhodes in 1310, the Knights of St John moved operations to Smyrna (now İzmir) in 1344. When Smyrna was lost to the Mongols, the knights moved down the coast to Bodrum.

The Knights of St John
The crests of English, French and German crusaders are carved into the walls of the Castle of St Peter at Bodrum.

Grand Master of the Teutonic Knights
The Teutonic Order held castles in Cilicia, in the Crusader-aligned Kingdom of Lesser Armenia (1198–1375).

Corinthian columns of the Temple of Zeus Olbios at Uzuncaburç

24 Silifke

105,000. İnönü Cad. Göksu Mahallesi, Gürten Bozbey Cad 6, (0324) 714 11 51. **Closed** weekends. Folklore and Culture Festival (3rd week in May).

Founded as Seleucia by one of Alexander the Great's generals, Silifke lies on an important route to Konya and the interior by way of the Göksu River valley. A temple of Jupiter, with its surviving columns topped by stork's nests, a Byzantine cistern and a Roman bridge can still be seen today. St Paul passed through here, and Thecla, his disciple, founded an underground church about 5 km (3 miles) east of Silifke. This is currently being restored. A Byzantine castle is accessible from the Konya road and, 9 km (6 miles) to the north, is a monument that points to where the Holy Roman Emperor Frederick Barbarossa drowned on 10 June 1190 while attempting to ford the deep Göksu River during the Third Crusade.

Silifke Museum, 1 km (0.5 mile) west of the town, houses the Gülnür hoard, a superb collection of 5,200 silver and gold coins dating from the reign of Alexander the Great.

Silifke Museum
Taşucu Cad. **Tel** (0324) 714 10 19. **Open** 8am–noon & 1–5pm Tue–Sun.

Environs

At **Uzuncaburç**, about 28 km (17 miles) north of Silifke, lie the remains of an impressive Roman city. Inhabited from Hittite times, the city was called Olba by the Greeks and Diocaesarea by the Romans.

Beside the road are several temple tombs, complete with sarcophagi. The centrepiece is the Temple of Zeus, with about 30 massive peristyle columns. However, the walls of the cella (which would have enclosed the statue of Zeus) were removed when the building was converted into a church. Other sights include a Greek theatre and two city gates. Also worth exploring are a Hellenistic tower, the necropolis and a pyramid-roofed mausoleum. Orchards surround the ruins today.

Uzuncaburç
Open Apr–Oct: 8am–8pm daily; Nov–Mar: 8am–5pm.

The romantic sea castle, off the coast near Kızkalesi

25 Kızkalesi

Kızkalesi is situated where the narrow coastal strip opens out onto the Çukurova plain. Its chief landmarks are two **castles**, one on the shore, and its sister, 200 m (656 ft) out to sea. Local fishermen will ferry you over to explore the ruins. The 12th-century castle on the shore was built on the ancient site of Korykos from the stones of Greek and Roman buildings preceding it.

In the early 19th century, a lighthouse was built on the site of an old sea castle, which lay on an island. Legend has it that a jealous father confined his daughter to this castle, but the fortress was more likely built for protection from the Mediterranean's fierce pirates.

Birds of the Göksu Delta

South of the main coast road near Silifke, where the Göksu River reaches the sea, 145 sq km (56 sq miles) have been designated as a region of outstanding environmental importance. The two lagoons are home to migrating and permanently residing water birds, including Dalmatian pelicans, pygmy cormorants, marbled and white-headed ducks, ospreys and terns. The marshlands provide food for wagtails, egrets, spoonbills and squacco, grey and purple heron. The best times to see the birds are at dawn and dusk in spring and autumn. Bird-watchers need their own transport to tour the Delta, which is also an important nesting area for loggerhead and green turtles.

Nesting storks, Göksu Delta

Three km (2 miles) east of Kızkalesi are the ruins of **Elaiussa Sebaste**. The area around the theatre is under excavation by an Italian team. There is a Byzantine church and harbour buildings to the south of the road. The town must have been important in classical times, for no less than three aqueducts and numerous reservoirs were built to supply it with water. 4 km (3 miles) further along the coast is Kanlıdivane ("Place of Blood"), a huge chasm 60 m (197 ft) deep, into which prisoners were thrown to their deaths. There are several churches and a Hellenistic tower around the chasm, which features carvings in niches in the side and has become a haven for local wildlife. From this point onwards, the coast abounds in ancient ruins, although the population is sparse until you reach the holiday villages associated with Mersin.

Castles
Open Apr–Oct: 9am–5pm daily; Nov–Mar: 8am–5pm daily.

Elaiussa Sebaste
Open 9am–6pm daily.

㉖ Mersin (İçel)

1,327,000. NE of city centre (service buses from train station). İstiklal Cad NE of city centre, (0324) 238 16 48. Near tourist office in the harbour area. İsmet İnönü Bul 5, (0324) 238 32 71. Mersin Arts Festival (Sep).

Mersin is a harbour city with relatively few tourist attractions. The main reason to stay here is to catch a ferry to Northern Cyprus. Accommodation is plentiful and restaurants varied, with good fish and fast food. Mersin's **museum** contains local archaeological remains such as glass, earthenware and bronze items.

Mersin means "myrtle" in Turkish, referring to the shrub found all along the coast. The city's official name is İçel (the name of the province of which it is the capital).

Compared to other Turkish cities, Mersin is fairly young, and was first incorporated in 1852, with a cosmopolitan population of Turks, Greeks and Armenians. The Turkish government had plans to turn Mersin into a strategic port, but this never happened.

In 1989, the government initiated a housing scheme here for Kurds displaced by ethnic fighting in the eastern provinces. But the transition to city life has been hard for these people, and many remain jobless. Mersin has the transient feel of a port, which many believe stems from the city not having enjoyed the benefits of a structured Ottoman administration.

About 12 km (8 miles) west of Mersin lie the ruins of Pompeiopolis, where the remains of a harbour and a column-lined street that date from the 2nd century AD survive. In 1812, Captain Francis Beaufort described this street, the city gates, a substantial theatre and a "beautiful harbour with parallel sides and circular ends" as being on the whole so imposing that even "the most illiterate seaman in the ship could not behold it without emotion".

The spectacular Selale Waterfall on the Tarsus River, outside Tarsus

Mersin Museum
Republic Square, Halkevi Binası.
Tel (0324) 231 96 18. **Open** 9am–noon & 1:30–4:30pm Tue–Sun.

㉗ Tarsus

245,000. Drop-off point at Cleopatra's Gate. from Adana.

Although St Paul is referred to in the Bible as "the man from Tarsus", this does not mean that there is a lot to see in the town. The museum has moved to a cultural centre, near an excavated portion of the old city. Here, a section of Roman street, complete with stoas (covered walkways), has been exposed to a depth of 2–3 m (6.5–10 ft) below today's street level. In the backstreets of the town is a covered well, named after St Paul, which is still a place of pilgrimage.

St Paul's well, Tarsus

Tarsus once controlled the Cilician Gates, a strategic pass through the Taurus Mountains into the Anatolian interior. The route is now bypassed by a motorway carrying oil tankers and other truck traffic to Ankara and beyond.

㉘ Adana

Adana is an important manufacturing centre, with its origins rooted in commerce and trade. The city lies on the Seyhan River, which is spanned by a Roman bridge. This bridge marks the lowest possible ford over the river, which bisected a crucial extension of the Silk Route through the Cilician Gates. The pass linked the coast with the interior of Anatolia. Adana was ruled by the Arabs, Seljuks, Armenians and Mamelukes until it came under Ottoman sovereignty in 1516. From 1918 until 1922, France held sway over Adana.

Exploring Adana

Adana's old quarter includes metal workshops, an 18th-century church and a clock tower. The Roman Stone Bridge, restful park and stunning Sabancı Central Mosque are all worth visiting, and the city makes a comfortable base if you are travelling further east.

Be sure to sample Adana's speciality kebab, which is made of highly spiced minced meat pressed onto a skewer and grilled. This is served with *şalgam*, a fiery blood-red drink made from red carrot pickles and turnip juice, or *aşlama*, a liquorice drink.

Ethnography Museum

Etnografya Müzesi

İnönü Cad (off Ziyapaşa Bulvarı). **Tel** (0322) 363 37 17. **Open** 8am–noon & 1–5pm Tue–Sun.

The museum is housed in a former church situated to the west of the old town, and includes a reconstruction of an old Adana house. There is a collection of ceremonial weaponry and firearms, while the displays of copper kitchenware illustrate a prominent local trade. Tents, carpets and textiles complete the display.

Colourful traditional *kilim* (rug) in the Ethnography Museum

The Archaeological Museum, with local finds displayed outside

Archaeological Museum

Adana Müzesi

Fuzuli Sok 10. **Tel** (0322) 454 38 55. **Open** 8:30am–5pm Tue–Sun.

The museum contains objects from excavations of local late Hittite sites, as well as Hellenistic and Roman remains from in and around the city. A highlight is the natural crystal figure of a Hittite god, Tarhunda, clad in a pointed hat, together with Eastern Anatolian Urartian belts from around 600 BC.

There is also a gold and silver ram-headed bracelet and a gold ring bearing the head of a woman. The fine Achilleus marble sarcophagus, from the 2nd century AD, has lively battle scenes; another sarcophagus is adorned with standing draped women. A Roman mosaic shows animals listening to lyre music.

Sabancı Central Mosque

Merkez Camii

Fuzuli Cad (near the Roman Stone Bridge). **Open** daily (except during prayer times). donation.

Completed in 1998, this is Turkey's largest mosque and rivals most in the Middle East for sheer size. The principal dome is 54 m (177 ft) high. The architectural style of the mosque follows that of the Blue Mosque *(see p92)* in Istanbul and Edirne's Selimiye Mosque *(see pp160–61)*. Only the Sabancı and Blue mosques feature the hallowed six minarets. All work on the mosque, down to state-of-the-art wireless acoustics, was carried out by Turkey's most prestigious craftsmen.

The massive Sabancı Central Mosque, with its six minarets

For hotels and restaurants in this area see pp335–6 and pp354–6

The Roman Stone Bridge, still in use after more than 18 centuries

Roman Stone Bridge

Taş Köprü

The graceful, 14-arch Roman Stone Bridge over the Seyhan River is 319 m (1,056 ft) long. Built in the 2nd century AD, during the reign of Emperor Hadrian, the bridge may be one of the oldest still used by vehicular traffic. It originally had 21 arches, but only 14 of these are visible and in use today. The bridge has been restored several times, first by Emperor Justinian in the 6th century and later under the Ottomans.

Great Mosque

Ulu Cami

Abidinpaşa Cad. **Open** daily (except during prayer times). donation.

The Great Mosque was begun in 1507 by Halil Ramazanoğlu, scion of a powerful dynastic clan; however, it was not completed until 1541. Its octagonal minaret is a particularly striking feature. The bands of black and white stone used for the mosque are a typical feature of Syrian religious architecture.

The impressive tomb of the Ramazanoğlu family, located inside the mosque, is finished in beautiful tiles. A *medrese* (Koranic seminary) is located in the east wing of the building.

The Great Mosque, decorated with black and white marble

VISITORS' CHECKLIST

Practical Information

2,300,000. Atatürk Cad 11, (0322) 363 14 48. Altın Koza Art and Culture Festival (May). daily.

Transport

Şakirağa, 3 km (2 miles) W of city centre. 6 km (4 miles) W of city centre, (0322) 428 20 47. N end of Ziya Paşa Cad, (0322) 453 31 72. Atatürk Cad, Osman Gazi Cad.

Covered Bazaar

Near the clock tower on Ali Münif Cad. **Open** dawn to dusk, daily.

Adana's medieval-looking clock tower was built in late Ottoman times. It overlooks the Covered Bazaar, where handicrafts, trinkets and food items are sold. Near the Covered Bazaar is the Çarşı Hamamı, a beautiful, domed Turkish bath with an exquisite marble interior. The baths are open to all.

Adana City Centre

1. Ethnography Museum
2. Archaeological Museum
3. Sabancı Central Mosque
4. Roman Stone Bridge
5. Great Mosque
6. Covered Bazaar

29 Karatepe

Karatepe is a late Hittite fortress dating from the 9th century BC built on a hill beside the Seyhan River. It was discovered by the German archaeologist H T Bossert and Turkish archaeologist Halet Çambel in 1946. When the team excavated the site, they found two entrances. Each was lined with relief carvings and featured an inscription in both ancient Phoenician and Hieroglyphic Hittite. As the Phoenician language had already been deciphered, this proved to be a vital clue to the interpretation of the hieroglyphic form of the Hittite language, which was found to be close to Luwian, an ancient Anatolian language.

Excavating the fortress became the life's work of Halet Çambel. Today, the pleasant hilltop site is well worth the 70 km (44 mile) drive from Adana. The site is open 8am–noon and 1–5pm daily, and there is an admission fee.

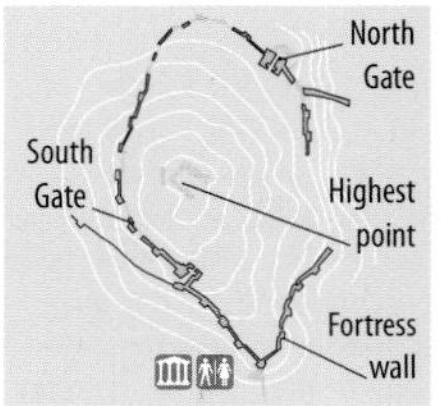

Karatepe Fortress

Karatepe Hill juts into the waters of a lake created by the construction of the Aslantaş Dam. Water from the lake irrigates the fertile farmlands around Adana.

The Karatepe site is believed to have been the fortified residence of the Hittite king of Adana, Azatiwatas. Entry was through formal gateways, one of which is shown right. Each was lined with *orthostats* (carved relief panels). The gateways are now roofed to protect the ancient stonework.

The orthostats consist of carvings of sacrificial, hunting and feasting scenes. There are numerous figures of gods and sphinxes, interspersed with scenes of ordinary people, all done in a cheerful cartoon style.

Relief carvings at Karatepe show influences from a number of cultures, including Assyria and ancient Egypt. Because of this, archaeologists believe the carvings were executed by foreign craftsmen recruited by King Azatiwatas to work on the site.

The remains of the theatre at Hierapolis (Castabala)

㉚ Hierapolis (Castabala)

22 km (14 miles) N of Osmaniye.
Open 8am–5pm daily.

On the road leading to the Hittite site of Karatepe, take some time to see the ancient Roman city of Hierapolis (Castabala) – not to be confused with the other Hierapolis *(see pp190–91)*, near Denizli. Hierapolis (Castabala) was mentioned by the elder Pliny (AD 23–79) around AD 70. There is a colonnaded street, theatre, baths and a hill fortress.

㉛ Yakacık

22 km (14 miles) N of İskenderun.
in the town hall. **Open** 8am–5pm daily.

Yakacık (Ancient Payas) is the site of the Sokollu Mehmet Paşa complex. This is not an especially well-known archaeological site, but it is run with great enthusiasm by the local municipality.
The complex features all the amenities that would have been required by Ottoman travellers, including a mosque, a bathhouse, a *kervansaray* and a theological college. The *kervansaray* was built in 1574 for Muslims making the *haj* (pilgrimage to Mecca).

The complex was the brainchild of Sokollu Mehmet Paşa, one of the most enlightened grand viziers ever to serve the Ottoman state. A Serb who rose to power from humble beginnings, Sokollu Mehmet Paşa served under three sultans between 1564 and 1579. It was under his initiative that Sultan Selim II (1524–74) seized Cyprus from the Venetians in 1571. However, Selim's fondness for the island's wine earned him the nickname "the Sot" and proved to be his undoing, as he allegedly slipped in the bath while inebriated and never regained consciousness.

Massive Atatürk memorial statue on the promenade at İskenderun

㉜ İskenderun

166,000. Atatürk Cad, (0326) 616 36 31. İstasyon Cad, (0326) 614 00 49. İskele Cad, (0326) 613 54 00. Atatürk Bulvarı 49/B, (0326) 614 16 20. İskenderun Culture and Fine Arts Week (1st week in Jul).

The city of İskenderun (formerly Alexandretta) was originally founded to commemorate Alexander the Great's victory over Persian emperor Darius at the Battle of Issus in 332 BC *(see pp50–51)*. It was a major trading centre in Roman times, and is still an important port. The people of İskenderun are proud of their multicultural city and of its remaining Christian and Jewish communities. The surviving Armenian, Catholic and Orthodox churches are hidden in the backstreets, along with mosques. None are particularly old, but all will welcome visitors on Sundays. The promenade, with its attractive French colonial architecture, is a favourite place for an evening stroll.

㉝ Antakya

Antakya was founded (as Antioch) by the Seleucids in 300 BC, and was their capital. Later, it became the third-largest city of the Roman Empire, and an important Christian centre. Antioch was devastated by earthquakes in the 6th century and fell into Arab hands in 638. Although recaptured by the Byzantines, its role was gradually displaced by the rise of Constantinople. In 1098, Antakya was captured by the Crusaders after a seven-month siege, and became capital of the Principality of Antioch. It passed to the Mamelukes in 1268 and the Ottomans in 1516, and eventually slipped into decline.

Exploring Antakya

Antakya is located on the Asi (Orontes) River. After World War I, it was part of French-ruled Syria. Following a plebiscite in 1939, it became part of Turkey, together with the rest of Hatay Province. The city's mixed population, Arab cultural influence and vestiges of French colonial rule give Antakya a distinct character. You are likely to hear Arabic spoken, and many local dishes, such as *şam oruğu*, a wheaten ball filled with minced meat and walnuts, have Arabic origins. Quite different to mainstream Turkish cuisine, one of the real joys of a trip to Hatay is to sample delicious *muhammara* (a spicy dip made from hot peppers, walnuts and breadcrumbs) and the broad bean and tahini dip *bakla*. Antakya is also famous for its *künefe*, a wonderful cheese-based pastry dessert.

St Peter's Grotto

Open Apr–Oct: 9am–7pm Tue–Sun; Nov–Mar: 8am–5pm Tue–Sun.

This cave church is thought to have been founded by St Luke. It is named, however, after Peter, who was at the forefront of the early church movement from his headquarters in Antioch. Rebuilt by the Crusaders, it is partially floored with mosaic, and the remains of frescoes can be seen. A tiny spring in the church was used for baptisms. The church was repaired in the 19th century by Capuchin monks, who are now its custodians. A festival is held here annually on 29 June.

Near the church is a relief portrait carved into the hillside. This is thought by some to be a representation of Charon,

The Grotto where St Peter preached to the early Christians

Antakya City Centre

① St Peter's Grotto
② Bazaar

A cobbler at his work bench in the Bazaar

the boatman who conveyed the dead to Hades. However, the image is more likely to be that of a member of the Seleucid dynasty, founders of the city.

Three other churches operate in the city – the central Greek Orthodox Church, a Capuchin Catholic church and a Korean Methodist church, the latter in the former French Embassy.

Bazaar

Open 9am–9pm Mon–Sat.

A warren of streets to the east of the Roman Bridge houses Antakya's bazaar. Here, you can see *hans* (warehouses) dating from Ottoman times, in which skilled metalworkers are hard at work. Donkeys are a common sight in the streets around the bazaar, and the aroma of exotic foods fills the air. The shops in the bazaar are a good place to sample *künefe*, a pudding made of cream cheese and spun wheat, baked in a sweet sauce and served warm.

This is only one of the local specialities to be savoured in the city. Many restaurants are located in the bazaar.

Habibi Neccar Camii is a mosque converted from a Byzantine church, which itself succeeded a Classical temple. The minaret was added in the 17th century. It is a place of pilgrimage in honour of a local saint, whose head is reputedly buried beneath it.

VISITORS' CHECKLIST

Practical Information

150,000. Şehit Mustafa Sevgi Cas 8/A, (0326) 216 60 98. St Peter's Catholic Church Festival (29 Jun). Mon–Sat.

Transport

Abdürrahman Melek Cad, NE of town centre, (0326) 214 91 97.

Archaeological Museum

Atatürk Cad. **Tel** (0326) 225 10 60. **Open** Apr–Oct: 9am–6:30pm Tue–Sun; Nov–Mar: 8:30am–4:30pm Tue–Sun.

Spurred on by the opening of the superb new museum in Gaziantep, built to house the mosaics retrieved from Zeugma *(see p311)*, Antakya opened its own state-of-the-art Archaeological Museum in 2014. As in Gaziantep, the star attractions are Roman-era mosaics, many of them found in situ at nearby Harbiye (ancient Daphne). The mosaics portray the deeds of Thetis, Orpheus, Dionysus, Heracles and other mythical figures in a lively style. Other exhibits on display include Roman sarcophagi and Neo-Hittite sculptures from nearby sites.

Statue in the Archaeological Museum

The museum is located northeast of the city centre, a couple of kilometres beyond St Peter's Grotto. The old Archaeological Museum, located in the centre of town, is closed for refurbishment.

Environs

South of Antakya lies **Harbiye**, famed for its forests of cypress and laurel, and for its waterfalls and trout streams. In antiquity, the valley was known as Daphne, after the mythical "queen of the nymphs" pursued by Apollo, and was a popular resort. However, the ruins of the temple to Apollo and the ancient pleasure gardens have all disappeared. Reachable by dolmuş from Antakya, there are several good restaurants here, and local gift shops sell the popular laurel soap.

34 Samandağ

25 km (15 miles) SW of Antakya. local *dolmuş* from Antakya.

Southwest of Antakya lies Samandağ, a modest, largely Arabic-speaking resort town near the border, where you will feel that you have already entered Syria. There are a couple of hotels and seaside restaurants along the somewhat scruffy beach.

North of the town is the site of Seleucia ad Piera (modern-day Çevlik), founded as the port of Antioch in around 300 BC. This was the site of an important temple to Zeus, which still stands above the coast and affords grand views over the sea.

Because ancient Antioch lay at the junction of important trading routes, Seleucia ad Piera became a major port, but the danger posed by the region's periodic but devastating floods led Emperor Vespasian to commission a tunnel to divert floodwaters from the town. The **Titus Tunnel** (Titus ve Vespasianyus Tüneli), completed by Vespasian's son, Titus, is an impressive feat of engineering, running 1,380 m (4,527 ft) through solid rock. The tunnel is 7 m (23 ft) high and 6 m (20 ft) wide.

Titus Tunnel

25 km (16 miles) SE of Antakya. **Open** daily. Only in summer.

The Titus Tunnel, a flood-control project built by the Romans

For hotels and restaurants in this area see pp335–6 and pp353–6

ANKARA AND WESTERN ANATOLIA

Ankara, the bustling capital of Turkey, can appear rather soulless and cold in its modernity as it rises from the plains of Western Anatolia. When Atatürk chose it as his capital in the 1920s, his determination to westernize led him to commission the German architect, Hermann Jansen, to build a thoroughly new city. Today, most tourists visit Ankara for its outstanding museums.

No doubt the most fascinating sight in Ankara is the superb Museum of Anatolian Civilizations, housing the greatest collection of Hittite antiquities in the world. The Hittite civilization flourished in central Anatolia during the second millennium BC, and for some time their empire almost rivalled that of ancient Egypt. The exquisite relief carvings and statues conjure up an intriguing picture of a civilization about which relatively little is known. Also worthy of a visit is the impressive Atatürk Mausoleum, the great leader's enduring symbol of immortality.

The western approach to Ankara winds over monochrome, flat, steppe country. Near Polatlı – the easternmost point reached by Greek forces in 1922 during the War of Independence – lies Gordion, capital of the ancient kingdom of Phrygia and seat of the legendary King Midas. The more picturesque route runs northwest from Ankara through the forests and mineral springs of Kızılcahamam National Park.

Much of the area encompassed by Eşkişehir and Afyon is inhospitable and forbidding. By comparison, the Lake District forms a welcome oasis with an abundance of birds attracted by its reeds and marshlands. Lake Eğirdir is an unspoiled resort area.

Kütahya owes its existence to an illustrious tile-making tradition on which the town still relies today.

Konya is the cultural gem of Western Anatolia. Its Seljuk architecture and the impressive Mevlâna Museum, home of the Whirling Dervish sect, make it one of the country's most visited sights. Konya's Karatay Museum houses an important tile collection.

Sunflowers thrive on the rolling Anatolian plain

◀ Colonnaded walkway with decorative ceiling at the Atatürk Mausoleum, Ankara

Exploring Ankara and Western Anatolia

Western Anatolia may seem somewhat bleak and inhospitable, yet the vast steppes, remote towns and salt lakes have much to offer the visitor. This is also where Turkey's administrative heart beats. Ankara, the efficient modern capital, has excellent transport links to the rest of the country and is a good starting point for tours of the region. Southeast of the pious city of Konya, former capital of the Seljuk Sultanate of Rum, lies the Bronze Age site of Çatalhöyük, widely regarded as the world's earliest urban settlement.

Houses painted in pastel shades, Afyon

Sights at a Glance

1 *Ankara pp244–51*
2 *Konya pp254–7*
3 Çatalhöyük
4 Beyşehir
5 Eğirdir
6 Afyon
7 Sivrihisar
8 Şeyitgazi Valley
9 Eskişehir
10 *Kütahya pp262–3*
11 Çavdarhisar

Sunset at tranquil Lake Eğirdir

Key

- Motorway
- Dual carriageway
- Major road
- Minor road
- Scenic route
- Main railway
- Minor railway
- △ Summit

For additional map symbols *see back flap*

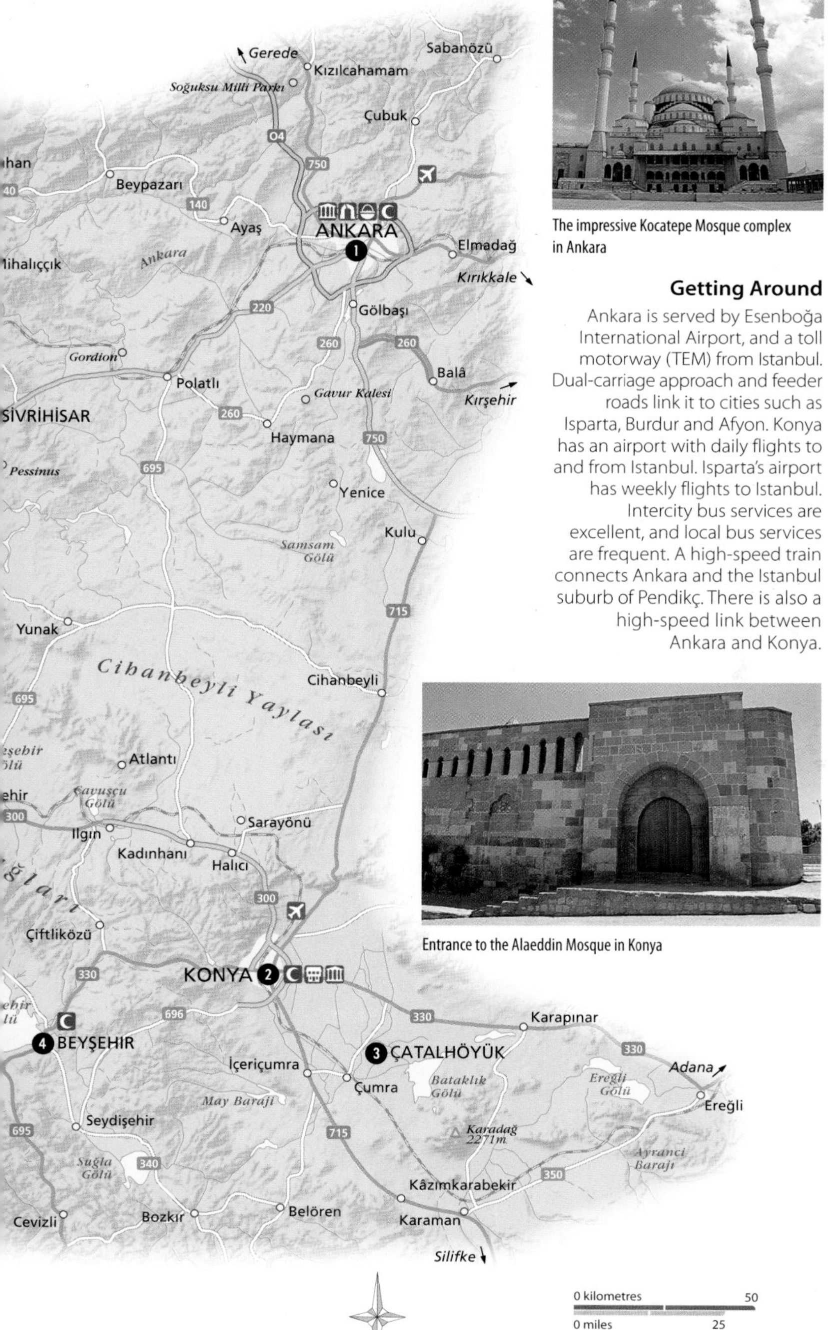

The impressive Kocatepe Mosque complex in Ankara

Getting Around

Ankara is served by Esenboğa International Airport, and a toll motorway (TEM) from Istanbul. Dual-carriage approach and feeder roads link it to cities such as Isparta, Burdur and Afyon. Konya has an airport with daily flights to and from Istanbul. Isparta's airport has weekly flights to Istanbul. Intercity bus services are excellent, and local bus services are frequent. A high-speed train connects Ankara and the Istanbul suburb of Pendikç. There is also a high-speed link between Ankara and Konya.

Entrance to the Alaeddin Mosque in Konya

❶ Ankara

Ankara, the modern capital of the Turkish Republic, occupies a strategic location on the east–west route across the Anatolian steppe. Believed to have been the site of a Hittite city, there is evidence of Phrygian settlement here in 1200 BC, when it was known as Ancyra. The city was occupied by the Lydians and Persians before its absorption into the Roman Empire in 24 BC. Annexed by the Seljuks in 1073, the city played a military and commercial role until Byzantine times. At this time, wool from the Angora (Ankara) goat became a major export. When Atatürk chose Ankara as the new capital in 1923, land values boomed and developments spread out across the surrounding hills.

View of Ankara, a modern capital with attractive, wide boulevards

Exploring Ankara

A metro system, state theatres and good museums combine with lush parks and good shopping in the Ulus/Hisar district to ensure a pleasant visit. Buses and *dolmuşes* cover the main routes in the city.

Roman Baths

Hamamları
Çankırı Cad, Ulus. **Tel** (0312) 310 72 80. Ulus. **Open** Apr–Oct: 9am–7pm daily; Nov–Mar: 8am–5pm daily.

Very little remains to be seen of these 3rd-century Roman baths. With the trademark features of frigidarium (cold room), tepidarium (warm room) and caldarium (hot room), these baths were built to honour Asclepius, the Greek god of medicine.

Temple of Augustus and Rome

Augustus Tapınağı
Ulus. Ulus. **Open** daily.

This temple was built in about 20 BC by King Pylamenes of Galatia to honour a visit by the great Roman emperor, Augustus. The inscription on the outer walls is one of the few surviving testaments to authenticate Augustus's accomplishments. The temple became a Byzantine church in the 4th century AD.

Adjoining the temple are the mosque (dating from 1425) and tomb of **Hacı Bayram Veli** (1352–1429), founder of the Bayrami religious sect. The fine Seljuk wooden interior, in particular, is worth seeing. Some renovation work was done in the 17th century by the famous architect Mimar Sinan *(see p105)*.

Nearby is the **Column of Julian**, reaching 15 m (49 ft) and dating from AD 362. The column commemorates a visit by this Roman emperor.

Hacı Bayram Veli

Ulus. **Open** daily (except during prayer times). donation appreciated.

Column of Julian

Jülyanüs Direği. Ulus.

A typical shop selling old carpets in the Hisar area

Museum of the War of Independence

Kurtuluş Savaşı Müzesi
Cumhuriyet Bulvarı, Ulus. **Tel** (0312) 310 71 40. Ulus. **Open** 9am–noon & 1–5pm Tue–Sun. (students, soldiers and teachers free).

Ankara City Centre

① Roman Baths
② Temple of Augustus and Rome
③ Museum of the War of Independence
④ Republic Museum
⑤ Bazaars and Markets
⑥ Ethnography Museum
⑦ *Museum of Anatolian Civilizations (see pp246–7)*
⑧ Çengelhan Rahmi M. Koç Museum
⑨ Citadel
⑩ Youth Park
⑪ Locomotive Museum
⑫ Atatürk Mausoleum
⑬ Kocatepe Mosque
⑭ Atatürk Boulevard
⑮ Kavaklidere
⑯ Turkish Grand National Assembly

The attractive museum building once served as the Grand National Assembly. A collection of photographs, ephemera and documents records the events that led up to the founding of the Republic (1919–23). Although captions are in Turkish, the exhibits are self-explanatory.

Republic Museum

Cumhuriyet Müzesi

Cumhuriyet Meydanı. **Tel** (0312) 310 53 61. Ulus. Ulus. **Open** Apr–Oct: 9am–7pm Tue–Sun; Nov–Mar: 8am–5pm Tue–Sun. (students, soldiers and teachers free).

The displays in the museum celebrate the advances and achievements that the Turkish Republic has made since its inception in 1923. Most of the labels are in Turkish.

Bazaars and Markets

Ulus. **Open** 9:30am–5:30pm daily.

The most interesting and "authentic" shopping districts are in the Ulus/Hisar area. The streets to look for are Salman Sokak, Konya Sokak and Çıkrıkçılar Sokak. Markets cater to tourists and sell a wide range of jewellery, carpets, herbal remedies, spices, iron and copper trinkets, as well as various textiles. Also look out for the Bakırçılar Çarşısı (Copperworkers' Bazaar) on Salman Sokak.

Local flea markets and produce markets are held in most districts at least once a week. One of the best takes place on Saturdays on Konya Sokak in the Ulus area.

Ethnography Museum

Ethnografya Müzesi

Talat Paşa Bulvarı. **Tel** (0312) 310 30 07. Ulus. **Open** 8:30am–12:30pm & 1:30–5:30pm Tue–Sun.

Set in a pretty, white marble kiosk (summerhouse), with beautiful Ottoman interiors, and carpets and mosque woodwork dating from Seljuk times onwards, the museum offers a charming record of Turkish costume and handicrafts through the years.

Triangular fountain outside the Turkish Grand National Assembly

Çengelhan Rahmi M. Koç Museum

Çengelhan Rahmi M. Koç Müzesi

Sutepe Mah, Depo Sokak 1, Altındağ, Ankara. **Tel** (0312) 309 68 00. **Open** 10am–5pm Tue–Thu, 10am–7pm Sat & Sun.

rmk-museum.org.tr

A sister museum to the Rahmi Koç Industrial Museum in Istanbul, the Ankara site is opposite the entrance to Ankara Castle in a restored 16th century *kervansaray*.

Eclectic exhibits range from toys, bicycles, prams and scientific instruments to air, rail and sea transport. Early motor cars include a 1918 Model T Ford. A replica of the Nile river boat from the film *The African Queen* is among the 1,200 items on display. There are two good on-site restaurants.

Turkish Grand National Assembly

TBMM (Türkiye Büyük Millet Meclesi

Ismet Inönü Bul. **Tel** (0312) 420 67 42. Bakanlıklar. **Closed** to the public.

This impressive complex, housing the legislature, is of a pre-World War II, German design. Visitors wishing to see the General Assembly Meeting Hall of the TGNA must call (0312) 420 68 87 to make an appointment.

VISITORS' CHECKLIST

Practical Information

4,630,000. Gazi Mustafa Kemal Bulvarı 121, Tandoğan, (0312) 231 55 72. daily in Ulus and Kale. International Ankara Music Festival (Apr); Film Festival (late Apr–early May); Cartoon Festival (2nd week in May).

Transport

Esenboğa International Airport, (0312) 398 00 00. Talatpaşa Bul, (0312) 311 06 20. Bahçelerarası Cad, Söğütözü, (0312) 224 10 00. east–west Ankaray line and north–south Metro line, with various stops; both operate from 6:15am–midnight.

For keys to symbols *see back flap*

Museum of Anatolian Civilizations

Anadolu Medeniyetleri Müzesi

Turkey's most outstanding museum occupies two renovated Ottoman-era buildings and is situated in the Atpazarı (horse market) district of the city, below the citadel. The museum displays the achievements of Anatolia's many diverse cultures. Exhibits range from simple Paleolithic stone tools to clay tablets inscribed in Assyrian cuneiform and exquisite Hellenistic and Roman sculptures. The displays are laid out in chronological order, and include a statuette of the Mother Goddess from Çatalhöyük *(see p258)*, Bronze Age treasures from the royal tombs at Alacahöyük *(see p298)* and superb Hittite sculptures and orthostat reliefs.

★ Serving Table
Found at Gordion *(see p251)*, this 8th-century BC folding wooden table is an outstanding example of Phrygian craftsmanship.

Lecture theatre

Urartian Lion Statuette
Unearthed at Kayalıdere, this small bronze lion shows the skill of the Urartian craftsmen.

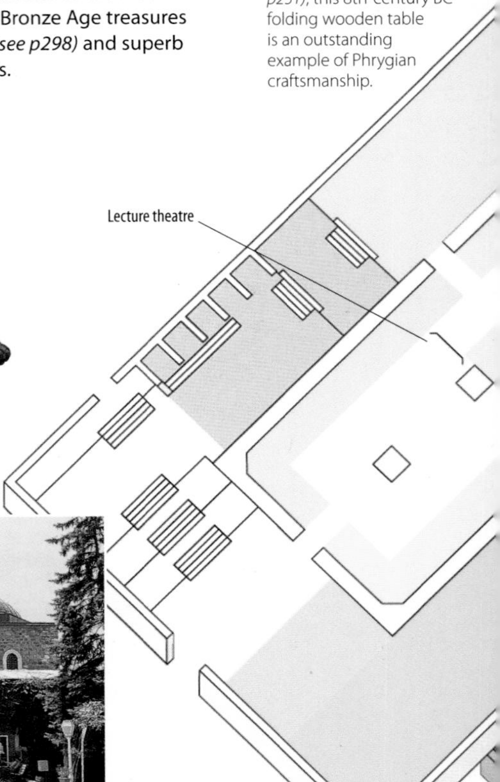

Museum Entrance
The main displays are housed in the Mahmut Paşa Bedesten, a bazaar warehouse built in the 15th century.

Terracotta Cooking Pot
Neolithic peoples favoured the use of terracotta. This small pot and stand, found at Çatalhöyük *(see p258)*, dates from approximately the 6th millennium BC.

★ Sphinx Relief
This well-preserved Neo-Hittite stone relief, dating from the 9th century BC, was found at Carchemish.

VISITORS' CHECKLIST

Practical Information
Saraçlar Sokak (below the Citadel). **Tel** (0312) 310 87 87. **Open** Apr–Oct: 8:30am–7pm Tue–Sun (to 5:30pm Nov–Mar).

Transport
Ulus.

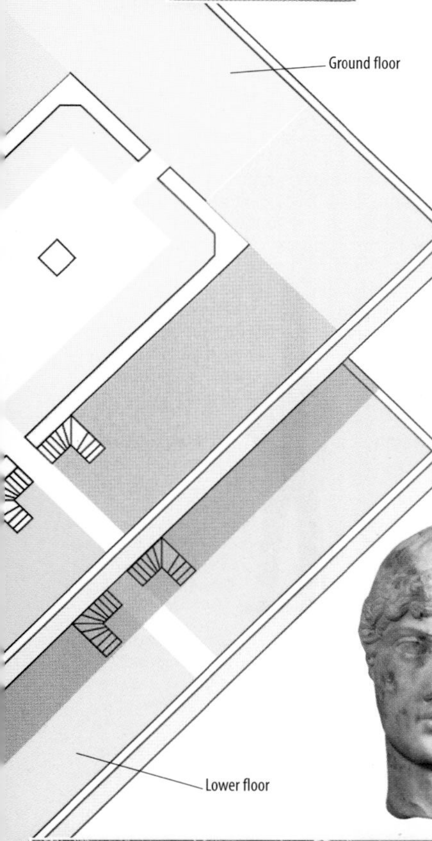

Interior
The uncluttered layout of the interior provides the perfect setting for the vast range of historic collections.

Golden Bowl with Studs
This early Bronze Age bowl from Alacahöyük dates from the 3rd millennium BC.

★ Roman Head
The spread of classical Greek and Roman civilization gave rise to more realistic works of art, such as this marble head.

Lower floor

Artifacts displayed in the museum gardens

Key

- Urartian Period
- Phrygian Period
- Hittite Period
- Assyrian Colonies
- Early Bronze Age
- Chalcolithic and Neolithic
- Palaeolithic
- Classical Period

Exploring Ankara

Visitors travelling to Ankara will notice the striking contrasts between the modern city centre and the old town. Wide, tree-lined boulevards, green parks, smart embassies, government buildings and universities make up the new administrative centre, while parts of the old town – particularly a number of streets around the citadel – are remarkably simple and traditional. Atatürk's striking mausoleum dominates the modern part of this capital city, symbolizing a fusion of ancient and modern concepts.

Aerial view of Ankara's Youth Park

Citadel

Hisar

Hisarparkı Cad. Hisar. **Open** daily.

The Hisar, or Byzantine citadel, dominates the northern end of Ankara. The walls enclose a ramshackle collection of wooden houses, with some passable restaurants, several carpet shops and junkyards filled with antiques and collectables. Salman Sokak, or "Copper Alley", lives up to its nickname, with plenty of old and new copper pieces on offer. You will find bargains and bric-a-brac here, but few real treasures.

Youth Park

Gençlik Parkı

Atatürk Bulvarı. Opera or Ulus. Ulus. **Open** dawn to dusk daily.

The Youth Park just south of Ulus is Ankara's liveliest and most popular area for urban recreation. Now extensively renovated, the park has a small lake with fountains. There are also a few pleasant cafés, where tea is served in a *samovar* (double-tiered pot) at tables overlooking the lake. There is also a funfair *(luna park)*, a sports stadium, tennis courts and a swimming pool.

The lovely Korean Garden, on the other side of Cumhuriyet Bulvarı, commemorates the oft-forgotten combat role played by Turkish soldiers during the Korean War (1950–54). The 45-m- (148-ft-) high Parachute Tower here was once popular with daredevils willing to pay to leap from its heights.

Turkish Railways Open-Air Steam Locomotive Museum

Açık Hava Buharlı Lokomotif Müzesi

Ankara Gar Sahası, Celâl Bayar Bulvarı üzeri. **Tel** (0312) 309 05 15. **Open** 9am–6pm daily.

This impressive open-air museum close to the Ankara Railway Station is bound to appeal to a broad audience, and not simply those visitors interested in steam traction. It should not be confused with the Turkish Railways (TCDD) Museum, which is located inside the station. Atatürk's personal railway carriage, a gift from Adolf Hitler, can be seen adjacent to the main station concourse. The open-air collection of steam-driven giants, located across the railway tracks to the left, includes a number of old German models which were used during the invasion of Russia in World War II.

If the museum is closed, ask one of the railway personnel in the station building to arrange for someone to open it.

Guard at the Atatürk Mausoleum

Atatürk Mausoleum

Anıtkabir

Anıt Cad, Anıttepe. **Tel** (0312) 231 79 75. Anıttepe. Tandoğan. **Open** Feb–mid-May: 9am–4:30pm; mid-May–Oct: 9am–7pm; Nov–Jan: 9am–4pm. Sound and light show (summer).

Ankara's most imposing site commands a hill to the west of the city. Construction of this monument, begun in 1944, was completed in 1953. Twenty-four stone lions flank the pathway leading to the mausoleum. To one side of the central courtyard, bronze doors open into the marble-lined hall and cenotaph, where visiting heads of state and vast numbers of ordinary Turks still come to pay their respects to Turkey's supreme leader. İsmet İnönü, second President of the Republic, is entombed opposite. A hall nearby houses some splendid vintage cars used by Atatürk, and visitors can also admire a display of personal possessions and gifts presented to Atatürk by fellow heads of state over the years.

Vintage steam engine at the Open-Air Steam Locomotive Museum

For hotels and restaurants in this area see pp336–7 and pp356–8

Kocatepe Mosque

Kocatepe Camii

Olgunlar Sok. Kocatepe. Kızılay. **Open** daily (except during prayer times). donations appreciated.

Kocatepe Mosque is a landmark in Ankara. One of the world's largest mosques, it is a four-minaret replica of the Blue Mosque *(see pp92–3)* in Istanbul. Underneath it is a western-style shopping centre called Beğendik, as well as a large car park.

Chandelier inside the Kocatepe Mosque

Atatürk Boulevard

Atatürk Bulvarı

Ankara's premier boulevard links the old city with the Presidential Palace and the official government buildings. Along the way is the original home of the Red Crescent (Kızılay), the Islamic equivalent of the Red Cross, as well as Turkey's first department store, Gima.

Kavaklıdere and Çankaya

Ankara's up-market shopping areas cater for the diplomatic corps and government elite. The best can be found south of Kızılay in the suburbs of Kavaklıdere and Çankaya, where many foreign embassies are located. Going south on Tunalı Hilmi Caddesi, parallel to Atatürk Bulvarı, you reach Kuğulu Park and Cinnah Caddesi. Both streets are studded with designer boutiques. Karum, opposite the park, is an exclusive shopping centre. Do not expect bargains here.

Atakule

Atatürk Bulvarı terminates in Çankaya Caddesi. A short stroll down this lively street will take you to the impressive Atakule tower and shopping complex. In good weather, the restaurant at the top of the 125 m- (410 ft-) high tower affords excellent views over the city.

Presidential Palace

Cumhurbaşkanlığı Köşkü

Çankaya Cad. **Tel** (0312) 470 11 00. Çankaya. **Open** 1–5pm Sun & national holidays only. no entrance fee, but passport or identity card required.

Set in a formal garden, the residence is not open to the public, but visitors can view Atatürk's house, which is now a museum, within the grounds. The father of the Turkish republic moved here in 1921 and this is where he planned the direction his country would take in years to come. The house has a slightly sombre atmosphere. The ground floor is decorated in a classic Ottoman fashion, while upstairs provides visitors with a glimpse of Atatürk's lifestyle and personal tastes.

Sign at Atatürk Farm

Atatürk Farm and Zoo

Atatürk Orman Çiftliği

Çiftlik Cad. **Tel** (0312) 211 01 70. Gazi. **Open** 9am–5pm Tue–Thu, Sat & Sun.

Ankara's many parks were established in the early years of the republic, since Atatürk believed that parks and natural recreation areas were part of his country's heritage.

His farm on the outskirts of Ankara is one such peaceful retreat and is a good destination for those with children.

There is a replica of Atatürk's boyhood home in Salonika (modern Thessaloniki), and there are large leafy grounds and orchards to explore and enjoy.

The farm grounds adjoin the railway line. It is most convenient to take the suburban train to Gazi Station and make your way from there. A controversial monumental presidential complex, known as the White Palace (Ak Saray), was completed in 2014, and is located inside the grounds.

The vast central courtyard and stark simplicity of Atatürk's mausoleum, housing his plain sarcophagus

Ankara: Further Afield

Life in the Turkish capital is enhanced by a number of green belts situated around the outskirts of the city. Here, the focus is on outdoor and leisure activities. These are made possible by the proximity of forests, ski centres, thermal spas and some attractive picnic areas. Most forest areas and parks are open from dawn to dusk; a guardian or ranger is generally in attendance and a small fee will be charged for vehicles. Taking your own vehicle is recommended for maximum enjoyment; the centres are clearly marked off the main roads. Note that camping is restricted to designated areas only. Most of the attractions listed here are day outings from Ankara, but if you want to "take the waters" at a spa, plan to spend a few days.

The town of Kızılcahamam, with the blue spa building on the left

Apple Mountain

Elma Dağı

23 km (14 miles) E of Ankara on the Sivas road.

Located at an altitude of 1,855 m (6,085 ft), this is the nearest ski centre to Ankara. On snowy weekends the slopes are crowded with locals skiing, skating and tobogganing. Although the season here is limited and the runs short and busy, Apple Mountain makes a good place to practise before heading eastwards to try the more challenging runs at Palandöken *(see p323)*.

Soğuksu National Park

Soğuksu Milli Parkı

82 km (51 miles) N of Ankara.
Tel (0312) 736 11 15 (national park office).

If you like walking and trekking in a beautiful and safe forest area, this is the ideal place to go. The forest park, situated at an altitude of 975 m (3,200 ft), has picnic places and well-marked hiking trails, and offers a relaxing retreat from the city.

The region's many natural hot mineral springs have been developed to create spa resorts. One of the best of these is **Kızılcahamam**. Of all the thermal spas scattered around Ankara, it is also the most suited to tourists. There are comfortable hotels and other facilities for visitors who want to stay for a few days. Some treatments involve not only bathing in, but also drinking, the mineral-rich waters, which contain bicarbonate, chloride, sodium and carbon dioxide.

Shady forest footpath in the Soğuksu National Park

A pleasant outdoor swimming pool at Kızılcahamam

Bolu

137 km (85 miles) NE of Ankara. Take toll motorway (E89) from Ankara to Istanbul, or highway (no toll) E80.
(0374) 212 22 54.

The Bolu area is known for its deciduous forests and a steep mountain pass, which affords splendid views. It also produces a delicious ewe's milk cheese. At Kartalkaya, 42 km (26 miles) east of the town of Bolu, one of Turkey's best ski centres is open from December to March.

Gölbaşı Lake and Çubuk Dam

25 km (16 miles) S of Ankara along the E90 towards Konya and 12 km (7.5 miles) N of Ankara on the D180 towards Çorum respectively.

Gölbaşı and the Çubuk Dam are popular with Turkish families for day outings, weekend picnics and informal waterside lunches. Both locations also offer excellent lakeside restaurants.

Haymana Hot Springs

Haymana Kaplıca

60 km (38 miles) S of Ankara.
Tel contact hotels directly for bookings. Hot Springs Festival (3rd week in Jun).

Haymana is one of six thermal spas within easy reach of Ankara, and its history extends as far back as Roman times. It is worth coming here for the

Municipal water fountain in the centre of Haymana

relaxing atmosphere and to experience the feeling of physical well-being after a good soak. At Haymana, the waters emerge at 45°C (113°F) and you can smell the calcium, magnesium, sodium and bicarbonate. There are several good hotels here, providing a wide range of facilities.

Infidel's Castle

42 km (26 miles) NE of Haymana
Open daily.

A sight worth visiting in this region is the **Infidel's Castle** (Gavur Kalesi). Strategically perched on a sheer cliff, it consists of an underground cult tomb with two adjoining tomb chambers, and was discovered in 1930. Gavur Kalesi depicts two gods standing opposite a sitting goddess. There are also remnants of a burial chamber 2 m (6.5 ft) underground.

Polatlı and Gordion

70 km (43 miles) W of Ankara. from Ankara to Polatı, then taxi. intercity bus between Ankara and Afyon, getting off at Polatı. Take a taxi or one of the infrequent dolmuşes from there.

The village of Yassıhöyük stands on the site of Gordion, the capital of ancient Phrygia, dating from around the 8th century BC. There are several sights worth seeing here, and you can easily tour the site in the course of a day trip from Ankara. If you wish to stay over, however, the nearby town of **Polatlı**, some 18 km (11 miles) to the southeast, is well supplied with hotels and some good restaurants.

Gordion was famous as the seat of the legendary King Midas, whose touch was said to have turned everything to gold. Legend has it that this power turned on Midas when he touched his daughter, as well as his food and drink. The problem was solved only when the god Dionysus took pity on him and granted him a cure. It is thought that Midas took his own life in 695 BC after a crushing military defeat.

Phrygia reached its zenith in the middle of the 8th century BC, but Gordion was made famous again by Alexander the Great *(see pp50–51)*. In 333 BC, after wintering in Lycia, Alexander led his army northward from Sagalassos to Gordion. Here, he came upon and cut the Gordian knot *(see p51)*, fulfilling a prophecy that whoever loosed the bond would become the ruler of the known world.

Phrygian mosaic, Gordion Museum

Today, little remains of the palace, but about 80 burial mounds of Phrygian kings have been excavated in the Gordion area over the past 40 years. The most interesting of these is the **Midas Tomb** (Midas Tümülusü), which lies within the grounds of the **Gordion Museum** (Gordion Müzesi). The large mound is thought to cover the chamber in which the king was buried, and is 50 m (164 ft) in height. When archaeologists opened the tomb they found the skeleton of a man of around 60 years of age, who is now believed to be another king from the same dynasty.

The acropolis has also been excavated, and shows layers of civilization from the Bronze Age to Greek and Roman times. Although the acropolis gives an idea of the size and extent of the historic settlements in the region, most of the mosaics found there have been moved and are now kept in the museum. In other places, simple roof structures have been erected to protect excavated mosaics from the elements.

The Gordion Museum was established in 1963, and has been nominated for several awards over the years. It displays Bronze Age, Hittite, Hellenistic, Greek and Roman finds, but its displays concentrate on the Phrygian period, and feature many superbly crafted artifacts. The exhibits include ceramics, woodwork and several bronze vessels found in the Midas Tomb, as well as musical instruments and more.

Midas Tomb

Open Apr–Oct: 9am–7pm daily; Nov–Mar: 8am–5pm daily.

Gordion Museum

9 km (5 miles) N of the town.
Tel (0312) 638 21 88.
Open 8:30am–5:30pm Tue–Sun.

Entrance to the burial mound said to house the tomb of King Midas

Sufi dervishes performing a mystic dance as part of the *sema* worship ceremony, Konya ▶

❷ Street-by-Street: Konya

Konya is set on a high, bleak plain in the middle of the Anatolian steppe. Known throughout Turkey for its pious inhabitants and strong Islamic leanings, this ancient city has an increasingly modern and prosperous appearance. Konya has been inhabited since Hittite times. It was known as Iconium to the Romans and Byzantines. The city's heyday was in the 12th century, when it was the capital of the Seljuk Sultanate of Rum.

At the heart of the city lies the circular Alaeddin Park (Alaeddin Parkı), a low hill dominated by the Alaeddin Mosque, Konya's largest. It was finished in 1220 by Alaeddin Keykubad I (1219–36), the greatest and most prolific builder of the Seljuk sultans.

Villa of Sultan Kılıç Arslan
A concrete arch covers the remains of this Seljuk landmark. Nearby are tea gardens.

★ Konya Fairground
Fairs are now held elsewhere, so the shady gardens are a cool, restful retreat.

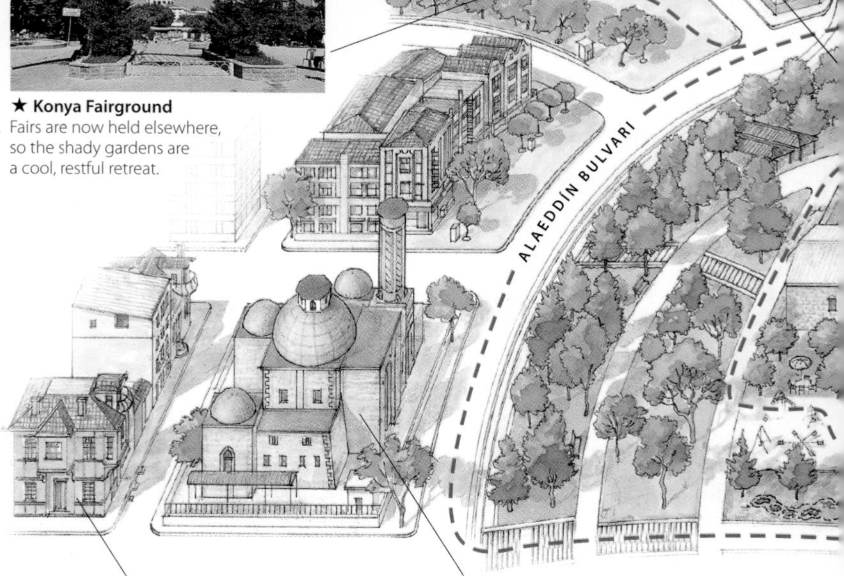

ALAEDDİN BULVARI

The Seminary of the Slender Minaret, now housing the Museum of Wood and Stone Carving, is named after its elegant tiled minaret.

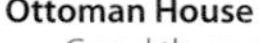

Ottoman House
Grand three-storey houses with projecting balconies are typical of middle-class homes built during the late Ottoman period.

0 metres 80
0 yards 80

For hotels and restaurants in this area see pp336–7 and pp356–8

★ Karatay Museum
Housed in the Great Karatay Seminary, a 13th-century Seljuk theological school, the Karatay Museum houses a superb collection of ceramics and tiles.

VISITORS' CHECKLIST

Practical Information
1,565,000.
Mevlâna Cad 65, (0332) 353 40 20 (ext 147/148). Mevlâna Festival (7–17 Dec). daily.

Transport
11 km (7 miles) NW of city centre, (0332) 265 02 44.
20 km (12 miles) N of city centre, (0332) 239 13 43. Ferit Paşa Cad, (0332) 332 36 70.

★ Alaeddin Mosque
The mosque is set in beautiful wooded surroundings on a site that has been used since prehistoric times.

Tiled mihrab
The *mihrab* in the Alaeddin Mosque is adorned with some of the finest Seljuk tilework.

Key

— Suggested route

Mevlâna Museum

Mevlâna Müzesi

The city of Konya has close links with the life and work of Celaleddin Rumi, or Mevlâna, the 13th-century founder of the Mevlevi Dervish sect – better known as the "Whirling" Dervishes *(see p259)*. Rumi developed a philosophy of spiritual union and universal love, and is regarded as one of the Islamic world's greatest mystics. He settled in Seljuk-ruled Konya and is believed to have died here in 1273.

The museum is an enlargement of the original dervish lodge *(tekke)*. It contains the tomb of Rumi, the ceremonial hall *(semahane)*, and displays of memorabilia and manuscripts. There are also galleries for spectators and musicians.

The entrance to the museum, with the famous green-tiled dome

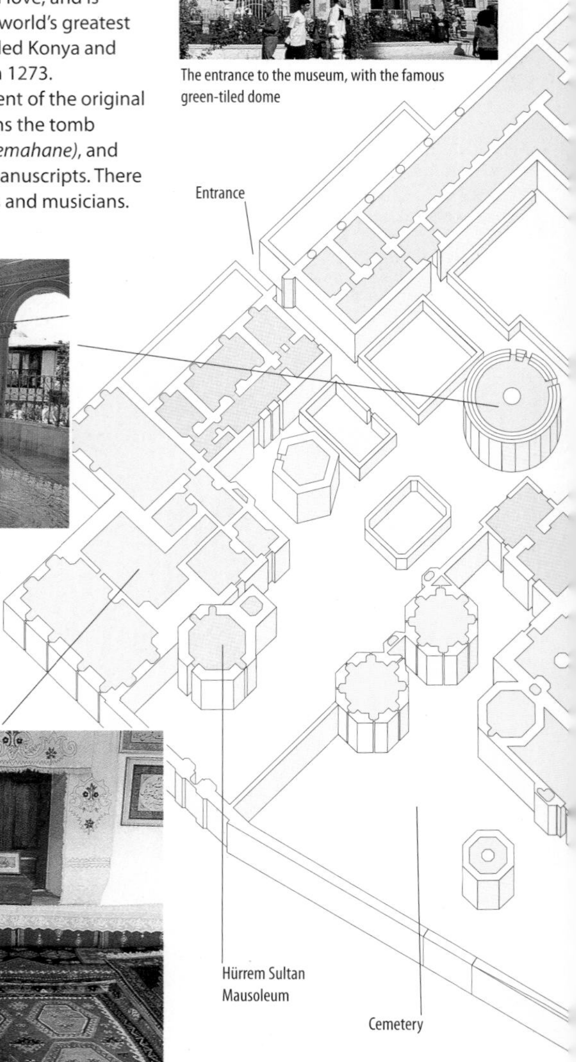

★ Ablutions Fountain

Used in the dervish cleansing ritual, the ablutions fountain (*şadırvan*) is pleasantly cooling on hot days.

Dervish Life

Life-like mannequins clad in authentic dress illustrate the spiritual aspects of the daily life of an initiate in the lodge.

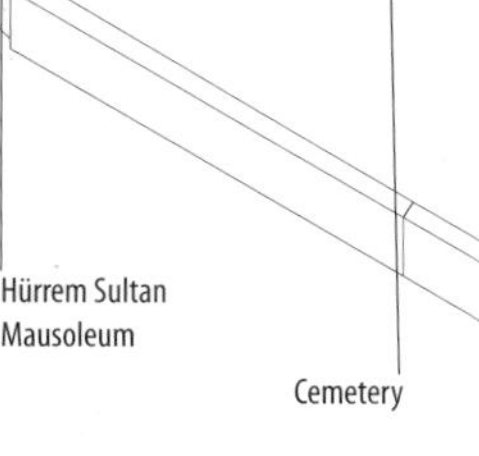

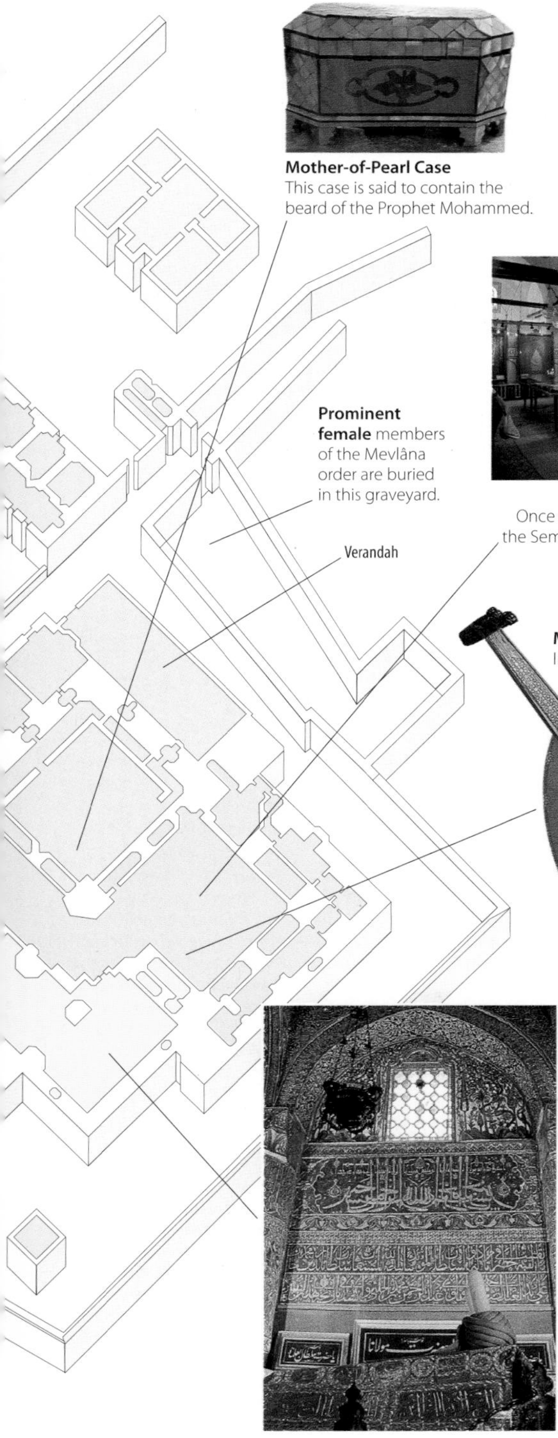

Mother-of-Pearl Case
This case is said to contain the beard of the Prophet Mohammed.

VISITORS' CHECKLIST

Practical Information
Selimiye Cad, Mevlâna Mahallesi. **Tel** (0332) 351 12 15. **Open** Apr–Oct: 9am–6:30pm daily (to 4:40pm Nov–Mar). Women should cover their heads and shoulders.

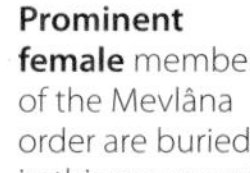

Prominent female members of the Mevlâna order are buried in this graveyard.

Verandah

★ Semahane (Ceremonial Hall)
Once the setting for the whirling ceremony, the Semahane now houses museum displays.

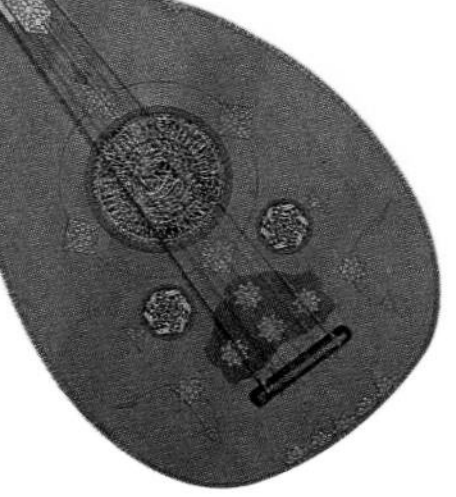

Musical Instruments
Instruments used by the dervishes include this *ud*, finely worked in ivory with a mother-of-pearl fretboard.

★ Mevlâna's Tomb
Gilded calligraphy adorns the walls around the sarcophagus. The tombs of Rumi's father and other dervish leaders are nearby.

Key

- Dervish Lodge
- Administrative Offices
- Dervish Assembly Chamber
- Monumental Fountain
- Recitation Room
- Mescid-Chapel Mosque
- Semahane (Ceremonial Hall)
- Tombs of Çelebi

❸ Çatalhöyük

60 km (36 miles) S of Konya. Own transport or taxi recommended. Turn left to Çumra, from the Karaman/ Mersin road. **catalhoyuk.com**

Dating from as early as 7000 BC, Çatalhöyük is one of the world's earliest urban settlements. It was originally discovered and excavated by James Mellaart in 1958. Research under the leadership of Ian Hodder resumed in 1993. The site is on the UNESCO World Heritage list.

It is thought that roughly 10,000 people lived here in flat-roofed square houses with rooftop entrances and high windows. The city was the focus of a culture that produced an array of mural decoration, decorative textiles and pottery.

Visitors can enter the site only when accompanied by an official museum guide. The **Çatalhöyük Museum** displays the latest finds, and there are "virtual reality" exhibits in houses and shrines. Artifacts displayed in the museum are reproductions; the originals are either in museums in Konya or the superb Museum of Anatolian Civilizations *(see pp246–7)* in Ankara.

Bronze bowl found at Çatalhöyük

Çatalhöyük Museum

Tel (0332) 452 56 21. **Open** Apr–Oct: 9am–7pm daily (to 5pm Nov–Mar).

Eğirdir Lake, a tranquil haven for naturalists

❹ Beyşehir

70,000. frequent buses from Konya, or intercity buses to Burdur.

Beyşehir is the largest of the freshwater lakes in what is known as Turkey's Lake District, and the third largest in the country. Its shallow waters contain carp, perch and pike. The town of the same name, at the southeastern corner of the lake, features an unusual combined weir and bridge.

One of the main reasons for coming to Beyşehir is to see the **Eşrefoğlu Mosque** (Eşrefoğlu Camii), dating from 1297. The wooden interior, with its 48 wooden columns and *mihrab* (prayer niche) decorated with cut tiles, is among the finest examples of this type of architecture remaining from the Beylik period *(see p57)*.

Eşrefoğlu Mosque

Beside the bus station, NW after crossing the weir-bridge. **Open** prayer times, but a guardian will let visitors in at other times. donation.

The unusual wooden interior of the Eşrefoğlu Mosque

❺ Eğirdir

17,000. daily to Istanbul via Afyon, (0246) 311 46 94. (0246) 311 40 36. 2 Sahil Yolu, (0246) 311 43 88. Thu. Apple Festival (Sep).

Ringed by mountains rising to 3,000 m (9,842 ft), Eğirdir Lake makes a good base for walkers, birders and flower enthusiasts. In May, the hills display many flowering bulbs, orchids and become a stop-over for migrating birds. Eğirdir makes an ideal base for exploring the northern sections of the St Paul trail, Turkey's second-longest long-distance walk.

Environs

Antiocheia-in-Pisidia is famous as the place where St Paul first preached to the Gentiles. The ruins of the city include the basilica of St Paul, a synagogue, Roman theatre, baths and a superb aqueduct.

Davraz Ski Centre is operational from December to April. There are two hotels at the centre itself, and more accommodation in Çobanisa village, some 7 km (4 miles) below.

Davraz Ski Centre

davrazkayakmerkezi.com for the most up-to-date information.

For hotels and restaurants in this area see pp336–7 and pp356–8

The Whirling Dervishes

The Mevlevi order, better known as the Whirling Dervishes, was founded by the Sufi mystic Celaleddin Rumi, also called Mevlâna. He believed that music and dance represented a means to induce an ecstatic state of universal love and offered a way to liberate the individual from the anxiety and pain of daily life. His greatest work, the six-volume *Mesnevi*, consists of 25,000 poems that were read in the *tekkes* (lodges) of the order. Central to the practice of the dervishes is the *sema*, or whirling ceremony. This consists of several parts, each with its own meaning. Love is the central theme of the mystical cycle of the *sema*, which symbolizes the sharing of God's love among earthly beings. For man, the dance is a spiritual ascent to divine love. The *sema* combines both spiritual and intellectual elements, emphasizing self-realization and the ultimate goal, which is perfect union with God.

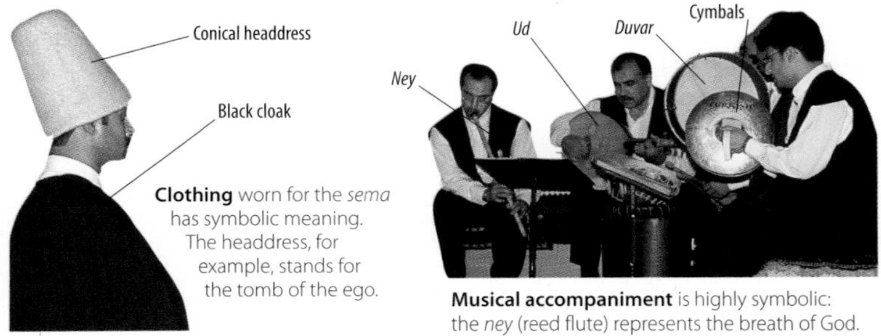

Clothing worn for the *sema* has symbolic meaning. The headdress, for example, stands for the tomb of the ego.

Musical accompaniment is highly symbolic: the *ney* (reed flute) represents the breath of God.

The Sema Ritual

The sema *consists of five parts, the first three of which are prayers, greetings, and musical improvisations. The ritual then moves into four salutes* (selams)*: truth through knowledge, the splendour of creation, total submission before God and coming to terms with destiny.*

Whirling is the climax of the *sema*. Its *selams* (salutes) represent stages during the rapture of submission to God.

The wide white skirt symbolizes the ego's shroud.

The movement concludes with a bow, signifying the return to a state of subservience.

The dervishes greet one another and salute the soul, which is "enslaved" by shapes and bodies.

The dervishes extend their arms, to allow divine energy to enter the right palm, move through the body and pass out through the left palm into the earth.

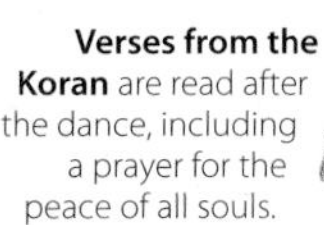

Verses from the Koran are read after the dance, including a prayer for the peace of all souls.

Cobbled street in the old quarter of Afyon

❻ Afyon

186,000. İsmet İnönü Cad, (0272) 212 09 63. (0272) 213 00 22. Cumhüriyet Meydani, Hükümet Konağı Yanı, (0272) 213 54 47.

The word Afyon means "opium", and it is difficult not to miss the fields of white and dark purple opium poppies if you visit the area in May. Opiates are extracted for medicinal purposes at a factory in nearby Bolvadın, using the special poppy straw method. The town museum has exhibits detailing various methods of opiate extraction.

Other local products are a white, soft marble, which is found in huge slabs along the roadsides and is used for everything from gravestones to kitchen basins. Afyon Kaymağı, a rich clotted cream, is typically served on small metal trays and eaten with honey for breakfast.

Towering over the town is a 225 m (738 ft) crag that can be reached by climbing 700 steps. The Hittites and Byzantines may have used its commanding position for a fortress, but exact dates are speculative.

The Seljuks left the greatest mark on Afyon's history. The major Seljuk building is the **Great Mosque** (Ulu Cami), completed in 1272. It features a geometric wooden ceiling and 40 wooden columns, some with traces of paint on the intricately carved capitals.

The **Archaeological Museum** contains a collection of largely Roman artifacts, which were excavated from around Isparta, Uşak, Burdur and Kütahya.

Afyon was Atatürk's headquarters for the final stages of Turkey's War of Independence *(see p62)*, which reached a climax with the victory over the advancing Greek army at Dumlupınar on 26 August 1922. The **Victory Museum** (Zafer Müzesi), known more for its classical Anatolian architecture than for its contents, recalls the heady days of national liberation. Most of the top Republican commanders stayed in this building during the campaign. There is also a war memorial at nearby Dumlupınar.

Great Mosque
Ulu Cami
Open during prayer, or ask the guardian on duty to let you in. donation.

Afyon Archaeological Museum
Kurtuluş Cad 96. **Tel** (0272) 215 11 91. **Open** Apr–Oct: 9am–7pm Tue–Sun; Nov–Mar: 8am–5pm Tue–Sun.

Victory Museum
Zafer Müzesi
In front of the Governor's Building. **Tel** (0272) 212 09 16. **Open** 9am–noon & 1–5pm Tue–Sun.

❼ Sivrihisar

32,600. along the E90 from Polatlı, then dolmuş to the town.

Sivrihisar is the ancient town of Justinianopolis, built by Emperor Justinian *(see p53)* to guard the western route to Ancyra (ancient Ankara). The modern town is spread out at the foot of a crag, on which lie the remains of the original Byzantine fortress. The Great Mosque (Ulu Cami), built in 1247, is an excellent example of a Seljuk mosque. Some of its 67 wooden pillars have intricately carved and painted capitals. A warren of pretty Ottoman houses surrounds the mosque, and the Sivrihisar area is famous for fine hand-woven kilims.

Environs
14 km (9 miles) to the south of Sivrihisar lie the ancient ruins of **Pessinus**, near the modern village of Ballıhisar (honey castle). During the 3rd century BC, Pessinus was an important Phrygian cult centre but was abandoned in around AD 500 or 600. Sights include the scant remains of a temple of Cybele, the Anatolian mother goddess. However, nothing is left of the stadium and theatre. At one time, it is believed that there were over 360 springs here, and the remains of hydraulic works can still be seen. The site is open to the public and access is free, if not easy.

The "forest of columns" in the Great Mosque in Sivrihisar

For hotels and restaurants in this area see pp336–7 and pp356–8

The Tomb of King Midas (left), cut from solid rock

❽ Şeyitgazi Valley

32,600. D or on foot.

The village of Şeyitgazi is named after Şeyyid Battal Gazi, an Arab commander and martyr *(şehit)*, and "warrior of the faith", who died during the siege of Afyon in about AD 750. His large tomb, and that of the Byzantine princess who fell in love with him, are housed in a beautiful *tekke* (monastery complex), built by Hacı Bektaş Veli *(see p297)* about 10 km (6 miles) to the northwest of the town centre.

The main attraction of the valley is the monumental tomb (5th or 6th century BC) of King Midas at Midasşehir, or Yazılıkaya. The tomb lies 65 km (40 miles) south of Eskişehir in a marvellous, open-air setting. The site is open from dawn to dusk and you can wander freely here and in the small museum.

Aslantaş, 35 km (22 miles) north of Afyon, was a major Phrygian cult centre. There are other Phrygian sites at Kümbet and Aslankaya, but the roads here are unpaved and there are few visitors.

❾ Eskişehir

872,650. from Istanbul and Ankara, (0222) 231 13 65. (0222) 225 80 94. Valilik Binası, ground floor, (0222) 230 17 52. International Yunus Emre Culture and Fine Arts Week (6–10 May), Meerschaum Festival (3rd week Sep). most days.

Commanding the main road from Istanbul to Ankara, Eskişehir (ancient Dorylaeum) has prospered from trade for centuries, but has also been ravaged by passing armies. It was badly damaged during the War of Independence and has few historical monuments. Today, it is a major railway junction, as well as the home base of the Turkish air force.

Eskişehir is also a mining centre, with supplies of borax, chrome and manganese, as well as meerschaum (or "sea foam"), a soft, porous, heat-resistant, light white clay used to make elaborate carved tobacco pipes *(see p364)*, which are popular among visitors to Turkey. The **Meerschaum Museum** (Lületaşı Müzesi) has displays of historic pipes and old photos of the mines. You can watch carvers at work on Sakarya Caddesi, and purchase pipes and other decorative items made from meerschaum.

Meerschaum pipe

Meerschaum Museum
Lületaşı Müzesi
İki Eylül Cad. **Tel** (0222) 233 05 82.
Open 10am–5pm daily.

❿ Kütahya

See pp262–3.

⓫ Çavdarhisar (Aezani)

60 km (37 miles) SW of Kütahya. D infrequent *dolmuş* to and from Kütahya. **Tel** (0274) 223 62 13. **Open** Apr–Oct: 9am–7pm daily; Nov– Mar: 8am–5pm daily.

The Phrygian site at Aezani (today's Çavdarhisar) does not feature on most tourists' itineraries, but a visit here will be highly rewarding.

Aezani reached its zenith in the 2nd century AD, when it was transformed from a minor settlement into a large, thriving city and sanctuary of Zeus, ruler of the gods. At this time, the legend of Zeus's birth in the nearby cave at Steunos reinforced the belief in pagan culture, even though such cult worship was at that time being challenged elsewhere by early Christian communities. Today, the cave can be reached only with a four-wheel-drive vehicle.

The most impressive remains are of the Temple of Zeus, built during the reign of Emperor Hadrian (AD 117–138). There is a crypt underneath the temple that is believed to have been the seat of the cult of Cybele, the mother goddess of Anatolia.

The scattered remains of a theatre, municipal gymnasium and stadium are visible today. These were envisaged on a scale that would rival cities like Ephesus or Pergamum. However, Aezani's influence had begun to wane by the 3rd century AD. In 1970, an earthquake demolished much of the site. Some fine mosaics of Phrygian gods can be seen in the ruins of the bathhouse and gymnasium.

Remains of the well-preserved Temple of Zeus at Aezani

⑩ Kütahya

Kütahya's earliest inhabitants were the Phrygians in the 7th century BC. Alexander the Great called the city Kotaeon and used it as his headquarters as he advanced on Gordion *(see p251)* in 332 BC. The Byzantines later occupied the fortress on the acropolis hill until it fell to the Seljuks. Kütahya's golden age was under Sultan Selim I (the Grim; 1512–20), when ceramic craftsmen from Persia were settled here. In 1833, the breakaway ruler of Egypt, Paşa Muhammad Ali, occupied Kütahya. In 1922, Greek forces were routed near here, marking a turning point in the War of Independence *(see p62)*. Today, this is a peaceful and devout town and most shops shut during prayer times on Fridays. The numerous splendid period houses hint at untapped tourist potential.

The double-walled fortress, built by the Ottomans

The Dumlupınar monument, honouring Turkish war dead

Exploring Kütahya

Almost all of the town's sites can be seen on foot. Allow at least an afternoon to see the scores of mansions and town houses.

Between the 15th and the 17th centuries, Kütahya was the rival of İznik *(see pp164–5)* in the painting and glazing of tiles and ceramics. By the early 20th century, the local ceramic industry had all but vanished. Now, Kütahya is again the focus of a revival of this skilled art. The town is acclaimed for beautiful hand-painted ceramic items, and workshops are found in many of the back streets.

The Dumlupınar monument, 50 km (31 miles) south of the town, is also worth visiting. It commemorates the soldiers who fell in the decisive battle of the War of Independence.

Kossuth House Museum

Kossuth Evi Müzesi
Macar Sokak (off Gediz Cad).
Tel (0274) 223 62 14. **Open** 9am–1pm & 2–6pm Tue–Sun.

This house/museum complex was the home of Hungarian freedom fighter Lajos Kossuth (1802–94), who sought refuge in Turkey after leading an unsuccessful revolt to free his homeland from the rule of the Habsburgs in 1848. Kossuth and his family stayed here as the guests of the Ottoman government in 1850–51, and the 19th-century stone-and-wood house where they lived has changed remarkably little since that time.

The statue of Kossuth in the rose garden was erected in 1982, and Hungarians renew friendship ties here annually on 5 April. The house is also referred to as "the House of the Hungarian Patriot".

Fortress

Kale
Proceed up Gediz Cad from the Kossuth House Museum.

The ruined fortress resembles many other Ottoman-period citadels. Not much is known about its history, but the Kütahya-born historian and traveller Evliya Çelebi (1811–82) wrote that it had 70 towers. One of the few remaining ones has been extensively restored. Most people come here for the delightful revolving restaurant, **Döner Gazino**, at the top.

Döner Gazino
Open dawn to dusk daily.

Kütahya Tile Museum

Kütahya Çini Müzesi
Gediz Cad. **Tel** (0274) 223 69 90.
Open Apr–Oct: 9am–7pm daily; Nov–Mar: 8am–5pm daily.

Since 1999, the Tile Museum has been housed in a restored 15th-century soup kitchen *(imaret)* located behind the Great Mosque (Ulu Cami). This is one of Turkey's most attractive small museums. The displays focus on tiles, vases, ewers and decorative porcelainware produced in the town from the 14th century to the present, and are arranged around a typical ornamental pool *(şadırvan)*.

Great Mosque

Ulu Cami
End of Cumhuriyet Cad, Börekciler Mahallesi. **Open** daily, except at prayer times. donation.

This is the biggest mosque in Kütahya, but not the oldest.

Restored mosque soup kitchen, now housing the Kütahya Tile Museum

Building started under Sultan Yıldırım Beyazıt early in the 15th century, but it was not finished until the time of Mehmet II (1451–81). Many of the marble columns come from Aezani *(see p261)*. The Sakahanesi (watersellers' square) near the mosque is a popular local gathering place.

Bazaars

Open 9am–6pm Mon–Sat.

Kütahya's bazaars occupy two buildings. The Grand Market (Büyük Bedesten) was built in the 14th century and stands on Çemberciler Caddesi. The 15th-century Small Market (Küçük Bedesten) is just next to it on Kavafiye Sokak (Shoemaker's Street). Don't miss the vaulted ceilings. Today, the bazaars sell chiefly vegetables and second-hand goods. More specialized traders overflow into the surrounding streets.

Spices and pulses for sale outside the Grand Market

Interior of the Great Mosque showing the women's balcony

Kütahya Archaeology Museum

Kütahya Arkeoloji Müzesi
Gediz Cad, Börekciler Mahallesi. **Tel** (0274) 223 62 13. **Open** Apr–Oct: 9am–7pm Tue–Sun; Nov–Mar: 8am–5pm Tue–Sun.

Adjoining the Great Mosque, the museum is housed in the mosque's former seminary, the Vacidiye Medresesi, built in 1314 by a local ruling clan. The museum was restored in 1999, and its centrepiece is a stunningly beautiful Amazon tomb dating from the 2nd century AD, found at Aezani in 1990. The displays also include fossils, Phrygian terracotta toys, Roman glass and sculptures and delicate earthenware figurines.

VISITORS' CHECKLIST

Practical Information
250,000. Hükümet, (0274) 223 62 13. Dumlupınar Fair, Turkey's largest handicraft fair (last 3 weeks of Jul); Culture and Tourism Fair (mid Jul for 3 days). Wed and Sat on Belediye Sok (central area). Local market (Thu) along Gediz Cad.

Transport
İstasyon Cad, (0274) 223 61 21. Atatürk Bulvarı, (0274) 224 33 00.

Historic Kütahya Manor Houses

Tarihi Kütahya Konakları

The town's spacious period houses date mainly from the 18th and 19th centuries. All are derelict and so only the exteriors can be seen. They usually have three storeys, projecting balconies and front and back entrances. Look near the Ulu Cami on Ahi Erbasan Sokak (in Gazi Kemal Mahallesi) and Germiyan Sokak for typical examples.

Kutahya Town Centre

1. Kossuth House Museum
2. Fortress
3. Kütahya Tile Museum
4. Great Mosque
5. Bazaars
6. Kütahya Archaeology Museum
7. Historic Kütahya Manor Houses

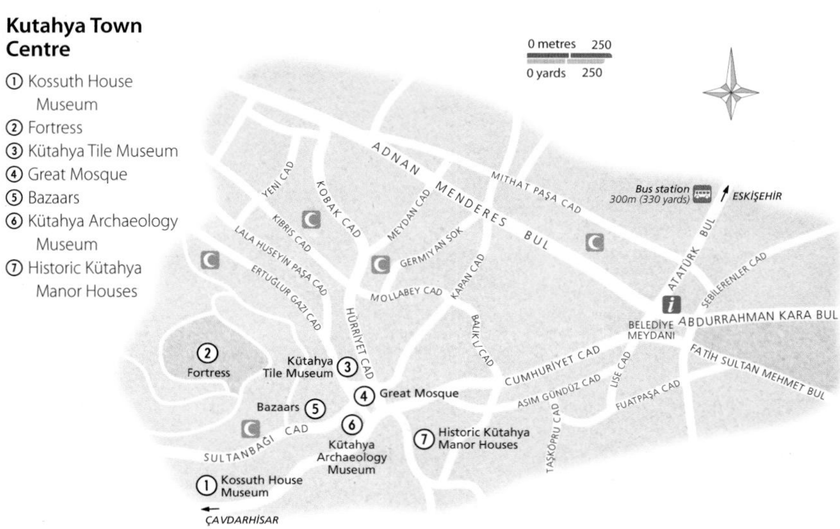

THE BLACK SEA

Although it is the least visited part of Turkey, the Black Sea region is one of the loveliest, most scenic and culturally authentic areas of the country. Take some time to explore the hidden treasures of this diverse region, which include the beautiful ports of Amasra and Sinop, the historic coastal city of Trabzon, and Safranbolu, a gem of Ottoman architecture and a UNESCO World Heritage Site.

Until the 1920s, the Black Sea coast was strongly influenced by Greek culture. Its major city, Trabzon, was once capital of a Byzantine state ruled by the Comnene family. The Genoese and Venetians were also active along the coast, as can be seen from the many ruined castles.

For travellers with an interest in religion and history, the region has many Christian sites to explore. Chief among these are Trabzon's church of Haghia Sophia and the Sumela Monastery, as well as the Georgian churches and monasteries in the Artvin area.

This is Turkey's wettest region, and the climate is moist and moderate even in summer. From the coastal highway, the coastal plain rises to lush tea and hazelnut plantations, virgin forests and the Pontic mountain ranges, which form an almost unbroken barrier. The peaks around Çamlıhemşin attract trekkers and mountaineers from all over the world.

A Black Sea sardine known as *hamsi* is the symbol of the region and the nickname for its people. The locals are generally down-to-earth and industrious. Smallholdings are common, and many of the owners have retained their Caucasian origins and traditions.

The region is poised for development: in 2011 the Turkish Petroleum Corporation joined forces with Shell to develop beds of untapped offshore oil and gas reserves.

The centre of Trabzon, around the historic castle

◀ Alpine scenery behind Uzungöl (Long Lake) in Trabzon

Exploring the Black Sea

With its mild, damp climate, the Black Sea region is suitable to visit all year round. The best time to go is in springtime, when the mountain valleys are carpeted with wild flowers. The high peaks of the coastal mountains are known for their luxuriant pine forests, alpine lakes and racing rivers which descend to the coastal plain. In the extreme northeast, the Kaçkar range is the highest of the Pontic mountain chain, which defines the region. These mountainous areas receive heavy snowfalls in winter. Safranbolu and Sumela Monastery are the outstanding sights of the region. There are many villages where locals still practise Ottoman-era crafts: Devrek, for example, is renowned for its decorative wooden canes.

Picturesque Amasra, built on a rocky promontory

Sights at a Glance

1. Amasra
2. *Safranbolu pp272–3*
3. Kastamonu
4. Samsun
5. *Trabzon pp274–5*
6. *Sumela Monastery p276*
7. Zigana
8. Gümüşhane
9. Bayburt
10. Uzungöl
11. Rize
12. Hemşin Valley
13. Hopa
14. Artvin
15. Yusufeli

Government House at Safranbolu

For additional map symbols *see back flap*

Getting Around

Renting a car, or even a four-wheel-drive vehicle, is probably the best way to see the Black Sea coast. This option offers the flexibility to explore minor roads and lanes. Take the central highway only when necessary, or risk missing much of what the region has to offer. Samsun and Trabzon are both served by non-stop flights from Istanbul and Ankara. Intercity buses run daily, or more frequently, to the major centres. Otherwise, visitors must rely on local minibuses, erratic *dolmuşes* or foot. Take walking shoes and rain gear in any season. Don't expect to find the same sophisticated, scheduled transport as in other parts of Turkey. But if you are adventurous and flexible, a Black Sea journey will be highly rewarding.

Breathtaking Sumela Monastery

Haghia Sophia, a well-preserved Byzantine church in Trabzon

Key

- Motorway
- Dual carriageway
- Major road
- Minor road
- Scenic route
- Minor railway
- International border

The small harbour at Amasra, with its Roman bridge and watch tower

❶ Amasra

8,200. Atatürk Meydanı. Büyük Liman Cad, (0378) 315 12 19.

The picturesque and tranquil town of Amasra is located about 15 km (9 miles) from Bartın. In the 6th century BC, Amasra was called Sesamus, and its inhabitants were known as Megara. By the 9th century, Amasra was of sufficient importance to be designated a bishopric. It was destroyed by Arab raiders, and then rebuilt in the 12th century by the Genoese.

They recognized the trading advantages that Amasra could give them and rented the castle and harbour from the Byzantines. The two fortresses built by the Genoese during the 14th century can still be seen today. One overlooks the main harbour and the other – no more than the remains of a small tower – sits at the harbour mouth. Amasra came under Ottoman rule in 1460.

Interesting places to see in the town include the **Fatih Mosque**, a former Byzantine church, and the 19th-century **İskele Mosque**. Some portions of the Byzantine city walls are still standing, as is a Roman bridge in the harbour.

Fatih Mosque
In the town centre. **Open** daily (except during prayer times).

İskele Mosque
On the harbour. **Open** daily (except during prayer times).

❷ Safranbolu

See pp272–3.

❸ Kastamonu

207,000. 10 min walk N of town centre. Nasrullah Meydanı, (0366) 212 01 62. Wed & Sat. Atatürk Hat Festival (23–30 Aug), Garlic Festival (1st week Sep). near Daday at Çömlekciler.

Kastamonu is well known for outdoor activities as well as for crafts. The pastures of nearby Daday offer some of the very finest trail riding in all of Turkey. The local women are famed for hand-printed tablecloths and upholstery fabrics made from cotton and flax. Other specialities of the area include colourful knitted wool socks and fruit jams.

Carved wooden implements, Amasra

During the 11th century, Kastamonu was controlled by the powerful Comnene family, rulers of Trabzon *(see pp274–5)*. Indeed, the town's name probably comes from Castra Comneni (Latin for "camp of the Comnenes").

The town fell under Ottoman rule in 1459. During this era, the region around Kastamonu produced rice, iron, cotton fabrics and mohair, mostly for export. Kastamonu Castle was built by the Byzantines in the 12th century and was kept in good repair by the Seljuks and Ottomans. Today, its remains serve as a fire tower and lookout point.

Displays at the Kastamonu **Ethnographic Museum** include Byzantine and Greek mementos and 17th-century agricultural tools. There is a library on the first floor and a coin display. The building itself is of historic importance, for it was here on 25 August 1925 that Atatürk delivered a famous speech forbidding the wearing of the fez (the old-fashioned conical felt hat).

The **Archaeology Museum** displays finds from Byzantine and Ottoman times, and has a room that commemorates Atatürk's 1925 visit to the town.

The town's main mosques are the Atabey Mosque (uphill, behind the Aşir Efendi Han shopping centre), with its 40 wooden pillars and stone door, and the İbni Meccar Mosque, built in 1353 by

Mahmut Bey Mosque, containing a beautiful wooden interior

the Çandaroğulları family. This lovely mosque in stone and wood is also known as *Eli güzel* ("beautiful hand").

Ethnographic Museum
Hepkebirler Mah, Sakarya Cad. **Tel** (0366) 214 01 49. **Open** 8am–5pm Tue–Sun.

Archaeology Museum
İsfendiyarbey Mahallesi, Cumhuriyet Cad 6. **Tel** (0366) 214 10 70. **Open** 8am–5pm Tue–Sun.

Environs
The Mahmut Bey Mosque is located some 17 km (10 miles) northwest of Kastamonu in the village of Kasaba. For a small donation, the local *imam* (Muslim priest) will open the mosque. Inside the well-preserved building are some beautiful paintings and fine calligraphy.

Cide, Abana and İnebolu are all easy day trips from Kastamonu. Cide is a pretty, unspoiled fishing village, and Abana is renowned for its fish restaurants and good, clean swimming. İnebolu has some well-preserved houses.

About 63 km (39 miles) south of Kastamonu is **Ilgaz Mountain National Park**, reachable by *dolmuş* or your own transport. Visitors to the park can see bears, foxes and deer. There is also a deer breeding and research station. This area offers excellent skiing from November until March. A culinary speciality here is whole lamb, cooked *tandır* style (in a wood-fired clay oven) for four to five hours until the meat falls off the bone. The dish is traditionally eaten with the fingers.

Ilgaz Mountain National Park
Tel (0336) 212 58 71.
Open all year. for vehicles.

❹ Samsun

840,000. Yaşar Doğu Spor Salonu, (0362) 431 12 28. from Ankara to Atatürk Bulvarı, (0362) 445 15 82. Yeni Garajlar 1, (0362) 238 11 70. direct from Ankara or Istanbul; 8 km (5 miles) from Samsun on the Amasya road. from Istanbul (30 hrs). Samsun Fair (Jul), Akdağı Annual Summer Migration Festival "Hıdrellez" (Jun or Jul depending on weather). Sat.

Apart from producing a popular cigarette brand, Samsun also holds a proud place in Turkish hearts as the place where Atatürk came after his escape from Istanbul on 19 May 1919, to draw up plans for a Turkish republic. Today, this anniversary is celebrated as a national holiday, Youth and Sports Day.

Samsun has two museums devoted to the revered memory of Atatürk and his legacy. The **Gazi Museum** occupies a former hotel where he stayed in 1919 and the **Atatürk Museum** has displays of his clothing, various personal items and a collection of photographs.

The **Archaeological and Ethnographic Museum** is a treasure-trove of antiquities from the surrounding villages. It has Bronze Age artifacts as well as ceramics, bronze and brass implements, glass and mosaics dating from the Hittite, Hellenic, Roman and Byzantine eras. There is also some beautiful gold and silver jewellery, as well as several fine handwritten books and hand-woven kilims.

About 80 km (50 miles) southwest of Samsun in the **Havza** district are a number of thermal springs *(kaplıca)* that are popular.

Gazi Museum
Tel (0362) 431 75 35. **Open** 9am–noon & 1–5:30pm Tue–Sun.

Atatürk Museum
Tel (0362) 435 75 35.
Open 9am–noon & 1–5:30pm.

Archaeological and Ethnographic Museum
Cumhuriyet Meydanı. **Tel** (0362) 431 68 28. **Open** Apr–Oct: 9am–7pm daily; Nov–Mar: 8am–5pm daily.

Men's section at a thermal spring in the Havza area

Environs
Near Bafra, about 40 km (25 miles) northwest of Samsun, excavations at a site called İkiztepe (or "Twin Hills") have revealed early Hittite bronze finds. The bronze items have been removed, but the site is open and there is no entrance fee. Hittite copper and bronze artifacts have also been uncovered at Dündartepe, 3 km (2 miles) outside Samsun, where excavations continue.

Atatürk and aides, Atatürk Museum

SATILI
KAZAN OCAGI
EV YEMEKLERI

❷ Street-by-Street: Safranbolu

Safranbolu's market area, a warren of narrow streets and merchant shops, has many restored Ottoman dwellings *(see p35)*. Because of its important architectural heritage, Safranbolu has been declared a World Heritage Site. In Ottoman times, the town lay on a major trade route. Its many handsome three-storey, stone-and-timber *konaks* (mansions) were erected by wealthy merchants and craftsmen. In summer they lived in the cool Bağlar district, and in winter they moved down to the more sheltered Çarşı (bazaar) quarter around the Kazdağlıoğlu Mosque.

Köprülü Mehmet Paşa Mosque
The mosque, located near the massive Cinci Hanı, opened for worship in 1661.

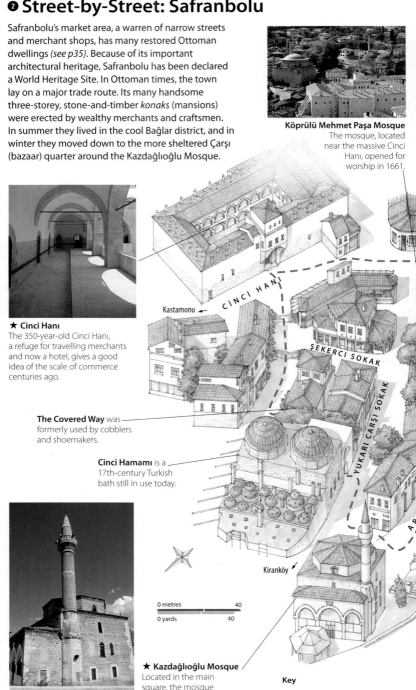

CİNCİ HANI
Kastamonu
ŞEKERCI SOKAK
YUKARI ÇARŞI SOKAK
Kiranköy

★ Cinci Hanı
The 350-year-old Cinci Hanı, a refuge for travelling merchants and now a hotel, gives a good idea of the scale of commerce centuries ago.

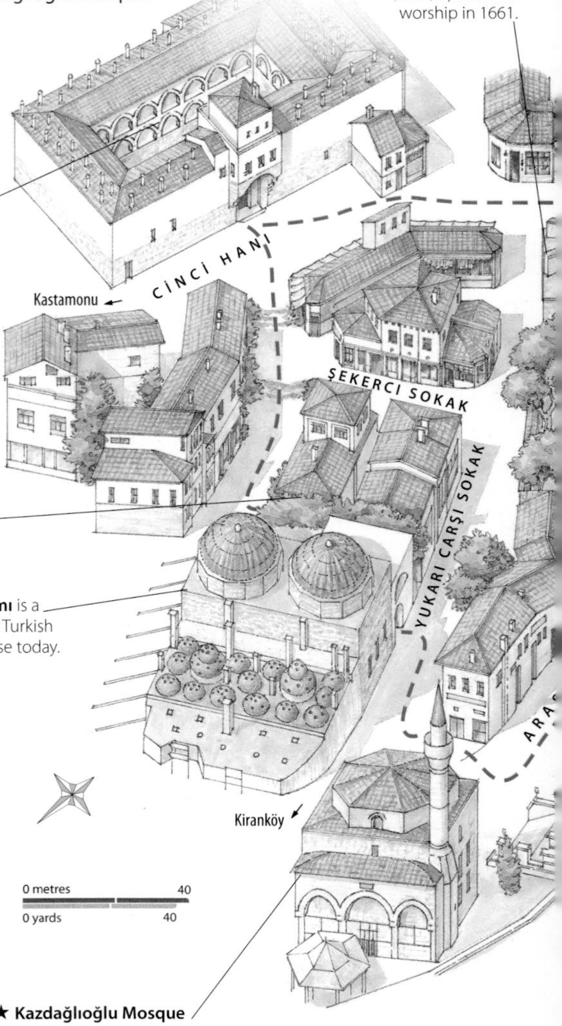

The Covered Way was formerly used by cobblers and shoemakers.

Cinci Hamamı is a 17th-century Turkish bath still in use today.

0 metres 40
0 yards 40

★ Kazdağlıoğlu Mosque
Located in the main square, the mosque was built in 1779.

Key
— Suggested route

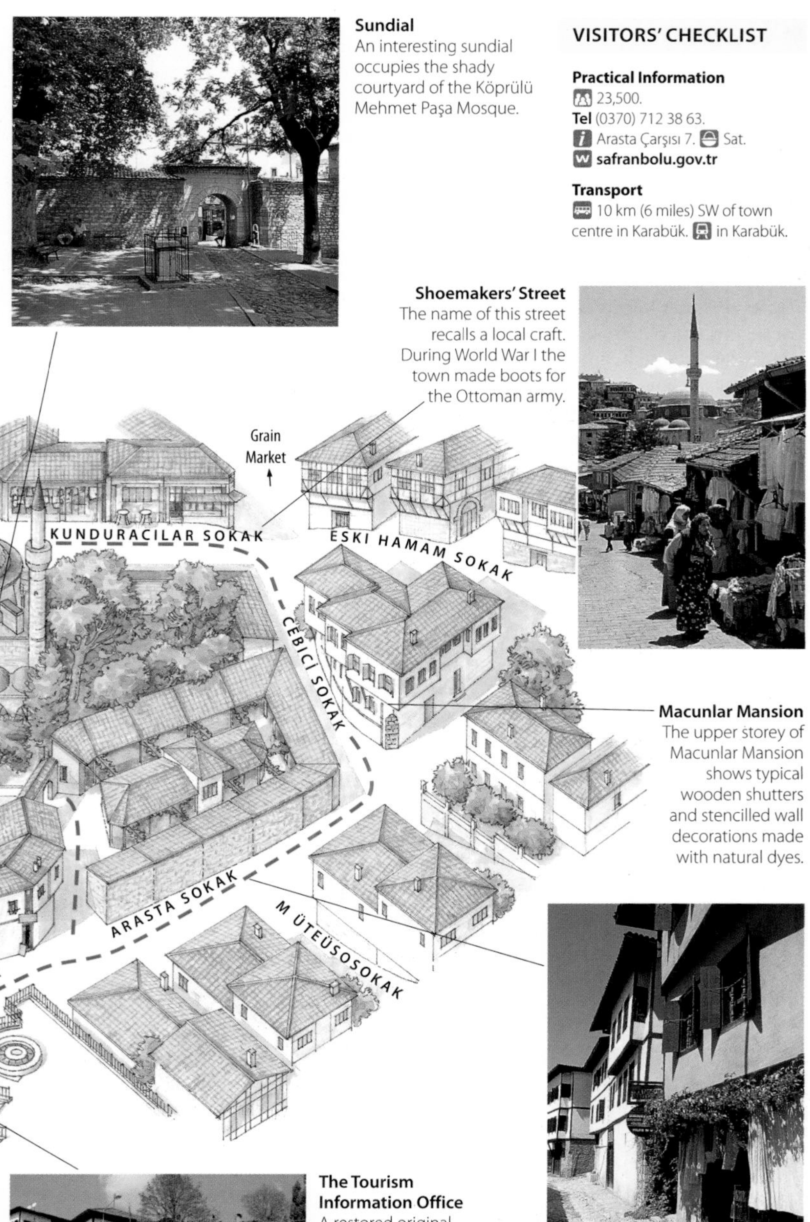

Sundial
An interesting sundial occupies the shady courtyard of the Köprülü Mehmet Paşa Mosque.

VISITORS' CHECKLIST

Practical Information
23,500.
Tel (0370) 712 38 63.
Arasta Çarşısı 7. Sat.
safranbolu.gov.tr

Transport
10 km (6 miles) SW of town centre in Karabük. in Karabük.

Shoemakers' Street
The name of this street recalls a local craft. During World War I the town made boots for the Ottoman army.

Macunlar Mansion
The upper storey of Macunlar Mansion shows typical wooden shutters and stencilled wall decorations made with natural dyes.

The Tourism Information Office
A restored original Ottoman house, built in the style that Safranbolu is famous for, houses the tourist office, located in the Arasta (market) area.

Market Street
Restored *konaks* line the narrow Arasta Sokak (Market Street). Some of these old houses have been turned into atmospheric guesthouses, complete with authentic decor and furniture.

5 Trabzon

Trabzon Castle, established in the 5th century BC

The earliest evidence of civilization in Trabzon dates from 7000 BC. Established as a Greek colony (with Amasra and Sinop), the town, then known as Trebizond, benefited from its position on the busy trade route between the Black Sea and the Mediterranean. It grew quickly and was a focal point for the Pontic kings.

At the beginning of the 13th century, the Comnene dynasty established a Byzantine state with its capital at Trabzon. During the Comnene era, the city gained a reputation as a beautiful, sophisticated cultural centre. The Genoese and the Venetians came here to trade, as Trabzon was the terminus of a northern branch of the Silk Route. In 1461, Trabzon fell under Ottoman rule.

Haghia Sophia

Aya Sofya

Follow İnönü Cad. **Open** dawn–dusk (avoid prayer times if possible).

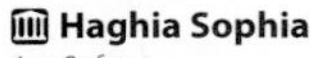

This restored 13th-century Byzantine church, situated just a kilometre from the city centre, is by far the most impressive sight in Trabzon. It was originally built by the Comnene emperor, Manuel VII Palaeologus. In 1577, it reverted to a mosque and, after serving as an ammunition depot and also as a hospital, became a museum in 1957. In 2013, the museum was controversially reconsecrated as a mosque.

The patterned mosaics here date from Byzantine times, and you can still see the original coloured marble covering of the floor. Restoration work on the old frescoes is intermittent. The best frescoes, in the narthex, are perfectly visible, while the faded ones in the nave are hidden behind a screen.

St Anne's Church

Küçük Ayvasıl Kilisesi

Kahraman Maraş Cad.

An Armenian church built in the 9th century, St Anne's has a beautiful exterior and the entrance is adorned with crucifixes and angels. With advance notice to the tourism office, groups are allowed inside to view the interior. Another Armenian church, St Basil's (Büyük Ayvasil), is also located nearby.

Trabzon Castle

Trabzon Kalesi

İç Kale Sok.

The castle is located on the flat-topped hill (*trapezus* in Greek) that gave Trabzon its name. Today, only a small portion of the castle walls remain, but the area originally had three distinct wards, each with its own mosque. The only one still standing is the Fatih Camii in the Ortahisar (middle castle) section. Before it became a mosque, this was the principal church of the Comnene dynasty and its dome was topped with gold. Sadly, the gold, like the mosaics and frescoes inside, is long gone.

Zağnos Bridge and Tower

Zağnos Köprüsü ve Kale Kule

Zağnos Cad.

Built in 1467, the Zağnos Bridge crosses the Kuzgun ravine. In Ottoman times, the bridge provided access to charitable institutions. The Zağnos Tower was formerly a much-feared prison. Today, there is little reminder of its grim past, and visitors can tour the site and enjoy a meal at the tower restaurant.

Gülbahar Mosque and Tomb

Gülbahar Hatun Camii

Tanjant Yolu.

Open except during prayer times.

Built in 1514 by Sultan Selim the Grim in memory of his mother, Gülbahar, this is one of the few mosques in the city that was not originally a church. Gülbahar was noted for her charity work, and the mosque was built as part of an *imaret*, an Ottoman social welfare institution consisting of a soup kitchen and hostel for students and the poor. The main place of worship was the black-and-white stone section, with its five cupolas. The mosque is all that remains of the complex. Just to the east is Gülbahar's octagonal tomb.

Fresco in Haghia Sophia, showing Jesus turning water into wine at Galilee

For hotels and restaurants in this area see pp337–8 and pp358–60

St Eugenius Church, turned into a mosque in 1461

St Eugenius Church

Yeni Cuma Camii

Follow signs from Fatih Hamamı on Kasım Sok. **Open** 9am–5pm.

In the 14th century, this was the Church of St Eugenius, named for the martyred 5th-century archbishop of Carthage. In Ottoman times, the church became a mosque.

Trabzon Museum

Uzun Sok, Zeytinlik Cad 10.
Tel (0462) 322 38 22. **Open** Apr–Oct: 9am–7pm Tue–Sun; Nov–Mar: 9am–5pm Tue–Sun.

Trabzon Museum occupies a mansion built in the late 19th century for a Greek banker. The finely restored house is decorated in Baroque style and contains displays of local archaeology and ethnography.

Environs

A few kilometres outside the centre of the city is **Atatürk's Villa**, an ornate three-storey mansion where Atatürk stayed several times after 1924. It was here that he made his will in 1937, the year before his death. The house was built in 1903, and is a typical example of upper-class Crimean archi-tecture. The city of Trabzon presented it to Atatürk, and he left it to his sister, Makbule Atakan, at his death. The interior has been left almost undisturbed.

Atatürk's Villa

Atatürk Köşkü

Soğuksu Cad, 4 km (2.4 miles) SW of city centre. **Tel** (0462) 231 00 28. **Open** 8:30am–4:30pm daily. on inquiry at the entrance.

VISITORS' CHECKLIST

Practical Information

763,000. İskenderpaşa Mahallesi, Ali Naki Effendi Sok 1/A, (0462) 326 47 60. Hıdrellez Summer Migration Festival (6 May). daily.

Transport

8 km (5 miles) from city centre, (0462) 325 99 52.
Değirmendere, 3 km (2 miles) from city centre, (0462) 325 23 43.
from Istanbul and Rize.

Atatürk's Villa, a handsome early 20th-century mansion

Trabzon City Centre

① Haghia Sophia
② St Anne's Church
③ Trabzon Castle
④ Zağnos Bridge and Tower
⑤ Gülbahar Mosque and Tomb
⑥ St Eugenius Church
⑦ Trabzon Museum

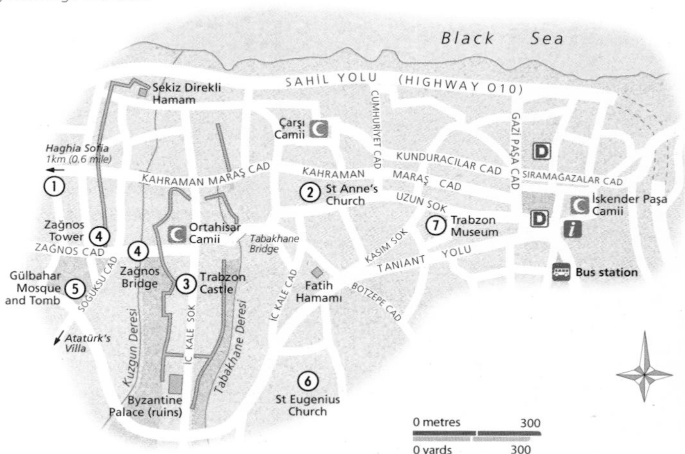

❻ Sumela Monastery

Sümela Manastırı

Sumela Monastery sits high up on the cliffs of Mount Mela, south of Trabzon. It was founded in the 4th century by two Greek monks, Barnabas and Sophronius, who were guided to the site by an icon of a "black" image of the Virgin, allegedly painted by St Luke. After their deaths, Sumela became a place of pilgrimage. It was decorated with frescoes, and its treasures included priceless manuscripts and silver plates. The monastery was rebuilt several times – the ruins seen by today's visitors date largely from the 19th century.

In the Ottoman era, Sumela enjoyed the protection of the sultans, but it was abandoned and badly damaged during the War of Independence. Extensive restoration work has been carried out to preserve the monastery.

VISITORS' CHECKLIST

Practical Information
55 km (34 miles) SE of Trabzon in Altındere National Park.
Tel (0462) 230 19 66 (lower entrance) and (0462) 531 10 64 (upper entrance).
Open Apr–Oct: 9am–6pm daily; Nov–Mar: 8am–4pm daily.

★ Frescoes
Though badly damaged by vandals, lovely fresco panels cover the walls of the church.

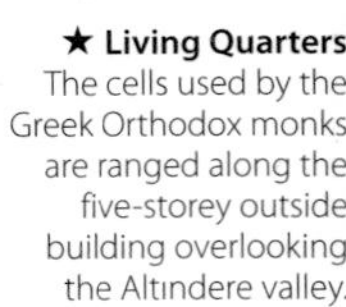

★ Living Quarters
The cells used by the Greek Orthodox monks are ranged along the five-storey outside building overlooking the Altındere valley.

Restoration
A fire in the 1920s left many of the monastery buildings roofless and exposed to the elements. Restoration work involves rebuilding the roof trusses and adding tiles.

Forest Path
A 1 km (0.5 mile) path winds through pine forest to the often mist-shrouded monastery. It takes 30 minutes to make the ascent.

For hotels and restaurants in this area see pp337–8 and pp358–60

❼ Zigana

Kadırga Festival: migration to high pastures and nomadic origins (usually held in spring and summer).

After visiting the Sumela Monastery, travellers can return to Trabzon or continue further southwest to reach the spectacular alpine area known as Zigana and situated in the Kalkanlı Mountains. There is some skiing here, but only day trips are possible as there are no hotels.

Fog and snow cover the Zigana area for about seven months of the year, and it is usually damp here. Heavy winter snowfalls make access difficult and even dangerous.

To get to Zigana, you can drive through the 1,500 m (4,291 ft) mountain tunnel, the longest in Turkey.

A more challenging, but much more scenic, route runs parallel to the main 885 road through Hamsiköy village. It is worth stopping here to sample the excellent local cuisine. The speciality is a nourishing, creamy rice pudding.

❽ Gümüşhane

70,000. Valilik Binası, Kat 4, (0456) 213 10 07.

Gümüşhane (silver works) takes its name from the rich deposits of silver ore found here. In the late 16th century, silver was more valuable than gold. However, by the late 19th century, the silver industry had declined.

Before World War I, the area was a focus of conflict between the Russians and the Ottomans, for Gümüşhane occupied a strategic position on the trade route between Anatolia and Persia (Iran).

Here, visitors can explore the surrounding castles, and several mosques. The most interesting of these is the Süleymaniye (or Küçük) Camii. There are also eight *hamams* (Turkish baths), which cater for men and women.

Gümüşhane is renowned for its rosehip *(kuşburun)* syrup and sweet cherry jam *(kiraz reçeli)*.

A ruined Byzantine church in the old section of Gümüşhane

The Çoruh River, running through the fortress town of Bayburt

❾ Bayburt

38,000. Hükümet Binası, Kat 4, (0458) 211 44 29. Mon. Dedekorkut Cultural Festival (2nd week in Jul).

Situated on the Çoruh River, Bayburt is the capital of the smallest of Turkey's 78 provinces. Bayburt Castle was probably built in Byzantine times, but there is evidence of an older fortress on the site.

The castle has a violent history. It had to be rebuilt by the Byzantine Emperor Justinian and was repaired by both Seljuks and Ottomans following various attacks. At its peak, there were 300 houses within the complex. Provision for daily needs included a bakery and flour mill. The community even produced its own paint.

Today, visitors can see a theological school, a mosque, *hamams* and kitchens, as well as a dervish lodge.

The eastern corner contains the remains of a church built between the 8th and 14th centuries.

Wild poppy near Bayburt

About 20 km (12 miles) northwest of Bayburt are the remains of underground cities dating from Byzantine times. These are usually open to visitors. For details, inquire at the tea garden at the entrance or at the tourism office in the town centre.

Outside Bayburt, on the way to Aşkale and Erzurum, travellers must negotiate a spectacular mountain pass which rises to the dizzying height of 2,302 m (7,552 ft). Around 45 km (28 miles) from Bayburt is the startlingly modern Baksi Museum (www.en.baksi.org), which displays a selection of contemporary art exhibitions and ethnographic displays.

Village on the shores of Uzungöl (Long Lake)

⑩ Uzungöl

tour bus from Trabzon or *dolmuş* from Of (90 min); *dolmuşes* are less frequent in the winter months.

For mountain scenery, few places in Turkey compare with this alpine lake, which was carved out during the Ice Ages. At an altitude of over 1,000 m (3,280 ft), Uzungöl (Long Lake) is a hidden gem surrounded by lush greenery and remote meadows.

At weekends, Uzungöl is popular with local people, who journey here by *dolmuş* from the coastal village, Of, but there is not much to do besides camping, hiking in the nearby hills, fishing and relaxing. The village has a few basic hotels, and the local lake trout is excellent.

⑪ Rize

104,000. 0.8 km (0.5 mile) west of town. Valilik Binası, A Blok, Kat 5, (0464) 213 04 07. Russian bazaar daily. Tea Festival (3rd week Jun).

In ancient times, Rize was ruled by the Pontic kings *(see p302)* and was known as Rhizus. The name means "rice", although the town is now better known for its tea.

Rize was strongly fortified by the Byzantines in the 6th century and later became part of the Comnene empire. Like Trabzon, it came under Ottoman control in 1461.

In Ottoman times, many people left Rize to seek work in Russia. There they learned the art of bread- and pastry-making, which they brought back with them when they returned. Today, many of Turkey's master pastry chefs and bakers come from Rize.

Visitors will notice many locals clad in the versatile *Rize bezi*, a light cloth made of silk, cotton or wool, in black and purple. It is mainly used as a head covering for women, but also doubles as a useful rain bonnet and a handy receptacle when the local women go out to gather tea leaves.

The small **Rize Museum** is not outstanding, but has some displays of local life and lore.

Rize Museum
Piri Çelebi Mahellesi, PTT Arkası.
Tel (0464) 214 02 35. **Open** 9am–noon & 1–5:30pm Tue–Sun.

⑫ Hemşin Valley

42 km (26 miles) E of Rize.

East of Rize, the road turns off to the Hemşin Valley. About 20 km (12 miles) further east a second turning goes to Çamlıhemşin. The road rises steeply and the air is filled with the smell of boxwood trees. This area lies deep within the Kaçkar Mountains (Kaçkar Dağları), at an altitude of 3,932 m (12,900 ft).

Continue on the same road signposted to Ayder, famous for its hot springs. The local inhabitants, the Hemşin, were once Christian Armenians who converted to Islam. They delight in their seasonal festivals, folklore traditions and distinctive ethnic costumes.

A staple food of the valley is *mıhlama* (corn bread), that is served hot from the baking pan. Sometimes, *lor* (white, unsalted cheese) is served alongside *mıhlama* as a breakfast dish.

Corn bread, Hemşin Valley

There are two castles near Çamlıhemşin. One is Kale-i Bala, above the village of Hisarcık Köyü, dating from 200 BC. Further up the valley is the lonely Zilkalesi (Bell Castle) with eight ramparts overlooking the valley of the Storm River (Fırtına Çayı).

Turkish Tea

Turkey's first tea plants were brought from Japan in 1878, but the industry did not take off until the 1930s. The moist climate of the Black Sea coast provides superb growing conditions. Rize is the centre of the Turkish tea industry, and the home of the country's Tea Institute (Çay Enstitüsü).

To sample the best tea, look for *tomurcuk* (the flowering bud of the tea bush). Leaves from other parts of the plant are not as flavourful. Turks prefer the black tea sold in local markets; green tea is exported. Specialized fragrant teas are also produced, again mostly for export.

Glasses, spoons, sugar and some good company are all part of enjoying Turkish tea, which is brewed in a double boiler. The leaves are scalded before brewing to impart an earthy, smoky flavour.

Turkish tea served in a typical "tulip" glass

Roads and driving in general are a challenge in the Hemşin Valley's short summer season. A four-wheel-drive vehicle is recommended, as local *dolmuş* transport can be daily, not hourly.

Because of the vertical valleys, local people have devised an ingenious transport solution: the *vargel*, a cable car on a pulley system. It is powered by electricity (or people power, if no electricity is available). It is a quaint solution, which offers a bird's-eye view of the isolated gorges.

Russian dolls for sale in Hopa, near the Georgian border

⓭ Hopa

on W bank of river.

Hopa is the last main town before the frontier with Georgia. It is a garrison town, and there is a strong military presence. Hopa was a major port in ancient times, and is still the main seaport (after Trabzon) on the eastern Black Sea coast. Today, the town is dominated by the boat-building industry and a large thermal power station.

⓮ Artvin

25,000. Katliotopark Binası, Kat 3, (0466) 212 30 71. Kafkasör Festival (Jun). **artvin.gov.tr**

Artvin receives more rain than any other place in Turkey, so everything grows wonderfully here. The people of Artvin are known for their many festivals, which feature traditional dancing, games, music, food and costumes. The major annual celebration is the Kafkasör (Caucasian) Festival in June, featuring the spectacle of fighting bulls.

Bulls fighting at the Kafkasör Festival in Artvin

Around Artvin are a number of beautiful villages. Şavşat, about 55 km (34 miles) to the east on the road to Ardahan, is a lovely alpine hamlet. The road goes on to Veliköy and, 19 km (11 miles) further on, reaches the **Karagöl-Sahara National Park**, which has extensive forests and lakes.

Environs

A series of fifteen dams have been built or are under construction in the mountains around Artvin and Yusufeli as part of the Çoruh River Development Plan. The largest are near Yusufeli, and will be completed in 2018. The dams will generate power for the region, but many are critical as construction work has destroyed parts of the local environment and threatened the survival of native plants and animals.

Karagöl-Sahara National Park
Tel (0466) 531 21 37. **Open** May–Oct: daily. for cars only.

⓯ Yusufeli

68 km (42 miles) S of Artvin or 150 km (93 miles) NE of Bayburt (difficult route). 4,000.

Yusufeli is a nature lover's paradise, with some of the most rugged scenery in Turkey. As it is a designated conservation area, hunting is strictly controlled and many wild species are protected.

Yusufeli is becoming well known for whitewater rafting *(see p372)* on the challenging Çoruh River. The best time to go is in spring when the wild flowers are in bloom. There are outstanding opportunities for photography, particularly around the deep, icy lakes.

Around Yusufeli, there are many Georgian and Armenian churches and out-of-the way castles. Dört Kilise (Four Churches) is a few kilometres southwest of the town, while İşhan is a superb 11th-century church in the mountains east of Yusufeli off the main road (signposted to Olur). A track leads to the church.

The churning waters of the spectacular Çoruh River

CAPPADOCIA AND CENTRAL ANATOLIA

Central Anatolia is one of Turkey's few completely landlocked regions. The ancient cities of Boğazkale and Alacahöyük reveal the Hittite presence in this area during the 1st and 2nd millennia BC. Most of the artifacts from these places are now housed in museums, but visitors can imagine the impact and extent of the impressive civilization that once flourished in the region.

In the ancient Persian language, Cappadocia meant "land of beautful horses", and in Roman times, brood mares from Cappadocia were so highly prized that a special tax was imposed on their sale.

Trying to describe Cappadocia in physical terms simply does not do justice to the air of mystery that pervades the area. Remarkable conical rock outcrops, called *peri bacaları* (fairy chimneys), are the region's most famous and characteristic feature. Carved into the rock are scores of hidden chapels adorned with exquisite frescoes – ample proof of the strength of the Christian faith that was established here by the 4th century AD.

Over the centuries, Central Anatolia has nurtured vast armies and great empires, and its history and prosperity have always been linked to the land and agriculture. Today, tourism has become the mainstay of the local economy, but the region still produces many of Turkey's cereal crops as well as grapes, vegetable oils and sugar beets. The diary of a 4th-century saint even records wine as a local product.

Kayseri, the major city, is known as much for its many varieties of *pastırma* (cured beef) as for its industrious but conservative inhabitants. A gentler side of the region is to be found near Amasya along the picturesque Yeşilırmak River.

Konaks (mansion houses) along the bank of the Yeşilırmak River

◀ Dwellings carved into the rocks in Güzelyurt, Cappadocia

Exploring Cappadocia and Central Anatolia

The majestic jewel of Central Anatolia is the Cappadocia region, a bewitching landscape of spectacularly eroded tuff (hardened volcanic ash). Mount Erciyes (Erciyes Dağı), an extinct volcano, looms over this haunting panorama. Volcanic deposits have made this a fertile area for agriculture, with grapes, apricots, cherries, sugar beets and chickpeas grown locally.

The main Hittite sites in Asia Minor are found at Boğazkale and Alacahöyük. Often neglected, Kayseri is a treasure-trove of Seljuk history and should not be missed. The Pontic kings *(see p52)* once ruled in Amasya, an unspoiled town in the valley of the Yeşilırmak River. The region's varied sights complement the country crafts, such as carpet weaving and the beautiful decorative pottery produced around Avanos.

Uçhisar village, overlooked by cave dwellings

Hot-air balloon drifting over the eroded tuff landscape

Sights at a Glance

1. Nevşehir
2. *Göreme Open-Air Museum pp288–9*
3. Mustafapaşa
4. *Kayseri pp294–5*
5. Bünyan
6. Mount Erciyes
7. Soğanlı
8. Niğde
9. Güzelyurt
10. Ihlara Valley
11. Aksaray
12. Kırşehir
13. Hacı Bektaş
14. Yozgat
15. *Boğazkale pp300–1*
16. Alacahöyük
17. Çorum
18. *Amasya pp302–3*
19. Tokat
20. Sivas

For additional map symbols *see back flap*

The King's Gate at Boğazkale, in Hattuşaş National Park

Key

- Major road
- Dual carriageway
- Minor road
- Scenic route
- Main railway
- Minor railway
- △ Summit

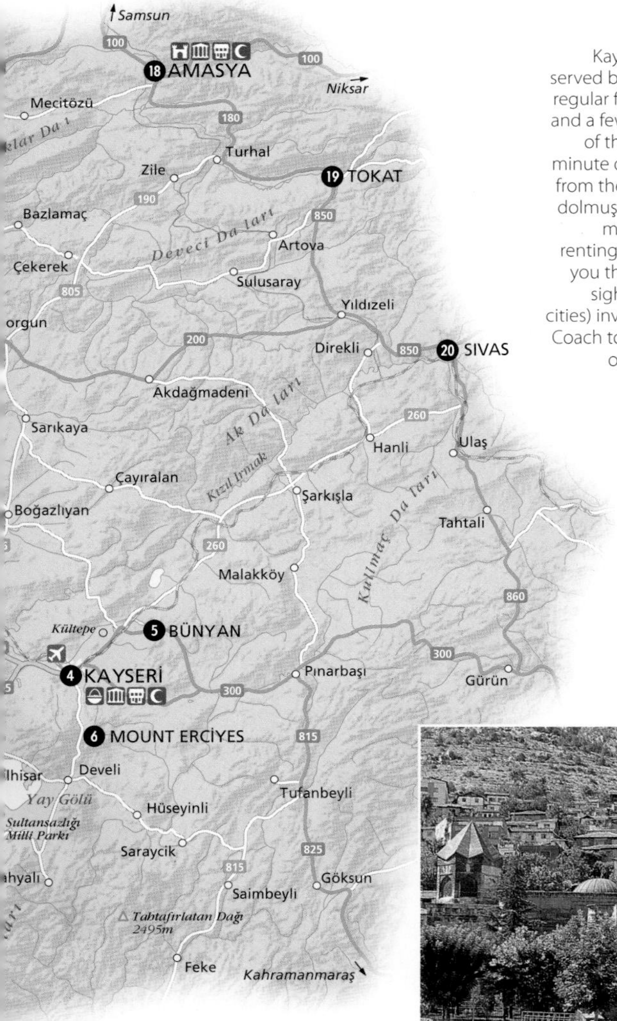

0 kilometres 50
0 miles 25

Getting Around

Kayseri and Nevşehir are both served by intercity buses, as well as regular flights to and from Istanbul and a few other Turkish cities. Most of the main sights are a 40–60-minute drive on good paved roads from these centres. Minibuses and dolmuşes run frequently between major tourist attractions, but renting your own vehicle will give you the greatest flexibility. Some sights (even the underground cities) involve quite a bit of walking. Coach tours from centres throughout Turkey serve the region.

The Blue Seminary (Gök Medresesi) in Amasya

Rock Formations of Cappadocia

The landscape of Cappadocia was created around 30 million years ago, when erupting volcanoes blanketed the region with ash. The ash solidified into an easily eroded material called tuff, overlain in places by layers of hard volcanic rock. Over time, the tuff was worn away, creating distinctive formations, including the capped-cone "fairy chimneys" near Ürgüp. Cappadocia covers a relatively small area – around 300 sq km (116 sq miles). It has become a popular area for tourists, and the area around Nevşehir, together with nearby Ürgüp and Göreme *(see pp286–7)*, offer the best opportunities to see the bewitching natural formations for which the region is celebrated.

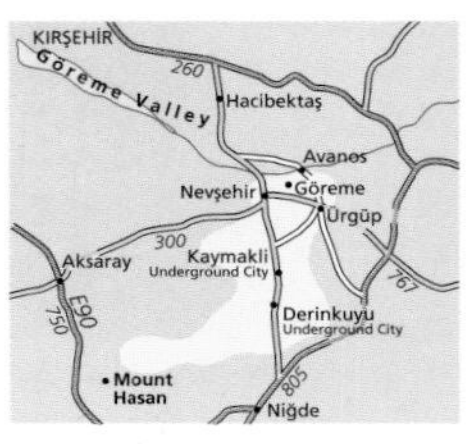

Locator Map

Tuff Formation

Erosion and Weathering

Cappadocia's extraordinary landscape is partly the result of erosion by water, wind and changes in temperature. Rainfall and rivers wear down the tuff and, like the wind, carry away loose material. In winter, extreme temperature changes cause the rocks to expand and contract and eventually to disintegrate.

Cavities below the hard layer are turned into dwellings.

Complete erosion wears away the protective caps and creates the conical shapes found in the Göreme Valley.

Mushroom Shape
This "mushroom" rock, an unusual example of erosion, is located near Gülşehir.

Fairy Chimneys

The extraordinary formations pictured below are called "fairy chimneys" because early inhabitants of Cappadocia believed that they were the chimneys of fairies, who lived under the ground. Some of them reach heights of up to 40 m (130 ft).

Elongated Shape These columns are capped with layers of slightly harder material.

Pedestal Shape Created when a lump of basalt rests atop a tuff column.

Cone Shape Erosion thins tuff beneath the basalt cap, which then falls off.

Eroded Tuff Field

In the triangle defined by Nevşehir, Ürgüp and Avanos, the tuff layer was originally up to 100 m (328 ft) thick. As the older tuff continues to erode, younger cones are formed. This process has been taking place for around 10 million years.

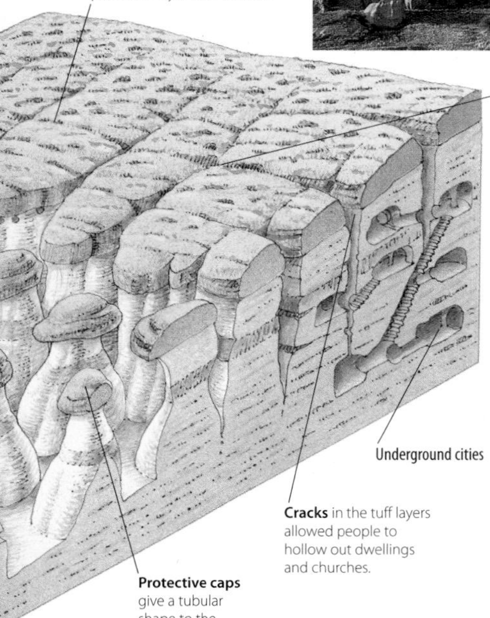
Lava flows harden into a protective layer over the tuff.
Erosion widens cracks and fissures, separating sections from the main body and allowing for the development of strange shapes.
Underground cities
Cracks in the tuff layers allowed people to hollow out dwellings and churches.
Protective caps give a tubular shape to the eroded formation.

Volcanoes of Anatolia

Snowcapped Mount Erciyes, 20 km (13 miles) southwest of Kayseri

Volcanic activity in Central Anatolia is a product of the region's position *(see pp22–3)* at the boundaries of two of the tectonic plates that make up the Earth's crust. Mount Erciyes is the largest in a chain of extinct volcanoes created by the collision of the heavy Arabian with the lighter Anatolian Plate. The collision pushed magma to the surface, building up immense pressure and eventually causing Mounts Erciyes, Hasan and others to erupt, spewing forth enormous amounts of rock and lava that greatly altered the landscape of Central Anatolia. The Hittites *(see pp48–9)* worshipped snow-covered Mount Erciyes. They called it "Harkassos" (White Mountain).

Underground Cities

The softness of the tuff made it easy to excavate in order to create dwellings. In some places, as at Derinkuyu (above), whole cities were constructed underground. These settlements had living quarters, stables, wells, ventilation systems, churches and storage rooms.

❶ Nevşehir

As the capital of Cappadocia, Nevşehir makes a very good starting point for touring the region. Known as Nyssa in antiquity, the town has the Kurşunlu Mosque and *medrese* *(see p36)*, dating from 1725, as well as a castle and a good museum. The surrounding tuff formations and troglodyte (underground) cities are the most popular attractions, but visitors are likely to leave the Nevşehir area with strong memories of sunflowers, chickpeas, donkeys and sugar beets, as well as apricots drying on rooftops. Christianity has a long history in the Nevşehir region, with monks and hermits inhabiting Cappadocia as early as the 4th century.

Passageway in Derinkuyu, showing "millstone" door

Zelve

10 km (6.2 miles) NE of Nevşehir.
Open Apr–Oct: 8am–7pm daily; Nov–Mar: 8am–5pm daily.

A secluded monastic retreat, Zelve lies in a series of deep valleys and is dotted with rooms and caves on many levels. Metal walkways and stairs lead to less accessible chapels and hide-aways which hold a few frescoes. In 1950 an earthquake shook the Çavuşın/Zelve area, and the cave dwellings remain somewhat unkempt today. The nature of the site will appeal to the fit and adventurous. Many of the caves and rooms are only accessed by clambering through dark holes and tunnels, so bring a torch and spare batteries.

Two small churches lie on the valley floor: the Üzümlü Kilise (Grape Church) and the Balık Kilise (Fish Church), both featuring ornate carvings. The latter is an Ottoman mosque, but with a stone steeple.

Derinkuyu

30 km (18.6 miles) S of Nevşehir.
Open Apr–Oct: 8am–7pm daily; Nov–Mar: 8am–5pm daily.

There are believed to be about 36 underground cities in this region, but only a few have been excavated. Of these, Derinkuyu (deep well) is the biggest, most popular and best lit. It is thought to have been home to around 20,000 people. The eight-level complex is 60 m (197 ft) deep. A long "transit" tunnel was supposed to have linked Derinkuyu with a similar "ant hill" settlement at Kaymaklı, about 10 km (6 miles) away. At peak times (11am–3pm) the tunnels can get somewhat uncomfortably crowded – anyone who tries to backtrack will be very unpopular.

The first levels include a stable, winepress and a large vault. Deeper down, there are living quarters, a kitchen and a church.

The heavy millstones recessed into the walls were, in fact, doors that could be rolled into place to seal off strategic areas of the settlement. Huge ventilation shafts still function, but damp is a problem. Living here for any extended period of time could not have been easy.

Ürgüp

12 km (7 miles) E of Nevşehir.
18,000. Parkı İçi, (0384) 341 40 59. Wine and Grape Festival (end Sep, early Oct).

Ürgüp is now so synonymous with the troglodyte cities built during Byzantine times that it is easy to overlook the town's

Spread over three valleys and with many fairy chimneys, Zelve was inhabited until 1952

House in Ürgüp dating from the period of Greek habitation

VISITORS' CHECKLIST

Practical Information
162,000. in front of the State Hospital, (0384) 212 95 73. Cappadocia Mountain Biking Festival (1st week Jul).

Transport
Kapadokya, (0384) 421 44 50. Gülşehir Cad, Nevtur, (0384) 213 11 71 and 213 12 29. Göreme Tur, (0384) 213 55 37 and 213 47 09.

Roman and Seljuk history. Ürgüp's ancient name was Assiana, and it was known as Başhisar under the Seljuks. Seljuk influence can be seen in the 13th-century remains of the Kadıkalesi (castle) and the Altıkapı Tomb. Near the Nükrettin Mausoleum is a library named after Tasinağa, a 19th-century town squire. Until 1923, when Turkey became a republic, the town had a large Greek population.

Ürgüp's **museum** contains ceramics and statues from prehistoric to Byzantine times, as well as displays of textiles, costumes, weapons and books.

Ürgüp is a convenient base to tour Cappadocia. There are plenty of pensions and hotels, yet the town has retained its village charm. This area has always been well-known for its farm produce, particularly for grapes. Ürgüp-labelled wine is refreshing and light. In general, the white wines are more authentic and interesting than the reds.

Several local spots offer impromptu entertainment in the evenings.

Museum
Kayser Cad 39. **Tel** (0384) 341 40 82.
Open 8am–noon, 1–5pm Tue–Sun.

Avanos
16 km (10 miles) NE of Nevşehir.
14,500. Atatürk Cad, (0384) 511 43 60.

Watered by the Kızılırmak (Red River), Avanos is a pretty, leafy town noted for its pottery and ceramics. Carpet-weaving and tapestry-making are equally important local skills.

In Roman times, Avanos was called Venessa. It fell under Ottoman suzerainty in 1466 along with Nevşehir. Today it is a typical country town, albeit with a lack of grand mosques or *medreses*. In the town centre is the Yeraltı (Ulu) Mosque, dating from the 15th century, and the Alaeddin Mosque, built by the Seljuks.

Ceramics and wine are the town's lifeblood. Visitors can purchase many serviceable pottery items, while exquisite porcelain designs are the stock in trade of places like Kaya Seramik Evi. These pieces are thrown by hand, then painted and glazed. The intricate designs are painstakingly reproduced from the İznik originals *(see p165)*.

About 5 km (3 miles) east of Avanos is Sarıhan, a Seljuk *han* or *kervansaray (see p28)* built in 1238 on the classic square plan. The repaired *han* gives a good idea of the accommodation facilities, as well as stables and a small mosque, available to traders making the long trek along the Silk Route *(see pp28–9)*. It also hosts atmospheric Whirling Dervish shows.

Shaping a jug in a pottery workshop in Avanos

Kaymaklı
20 km (12 miles) S of Nevşehir.
Open Apr–Oct: 8am–7pm daily; Nov–Mar: 6am–5pm daily.

Discovered in 1964, Kaymaklı is the second most important underground city in the region. It is believed to have housed thousands of people from the 6th to 9th centuries. Although five levels are open to visitors, experts believe Kaymaklı has eight levels. The underground area is thought to cover an area of about 2.5 sq km (1 sq mile).

Being smaller and less crowded than many of the region's other underground cities, the rooms and their various functions seem more convincing. It is advisable to arrive there early.

Göreme
10 km (6 miles) NE of Nevşehir.
1,100. Next to the bus station, (0384) 271 25 58.

At the heart of northern Cappadocia's fairytale landscape, the small village of Göreme is extremely popular with backpackers and other tourists. There are dozens of pensions and hotels here (many with cave rooms) and restaurants to suit all budgets. It is also a good place from which to arrange tours of the region and to take part in outdoor activities ranging from walking the valleys to hot-air ballooning. The main attraction is the village's open-air museum *(see pp288–9)*.

❷ Göreme Open-Air Museum

The Göreme Valley holds the greatest concentration of rock-cut chapels and monasteries in Cappadocia. Dating largely from the 9th century onwards, the valley's 30 or more churches were built out of the soft volcanic tuff. Many of the churches feature superb Byzantine frescoes depicting scenes from the Old and New Testaments, and particularly the life of Christ and deeds of the saints. The cultural importance of the valley has been recognized by the Turkish government and they have restored and preserved the many caves to create the Göreme Open-Air Museum. UNESCO has declared the Göreme Valley a World Heritage Site. A 2006 excavation of tombs uncovered human skeletons.

Tokalı Church
The Tokalı Church, located near the entrance to the museum, contains some of the most beautiful frescoes in the Göreme Valley.

★ Kızlar Monastery
Monks lived and worked in this hollowed-out formation. Ladders or scaffolding were probably used to reach the upper levels.

Camel Tours
Portions of the Göreme Valley and surrounding area can be viewed from atop a camel on guided tours.

For hotels and restaurants in this area see pp338–9 and pp360–61

★ **Karanlık Church**
A pillared church, built around a small courtyard, the Karanlık Church contains frescoes depicting the ascension of Christ.

VISITORS' CHECKLIST

Practical Information
15 km (9 miles) E of Nevşehir.
Tel (0384) 271 21 67.
Open Apr–Oct: 8am–7pm; Nov–Mar: 8am–5pm.
extra fee for Tokalı Church and Karanlık Church.

Transport
Nevşehir Kapadokya Havalimanı (30 km/19 miles from Nevşehir) (0384) 421 44 55.

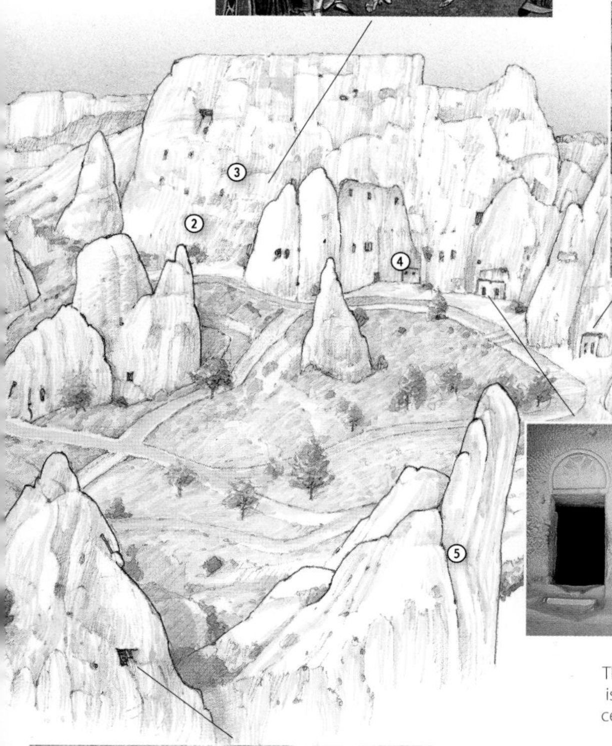

Yılanlı Church
The barrel-vaulted church has painted panels devoted to a number of saints.

Entrances to Monks' Cells
The southern end of the valley is honeycombed with the tiny cells once occupied by monks.

★ **Elmalı Church**
Noted for the sophistication of its frescoes, the church dates from the 11th century.

KEY

① **The walking route** starts at the car park near the entrance.

② **Çarıklı Church**

③ **Katherina Church**

④ **Dining Hall**

⑤ **Barbara Church** takes its name from a fresco on the west wall, which is thought to depict St Barbara. A seated figure of Christ occupies the central apse. Saints Georgius and Theodorus are depicted killing the dragon.

The Church of Constantine and Helen, in Mustafapaşa

❸ Mustafapaşa

6 km (4 miles) S of Ürgüp. 3,800.

Formerly known as Sinasos, Mustafapaşa is a perfectly preserved Greek village, whose inhabitants left during the exchange of populations between Greece and Turkey in 1923. The houses have a wealth of carved stonework, wall paintings and reminders of the former inhabitants' lifestyles. Although some houses are neglected, the balconies and sculptured windows are sure to delight. The large, 18th-century Church of Constantine and Helen contains some faded frescoes and draws pilgrims from Greece. Of note are the monastery of St Nicholas and the Church of St Basil, the latter located outside the village.

Several pensions and a few hotels have been restored to their former Greek appearance.

❹ Kayseri

See pp294–5.

❺ Bünyan

35 km (22 miles) E of Kayseri. 5,780. Yogurt Festival (18 May).

Bünyan lies east of Kayseri, off the main highway to Sivas. This is a good place for a relaxed outing for a few hours or an afternoon, and often features on sightseeing tours to the region.

The economic mainstay of the town is handicrafts, mainly the carpets hand-woven by the women. You can see them at work on the looms and learn about the designs and the amount of work involved. A particular feature of carpets from Bünyan is the use of thin, high-tensile mercerized cotton to make bedspreads, floor rugs and prayer mats. This ensures that the finished carpet always lies flat.

❻ Mount Erciyes

Erciyes Dağı

Mount Erciyes, at a height of 3,916 m (12,848 ft), is Cappadocia's dominant natural landmark. Locals regard this extinct volcano with respect because of its role in shaping the landscape when it buried the area in volcanic dust and ash millions of years ago. The residual tuff – fine-grained, compressed volcanic ash – is the area's major geological feature *(see pp284–5)*. The calcium in the tuff enriches the soil, encouraging the growth of trees and vines.

Between the two peaks (Greater and Lesser Erciyes) are two lovely moraine lakes, Cora and Sarı. Mount Erciyes is also a ski centre *(see p372)* with a chairlift and a lodge. The season runs from November to May. Hiking is possible in summer, but you will need experience and proper equipment.

❼ Soğanlı

38 km (24 miles) S of Ürgüp. 4,650. **Open** 8:30am–5:30pm daily.

The main attraction of the Soğanlı Valley is that it is quiet and undisturbed. It is possible, even, to think of this valley as a microcosm of the whole

Pigeon coops cut into the rocks at Soğanlı, marked with white rings to attract the birds

◄ Preparations for evening festivities in the Cappadocian town of Göreme

Göreme Valley. There are six interesting churches to visit here, though it is thought that more than 100 flourished at one time. All six are in good condition and can be seen on foot during the course of a day trip.

The delicate, pastel tones of Soğanlı's frescoes differ from the harsher hues to be seen in the churches at Göreme, where ongoing restoration has produced stronger colours.

The distinctive, colourful cloth dolls sold throughout Cappadocia are produced by Soğanlı's handicraft industry.

❽ Niğde

182,000. Adana Yolu, 1.5 km (1 mile) east of the city centre. end of İstasyon Cad, 1 km (0.5 mile) from town centre, (0388) 232 35 41. Belediye Sarayı, (0388) 232 33 93. Women's Handicraft Market (Sat). Tepecuması Folklore and Country Festival (27 May).

Known in Hittite times as Nahita, Niğde survived 10th-century Arab raids better than its neighbours. Its position on a major trade route to the Mediterranean appealed to the enterprising Seljuks, and so Niğde flourished as a regional capital until the time of the Mongol invasions *(see p57)*.

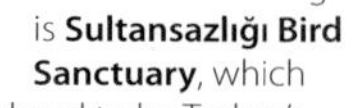

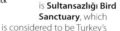

White-headed duck

The Seljuks filled the town with fine architecture, notably the Alaeddin Mosque (1223), distinguished by its superb stonework, ornate portal and typical squat minaret, and the Great Mosque (Ulu Cami), which was built around 1335. There is also a Seljuk tomb, the Hüdavend Hatun Türbe, featuring the octagonal forms typical of Seljuk architecture.

Niğde's bazaar *(bedesten)*, with its fine clock tower, is a vestige of the town's heyday. The museum has sections on ethnography and Asian civilizations, and displays the mummified remains of a nun from the Ihlara Valley *(see p296)*.

Do try and taste Niğde's deliciously creamy ewe's milk cheese, which comes "packaged" in a woolly sheepskin. Such local cheeses are called *tulum peynırı*.

A narrow gorge in the spectacular Aladağlar Mountains, near Niğde

Environs

There are several interesting places near Niğde. The best are **Bor**, a carpet-weaving centre that lies 15 km (9 miles) to the southwest, and **Kemerhisar**, which is 20 km (12 miles) to the south. This Hittite site dates from about 1200 BC. At the site, you can see the arches of an aqueduct and a mineral spring.

The Byzantine monastery church at **Eski Gümüş** was restored in the early 1990s and is one of the best-kept secrets in Turkey. The frescoes here are outstanding.

If you are a mountaineer, the **Aladağlar Mountains** offer some excellent climbing and include Demirkazık, the highest peak in the region. To reach the summit, the best starting point is the village of the same name, which lies 65 km (40 miles) east of Niğde.

Northeast of Niğde is **Sultansazlığı Bird Sanctuary**, which is considered to be Turkey's most important bird sanctuary after Lake Manyas (Kuşcenneti; *see p163*). With a total area of 172 sq km (66 sq miles), the marshes are regarded as some of the largest and most important wetlands in Europe and the Middle East. The area is protected by the Ramsar Convention, an agreement signed in Iran in 1971 to conserve wetlands and their resources. The reserve is a haven for around 300 species of bird, including ducks, flamingoes, terns, cranes, egrets and plovers. Partridges, swordbeaks, whimbrels and pelicans all come here to breed. The best bird-watching spot is the lookout at Ovaçiftlik.

Sultansazlığı Bird Sanctuary
70 km (44 miles) SW of Kayseri. **Tel** (0352) 658 55 49. **Open** Mar–Dec: 5am–midnight daily.

Eski Gümüş
9 km (6 miles) NE of Niğde. **Tel** (0388) 232 33 90. **Open** Apr–Oct: 8am–7pm daily; Nov–Mar: 8am–5pm daily.

The Sultansazlığı Bird Sanctuary, a bird-watcher's paradise

4 Kayseri

Dominated by Mount Erciyes, Kayseri has been fought over by Persians, Arabs, Mongols and Ottomans. Its most prosperous era was undoubtedly under the Romans – when it was known as Eusebeia/Mazaka and then Caesarea – but it also flourished under the Seljuks. At the junction of five roads, the city was a key point on the Roman road system, and the Romans established an imperial munitions factory here. By the 4th century Kayseri was a focal point of Christian life and faith. Its most famous cleric (and bishop) was St Basil the Great (around AD 329–379), who defended church doctrine against heretical movements.

Entrance to the Twin-Turreted Theology Complex

Exploring Kayseri

Kayseri was once a prominent centre of education, and has many religious institutions, tombs and mosques to visit. Agriculture, textiles and manufacturing are all crucial to the local economy, but it has preserved traditional crafts such as carpet-making. In addition the best *sucuk* (salami) in Turkey comes from here and the 20 varieties of *pastırma* (cured beef) are also a regional speciality.

Twin-Turreted Theology Complex

Çifte Medresesi

Sinan Park. **Tel** (0352) 231 35 65. **Open** 8am–5pm Wed–Sun.

The complex consists of two adjoining theological centres, the Gıyasiye Medresesi and the Şifahiye Medresesi. The Seljuks placed great emphasis on learning – this extended to anatomy and medicine. This was the first Seljuk academy of medicine and is now called the Gevher Nesibe Medical History Museum. Here you can learn more about Seljuk medical practices. There is an operating theatre and accommodation for psychiatric patients.

The architectural scheme incorporates arches, vaulted antechambers *(eyvan)* and an open courtyard.

Three Bazaars

Behind the Ulu Camii. **Closed** Sun.

Kayseri's three bazaars offer a contrast to the city's wealth of tombs and mausoleums. The Covered Bazaar (Kapılı Çarşı) dates from 1859, but the other two, the Bedesten and Vizir Han, date from the 15th and 16th centuries respectively.

There are few places that capture the keen spirit of age-old trading better than the bazaars of Kayseri. All three are still patronized by local people and traders, who barter and haggle in a lively atmosphere. Many of the local specialities, such as textiles and carpets, can be bought in the bazaars.

Citadel

Kale

The north wall and ramparts of the Citadel were built by Emperor Justinian in the 6th century. However, little of the outer fortifications can be seen today. The black basalt structure originally had 195 bastions, and it is still an imposing sight – albeit as a shopping centre today.

The 13th-century Citadel, now a busy shopping centre

Güpgüpoğlu Stately Home

Güpgüpoğlu Konağı

Tennuri Sok, Cumhuriyet Mahallesi. **Tel** (0352) 222 95 16. **Open** 8am–5pm Tue–Sun.

A family home built between 1417 and 1419, the house has been carefully preserved and restored to its former glory, with each room highlighting specific aspects of Ottoman life. There are guest rooms, a bridal chamber, meeting areas for family gatherings and men's and women's quarters. Notable features are the built-in cupboards *(yüklük)* for storing mattresses, and the kitchen area, which consists of a pantry and a large main kitchen *(tokana)*.

Hunat Hatun Mosque Complex

Hunat Hatun Camii ve Medresesi

Behind tourism information office. **Open** 9am–5:30pm daily.

This *külliye* (religious and educational institution adjoining a mosque) was one of the first mosque precincts the Seljuks built in Anatolia, although the minaret was erected in 1726. The complex has a mosque, training centre and *hamam* (Turkish bath) for

For hotels and restaurants in this area see pp338–9 and pp360–61

Owner of a typical *pastırma* (cured beef) shop in Kayseri

men and women, and also includes the substantial mausoleum of Mahperi Hunat Hatun, wife of Alaeddin I Keykubad *(see p254)*. Her inscription on the east door dates back to 1238.

Octagonal Tomb

Döner Kümbet

Talas Cad.

There are many grand tombs to be found all around Anatolia, but the elegance and pure simplicity of the Döner Kümbet makes it one of the most impressive. The tomb was constructed around 1250 as the final resting place of Şah Cihan Hatun, who was a Seljuk princess.

The Octagonal Tomb

Archaeology Museum

Arkeoloji Müzesi

Gültepe Mah. Kışla Cad 2. **Tel** (0352) 222 21 49 and 232 48 12. **Open** Apr–Oct: 9am–7pm daily; Nov–Mar: 8am–5pm daily.

The museum consists of two large halls and a pleasant garden. The displays run in chronological sequence from the Bronze Age to the Byzantine period. By far the most valuable and interesting items are the series of cuneiform tablets documenting the commercial transactions of the Assyrian trading colony which flourished here during the late Hittite era *(see pp48–9)*.

VISITORS' CHECKLIST

Practical Information

295,000.

Cumhuriyet Meydanı, Sivas Cad (0352) 222 39 03 and 222 03 63. Culture and Art Week (1st week Apr), Pastırma Festival (15 Sep).

Transport

Osman Kavuncu Cad, (0352) 327 45 00. North end of Atatürk Bulvarı, 1 km (0.5 mile) from city centre, (0352) 231 13 13. Erkilet, (0352) 337 52 44.

Environs

Kültepe, formerly known as Kanesh or Kanış, and now Karum, is one of the most important Bronze Age sites in Turkey. In the second millennium BC, Kültepe was the foremost Assyrian trading colony. Most of the objects found here can now be seen in the museum in Kayseri or in the Museum of Anatolian Civilizations in Ankara *(see pp246–7)*.

Kültepe

21 km (13 miles) NE of Kayseri on the Sivas highway.

Open 8am–5pm daily.

Kayseri City Centre

① Twin-Turreted Theology Complex
② Three Bazaars
③ Citadel
④ Güpgüpoğlu Stately Home
⑤ Hunat Hatun Mosque Complex
⑥ Octagonal Tomb
⑦ Archaeology Museum

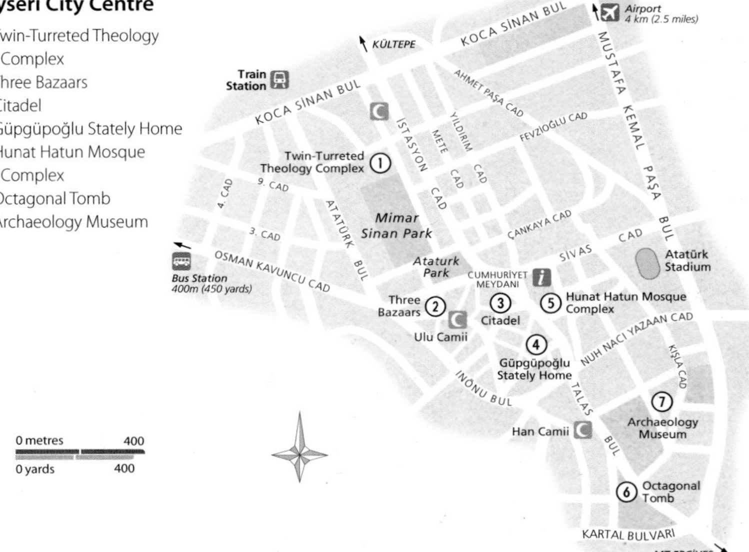

9 Güzelyurt

28 km (17 miles) SE of Aksaray. 4,380. infrequent from Aksaray or Ihlara Valley.

Güzelyurt means "beautiful country" and is an apt description of this charming and friendly town, which is surrounded by citrus groves. This is a popular area for horseback riding and mountain biking. The latter is a restful alternative to driving.

It is estimated that there were over 50 Greek Orthodox churches here once, though only a few endure today. The church of St Gregory of Nazianzus, one of the four founders of the Greek Orthodox Church, has been converted into a mosque. It was first built in AD 385, but the current church dates from 1896.

A government protection order is in force in Güzelyurt, so all restoration and construction work must conform to official guidelines. Local stone must be used and the buildings must be appropriate to the town.

The valley 4 km (2 miles) to the northeast of the town, also known as the Monastery Valley, has an abundance of rock-carved churches.

10 Ihlara Valley

To many people, the Ihlara Valley is more compelling than the rock churches and dwellings in the region. The setting is dramatic, with the Melendez River winding along the canyon floor.

The main part of the valley lies between the village of Selime to the north and the town of Ihlara to the south. You could spend an entire day exploring the 15-km- (9-mile-) canyon.

Of the 60 or so original churches in the valley, which was known as Peristrema in Greek times, only about 10 can be seen and some of the interior frescoes are in less than pristine condition.

Most of the churches in the valley date from the 11th century. Their unusual names signify their use or a peculiar feature: Hyacinth, Black Deer, Crooked Stone and Dovecote. Many of the interior frescoes depict scenes from the lives of the saints, the lives of the ascetic monks or punishments for wrongdoing.

It was once thought that a medical school, where the art of mummification was taught and practised, was located between the villages of Belisırma and Yaprakhisar.

The Eğri (Leaning) Minaret, built by the Seljuks in the 13th century

11 Aksaray

239,000. 0.5 km (0.3 mile) from main square. Taşpazar Mahallesi, Kadıoğlu Sok 1, (0382) 213 24 74 and 212 46 88.

In Roman times, Aksaray was known as Archelais, after Archelaus II, the last king of Cappadocia. By 20 BC, the kingdom had been reduced to a virtual protectorate of Rome and the king enjoyed only token status.

From the south, Aksaray is overlooked by the twin peaks of Mount Hasan (Hasan Dağı), an extinct volcano known as "little

The spectacular Ihlara Valley, one of Central Anatolia's best hiking areas

For hotels and restaurants in this area see pp338–9 and pp360–61

sister" to Mount Erciyes. Aksaray is close to the eastern end of the Tuz Gölü (Salt Lake). In Ottoman times, the lake brought prosperity to Aksaray as it was the main source of salt for almost the whole of Anatolia.

Aksaray might appear to be a sleepy base for tourists, but spare some time to view the fine Seljuk building styles and architecture, with vestiges of the original ochre-coloured sandstone. Worth seeing are the Great Mosque (1314), with its beautifully carved *minbar* (pulpit), and the **Zinciriye Medresesi**, a 14th-century Koranic school, that now serves as the museum.

Aksaray has its own leaning tower, the Eğri (Leaning) Minaret, on Nevşehir Caddesi. The minaret is part of the Kızıl (Red) Minare Mosque, which was built in 1236 during the reign of the great Seljuk Sultan Alaeddin I Keykubat *(see p254)*. The mosque was built on sand, which has shifted over time, causing the minaret to lean.

Zinciriye Medresesi
Muhsin Çelebi Sokak. **Tel** (0382) 213 16 67. **Open** 8am–noon & 1–5pm daily.

⓬ Kırşehir

160 km (100 miles) SE of Ankara. 83,450. Terme Cad, Ulucan I Apartman, Kat 1, (0386) 213 14 16.

In Byzantine times, Kırşehir was known as Mokyssos. It prospered under the Seljuks, who renamed it Gülşehir, or Rose Town. One of the finest of the city's Seljuk buildings is the Cacabey Mosque, built in 1272 as an astrological observatory and theological college. The Alaeddin Mosque, built in 1230, and the Ahi Evran Mosque are also located in Kırşehir. The latter contains the tomb of Ahi Evran, founder of a *tarikât* (religious brotherhood) whose members helped to spread the message of Islam to the Christian communities of Anatolia.

Various artifacts from Kalehöyük, an important Hittite archaeological site 55 km (34 miles) to the northwest of Kırşehir, are on display in the excellent **Archaeology Museum**. Kalehöyük is one of the many Hittite centres that are being excavated in the area. The museum has more than 3,300 artifacts on display, including coins, ethnographic items and archaeological materials.

Another prime reason for visiting the area is a Japanese arboretum, the **Mikasonmiya Memorial Garden** (Mikasonmiya Anı Bahçesi). One of the largest and most pleasant parks in Turkey, it is planted with some 16,500 trees, made up of 33 different species.

Archaeology Museum
Ahi Evren Cad 10. **Tel** (0386) 213 33 91. **Open** 8am–5pm daily.

Mikasonmiya Memorial Garden
Contact the Kırşehir tourist office, (0386) 213 1416, for opening hours.

⓭ Hacı Bektaş

9,348. Opposite the Museum, (0384) 441 36 87. Hacı Bektaş Veli Commemoration Festival (16–18 Aug).

The mystic and spiritual philosopher Hacı Bektaş arrived in this area from Iran, via Mecca, in the late 13th century, and founded a centre of learning. His ideas were an offshoot of the Shi'ite sect of Islam, and rested on a belief in natural harmony that was bolstered by mysticism and divine love. The teachings of Hacı Bektaş offered an approachable and compassionate alternative to the main current of Islam. The Bektaşi doctrine, as set out in his book the *Malakat*, is based on both Islamic and Christian principles. This made it a popular belief. He attracted many devotees, most notably among the Janissaries, who were the elite fighting force of the Ottoman sultans *(see p60)*.

Gravestone at Hacı Bektaş

Doorway into the tomb of Hacı Bektaş, in the third courtyard

The **Hacı Bektaş Museum** (Pirevi, or "founder's house") is the chief attraction, along with the stunning wood carvings of the archaeological museum. Be sure you allow sufficient time to see the whole complex: there are tombs, courtyards, initiation cells, pools and a refectory (dining room) with authentic kitchen cauldrons. The tomb of Hacı Bektaş, in the third courtyard, has seven doors, and is particularly striking. Some of the inscriptions were done with natural dyes from the madder root, and later restored with oil-based paint.

Atatürk came through here in 1919 on his way from Sivas to Ankara; his visit is marked on 22 and 23 December each year. Admiration for the order did not prevent him banning all mystical sects and dervish lodges in 1925, because they were contrary to Turkey's secular state dogma.

The symbol of the order is the rose and blond onyx that is found in the area. It is known as Hacı Bektaş stone.

Hacı Bektaş Museum
Nevşehir Cad. **Tel** (0384) 441 30 22. **Open** Apr–Oct: 9am–7pm daily; Nov–Mar: 8am–5pm daily.

The 19th-century clock tower in the main square in Yozgat

⓮ Yozgat

264,000. İl Özel İdare Hizmet Binası, Kat 3, (0354) 212 64 23. (0354) 212 41 15. Tue. Summer Folklore and Culture Festival (10–15 Jun).

Research shows that there were settlements here as early as 3,000 BC. However, the tides of history barely affected Yozgat until it fell to the Ottomans in 1408 and the influential Çapanoğlu dynasty made the town their seat. The Çapanoğlus built or repaired many fine mosques, including the Ulu (Çapanoğlu) Camii. The **Yozgat Ethnographic Museum** is housed in a 19th-century *konak* (mansion), the Nizamoğülu Konağı.

In the centre of the town there is an interesting, though garish, clock tower built in 1897 by Ahmet Tevfikzade, the mayor of the town. Ask to see the mechanism if you are interested in timepieces.

Yozgat Ethnographic Museum
Emniyet Cad. **Tel** (0354) 212 27 73.
Open 8am–5pm Tue–Sun.

Environs
Çamlık National Park, located about 5 km (3 miles) south of Yozgat, covers 8 sq km (3 sq miles) of woodland, and has abundant fauna and flora, picnic areas, mineral springs and a hotel.

Çamlık National Park
Tel (0354) 212 10 84. **Open** daily

⓯ Boğazkale

See pp300–1.

⓰ Alacahöyük

30 km (19 miles) SE of Çorum.

Located between Sungurlu and Çorum, Alacahöyük is the third and most important site (after Boğazkale and Yazılıkaya) in the Hattuşaş complex of Hittite sites in this region. Most of the artifacts found at the site are displayed in museums in Ankara *(see pp246–7)* and Çorum.

Excavations at Alacahöyük have yielded items ranging from the Chalcolithic period (5500 BC–3000 BC) up to the Phrygian period (750 BC–300 BC) – a staggering time span that makes the site one of Turkey's most important archaeological centres.

At the site itself, the Sphinx Gate is an imposing reminder of cult power, its half-man, half-animal statues displaying striking Egyptian influences. The royal tombs can also be seen. The **Alacahöyük Museum** displays some of the earthenware pots that were used for burial rites.

Alacahöyük Museum
Tel (0364) 422 70 11.
Open 8am–5pm daily.

One of the carved sphinxes that guard the gate at Alacahöyük

⓱ Çorum

Yeni Hükümet Binası, A Blok, Kat 4, (0364) 213 85 02. Hittite Festival (mid-Jun).

The town of Çorum dates from Roman times, when it was known as Niconia. The surrounding area is rich in Hittite history, making it likely that the site was inhabited as early as 1400 BC. Throughout Turkey, the name of Çorum is associated with roasted chickpeas *(leblebi)*, one of the many snacks that Turks munch compulsively. A particularly delicious local cheese is Kargi, made from cow's milk. Çorum makes a good base from which to tour two major Hittite

Shop in Çorum specializing in the famous local produce, chickpeas

For hotels and restaurants in this area see pp338–9 and pp360–61

sights, Boğazkale *(see pp300–301)* and Alacahöyük. Both are located to the southwest of the town.

The **Çorum Museum** sprawls over several buildings. It is a serious and informative place with many artifacts and ethnographic displays, among them very good Hittite objects, as well as local *kilims* (rugs).

Çorum Museum
Town centre. **Tel** (0364) 213 15 68.
Open Apr–Oct: 9am–7pm daily; Nov–Mar: 8am–5pm daily.

⓲ Amasya

See pp302–3.

⓳ Tokat

358,000. Valilik Binası, Kat. 3, (0356) 214 37 53. 2 km (1 mile) from main square, (0356) 214 22 20. Pinecone Festival (mid-Sep).

Tokat deserves a place on visitors' itineraries because there is a lot more to see here than ankle-high ruins. The Seljuks left the most to see, but the town is also known for resisting Ottoman rule. In protest at Ottoman authority, Turcoman tribesmen took to wearing distinctive red headgear, thus earning the name of Kızılbaşı (redheads), which became a term for "rebels".

The town flourished after Sultan Beyazıt I won control of trade routes to Erzincan. Trade caravans then began to use the Amasya–Tokat route, skirting Trabzon (Trebizond), to reach Bursa *(see pp166–71)*, the commercial jewel of the 15th and 16th centuries.

The Seljuks and Ottomans endowed Tokat with many fine buildings, especially the Blue Seminary (Gök Medrese) and two restored 19th-century Ottoman *konaks* (mansions): the Madımağın Celal'ın House and the Latifoğlu House. If time is limited, Tokat's interesting **Archaeological Museum** is the place to go.

Tokat has a proud 300-year tradition of hand-printed textiles *(yazmacılık)*. The craft still thrives in the Gazi Emir Han near the business hub of Sulu Sokak. The town is also renowned for copper-working and ceramics in bold primary colours.

Specialities include *pekmez*, a delicious drink made from concentrated grape juice, and the full-bodied, fruity Karaman red wine.

Archaeological Museum
Gaziosmanpaşa Bulvarı 143.
Tel (0356) 214 15 09. **Open** 8am–noon & 1–5pm Tue–Sun.

Environs
The ruined city of Sebastopolis is located 68 km (42 miles) southwest of Tokat. The modern name, Sulusaray (watery palace), comes from the thermal springs, which bubble water at 50°C (122°F). Interesting finds here include a city wall, bath chambers and a temple.

Shop selling hand-printed textiles in Tokat

The Heavenly Seminary in Sivas, showing filigree stonework

⓴ Sivas

318,000. Atatürk Kültür Merkezi, (0346) 223 92 99. İstasyon Cad, (0346) 221 10 91. 3 km (2 miles) SE of main square, (0346) 226 15 90. Nevruz (21 Mar). **sivas.gov.tr**

Situated at an altitude of 1,275 m (4,183 ft), Sivas is the highest city in Central Anatolia. Known as Sebasteia in Roman times, its position on a caravan route made it an important trade centre.

Sivas boasts the cream of Seljuk architecture, with tiles, intricately etched stonework, star mosaics, honeycombed decorative motifs and bold blue hues all in evidence. The Heavenly Seminary (Gök Medresesi), built in the 1200s, and Twin Minaret Seminary (Çifte Minareli Medresesi), with its outstanding carved details, should not be missed. The Darüşşifası (Medical Hospice) housed a hospital. The Bürüciye Medresesi (1271) has a quiet courtyard and some excellent tilework.

The Sivas Congress (to consolidate Atatürk's plans to free Turkey from foreign domination) was held in a schoolroom here in 1919. The room is preserved in the **Ethnography Museum**. Local artisans are known for long-stemmed wooden pipes, penknives and bone-handled knives.

Ethnography Museum
Istasyon Cad. **Tel** (0346) 221 04 46.
Open 8am–5pm Tue–Sun.

15 Boğazkale

Hattuşaş National Park

Boğazkale is the modern name for the ancient Hittite capital city of Hattuşaş, built around 1600 BC on a strategic site occupied since the third millennium BC. An Assyrian trading colony was also active here early in the 2nd millennium BC. A UNESCO World Heritage Site, it is one of the most important ancient sites to be found in Anatolia. The many thousands of clay and bronze tablets discovered here have provided scholars with a wealth of information about the ancient Hittite civilization.

The city occupies an extensive site bordered on three sides by steep ravines. Sections of the walls, including the impressive Lion's and King's gates, are still standing. The builders adapted the fortifications in masterly fashion to take advantage of topographical features.

Bronze Plaque
This plaque found at Boğazkale records a treaty between the Hittite king, Tudhaliyas IV, and another ruler.

★ Lion's Gate (Aslanlıkapı)
The Lion's Gate takes its name from the two lion statues that guarded the city over 3,000 years ago. The lions here are only replicas – the originals are now in the Museum of Anatolian Civilizations in Ankara *(see pp246–7)*.

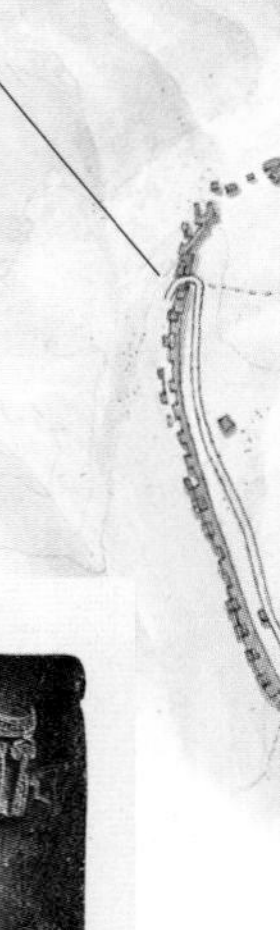

Hittite Civilization

A people of Indo-European origin, the Hittites arrived in Anatolia from the Caucasus region around 2000 BC. Over the next few centuries, they built up a powerful state, with a capital at Hattuşaş (now known as Boğazkale). At its height, the Hittite kingdom controlled much of Anatolia, rivalling both Egypt and Babylon. Hittite art reached its peak between 1450 BC and 1200 BC, and Hittite artisans were renowned as superb carvers and metalworkers.

One of the 12 gods in stone relief at Yazılıkaya, near Boğazkale

★ Great Temple (Büyük Mabet)
One of the best-preserved Hittite temples, the Great Temple was built around 1400 BC, and was dedicated to the storm god, Teshub. The temple complex contains ritual chambers, administrative areas and storage rooms.

VISITORS' CHECKLIST

Practical Information
Part of Çorum Museum, within Hattuşaş National Park.
Tel (0364) 452 20 06.
Open 8am–5pm Tue–Sun.
Admission includes entry to the Yazılıkaya site nearby.

The Citadel (Büyükkale)
The walled citadel was the seat of government at Hattuşaş. A monumental staircase led up to three courts, one of which contained the living quarters of the royal household.

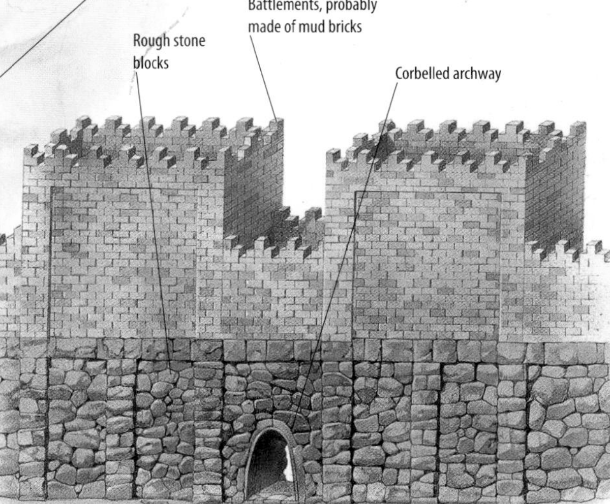

KEY

① **The Sphinx Gate** (Yerkapı) is built into an artificial hill, and incorporates a tunnel 70 m (230 ft) in length.

② **Yenice Citadel**

③ **Modern village of Boğazköy**

④ **Sarı Citadel**

⑤ **King's Gate**

★ Reconstruction of the King's Gate

The King's Gate (Kral Kapı) was named after the regal-looking Hittite war god on the stone relief guarding the entrance. The city wall is built with huge, roughly worked stone blocks, and totals about 7 km (4 miles) in length. The height of the stone portion was about 6 m (20 ft). Like the other structures in the city, this would have been overlaid with sun-dried brick.

⓲ Amasya

Lying in a secluded valley of the Yeşilırmak River, Amasya has seen the passage of nine civilizations, from the Hittites to Ottomans. Its most prosperous era was as royal capital of the Roman kingdom of Pontus, when it was called Amaseia; the tombs cut into the cliffs above the town contain the graves of the Pontic kings. However, a glance at Amasya's many fine Ottoman buildings will confirm that the four centuries of Ottoman rule were equally illustrious. In the 15th century, Amasya was second only to Bursa in cultural and trading importance. By the 1800s, the city excelled as the empire's leading centre for Islamic education.

Exploring Amasya

Its dramatic location and air of tranquillity aside, Amasya is known for the tasty apples grown on the surrounding farms and for colourful hand-knitted socks. All main sights are conveniently accessible on foot. The citadel is the only exception, but it can be reached by car.

The Citadel, perched dramatically on a hilltop

Great Lord's Seminary

Büyük Ağa Medresesi

Zubediye Hanım Sok.
Closed during lessons.

The wonderful airy symmetry and octagonal plan of this complex, also known as the Kapıağası, are its outstanding features. It was built in 1488 by Hüseyin Agha, a private consort of Sultan Beyazıt II. The vaulted porticoes and domed rooms are now used by Koranic students, who adhere to exactly the same rigorous discipline as their predecessors did two or three centuries ago.

Citadel

Kale

Can be reached by 2-hour climb from the front, or by a road from behind.

The original Hittite fortress was reinforced by the Pontic king, Mithridates *(see p52)*. He built eight layers of walls, with 41 towers, to protect a self-sustaining complex with a palace, cisterns, storage areas, powder magazine and cemetery. From the Citadel there are stupendous views of the nearby Rock Tombs.

Rock Tombs

Kral Kaya Mezarları

Entrance under the railway line off Hazeranlar Sok. **Open** 8am–5pm (7pm in summer).

The tombs of the Pontic kings date from 333 BC to 44 BC, covering the Hellenistic and Roman periods. The Mirror Cave (Aynalı Mağrası), about 1 km (0.5 mile) from the main tombs, has a coloured painting showing the Virgin Mary and the Apostles.

The carved portal of the Teaching Hospital Complex

Teaching Hospital Complex

Daruşşifa/Bimarhane Medresesi

Atatürk Cad. **Open** 9am–6pm daily.

The outer walls of the original asylum date from 1308. The complex served as a medical research centre, a school for interns and a hospice for mental patients. Music and speech therapy were used to calm disturbed patients. The carved front portal is wonderfully detailed and represents a rare architectural remnant of the Ilhanid Persian empire of the 13th century. The building houses a café and the offices of the local Music and Fine Arts Directorate.

Hazeranlar Mansion

Hazeranlar Konağı

Hattuniye Mahallesi. **Tel** (0358) 218 40 18. **Open** Apr–Oct: 9am–7pm daily; Nov–Mar: 8am–5pm daily.

This restored mansion dates from 1865. It was built by a local treasury officer, Hasan Talat Efendi, in memory of his sister, Hazeran Hanım (Lady Hazeran). The layout, typical of the time, features separate areas for men and women. The carpets, from the late Ottoman period, are particularly fine.

The tombs of the Pontic kings, carved into the limestone cliffs

Konaks (mansion houses) along the Yeşilırmak River

Sultan Beyazıt Mosque and Theological College

Sultan Beyazıt II Külliyesi
Mustafa Kemal Paşa Cad.
Closed during prayer times.
donation.

This was Amasya's primary theological complex, eclipsing all other places of religious learning. It was a product of the prosperity and social stability that prevailed under Sultan Beyazıt II (1481–1512). In that era, Muslim principles and obedience to the state were instilled at an early age. The wonderful domes and portals are inspirational in themselves, and the oak trees in the garden are said to be as old as the mosque itself.

Archaeology and Ethnography Museum

Arkeoloji ve Etnografik Müzesi
Mustafa Kemal Paşa Cad 91. **Tel** (0358) 218 45 13. **Open** Apr–Oct: 9am–7pm daily; Nov–Mar: 8am–5pm daily.

The museum has been improved and modernized, and so the concept of space is much enhanced. Notable among its exhibits is the bronze statue of the Hittite storm god, as well as a collection of Roman coins minted in the town.

The museum is best known for its collection of mummies, which were found in Anatolia and date from the Ilhanid period (around the 14th century). Previously housed in a dank tomb adjacent to the museum, these now have much more prominence in their display cases.

The Sultan Beyazıt Mosque, completed in 1486, with its famous rose garden

VISITORS' CHECKLIST

Practical Information
215,000. Atatürk Cad, Pirinç Mah (opposite Bimarhane), (0358) 218 50 02.

Transport
2 km (1 mile) W of town centre, (0358) 218 12 39.
2 km (1 mile) NE of town centre, (0358) 218 80 12.

Blue Seminary

Gök Medresesi
Mustafa Kemal Paşa Cad (Torumtay Sok). **Open** contact a guardian to let you in. **Closed** during prayer time.
donation.

A theological complex dating from 1267, the Blue Seminary is typical of 13th-century Seljuk architecture. It was formerly used as a mosque and Koranic school, and takes its name from the turquois and blue tiles and the glazed bricks used in its construction. The elaborately carved wooden doors contrasted with the austere interior and are now housed in the Archaeology and Ethnographic Museum.

Adjoining the complex is the Torumtay Türbe, a square tomb built in 1279 in memory of the Emir Torumtay, Seljuk governor of the province and founder of the seminary.

Amasya City Centre

① Great Lord's Seminary
② Citadel
③ Rock Tombs
④ Teaching Hospital Complex
⑤ Hazeranlar Mansion
⑥ Sultan Beyazıt Mosque and Theological College
⑦ Archaeology and Ethnography Museum
⑧ Blue Seminary

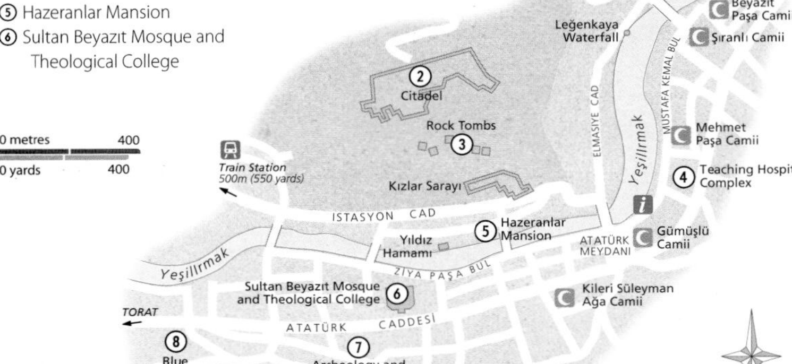

For keys to symbols *see back flap*

EASTERN ANATOLIA

The vast, high plateau of eastern Turkey is dominated by the extinct volcano of Mount Ağrı (Ararat), which soars to a height of 5,165 m (16,945 ft). The surface of Lake Van reflects the summits of the surrounding peaks. Trapped by the mountains, the lake has no outflow. In the south, the eastern extension of the Taurus range crumbles suddenly into the sun-baked Mesopotamian plain.

The region is drained by two great rivers – the Euphrates (Fırat) and Tigris (Dicle) – as well as their tributaries. For centuries, the Euphrates demarcated the eastern frontier of the Roman and Byzantine empires. Today, the rivers have been harnessed by the Southeast Anatolian Project (GAP) to supply the southeastern part of the country with irrigation water and hydro-electric power.

This border zone has always been a cultural melting pot – Monophysite Christian Armenians and Syrians lived alongside Orthodox Greeks and later Arabs and Turks, while Kurds have long occupied the highlands.

Historic Gaziantep is the gateway from the southeast, leading to the golden apricot orchards of Malatya, the huge stone heads on the summit of Mount Nemrut (Nemrut Dağı) and Abraham's legendary birthplace at Şanlıurfa. Diyarbakır's austere basalt walls loom dramatically over the Tigris, guarding the road north to the interior plateau. Van was once the seat of the sophisticated Urartian kingdom. The rough frontier town of Doğubayazıt was home to fiercely independent Kurdish princes. Kars, 10th-century capital of Armenia and access point for Ani, has been fought over many times by Russians and Turks. During World War I, Russian forces reached as far west as Erzurum, a Seljuk city with imposing medieval tombs and religious buildings, which guards the strategic highway into central Anatolia.

Snowcapped Mount Ağrı (Ararat), legendary resting place of Noah's Ark

◀ The Armenian Church of the Holy Cross on Akdamar Island, Lake Van

Exploring Eastern Anatolia

From the baking plains of Upper Mesopotamia to the icy heights of Mount Ağrı (Ararat), this vast region of Turkey is relatively undeveloped and unspoiled, making it a natural target for the more adventurous traveller. It is a land of frontiers, from cold and lonely Kars – a short step away from Armenia – through the Turkish-Iranian border town of Doğubayazıt, to the bustling bazaar city of Şanlıurfa close to Syria. Many peoples have lived in and fought over this land. Visitors can see Armenian churches and Kurdish castles, Arab houses, Syrian Orthodox monasteries and both Seljuk and Ottoman mosques vying with ruins from the Urartian and Roman eras. Late spring and early autumn are the best seasons to visit.

The citadel at Şanlıurfa

Stone head on Mount Nemrut

Sights at a Glance

1. Kâhta
2. *Mount Nemrut p310*
3. Malatya
4. Kahramanmaraş
5. Gaziantep
6. Şanlıurfa
7. Mardin
8. *Diyarbakır pp314–15*
9. Lake Van
10. Doğubayazıt
11. Kars
12. *Ani pp320–21*
13. *Erzurum pp322–3*
14. Erzincan
15. Divriği

Amasya
Sußehri
100
Zara
200
Refahiye
Sivas
Tecer Da ları
ERZİNCAN 14
Euphrates (Fırat Nehri)
DİVRİĞİ 15
Kemaliye
Karag
Tunceli
260
Keban Barajı
Hekimhan
Kayseri
850
Elazığ
Karakaya Barajı
Tohma Çayı
Darende
300
Eski Malatya
300
3 MALATYA
Elbistan
Ergani
Doğanşehir
Çerm
MOUNT NEMRUT 2
Göksun
Devegeçidi Barajı
Gölbaşı
Adıyaman
1
850
KÂHTA
Siverek
4 KAHRAMANMARAŞ
Atatürk Barajı
Pazarcık
Euphrates (Fırat Nehri)
Bozova
anlıurfa Yaylası
Adana
400
5 GAZİANTEP
052
400
6 ŞANLIURFA
Birecik
Nizip
835
Kilis
0 kilometres 80
0 miles 40

For additional map symbols *see back flap*

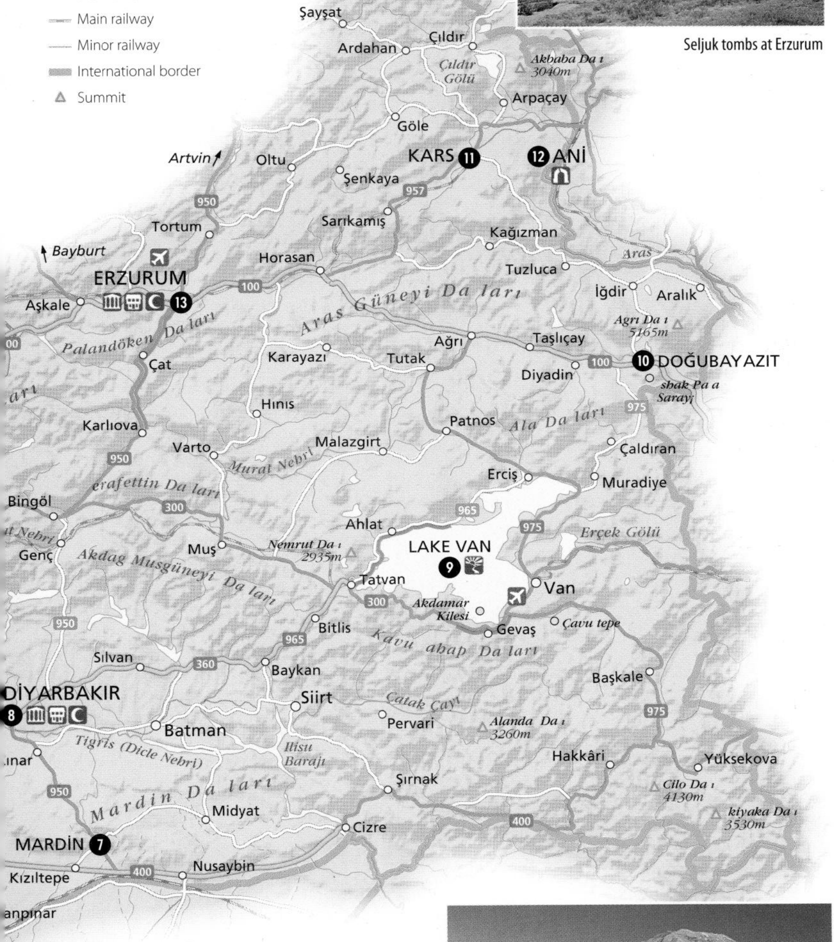

Key

- Motorway
- Dual carriageway
- Major road
- Minor road
- Scenic route
- Main railway
- Minor railway
- International border
- Δ Summit

Seljuk tombs at Erzurum

Getting Around

Comfortable intercity coaches connect all the major cities in the region, and are reasonably priced. For rural areas or out-of-the-way sites, the best option is a locally hired taxi. Rental cars are available in major cities such as Gaziantep, Şanlıurfa and Van, as well as in smaller tourist towns such as Mardin. Non-stop flights from Istanbul and Ankara serve Şanlıurfa, Mardin, Erzincan and Kars. Rail travel between Erzurum and Kars, and Malatya and Tatvan, on Lake Van, is slow but scenically rewarding.

The island of Akdamar, in Lake Van

The Atatürk Dam, centrepiece of the GAP (Southeast Anatolian Project)

❶ Kâhta

43 km (27 miles) E of Adıyaman. Kâhta Kaymakamlik, (0416) 725 50 05 (all year); (0416) 725 50 07 (summer only). International Kâhta Kommagene Festival (last week in Jun).

Although it is located close to the lake created by the monumental **Atatürk Dam** (Atatürk Barajı), Kâhta's main attraction is its proximity to Mount Nemrut (Nemrut Dağı), located 70 km (44 miles) northeast.

Environs

The Atatürk Dam, part of the GAP project, has intruded into the Euphrates basin's ancient past. Building of this and other dams has flooded important historic treasures and sites.

The town of **Adıyaman** is slightly further away from Mount Nemrut (about a half-hour drive west of Kâhta), and makes an alternative base.

The lush, green village of Karadut (Black Mulberry), set in dramatic mountain scenery 12 km (7 miles) below the summit. There are good options for accommodation nearby.

Adıyaman

Atatürk Bul 184, (0416) 216 10 08.

❷ Mount Nemrut

Nemrut Dağı

See p310.

❸ Malatya

762,000. 4 km (2.5 miles) W of city centre, off Turgut Özal Bul, (0422) 238 47 68. 2 km (1 mile) W of city centre, (0422) 212 40 40. 23 km (14 miles) W of city centre. Valilik Binası, (0422) 323 30 25/29 42. daily. Cherry Festival (18 Jun); Apricot Festival (3rd week Jul).

Malatya is famous for its apricots, grown in the vast surrounding orchards. It was also the birthplace of two Turkish presidents: İsmet İnönü, Atatürk's right-hand man during the War of Independence; and Turgut Özal, an economist who served first as Prime Minister, and then President, from the mid-1980s *(see p63)*.

Malatya is a pleasant and fairly prosperous town with a university and a military base, but makes a less convenient base than Kâhta for trips to Mount Nemrut.

Apricot vendor in Malatya's Apricot Bazaar

The town's most interesting sights are its bazaars. The **Apricot Bazaar** specializes in locally grown and dried apricots. Trading takes place after the harvest, and during the Apricot Festival in July. Around the central mosque is the **Copper Bazaar**, a group of copper-beating workshops where you can buy handmade trays, pots and vases.

Aslantepe, a HIttite site located 4 km (3 miles) northeast of Malatya was flooded as a result of the GAP project. Dating back to the 4th millennium BC this artificial settlement mound, which has been excavated by Italian teams since the 1960s, is now an open-air museum. Complete with walkways and informative signboards, it gives valuable insights into the Chacolithic, Hittite, Roman and Medieval periods and is set in delightful apricot orchards.

Finds from Aslantepe are on display in the **Malatya Archaeological Museum**. Items including Hittite stone god statues, cuneiform seals, bone idols and early bronze swords were transferred to the museum. There are over 15,500 items spanning most historic periods. The Neolithic sculptures from 8000 BC are particularly impressive, as are the obsidian knives.

Local carpets and *kilims* (rugs) have distinctive features, such as the rectangular "tower bastion" motif. The *yedi dağ çiçeği* (seven-point flower) motif can be found on *kilims*. Carpets generally have simpler designs in strong, primary colours, with borders featuring stylized flowers, rams, medallions or dragons. Small hand-loomed carpets and goat-hair rugs are also found in and around Malatya.

Apricot Bazaar
New Malatya Quarter. **Open** Mon–Sat.

Copper Bazaar
New Malatya Quarter. Adjoining the Apricot Bazaar. **Open** Mon–Sat.

Aslantepe
4 km NE of Malatya.
Tel (0422) 321 30 06. **Open** 8am–5pm Tue–Sun.

Malatya Archaeological Museum
Dernek Mahallesi, Kanal Boyu. **Tel** (0422) 321 30 06.
Open 8am–5pm Tue–Sun.

Copper teapot from Malatya

Environs
Eski Malatya, the old part of town, lies about 12 km (7.5 miles) north of the modern centre. A little village of 2,000 inhabitants has developed inside these walls, once an important Roman and then Byzantine stronghold. The 17th-century Silahtar Mustafa Paşa Caravanserai had been restored, but is now sadly neglected and visitors have to wander around among chickens and donkeys.

The much-restored **Great Mosque** (Ulu Cami) is built around a tiny courtyard, its graceful interior divided into separate summer and winter areas. The winter area is supported by massive pillars and enclosed by thick walls, while the summer section has a beautifully carved wooden pulpit, and amazing herring-bone brick vaulting decorated with scattered turquoise tiles.

Great Mosque
Ulu Cami
Opposite the bus station. **Open** daily (except during prayer times).

❹ Kahramanmaraş

675,000. W of main highway on Azerbaycan Bulvarı, (0344) 235 30 06. Cumhuriyet Cad, (0344) 235 00 75. Valilik Bahçesi, (0344) 223 03 55.

Like many other Turkish towns, Kahramanmaraş has a deceptive air of calm and tranquillity that conceals a turbulent past. The first part of its name (meaning "heroic") was added by Atatürk in recognition of the town's successful expulsion of French and British troops in 1920.

It is, however, often just called "Maraş", after its particularly famous product, Maraş Dondurması – a delicious type of ice cream containing gum arabic that is pounded or whipped into glutinous form. It is sold all over Turkey by costumed vendors. Locally, it is sold by the metre and cut with a knife. You can also buy it served in a cone.

The pleasant park below the citadel at Kahramanmaraş

The town's citadel, probably used as defence against Arab raiders in the 7th century, is now a popular tea garden and park. Two mosques, the Great Mosque and the Hatuniye Camii, date from the 15th- and 16th-century Beylik period. Their interiors feature fine wooden carvings.

The local **Archaeological and Ethnographic Museum** displays Hittite statues, ceremonial costumes, *kilims* and textile items from various eras.

Archaeological and Ethnographic Museum
Azerbaycan Bul. **Tel** (0344) 223 44 88.
Open Apr–Oct: 9am–7pm daily; Nov–Mar: 8am–5pm daily.

The 17th-century Silahtar Mustafa Paşa Caravanserai in Eski Malatya

❷ Mount Nemrut

Nemrut Dağı

The huge stone heads on the summit of Mount Nemrut (Nemrut Dağı) were built by King Antiochus I Epiphanes, who ruled the Commagene kingdom between 64 and 38 BC. To glorify his rule, the king had three enormous terraces (east, west and north) cut into the mountaintop. Colossal statues of himself and the major gods (both Greek and Persian) of the kingdom were placed on the terraces, and the summit became a sanctuary where the king was worshipped. Today's visitors can still see the remains of the east and west terraces (not much is left of the north terrace), which also feature large, detailed stone reliefs.

The enigmatic site was discovered in 1881 by a German engineer, Karl Sester, but was not fully documented until the 1990s.

VISITORS' CHECKLIST

Practical Information
70 km (44 miles) from Kâhta, 84 km (52 miles) from Adıyaman in Nemrut Dağı National Park.
Tel (0416) 725 50 07.
Open May–Oct: 8am–7pm daily.
Closed Nov–Apr.

★ East Terrace
The site affords superb views of the surrounding region. Behind the sanctuary rises a 50 m- (165 ft-) high mound rumoured to contain the tumulus of King Antiochus.

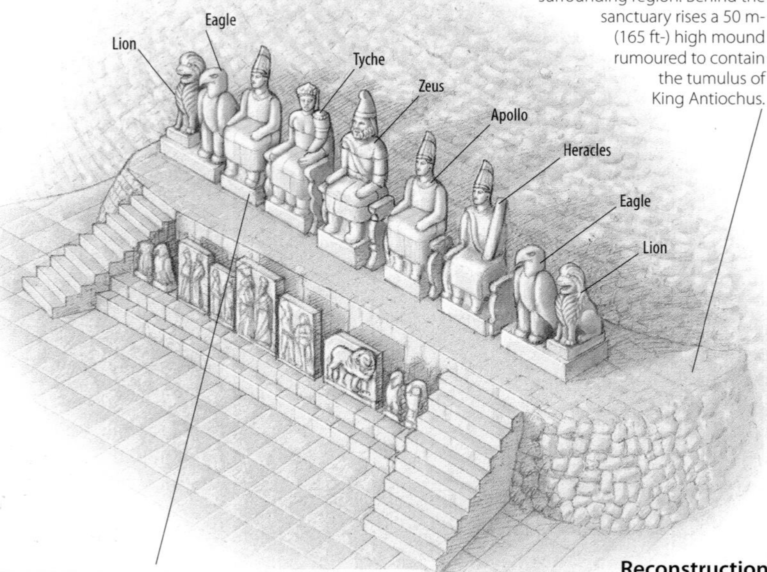

Reconstruction
This artists' impression depicts the East Terrace as it probably looked in the 1st century BC. The limestone figures were 8–10 m (26–33 ft) in height.

Head of Antiochus
The re-erected head of King Antiochus stands near the tumbled one of Tyche, Commagene goddess of fortune.

For hotels and restaurants in this area see p339 and p361

❺ Gaziantep

1,604,000. İstasyon Cad, (0342) 323 31 96. Sazgan, 18 km (11 miles) from city centre, (0342) 582 11 11. 5 km (3 miles) North of city centre, (0342) 328 92 46. Yüzyıl Atatürk Kültür Parkı, (0342) 230 59 69. Pistachio Festival (1st week in Sep).

Named Ayntap, or pure spring, by the Byzantines, Gaziantep's modern prefix of *gazi* (war hero) derives from heroic resistance to French and English invaders in 1920. The site has been occupied for 8,000 years and was a strategic defence hub in Hittite times (1200–700BC). The city sprawls around an imposing castle (*kale*) perched atop a partly man-made mound. On the approach to the castle is the Panorama Museum (open daily), which gives a vivid insight into the Turks' defence of the city from the invading French in 1920. After decades of economic decline the city has boomed, not least because of its proximity to the Southeast Anatolian Project *(see p25)*.

Just below the citadel is a bazaar, where craftsmen produce and sell copperware and furniture inlaid with mother-of-pearl, a craft for which the town is famous.

Stroll around the old town to see traditional architecture adapted for regional life, like the *hayat*, or summer courtyard, seen in the **Hasan Süzer Ethnographic Museum**. The central **Gaziantep Archaeological Museum** is worth a visit to see Hittite and Roman statuary as well as Assyrian, Babylonian and Urartian artifacts.

Gypsy girl mosaic, Gaziantep Zeugma Mosaic Museum

The jewel of the city's museums is the state-of-the-art **Gaziantep Zeugma Mosaic Museum**. Spread over three floors, it is the world's largest mosaic museum, housing more than 3,500 sq m of largely 2nd- and 3rd-century mosaics rescued from the floodwaters of a dam on the nearby Euphrates. The mosaics once adorned the villas of the wealthy citizens of Zeugma, a frontier city that controlled trade along an arm of the Silk Route. Of particular note are the statue of Mars and the gypsy girl mosaic, which is a regional idol and symbol of the Zeugma excavations. Also housed in the museum are superb reconstructions of courtyard villas complete with mosaic floors, frescoes and columns and the remains of a Roman bathhouse.

Statue of Mars, Gaziantep Zeugma Mosaic Museum

Gaziantep is an important agricultural and industrial centre, and olives, grapes and pistachio nuts are grown around the city. The city's distinctive cuisine is famed throughout the country, particularly sweet pastries such as pistachio-filled *baklava*. To find out more about the city's cuisine, it is worth visiting **Emine Göğüş Culinary Museum** in the bazaar quarter below the castle.

Hasan Süzer Ethnography Museum
Eyüboğlu Mah, Hanifioğlu Sok 64. **Tel** (0342) 230 47 21. **Open** 8:30am–noon & 1–4:30pm Tue–Sun.

Gaziantep Archaeological Museum
Istasyon Cad. **Tel** (0342) 324 88 09. **Open** 8:30am– noon & 1–6pm Tue–Sun.

Gaziantep Zeugma Mosaic Museum
Konukoğlu Bulvarı. **Tel** (0342) 325 27 27. **Open** Apr–Oct: 9am–5pm; Nov–Mar: 9am–5:30pm Tue–Sun.

Emine Göğüş Culinary Museum
Hasırcı Sok. **Tel** (0342) 220 08 88. **Open** 9am–6pm daily.

Gaziantep's bazaars, colourful and brimming with local goods

❻ Şanlıurfa

975,000. 5 km (3 miles) N of city centre, (0482) 412 15 49. 6 km (4 miles) S of city centre, (0414) 313 78 23. Atatürk Bul, Vilayet Binası, Kat 3, (0414) 312 53 32.

The city of Şanlıurfa is one of the most interesting and colourful in the region. First settled by the Hurri peoples around 5,500 years ago, it was occupied by a succession of peoples, such as the Hittites, Assyrians, Greeks and Romans.

Alexander the Great named it Edessa, and the Ottomans renamed it Urfa. The city acquired the prefix *şanlı* (glorious) through the role it played in resistance to the French in 1920.

Şanlıurfa was a major centre for the Nestorian branch of Christianity, and later became the capital of a Crusader state (1097–1144). Churches, now mosques, in the old town include the Selahattin Eyubi Camii, once the church of St John.

Most visitors, however, come here to see the Gölbaşı (lakeside) area at the foot of the citadel. This pleasantly landscaped garden contains the Pool of Abraham, said to be the site where the biblical prophet was saved from the vengeful Assyrian king, Nimrod (Nemrut). A small cave nearby is said to be the birthplace of Abraham.

The stone covered bazaar, or Kapalı Çarşı, is an Ottoman structure, with designated rows of streets devoted to particular trades. Traditional crafts and skills predominate, and it is a good place to shop for locally produced cloth. Don't miss the Gümrük Hanı in the bazaar. This beautifully shady Ottoman-era courtyard building is full of locals drinking tea and coffee, and playing endless games of backgammon.

People playing games and relaxing in Gümrük Hanı, a lovely courtyard in Sanliurfa's bazaar

The Haleplibahçe Museum Complex is scheduled to open in the spring or summer 2015. Situated just west of the Gölbaşı area, this huge museum is built around some superb 3rd- to 5th-century late Roman and Byzantine mosaics, which were discovered in situ in 2007 during excavations for an urban infrastructure project. Some 10,000 objects will be displayed in the museum, including finds from one of the world's most important archaeological sites, Göbekli Tepe. A replica of the temple complex at Göbekli will form a focal attraction, along with audio-visual presentations.

Beehive-shaped hosues in Harran

Environs

Set on a rounded hilltop some 15 km (9 miles) northeast of Şanlıurafa, **Göbekli Tepe** *(see p312)* is one of the most exciting sights in Turkey. A temple complex of immense significance, its discovery in 1995 challenged traditional concepts that mankind was only able to produce monumental buildings after the transition had been made from a hunter-gatherer to a settled society. Some of the monolithic, anthropomorphic T-shaped stones here are 5 m (16 ft) tall and the earliest predate Stonehenge by nearly 8,000 years. Arranged in circles in chambers hollowed from the hilltop, most of the stones are decorated with raised relief carvings of foxes, wild boars, snakes and lions. Walkways allow visitors to examine the temple complex. The site is open between sunrise and sunset, and there is a small entrance fee.

It is worth making the 45-km (28-mile) trip southeast of Şanlıurfa to see the curious beehive houses of **Harran**, once an important city but which was destroyed by the Mongols in the 13th century. Most of the inhabitants of this austerely beautiful place are Arabs, and some still live among the ruins of old Harran in houses made from mud-plastered stone. Substantial remains include the citadel and Ulu Cami, a massive (though now ruined) mosque denoted by a square minaret.

The Pool of Abraham in Şanlıurfa

For hotels and restaurants in this area see p339 and p360–61

7 Mardin

88,000. Valilik Binası, (0482) 212 18 52 and (0482) 212 37 76. Kite Festival (3rd week Jun).

Superbly situated atop a limestone crag overlooking the Mesopotamian plain, Mardin is justly famed for its beautiful vernacular architecture. Many of its superb stone houses have been converted into boutique hotels and, after Gaziantep, it is the arguably the most tourist-friendly city in southeast Turkey. The city was captured by Muslims in about AD 640 and ruled by various Arab and Kurdish states until the 11th century. Some exceptional theological buildings, like the Zinciriye Medresesi and the Kasımiye Medresesi, date from the 14th and 15th centuries respectively.

The unusual terrace-style dwellings and narrow, labyrinth-like streets invoke the style and form of their Arab heritage. A city landmark is the **Mardin Museum**, whose archaeological section displays works from 4000 BC until the 7th century BC.

The Ulu Cami, a 12th-century Syrian-style mosque, built by an Artukid chieftain, is another city symbol. It is noted for its huge minaret, which soars above the city and is decorated with teardrop-shaped relief carvings and has inscriptions in Kufic Arabic script. There is a fascinating bazaar surrounding the mosque.

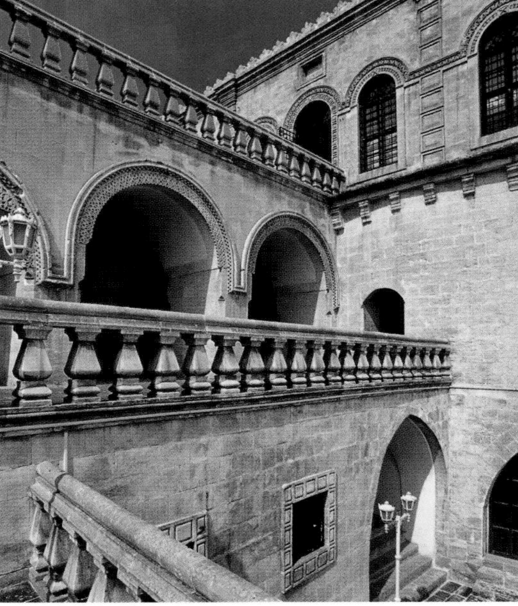

Mardin Museum, which was formerly the Syrian Catholic Patriarchate

A state-of-the-art ethnography museum housed in a beautifully restored period stone building, **Sakip Sabancı City Museum** is the place to find out about the traditional way of life in Mardin. Exhibits range from audiovisual presentations on metalworking and fabric printing to superb photographs of the town's myriad mosques and churches. Temporary exhibitions are also held at the museum.

Mardin Museum
Cumhuriyet Meydani, Latifiye Mah, Mardin. **Tel** (0482) 212 16 14.
Open 9am–6pm Tue–Sun.

Sakip Sabancı City Museum
Gül Mahallesi Eski Hükümet Cad, Mardin. **Tel** (0482) 212 93 96.
Open 8am–5pm Tue–Sun.

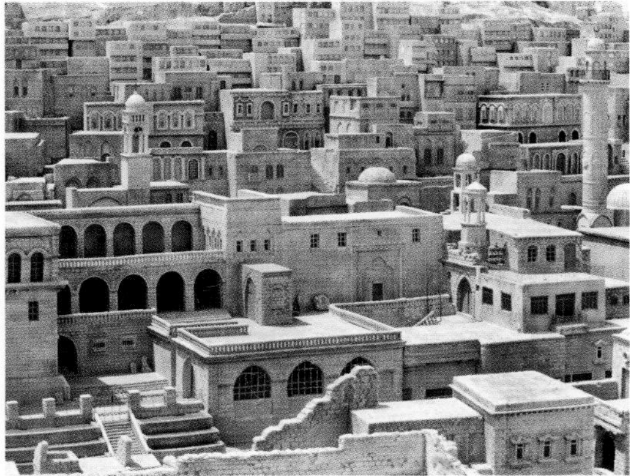

Traditional stone houses in Mardin

Environs

Mardin, and the Tör Abdin plateau east of it, has long been a stronghold of the Syrian Orthodox Church. **Deyr-az-Zaferan**, known as the Saffron Monastery due to the colour of the yellowish stones it is built with, is the showcase of a much persecuted minority, and is beautifully set in a peaceful valley below dramatic bluffs some 6 km (4 miles) southeast of Mardin. A guide accompanies visitors around the picturesque stone-built monastery dating back to the 5th century and still in operation. There is a also a café, and one guestroom is available for overnight stays.

Deyr-az-Zaferan
6 km (4 miles) SE of Mardin.
Open 8am–noon, 1–5pm daily. 

❽ Diyarbakır

Southeastern Turkey's liveliest city, Diyarbakır is situated on the edge of a high bank dropping down to the Tigris River. Its 6 km (4 miles) of black basalt walls encircle an old centre of cobbled streets and alleys, mosques, churches and mansions.

As the unofficial capital of Turkey's Kurdish-dominated southeast, political feelings can run high here. However, the inhabitants are generally warm and open to visitors, and justly proud of their atmospheric but economically deprived home city.

Diyarbakır is renowned for the gigantic watermelons sold in its markets. Watered by the Tigris River and fertilized with pigeon droppings, the melons can reach weights of up to 50 kg (112 lb).

Vendor offering one of the region's famous watermelons

Exploring Diyarbakır

Most of the city's sights are concentrated in the central area and can be seen on foot. Walking alone around the walls is not recommended.

Diyarbakir's Churches

Diyarbakır'ın Kilise

Church of the Virgin Mary. **Open** daily; services 8am–noon Sun. Church of St George. **Open** admission via caretaker.

The city's oldest church is the Syrian Orthodox Church of the Virgin Mary (Meryaman Kilise), possibly dating back to the 4th century. Restored to its former splendour, the Armenian Apostolic Church of St George (St Giargos Kilesesi) is reckoned to be one of the largest churches in the Middle East.

Hasan Paşa Hanı

Gazi Cad. **Open** Mon–Sat.

Located opposite the Great Mosque (Ulu Cami), and built by governor Verizade Hasan Paşa, this 16th-century *han (see pp28–9)* is still used by traders, and has some decent jewellery, carpet and antique outlets, and a couple of great places to go to for a traditional Kurdish breakfast. The black basalt façade is dignified by a bold white limestone frieze.

Great Mosque

Ulu Cami

Gazi Cad. **Open** daily.
Closed during prayer times.

A fairly plain building with a basilica-plan style, the Great Mosque is the most significant building in Diyarbakır, and is regarded as one of the holiest places in the Islamic world. It was built on the site of a church around AD 639 after the Arabs captured the city. In 1091–2, the Seljuk ruler Malik Şah remodelled the building, using the revered Great Ummayad Mosque in Damascus as a model.

The Great Mosque, originally built by the Arabs in the 7th century

The interior is spacious and austere, while the courtyard buildings are built from black basalt with bands of white limestone, faced with blind arches supported by Roman columns interspersed with Seljuk friezes.

Ziya Gökalp Museum

Ziya Gökalp Müzesi

Ziya Gökalp Bul. **Tel** (0412) 228 13 26.
Open 8:30am–noon & 1–5pm Tue–Sun.

Ziya Gökalp, one of the chief ideologues of Turkish nationalism during the period of the Young Turks *(see p61)*, was born in Diyarbakır. His house is now a museum.

Kasım Padişah Mosque

Dört Ayaklı Camii

Yeni Kapı Cad. **Open** daily.
Closed during prayer times.
donation.

This was the last of the great mosques built under the reign of the Akkoyunlu (White Sheep) Turkomans. It is unusual for its free-standing minaret supported by four 2-m- (6.5-ft-) high basalt pillars carved from a single block of stone, known as the Dört Ayaklı Minare (four-legged minaret). It is said that your wish will be granted if you walk seven times around its pillars.

Behram Paşa Mosque

Behram Paşa Camii

Melik Ahmet Cad. **Open** daily.
Closed during prayer times.
donation.

Built in 1572 on the orders of the governor, Behram Paşa, this centrally located mosque is the city's largest. The black basalt exterior is enlivened by white stone banding, and the interior is light and graceful. The central ceiling has a calligraphic frieze of inlaid mother-of-pearl.

Black-and-white banding on the Behram Paşa Camii

For hotels and restaurants in this area see p339 and pp360–61

The impressive walls surrounding the old city

VISITORS' CHECKLIST

Practical Information
835,000. Dağ Kapısı Burçu Giriş Bölümü, (0412) 228 17 06. Watermelon Festival (Sep); Nevruz (21 Mar); Hıdrellez Festival celebrating spring migration (6 May, depending on weather).

Transport
Kaplaner, 3 km (2 miles) SW of city centre, (0412) 233 27 19. 10 km (6 miles) W of city centre, (0412) 221 87 87/87 86.

City Walls

Diyarbakır Surları

The black walls encircling the city – said to be visible from space – were originally built by the Romans (who captured Diyarbakır from the Sassanids in the 3rd century AD), since the city lacked natural defences. The Byzantines added to the structure, but what can be seen today is mainly the work of Seljuks, who captured the city in 1088.

Constructed from blocks of black basalt, the walls are pierced by four major gates (Harput, Yenikapı, Mardin and Urfa) and studded with 72 towers. The walls are 12 m (39 ft) high and more than 5 km (3 miles) in length. It is possible to walk along the top for much of the way.

The most impressive views are from the southern walls, looking down over the Tigris River winding its way towards Iraq. The Tower of the Seven Brothers (Yedi Kardeş Burçu), located between the Mardin and Urfa gates and built in 1208, provides a particularly good vantage point.

Environs

The **Atatürk Villa** was given to the founder of the Turkish Republic in 1937 by the citizens of Diyarbakır. On display are period photographs and personal effects. It is situated a few kilometres south of the city, off the road to Mardin, and has expansive views of the Tigris and the Dicle Köprüsü (Tigris Bridge). Built in 1065 on the site of an older structure, the bridge spans the river in 10 arches.

Atatürk Villa

Atatürk Köşkü

Open 8:30am–noon & 1:30–5pm daily.

Diyarbakır City Centre

① Hasan Paşa Hanı
② Great Mosque
③ Ziya Gökalp Museum
④ Kasım Padişah Mosque
⑤ Behram Paşa Mosque
⑥ City Walls

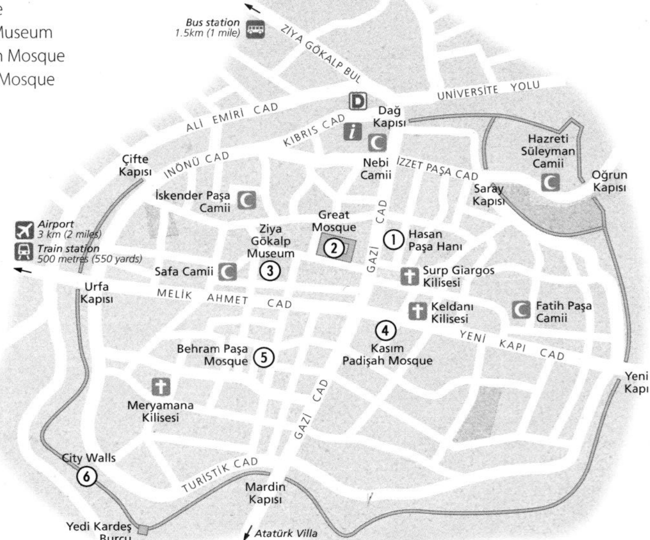

9 Lake Van

548,000. 6 km (4 miles) S of city centre, (0432) 216 10 19. Ipek Yolu, NW of town centre. to Tatvan, (0432) 223 41 38. 5 km (3 miles) from town centre. Cumhuriyet Cad 105, (0432) 216 20 18.

The Rock of Van, with an ancient Urartian citadel at the summit

The startlingly blue waters of Lake Van (Van Gölü) mirror the surrounding peaks, the highest of which soars to a dizzying 4,058 m (13,313 ft). The lake is seven times larger than Lake Geneva and may be up to 400 m (1,312 ft) deep. The lake has a salinity level well above that of sea water. It is so alkaline that locals can wash dirty laundry in the lake without the need for any soap.

The Van basin was once the centre of the Urartian civilization (contemporaries and foes of the Assyrians). The remnants of their fortified capital straddle the imposing **Rock of Van**, located close to the eastern shore of the lake. This spectacular rock outcrop, sheer on its southern side, was once the premier settlement of the Kingdom of Urartu. The most obvious remains left by this remarkable civilization are their cuneiform inscriptions, seen most obviously on the entrance to the Tomb of Argishti, which is reached by steps from near the top of the rock. The remains of an Ottoman mosque now crown the rock, while at its feet spread the remnants of old Van, a walled settlement destroyed in World War I. A few kilometres away is the modern city of Van. Although the centre lacks historical interest, it has plenty of decent restaurants. Try the famed Van breakfast, which includes clotted cream and honey, plus fried eggs and strips of lamb. The region is also proud of the Van Cat, a rare breed of cat noted for having one blue eye and one amber, and for demonstrating an unusual fascination with water.

Rock of Van
Van Kalesi. **Open** Apr–Oct: 9am–7pm daily; Nov–Mar: 8am–5pm daily.

Environs
Çavuştepe, 35 km (22 miles) southeast of Van, is another Urartian site, with a palace, sacrificial altar and inscriptions. It is best visited en route to the stark and hauntingly beautiful 17th-century castle at Hoşap, 60 km (37 miles) from Van on the same road.

The high point of a visit to the Lake Van area is the exquisite 10th-century Armenian **Church of the Holy Cross** (Akdamar Kilise), on a small island a few kilometres from the southern shore of the lake. Beautifully restored, the exterior boasts a remarkable series of bas-relief carvings and friezes showing biblical scenes. Cruciform in plan, and just 15 x 12 m (49 x 39 ft) in size, the church is topped by a conical roof.

Its classical beauty makes this church one of the most photographed buildings in eastern Anatolia. The frescoes that adorn the interior walls and cupola are unique in their artistic merit. Following the restoration of the church, services have been held, attracting many worshippers from both the Armenian community in Istanbul and from Armenia itself.

On the lake's northwestern shore is the crescent-shaped crater lake on Nemrut Dağı (not the mountain with the statues near Kâhta) and the Seljuk cemetery and *kümbet* (domed tombs) at Ahlat. Both are worth a visit and can be accessed from Tatvan.

The local cheese, *otlu peynir*, is a real delicacy. A whole-milk cheese flecked with nutritious and flavoursome mountain herbs, it is now rarely found outside the Van area.

Frieze on the wall of the Church of the Holy Cross

Church of the Holy Cross
40 km (25 miles) SW of Van. from quay, opposite the island. **Open** Apr–Oct: 9am–7pm daily; Nov–Mar: 8am–5pm daily.

◀ Collosal statues on the Eastern terrace of Mount Nemrut

⑩ Doğubayazıt

73,000. Belediye Cad, W of town centre.

Situated on the main road between Turkey and Iran, Doğubayazıt is a half-hour drive from the border. It is a typically untidy frontier town, with a large military base on its eastern outskirts, and few visitors spend more than a night here. Mount Ağrı (Ararat), Turkey's highest mountain, rises 5,165 m (16,945 ft) above the landscape. Although said to be the resting place of Noah's Ark, little evidence has ever been found to support this claim. Access is difficult and prospective climbers need to obtain permission from the Ministry of Culture and Tourism in Ankara *(see p375)* in advance.

The impressive **İshak Paşa Sarayı** lies 8 km (5 miles) southeast of Dogubayazıt. The fortress-like palace was constructed from honey-coloured sandstone by an Ottoman governor in the late 18th century, although the variety of building styles (Ottoman, Persian, Armenian/Georgian and Seljuk) makes it difficult to attach an exact date. In Ottoman times, the palace lay on an important caravan route, explaining why such an opulent structure was erected in this lonely and remote part of the country.

The lavish arrangement of 366 rooms includes a harem with 14 bedrooms, *selamlık* (men's quarters) and a small but beautiful mosque, the interior of which has been badly damaged over the years. A roof made of steel and glass has now been installed to preserve the structure. Ottoman and Russian troops have occupied **İshak Paşa Sarayı** at various times.

Nearby attractions, best visited on a *dolmuş* tour from Dogubayazıt, are the sulphur springs at Diyadin, and the Meteor Çukuru (meteor crater), just before the Iranian border.

İshak Paşa Sarayı
Open 9am–noon & 1–5:30pm Tue–Sun.

İshak Paşa Sarayı, on a hillside southeast of Doğubayazıt

⑪ Kars

78,000. 2 km (1 mile) SE of town centre, (0474) 223 14 45. off Cumhuriyet Cad, (0474) 223 43 99/43 98. (0474) 223 06 74. Cumhuriyet Mah, Lise Sokak 15, (0474) 212 68 17.

Remote but strategically very important, Kars is set on a grassy plain that is backed by distant peaks. The word *kar* means "snow" in Turkish and winters here are long and cold, while the spring and autumn rains turn streets to mud. The brief summer season is hot, dry and dusty.

Founded in the 10th century by the Armenian King Abas I, Kars was once a metropolis of around 100,000 inhabitants. In 1064, it was captured by the Seljuks, and subsequently came under Georgian and Ottoman rule. It was held by the Russians from 1878 to 1919, and the grid plan and numerous run-down Neo-Classical houses are significant reminders of their presence here.

The citadel (Kars Kalesi) was built by the Ottomans, as was the 15th-century Taş Köprü (stone bridge) over the River Kars. The 10th-century Armenian Church of the Apostles is today a mosque.

The small **Archaeological Museum**, just east of the town centre, is surprisingly good, particularly its displays of *kilims* (rugs) and carpets.

Kars is known for its huge wheels of Kaşar, a classic cow's milk cheese. One of the city's gourmet secrets is its Gruyère, which is produced by one cheesemaker using authentic Swiss techniques.

Archaeological Museum
Cumhuriyet Cad 365. **Tel** (0474) 212 14 30. **Open** 8am–noon & 1–5pm Tue–Sun.

Environs

Most visitors visit Kars to see Ani *(see pp320–21)*, a visually dramatic, ruined 11th-century Armenian city 43 km (27 miles) away to the east, on the border with Armenia.

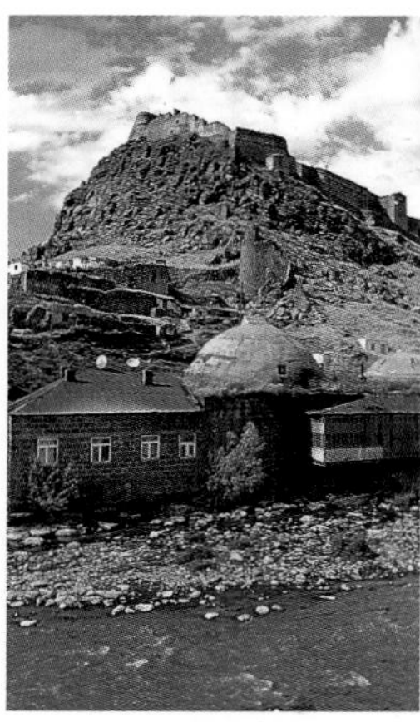

The citadel at Kars, overlooking a Turkish bath

For hotels and restaurants in this area see p339 and pp360–61

⓬ Ani

The ruined city of Ani, on the border with Armenia, is one of the most evocative historical sites in Turkey. Set on a windswept, grassy plateau along the Barley River (Arpa Çayı), the site contains important remnants of Armenian architecture, including the city walls protecting its northern border, parts of which are still intact.

In 961, Ani became the capital of the Bagratid kings of Armenia. It reached its apogee under King Gagik I (990–1020), when it was known as "the city of a thousand and one churches". Sacked by the Turks in 1064, Ani eventually recovered, only to be razed by an earthquake in 1319.

Located on the sensitive Turkish-Armenian border, parts of the site are off-limits to visitors – stick to the marked trail. Photography is also restricted, so avoid pointing your camera across the border.

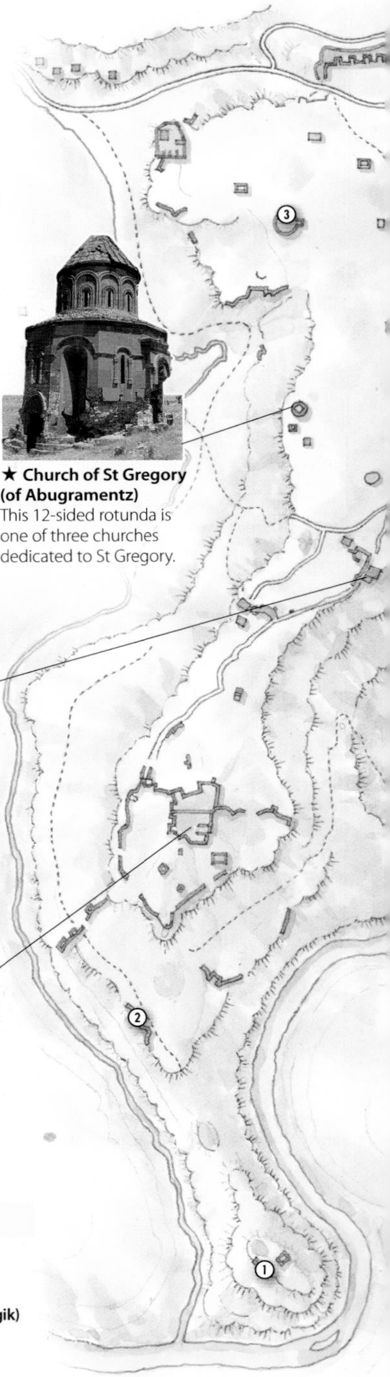

★ Church of St Gregory (of Abugramentz)
This 12-sided rotunda is one of three churches dedicated to St Gregory.

View from Menücehir Mosque
This bridge, now ruined, spanned the Barley River (Arpa Çayı) in a single arch 30 m (32 yards) in length. The river demarcates the border between Turkey and Armenia.

Citadel
The Citadel is the oldest part of Ani and housed most of its residents until 961, when the Bagratids moved their capital here from Kars. It contains the ruined palace of the Bagratid kings.

KEY

① **Maiden's Castle**
② **City Walls**
③ **Church of St Gregory (of Gagik)**
④ **Ruined Bridge**

For hotels and restaurants in this area see p339 and p361

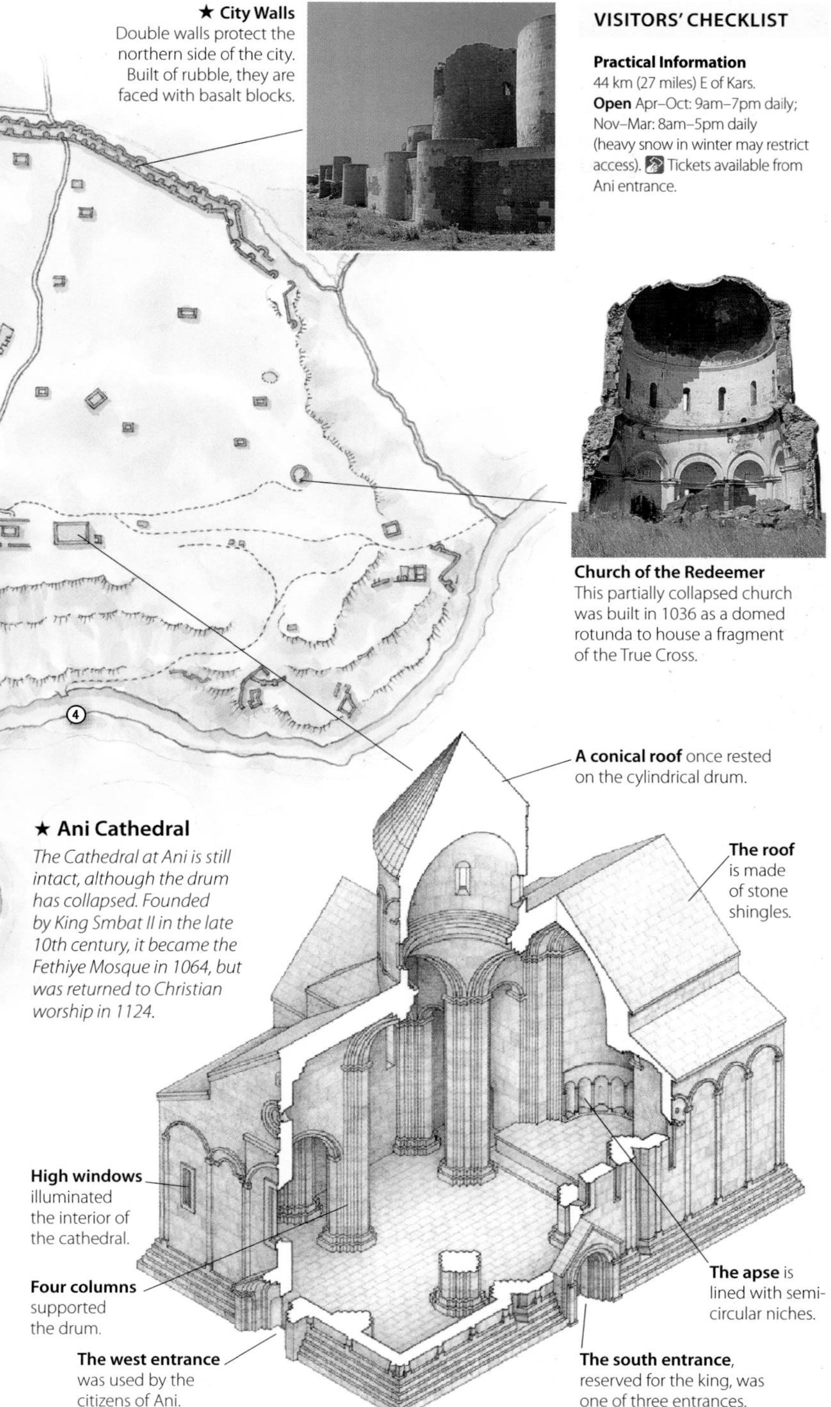

★ City Walls
Double walls protect the northern side of the city. Built of rubble, they are faced with basalt blocks.

Church of the Redeemer
This partially collapsed church was built in 1036 as a domed rotunda to house a fragment of the True Cross.

A conical roof once rested on the cylindrical drum.

★ Ani Cathedral

The Cathedral at Ani is still intact, although the drum has collapsed. Founded by King Smbat II in the late 10th century, it became the Fethiye Mosque in 1064, but was returned to Christian worship in 1124.

The roof is made of stone shingles.

High windows illuminated the interior of the cathedral.

Four columns supported the drum.

The west entrance was used by the citizens of Ani.

The apse is lined with semi-circular niches.

The south entrance, reserved for the king, was one of three entrances.

VISITORS' CHECKLIST

Practical Information
44 km (27 miles) E of Kars.
Open Apr–Oct: 9am–7pm daily; Nov–Mar: 8am–5pm daily (heavy snow in winter may restrict access). Tickets available from Ani entrance.

⓭ Erzurum

Sprawling across a vast plain at an altitude of almost 2,000 m (6,560 ft) and ringed by mountains, Erzurum is Turkey's coldest city. It is also by far the most developed city in the region. Because it was located astride the main caravan route from India to Europe, and controlled the passage between the Caucasus and Anatolia, Erzurum was fought over and ruled by many peoples – Byzantines, Sassanids, Arabs, Armenians, Seljuk Turks, Mongols and Ottomans. Its most famous sights date from Seljuk times. Like Kars, the city was in Russian hands for over 40 years. In 1919, Atatürk's Nationalists met here to map out the frontiers of modern Turkey.

Exploring Erzurum
Erzurum has a university and a large garrison population. It hosts a rough-and-ready horseback competition *(cirit)*, which involves throwing a spear at a target.

Archaeological Museum
Arkeoloji Müzesi
Paşalar Cad 11. **Tel** (0442) 233 04 14.
Open Apr–Oct: 9am–7pm daily; Nov–Mar: 8am–5pm daily.

Exhibits here range from Urartian metalwork and pottery to the jewellery and glassware of the Hellenistic and Roman eras.

Lala Mustafa Paşa Mosque
Cumhuriyet Caddesi. **Open** daily.

This charming Ottoman mosque, built in 1562, conforms to a typical square-plan design, with columns and cupolas around a courtyard with a fountain. Original tile work adorns the interior.

Yakutiye Seminary
Yakutiye Medrese
Cumhuriyet Cad. **Open** 8am–noon & 1–5pm Tue–Sun.

Built in 1310 by Hoca Yakut, governor of the İlhan Mongols, this ornate Koranic school is regarded as the city's most beautiful building. The carved stonework around the entrance is very appealing and the short minaret features an elaborate lattice of brick and turquoise tiles. The building houses the Museum of Islamic Artefacts.

The ornate entrance portal of the Yakutiye Seminary

Citadel
Kale
N of Çifte Minareli Medresesi.
Open Apr–Oct: 9am–7pm daily; Nov–Mar: 8am–5pm daily.

The citadel was built in the 5th century, during the reign of Byzantine Emperor Theodosius. It was restored in 1555 by Sultan Süleyman I (the Magnificent) and served as the eastern base of the Janissaries *(see p60)*. Inside is a ruined clocktower and also a mosque. There are fine views over the city from the walls.

Twin Minaret Seminary
Çifte Minareli Medresesi
Cumhuriyet Cad.
Open 8am–5pm daily.

The two minarets that flank the portal of the Çifte Minareli Medresesi have become the

Erzurum City Centre

① Archaeological Museum
② Lala Mustafa Paşa Mosque
③ Yakutiye Seminary
④ Citadel
⑤ Twin Minaret Seminary
⑥ Three Tombs

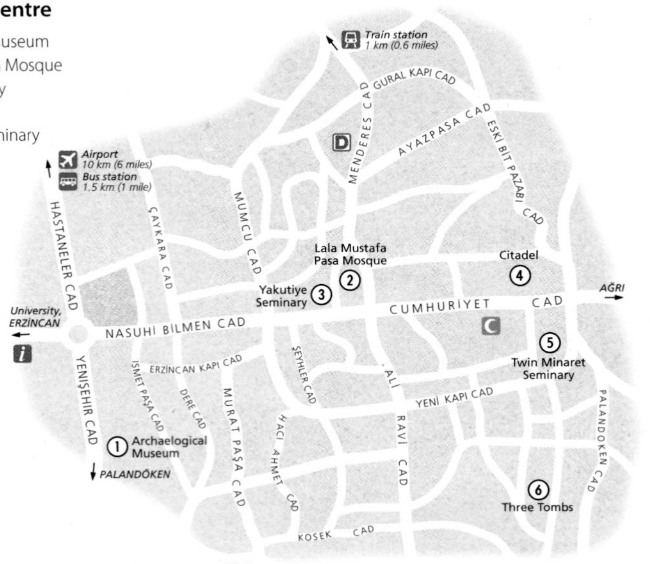

VISITORS' CHECKLIST

Practical Information
385,000. Cemal Gürsel Caddesi 9, (0442) 233 71 99 and 235 09 25. Atatürk Congress and Festival (23 Jul). most days.

Transport
10 km (6 miles) NE of city centre, (0442) 327 28 35. 3 km (2 miles) NW of city centre. 1 km (0.5 mile) N of city centre.

symbols of Erzurum. They are thought to have been built in 1253 on the authority of Hunat Hatun, daughter of Seljuk Sultan Alaeddin Keykubad II. At the rear of the complex is the 12-sided cylinder tomb that contains her remains.

Twin Minaret Seminary

Three Tombs
Üç Kümbet
S of Twin Minaret Seminary.
Open daily.

Built by the Seljuks, the oldest of these conical mausoleums dates from the early 12th century. It is distinguished by the use of contrasting light and dark stone and by its truncated cone.

Environs
Erzurum has a reliable ski season that runs from November to May. Palandöken Ski Centre *(see p388)*, situated 8 km (5 miles) southwest of the city centre, has several hotels and six ski lifts serving 30 km (19 miles) of piste.

The gorge of the Euphrates (Firat) near Kemaliye

⓮ Erzincan

280,118. Atatürk Mah, Bariş Manço Parkı içi, Kültür Sitesi, (0446) 214 30 79 or 223 06 71.

Erzincan's history has been marked by earthquakes, notably in 1939 and 1992. It was once considered one of Turkey's most impressive cities, but rebuilding work over the years has left it with few historic attractions.

Erzincan's specialities include decorative copperware and *tulum peynır*, and a cheese made from raw milk and sold encased in a sheep skin.

Environs
Altıntepe (Golden Hill), a Urartian site 27 km (17 miles) east of Erzincan, dates from around 700 BC. Many of the objects found here are now on display in Ankara's Museum of Anatolian Civilizations *(see p246–7)*. One of the best of these is a bronze cauldron with handles in the shape of bulls' heads.

The little town of **Kemaliye** (formerly known as Eğin) lies in the Munzur Mountains not far from Erzincan. Founded in the 11th century, Kemaliye's pebbled streets, wild streams and trim wooden buildings offer a charming snapshot of life in Ottoman times. The Village Life Museum in Ocakköyü, near Kemaliye, is the only private ethnographic museum in Turkey.

Village Life Museum
Köy Müzesi
Ocakköyü. **Tel** (0446) 754 40 65.
Open 9am–noon & 1–5pm Tue–Sun.

⓯ Divriği

18,000. S of town centre, on road to Elaziğ. from Sivas, Erzincan or Malatya.

After the Seljuk victory at Manzikert (Malazgirt) in 1071 *(see p56)*, Divriği became the seat of the Mengüçek state and was ruled by the Mengüç family from 1142 to 1252. Among many fine buildings they left behind is the *külliye* (mosque-hospital complex), the best example of 13th-century Seljuk stonecarving in Turkey, and now a UNESCO World Heritage Site. The ornate portals of the **Ulu Cami**, or Great Mosque (built around 1229) and the adjoining *daruşşifa* (hospital) – easy to spot as you come into town – display exceptionally rich decoration.

Carving detail, Divriği

Ulu Cami
Open during prayer times daily.

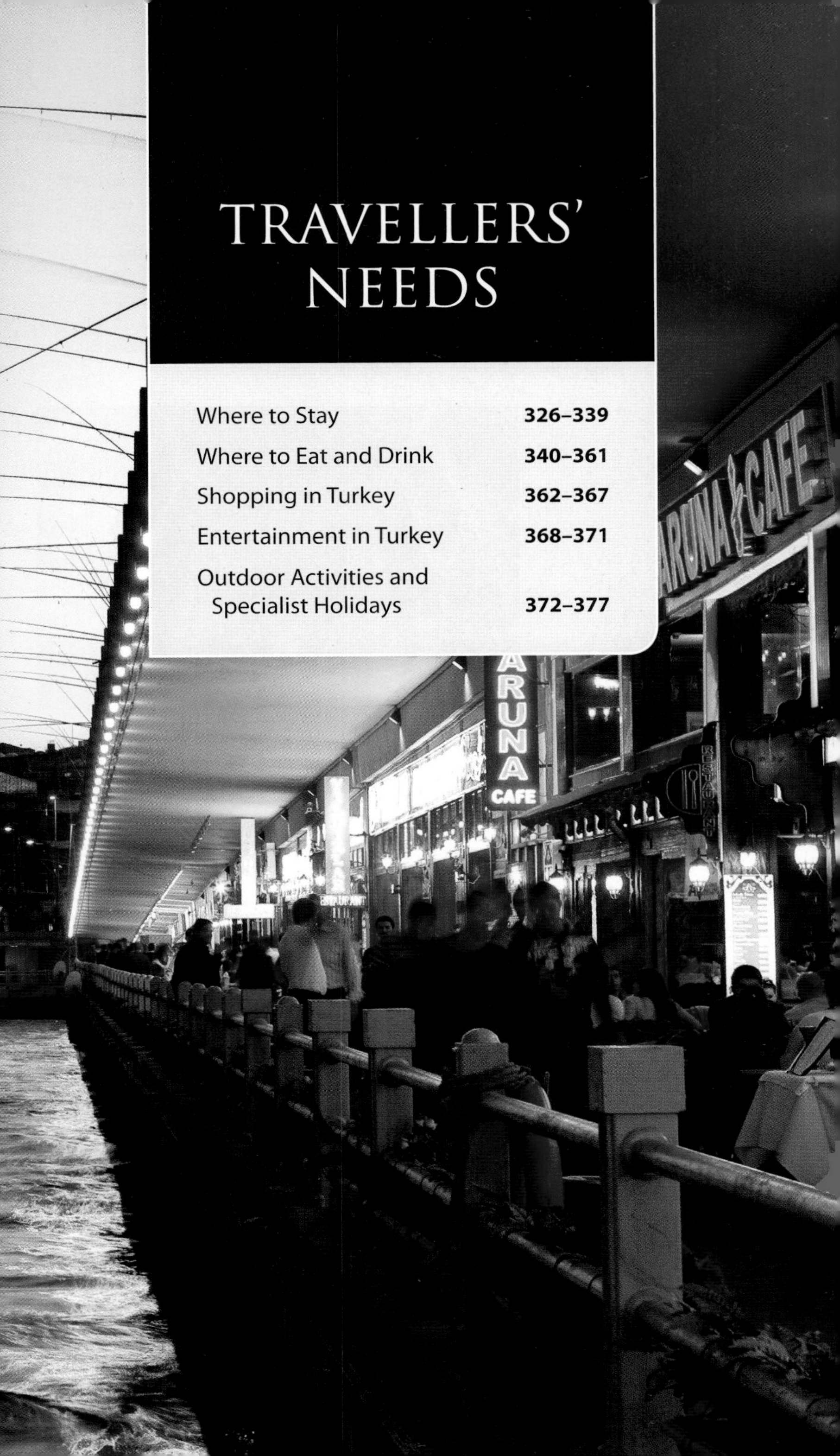

TRAVELLERS' NEEDS

Where to Stay **326–339**

Where to Eat and Drink **340–361**

Shopping in Turkey **362–367**

Entertainment in Turkey **368–371**

Outdoor Activities and Specialist Holidays **372–377**

WHERE TO STAY

Whether you wish to stay in an Ottoman sultan's opulent palace, a quaint *yalı* (traditional wooden waterfront mansion) on the Bosphorus or in a comfortable family home, it is fairly easy to find the accommodation of your choice in Turkey. The country's hotels and guesthouses cater for a wide range of budgets and, in general, these are found clustered around the main sightseeing areas. Some of the old towns, notably Safranbolu *(see pp272–3)*, offer accommodation in restored mansions and family homes around the historic town centre. The choice of hotels in Turkey's eastern provinces is more restricted, though accommodation options in all price ranges are steadily improving. The hotel listings provided on pp330–39 will help visitors to find accommodations to suit all budgets.

Choosing a Hotel

Many hotels in Turkey are rated by the Ministry of Tourism according to a star system – from one to five – with five stars representing the most luxurious. However, try not to make a choice exclusively on the basis of star ratings – the comfort and service levels may vary regardless of such ratings based on technical criteria.

Most hotels can be easily reached by public transport from the airport, bus or train station. With advance notice, many hotels will also ferry guests to and from the airport.

A lot of hotels in resort areas close from late October to March or April. Check when booking or on the hotel's website. Most hotels also have direct reservation pages on their websites.

Summer is hot and humid in the southern coastal areas, so it is worth paying extra for an air-conditioned room. Water shortages are not uncommon, and in cheaper hotels reliant on solar heating hot water may run out at busy times.

The impressive lobby of the Zorlu Grand Hotel, Trabzon *(see p338)*

In Turkey you may come across "Special Class" hotels. These are generally considered to be establishments that comply with strict standards of hospitality and service. So, even if it is listed as a *pansiyon* (pension), the comfort levels, decor and food will be first-rate. It is advisable to book well in advance at these establishments.

Luxury Hotels

Upmarket international hotel chains are well represented in Istanbul, Ankara, İzmir and other large cities. Almost all five-star hotels offer fine views over the city or the Bosphorus, in the case of Istanbul.

Luxury hotels also typically have pools, fitness and health facilities, *hamams* (Turkish baths) and conference facilities. Resort hotels and holiday villages feature nightly entertainment, such as traditional music and dancing. Most hotels will gladly arrange city or boating tours, as well as day trips to local attractions. Visitors can also organize these trips personally to get reasonably lower rates.

A good reference point for plush properties is **The Luxury Hotels of Turkey**, an organization that offers an exclusive selection of luxury establishments – the Turkish counterpart of "World's Leading Hotels".

The Baylo Suites' garden terrace boasts superb views of the Golden Horn *(see p331)*

Holiday Villages

The coastal areas of Turkey have numerous holiday villages and self-contained resorts (many of them all-inclusive) that offer a full range of holiday options for visitors, usually with access to their private stretch of beach. Staying in a holiday village can be very economical, especially for families with children, as the activities on offer are included in the price of the holiday.

Most holiday villages offer programmes for children, as well as babysitting services and nightly entertainment.

◀ Restaurants and cafés under the Galata Bridge which spans the Golden Horn, Istanbul

Beautifully decorated suite at the Museum Hotel in Uçhisar *(see p338)*

Budget Hotels

There is a wide range of inexpensive accommodation in Turkey, from hotels and motels to family-run pensions (*pansiyons*).

Some of the budget hotels are not rated by the Ministry of Tourism but by the local municipality, whose standards depend on the region. Therefore, when choosing one of these hotels, take care not to make a decision solely on the basis of what you see in the newly renovated lobby; it is always best to see if the carpet runs past the first stairs. Most budget hotels provide only minimal services, which could mean communal rather than private washing facilities.

A far better option than a one-star hotel is a *pansiyon*. The vast majority of these are family-run establishments offering friendly, good-value accommodation. Most have comfortable rooms with air-conditioning, television and en-suite facilities.

Boutique Hotels

Boutique hotels are usually historic buildings that have been restored and transformed into quaint hotels full of character. Or, they may have outstanding features such as unique architecture, innovative design, artistic value, an exceptional view or an excellent location. Facilities may vary from the grand and luxurious to the more basic. In Istanbul, most such hotels are found in the older quarters, and give guests a chance to experience closely the lifestyle of the late Ottoman era. Cappadocia is another region where some outstanding boutique hotels can be found clustered together.

The **Association of Small Hotels** pulls together a refined group of boutique hotels, and offers booking facilities online.

What to Expect

In the popular regions, front desk staff can be expected to speak English, but this is less likely when staying in more remote areas. The average rooms may not be very spacious, especially for those travelling with family. Single occupancy rooms can be difficult to find, and travellers requiring a single room usually end up paying for single occupancy in a double or twin room. A double bed is usually queen-sized. King-sized beds are rare, except at international five-star hotels, and in some boutique hotels. A triple room is usually a double room with enough space for a cot, a roll-out or a divan. Quads are almost unheard of, but many hotels offer connecting rooms or family suites that can accommodate four people.

Most multistorey hotels have lifts but this will not be the case in older buildings converted into boutique hotels. Facilities for wheelchair users and other disabled guests are also only found in the more expensive hotels.

Noise can be quite a problem in downtown areas, even in the luxury hotels, so be sure to ask for a quiet room when you make your reservation.

All hotels must provide floors or sections where smoking is forbidden – all public areas are non-smoking by law.

The price of the room usually includes breakfast and this will be either a set Turkish breakfast that includes fresh bread, butter, jam, soft white cheese, tomatoes, cucumbers and black olives, or a self-service buffet with more choice. Coastal hotels and holiday villages offer half-board, with an evening meal thrown in. This is usually another buffet spread.

Internet access is widespread. Most of the hotels across the country offer high-speed Wi-Fi either for free or for an additional charge.

Yeşil Ev, a boutique hotel in Istanbul *(see p330)*

The elegant reception area at the Ferahi Evler Butik Otel, Ayvalık *(see p333)*

Prices and Discounts

Hotel prices are quoted per room, not per person in Turkish lira, euros or US dollars. Bargaining when booking a room is perfectly acceptable, and discounts are often available if you pay in cash or book ahead online. Luxury hotels may also offer a discount to business travellers; ask for the corporate rate. In general, your success in bargaining will depend on how busy the hotel is at the time. Expect to pay premium prices during religious or national holidays, when virtually all accommodation is booked. Check individual hotel websites to find their latest discounts and promotions – hotels usually offer their best rates on the Internet.

Booking a Room

It is always a good idea to book early, especially in Istanbul or other popular destinations, and during high season between May and October. Telephone and email bookings are both accepted. If you haven't prebooked accommodation, or you have changed your itinerary to get off the beaten track, visit any of the tourist information offices to inquire about available places to stay. Tourist offices can also give you advice on approximate prices. Don't be shy about looking around, seeing rooms and comparing prices.

If travelling with an organized tour group, your agent should handle all the arrangements.

Checking Out and Paying

Guests are expected to check out by noon, but on request most hotels will agree to hold luggage for collection later.

Except for the very remote or low-cost establishments, most hotels listed in this guide accept major international credit cards. Travellers' cheques, however, are almost obsolete.

Value-added tax (VAT) is known as KDV in Turkish *(see p384)* and is generally included in the price of a room. When registering at a hotel, you may be asked for your credit card, which will then be swiped through an authorization machine. Sign the transaction form and the card is then resubmitted for payment when your account is settled.

Luxurious room at the Hilton Bursa, with views of Bursa City and the Uludağ Mountains *(see p332)*

Tips for the staff are always appreciated. A few dollars should suffice for junior personnel, while a little more is good for the front desk if they have done something special. Remember that phone calls and minibar drinks are additional charges that can increase the overall bill substantially.

Children

In most hotels, children up to the age of six years can stay in their parents' room at no extra charge. Many hotels also offer up to 50 per cent discount for 12- to 15-year-olds sharing a room with their parents. Some smaller boutique-style hotels may not take children under 12 years, so check when booking. Cots for babies are willingly provided even by mid-range hotels. Children's menus are usually available in family resort areas and holiday villages. In Turkey, children generally eat when their parents do and they also tend to stay up late, particularly during the hot summer months.

Hostels

Hostels are a budget option worth exploring. Turkey has a growing number of decent hostels welcoming travellers of all ages. Membership to these establishments is not required. Hostels are usually clustered in Istanbul's Old Town and other popular destinations, including the smaller resort towns such as Çanakkale and Fethiye. They generally offer basic comforts in shared dormitories; however, many also have private rooms with or without private facilities. The majority of hostels have a good range of amenities, including free Wi-Fi and breakfast. Some also organize local tours and excursions. **Hostel World** is an international booking portal with a good listing of Turkish hostels.

The major advantages of using a hostel are that you are guaranteed to meet like-minded travellers.

Camping and Caravanning

Caravanning and camping holidays are becoming increasingly popular and many new areas are being developed into well-equipped, highly organized camp sites that provide ample space for tents or trailers, as well as for washing or other facilities.

However, visitors should note that camping is only allowed in designated areas, so be sure to check with the **Turkish Camping and Caravanning Association**, who will be able to provide a comprehensive list of approved sites.

Parking a caravan or pitching a tent on any deserted beach, or simply pulling over to the side of the road in a caravan, is strongly discouraged.

In some parts of the country, cozy, furnished bungalows may be available for self-catered holidays in a natural environment.

Self-catering

Most major cities and coastal resorts in Turkey have plenty of apartments for short-term rental. Pensions, too, often include cooking facilities, but these are usually shared with other guests. For tax reasons, many self-catering apartments do not advertise openly, and word of mouth is the best way to locate these places. This is not the case in Istanbul and Ankara. Some travel agents have lists of apartments that they own and maintain. These are available for self-catering holidays.

A quaint, old-fashioned pension in the back streets of Selçuk

Recommended Hotels

The hotel listings in this book offer a selection of places to stay throughout the country across a range of budgets. Divided into eight geographical areas corresponding to the chapters in this guide, the entries are then organized by town and price. The accommodation options have been selected for their excellent facilities and value for money and cover a diverse array of places to stay from no-frills budget options to luxury properties that take hospitality standards to a high level.

Choose from historic hotels that exude the charm of a bygone era or opt for strikingly designed modern hotels that offer all the latest conveniences and amenities. To enjoy the comforts of home, try a family-run pension *(pansiyon)*.

Boutique hotels are usually smaller establishments that offer a unique stay. Amenities may be limited in some, but the experience and warm staff more than make up for the missing extravagances found in the larger chain hotels. These establishments often only have a handful of rooms, so it's worth booking in advance.

Entries highlighted as DK Choice offer something extra special. They may be nestled within beautiful surroundings, be in historically important buildings, have a noteworthy sustainable outlook, be incredibly charming or offer exceptional service. Whatever the reason, it is a guarantee of a memorable stay.

DIRECTORY

Luxury Hotels

The Luxury Hotels of Turkey
W turing.org.tr

Boutique Hotels

Association of Small Hotels
W smallhotels.com.tr

Hostels

Hostel World
W hostelworld.com/hostels/Turkey

Camping and Caravanning

Turkish Camping and Caravanning Association
Bestekar Sok 62/12, Kavaklıdere, Ankara.
Tel (0312) 466 19 97.
Istanbul Cad, Pelin Iş Hani K3 91–92, Bakırköy, Istanbul.
Tel (0212) 571 42 44.
W kampkaravan.org.tr

Brightly coloured façade of the Kybele Hotel, Istanbul *(see p330)*

Where to Stay

Istanbul

Seraglio Point

Gulhane Park Hotel ₺₺
Modern **Map** 5 E3
Nöbethane Cad 1, 34112 Sirkeci
Tel *(0212) 519 68 68*
W gulhaneparkhotel.com.tr
Overlooking the Topkapı Palace gardens, facilities at this hotel include a gym and *hamam*.

Neorion Hotel ₺₺₺
Modern **Map** 5 E3
Orhanıye Sok 14, Sirkeci, 34112
Tel *(0212) 527 90 90*
W neorionhotel.com
Enjoy great views and breakfast at the roof terrace or relax at the pool or sauna. Wonderful service.

Sultanahmet

Akdenız Hotel Guest House ₺
Budget **Map** 5 D4
Divanyolu Cad, Haci Tahsin Bey Sok 7, 34410
Tel *(0212) 520 20 99*
W istanbulakdenizhotel.com
A modest hotel up a flight of stairs with clean, comfortable rooms. It is located close to the T1 tram.

Aruna ₺
Boutique **Map** 5 E5
Cankurtaran Mah, Ahirkapi Sok 74, 34122
Tel *(0212) 458 54 88*
W arunahotel.com
Inviting hotel with sauna and *hamam*. Suites have private Jacuzzis. Good breakfast spread.

Cheers Hostel ₺
Hostel **Map** 4 B4
Zeynep Kamil Sok 21, 34400
Tel *(0212) 526 02 00*
W cheershostel.com
Situated in the heart of the old city, this hostel offers comfortable dorms, private rooms and a roof top bar with great views of Haghia Sophia.

Hotel Nomade ₺
Boutique **Map** 5 E4
Ticarethane Sok 15, 34410
Tel *(0212) 513 81 72*
W hotelnomade.com
Well-appointed rooms with a cosy atmosphere. Enjoy breakfast or drinks on the terrace.

Hotel Sultanahmet ₺
Budget **Map** 5 D4
Divanyolu Cad 20, 34110
Tel *(0212) 527 02 39*
W hotelsultanahmet.com
Inexpensive hotel with lovely views, a great location and friendly service. Enjoy delicious food and a glass of wine at the lovely terrace restaurant.

Sultan Hostel ₺
Hostel **Map** 5 E5
Akbıyık Cad 17, 34122
Tel *(0212) 516 92 60*
W sultanhostel.com
A backpacker's haven. Helpful staff, neat dormitories and private rooms. Close to all the main sights, and there is even a pub downstairs.

Dersaadet ₺₺
Boutique **Map** 5 D5
Küçük Ayasofya Cad, Kapıağası Sok 5, 34400
Tel *(0212) 458 07 60*
W dersaadethotel.com
Impressive wooden Ottoman mansion near the Blue Mosque. Turkish carpets run throughout.

Hippodrome Hotel ₺₺
Boutique **Map** 5 E4
Mimar Mehmet Ağa Cad 38, 34400
Tel *(0212) 517 68 89*
W hippodromehotel.com
A wide range of rooms to choose from, including an apartment that can accommodate six adults.

DK Choice

The Kybele Hotel ₺₺
Boutique **Map** 5 E4
Yerebatan Cad 23, 34410
Tel *(0212) 511 77 66*
W kybelehotel.com
Although decorated with 4,000 coloured-glass lamps, rich fabric and wallpaper, this wooden town house never feels kitch or over done. The relaxing ambience and friendly staff ensure a great stay.

The bright-yellow building of the Ottoman Hotel Imperial sits in front of Haghia Sophia

Price Guide
Prices are based on one night's stay in high season for a standard double room, inclusive of service charges and taxes.

₺	under ₺250
₺₺	₺250 to ₺400
₺₺₺	over ₺400

Ottoman Hotel Imperial ₺₺
Boutique **Map** 5 E4
Caferiye Sok 6/1, 34400
Tel *(0212) 513 61 51*
W ottomanhotelimperial.com
Sheer opulence; some rooms have private *hamams* and close-up views of Haghia Sophia.

Spectra ₺₺
Boutique **Map** 5 D5
Şehit Mehmetpaşa Yokuşu 2, 34400
Tel *(0212) 516 35 46*
W hotelspectra.com
A converted Ottoman house with all the basic amenities at good prices. Comfortable, no-frills rooms, most with views of Hippodrome Square and the Blue Mosque.

DK Choice

White House Hotel ₺₺
Boutique **Map** 5 E4
Çatalçeşme Sok 21, 34110
Tel *(0212) 526 00 19*
W istanbulwhitehouse.com
Gorgeous golden colours make this lovely hotel stand out. The rooms are elegant and well decorated. Enjoy breakfast on the terrace, with views of the Bosphorus. Free Wi-Fi.

Yeşil Ev ₺₺
Boutique **Map** 5 E4
Kabasakal Cad 5, 34122
Tel *(0212) 517 67 85*
W yesilev.com.tr
Velvet curtains and oil paintings adorn attractive rooms. In summer, breakfast is served in the garden.

Aren Suites ₺₺₺
Boutique **Map** 5 D5
Küçük Ayasofya Cad, Gelinlik Sok 13, 34122
Tel *(0212) 517 31 26*
W arensuites.com
Rooms are stylish and kept meticulously clean. The terrace and many of the rooms overlook the Sea of Marmara.

Ayasofya Konakları ₺₺₺
Boutique **Map** 5 E4
Soğukçeşme Sok, 34400
Tel *(0212) 513 36 00*
W ayasofyakonaklari.com
A leafy cobbled street leads to nine wooden 19th-century

Ottoman mansions with basic rooms. Relax at the pretty courtyard café.

Blue House–Mavi Ev ₺₺₺
Boutique **Map** 5 E5
Dalbasti Sok 14, 34110
Tel *(0212) 638 90 10*
W bluehouse.com.tr
Family-run hotel with tasteful rooms. The suites have great views of the Sea of Marmara.

Deluxe Golden Horn Hotel ₺₺₺
Boutique **Map** 5 D4
Binbirdirek Meydanı Sok 1, 34400
Tel *(0212) 518 17 17*
W deluxegoldenhornhotel.com
The ambience at this hotel is reminiscent of the Orient Express era. Ornately decorated lobby.

Four Seasons Sultanahmet ₺₺₺
Historic **Map** 5 E4
Tevkifhane Sok 1, 34110
Tel *(0212) 402 30 00*
W fourseasons.com/istanbul
This top-notch hotel is housed in an old and atmospheric Ottoman prison building. Herb-scented courtyard and good restaurants.

Hagia Sophia Hotel Istanbul Old City ₺₺₺
Modern **Map** 5 E4
Yerebatan Cad 13, 34110
Tel *444 93 32*
W hsoldcity.com
A surprisingly sleek option in the heart of the Old City with an English-style pub.

Ibrahim Pasha ₺₺₺
Boutique **Map** 5 D4
Terzihane Sok 5, 34110
Tel *(0212) 518 03 94*
W ibrahimpasha.com
Stylish and well-run hotel housed in a pair of atmospheric town houses located just a few metres away from the Hippodrome.

Pierre Loti Hotel ₺₺₺
Modern **Map** 5 D4
Piyer Loti Cad 1, 34400
Tel *(0212) 518 57 00*
W pierrelotihotel.com
A range of well-designed rooms ensure a comfortable and hassle-free stay. Excellent spa and *hamam* facilities on site. Scenic views.

The Bazaar Quarter

Antik Cisterna ₺₺
Historic **Map** 4 C4
Sekbanbaşı Sok 10, 34130
Tel *(0212) 638 58 58*
W antikhotel.com
An extraordinary hotel with a fascinating history – the restaurant is set in a basement cistern, which dates back to 450–500 AD.

Beyoğlu

DK Choice

#Bunk ₺
Budget **Map** 1 A4
Balik Sok 7, 34435
Tel *(0212) 244 88 08*
W bunkhostels.com
Launched by an international group of friends, #Bunk is a unique establishment offering low-cost accommodation with a seriously cool design. They also sell their own brand of quirky T-shirts.

Chill Out Hostel and Cafe ₺
Budget **Map** 1 A5
Balyoz Sok 3, 34445
Tel *(0212) 249 47 84*
W chillouthostelistanbul.com
No curfew, friendly staff and a choice of private rooms or dorms. Close to the best nightlife spots.

Adahan Istanbul ₺₺
Historic **Map** 1 A5
General Yazgan Sok 14, 34430
Tel *(0212) 243 85 81*
W adahanistanbul.com
Sensitively restored hotel with a homely feel, in the heart of the European Quarter.

DK Choice

Baylo Suites ₺₺
Apartments **Map** 5 D1
Galata Kulesi Sok 24, 34420
Tel *(0212) 245 98 60/61*
W baylosuites.com
Four individually decorated apartments inside a historic 19th-century Galata building, lovingly restored by a mother-daughter team. Energy-saving systems have been installed throughout the building. Wonderful views from the terrace. Booking is required for a minimum of three nights' stay.

Galata Flats ₺₺
Apartments **Map** 1 A5
Tünel Meydani 84, 34430
Tel *(0212) 244 26 76*
W galataflats.com
Comfortable apartments that are serviced daily. The larger options have terraces and balconies.

Georges Hotel Galata ₺₺₺
Boutique **Map** 1 A5
Serdar-ı Ekrem Cad 24, 34425
Tel *(0212) 244 24 23*
W georges.com
Set in a grand old town house, Georges Hotel Galata offers first-rate services and stunning views.

Many coloured-glass lamps adorn the ceiling of a room at the Kybele Hotel *(see p330)*

Istanbul! Place ₺₺₺
Apartments **Map** 1 A5
Serdar-ı Ekrem Cad, Galata, 34430
Tel *(0772) 925 16 76*
W istanbulplace.com
A range of beautifully restored period apartments located in the fashionable neighbourhoods of Galata and Beyoğlu. Friendly service.

The Marmara Taksim ₺₺₺
Modern **Map** 1 B3
Taksim Meydani, 34437
Tel *(0212) 251 46 96*
W taksim.themarmarahotels.com
Landmark hotel towering over much of the modern city. Great views from the gym and pool area.

Palazzo Donizetti ₺₺₺
Historic **Map** 1 A5
Asmali Mescit Sok 55, 34400
Tel *(0212) 249 51 51*
W palazzodonizetti.com
Similar to a European château, Palazzo Donizetti is all about elegance and luxury.

Pera Palace Hotel Jumeirah ₺₺₺
Historic **Map** 1 A5
Meşrutiyet Cad 52, Tepebaşı, 34430
Tel *(0212) 377 40 00*
W jumeirah.com
The elegant suites here are named after famous guests such as Agatha Christie and Hemingway.

Sub Hotel ₺₺₺
Boutique **Map** 5 E1
Necatibey Cad 91, Karaköy, 34435
Tel *(0212) 243 00 05*
W subkarakoy.com
An ultra-stylish hotel with well-appointed rooms. It also has a roof-top bar and serves a hearty organic breakfast buffet spread. Free Wi-Fi.

Witt Istanbul Suites ₺₺₺
Boutique **Map** 1 B5
Defterdar Yokuşu 26, Cihangir, 34433
Tel *(0212) 293 15 00*
W wittistanbul.com
One of the city's first designer hotels Witt Istanbul Suites has enormous rooms with retro design touches.

Luxurious Turkish *hammam* at the Hilton Bursa Convention Center & Spa, Bursa

Further Afield

Kariye Hotel ₺
Boutique
Kariye Camii Sok 6, Edirnekapi, 34080
Tel *(0212) 534 84 14*
W kariyeotel.com
Tastefully restored 19th-century mansion close to the famous Chora Church, near the city walls.

Çırağan Palace Kempinski ₺₺₺
Historic
Çırağan Cad, Beşiktaş, 34349
Tel *(0212) 258 33 77*
W kempinski.com
The only hotel in Istanbul set in a royal Ottoman palace. Waterside terrace and heated infinity pool.

DK Choice

The Edition ₺₺₺
Luxury
Büyükdere Cad 136, 34330
Tel *(0212) 317 77 00*
W editionhotels.com
Enter a private world of luxury in the heart of Istanbul's busy business district. There is a stunning full-floor penthouse and a top-notch restaurant. Good transport connections to the main tourist sites.

Hilton Istanbul ₺₺₺
Modern
Cumhuriyet Cad, Harbiye, 34367
Tel *(0212) 315 60 00*
W placeshilton.com
The Hilton group's first step outside the USA – hence the footprint-shaped swimming pool. All rooms have private balconies.

The House Hotel Bosphorus ₺₺₺
Boutique
Salhane Sok 1, Ortaköy, 34347
Tel *(0212) 327 77 87*
W thehousehotel.com
This hotel is a favourite with celebrities and is located close to the city's most exclusive nightspots.

DK Choice

Sumahan on the Water ₺₺₺
Historic
Kuleli Cad 51, 34684
Tel *(0216) 422 80 00*
W sumahan.com
A multi-award-winning gem in a converted distillery. Every room boasts superb sea views and some open onto a lawn terrace. Unwind at the fully equipped spa or grab a bite at the excellent on-site restaurant.

Thrace and the Sea of Marmara

BURSA: Atlas Termal ₺
Budget
Hamamlar Cad 35, Çekirge, 16070
Tel *(0224) 234 41 00*
W atlasotel.com.tr
Traditionally decorated comfortable rooms, a good restaurant and two Turkish baths make this an ideal spa hotel.

DK Choice

BURSA: Kitap Evi Hotel ₺
Boutique
Kavaklı Mah, Burç Üstü 21, 16040
Tel *(0224) 225 41 60*
W kitapevi.com.tr
Choose from 13 comfortable rooms at this delightful place. The rooms are all charming and uniquely decorated. There is an elegant restaurant on site that opens onto a beautiful garden.

BURSA: Hilton Bursa Convention Center & Spa ₺₺
Modern
Yeni Yalova Cad 347, 16210
Tel *(0224) 500 05 05*
W bursa.hilton.com
A 35-floor tower hotel boasting an ultra-smart spa. Good gym facilities and excellent service.

BURSA: Marigold Thermal Spa Hotel ₺₺
Boutique
1 Murat Cad 47, Çekirge, Osmangazi, 16070
Tel *444 40 00*
W marigold.com.tr
A thermal therapy hotel on a hilltop. Rooms are large with comfortable beds.

EDIRNE: Aksaray Hotel ₺
Budget
Alipaşa Ortakapı Cad 8
Tel *(0284) 225 68 06*
W hoteledirnepalace.com
Located in the centre of the town, this charming 19th-century town house offers modest rooms.

EDIRNE: Edirne Antik Hotel ₺
Boutique
Marif Cad 6, Kaleiçi, 22030
Tel *(0284) 225 15 55*
W edirneantikhotel.com
This is a delightful hotel in the historic centre and has a small on-site restaurant.

EDIRNE: Otel Şimşek ₺
Budget
Trakya Üniversitesi Tıp Fakültesi Karşısı, 22000
Tel *(0284) 236 60 00*
W hotelsimsek.com.tr
Located just across from the university campus, this hotel includes a playground for kids and a simple fitness centre.

EDIRNE: Taş Odalar Hotel ₺
Historic
Selimiye Camii Arkası Merkez, 22000
Tel *(0284) 212 35 29*
W tasodalar.com
A 15th-century mansion converted into a lovely hotel. Ottoman sultan Mehmet II was born here.

İZNIK: Cem Otel ₺
Budget
Mustafa Kemal Paşa Mah, Göl Sahili Cad 34, 16860
Tel *(0224) 757 16 87*
W cemotel.com
This hotel offers simple rooms, some with lake views. The on-site restaurant serves superb food.

İZNIK: İznik Otel ₺
Budget
Selçuk Mah, Göl Sahil Yolu 22, Liman Karşısı, 16860
Tel *(0224) 757 22 55*
W iznikotel.com
This no-frills hotel is set beside İznik Lake. It offers basic rooms, with air conditioning and free Wi-Fi.

Key to Price Guide *see p330*

The Aegean

ASSOS: Assosyal Butik Otel ₺₺
Budget
Alan Meydani, 8 Behramkale, 17860, Çanakkale
Tel *(0286) 721 70 46*
W assosyalotel.com
A small but beautifully maintained hotel offering great views of Edremit Bay.

ASSOS: Nazlıhan Hotel ₺₺
Budget
Behramkale Köyü Antik İskele Mevkii Ayvacık, 17860, Çanakkale
Tel *(0286) 721 73 85*
W assosnazlıhan.com
Idyllic location on the ancient harbour. Spacious, well-furnished rooms in the wing.

AYVALIK: Butik Sızma Han ₺
Boutique
Gümrük Cad 2, Sok 49, 10400
Tel *(0266) 312 77 00*
W butiksizmahan.com
Set in a former olive-oil press, this hotel has a lovely waterfront location and comfortable rooms.

AYVALIK: Ferahi Evler Butik Otel ₺
Boutique
Sakarya Mah, Atatürk Bulv 20, Sok 1, 3, 5, 10400
Tel *(0266) 312 33 55*
W ferahievler.com
A small hotel with sea views, traditional decor and volcanic stone walls. Close to Lesbos ferries.

BERGAMA: Hera Hotel ₺
Boutique
Talatpaşa Mah, Tabak Köprü Cad 21, 35700
Tel *(0232) 631 06 34*
W bergama.hotelhera.com
Two historic buildings have been converted to house ten rooms named after Greek deities.

DK Choice

BODRUM: El Vino Bodrum ₺₺
Boutique
Omurça Mah, Pamili Sok 14, 48400
Tel *(0252) 313 87 70*
W elvinobodrum.com
A small but charming hotel overlooking Bodrum Castle, with spacious, tasteful rooms. The garden level rooms have a private patio; most others have balconies. Relax at the pool or in the garden, or watch spectacular sunsets on the rooftop. Excellent and efficient service.

BODRUM: The Marmara Bodrum ₺₺
Boutique
Yokusbaşı Mah, Suluhasan Cad 18, 48400
Tel *(0252) 999 10 10*
W bodrum.themarmarahotels.com
Rooms boast breathtaking views of the city and the castle and there is an art gallery in the lobby.

BODRUM: Vogue Hotel Bodrum ₺₺₺
Luxury
Bodrum, Milas, Torba, 48400
Tel *(0252) 337 10 70*
W voguehotel.net
An up-market hotel with smart rooms, suites and villas. A host of pools and an aquapark.

BODRUM PENINSULA: Divan Bodrum Palmira Hotel ₺₺
Boutique
Kelesharim Cad 6, Göltürkbükü, 48483
Tel *(0252) 377 56 01*
W divan.com.tr
Upscale choice with landscaped gardens. Complimentary fresh fruit in all the elegant rooms.

BODRUM PENINSULA: Casa dell'Arte ₺₺₺
Luxury
İnönü Cad 66 Torba, Muğla, 48400
Tel *(0252) 367 18 48*
W casadellartebodrum.com
Artworks are exhibited in the rooms of this stylish hotel. Guests can also choose to stay on a luxurious yacht.

BODRUM PENINSULA: Kempinski Hotel Barbaros Bay ₺₺₺
Luxury
Kizilağaç Köyü, Gerenkuyu Mevkii, Yaliciftlik, 48400
Tel *(0252) 311 03 03*
W kempinski.com
Plush hotel with private beach and a variety of watersports on offer. Luxurious spa on site.

ÇANAKKALE: Grand Anzac Hotel ₺
Budget
Kemalpaşa Mah, Kemalyeri Sok 11, 17100
Tel *(0286) 217 77 77*
W grandanzachotel.com
Centrally located, with decent rooms and friendly staff. Street facing rooms can be noisy.

ÇANAKKALE: Helen Otel ₺
Budget
Kemalpaşa Mah, Cumhuriyet Meydanı 57, 17100
Tel *(0286) 212 18 18*
W helenhotel.com
Modern hotel with clean, simple and well-appointed rooms. Good restaurant on site.

ÇANAKKALE: Kervansaray ₺
Boutique
Fetvahane Sok 13
Tel *(0286) 217 81 92*
W kervansarayhotel.com
Housed in a 19th-century brick mansion, this is a comfortable and well-organized hotel.

ÇANAKKALE: Hotel des Etrangers ₺₺
Boutique
Yalı Cad 25–27
Tel *(0286) 214 24 24*
W hoteldesetrangers.com
This 19th-century, atmospheric hotel has hosted Heinrich Schliemann, the archaeologist who is believed to have discovered Troy.

ÇEŞME: Albano Hotel ₺
Budget
Açık Hava Tiyatrosu Karşısı Çevre Yolu, 35930
Tel *(0232) 712 82 02*
W cesmealbanohotel.com
Half-board lodging option with comfortable rooms. A varied breakfast spread and conveniently close to the city centre.

ÇEŞME: Grand Hotel Ontur Çeşme ₺₺₺
Modern
Cumhuriyet Mah, 4330/3 Sok 63/A, Dalyan, 35280
Tel *(0232) 724 00 11*
W onturhotels.com/onturcesme
Beachside hotel offering spacious rooms with balconies. The on-site spa offers a range of treatments.

ÇEŞME: Ilıca Hotel Spa & Wellness Resort ₺₺₺
Luxury
Boyalık Mevkii Ilıca, 35937
Tel *(0232) 723 31 31*
W ilicahotel.com
Plush rooms and a beautiful location on a pristine beach. Excellent spa treatments.

The pretty, tranquil pool area at the El Vino hotel, Bodrum

CUNDA ISLAND: Taş Konak ₺₺
Boutique
Mithat Paşa Mah, Şafak Sok 15, Alibey, Ayvalik, 10400
Tel *(0266) 327 26 33*
W taskonak.com.tr
Situated on a cobbled street lined with historic homes, this place has lovely rooms, some with sea views.

CUNDA ISLAND: Yund Antik Cunda Konakları ₺₺
Boutique
Namık Kemal Mah, Hayat Cad 27, Alibey Adası, Ayvalik, 10405
Tel *(0266) 327 30 60*
W yundantik.com
Elegant hotel with immaculate and comfortable rooms set in a beautifully restored Greek mansion. Closed Nov–Mar.

DATÇA: Han Royal Villa Datça ₺₺
Boutique
İskele Mah, Pir Sultan Abdal Sok 7, Datça, Muğla, 48900
Tel *(0252) 712 29 52*
W hanroyalhotels.com/datca
Family-run establishment, perfect for a cosy stay. Located close to a public beach with clear and pristine waters.

İZMIR: Met Boutique Hotel ₺
Boutique
Gazi Bulv 124, Çankaya, 35210
Tel *(0232) 483 01 11*
W metotel.com
Stylish hotel with comfortable beds in the business district. The hotel takes pride in its good quality Aegean cuisine and friendly service.

İZMIR: Mövenpick Hotel ₺
Modern
Cumhuriyet Bul 138, 35210
Tel *(0232) 488 14 14*
W movenpick-hotels.com
Award-winning hotel geared towards corporate travellers. Stylish, contemporary rooms.

İZMIR: Key Hotel ₺₺₺
Historic
Mimar Kemalettin Cad 1, Konak, 35260
Tel *(0232) 482 11 11*
W keyhotel.com
An old building on the waterfront, with smart rooms, a wellness centre and a restaurant.

İZMIR: Swissotel Büyük Efes ₺₺₺
Luxury
Gaziosmanpaşa Bulv 1, Alsancak, 35210
Tel *(0232) 414 00 00*
W swissotel.com/izmir
Well-located in the lively waterfront quarter of Alsancak, this hotel is an opulent landmark of İzmir with a huge garden and an excellent spa.

KUŞADASI: Alkoçlar Adakule Hotel ₺
Modern
Bayraklıdere Mevkii, 09400
Tel *(0256) 618 11 43*
W kusadasiadakulehotel.com
This seafront hotel, with a private beach, an outdoor pool and an aquapark, ensures a fun stay.

KUŞADASI: Club Caravanserai ₺
Historic
Atatürk Bulv 2, 09400
Tel *(0256) 614 41 15*
Built in 1618, this former *kervansaray* offers basic rooms around a spacious courtyard.

KUŞADASI: Hotel Carina ₺
Budget
Yılancıburnu Mevkii 1, 09400
Tel *(0256) 612 40 21*
W hotelcarina.com.tr
Pretty gardens and an outdoor pool charm guests. Some rooms have balconies with sea views.

KUŞADASI: Efe Boutique Hotel ₺₺
Boutique
Güvercinada Cad 37, 09400
Tel *(0256) 614 36 60*
W efeboutiquehotel.com
Comfortable rooms, most with balconies, but can be slightly noisy due to the lively promenade.

KUŞADASI: Kısmet Hotel ₺₺
Luxury
Gazi Beğendi Bulv 1, 09400
Tel *(0256) 618 12 90*
W kismet.com.tr
Views of the Aegean Sea can be enjoyed in every room. Private beach area and an outdoor pool.

KUŞADASI: Charisma Deluxe Hotel ₺₺₺
Luxury
Akyar Mevkii 5, 09400
Tel *(0256) 618 32 66*
W charismahotel.com
Breathtaking infinity pool with sweeping views of the Aegean Sea. All rooms have Jacuzzis.

A luxurious superior room with a spacious sitting area at the Key Hotel, İzmir

KUŞADASI: Korumar Hotel DeLuxe ₺₺₺
Luxury
Gazi Beğendi Mevkii PK 18, 09400
Tel *(0256) 618 15 30*
W korumar.com.tr
Great sea views, two private beaches, pools and a spa – one of the best five-star hotels in town.

MARMARIS: D-Hotel Maris ₺₺₺
Luxury
Datça Yolu, Hisaronu Mevkii, PO Box 119, 48700
Tel *(0252) 441 20 00*
W dhotel.com.tr
A romantic getaway inside a natural reservation with refined service. Open in summer only.

MARMARIS: Martı Hemithea Hotel ₺₺₺
Boutique
Martı Marina & Yacht Club, Orhaniye Köyü Keçibükü Mevkii, 48700
Tel *(0252) 487 10 55*
W martihemitheahotel.com
Beautifully decorated hotel with a yacht marina and classy rooms. Sample delicious food at the Mistral Restaurant.

PAMUKKALE: Venus Hotel ₺
Pension
Pamuk Mah, Hasan Tahsin Cad 16, 20280
Tel *(0258) 272 21 52*
W venushotel.net
A friendly, family-run place with bright, tastefully decorated rooms. Relax on the large patio or in the beautiful gardens.

PAMUKKALE: Spa Hotel Colossae Thermal ₺₺
Luxury
Fatih Mah 112, Sok 4, Pamukkale Mevkii Karahayıt, Denizli, 20290
Tel *(0258) 271 41 56*
W colossaehotel.com
One of the best hotels in town, with vast gardens, huge pools, and excellent spa and thermal services.

SELÇUK: Ephesus Suites ₺₺
Budget
İsabey Mah, Anton Kallinger Cad 1056, 35920
Tel *(0232) 892 63 12*
W ephesussuiteshotel.com
Four basic but comfortable rooms, close to the main sites. A delicious breakfast is served in the garden.

SELÇUK: Güllü Konakları ₺₺
Boutique
Şirince Köyü 44, 35920
Tel *(0232) 898 31 31*
W gullukonak.com
Elegant hotel in a charming village, 20 minutes from Ephesus. Lovely public spaces.

Key to Price Guide *see p330*

Mediterranean Turkey

ADANA: Hotel Seyhan ₺
Budget
Turhan Cemal Beriker Bulv 20/A, 01120
Tel *(0322) 455 30 30*
W otelseyhan.com.tr
This sleek hotel, located close to the major sights, offers great views from the dining room.

ADANA: Riva Reşat Bey Boutique & Business Hotel ₺
Boutique
Reşatbey Mah, Adalet Cad 20, Seyhan, 01170
Tel *(0322) 401 00 00*
W adanariva.com
Eco-friendly hotel with unique architecture and modern decor. It offers a great buffet breakfast.

ADANA: Adana Hilton SA Hotel ₺₺
Luxury
Sinanpaşa Mah, Hacı Sabancı Bulv 1, 01220
Tel *(0322) 355 50 00*
W hilton.com.tr
Spacious rooms and an attractive lobby at this riverside hotel. Good on-site restaurant and bar.

ADRASSAN: Ottoman Palace Hotel ₺
Budget
Deniz Mah, Çavuşköy Beldesi Kumluca Antalya, 07100
Tel *(0242) 883 14 62*
W jonnyturk.com
Run by a hospitable couple who also organize walks on the Lycian Way. Excellent service.

ALANYA: Hotel Villa Turka ₺
Boutique
Tophane Mah Kargı Sok 7, Alanya, Antalya, 07400
Tel *(0242) 530 54 76 41*
W hotelvillaturka.com
Stylish and homely Ottoman-period hotel perched above the sea within the walls of the citadel.

ALANYA: Sentido Gold Island Hotel ₺₺₺
Modern
Fuğla Mah, Gölcük Cad 27, 07400
Tel *(0242) 510 03 00*
W goldhotels.com.tr
This hotel is located on a peninsula surrounded by beaches. Many on-site restaurants and bars and courteous staff.

ANTAKYA: The Liwan Hotel ₺
Boutique
Silahlı Kuvvetler Cad 5, 31070
Tel *(0326) 215 77 77*
W theliwanhotel.com
Charmingly converted from a 1920s building, this hotel has elegant rooms. Great breakfasts and a good central location.

The indoor pool area at the Adana Hilton SA Hotel, Adana

ANTAKYA: Savon Hotel ₺₺
Boutique
Kurtuluş Cad 192, 31070
Tel *(0326) 214 63 55*
W savonhotel.com.tr
A soap factory converted into a fine hotel. Most rooms are large and luxurious. The hotel lobby has plush sofas and a grand piano.

ANTALYA: Hotel Villa Perla ₺
Boutique
Barbaros Mah, Hesapçi Sok 26, Kaleiçi, 07100
Tel *(0242) 248 97 93*
W villaperla.com
A small Ottoman-period hotel with a handful of rooms set around a courtyard and pool.

ANTALYA: Ninova Pension ₺
Pension
Barbaros Mah, Hamit Efendi Sok 9, Kaleiçi, 07100
Tel *(0242) 248 61 14*
W ninovapension.net
This establishment in the Old Town has been converted from an old, traditional house. Quiet rooms and a lovely garden.

ANTALYA: Mardan Palace ₺₺₺
Luxury
Kundu Koyu, Oteller Mevkii, 07110
Tel *(0242) 310 41 00*
W mardanpalace.com.tr
Gold and marble opulence at every corner in this hotel out on Lara Beach, east of the city centre.

ANTALYA: Tuvana ₺₺₺
Boutique
Karanlık Sokak, Kaleiçi, 07100
Tel *(0242) 247 60 15*
W tuvanahotel.com
Set in a series of Ottoman mansions overlooking a central pool and lush gardens, this hotel is one of the best in Antalya's charming Old Town.

BELEK: Cornelia Diamond Golf Resort & Spa ₺₺₺
Luxury
İskele Mevkii, 07500
Tel *(0242) 710 16 00*
W corneliaresort.com
An all-inclusive golf resort on the Mediterraean with several restaurants and bars. Spacious, elegant rooms.

BELEK: Maxx Royal Belek Golf & Spa ₺₺₺
Luxury
İskele Mevkii, 07505
Tel *(0242) 710 27 00*
W maxxroyal.com
Exclusive deluxe 18-hole golf resort with an aqua park. There is also a spa, a private beach and several swimming pools.

BELEK: Susesi Luxury Resort ₺₺₺
Luxury
İskele Mevkii, 07506
Tel *(0242) 710 24 00*
W susesihotel.com
A large and luxurious resort found right on the beach with well-manicured gardens.

DALYAN: Midas Pension ₺
Pension
Maraş Cad, Kaunos Sok 32, 48840
Tel *(0252) 284 21 95*
W midasdalyan.com
Set by the river, this small and charming place offers comfortable rooms with wonderful views.

FETHIYE: Villa Daffodil ₺
Boutique
Fevzi Çakmak Cad 115, Ikinci Karagözler
Tel *(0252) 614 95 95*
W villadaffodil.com
Small, traditional-style but modern hotel found on a quiet street just outside the centre of the town.

FETHIYE: Yacht Boutique Hotel ₺
Boutique
1 Karagözler Mevki Fevzi Çakmak Cad, 48300
Tel *(0252) 614 15 30*
W yachthotelturkey.com
Close to the water-front promenade, this place offers modern rooms decorated in warm colours.

GÖCEK: Dalya Life ₺
Boutique
Şerefler Köyü, Tersakan Mah 37, PK 36, Dalaman, 48770
Tel *(0252) 791 10 40*
W gocekotel.com
Off-the-beaten-track bungalows and suites surrounded by a pine forest. Organic food available.

For more information on types of hotels *see p329*

GÖCEK: Yonca Resort ₺
Budget
Cumhuriyet Mah, 48310
Tel *(0252) 645 22 55*
W yoncaresort.com
Run by a welcoming couple, this peaceful gem has pleasant rooms, a private pool and pleasant gardens.

KALKAN: Allegra Hotel ₺
Boutique
Zeytinlik Cad, 07960
Tel *(0242) 844 24 36*
W allegrahotel.com
Charming small-sized hotel on a mountain slope. Simple rooms with balconies and an infinity pool.

KALKAN: Ekinhan Hotel ₺
Boutique
Kalamar Yolu, 07960
Tel *(0242) 844 10 50*
W ekinhan.net
Exotic flowers and olive trees fill the garden of this tranquil hotel. Some rooms offer lovely views over the town and bay.

KALKAN: White House ₺₺₺
Boutique
Menteşe Mah, 5 Nolu Sok, 07960
Tel *(0242) 844 37 38*
W whitehousekalkan.com
A restored old Greek house that combines period charm with all mod cons. Welcoming hosts.

KAŞ: Aqua Princess Hotel ₺
Budget
Hükümet Cad 71, 07580
Tel *(0242) 836 20 26*
W aquaprincess.com
Small hotel with a resort feel set on a quiet beach. Half-board option is available.

KAŞ: Gardenia ₺₺
Boutique
Küçük Çakil, Hükümet Cad 41, Kaş, 07580
Tel *(0242) 836 23 68*
W gardeniahotel-kas.com
Stylish hotel above a small beach with views to the island of Meis. Very friendly owners.

DK Choice

KAŞ: Lukka Exclusive Hotel ₺₺
Boutique
Çukurbağ Yarımadası Oteller Bölgesi Bülent Kalkavan Sok 16, 07580
Tel *(0242) 836 14 20*
W lukkahotel.com
A beautiful cliffside location makes Lukka one of the most romantic sunset spots in the area. There is a private beach and an infinity pool with wonderful views. The sleek rooms offer sea or garden views.

The large resort of Rixos Sungate set on the coast right by the beach, Kemer

KAŞ: Doria Hotel Yacht Club ₺₺₺
Boutique
Uğur Mumcu Cad, Bucak Denizi Acisu Mevkii, 07580
Tel *(0242) 836 42 04*
W doriahotelkas.com
Set on a peaceful Blue Flag beach this hotel boasts impressive architecture. Some rooms have Jacuzzis.

KEMER: Rixos Sungate ₺₺₺
Luxury
Çifteçeşmeler Mevkii, Beldibi 3, 07985
Tel *(0242) 824 00 00*
W rixos.com
Offering all-inclusive vacations and the deluxe amenities associated with the Rixos hotel chain. Service may be downsized in the winter.

ÖLÜ DENIZ: Morina Hotel ₺
Budget
Belceğiz, Fethiye, 48340
Tel *(0252) 617 02 55*
W morinahotel.com
Set in an attractive olive grove, close to Ölü Deniz lagoon. Choose from a variety of basic rooms.

ÖLÜ DENIZ: Oyster Residences ₺₺
Boutique
Belceğiz Mevkii 1, Sok Ölü Deniz Fethiye, 48340
Tel *(0252) 617 07 65*
W oysterresidences.com
Beautifully decorated hotel set in lush gardens in the heart of a lively resort. Close to the beach.

SIDE: Beach House Hotel ₺₺
Boutique
Barbaros Cad
Tel *(0242) 753 16 07*
W beachhouse-hotel.com
Very atmospheric accommodation overlooking the small western beach on Side's old quarter. Enjoy the company of the friendly owners and their cute pets.

Ankara and Western Anatolia

AFYON: İkbal Thermal Hotel ₺
Modern
İzmir Karayolu 9 km, 03000
Tel *(0272) 252 56 00*
W ikbal.com.tr
İkbal offers simple, chic rooms with marble bathrooms. Some rooms have balconies.

AFYON: Güral Afyon Wellness & Convention ₺₺
Modern
İzmir Karayolu 7 km, 03000
Tel *(0272) 220 22 22*
W nghotels.com.tr
Unwind at the immaculately kept pool and enjoy warm Turkish hospitality at this large hotel.

ANKARA: And Butik Hotel ₺
Boutique
Içkale Mah Istek Sok 3, Altındağ, 06680
Tel *(0312) 310 23 04*
W andbutikhotel.com
Located in the heart of the city, with bright modern rooms. Breakfast is available for an extra charge.

ANKARA: No 19 ₺
Boutique
Birlik Mah 457, Sok 19, 06000
Tel *(0312) 495 00 00*
W no19hotel.com
Sleek, minimalist hotel in a trendy neighbourhood. The spa is owned by top model Adriana Karambeau.

DK Choice

ANKARA: Divan Çukurhan ₺₺
Boutique
Ankara Kalesi Necatibey Mah, Depo Sok 3, Ulus, 06240
Tel *(0312) 306 64 00*
W divan.com.tr/TR
Located close to Ankara Castle and the Museum of Anatolian Civilizations, this superb period hotel is the pride of the wealthy Koç family. Rooms are individually decorated and have high-quality furnishings. There's also a great library for guests.

ANKARA: Sheraton Hotel & Convention Centre ₺₺
Modern
Noktalı Sok, Kavaklıdere, 06700
Tel *(0312) 457 60 00*
W sheratonankara.com
This hotel with striking cylindrical architecture offers tastefully decorated and well-appointed rooms and suites. Some rooms offer stunning views. Relax at the on-site restaurants and bars or rejuvenate at the health club.

Key to Price Guide *see p330*

ANKARA: JW Marriot Hotel ₺₺₺
Luxury
Kızılırmak Mah, Muhsin Yazıcıoğlu Cad 1, Söğütözü, 06520
Tel *(0312) 248 88 88*
W jwmarriottankara.com
Spacious rooms complemented with excellent service and amenities. Expect all the plush frills from this top-notch establishment.

ESKİŞEHIR: Abacı Konak Hotel ₺₺
Boutique
Akarbaşı Mah, Türkmen Hoca Sok 29, Odunpazarı, 26000
Tel *(0222) 333 03 33*
W abaciotel.com
Considered one of the most atmospheric places to stay in Eskişehir, this hotel comprises several beautifully restored town houses.

ISPARTA: Barida Hotels ₺₺
Modern
102 Cad 81, 32040
Tel *(0246) 500 25 25*
W baridahotels.com
Hospitable and friendly hotel that aims to cater for every need. Superb view from the rooftop restaurant.

KONYA: Paşapark Hotel ₺
Modern
Şems-i Tebrizi Mah, Sultan Veled Cad 3, Karatay, 42030
Tel *(0332) 444 57 05*
W pasapark.com.tr
Smart hotel with traditional touches. Bathrooms have hydro-massage shower heads.

KONYA: Rumi Hotel ₺
Modern
Fakih Sok
Tel *(0332) 353 11 21*
W rumihotel.com
Very tastefully done hotel in a great location overlooking the Mevlâna Museum. Rejuvenate at the spa and fitness centre.

KONYA: Hilton Garden Inn ₺₺
Modern
Aziziye Mah, Kışlaönü Sok 4, Karatay, 42020
Tel *(0332) 221 60 00*
W hilton.com.tr
Smart, modern hotel located close to the Mevlâna Museum and city centre. Spacious rooms and a good grill restaurant.

KONYA: Dedeman Konya Hotel Convention Center ₺₺₺
Modern
Isparta Beyşehir Yolu Yeni Sille Cad, Özalan Mah, Selçuklu, 42080
Tel *(0332) 221 66 00*
W dedeman.com
Though outside the city centre, this large stylish hotel has all the usual amenities, a great spa and good service.

KÜTAHYA: Hilton Garden Inn ₺
Modern
Servi Mah, Atatürk Bulv 21, 43030
Tel *(0274) 229 55 55*
W kutahya.hgi.com
Centrally located, good-value chain hotel offering comfortable rooms, a cooked-to-order breakfast and a fitness centre.

The Black Sea

AYDER PLATEAU: Bukla Oberj ₺
Pension
Ayder Yaylası, Çamlıhemşin, 53750
Tel *(0464) 657 20 55*
W oberj.com
Set across a waterfall with a huge spruce forest in the backdrop. Popular with hikers.

AYDER PLATEAU: Natura Otel ₺
Pension
Ayder Yaylası Turizm Merkezi, Rize, Çamlıhemşin, 53780
Tel *(0464) 657 20 35*
W naturaotel.com
Wooden, Alpine-style chalet with views of the valley and mountain. Simple, en-suite rooms with central heating and flat-screen TVs.

BOLU: Büyük Abant Hotel ₺₺
Modern
14800 Bolu
Tel *(0374) 224 50 33*
W buyukabantoteli.com
Large hotel set beside Abant lake and surrounded by pretty pine forests. Modern, comfortable rooms. There is also has a pool and a tennis court.

DK Choice

BOLU: Kartal Hotel ₺₺₺
Ski lodge
Kartalkaya Mevkii PK 5, 14200
Tel *(0374) 234 50 05*
W kartalotel.com
This upmarket ski resort has direct access to the south-facing slopes of Mount Bolu. Heated indoor pool and a large and comfortable lobby. Range of accommodation available from basic rooms to spacious suites. Higher prices on weekends.

MAÇAHEL: Maçahel Konukevi ₺
Guesthouse
Camili Köyü, Maçahel Borçka, 08400
Tel *(0466) 485 24 04*
W macahelkonukevi.com
Eco-friendly, stone-built guest-house set in a pretty green valley on the frontier with Georgia. Foreigners need military permission to stay.

RIZE: Dedeman Hotel ₺
Modern
Ali Paşa Köyü, 53100
Tel *(0464) 223 44 44*
W dedeman.com
Set on a rocky cliff on the Black Sea. Most rooms have sea views. Good buffet dinners.

SAFRANBOLU: Cinci Han ₺
Boutique
Cinci Han Sokak, Safranbolu, 78600
Tel *(0370) 712 06 90*
W cincihan.com
This stunning 17th-century *kervansaray* offers superb upper-floor suite rooms. The standard rooms overlooking the courtyard are almost as good.

DK Choice

SAFRANBOLU: Gülevi ₺₺
Boutique
Hükümet Sokak 46, TR - 78600
Tel *(0370) 725 46 45*
W canbulat.com.tr
A UNESCO World Heritage Site, Gulevi was converted from an 18th-century mansion. Delicate wood-carvings adorn the walls, and all rooms have fireplaces and window shutters. Sleek, modern bathrooms.

SAMSUN: Venn Boutique Hotel ₺₺
Boutique
Cumhuriyet Mah, Adnan Menderes Bulv 325, Atakum, 55200
Tel *(0362) 407 00 01*
W vennbutikotel.com
This contemporary-style hotel offers a range of spacious rooms and lovely sea views. Superb roof-top restaurant.

Beautifully decorated library at Divan Çukurhan, Ankara *(see p336)*

SINOP: Zinos Hotel ₺₺
Budget
Ada Mah, Enver Bahadır Yolu 69, Karakum, 57000
Tel *(0368) 260 56 00*
W zinoshotel.com.tr
This hotel has two sections: country and business. Rooms are either homely or modern in style.

TRABZON: Taş Konak Hotel ₺₺
Boutique
Esentepe Mah, Y Selim Bulv 89, 61100
Tel *(0462) 325 77 17*
W taskonakbutikotel.com.tr
Converted from a historic house, this stylish establishment has cosy rooms. Some rooms have sea views.

TRABZON: Zorlu Grand Hotel ₺₺₺
Luxury
Maraş Cad 9, 61110
Tel *(0462) 326 84 00*
W zorlugrand.com
This hotel has comfortable rooms and offers a great breakfast buffet. The impressive lobby has a stunning glass ceiling.

Cappadocia and Central Anatolia

AMASYA: Lalehan Hotel ₺
Boutique
Pirinççi Mah, Mehmet Paşa Sok 31, 05000
Tel *(0358) 212 77 77*
W lalehanotel.com
Clean, well-appointed rooms in a characterful Ottoman mansion. Some rooms have balconies overlooking the river. Near the Pontic tombs.

GÖREME: Kookaburra Pension ₺
Guesthouse
Orta Mah, Konak Sok 10, 50180 Nevsehir
Tel *(0384) 271 25 49*
W kookaburramotel.com
Long-established, old village house with an enviable location and a charming roof-terrace. This immaculately well-presented and well-run place is ideal for budget travellers.

GÖREME: Melek Cave Hotel ₺
Budget
Gaferli Mah, Ünler Sok 28, 50180
Tel *(0384) 271 22 33*
W melekcave.com
Inexpensive, cheerful village hotel offering a choice of Ottoman-era and cave rooms. Lovely garden.

GÖREME: Anatolian Houses ₺₺
Boutique
Gaferli Mah, Nevşehir, 50180
Tel *(0384) 271 24 63*
W anatolianhouses.com.tr
The best conversion of a series of rock-cut cave dwellings in the village. Lovely courtyard and spa/ Turkish bath complex.

GÖREME: Cappadocia Cave Suites ₺₺
Boutique
Gafferli Mah, Ünlü Sok19, 50180
Tel *(0384) 271 28 00*
W cappadociacavesuites.com
Decent sized cave rooms but the fairy-chimney rooms are smaller. The restaurant uses local produce.

KAYSERI: Bent Hotel ₺
Budget
Gevher Nesibe Mah, Atatürk Bulv 40, Kocasinan, 38020
Tel *(0352) 221 24 00*
W benthotel.com
Located in the historic centre of the city. Rooms are decorated with warm colours.

KAYSERI: Novotel ₺
Modern
Yeni Pervane Mah, Kocasinan Bulv 163, Kocasinan, 38110
Tel *(0352) 207 30 00*
W novotel.com
A typical Novotel conveniently located close to the historic city centre. On-site restaurant and some rooms have views of Mount Erciyes.

KAYSERI: Radisson Blu ₺
Modern
Sivas Cad 24
Tel *(0352) 315 50 00*
W radissonblu.com.tr
Located at the city centre, this is a good-value, modern hotel. Sample a great breakfast and enjoy fine views at the rooftop restaurant.

Selection of tasty savoury and sweet treats served in the Zorlu Grand lobby, Trabzon

MUSTAFAPAŞA: Gül Konakları ₺
Historic
Sümer Cad, Ürgüp, 50401
Tel *(0384) 353 54 86*
W gulkonaklari.dinler.com
A pair of beautifully restored mansions with a lovely garden. The rooms are full of character and many rooms have stone-vaulted ceilings.

DK Choice

MUSTAFAPAŞA: Cappadocia Estates ₺₺
Boutique
Şahin Bey Cad, Vezir Sok 12, 50420
Tel *(0384) 535 50 20*
W cappadociaestates.com
An elegant little gem converted from registered historical properties. Exquisitely decorated with antiques, custom-made furniture and original works of art. Spacious cave rooms with high ceilings and tall windows.

NEVŞEHIR: Dedeman Cappadocia Convention Centre ₺₺
Modern
Ürgüp Yolu, 2 km, 50200
Tel *(0384) 213 99 00*
W dedeman.com
Huge hotel with an array of facilities including indoor and outdoor pools, a Turkish bath, a fitness centre and a wine bar.

ORTAHISAR: Hezen Cave Hotel ₺₺₺
Boutique
Tahir Bey Sok 87, Ortahisar/ Ürgüp, 50400
Tel *(0384) 343 30 05*
W hezenhotel.com
Very stylish ten-room cave hotel with a tasteful mix of antique and contemporary decor and furnishings. Enjoy a hearty breakfast at the vine-shaded terrace along with superb views of Ortahisar's towering citadel rock pinnacle.

UÇHISAR: Argos in Cappadocia ₺₺₺
Boutique
Uçhisar, 50240
Tel *(0384) 219 31 30*
W argosincappadocia.com
Located on a sloped hillside, this charming hotel offers great views of Uçhisar Castle.

UÇHISAR: Museum Hotel ₺₺₺
Boutique
Tekelli Mah 1, 50240
Tel *(0384) 219 22 20*
W museum-hotel.com
Cappadocia's oldest cave hotel is a registered museum, so it is full of interesting artifacts.

Key to Price Guide *see p330*

Rooms feature whirlpool baths and many have great views.

ÜRGÜP: Ürgüp Esbelli Ev ₺₺
Boutique
Dolay Sok 8, 50400
Tel *(0384) 341 33 95*
W esbelli.com
One of the first, and still one of the best, period boutique hotels in Cappadocia. Lovely cave rooms and great breakfasts.

Eastern Anatolia

DIYARBAKIR: Dedeman Diyarbakır Hotel ₺
Modern
Elazığ Cad, Büyükşehir Belediyesi Yanı, 21400
Tel *(0412) 229 00 00*
W dedeman.com
Next to one of the biggest malls in town, this is a large hotel with many rooms and good facilities.

DIYARBAKIR: Büyük Kervansaray Diyarbakır ₺₺
Boutique
Sur Içi Gazi Cad, Deliler Han, 21200
Tel *(0412) 228 96 06*
W kervansarayotel.com.tr
Well-established hotel beautifully fashioned from a *kervansaray*. Small but well-appointed rooms. It can be noisy at weekends as there are sometimes wedding functions held in the courtyard.

DOĞUBEYAZIT: Simer Hotel ₺
Budget
İran Transit Yolu, 3 km, Doğubeyazıt, Ağrı, 04400
Tel *(0472) 312 48 48*
W simerotel.com
A modest hotel east of town on the road to Iran. Stunning views of Mount Ararat. Friendly staff and a good buffet breakfast, but some of the rooms are dark and dull.

ERZURUM: Grand Hitit Hotel ₺
Budget
Mehmet Akif Ersoy Mah 26, Sok, 25200
Tel *(0442) 233 50 01*
W grandhitithotel.com.tr
Centrally located hotel with a large lobby. Functional rooms with a safe, a minibar and a spacious en-suite bathroom. Friendly service.

ERZURUM: Dedeman Palandöken Ski Lodge Hotel ₺₺
Boutique
PK 115, 25000
Tel *(0442) 317 05 00*
W dedeman.com
This small hotel has direct access to the ski slopes and a dedicated room to store ski equipment.

GAZIANTEP: The Anatolian Hotel ₺
Modern
Mücahitler Mah, Gazimuhtarpaşa Bulv 50, Şehitkamil, 27010
Tel *(0342) 211 40 40*
W theanatolianhotel.com
Hotel with clean and comfortable rooms and a wellness club in an up-market neighbourhood. On-site restaurants, cafés and bars.

GAZIANTEP: Zeynep Hanım Konağı ₺
Boutique
Bey Mah, Atatürk Bulv, Eski Sinema Sok 17, 27010
Tel *(0342) 232 02 07*
W zeynephanimkonagi.com
Charming pension set in a historic building with lots of character. Rustic and traditional with nice amenities such as tea- and coffee-making facilities in all rooms.

KAHTA: Zeus Hotel ₺
Modern
M Kemal Cad 20, Adiyaman
Tel *(0416) 725 56 94*
W zeushotel.com.tr
Modest hotel with friendly staff, lovely gardens and a fine pool. Located at the foot of Mount Nemrut. Amenities include a swimming pool, sauna and a Turkish bath. Free Wi-Fi.

KARS: Kar's Hotel ₺₺
Historic
Yusufpaşa Mah, Halitpaşa Cad 31, 36100
Tel *(0474) 212 16 16*
W karsotel.com
Stately old Russian mansion now converted into an elegant hotel. Beautifully furnished rooms with modern amenities. Breakfasts feature local produce.

Spacious and cosy common living room at Ürgüp Esbelli Ev, Ürgüp

MARDIN: Antik Tatlı Dede Konağı ₺
Boutique
Ulucami Mah 104, Sok 27, 47100
Tel *(0482) 213 27 20*
W tatlidede.com.tr
Delightful hotel near the Ulu Cami. The spacious rooms have barrel vaulted ceilings and decorative carvings.

MARDIN: Reyhan Kasrı ₺₺
Boutique
Birinci Cad 163
Tel *(0482) 212 13 33*
W erdobaelegance.com
Well located in the heart of old Mardin, this hotel features traditional style rooms with all mod cons including tea- and coffee-making facilities in rooms. The rear rooms have great views over the Mesopotamian plains.

DK Choice

MIDYAT: Kasr-ı Nehroz Hotel ₺
Boutique
Işıklar Mah 219, Sok 14, 47500
Tel *(0482) 464 25 25*
W hotelnehroz.com
A wonderful find in the historical centre of Midyat, this hotel is in a lovingly and tastefully converted honey-coloured mansion house where no expense has been spared. Combines period charm with modern conveniences.

ŞANLIURFA: Dedeman Hotel ₺
Modern
Atatürk Mah, Hastane Cad, 63100
Tel *(0414) 318 25 00*
W dedeman.com
Stylish tower block on the edge of the city with fine views of the city. Comfortable and contemporary-style rooms. Spa and gym facilities.

ŞANLIURFA: Manici Otel ₺₺
Boutique
Balıklıgöl Civarı Şurkav Alışveriş Merkezi 68, 63200
Tel *(0414) 215 99 11*
W maniciurfa.com
Spacious, elegant rooms featuring painted furniture. Relax at the coutyard bar or enjoy evening meals featuring local specialities. Conveniently located for the Pool of Abraham and citadel.

VAN: Ada Palas Hotel ₺
Modern
Şerefiye Mah, Cumhuriyet Cad, 65100
Tel *(0432) 216 27 16*
W vanadapalasoteli.com
This spotless place is the best budget option in Van. Front rooms may get some street noise. Very friendly.

For more information on types of hotels *see p329*

WHERE TO EAT AND DRINK

Restaurants in Turkey range from the informal *lokanta* and kebab houses, found on every street corner, to upscale gourmet restaurants. In Istanbul, and in most major tourist centres, the restaurants cover a wide variety of cuisines, from French to Korean. Restaurants on the Mediterranean and Aegean coasts specialize in seafood dishes, and Cappadocia is famous for its wines and traditional cuisine. A range of interesting local dishes can be found along the Black Sea coast and in the interior of Anatolia. Every region presents its own culinary specialities: you can sample thick, clotted cream in Afyon, spicy meatballs in Tekirdağ, chewy ice cream in Kahramanmaraş and whole-milk yogurt in distant Erzurum. As you move further away from Istanbul, finding vegetarian options on the menu becomes a little tricky.

Where to Look

The smartest and most expensive restaurants are usually located in upmarket neighbourhoods of major cities, often as part of renowned international hotel chains. The main roads and central business districts of most towns have a selection of fast-food eateries, cafés and inexpensive restaurants where the locals go to eat – most of these towns also have a number of cafés, patisseries and pudding shops which specialize in *muhallebi* (traditional sweet milk puddings). In the interiors, most restaurants focus on regional food and the menu caters to locals more than tourists. However, coastal resorts cater to all ages and tastes, and offer a wide variety of dishes from across the world.

The sumptuous Beyti restaurant in Florya, Istanbul *(see p349)*

Types of Restaurant

The most common type of restaurant in Turkey is the traditional *lokanta*. These establishments serve a variety of dishes, often listed on a board near the entrance. They offer *hazır yemek* (ready-to-serve food), usually consisting of hot meat and vegetable dishes that are displayed in a *bain marie*, or steam table. Other dishes on the menu may be *sulu yemek* (stews) and *ızgara* (grilled meat and kebabs).

Slicing meat from a revolving grill for a *döner* kebab

Equally popular eating joints include the *kebapcı* or *ocakbaşı* (kebab house). Most kebab houses also serve the popular *lahmacun*, a thin dough base topped with fried onions, minced meat and tomato sauce – this dish is the Turkish version of a pizza. Some also serve *pide*, a flat-bread base with various toppings such as eggs, cheese and cured meat. If you have had too much to drink, you may need a bowl of *işkembe* (tripe soup), the traditional Turkish cure for a hangover, before going to bed. *İşkembe* restaurants stay open until the early hours of the morning.

Fish restaurants are sometimes concentrated along the same street, creating a lively atmosphere and making the street seem like one large restaurant. The meals here typically consist of a selection of *mezes* (appetizers) *(see p344)*, followed by the catch of the day, which might include *palamut* (bonito), *lüfer* (bluefish), *kalkan* (turbot), *kılıç balığı* (swordfish) and *levrek* (sea bass). Also popular are Black Sea *hamsi* (a kind of anchovy) and deep-fried *barbun* (red mullet). Wild-caught fish is much more expensive than farmed fish, the latter of which is widely available in many restaurants that do not specialize in fish. The most common varieties of farmed sea fish are a type of bream known as *çipura* and *levrek* (sea bass). *Alabalık* (trout) is also popular from fish farms by rivers. Fish is served grilled or fried, and is usually accompanied by salad and *rakı (see p345)*, an anise-flavoured spirit.

A trout restaurant on the river at Saklıkent

When choosing a place to eat, remember that many of the cheaper restaurants and kebab houses do not serve alcohol. Alcoholic drinks are generally expensive due to high taxes – this can double the cost of the overall bill. The more conservative places may have a separate section for families or women. These are designated by a sign with the words *aile salonu* (family room), and single men do not enter.

Turks are proud of their hospitality and service. Good service is always found in the upmarket restaurants with well-trained, professional waiters and kitchen staff, and the same level of attentive service is also present at cheaper eateries. It is natural for Turks to call a waiter by saying, *bakar mısınız* (service, please).

Meyhanes are also quite popular in Turkey – they are similar to taverns, serving alcohol and *mezes*, and often have live music.

International culinary influences are encouraging local chefs to be more adventurous and innovative. Wealthier Turks frequent the foreign restaurants found in a number of Istanbul neighbourhoods, while global icons such as Starbucks and Gloria Jean's have become part of everyday life in major cities and coastal resorts.

Opening Hours

Turks eat when they are hungry, without looking at the clock, and will simply drop in at the most convenient place around. Restaurants and kebab houses open at about 11am and stay open for business until the last customer leaves in the evening.

During Ramadan Muslims fast from sunrise to sunset. Hence restaurants in rural Turkey remain closed during the day, or they may serve only a special *iftar* (fast-breaking) menu in the evening. There are no firm guidelines on opening hours. Restaurants in many of the tourist resorts grind to a halt by the end of October, to re-open in March or April when the weather improves.

What to Expect

In Turkey, a meal is always an occasion and, for special meals, it is best to book ahead. In large centres vegetarians can enjoy variety, but the options become scarcer as you travel further east.

Service Charges and Paying

All major credit cards are widely accepted, except in the cheaper restaurants, kebab houses, local *bufes* (snack kiosks) and some *lokantas*. Value-added tax (KDV in Turkish) is always included in the bill, but the policy on service varies. Some restaurants may add a service charge of 10 per cent or more, while others leave it to the discretion of the customer. Some restaurants charge a *kuver* (cover) of a few liras per person for sitting down, which usually includes bread and water. Always check the bill and make sure you are being charged only for the things you ordered and received.

Recommended Restaurants

The restaurants recommended on the following pages have been carefully selected for their quality food, good value and decent service. They range from understated local cafés to glitzy restaurants serving international dishes. Divided into eight geographical areas corresponding to the chapters in this guide, the entries are then organized by town.

The listings cover the various types of restaurant in Turkey including *lokantas*, kebab restaurants and *meyhanes*. Restaurants listed with the name of a particular region of the country usually specialize in the cuisine from that area. Look out for South East Anatolia cuisine – a vibrant mix of Kurdish, Arabian, Syrian and Turkish flavours. Black Sea fare is also worth sampling, and is usually made up of Black Sea fish (mainly anchovy), corn and corn flour, collard greens, milk, cream, butter and cheese. Some restaurants, especially in Istanbul, have revived the art of preparing Ottoman Turkish dishes, with main meat dishes often cooked with fruit.

Restaurants labelled as DK Choice offer something extra special. This may be their superb location, inviting or romantic ambience, sensational cuisine, or impeccable service.

Waterside restaurant on Bird Island, near the Aegean resort of Kuşadası

The Flavours of Turkey

The wide range of climatic zones across Turkey make it one of the few countries that can grow all its own food. Tea is cultivated in the mountains by the Black Sea, and bananas in the sultry south. The Anatolian plain in between is criss-crossed by wheat fields and rich grasslands on which cattle graze, providing top-quality meat and dairy produce. Fruit and vegetables flourish everywhere and fish abound in the salty seas that lap the nation's shores. Freshness is the hallmark of this varied cuisine, drawn from the many cultures that were subject to nearly five centuries of Ottoman rule.

Pomegranates

A stall in the Egyptian Bazaar, one of Istanbul's oldest markets

The Anatolian Steppe

The steppe stretching from Central Asia to Anatolia is one of the oldest inhabited regions of the world. Dishes from this vast area are as varied as the different ethnic groups that live here, but are mainly traditional and simple. To fit in with a mainly nomadic way of life, food generally needed to be quick and easy to prepare. Turkey's most famous culinary staples – yogurt, flatbread and the kebab – originate in this region.

The common use of fruits, such as pomegranates, figs and apricots, in Turkish savoury dishes stems from Persian influences, filtering down with the tribes that came from the north of the steppe. From the Middle East, further south, nomads introduced the occasional fiery blast of chilli. Its use was once an essential aid to preserving meat in the searing desert heat.

Ottoman Cuisine

It was in the vast, steamy kitchens of the Topkapı Palace in Istanbul that a repertoire of

A selection of typical Turkish kebabs

Local Dishes and Specialities

Turkish Delight

Fish has been caught and consumed in abundance in Turkey since Greek times and is usually prepared very simply. Since ancient times the Bosphorus has been known for its excellent fishing and in the winter months especially, there is a bounty of oil-rich fish, such as bluefish, bream, bonito tuna, sea bass, mullet and mackerel, waiting to be reeled in. The Black Sea in the North is also provided with a steady supply of juicy mussels and *hamsi*, a type of anchovy. Sweets are also popular and eaten throughout the day, not just after a meal. They are sold in shops, on stalls and by street vendors. Turkey is renowned for its *baklava*, sweet pastries coated with syrup and often filled with nuts.

Midye Dolması Mussels are stuffed with a spiced rice mixture, steamed and served with a squirt of lemon juice.

A splendid array of fruit, vegetables and dried goods in the Egyptian Bazaar

mouthwatering dishes to rival the celebrated cuisines of France and China grew up. At the height of the Ottoman Empire, in the 16th and 17th centuries, legions of kitchen staff slaved away on the Sultan's behalf. Court cooks usually specialized in particular dishes. Some prepared soups, while others just grilled meats or fish, or dreamed up combinations of vegetables, or baked breads, or made puddings and sherbets. As Ottoman rule expanded to North Africa, the Balkans and parts of southern Russia, influences from these far-flung places crept into the Turkish imperial kitchens. Complex dishes of finely seasoned stuffed meats and vegetables, often with such fanciful names as "lady's lips", "Vizier's fingers" and the "fainting Imam", appeared. This imperial tradition lives on in many of Turkey's restaurants, where dishes such as *karnıyarık* (halved aubergines or eggplants stuffed with minced lamb, pine nuts and dried fruit) and *hünkar begendili köfte* (meatballs served with a smooth purée of smoked aubergine and cheese) grace the menu.

Fresh catch from the Bosphorus on a fish stall in Karaköy

Bazaar Culture

A visit to the food markets in Turkey, especially Istanbul's Egyptian Bazaar (*see p102*) is a must. A cornucopia of fine ingredients is brought here daily from farms that surround the city. Apricots, watermelons, cherries and figs sit alongside staple vegetables, such as peppers, onions, aubergines and tomatoes. Fine cuts of lamb and beef, cheeses, pickles, herbs, spices and honey-drenched pastries and puddings are also on offer.

Know Your Fish

The profusion of different species in the waters around Turkey makes the country a paradise for fish lovers:

Barbun Red mullet

Çipura Sea bream

Dilbalığı Sole

Hamsi Anchovy

Kalamar Squid

Kalkan Turbot

Kefal Grey mullet

Kılıç Swordfish

Levrek Sea bass

Lüfer Bluefish

Midye Mussels

Palamut Bonito tuna

Uskumru Mackerel

İmam Bayıldı Aubergines, stuffed with tomatoes, garlic and onions, are baked in the oven until meltingly soft.

Levrek Pilakisi This stew is made by simmering sea bass fillets with potatoes, carrots, tomatoes, onions and garlic.

Kadayıf Rounds of vermicelli are stuffed with nuts and doused with honey to make a sumptuous dessert.

Mezes

As in many southern European countries, a Turkish meal begins with a selection of appetizing starters known as *mezes*, which are placed in the middle of the table for sharing. In a basic *meyhane* restaurant, you may be offered olives, cheese and slices of melon, but in a grander establishment the choice will be enormous. Mainly consisting of cold vegetables and salads of various kinds, *mezes* can also include a number of hot dishes, such as *börek* (cheese pastries), fried mussels and squid. *Mezes* are eaten with bread and traditionally washed down with *rakı* (a clear, anise-flavoured spirit).

Humus with *pide* bread

Turkish Breads

Bread is the cornerstone of every meal in Turkey and comes in a wide range of shapes and styles. Besides *ekmek* (crusty white loaves), the other most common types of Turkish bread are *yufka* and *pide*. *Yufka*, the typical bread of nomadic communities, is made from thinly rolled sheets of dough which are cooked on a griddle, and dried to help preserve them. They can then be heated up and served to accompany any main meal as required. *Pide* is the type of flatbread that is usually served with *mezes* and kebabs in restaurants. It consists of a flattened circle or oval of dough, sometimes brushed with beaten egg and sprinkled with sesame seeds or black cumin, that is baked in an oven. It is a staple during many religious festivals. In the month of Ramadan, no meal is considered complete without *pide*. Another popular bread is *simit*, a crisp, ring-shaped savoury loaf that comes covered in sesame seeds.

A delivery of freshly baked *simit* loaves

What to Drink in Turkey

The most common drink in Turkey is tea *(çay)*, which is normally served black in small, tulip-shaped glasses. It will be offered to you wherever you go: in shops and bazaars, and even in banks and offices. Breakfast is usually accompanied by tea, whereas small cups of strong Turkish coffee *(kahve)* are drunk mid-morning and also at the end of meals. Cold drinks include a variety of fresh fruit juices, such as orange and cherry, and refreshing syrup-based sherbets. Although Turkey does produce its own wine and beer, the most popular alcoholic drink is rakı, which is usually served to accompany *mezes*.

Soft-drink seller

Soft Drinks

Bottled mineral water *(su)* is sold in corner shops and served in restaurants everywhere. If you're feeling adventurous, you might like to try a glass of *ayran*, salty liquid yogurt. *Boza* is made from bulgur wheat or millet and is another local drink to sample. There is always a variety of refreshing, cold fruit and vegetable juices available. They include cherry juice *(vişne suyu)*, turnip juice *(şalgam suyu)* and *şıra*, a juice made from fermented grapes.

Vişne suyu *Ayran*

Alcoholic Drinks

Turkey's national alcoholic drink is *rakı*, a clear, anise-flavoured spirit that turns cloudy when water is added and is drunk with fish and mezes. The Turkish wine industry has yet to realize its full potential. Kavaklıdere and Doluca, the best-known brands, are overpriced for table wines. Villa Doluca is preferable. Sevilen offers several interesting wines, such as Majestic, and an outstanding Merlot. All alcohol is heavily taxed, making simple table wine a luxury. The locally brewed Efes Pilsen beer, also widely available on draught, is quite drinkable but note that alcohol is not usually served in cheaper restaurants and kebab houses.

Rakı Beer Red wine White wine

Coffee and Tea

Turkish coffee is dark, strong and served in tiny cups, with the grounds left in the bottom. It is ordered according to the amount of sugar required: *az* (little), *orta* (medium) or *şekerli* (a lot). Insist on Turkish coffee, or the waiter may assume you want Nescafé. Tea *(çay)* is served with sugar but without milk, and it comes in a small, tulip-shaped glass. Also popular are apple- *(elma-)*, rosehip- *(kuşburnu-)* and mint- *(nane-)* flavoured teas.

Traditional *samovar* for tea

Turkish coffee is a very strong drink and an acquired taste for most people.

Apple tea Limeflower tea

Sahlep is a winter drink made from orchid root.

Where to Eat and Drink

Istanbul

Seraglio Point

Bizim Mutfak ₺
Lokanta **Map** 5 D3
Şeyhülislam Hayri Efendi Cad 2, Eminönü, 34110
Tel (0212) 522 78 46
Locals flock to this modern dining establishment to enjoy a variety of home-cooked style soups, meats, vegetarian delights and desserts.

Şehzade Erzurum Cağ Kebabi ₺
Kebab **Map** 5 E3
Hocapaşa Sok 3A, Sirkeci, 34400
Tel (0212) 520 33 61
Unpretentious restaurant that serves a delicious, succulent marinated lamb kebab on warm *lavaş* (flatbread). A speciality dish from northeastern Anatolia.

Can Oba ₺₺
Turkish **Map** 5 E3
Hocapaşa Sok 10, Sirkeci, 34400
Tel (0212) 522 12 15
A lively *lokanta* specializing in kebabs, but also does a wide range of other dishes, from fish soup to chocolate puddings.

DK Choice

Imbat ₺₺
Regional/Turkish **Map** 5 E3
Hudavendigar Cad 34, Sirkeci, 34410
Tel (0212) 520 71 91
A very popular restaurant atop the Orient Express Hotel. The lamb is highly recommended, and the menu also caters to vegetarians. Attentive staff ensure a pleasant dining experience. Reserve ahead to secure a coveted Bosphorus-facing spot on the terrace.

Paşazade ₺₺
Ottoman Turkish **Map** 5 E3
İbn-i Kemal Sok 5A, Sirkeci, 34110
Tel (0212) 513 37 50
Smart ground-floor place that offers a variety of Ottoman-style dishes at affordable prices. Try the tasty *mahmudiye* (a fruity chicken dish).

Balıkçı Sabahattin ₺₺₺
Seafood **Map** 5 E5
Seyit Hasan Kuyu Sok 1, Cankurtaran – Eminönü
Tel (0212) 458 18 24
Housed in a restored wooden mansion near the Armada hotel, this old Istanbul favourite specializes in seafood. In summer the crowd of diners spills out onto garden tables.

Karakol ₺₺₺
Turkish **Map** 5 F3
Inside Topkapı Palace grounds, next to Aya Irene
Tel (0212) 514 94 94
Housed next to the 6th-century church Haghia Eirene, Karakol presents Turkish cuisine at its best. Dining is mainly outdoors, but in winter patrons can sit inside the restored sentry-post building.

Sultanahmet

Fes Café ₺
Café **Map** 5 D4
Ali Baba Türbe Sok 25, Nuruosmaniye, 34200
Tel (0212) 526 30 71
An unusually contemporary café in a street near the bazaar. Fruit sherbets, tasty coffees and modest lunch options in cool retro surroundings.

DK Choice

Tarihi Sultanahmet Koftecisi ₺
Kebab **Map** 5 D4
Divanyolu Cad 12, 34400
Tel (0212) 520 05 66
This place is famous for its delicious grilled *köfte* (meatballs), which have garnered many famous admirers over the years – find their written reviews framed on the walls. Eat *köfte* with *piyaz* (bean salad), and follow it up with *semolina helva* for dessert.

Amedros ₺₺
Turkish/International **Map** 5 D4
Hoca Rüstem Sok 7, Divanyolu,
Tel (0212) 522 83 56
Stylish little place with unusually good service and a great ambience, offering a range of traditional Turkish and Ottoman dishes, along with a variety of pastas and steaks.

Beautifully cooked lamb cutlets at Karakol served outdoors in summer

Price Guide
Prices categories include a three-course meal for one (excluding alcohol), and all extra charges including service and tax.

₺	under ₺35
₺₺	₺35 to ₺50
₺₺₺	over ₺50

Sultanahmet Fish House ₺₺
Seafood/Kebab **Map** 5 D4
Prof Kasim Ismail Gürkan Cad 14, 34400
Tel (0212) 527 44 45
Great place for fish and seasonal specials including salt-baked sea bass. Wide range of *mezes* along with a number of kebab choices.

DK Choice

Giritli Restaurant ₺₺₺
Cretan Meyhane **Map** 5 E5
Keresteci Hakkı Sok, Cankurtaran, 34122
Tel (0212) 458 22 70
A Cretan restaurant housed in a charming 19th-century wooden mansion, with a lovely courtyard for summer dining. A good-value all-you-can-eat menu, which includes unlimited alcoholic drinks and about 20 different kinds of *meze*. Grilled seasonal fish features in the main course.

Seasons Restaurant ₺₺₺
International **Map** 5 E4
Four Seasons Hotel, Tevkifhane Sok 1, Cankurturan
Tel (0212) 402 31 50
Located inside the hotel, converted from a late Ottoman prison, this popular restaurant offers everything from sushi and antipasti to classic Turkish fare.

The Bazaar Quarter

Can Restaurant ₺
Lokanta **Map** 4 C4
Sorguclu Han 19–26, Kapalicarsi
Tel (0212) 511 91 53
Workers and shoppers from the Bazaar come here to get their fill of hearty home-style cooking. The delicious meat broth, thickened with egg, is worth the trip.

Gaziantep Burç Ocakbaşı ₺
Kebab/Southeast Anatolian **Map** 4 C4
Parçacılar Sok 12, Kapalıçarşı
Tel (0212) 527 15 16
This delightful bazaar restaurant serves meat dishes from the southeastern region of Turkey, famed for its flavourful kebabs. Stuffed and dried vegetables are a delicious alternative.

The spacious dining area and one of the counters displaying tasty treats at Nar Lokanta

Havuzlu ₺₺
Lokanta **Map** 4 C4
Gani Çelebi Sok 3, Grand Bazaar, 36420
Tel (0212) 527 33 46
A rare dining option in the Grand Bazaar, Havuzlu is a pleasant restaurant serving freshly cooked local food. Try the soups.

Darüzziyafe ₺₺₺
Ottoman Turkish **Map** 4 B3
Şifahane Sok 6, Süleymaniye, 36420
Tel (0212) 511 84 14
Located in the former *imaret* (soup kitchens) of the Süleymaniye Mosque complex, this atmospheric restaurant offers a wide range of traditional Turkish dishes.

DK Choice

Nar Lokanta ₺₺₺
Lokanta **Map** 5 D4
Armaggan store 5th Floor, Nuruosmaniye Cad 65
Tel (0212) 522 28 00
An excellent choice tucked away in the Grand Bazaar, Nar makes a point of only using seasonal ingredients, from which they fashion 50 dishes daily. Step into the glamorous dining room inside and take your pick from an open buffet of vegetable specials. There is also an extensive list of Turkish wines.

Beyoğlu

Café Privato ₺
Café **Map** 1 A5
Timarcı Sok 3/B, Galata
Tel (0212) 293 20 55
Run by a friendly woman from Turkey's northeastern neighbour country, Georgia, this homely little café serves one of the best breakfast spreads in Turkey.

DK Choice

Canim Cigerim ₺
Kebab **Map** 1 A4
Minare Sok 1, 34430
Tel (0212) 252 60 60
Famous for its skewers of liver, this inexpensive and welcoming restaurant is popular with locals and tourists alike. Get succulent meat pieces wrapped up with onions and greens. Try the mouthwatering *kunefe* (sweet cheese pastry) for dessert.

Datlı Maya ₺
Lokanta **Map** 1 B5
Türkgücü Cad 59/A, Cihangir
Tel (0212) 292 90 56
Exuberant chef Dilara Erbay leads this restaurant, which features a menu of creatively reimagined Turkish street-food staples.

Fasuli ₺
Regional/Lokanta **Map** 5 F1
Kılıçalipaşa CD 6, Tophane, 34425
Tel (0212) 243 65 80
Famous for the Black-Sea-style beans after which it is named, the menu at Fasuli also features cornbread, *mihlama* (fondue) and salads.

Furreyya ₺
Seafood **Map** 1 A5
Serdari Ekrem Sok 2B
Tel (0212) 252 48 53
This miniature restaurant, a stone's throw from the Galata Tower, serves tasty fish soups, wraps and sandwiches.

Helvetia ₺
Lokanta **Map** 1 A5
Asmalı Mescit Mh, Gen Yazgan Sok 12
Tel (0212) 245 87 80
Good place for vegetarians, though there are a number of choices for meat lovers as well. After eating, enjoy an aromatic herbal tea.

Lale Işkembecesi ₺
Lokanta **Map** 1 A4
Tarlabaşı Bulvarı 13, 34437
Tel (0212) 252 69 69
Open 24/7, this restaurant is one of the oldest in the city. It is popular with late-night diners for its *işkembe*, a tripe soup that is known locally as a hangover cure.

Mandabatmaz ₺
Café **Map** 1 A4
Olivia Geçidi 1/A, off İstiklal Cad
Established in 1967 and set in a tiny hole in the wall, down an alley off the busy Caddesi, this is the best place in Istanbul for thick and rich Turkish coffee.

Van Kahvaltı Evi ₺
Kurdish **Map** 1 B5
Defterdar Yokusu 52 A
Tel (0212) 293 64 37
This hip Kurdish breakfast joint offers a lot of regional specialities. There can be a wait to get in, but the food is worth it.

49 Cukurcuma ₺₺
International **Map** 1 B4
Turnacıbaşı Sok 49, 34433
Tel (0212) 249 00 48
Scrumptious pizza and excellent Turkish wines from the island of Bozcaada are available at this cool café with exposed-brick decor. Friendly service.

Antiochia ₺₺
Kebab **Map** 1 A5
Asmalı Mescit, Gen Yazgan Sok 3
Tel (0212) 244 08 20
A great spot to come for delicious southeastern Turkish food, including spicy dips, tangy salads with wild thyme, pistachio kebabs and much more.

Ara Kafe ₺₺
Turkish/International **Map** 1 A4
Tosbağ Sok 8, 34433
Tel (0212) 245 41 05
The black-and-white photos on the walls are the works of Istanbul-Armenian Ara Güler, Turkey's best-known photographer. No alcohol but milky Indian teas and home-made lemonades won't disappoint.

Culinary Institute ₺₺
Fusion **Map** 1 A5
Meşrutiyet Cad 59, Asmalı Mescit, 34437
Tel (0212) 251 22 14
Feast on persimmon martinis, dried aubergine (eggplant) stuffed kebabs and bean and rice dishes in the dining room of this cookery school.

For more information on types of restaurants *see p340–41*

The entrance to Akdeniz Hatay Sofrasi, Istanbul

Fıccın ₺₺
Meyhane **Map** 1 A4
Kallavi Sok 7/1–13/1
Tel (0212) 293 37 86
This Circassian-influenced *meze* place comprises a series of eateries set on the same street. Try the *çerkez tavuk* (a garlicky chicken and walnut dish) or the signature meat pie.

Imroz ₺₺
Meyhane **Map** 1 A4
Nevizade Sok 24
Tel (0212) 249 90 73
This friendly *meyhane* is one of the longest-established on Istanbul's liveliest street, Nevizade Sokak. Sample the *meze* and grilled fish while enjoying the ambience.

Jash ₺₺
Meyhane **Map** 1 C4
Pürletaş Mah, Cihangir Cad 9
Tel (0212) 244 30 42
Armenian *mezes* are served in this cozy *meyhane*. It can get a bit raucous when musicians arrive with their accordions.

DK Choice

Kahve 6 ₺₺
Breakfast **Map** 1 B5
Anahtar Sok 13, Cihangir
Tel (0212) 293 08 49
A great place for breakfast, Kahve 6 offers poached eggs with spinach and garlic sauce and "life-saver *simit*" – a seeded bread ring with all the essential Turkish breakfast jams, cheeses and olives. A trendy Cihangir hangout with creative versions of old favourites.

Karaköy Lokantası ₺₺
Lokanta/Meyhane **Map** 5 E1
Kemankeş Cad 37, Karaköy, 34425
Tel (0212) 292 44 55
Beautiful tiled interiors at this hip *lokanta*. Popular lunch choice for businessmen in the area. Try *mezes* or the chicken and lemon pasta served with dried mint and paprika. A refined *meyhane* in the evening.

Kiva ₺₺
Kebab **Map** 5 D1
Galata Kulesi Meydanı 4
Tel (0212) 292 00 37
A huge range of Anatolian dishes to try at this vibrant restaurant. Excellent beef casseroles and a choice of rice items on the menu.

Lokanta Maya ₺₺
Lokanta **Map** 5 E1
Kemankeş Cad 35 A
Tel (0212) 252 68 84
Didem, the French-Culinary-Institute trained chef at this charming restaurant, creates a well presented menu of daily specials, offering standard Turkish dishes with a contemporary twist.

Mekan ₺₺
Meyhane **Map** 1 A4
Eski Çiçekçi Sok 3, 34250
Tel (0212) 252 60 52
An Armenian *meyhane* just off Istiklal Caddesi offering *mezes* such as *topik*, which is made with chickpeas, currants and cinnamon.

Zencefil ₺₺
Lokanta **Map** 1 B3
Şht Muhtar Mh, Kurabiye Sok 8, 34430
Tel (0212) 243 82 34
A very pretty vegetarian café set in a glasshouse building. A calm oasis away from the noise and traffic of Taksim's busier end.

Diners relaxing in the gently lit interiors at Lokanta Maya

Çok Çok Thai ₺₺₺
Thai **Map** 1 A4
Mesrutiyet Cad 51, 34420
Tel (0212) 292 64 96
Up-market restaurant with a hip ambience and friendly staff. The honey-grilled salmon with mung bean salad is a winner.

Leb-i derya ₺₺₺
International **Map** 1 A5
Richmond Otel Kat 6, İstiklal Cad 227
Tel (0212) 243 43 75
Sample a modern take on traditional Turkish cuisine on the top floor of the refined Richmond Hotel. A good breakfast buffet.

Meze by Lemon Tree ₺₺₺
Meyhane **Map** 1 A4
Meşrutiyet Cad 83/B
Tel (0212) 252 83 02
Very chic and upmarket *meyhane* offering imaginative twists on traditional Turkish dishes. Great variety of *mezes*, tender fish and a wide range of wines.

La Mouette ₺₺₺
Turkish **Map** 1 A5
Tomtom Kaptan Sok 18, 34433
Tel (0212) 292 44 67
A smart restaurant with an impressive *dégustation* menu – sample a gamut of creative dishes. Superb city views.

Munferit ₺₺₺
Mediterranean **Map** 1 A4
Yeni Çarşı Cad 19, Galatasaray, 34425
Tel (0212) 252 50 67
Cutting-edge interiors and great food combine at Munferit. At the weekends this hip restaurant turns into an impromptu club.

Ninja ₺₺₺
Japanese **Map** 1 C4
Inonu Cad 43, Gümüşsuyu, 34398
Tel (0212) 237 23 28
Ninja serves grills as well as noodles and sushi. Smaller booths for private parties.

Further Afield

Asude ₺
Lokanta
Perihan Abla Sok 4, Kuzguncuk, Üsküdar
Tel (0216) 334 44 14
A crowded family-run lunch spot with a few revolving specials. Home-made Turkish ravioli is the speciality on Mondays.

Kanaat ₺
Lokanta
Selmanipak Cad 9, Üsküdar
Tel (0216) 341 54 44
One of Üsküdar's favourite restaurants, Kanaat was established back 1931,

Key to Price Guide *see p346*

and offers a wide range of lunch specials. Delicious milky pudding for dessert.

Pierre Loti Coffee House ₺
Café
Gümüşsuyu Balmumcu Sok 1, Eyüp
Tel (0212) 581 26 96
Named after the French novelist, Pierre Loti, this is a modest tea spot, famous for its spectacular views up the Golden Horn.

DK Choice

Akdeniz Hatay Sofrası ₺₺
Kebab
Ahmediye Cad 44, Fatih, 34091
Tel (0212) 444 72 47
This restaurant is a showcase of the Antakya region's flavourful cuisine. Try the sour minced meat, chickpea and pomegranate soup or the home-made bread cooked in an infusion of cheese and herbs. Call ahead to sample the special salt-baked chicken.

DK Choice

Çiya ₺₺
Kebab/Regional Turkish
Güneşli Bahçe Sok 48/B, Caferağa, Kadıköy
Tel (0216) 330 31 90
A humble trio of kebab houses make up Çiya, all located along the same Kadıköy street. The *lokanta*-style café offers a plethora of *meze* and salads, while the other two restaurants concentrate on a wide range of tender kebabs.

Incir Altı ₺₺
Meyhane
Arabacılar Sok 4, Beylerbeyi, 34398
Tel (0216) 557 66 86
A beautiful walled garden surrounds this lovely restaurant. Classic Istanbul *mezes* line the menu. The grilled octopus and fish in vine leaves are highlights.

Kosinitza ₺₺
Meyhane
Bereketli Sok 2, Kuzguncuk, Üsküdar
Tel (0216) 334 04 00
Tickle your taste buds with an interesting combination of flavours – relish delicately spiced fish stew or go for the usual plain grilled offerings.

Suna'nın yeri Suna Balık ₺₺
Meyhane
Kandilli İskele Cad 4, Kandilli
Tel (0216) 332 32 41
An unpretentious fish restaurant offering delicious food. There is no wine list, but ask the waiters for their recommendations.

DK Choice

360 East ₺₺₺
Fusion
Albay Faik 31, Sozdener Cad, Kadıköy
Tel (0216) 542 43 50
Take a boat ride to this sleek, upmarket establishment that is part of the 360 Istanbul chain. It doubles up as a refined dining space and a nightclub joint in the fashionable neighbourhood of Moda. The sea bass and the lamb are cooked to perfection. 360 East also has wonderful views and offers entertainment in the form of international DJs and world-class musicians.

Angel ₺₺₺
Meyhane
Salacak Sahil Yolu 46, Üsküdar, 34470
Tel (0216) 553 04 26
A smart *meyhane* which looks out towards Seraglio Point. Fish *mezes* are a big draw here, as well as salt-baked John Dory, which is wheeled to the table girded by blue flames.

Beyti ₺₺₺
Kebab
Orman Sok 8, Florya, 34153
Tel (0212) 663 29 90
A pilgrimage site for meat lovers, Beyti delights with its big portions. Do not miss the mixed grill.

Lacivert ₺₺₺
Meyhane
Körfez Cad 57, Anadolu Hisarı, 34410
Tel (0216) 413 37 53
Practically under the second Bosphorus bridge, Lacivert was the locale for a set of 1970s Turkish films. Good seafood.

Patrons sitting outside one of Çiya's establishments on Kadıköy street

Beautiful sunset view from the funky rooftop dining area at 360 East

Thrace and the Sea of Marmara

BURSA: Çıcek Izgara ₺
Kebab
Belediye Cad 5, Heykel
Tel (0224) 221 12 88
Fantastic range of tender kebabs, *köfte* (meatballs) and delicious soups all elegantly served in a period house in central Bursa.

BURSA: Çırağan Restaurant ₺
Turkish/International
Çekirge Cad, Süleyman Çelebi Parkı No 155, 16150
Tel (0224) 234 03 25
There is something to suit the taste of each family member here. The large bakery furnace turns out traditional *pides* (Turkish flatbread).

DK Choice

BURSA: Kebapçı İskender ₺
Kebab
Tayyare Kültür Merkezi yanı, Atatürk Cad 60, 16330
Tel (0224) 221 10 76
A national favourite, *İskender* kebab restaurants are found all across Turkey, and this place is where the dish was born. *İskender* is *döner* kebab served with a tomato dressing and melted butter on a single layer of diced *pide* bread – heavenly.

BURSA: Zeynel İnegöl Köftecisi ₺
Kebab
İzmir Yolu üzeri, 16500
Tel (0224) 618 03 16
Feast on *inegöl köfte*, a special meatball made with minced meat and red onions, cooked on oak-wood grills.

For more information on types of restaurants *see p340–41*

Informal indoor and outdoor dining at Yelken Café, Ayvalık

BURSA: Darüzziyafe Bursa ₺₺
Ottoman Turkish
II Murat Cad 36, Muradiye Cami Karşısı, 16050
Tel (0224) 224 64 40
Located in the former soup kitchen of Ottoman-era Muradiye Mosque, this restaurant's specialities include *Yufkalı Darüzziyafe köfte* (meatballs). Good desserts.

BURSA: Uludağ Kebapçısı ₺₺
Kebab
Uluyol Şirin Sok 12, 16050
Tel *(0224) 251 45 51*
One of the oldest and longest-established kebab restaurants in Turkey, this place is a city landmark for good reason. Simply delicious kebabs.

BURSA: Skylight Restaurant ₺₺₺
Mediterranean
Hilton Hotel, Yeni Yalova Cad 347, 16210
Tel (0224) 500 05 05
An elegant restaurant offering creative fish, meat and vegetable dishes. Gorgeous views of the city from its top-floor location.

ÇANAKKALE: Cafe Du Port ₺₺
International
Yalı Cad 12, 17100
Tel (0286) 217 29 08
French toasts and omelette for breakfast, and freshly brewed Turkish tea and cakes in mid-afternoon. Good hearty food.

ÇANAKKALE: Rıhtim Restaurant ₺₺
Seafood
Eski Balıkhane Sok 7–9, 12100
Tel (0286) 212 53 67
Peaceful waterfront location with fantastic seafood. The daily catch is displayed on a counter by the entrance.

ECEABAT: Maydos Restaurant ₺
International
İsmetpaşa Paşa Mah, Kilitbahir Yolu, İstiklal Cad 105
Tel (0286) 814 14 54
This Australian-run restaurant in Maydos offers a very varied menu. Its location by the water-front encourages outdoor dining on fair days. Also runs tours of the Gallipoli World War I battlefields.

ECEABAT: Liman Restaurant ₺₺
Seafood
İsmet Paşa Mah, İstiklal Cad 67, 17900
Tel (0286) 814 27 55
A low-key seafood restaurant with a coffee shop feel, especially on the outdoor terrace. One speciality is *paçanga* – a savoury filo roll, deep fried with pastrami and cheese, though most people come here to enjoy the seafood.

EDIRNE: Cigerci Kemal Üsta ₺
Traditional Turkish
Ortakapı Cad 3
A humble option and a great place to try Edirne's signature dish of tender liver, best eaten with fried red peppers, *sumac* smothered onions and yogurt.

EDIRNE: Sivrikaya Restaurant ₺
Turkish/Seafood
Migros Kavşağı, Tren İstasyonu Cad, 22100
Tel (0284) 236 21 64
Sivrikaya partners a dairy farm known for its delicious dairy products, which are incorporated into the restaurant's menu.

EDIRNE: Hanedan Restaurant ₺₺
Turkish
Karaağaç Yolu üzeri, Iki Köprü Arası, Tunca Köprüsü yanı, 22100
Tel (0284) 214 21 22
A renowned and large facility located on the Tunca River. Besides the *mezes*, they serve great fish and meat dishes.

GELIBOLU: Gelibolu Osmanlı Mutfağı ₺
Ottoman Turkish
Atatürk Cad 34, 17500, Çanakkale
Tel (0286) 566 12 25
Dishes once made to please the sultans are now enjoyed by all food lovers. Aubergine fillet or deep-fried dumplings dipped in honey syrup are favourites.

GELIBOLU: Gelibolu Restaurant ₺₺
Seafood
İskele Meydanı, Vapur İskelesi yanı, 17500
Tel (0286) 566 12 27
Conveniently located by the port, this eatery serves delicacies such as octopus, calamari, grilled fish and anchovies in Black Sea style.

İZNIK: Köfteci Yusuf ₺
Kebab
Selçuk Mah, Atatürk Cad 73, 16860
Tel (0224) 444 61 62
Inexpensive eatery rustling up delectable grilled meat, chicken and *köfte* (meatballs) served with pepper, garlic and parsley paste.

İZNIK: Umut Restaurant ₺₺
Seafood
Göl Sahil Yolu 24, 16860
Tel (0224) 757 07 38
Situated on the lakefront, with an outdoor section shaded with vines. Expect to find freshwater fish dishes such as skewered catfish and carp.

The Aegean

ASSOS: Nazlıhan Restaurant ₺₺
Turkish
İskele Mevkii, Behramkale, 17860
Tel (0286) 721 73 85 86
The usual Turkish fare, in a truly romantic setting. Enjoy a special meal on the waterfront of the ancient harbour of Assos.

The tasteful, softy lit interior at Skylight Restaurant, Bursa

Key to Price Guide *see p346*

Picturesque setting of Mimoza Restaurant, Bodrum Peninsula

AYVALIK: Avşar Büfe ₺
Fast Food
Barbaros Cad, 10400
Tel (0266) 312 98 21
One of the most well-known sandwich kiosks in the country. Try the famous Ayvalık Tostu, a toasted cheese, sausage and pickle sandwich. Food is served from a 1960s-style minibus.

AYVALIK: Paşalı Restaurant ₺
Lokanta
Talatpaşa Cad 14, 14000
Tel (0266) 312 50 18
Relish hearty food at the centre of Ayvalık's market district. Popular for its soups.

DK Choice

AYVALIK: Yelken Café ₺₺
International
Çamlık Mevkii İnönü Cad 14, 10400
Tel (0266) 312 77 82
In an area full of touristy restaurants, Yelken is a gem and a local favourite. Located on the waterfront, away from the bustle of the town, this casual restaurant rustles up delicious Aegean, Italian and seafood dishes cooked in high-quality virgin olive oil. Fine service.

AYVALIK: Şehir Kulübü ₺₺₺
Seafood
Gazinolar Cad, Ayvalık Merkez, 10400
Tel (0266) 312 36 76
An elegant city-centre restaurant on the waterfront. Try *karagöz* – a kind of sea bream rarely available elsewhere. Reservations recommended at the weekend.

BEHRAMKALE: Kale Restaurant ₺
Turkish
Akropol Yolu, Behramkale Köyü, Çanakkale
Tel (0543) 317 49 69
Built against the ancient walls of Assos, Kale serves *gözleme* (stuffed wrap), *mantı* (Turkish ravioli) and *ayran* (yogurt drink).

BERGAMA: Kardeşler Restaurant ₺
Turkish
İzmir Yolu Üzeri, 35700
Tel (0232) 631 08 56
On the Izmir highway leading to Bergama and its acropolis, Kardeşler offers a daily buffet of traditional food. Grilled meat dishes are made to order.

BERGAMA: Meydan Restaurant ₺
Lokanta
Mustafa Yazıcı Cad 17/A, 35700
Tel (0232) 631 52 25
A short walk from the museum this restaurant is a no-frills local favourite. It offers daily cooked dishes that change by the season.

BODRUM: Bodrum El Vino Restaurant ₺₺
Regional/Seafood
Omurça Mah, Pamili Sok 14, 48400
Tel (0252) 313 87 70
Terrace restaurant in a peaceful backstreet with delicious seafood and awesome views overlooking the town and Crusader castle.

BODRUM: Meyhane Evgenia ₺₺
Aegean/Seafood
Çarşı Sok, 48400
Tel (0533) 305 54 19
Informal, family-run restaurant tucked away behind the fish market. The *mezes* are all full of flavour; ask the owners for their recommendations – you won't be disappointed.

BODRUM: Marina Yacht Club ₺₺₺
Seafood/International
Neyzen Tevfik Cad, 48000
Tel (0252) 316 12 28
A restaurant and club in the Marina with an all-day menu to choose from. Good food, cocktails and fine jazz musicians perform in the club section. A great place to chill out with friends and soak up the view.

BODRUM PENINSULA: Bodrum Mantı & Cafe ₺₺
Turkish
Bodrum Yarımadası, Göltürkbükü, İnönü Cad147, 48483
Tel (0252) 377 51 00
A pretty Mediterranean restaurant famous for its *mantı* (Turkish dumplings), which come with a variety of toppings and fillings. A wide choice of omelettes is also available.

BODRUM PENINSULA: Limon Cafe ₺₺
Café/Turkish
Bodrum Yarımadası, Gümüşlük Yalı Mevkii 1, 48400
Tel (0252) 394 40 44 **Closed** *winter*
A half-hour drive from Bodrum, in the village of Gümüşlük, this café serves cakes and lemonade in the afternoon, as well as a wide range of Turkish *mezes* and seafood.

BODRUM PENINSULA: Mimoza Restaurant ₺₺₺
Seafood
Bodrum Yarımadası, Gümüşlük, 48970
Tel (0252) 394 31 39 **Closed** *winter*
Elegant beach restaurant. Highlights on the menu include grilled octopus and clams, and shrimps on vine leaves.

ÇEŞME: İmren Lokantası ₺₺
Lokanta
16 Eylül Mah, 3004 Sok 81, 35940
Tel (0232) 712 76 70
Sample classic kebabs and Turkish food at İmren Lokantası. The menu offers a lot of options including *mezes* and stews.

ÇEŞME: Ferdi Baba Restaurant ₺₺₺
Seafood
5464 Sok 3 Şifne, 35950
Tel (0232) 717 21 45 **Closed** *winter*
An excellent seafood restaurant. The sea bass in liquor and deep-fried fish are delicious. Ask for the waiter's daily recommendations. Reservations required.

For more information on types of restaurants *see p340–41*

The exterior of İdaköy Çiftlik Evi, Edremit

ÇEŞME: Maria'nın Bahçesi ₺₺₺
Seafood
Kemalpaşa Cad 1, 35937
Tel (0232) 716 05 76
The menu here celebrates Aegean delicacies, plus clams, sea urchins, and fish cooked with fresh herbs. There are the usual fish dishes for the more conservative.

CUNDA ISLAND: Taş Kahve ₺
Turkish/International
Sahil Boyu, Mevlana Cad 20, Alibey Adası, 10400
Tel (0266) 327 11 66
Atmospheric restaurant, housed in a lofty, Neo-Classical building, much frequented by locals. It offers an excellent breakfast buffet and outdoor tables on the waterfront.

CUNDA ISLAND: Bay Nihat Restaurant ₺₺₺
Seafood
Sahil Boyu, Mevlana Cad, 10400 Alibey Adası Ayvalık
Tel (0266) 327 10 63
The most famous and expensive seafood restaurant in Cunda Island. Seafood *mezes* are made with local shellfish and fresh herbs. Go for the *kidonya* (a local clam cooked in white wine and spices).

DENIZLI: Kebapçı Halil ₺
Kebab
Eski Sarayköy Cad 357, Sok 11, Bayramyeri, 20100
Tel (0258) 261 13 57
The speciality of the kebab chef and former butcher here is the *denizli* kebab – made with lamb and slow-grilled on mastic gum tree wood.

DIDIM: Circus Restaurant ₺₺
Italian
Ataürk Bulv 221, 09270
Tel (0256) 813 74 17
Delightful, cosy place serving a varied menu of zesty dishes. The garlic prawn starter is a must. Attentive service.

DIDIM: Lush Café and Restaurant ₺₺
International
Çamlık Mah Sok 445, 09270
Tel (0256) 813 33 61
Best known for both its steaks and friendly staff, this well-located restaurant is a firm favourite with tourists and locals alike.

EDREMIT: İdaköy Çiftlik Evi ₺₺
Regional/Aegean
Çamlıbel Köyü, 10300
Tel (0535) 222 56 66
Seasonal delicacies, including *mezes* that incorporate locally grown herbs and cooked in home-made virgin olive oil. Reservations are required.

FOÇA: İğdeli Cafe ₺
Café
Reha Midlii Cad 40, 35680
Tel (0232) 812 81 27
Sample Aegean coffee made with mastic gum or go for Mesopotamian-style coffee, known locally as *dibek kahvesi*.

The attractive interior with Chinese lamps at Fondragonpearl, Adana

FOÇA: Celep Restaurant ₺₺₺
Seafood
Fevzipaşa Mah, Reha Midilli Cad 48, 35000
Tel (0232) 812 14 95
Located in one of the most pleasant northern Aegean towns, the daily catch at Celep is kept in a pool in the restaurant, and diners can choose their fish to be cooked.

İZMIR: Kır Çiçeği Restaurant ₺₺
Kebab
Kıbrıs Şehitleri Cad 83, Alsancak
Tel (0232) 464 30 90
Near the Hilton hotel, in the trendy Alsancak neighbourhood, this restaurant offers an amazing array of kebabs, *pides* (Turkish pizza), fresh salads and desserts.

İZMIR: Mezzaluna Restaurant ₺₺
Italian
Konak Pier, Atatük Cad 19, 35260
Tel (0232) 489 69 44
Housed inside a historic customs office designed by Gustave Eiffel, Mezzaluna is a good chain restaurant offering delicious and authentic Italian food. Try the gnocchi and veal carpaccio served with fresh arugula

İZMIR: Deniz Restaurant ₺₺₺
Seafood
Izmir Palas Hotel, Atatürk Cad 188, Alsancak
Tel (0232) 464 44 99
This long-standing seafood joint is much favoured by locals for its succulent fish dishes, *mezes* and refined atmosphere. Reservations are essential for Friday and Saturday evenings.

İZMIR: Körfez Restaurant ₺₺₺
Seafood
Atatürk Cad 182/A 1, Kordon, 35200
Tel (0232) 421 01 90
Upscale, elegant and famous establishment. Sample the grouper, slowly cooked in a thick layer of salt. There is a great selection of starters and a wide range of desserts on offer, too.

KARACASU: Anatolia Restaurant ₺
Regional
Geyre Köyü, Karacasu, 09385
Tel (0256) 448 81 38
Anatolia feels like an oasis as it houses a lush garden of flowers. Waiters present beautifully prepared dishes in large trays. Located very near to the ancient city of Aphrodisias.

Key to Price Guide *see p346*

KÜÇÜKKUYU ADATEPE KÖYÜ: Dut Dibi Kahvesi ₺
Café
Adatepe Köyü, 17980
Tel (0286) 752 65 37
Situated in the centre of sleepy Adatepe village, this is a typical village café serving *mantı* (dumplings), *gözleme* (stuffed wrap), tea and *ayran* (yogurt drink). A casual and refreshing outdoor setting.

KUŞADASI: Antepli Restaurant ₺₺
Kebab/Southeast Anatolian
Akyar Mevki Ege Vista Alış Veriş Merkezi 4/4, 09400
Tel (0256) 618 10 08
The chef at Antepli, located slightly away from the centre of Kuşadası, makes delicious pistachio kebabs, cooked on a skewer.

KUŞADASI: Ayhan Usta Restaurant ₺₺
Turkish/Seafood
Setur Marina, 09460
Tel (0256) 618 04 59
Amazing views of the marina and Aegean Sea accompany the great mix of seafood and succulent kebabs. Fresh *mezes* are prepared daily.

KUŞADASI: Kazım Usta Restaurant ₺₺₺
Seafood
Liman Cad 4, 09400
Tel (0256) 614 12 26
Select delicious seafood from a refrigerated counter or choose from a wide array of *meze*. The outdoor seating area is found under a lovely canopy of green vines.

PAMUKKALE: Ece Restaurant ₺
Turkish
Karahayıt Village, 20290
Tel (0258) 271 45 02
A short walk from most hotels in Pamukkale, this is a good budget choice. Choose potato, spinach or cheese filling with home-made *gözleme* (stuffed wrap).

PAMUKKALE: Kayas Restaurant ₺
Kebab
Atatürk Cad 3, 20280
Tel (0258) 272 29 35
Centrally located restaurant with friendly staff and service. Go for *köfte* (meatballs) and şiş kebab.

PAMUKKALE: Yörük Evi Restaurant ₺
Turkish
Karahayıt Village, Atatürk Cad, 20180
Tel (0258) 271 42 43
Gözleme (stuffed wrap) is the main dish here, with a choice of fillings. They also have *saç kavurma* (diced lamb cooked on an iron plate).

SELÇUK: Petek Çöp Şiş ₺
Kebab
Atatürk Cad, Selçuk Devlet Hastanesi Karşısı, 35920
Tel (0232) 892 40 77
The local delicacy here is *çöp şiş* – small pieces of lean lamb grilled on tiny wood chops, served with grilled tomatoes, peppers and rice.

SELÇUK: Artemis Restaurant ₺₺
Aegean
Şirince Village, 35920
Tel (0232) 898 32 40
Wine house producing grape and fruit wines. There is a cheese- and wine-tasting table in the garden.

TIRE: Kaplan Dağ Restaurant ₺
Aegean
Kaplan Köy, 35900
Tel (0232) 512 66 52
Good vegetarian restaurant offering *keşkek* (a beaten wheat and meat dish served at traditional weddings).

TROY: Hisarlık Restaurant ₺
Lokanta
Truva Sit Alanı Girişi, Tevfikiye Köyü, 17060, Çanakkale
Tel (0542) 243 93 59
Casual place with fresh Turkish food. The only restaurant before the entrance of the ancient city of Troy. The owner is known to be the best tour guide of Troy.

Kazım Usta Restaurant in Kuşadasi, a haven for seafood lovers

Innovative setting at Kaplan Dağ Restaurant, Tire

Mediterranean Turkey

ADANA: Yüzevler Kebap ₺₺
Kebab
Ziyapaşa Bulvarı Kurtuluş Mah, Yüzevler Apt 25, Seyhan, 01030
Tel (0322) 454 75 13
Savour mouthwatering *beyti* kebab (meat on a skewer) or go for the sizzling Adana-style kebab with garlic served in *pide* and with yogurt. Fine service.

ADANA: Fondragonpearl Restaurant ₺₺₺
Chinese
Hilton Hotel, Sinanpasa Mah, Haci Sabanci Bul, 01180
Tel (0322) 355 50 00
Chic restaurant serving excellent Chinese food – the style here is mainly Cantonese. Do not miss the sweet and sour chicken.

ALANYA: Red Tower Brewery and Restaurant ₺₺
International
Iskele Cad 80
Tel (0242) 513 66 64
Sample a range of traditional Turkish dishes and international spread including pastas and pizzas. Great views, sushi bar, live music and decent beer brewed on site.

ALANYA: Harbour Restaurant ₺₺₺
Seafood
Rıhtım Cad, İskele Meydanı, Kızıl Kule yanı, 07400
Tel (0242) 512 10 19
A local favourite, with a wide choice of seafood prepared by experienced chefs. Reservations are recommended, especially at weekends.

For more information on types of restaurants *see p340–41*

ANTAKYA: Anadolu Restaurant ₺
Southeast Anatolian
Hürriyet Cad 30/A, 31070
Tel (0326) 215 33 35
Try hummus, oregano or pepper salad with walnuts. The more adventurous can try *mumbar* – sheep intestines stuffed with rice, onions and herbs.

ANTAKYA: Sultan Sofrası ₺
Southeast Anatolian
İstiklal Cad 20/A, 31000
Tel (0326) 213 87 59
Very popular restaurant serving flavourful fare such as *kabak borani* – a zucchini dish with chick-peas, diced veal, onion, garlic and peppermint. Or sample delicious *semirsek* (a savoury pastry).

ANTALYA: Castle Restaurant ₺₺
Turkish/International
Hıdırlık Kulesi Sokak 75, Kaleiçi, 07040
Tel (0242) 248 65 94
Located on the cliff-edge next to a Roman watch-tower, offering fantastic sunset views, the food mixes Turkish and international classics, all lovingly prepared.

ANTALYA:
Stella's Manzara Restaurant ₺₺
Mediterranean
Eski Lara Yolu, 40 07230
Tel (0242) 316 35 96
A former Italian trattoria and now a glorious Mediterranean restaurant. Great service, menu and wine.

DK Choice

ANTALYA: 7 Mehmet ₺₺₺
Kebab/Seafood
Atatürk Kültür Parkı 201, 07200
Tel (0242) 238 52 00
Located west of the city centre, 7 Mehmet has been the most prominent local restaurant of Antalya for a number of generations. The daily *mezes* are exceptionally good, as is the tandoori lamb and the salad with avocado and plum. Both indoor and outdoor dining options are available. Great place for families.

ANTALYA:
Seraser Restaurant ₺₺₺
International
Tuzcular Mah, Karanlık Sok 18, 07100
Tel (0242) 247 60 15
Set in a historic building with indoor and outdoor seating, Seraser boasts exceptional service. Avocado salad, quail, mussels, beef carpaccio, salmon quartet and rum baba all stand out.

DALYAN: Saki ₺
Turkish
Gülpınar Mah. Geçit Sokak 21, 48840
Tel (0541) 284 52 12
Saki is a great value place in the heart of the town. Located on the river, it overlooks ancient Kaunos. There is no formal menu, but there are plenty of freshly prepared starters to choose from, as well as tender meat dishes.

DALYAN: Gel Gör Restaurant ₺₺
Seafood
Maraş Mah, Dalko Çarşısı, 48840
Tel (0252) 284 50 09
A great place that benefits from its quiet location by the river, on the outskirts of town. Choose from a staggering menu of 50 types of starters and wild or farmed fish mains.

DALYAN: Ramazan Han ₺₺
Turkish/International
Maraş Cad, Çarşı İçi, 48840
Tel (0252) 284 41 83
A wide variety of starters, main courses and desserts feature on the menu here. Relish the *Incik* kebab (lamb with vegetables); a popular draw. There is a special menu for children.

FETHIYE: Alarga Restaurant ₺₺
Turkish/International
Yat Limanı 17, 48300
Tel (0252) 601 00 00
Located just opposite the marina, Alarga is one of the few restaurants with a clear view of the Fethiye gulf. Tuck into the delicious swordfish kebab while enjoying beautiful sunset views.

Inviting, peaceful ambience of Stella's Manzara Restaurant, Antalya

DK Choice

FETHIYE: Balıkçılar Hali (Fish Market) ₺₺
Seafood
Balıkçılar Hali 46, 48300
Tel (0252) 612 28 06
For a different dining experience head to this famous fish market set in an atrium surrounded by restaurants. Buy the fish from the marble slab at the centre and have the fishermen clean and deliver it to a particular restaurant to be cooked to your liking. Usually there are 30 kinds of fish and 40 kinds of shellfish to choose from.

FETHIYE: Ocakbaşı İskele Restaurant ₺₺
Kebab/Seafood
Fevzi Çakmak Cad, Karagözler, 48300
Tel (0252) 614 94 23
On the harbour, just in front of the ancient theatre by the marina, this is one of the best local restaurants for kebabs and seafood.

GÖCEK:
Blue Restaurant & Bar ₺₺
International
Turgut Özal Bulv, 48310
Tel (0252) 645 17 42
A trendy bar and restaurant frequented by yacht owners. Sample seafood, Turkish and international dishes, from pizzas and burgers to wholesome dinners.

GÖCEK: Upper Deck ₺₺
Seafood/International
Büngüş Koyu, Club Marina, 48310
Tel (0252) 645 14 56
Good food at a beautiful waterfront location, with tables set out on the jetty. There is also a private beach for guests. Extensive menu to choose from.

GÖCEK:
The Galley Restaurant ₺₺₺
Turkish/International
Port Göcek Marina, 48310
Tel (0252) 645 25 35
Owned and run by famous chef Uğur Vata, who also has a restaurant in the UK. Delicious food, a relaxed and informal atmosphere and amazing views.

KALKAN: Iso's Kitchen ₺
Turkish/Seafood
Süleyman Yıldız Cad 39, 07960
Tel (0242) 844 24 15
Excellent value for this expensive resort. The standard Turkish fare includes great starters and grills. Set in an atmospheric old Greek house with beautiful sea views from the terrace.

Key to Price Guide *see p346*

The beautiful beach location of Buzz Grill & Beach Bar, Ölü Deniz

KALKAN: Korsan Balık ₺
Seafood
Atatürk Cad, 07960
Tel (0242) 844 36 22
Arguably one of the best places in town for a traditional fish meal made with fresh catch of the day. It offers delicious *mezes*, a decent selection of wines, along with good sea views.

KALKAN: Aubergine Restaurant ₺₺
International
Yalıboyu Mah 25–27, 07960
Tel (0242) 844 33 32
With a lovely harbourside location and great ambience, Aubergine offers a memorable dining experience. Chef's specials include wild boar and stuffed sea bass. Excellent wine menu.

KAŞ: Bi Lokma ₺
Turkish
Hükümet Cad 20, 07580
Tel (0242) 836 39 42
Bi Lokma means "one bite" in Turkish. It is a small family-owned restaurant serving tasty food and refreshing lemonade.

KAŞ: Hayta Meyhane ₺
Meyhane
Zumrut Sok 5, Merkez, 07580
Tel (0242) 836 37 76
Low-key *meyhane* in which the starters and *raki* (aniseed-flavoured apéritif) are as important as the grilled mains. Lovely old Greek house setting.

KAŞ: Mercan Restaurant ₺₺
Seafood
Balıkçı Barınağı Marina, 07580
Tel (0242) 836 12 09
An exceptionally clean restaurant with great sea views. Offers an array of fresh fish and other seafood dishes. The portions are huge, so bring an appetite.

KAYAKÖY: Çin Bal Restaurant ₺₺
Turkish
Kayaköy, 48300
Tel (0252) 618 00 06
Choose your own piece of lamb or fish and have it grilled over charcoal. Dine at shady outdoor tables in summer or inside with the roaring log fire in winter.

KAYAKÖY: Levissi ₺₺
Turkish
Kayaköy, 48300
Tel (0535) 275 01 73
Set in a restored period Greek property at the foot of the ghost town, this is an atmospheric dining spot. Lovely terrace and a log fire inside on cooler days.

MERSIN: 20. Cadde ₺₺
International
Adnan Menderes Bulvarı, Mersin 33200
Tel (0324) 330 00 60
This lively venue hosts meetings of Mersin's Gourmet Club. Delicious *mezes* can make a whole meal – stuffed dried aubergine (eggplant) and salads served with pomegranate molasses are regional specialties.

MERSIN: Big Chef's ₺₺
International
Adnan Menderes Bulv, Mersin Marinası, 33140
Tel (0324) 330 02 30
A local chain that has become incredibly popular with its trendy decor, a varied menu and good service. Fabulous choice of home-made breads, as well as olive oil and wines.

MERSIN: İskele Marin Restaurant ₺₺
Seafood
Adnan Menderes Bulv, Mersin Marinası, 33160
Tel (0324) 330 00 55
An elegant seafront restaurant. White grouper is a popular main, while the semolina pudding with ice cream makes a fine ending to a delicious Mediterranean meal.

ÖLÜ DENIZ: Buzz Grill & Beach Bar ₺₺
International
Ölüdeniz Sahil Fethiye Muğla, 48300
Tel (0252) 617 05 26
A renowned bar and arguably one of the world's most attractive dining establishments. Wraps, paninis, margaritas and ice cream cocktails are available and can all be enjoyed on the atmospheric outdoor rooftop deck.

ÖLÜ DENIZ: Sultan Ahmet Restaurant ₺₺
Turkish/ International
Çarşı Cad, Belceğiz
Tel (0546) 267 50 30
An extensive menu which includes pizzas, kebabs, fresh seafood and traditional Turkish dishes such as *lavaş* (puffy bread).

SAKLIKENT: Paradise Park ₺
Turkish/Italian
Fethiye Muğla, 48300
Tel (0252) 659 02 03
Tasty omelettes, salads, pastas and pizzas line the varied menu at Paradise Park. This restaurant proves to be a great base for hikers and rafters.

SIDE: Ocakbaşı Restaurant ₺₺
Kebab
Zambak Sok 8, 07600
Tel (0242) 753 18 10
For finely prepared kebabs grilled over charcoal right in front of you, this is *the* place. It is right in the heart of the Old Town and is good value compared to Side's frequently overpriced restaurants.

For more information on types of restaurants *see p340–41*

TARSUS: Şelale Restaurant ₺
Southeast Anatolian
Şelale Mevki, 33640
Tel (0324) 624 80 10
Just a short drive from the city centre, this eatery enjoys lovely views of Tarsus waterfall. Serves rich local delicacies such as *künefe* (a shredded wheat dessert with unsalted cheese) and hummus.

Ankara and Western Anatolia

AFYON: İkbal Lokantası ₺₺
Turkish
Uzun Çarşı 21, 3200
Tel (0272) 215 12 05
This venerable place is a local institution famed for its grills, home-produced spiced sausage and desserts topped with the local buffalo-milk clotted cream.

AFYON: Meşhur Aşçı Bacaksız ₺₺
Kebab
Karaman Mah, Yeni Saraçlar Çarşısı 6
Tel (0272) 215 20 97
Late 19th-century restaurant that specializes in kebabs and lamb roasted to tender perfection in a traditional tandoor oven.

ANKARA: Beykoz Restaurant ₺
Turkish
Hoşdere Cad 193/A, Y Ayrancı, 06550
Tel (0312) 442 68 68
The ideal restaurant for wholesome Turkish food. Savour tripe soup, cooked in broth with garlic and dressed with vinegar and lemon. The menu is seasonal but includes a wide variety of vegetables, stews and kebabs.

DK Choice

ANKARA: Boğaziçi Lokantası ₺
Lokanta
Ulus, Denizciler Cad 1/A, 06240
Tel (0312) 311 88 32
Since the 1950s, this has been the prime choice for Turkish cuisine in Ankara. The restaurant has a long menu, and each dish is as good as the other. Try the lamb shanks with aubergine (eggplant), lamb chops or go for Ankara *tava* with rice.

ANKARA: Çiftlik Merkez Lokantası ₺
Lokanta
Emniyet Mah, AOÇ, 06560
Tel (0312) 211 02 20
A locals' and expats' secret. Some of the tasty specials include chicken stuffed with spicy rice, and aubergine (eggplant) purée with yogurt served with seasoned ground meat.

ANKARA: Tavacı Recep Usta ₺
Southeast Anatolian
Dikmen Vadisi Hoşdere Girişi 5, Kapı Çankaya, 06540
Tel (0312) 442 29 45
Welcoming eatery offering such fare as stuffed lamb ribs served in a bed of pilaf cooked with onions – a rare dish to find. The stuffed turkey is also particularly well prepared.

ANKARA: Uludağ Kebapçısı ₺
Kebab
Altındağ, Denizciler Cad 54, 06240
Tel (0312) 309 04 00
Excellent *döner* kebabs in the historic centre of Ankara. Mushroom pilaf rice, slow roasted lamb shanks and Turkish coffee slowly cooked in a bed of hot sand are specialties.

ANKARA: Çiçek Lokantası ₺₺
Turkish
2176 Sok, Söğütözü, 06510
Tel (0312) 284 08 88
Fresh meat and vegetable dishes cooked in a traditional Ankara wok-like pan. Both indoor and outdoor dining available.

ANKARA: Gar Lokantası ₺₺
Turkish
Filistin Sok 35, Gaziosmanpaşa, 06700
Tel (0312) 447 29 96
Lively restaurant in a trendy and upmarket neighbourhood. Try the lamb roast, rolled cabbage leaves or monkfish. Popular with locals.

ANKARA: Kınacızade Konağı ₺₺
Turkish
Kale Mah Kalekapısı Sok 28, 06240
Tel (0312) 324 57 14
Tasty cuisine in a beautifully restored Ottoman period house. A great spot for breakfast, lunch or dinner.

The exterior of the Ottoman house where Kınacızade Konağı is located, Ankara

BEYŞEHIR: Beyatik Restaurant ₺
Turkish
Hacı Armağan Mah, Orman İşletmesi Karşısı, Vuslat Park yanı, 42700
Tel (0332) 512 91 77
This spacious restaurant has a large garden. Choose from traditional dishes such as fried carp, crayfish and other lake products. Good selection of desserts as well. Popular venue for local events.

BEYŞEHIR: Yusuf Ustanın Yeri ₺
Turkish
Hacı Armağan Mah, Köprübaşı Cad 53, 42700
Tel (0332) 512 54 47
Simple, no-frills restaurant offering a choice of stews and home-made dishes. This place remains one of the most prominent dining establishments in town. No alcohol is served.

EĞIRDIR: Derya Restaurant ₺
Turkish
Cami Mah 1, Sok 1, 32500
Tel (0246) 311 40 47
A spacious restaurant on the north shore of the peninsula, with amazing mountain and lake views. Don't miss the lake fish stews. Friendly, attentive service.

EĞIRDIR: Pehlivan Restaurant ₺
Turkish
Yeşil Ada Mah Kilise Arkası 18
Tel (0246) 311 58 81
Set on a quiet northeast corner of the island, this simple place serves up delicious *gözleme* (stuffed wraps) for lunch, and fish and meat grills in the evening. Generous portions. No alcohol.

ESKIŞEHIR: Mezze Restaurant ₺
Seafood
Kızılcıklı Mahmut Pehlivan Cad, Nazım Hikmet Sok 2, 26060
Tel (0222) 230 30 09
A wide array of *mezes* to choose from and full fish dinners; the grilled fish is a must. Octopus and prawns are other house specialities. Service is good, but it can get crowded, so reserve in advance.

ESKIŞEHIR: 222 Park Club and Restaurants ₺₺
International
Hoşnudiye Mah, İsmet İnönü-1, Cad 103, 26130
Tel (0222) 320 11 11
Trendy complex of clubs and eateries, including an excellent grill restaurant, an American restaurant and a wine house. Attracts a younger crowd.

Key to Price Guide *see p346*

ESKIŞEHIR: Ada Cafe ₺₺
International
Kentpark, 26000
Tel (0222) 217 72 73
An elegant restaurant located on an island on the Porsuk river. Great food – from hearty breakfasts to wholesome dinners. There is a choice of crêpes, juicy steaks, schnitzel, kebabs and *mezes*.

ESKIŞEHIR: Sempre Restaurant ₺₺
Italian
Gaffar Okkan Cad, Pehlivanlar Sok 11, 26120
Tel (0222) 221 04 31
A popular Italian restaurant attracting mainly university students and professors. It has a garden and, frequently, live music on weekends during the spring and summer months.

GÖLBAŞI: Beykoz Gölbaşı ₺
Kebab
Haymana yolu 105, Karşıyaka Mah, 06830
Tel (0312) 484 44 46
This eatery acts as a tranquil escape destination for locals. The house speciality is *kuzu tandır* – lamb slow-cooked inside an earthenware pit in the ground.

GÖLBAŞI: Şövalye Restaurant ₺
International
Karşıyaka Mah, Sahil Cad 392, Sok 3
Tel (0312) 484 27 64
Locals flock to this popular eatery in a peaceful riverside location. The recipes here have a French touch. There's an excellent selection of wines.

GÖLBAŞI: Chez Le Belge ₺₺₺
Belgian
Sahil Cad 24, 06830
Tel (0312) 484 14 78
Situated by Mogan Lake, this fine establishment has been in business since the 1980s. Crayfish dishes are its signature offering. Good wine selection.

ISPARTA: Doğu Karadeniz Pide & Kebab ₺
Turkish/Regional
Ziraat Bankası yanı, Valilik Karşısı 1, 32100
Tel (0246) 212 15 19
This establishment specializes in Black-Sea-style *pides* (Turkish pizza) and grills, all enriched with butter. The best is *kavurmalı pide*, for which *kavurma* (dried mutton) is stewed in its own juice for 12–14 hours.

A chef serving tasty Turkish food at Çiçek Lokantası, Ankara *(see p356)*

ISPARTA: Özsüt ₺
Turkish
İstasyon Cad 23, Çağlar Ap, 32100
Mimar Sinan Cad 38, 32100
Tel (0246) 223 16 83
Part of a nationwide chain that originally served only desserts, this restaurant now offers a wide choice of soups, salads and grills in addition to delicious French- and Russian-style cakes.

ISPARTA: Etopia Restaurant ₺₺
Turkish
İstanbul Cad, Toptancılar Sitesi 3, Blok 3, 32200
Tel (0246) 228 52 28
A meat lover's paradise. Specialities include meatballs with raisins, marinated T-bone steak and roast beef with puréed vegetables.

KONYA: Cemo Etli Ekmek ₺
Central Anatolian
Turkuaz İş Merkezi Selçuklu, 42060
Tel (0332) 249 66 66
Sample a Konya trademark, the *etli ekmek* – hand-chopped pieces of lamb or beef on a thin *pide* bread with tomatoes and onions. The restaurant also serves the usual grilled meat options.

KONYA: Hacı Şükrü ₺
Central Anatolian
Devricedid Mah, Cem Sultan Cad 327/A, 42000
Tel (0332) 352 76 23
Visit Hacı Şükrü to try the *tandır kebabı* – the city's famous lamb tandoori cooked in an earthen pit for several hours. Traditionally the dish is eaten directly by hand, but the restaurant does provide cutlery on request.

KONYA: Havzan Etli Ekmek ₺
Central Anatolian
Musalla Bağları Telgrafçı, Hamdibey Cad 8/A, 42060
Tel (0332) 236 14 14
Sample an interesting version of *etli ekmek* (Turkish-style pizza) laced with oregano or plain cheese. Also try the refreshing beet juice.

KONYA: Köşk Restaurant ₺
Central Anatolian/Turkish
Akçeşme Mah, Topraklık Cad 66, 42100
Tel (0332) 352 85 47
Set in an historic 19th-century house, this restaurant has lots of local delicacies, including okra stew, which is a regional favourite. The honey and vinegar sherbet is delicious.

KONYA: Gül Bahçe ₺₺
Central Anatolian
Mevlana Külliyesi yanı, Karatay, 42010
Tel (0332) 353 07 68
Located next to the Mevlâna Museum, this restaurant serves excellent local Konya dishes. The grills, kebabs and oven-baked lamb are all tender and tasty. There are great views over the beautiful and peaceful Mevlana.

KÜTAHYA: Antepli Seyfi ₺
Southeast Anatolian
Cumhuriyet Cad 23, 43000
Tel (0274) 216 43 26
Gorge on aubergine and pistachio kebabs, *künefe* (a shredded wheat dessert with cheese), and *baklava* (sweet pastry), along with yogurt drinks and *şalgam suyu* (beet juice).

KÜTAHYA: Güral Sofrası ₺
Turkish
Perli Mah, Eskişehir Kütahya yolu, 43000
Tel (0274) 225 06 06
A wide selection of scrumptious Turkish dishes is available at this friendly restaurant owned and operated by the people behind the leading porcelain brand of Turkey. You can buy porcelain from the nearby shop.

For more information on types of restaurants *see p340–41*

KÜTAHYA: Ispartalılar Konağı ₺
Turkish
Pirler Mah, Germiyan Cad 58, 43000
Tel (0274) 216 19 75
Housed in a restored period dwelling, this atmospheric place serves up standard Turkish fare such as *tutmaç* (green lentil soup) and *cimcik* (local *farfalle* served with a yogurt dressing).

KÜTAHYA: Konağ ₺
Turkish
Kurşunlu Sok 13
Tel (0274) 223 88 44
Delightfully located in a converted Ottoman Turkish house, this great place features traditional favourites, including heart-warming stews and desserts such as figs stewed in milk. No alcohol.

POLATLI: Kanca Lokantası ₺
Lokanta
Cumhuriyet Mah, Bozkurt Cad, Ünal Ap 57, 06900
Tel (0312) 621 38 96
Relish wholesome Turkish home food. One of Turkey's most popular dishes, lima bean soup, is cooked beautifully here. This delicious soup, with tomato paste and veal, is served with pilaf rice.

POLATLI: Kebap 49 ₺
Kebab
Cumhuriyet Mah, Sümer Cad 48
Tel (0312) 623 69 70
A good choice for those going on a daily excursion to the ancient city of Gordion. Expect standard Turkish fare such as kebabs and *pides*. Delicious food at reasonable prices.

The Black Sea

AMASRA: Canlı Balık ₺
Seafood
Küçük Liman Cad 8, 74300
Tel (0378) 315 26 06
Fresh flowers decorate tables at this elegant, waterfront restaurant. The salad made with 29 different herbs and vegetables is a popular draw. Interesting selection of desserts too – try the yogurt with honey and hazelnuts

AMASRA: Sahil Balık ₺₺
Seafood
Küçük Liman Cad15, 74300
Tel (0378) 315 34 65
The menu in the café area features omelettes, sandwiches and simple *mezes*, while the main restaurant offers a haven for seafood lovers with its extensive variety of dishes.

The informal, simple interior of Koru Restaurant, Artvin

ARTVIN: Bizim Döner ve Köfte Salonu ₺
Kebab
İnönü Cad 77/C, 08000
Tel (0466) 212 15 51
Super kebabs and lamb specialities. Sometimes they also serve *baklava* (sweet pastry) or *kadayif* (a shredded wheat dessert). Lunch usually runs out by mid-afternoon, so come early.

ARTVIN: Koru Restaurant ₺
Northeast Anatolian
Koru Hotel Yeni Mah 19, Mayıs Cad, 08000
Tel (0466) 212 65 65
Sizzling grills and local delicacies are on the menu at Koru, such as *kuymak* (local fondue with cheese, butter and cornflour) and *silor* (a crispy *meze* made with filo, yogurt and butter).

ÇAMLIHEMŞIN: Osmanlı Restaurant ₺
The Black Sea
Ayder Yolu üzeri, Tarihi Köprü yanı Hoşdere Köyü Ardeşen, 53400
Tel (0464) 752 42 23
En route to the Ayder plateau, this is mostly a seasonal restaurant serving hikers in summer. A delicious range of Black Sea dishes, not forgetting wonderfully cooked farm-raised trout.

ÇAMLIHEMŞIN: Yeşil Vadi Restaurant ₺
The Black Sea
Merkez Mah, 53750
Tel (0464) 651 72 82
A spectacular location over the Fırtına River at the end of the valley. Sample traditional corn-bread, *muhlama* (local fondue) and collard greens – the basis of their menu.

ÇAYELI: Hüsrev Lokantası ₺
The Black Sea
Çayeli çıkışı, Hopa istikameti, Karayolu Üzeri, 53200
Tel (0464) 532 70 37
The restaurant advertises itself as the "master of beans". Serves a rich selection of Black Sea cuisine. Ask for the cannellini bean soup prepared with diced beef, which this establishment is renowned for.

HOPA: Terzioğlu Restaurant ₺
The Black Sea
Sundura Mah, Rize Cad 27, 08600
Tel (0466) 351 51 11
Located in the Terzioğ lu Hotel close to the shore, this place is one of the few restaurants in Hopa. Come here to try the famous anchovy rice pilaf and sweet *laz böreği* (pastry with peppers). Great service.

KASTAMONU: Münire Sultan Sofrası ₺
Regional
Hepkebirler Mah, Fevzi Efendi Cad, Münire Medresesi girişi, 37100
Tel (0366) 214 96 66
Housed inside a *madrassa* built in 1746, this restaurant serves delectable local fare. Order the *tirit* (bread rolls dipped in grape molasses) or savour the tasty broth with ground beef, garlic, yogurt and butter.

DK Choice

MAÇKA: Coşandere Tesisleri ₺
The Black Sea
Sümela Yolu Üzeri 5km, Coşandere Köyü, 61750
Tel (0462) 531 11 90
A rustic restaurant on the way to Sumela Monastery by the Coşandere River. Don't let the simple interior of the venue dissuade you from dining here. The menu features delicious trout, rice pudding, *kuymak* (local fondue with cheese, butter and cornflour) and stuffed collard greens. There is a good selection of desserts on offer. They also organize local tours to the monastery and nearby uplands.

RIZE: Evvel Zaman Yöresel Yemek Lokantası ₺
The Black Sea
Piri Çelebi Mah, Şeyh Cami Arkası Eski Rize Evi, 53100
Tel (0464) 212 21 88
A lovely restaurant set in a historic house at the centre of town, offering traditional

Black Sea cuisine, which includes *laz böreği* (pastry with peppers).

SAFRANBOLU:
Kadıoğlu Şehzade Sofrası ₺
Turkish
Arasta Sok 8, 78600
Tel (0370) 712 56 57
Excellent *pides* and soups are served in a traditional home. The town name comes from the rare plant of the region, saffron – used in the preparation of the exquisite *zerde* (rice pudding).

SAFRANBOLU:
Havuzlu Köşk ₺₺
Turkish
Dibekönü Cad 32, Bağlar, 78600
Tel (0370) 725 21 68
With tables placed around a small pool in the atrium, this intimate eatery has consistent service and focuses on traditional meat dishes.

SAFRANBOLU:
Taş Ev Sanat ve Şarap Evi ₺₺
International
Baba Sultan Mah, Hidirlik Yokusu 14, 78600
Tel (0370) 725 53 00
Popular wine bar and restaurant set in a historic stone house. It offers steaks, salads, pastas, and cheeses from Kars.

SAMSUN:
Venn Café & Bistro ₺₺
International
Cumhuriyet Mah, Adnan Menderes Bulv 325, 55200
Tel (0362) 407 00 01
Housed in the Venn boutique hotel, this place has a wide choice of international dishes. The service is attentive and the views are good. Look out for the weekly specials.

TRABZON:
Ustad Lokantasi ₺
Lokanta
Atatürk Alanı 18
Tel (0462) 321 54 06
Small *lokanta* overlooking Trabzon's noisy but atmospheric central square. It dishes up traditional staples, including white bean stews, lentil soup, meatballs and kebabs.

TRABZON: Bey Konağı ₺₺
The Black Sea
Sahil Yolu Üzeri Bölge Trafiğe 300m Akyazı Beldes, 61195
Tel (0462) 273 25 14
Great place to sample Black Sea cuisine and seafood. Choose from a variety of anchovy dishes and vegetable specials made with collard greens.

Diners feasting on superb seafood in the restaurant at Sahil Balık, Amasra

TRABZON:
Süleyman Restaurant ₺₺
Seafood/Kebab
Devlet Sahil Yolu Cad, Forum AVM, 61100
Tel (0462) 330 03 64
An upscale restaurant with a wide range of *mezes* and wines. There is occasional live music at the bar.

UZUNGÖL:
İnan Kardeşler Restaurant ₺
Regional
In Uzungöl village, 61960
Tel (0462) 656 62 97
Rustic restaurant part of the İnan Kardeşler Hotel. Try the rare *benekli alabalık* (fried brown trout cooked with tomato and peppers).

YUSUFELI:
Hacıoğlu Cağ Döner Salonu ₺
Kebab
İnönü Cad, 08800
Tel (0466) 811 36 31
The *çağ* kebab – a döner kebab skewered over a charcoal fire – is the only option here. Shepherd's salad or aubergine salad are good accompaniments to this dish.

YUSUFELI:
Yusufeli Saray Lokantası ₺
Lokanta
Halitpaşa Cad 11, 08800
Tel (0466) 811 28 16
The restaurant is close to the Çoruh River, the mecca of river-rafters. Tasty, nourishing fare such as lentil soup, cannellini beans, rice pilaf and shepherd's salad.

Cappadocia and Central Anatolia

AMASYA:
Ali Kaya Restaurant ₺
Kebab
Çakallar Mevkii, Amasya Merkez, 05100
Tel (0358) 218 13 16
Relish a mixed kebab platter while enjoying views of the river valley, mountains and the rock-cut tombs of the Pontic kings. Lamb and aubergine kebab is the signature dish.

AMASYA:
Amasya Şehir Restaurant ₺₺
Kebab
Hatuniye Mah, H Teyfik Hafız Sok 1, 05100
Tel (0358) 218 10 13
Do not miss the *baklalı dolma* (rolled grape leaves stuffed with fava beans and wheat) here. Positioned on the banks of the Yeşilırmak.

BOĞAZKALE:
Aşıkoğlu Restaurant ₺
Turkish
Before the entrance of Hattuşaş city gate, 19310
Tel (0364) 452 20 04
Located near the capital city of the ancient Hittites, this is a spacious refectory-style cafeteria with self service. Phone ahead if you want to try the delicious grilled quail.

The dining area at Coşandere Tesisleri, Maçka

For more information on types of restaurants *see p340–41*

BELISIRMA: Belisırma ₺
Turkish
Ihlara Vadisi, Belisırma Köyü, 68570
Tel (0382) 457 30 57
A no-frills restaurant with simple but tasty food. The menu has a choice of soups, grills (including trout) and salads.

GÖREME: Dibek ₺
Central Anatolian/Turkish
Meydan Nevşehir, 50180
Tel (0384) 271 22 09
This cave-set restaurant is the place to try *testi* kebab, a tasty meat and vegetable dish stewed in its own juices in a clay pot.

GÖREME: A'la Turca Restaurant ₺₺
Central Anatolian/Turkish/International
Gaferli Mah, Cevizler Sok 6, 50180
Tel (0384) 271 28 82
Highlights include delicious local *zülbiye* (chunks of lamb, pearl onions, tomato and garlic) and *calla* (veal, aubergine, tomato, pepper and garlic).

GÖREME: Cappadocian Cuisine ₺₺
Central Anatolian
Yani Uzundere Caddesi, Göreme, 50180
Tel (0384) 271 27 01
Home cooking at its best makes this the place to try local dishes at reasonable prices. You can watch the chef rustle up the dishes in her own kitchen.

GÜZELYURT: Karballa Restaurant ₺
Turkish
Karballa Hotel, Çarşı içi, Aksaray, 68100
Tel (0382) 451 21 03
The only real restaurant in Güzelyurt, Karballa is located in a former monastery with an impressive barrel-vaulted ceiling. Book ahead.

KAYSERI: Kaşıkla ₺
Turkish
Şeker Mah, Osman Kavuncu Bulv 370, Kocasinan, 38070
Tel (0352) 326 30 75
Feast on delicious *mantı* – the Turkish version of minced meat-filled ravioli, smothered in a rich, creamy yogurt and garlic sauce spiced up with sumac. There are also grills and stews as alternatives.

KAYSERI: Beştepe Restaurant ₺₺
Turkish
Karacaoğlu Mah, Beştepeler Parkı, 38500 Melikgazi
Tel (0352) 347 18 18
This is a revolving restaurant with good views of the city and Mount Erciyes. The menu features local dishes with a focus on seafood. No alcohol.

KIRŞEHİR: Ahi Teras Restaurant ₺
Turkish
Terme Cad 8, 40000
Tel (0386) 214 14 24
Perfect combination of a bakery and restaurant. The café section of Ahi Teras offers *simit* (seeded bread ring) or *poğaça* (Balkan leavened bread).

DK Choice

MUSTAFAPAŞA: Old Greek House ₺₺
Turkish
Mustafapaşa Kasabası, 50420
Tel (0384) 353 53 06
A beautiful 19th-century Greek house with many preserved features. Original frescoes adorn the arches in the main courtyard shaded by grape vines. Enjoy authentic dishes cooked by local chefs. Seating is either at tables in the courtyard, or on cushions around low tables indoors. A very popular place with the locals.

Low tables and cushions in one of the dining areas at the Old Greek House, Mustafapaşa

UÇHİSAR: Café Centrum ₺
International
Belediye Meydanı, 50200
Tel (0384) 219 31 17
Though it looks more like a teahouse, the food at Café Centrum is surprisingly good. Try the vegetable and seafood pasta cooked in a traditional earthenware pot.

UÇHİSAR: Elai Cappadocia ₺₺
International
Tekelli Mah, Eski Göreme Cad, 50240
Tel (0384) 219 31 81
A chic restaurant in sophisticated Uçhisar. The indoor section is a cave and the terrace offers superb views of the valley. The dishes are artfully prepared. Smart dress preferred for dinner.

ÜRGÜP: Dimrit Café & Restaurant ₺₺
Turkish
Yunak Mah, Teyfik Fikret Cad 40, 50400
Tel (0384) 341 85 85
Most main courses at Dimrit have a meat base but they also carry some seafood *mezes* and a fish-of-the-day option. Lemon kebab and *testi* kebab (meat and vegetables cooked in a clay pot) are their specialities.

ÜRGÜP: Han Çırağan Restaurant ₺₺
Turkish/French
Cumhuriyet Meydanı 4, 50400
Tel (0384) 341 25 66
Owned and run by Francophiles settled in Cappadocia. Casual bar downstairs and a fine dining terrace space upstairs. Good cocktails.

ÜRGÜP: Şömine Restaurant ₺₺
Turkish
Cumhuriyet Meydanı 9, 50400
Tel (0384) 341 84 42
This is one of the most popular restaurants in Cappadocia. The menu features kebabs and other Turkish classics.

Eastern Anatolia

DİYARBAKIR: Kaburgacı Selim Amca ₺₺
Southeast Anatolian
Ali Emiri Cad 22/B Merkez
Tel (0412) 224 44 47
The original of a small chain with others in Mardin, Istanbul and Ankara, this place offers superb lamb ribs stuffed with piquant rice pilaf. No alcohol is served.

Key to Price Guide *see p346*

The elegant interior at Cerciş Murat Konağı, Mardin

ERZURUM:
Güzelyurt Restaurant ₺
Turkish
Cumhuriyet Cad 42, 25100
Tel (0442) 234 50 01
This modern restaurant is popular with local businessmen. The menu features excellent *mezes*, kebabs and seafood. Good service.

GAZİANTEP: Imam Çağdaş ₺
Southeast Anatolian
Kale Cıvarı Uzun Çarşısı 49, 27100
Tel (0342) 231 26 78
A long-established place that serves the city's best *lahmacun* (a thin, unleavened bread topped by spicy meat) and *baklava* (sweet pastry), as well as tender kebabs.

GAZİANTEP: Tahmis Kahvesi ₺
Café
Arasa Meydanı Elmacı Pazarı Şahinbey, 27000
Tel (0342) 232 89 77
Beautifully restored 17th-century café serving traditional Turkish coffee. Try *menengiç* coffee, made with roasted pistachios and milk.

GAZİANTEP:
İncilipınar Antep Sofrası ₺₺
Regional
100 Yıl Kültür Parkı İçi, Ulu Cami yanı, 27100
Tel (0342) 234 26 57
Lovely place serving sour wheat balls in broth, *fındık lahmacun* (small, thin pizzas) and pistachio-filled *baklava* (sweet pastry).

KAHRAMANMARAŞ:
Küçük Ev Et Lokantası ₺
Turkish
İsmet Paşa Mah, Borsa Cad 11, 46000
Tel (0344) 223 25 55
Relish traditional stews with vegetables as well as kebabs. Simple setting and good service.

KAHRAMANMARAŞ:
Yaşar Pastanesi ₺
Ice cream
İsmet Paşa Mah, Trabzon Bulv, 27100
Tel (0344) 225 08 08
The original shop of the national chain Mado that popularized beaten ice cream made from goat's milk and roots of wild orchid.

KARS: Hanımeli Lokantası ₺
Regional
Orta Kapı Mah, Ordu Cad 65, 36100
Tel (0474) 212 61 31
Tasty vegetarian fare such as *mantı* (Turkish ravioli) with caramelized onions and *bulgur* (wheat) pilaf with herbs.

KARS: Kars Kaz Evi ₺
Northeast Anatolian
Orta Kapı Mah, Şehit Polis Nuri Yıldız Sok 17, 36100
Tel (0474) 212 37 13
Come here for yogurt soup, goose roast and hot pickled vegetables. Book ahead.

MALATYA: Kaburga Sofrası ₺
Kebab
Cevatpaşa Mah, Karakavak, 44100
Tel (0422) 238 11 35
A no-frills, city-centre eatery specializing in stuffed ribs, kebabs and meat dishes.

The famous *menengiç* coffee at Tahmis Kahvesi, Gaziantep

DK Choice

MARDIN:
Cerciş Murat Konağı ₺₺
Southeast Anatolian
Merkez 1, Cad 517, 47100
Tel (0482) 213 68 41
Housed in a beautifully restored mansion house, this is one of the best restaurants in Eastern Turkey. A trendsetter in excellent and unusual fare, this place offers distinctive dishes that will delight the taste buds. Go for the set menu. Also on offer are unique Syrian Orthodox wines made from endemic Öküzgözü & Boğazakere grapes. Stunning views of the Mesopotamian Plain.

ŞANLIURFA:
Cevahir Konukevi Restaurant ₺
Southeast Anatolian
Büyükyol Cad, Selahaddin Eyyubi Cami Karşısı, 63000
Tel (0414) 215 93 77
Set in a historic building, Cevahir rustles up fiery Urfa dishes using Turkish hot pepper "Isot". Also organizes traditional folk evenings, which are a lot of fun.

ŞANLIURFA: Gülhan ₺
Lokanta
Atatürk Bulvarı, Urfa Merkez, 63200
Tel (0414) 313 33 18
This no-nonsense businessmen's establishment knocks out quality food at bargain prices – everything from hearty stews to soups and kebabs.

VAN: Firavin ₺
Kurdish
Hastane Cad, Urartu Oteli Karşısı
Tel (0432) 216 66 86
Completely run and managed by women, this place specializes in traditional, home-cooked food with a small range of local Kurdish dishes and a greater range of standard Turkish dishes.

VAN: Sütçü Kenan ₺
Breakfast
Cumhuriyet Cad, Kahvaltıcılar Sok 7/A, 65100
Tel (0432) 216 84 99
Enjoy an elaborate breakfast buffet here. Also on offer is the famous Van honey as well as a selection of local cheeses, including some with herbs and some that have been smoked.

SHOPPING IN TURKEY

Even if you are not a shopper by nature, the varied and unusual selection of gifts found in Turkey's markets will easily tempt you. The grand shops and teeming streets of Istanbul are a world away from the ateliers and craft shops of smaller towns in rural areas. Outside Istanbul, you will also find bargaining *(see p134)* a less cut-throat pursuit. However, you are sure to encounter high-pressure sales pitches wherever you travel. The weekly market is a unique aspect of regional shopping. These markets are a holdover from the days of trading caravans, when shops as we know them did not exist. Traders still pay taxes to have a market stall, as they did 400 years ago. And the *zabıta* (municipal market police) still control weights, measures and prices.

Upmarket clothing boutique in Bodrum

Opening Hours

In large cities, shops are usually open from 9am to 7pm or 8pm. But hours can be much extended in tourist and coastal areas, where many shops will stay open until midnight, seven days a week, particularly during the summer months, when the daytime heat discourages all but the most dedicated shoppers. Shopping malls are ubiquitous in most Turkish cities, and are usually open from 10am to 10pm.

In general, opening hours are much more flexible in rural areas. If you find a shop closed, you can ask where the owner is and it will not take long before someone tells him/her that there is a potential customer. Note that some shops may close during Muslim religious holidays.

How to Pay

Most shops that cater to tourists will be happy to accept foreign currency. If you can pay in cash, you can usually get a discount on most goods. Exchange rates are often displayed in shops, and also appear in daily newspapers.

Credit cards are widely accepted for purchases (except in markets and smaller shops), and most vendors do not charge a commission. Visa, MasterCard and American Express are the most common, Diners Club less so. Vendors who accept credit cards may try to tell you that they will not be reimbursed for the transaction for several days, and ask you to pay a small compensatory commission. Resist this, and insist on paying without a commission. It is common for a vendor to ask you to go to the bank with him to draw the money out on your credit card. There is nothing wrong with this, but you will pay interest on your card for a cash advance. Note that very few shops in Turkey now accept travellers' cheques.

In rural markets, you will be expected to pay in cash. Some merchants will happily accept foreign currency.

Merchants in bazaars and markets expect customers to bargain. If you see something you want to buy, offer half the asking price. Increase the offer slightly if the merchant resists. He will then indicate whether he thinks that the bargaining should continue.

VAT Exemption

If you spend at least ₺118 in one shop, you can claim back the 18 per cent VAT (KDV in Turkey). VAT exemption is now widely available – look for the Tax Free Shopping logo displayed in the shop. The retailer gives you a Global Refund Cheque, which you should present to customs officials with your invoices and purchases for a cash refund when leaving Turkey.

Fresh herbs and spices, sold by weight at Kadıköy Market in Istanbul

Locally produced copper and brassware in the old quarter of Safranbolu

Buying Antiques

Before purchasing antique items, it is important to know what can and cannot be taken out of Turkey. The rule is that objects which are over 100 years old may be exported only with a certificate stating their age and granting permission to remove them from the country. Museums issue these certificates, as does the Culture Ministry in Ankara, who will also authenticate the correct age and value of an object, if necessary. The shopkeeper from whom you bought your goods will often know which museum will be authorizing your purchases for export. In theory, a seller should register with a museum all goods that are over 100 years old. In practice, sellers usually only seek permission after a particular item has been sold. In the past, antiques could be removed from Turkey without a certificate. Although this has changed, the export of antiques is not forbidden, as some believe. If the relevant authorities permit your purchase to be exported, you can either take it with you or send it home, whether or not it is over 100 years old. Do take note, however, that taking antiques out of Turkey without proper permission is regarded as smuggling, and is a punishable offence.

Ornate ceramic vase and saucer

Van cats and Kangal dogs are now also included in this category.

How to Send Purchases Home

If you have bought items from a reputable and trustworthy supplier, he or she will have an arrangement with an international courier company who can ship goods to your home address. Try to get your own copy of any shipping documents and an air waybill number. Do not use the post office (PTT) to send such items. Be aware that there are also some disreputable dealers, especially in carpets, who will either substitute an inferior item in place of the one you have bought or who will fail to send the goods. Beware of traders who advise you to ignore official rules.

Sizes and Measures

Turkey uses continental European sizes for clothes and shoes. Food and drink are sold in metric measures.

DIRECTORY

VAT Exemption

Global Refund
Tel (0212) 232 11 21.
W globalblue.com

Antiques

Motif Handicrafts
Şirince Koyü, Selçuk, İzmir.
Tel (0232) 898 30 99.
W motiftr.com

Handicrafts and Gifts

Çeşni Turkish Handicrafts
Tunalı Hilmi Cad, Ertuğ Pasajı 88/44, Ankara.
Tel (0312) 426 57 87.

Gallery Anatolia
Hükümet Cad, Kaş.
Tel (0242) 836 19 54.
W gallery-anatolia.com

Homer Kitapevi
Yeni Çarşısı Cad 28, Beyoğlu, Istanbul. **Tel** (0212) 249 59 02. **W homerbooks.com**

Yörük Collection
Yerebatan Cad 35, Sultanahmet, Istanbul.
Tel (0212) 511 77 66.
W yorukcollection.com

Jewellery

Urart
Abdi Ipekçi Cad 18/1, Nişantaşı, Istanbul.
Tel (0212) 246 71 94.
W urart.com.tr

Carpets/Kilims

Gallery Shirvan
Halıcılar Sok 50–54, Kapalıçarşı (Grand Bazaar) Istanbul.
Tel (0212) 522 49 86.

Istanbul Handicraft Center
Kabasakal Cad 5, Sultanahmet, Istanbul.
Tel (0212) 517 67 48.
W istanbul handicraft center.com

Kaş and Carry
Liman Cad 10, Kaş.
Tel (0242) 836 16 62.
Fax (0242) 836 23 89.

Tribal Collections
Müze Yolu 24/C, Göreme, Nevşehir.
Tel (0384) 271 24 00.
W tribalcollections.net

Hand-worked Copperware

L'Orient
İçbedesten, Şerif Ağa Sok 22–23, Kapalıçarşı (Grand Bazaar), Istanbul.
Tel (0212) 520 70 46.

Linens

Özdilek
Yeni Yalova Yol, Bursa.
Tel (0224) 219 60 00.
W ozdilek.com.tr

Afyon
(on main highway junction of Ankara and Afyon road).
Tel (0272) 252 54 00.

Spices and Herbs

Ayfer Kaun
Mısır Çarşısı (Egyptian Bazaar) 7, Istanbul.
Tel (0212) 522 45 23.

Ucuzcular Kimya Sanayii
Mısır Çarşısı (Egyptian Bazaar) 51, Istanbul.
Tel (0212) 520 64 92.

What to Buy in Turkey

When it comes to shopping, nothing can compare with Istanbul's bustling bazaars, markets, shops and stalls. In contrast, the rural markets have an unhurried feel and unique products that often don't travel much beyond provincial boundaries, such as stout walking sticks made in Devrek (near Zonguldak), ceremonial pipes produced in Sivas and the angora goat-hair bedspreads and rugs made in Siirt. Markets are lively and colourful, and the best places to find handmade items that are produced in small quantities.

Pipes

Classic, beautifully crafted *nargiles* (water pipes) are still widely used in special cafés. They can make very attractive ornaments, even if you do not smoke.

Copper goblets

Copperware

Antique copperware can be very expensive. Newer items, however, are also available, at more affordable prices.

Antique copper water ewer

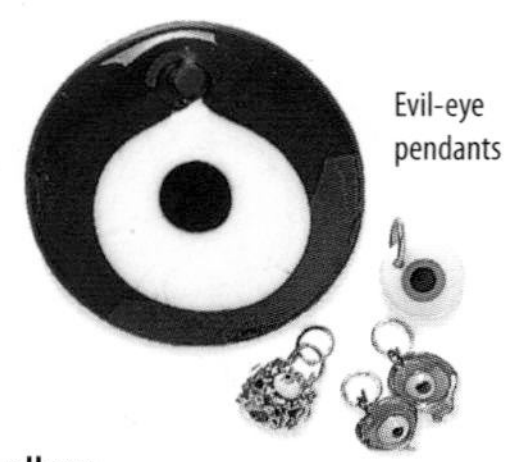

Evil-eye pendants

Jewellery

Turkey produces stunning gold jewellery in original designs. Silver is also popular, and rings and necklaces are often set with precious stones. A simple blue glass eye *(boncuk)* is said to ward off evil.

Box inlaid with mother-of-pearl

Box with painted scenes on bone inlay

Inlaid Wood

Jewellery boxes crafted from wood or bone, and then inlaid or painted, make unusual souvenirs. Backgammon players will be delighted at the delicate, inlaid rosewood backgammon *(tavla)* sets available in markets and shops around Turkey.

Green jugs from Çanakkale

Blue and white decorated ceramic plate

Ceramics

Ceramics are an important artistic tradition. The style varies according to the area of origin. İznik, Kütahya and Çanakkale are famous for ceramic production, but Avanos is also known for hand-painted pottery and porcelain.

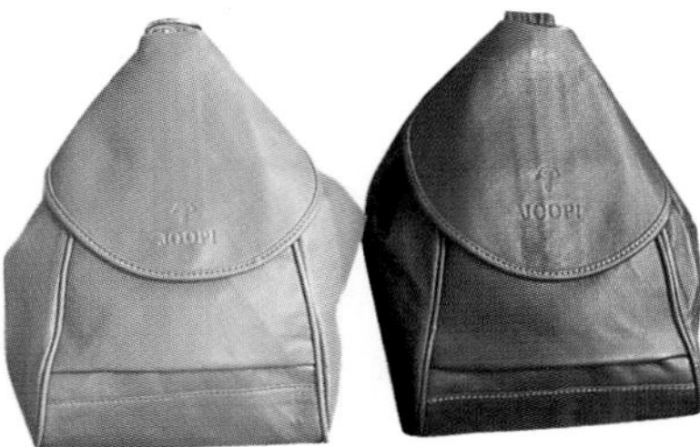

Leather Goods
Shoes, handbags, briefcases and other leather accessories are good buys, as are jackets. For high-fashion, Istanbul is the place. Desa Deri is a good name all over Turkey. For accessories, look for the Matraş or Tergan brands.

Glassware
This elegant lamp is an example of the blue and white striped glassware called *çeşmibülbül*, which is made in the famous Paşabahçe works. The firm makes many utilitarian designs as well as an up-market range in fine lead crystal. Paşabahçe glassware makes a wonderful gift.

Çeşmibülbül lamp

Textiles
Hand-woven cloths, including *ikat* work (where the cotton is dyed as it is woven), and fine embroidery are just some of the range of textiles that can be bought. Turkey is also a leading producer of top-quality garments and knitwear. Bathrobes and towels are of high quality. Look for the Altınyıldız label for finest woollens and fabrics by the metre or yard.

Cotton *ikat* work

Embroidered scarves known as *oyalı*

Hand-printed *yazma* (shawls) from Tokat

Local Delicacies
Delicious sweets such as halva, Turkish delight and baklava are always popular. Many fragrant spices, as well as dried fruit and nuts, are sold loose by weight in most markets and tourist shops throughout Turkey.

Halva

Nuts in honey

Turkish delight

Dried red peppers and aubergines

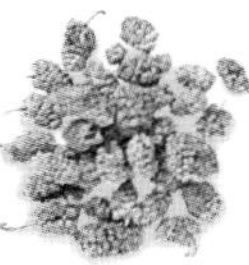

Mulberries

Sunflower and pumpkin seeds

Apricots

Chickpeas

Almonds

Pistachios

Turkish Carpets and Kilims

The ancient skill of weaving rugs has been handed down from generation to generation in Turkey. Rugs were originally made for warmth and decoration in the home, as dowry items for brides, or as donations to mosques. There are two main kinds of rug: carpets *(halı)*, which are knotted, and kilims, which are flat-woven with vertical (warp) and horizontal (weft) threads. Many foreign rugs are sold in Turkey, but those of Turkish origin come in a particularly wide range of attractive colours. Most of the carpets and kilims offered for sale will be new or almost new; antique rugs are rarer and far more expensive.

A carpet may be machine-made or handmade. Fold the face of the rug back on itself: if you can see the base of the knots and the pile cannot be pulled out, it means that it is handmade.

Wool is the usual material for making a rug, although some carpets are made from silk.

Carpet

This reproduction of a 16th-century Uşak carpet is known as a Bellini double entrance prayer rug.

Weaving a Carpet
Wool for rugs is washed, carded, spun and dyed before it is woven. Weaving is a cottage industry in Turkey; rural women often weave in winter, leaving the summer months for farming duties.

Rug-making Areas of Western Turkey

The weaving industry in Turkey is concentrated into several areas of production, listed below. Rug designs are traditional to their tribal origins, resulting in a wide range of designs and enabling a skilled buyer to identify the area of origin.

Carpets

① Hereke
② Çanakkale
③ Ayvacık
④ Bergama
⑤ Yuntdağ
⑥ Balıkesir
⑦ Sındırgı
⑧ Milas
⑨ Antalya
⑩ Isparta

Kilims

⑪ Denizli
⑫ Uşak

Carpets and Kilims

⑬ Konya

Indigo

Madder

Camomile

Dyes
Before chemical dyes were introduced in 1863, plant extracts were used: madder roots for red; indigo for blue; and camomile and other plants for yellow.

The "prayer design" is inspired by a *mihrab*, the niche in a mosque that indicates the direction of Mecca *(see pp36–7)*.

The tree of life motif at the centre of the kilim is symbolic of immortality.

Kilim

Kilims are usually made using the slit-weave technique by which a vertical slit marks a colour change.

The width of a rug is limited by the size of the loom. Most rugs are small because a large loom will not fit into a village house.

Buying a Rug

Before you buy a rug, look at it by itself on the floor, to see that it lies straight – without waves or lumps. Check that the pattern is balanced, the borders are of the same dimensions, and the ends are roughly the same width. The colours should be clear and not bleeding into one another. Bargaining is essential *(see p134)*, as the first price given is likely to be at least 30 per cent higher than the seller really expects.

Buying a good-quality old rug at a reasonable price, however, is a job for an expert. The age of a rug is ascertained from its colour, the quality of the weaving and the design. Check the pile to make sure that the surface has not been painted and look for any repairs – they can easily be seen on the back of the rug. The restoration of an old carpet is acceptable but the repair should not be too visible. Make sure the rug has a small lead seal attached to it, proving that it may be exported, and ask the shop for a receipt.

Kilim pieces are used to make a variety of smaller craft objects, also for sale in carpet shops.

Burdock motif

Chest motif

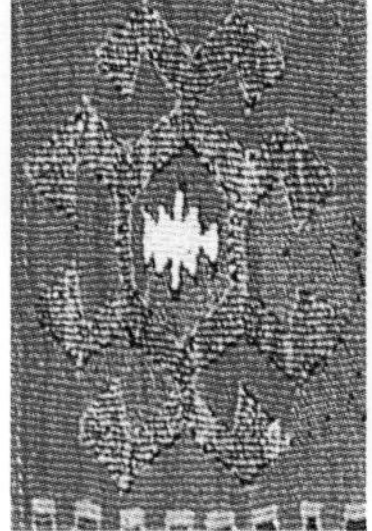

Motif from wolf track, crab or scorpion

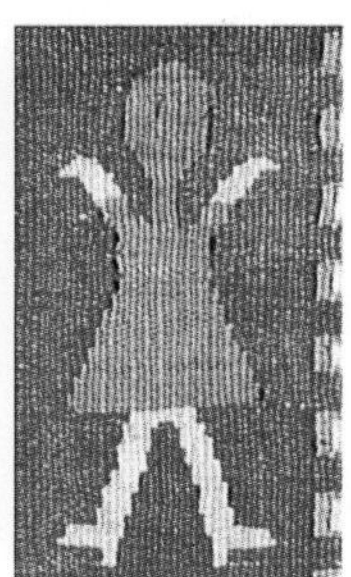

Modern motif of a human figure

Motifs

The recurring motifs in rugs – some of them seemingly abstract, others more figurative – often have a surprising origin. For instance, many are derived from marks that nomads and villagers used for branding animals.

ENTERTAINMENT IN TURKEY

Almost every town and village in Turkey enjoys an annual celebration – be it grease wrestling, bull butting or simply an agricultural festival where farmers can show off their new tractors. Some of these events hark back to ancient seasonal rites, such as the Giresun Aksu Festival on the Black Sea in May. Even though most of these activities are aimed at locals, you are sure to be made welcome or even be a guest of honour. Spectator sports have a very long history in Turkey. In classical times, the many amphitheatres of Anatolia hosted wrestling matches, circuses and risqué theatricals, which were entertainment as much as sport. Today, the average Turk identifies more with football (soccer) than any other type of sport. Visitors will soon notice the coloured banners and car horns blasting in support of favoured Istanbul teams such as Beşiktaş, Galatasaray and Fenerbahçe.

Entertainment Guides

A number of magazines list events and entertainment in Istanbul and elsewhere in the country. Visitors to Istanbul and Bodrum should look for *The Guide* and *Time Out Istanbul*, while *The Gate* magazine is available for free at airports. Turkish Airlines also has its own publication, *Skylife*. *Jazz*, the quarterly Istanbul magazine, is a good source of information on various local jazz clubs, events and musicians.

Bodrum events guide

Art, Cinema, Theatre and Music Festivals

Turkey has a large cinema-going public. Most foreign films (except those for children) are shown in their original language with Turkish subtitles. The **Golden Orange Film Festival** is held annually in Antalya *(see pp222–3)*. Other items on the arts calendar are the **International Opera and Ballet Festival** *(see p39)* held at Aspendos and the **Istanbul Biennial**, a multimedia arts festival that takes place on odd years (2017 and 2019). There is also an exciting series of Istanbul events that focus on theatre, classical music, film and jazz. Among these is the Istanbul Theatre Festival, held in May–June *(see p136)*.

Music festivals include the Akbank Jazz Festival, held in April and May in Istanbul, Ankara and other cities; the touring Efes Pilsen Blues Festival, held in the autumn; and the **Istanbul International Music Festival**, held each June and July.

Borusan Istanbul Philharmonic Orchestra performing at the International Music Festival

Discos, Night Clubs and Belly Dancing

You will find huge, open-air discos in most summer resorts – Bodrum's Halikarnas *(see p198)* is the best known, with pillars and torchlight reminiscent of ancient times.

Despite a somewhat seedy reputation – especially in the back alleys of Istanbul – belly dancing *(see p371)* is outdoor family entertainment for Turks at seaside resorts in summer, and this is where you are likely to see the most authentic displays.

Special tourist floor shows at hotels and holiday villages in season frequently include folk dancing and traditional music. Folkloric Whirling Dervish performances are frequently staged but these are not the authentic troupe who perform during the Mevlâna Festival in Konya in December *(see p41)*.

Halikarnas disco in Bodrum

Spectator Sports

Although football *(futbol)* is hugely popular, grease wrestling, or *yağlı güreş*, is Turkey's most time-honoured sport *(see p158)*. The main event is the four-day festival at **Kırkpınar**, near Edirne, in June. Wearing nothing but *kıspet* (black leather trousers soaked with olive oil), up to 1,000 men compete according to weight groups.

Camel wrestling *(see p41)* takes place every January and February. The biggest camel wrestling festivals are in Selçuk and around İzmir.

The Camel Classic Motor Racing series, which is held in the summer months, starts in Istanbul and follows a circuit that includes most of the western resort areas.

The major events on the horse racing calendar include the Gazi Race, held at the **Veli Efendi Hippodrome** in Istanbul at the end of June, and the

Presidential Cup in Ankara at the end of October.

The Mediterranean coastal town of Alanya *(see p230)* is the venue for the **Alanya International Triathlon** (swimming, cycling and foot races) in October.

Theme Parks

Theme parks are growing in popularity in Turkey. **Minicity Antalya** *(see p222)* is a cross-cultural attraction that enchants visitors young and old, as does the original Istanbul version of a scale-model theme park, **Miniatürk**, which is located on the banks of the Golden Horn.

Some of the big holiday villages around Kemer or Alanya even have their own mini theme parks tucked away within the hotel complex, but access to these is usually reserved for resident guests only.

At **Antalya Aqualand**, there is a good aquapark, with slides, pools and a dolphin park.

Folk dancers performing at Ephesus

Traditional Turkish Music and Dance

Traditional Turkish music is regularly performed at the Cemal Reşit Rey Concert Hall in Istanbul. In summer, recitals of Turkish music are occasionally organized in the Basilica Cistern *(see p90)*, which has wonderful acoustics. Traditional *Fasıl* music *(see p371)* is best enjoyed live in *meyhanes* (taverns) such as Ece, Kallavi and Hasır in Istanbul. *Fasıl* is performed on instruments which include the violin, *kanun* (zither), *tambur* and *ud* (both similar to the lute).

Miniature versions of Turkey's sights at Minicity Antalya

Children

Children are welcome and will be fussed over almost everywhere. However, there are relatively few attractions that have been planned with children in mind. Beaches and theme parks are good bets, and holiday villages always have programmes for children. In Istanbul, there are large parks at Yıldız *(see p125)* and Emirgan *(see p140)*. Also near Emirgan is Park Orman, with picnic areas, a pool, a giant walk-on chessboard and a theatre.

DIRECTORY

Art, Cinema, Theatre and Music Festivals

Ankara International Music Festival
Tel (0312) 427 23 53.
W **ankarafestival.com**

Ankara Theatre Festival
Tel (0312) 419 83 98.
W **ankaratiyatro festivali.org**

Aspendos International Opera & Ballet Festival
Near Antalya.
W **aspendosfestival. gov.tr**

Golden Orange Film Festival
Kültür Parkı İçi, Antalya.
Tel (0242) 238 54 44.
W **altinportakal.org.tr**

Istanbul International Music Festival
Tel (0212) 334 07 34.
W **iksv.org**

Istanbul Biennial
W **bienal.iksv.org**

Spectator Sports

Alanya International Triathlon
Alanya Municipality.
Tel (0242) 513 10 02.
W **triathlon.org**

Kırkpınar Grease-Wrestling
Edirne tourism office.
Tel (0284) 213 92 08.
W **kirkpinar.org**

Veli Efendi Hippodrome
Türkiye Jokey Kulübü, Osmaniye, Bakırköy, Istanbul.
Tel (0212) 543 70 96.
Tel (0212) 444 08 55.
W **veliefendi.com**

Theme Parks

Antalya Aqualand
Several locations.
W **aqualand.com.tr**

Miniatürk
Imrahor Cad, Sütlüceö, Istanbul.
Tel (0212) 222 28 22.
W **miniaturk.com.tr**

Minicity Antalya
Arapsu Mahallesi, Konyaaltı, Antalya.
Tel (0242) 229 45 45.
W **minicity.antalya net.de**

Music and Dance

Turkish music and dance are deeply rooted in history and tradition, having been influenced by Ottoman classics, mystical Sufi chants and Central Asian folk tunes, as well as jazz and pop. The result is a vibrant mosaic of old and new culture, an eclectic mixture of styles. In Turkey, visitors are treated to variety, from the meditational trance of Whirling dervishes and the merry twirling of folk dancers to the steady beat of *mehter* bands, undulating rhythms of belly dancers and the stirring strains of *zurna* buskers. The country offers a musical and dance extravaganza second to none.

The *zurna* (shawm) is a member of the oboe family. Its characteristic, strident sound features strongly in Turkish folk music.

Traditional Instruments

Turkish instruments can be classified into three main groups. Stringed instruments include the *saz* and *ud*, wind the *kaval* and *ney*, and percussion the *davul* and *darbuka*.

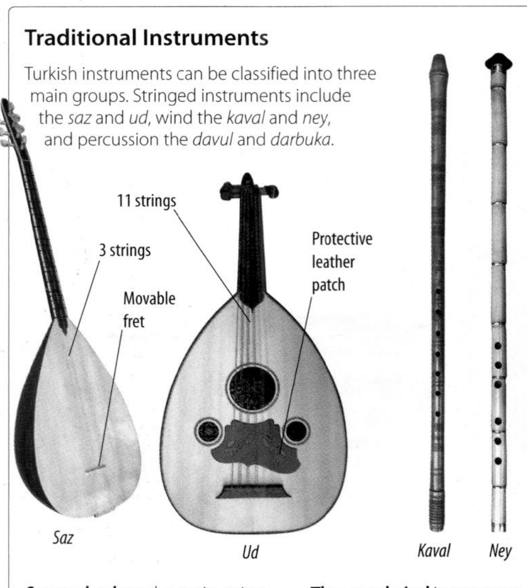

Saz* and *ud are the main string instruments. The *saz* is plucked. A piece of leather protects the belly of the *ud* from the strokes of the plectrum.

The woodwind instruments *ney* and *kaval* have ancient origins. The *ney* is made from reed, while the *kaval* is carved from the wood of the plum tree.

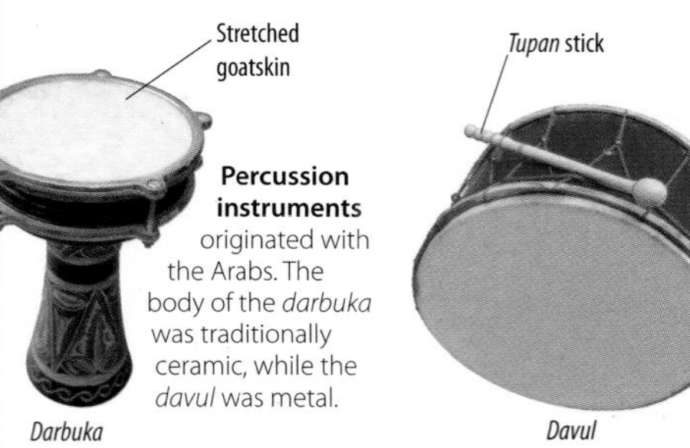

Percussion instruments originated with the Arabs. The body of the *darbuka* was traditionally ceramic, while the *davul* was metal.

A saz player entertains villagers in this 1950s photograph. Although tastes have changed, Turks remain proud of their musical traditions.

Sufi music uses the sounds of the *ney*, *ud* and *kanun* to interpret secular pieces based on the mode system and accompany poems that are chanted by a chorus. Through whirling motions, the dancers attain a trance-like state *(see p259)*.

The *Kılıç Kalkan*, or spoon dance, of the Black Sea region is performed to the rhythmic beating of two wooden spoons. Traditional folk dancing is an important part of Turkish culture, as are colourful regional costumes.

Belly dancing is popular in Turkey and remains a firm favourite with tourists. The sensuous rippling body movements, and gyrations of the hips, require impressive muscle control.

Arabesque and pop music are big business in Turkey, its heroes and heroines attaining cult status. Ibrahim Tatlıses is a much-loved performer of *arabesk*, Oriental-style music with lyrics that bemoan human hardship, while art-music-trained Sezen Aksu is one of the top-selling pop stars.

Fasíl Music

Fasıl music is considered semi-classical and is performed in meyhane (see p341) *or concert halls. Its distinctive single harmony is similar to gypsy* (Çingene) *music, and both display a masterful control of traditional wind, string and percussion instruments. Fasıl music is intended to be listened to, but gypsy music is often accompanied by dancing.*

Mehter: Music of the Janissaries

Mehter Troop performance

From 1299 until the dissolution of the Janissary corps in 1826, *mehter* music accompanied the armies of the Ottoman empire into battle, with a distinctive marching step to the rhythm of the words, "Gracious God is good. God is compassionate." Today the revived Mehter Troop performs at the Istanbul Military Museum *(see pp124–5)* and at Topkapı Palace.

OUTDOOR ACTIVITIES AND SPECIALIST HOLIDAYS

Turkey's geographical and climatic diversity presents almost limitless possibilities for outdoor enthusiasts. Anatolian winters are ideal for skiers and mountaineers, and the long, hot Mediterranean summers are perfect for yacht cruises, diving and windsurfing. Although spring and autumn are quite short, the temperate conditions are pleasant for walking and cycling. Turkey also has many options for themed holidays suitable for individuals or groups with particular interests, or those who prefer a more in-depth slant on historic events or sporting activities.

Walking and Trekking

Turkey's spectacular basalt and limestone mountain ranges provide ample opportunity for hiking. Since the opening of the first marked long-distance trek, the Lycian Way, in 1999 *(see pp210–11)*, marked walking trails have proliferated. The St Paul Trail across the western Taurus, Abraham's Path in remote southeast Turkey and the Carian Way on the southern Aegean coast are just some of the routes. Non-marked hiking areas include the landscape of Cappadocia, with its celebrated "fairy chimneys" *(see pp284–5)*.

Areas for good day walks include the mountains of Lycia on the Mediterranean coast, as well as the Turkish Lake District around Eğirdir *(see p258)*. For more serious walking on unmarked trails, the Bolkar range and, in particular, the Aladağlar range (part of the Taurus Mountains), is superb, as are the Kaçkar Mountains in the northwest. The highest peak in Turkey is Mount Ağrı (Ararat) *(see p319)*, near the eastern border with Armenia, rising to 5,165 m (16,945 ft). Adventure outfits like **Exodus, Mithra Travel** and **World Expeditions** can organize guided treks. **Türkü Turizm** offers high-altitude trekking expeditions in the Kaçkar Mountains south of Rize *(see p278)*. **Demavend Travel** is an excellent local outfit, with treks on Ararat, the Kaçkar and the Aladağlar, as is **Middle Earth Travel**, with treks on the Lycian, St Paul and Carian trails among the routes on offer.

Mountaineering, Climbing and Canyoning

Turkey's mountain ranges offer fantastic opportunities for serious climbers. Deep snow in the Aladağlar and Kaçkar makes for great winter ski-mountaineering. **Bukla Tour** can organize treks and guides. **Bougainville** and **Get Wet** offer canyoning excursions.

Skiing

Turkey's most popular ski centre is Uludağ, near Bursa *(see p163)*. It has many lifts and a range of runs. Kartal, between Istanbul and Ankara, offers newer facilities and less crowded runs. Near Isparta, the Davraz ski centre has reliable snow, two chairlifts, a couple of good hotels and more accommodation in Eğirdir. Erciyes, near Kayseri, has hotels, reliable snowfalls and long runs. Though remote, Palandöken *(see p323)* combines a long season with 45 km (28 miles) of piste well served by chairlifts and several very good hotels. **İçem Tour** will make bookings at most ski resorts.

The popular Palandöken ski resort near Erzurum

The rapids of the Çoruh River are only for experienced rafters

Whitewater Rafting

In the northeast, the Çoruh River has Grade-5 rapids and is the ideal testing ground for serious rafters. Several overseas agencies offer trips. In contrast, day trips on the Köprülü River (between Antalya and Side), or the Dalaman River near Fethiye, are suitable for families and novices. Local agencies and hotels near to both rafting rivers offer day rafting packages on the rivers. **Adrift** offers Çoruh rafting tours; **Medraft** and others run day tours on the Köprülü River.

Paragliding

Few activities combine the serenity and high altitude scenery of paragliding. Babadağ Mountain, above the coastal resort of Olü Deniz *(see pp216–17)* and the

Paragliding above the Mediterranean coast near Ölü Deniz

mountain ridge above Kaş *(see p218)* both have the ideal updrafts, vistas and landing pads needed for this breath-taking sport. **Skysports** is an experienced and reputable company, offering expert tuition and equipment hire.

Horse Riding and Pony Trekking

Cappadocia's trails weave through valleys and uplands. One of the best companies to go with is **Kirkit Voyage**, based in Avanos. In Istanbul, the **Klassis Golf and Country Club** has an indoor ring and jumping facilities. The best place for trail riding is the Equestrian Centre at Daday, a village near Kastamonu *(see pp268–9)*.

Sailing and Cruising Holidays

The Aegean and western Mediterranean coasts are perfect for cruises aboard comfortable *gulets* (traditional wooden sailing vessels). One- or two-week cruises (called "blue voyages") are an excuse to relax, swim and sunbathe, with occasional forays ashore for shopping or dining. Those with a historical bent can combine one of these cruises with visits to the many fascinating ancient sites along the coast, guided by an expert in Greek and Roman history. The chain of marinas, each about a day's sailing apart, also offer secure moorings and facilities for private yachts. **Arya Yachting** in Bodrum or the UK's **Alternative Travel Group** offer cruises. **Westminster Classic Tours** have cruises with lectures and site visits. **Gino Group** in Marmaris rents and sells new and good-value reconditioned sailing yachts.

Diving

Marmaris, Bodrum, Fethiye Kaş and Alanya are all leading diving resorts, offering warm water and perfect conditions with splendid visibility. Here, qualified scuba instructors who are accredited to the Professional Association of Diving Instructors (PADI) offer tuition which takes novices as well as more experienced divers through an internationally recognized diving certificate course.

The **European Diving Centre** in Fethiye and **Ayışığı Diving** in Istanbul both offer high quality tuition and can be recommended.

Beaches

Turkey's Mediterranean, Aegean and Black Sea coasts have many beaches, offering a wide range of seaside pursuits.

Conditions are generally warm, though the Black Sea can be rough at times, with big waves. The Bodrum peninsula has ideal conditions for sailing and dinghy racing. Water-skiing, water parasailing and jet-skiing are offered at major beachside hotels and resorts.

The best place near Istanbul for swimming and watersports such as water-skiing and windsurfing is the Princes' Islands *(see p162)*.

Hotel-Based Sports

Five-star hotels in the major resorts have good hard tennis courts. Most four- and five-star hotels also organize table tennis, billiards, archery, step dancing and aerobics; even some three-star hotels offer beach volleyball and excellent swimming pools.

Golf

The mild winter and early spring make golf a year-round sport in Turkey. There are more than 10 purpose-built courses at Belek, east of Antalya *(see p228)*. **Pamfilya Travel Agency** can arrange tailor-made tours for amateurs or championship golfers. Near Istanbul, the **Kemer Golf and Country Club** has a championship course.

Diving school in Marmaris, offering courses at all skill levels

Historical and Cultural Tours

Given Turkey's wealth and variety of historic sites, it is no surprise that these are what attract most visitors to the country. Tourists who wish to visit ancient and classical sites can do so in the company of an expert in the field. The classical sites of the west and south, Ephesus *(see pp186–7)* and Pergamum *(see pp180–81)* in particular, draw large crowds of visitors, especially in the summer months. Others under excavation, such as Sagalassos and Aphrodisias *(see pp192–3)*, are also very impressive and may be less congested. Some sites, such as Patara and Xanthos *(see p218)* – whose chief tombs are on view in the British Museum – can be visited as part of a *gulet* tour *(see p373)*.

Istanbul deserves careful exploration, particularly its churches, mosques and museums. Since the major sites in Istanbul and around Göreme in Cappadocia are situated fairly close together, walking tours are an attractive option.

Marble head of Athena

Much more recent history is movingly commemorated on the Gallipoli peninsula *(see pp172–3)*, site of some of the fiercest and most tragic battles of World War I.

The Traveller, **Andante Travels** and **Martin Randall** all offer tours of the classical sites, with Andante also covering much of the rest of the country. **Gallipoli and Troy Tours** operates tours to the Dardanelles and Gallipoli.

Memorial cemetery, Gallipoli

Wildlife Tours

Turkey's diverse habitats support many endemic plant species, especially of orchids and bulbs, with tulips being perhaps the best-known examples. This diversity, coupled with the country's pivotal position along migration routes between Europe, Asia and Africa, assures the presence of numerous bird species from three continents. In spring and autumn, over 200 species can be spotted in the course of a two-week holiday. DHKD, a local conservation group, records observations and works to preserve habitats such as wetlands. In-depth birding holidays are available from **Greentours**.

The House of the Virgin Mary, near Ephesus *(see p186)*

Religious Tours

Modern-day pilgrims can follow in the footsteps of the Apostle Paul, whose faith led him from Tarsus to Ephesus and beyond. Visitors can tour the "Seven Churches" founded by Paul, and see the small house near Ephesus where the Virgin Mary is said to have spent her last days.

There are also quite a few Armenian and Greek Orthodox churches in Istanbul *(see p118)* that are still active. In southeastern Turkey, there are haunting Syrian Orthodox churches and monasteries.

Pacha Tours offer specialist itineraries for pilgrims who would like to trace the wanderings of St Paul.

A bird hide in the Göksu Delta, near Silifke

Food Tours

Turkish food is regarded as some of the best in the world, with more and more people eager to sample its range of delicacies and try their hands at preparing traditional dishes. **Istanbul Eats** offers excellent day tours around off-the-beaten-track areas of the city, where visitors can sample a variety of local cuisine and street food. Visitors can learn how to cook traditional Turkish with **Cooking Alaturka**, or they can enjoy a gastronomic gulet cruise along the Aegean and Mediterranean coast with **Peter Sommer Travels**.

Other Specialist Holidays

Several operators offer more specialized holidays that involve particular pursuits such as photography, or painting and sketching. **Kaş Eflatun Art Camp**, for example, runs weekly residential painting courses, while **Fotografevi** offers photographic tours.

A range of companies also use Turkey's relaxed atmosphere and natural beauty to offer breaks that include such activities as yoga, massage, tai chi and meditation. For details on active holidays, try **Exclusive Escapes**.

DIRECTORY

Ministry of Culture and Tourism

(For general information)
Atatürk Bul 29, Ankara.
Tel (0312) 309 08 50.
Fax (0312) 312 43 59.
W **kulturturizm.gov.tr**

Adventure Travel Companies

Bougainville
Çukurbağlı Cad 10, Kaş.
Tel (0242) 836 37 37.
W **bt-turkey.com**

Demavend Travel
Esenbey Mah, Sefik Soyer Meydani, Niğde.
Tel (0388) 232 73 63.
W **demavendtravel.com**

Exodus
Grange Mills, Weir Road, London, SW12 ONE, UK.
Tel (44) 020 8772 3936 or 0845 869 8254.
W **exodus.co.uk**

Mithra Travel
Kılıçaslan Mah, Hesapçı Sok 70.
Tel (0242) 248 77 47.
W **mithratravel.com**

Türkü Turizm
İnönü Cad 47, Çamlıhemşin, Rize.
Tel (0464) 651 72 30.
W **turkutour.com**

Walking and Trekking

Demavend Travel
(See Adventure Travel Companies).

Exodus
(See Adventure Travel Companies).

Middle Earth Travel
Karşı Bucak Cad, Göreme.
Tel (0384) 271 25 59.
W **middleearth travel.com**

Türkü Turizm
(See Adventure Travel Companies).

World Expeditions
81 Craven Gardens, London SW19 8LU, UK.
Tel (44) 20 8545 9030.
W **worldexpeditions.com**

Mountaineering, Climbing and Canyoning

Bougainville
(See Adventure Travel Companies.)

Bukla Tour
İstiklâl Cad, Postacilar Sok 1/2, Beyoğlu, Istanbul.
Tel (0212) 245 06 35.
W **climbararat.com**
W **bukla.com**

Get Wet
Eski Lara Yolu 198/1, Şirinyalı, Antalya.
Tel (0242) 324 08 55.
W **getwet.com.tr**

Skiing

İcem Tour
Mimar Mehmet Ağa Cad 34, Sultanahmet, Istanbul.
Tel (0212) 638 19 86.
W **icemtour.com**

Whitewater Rafting

Adrift
127 High St, Hungerford RG17 0DL, UK.
Tel (44) 1488 711 52.
W **adrift.co.uk**

Medraft
Meydankavağı, Şehıtler Cad, Antalya.
Tel (0242) 312 57 70.
W **medraft.com.tr**

Paragliding

Skysports
Carsi Cad, Tonoz Otel Alti, Ölü Deniz, Fethiye, Muğla.
Tel (0252) 617 05 11.
W **skysports-turkey.com**

Horse Riding and Pony Trekking

Kirkit Voyage
Atatürk Cad 50, Avanos.
Tel (0384) 511 32 59.
W **kirkit.com**

Klassis Golf and Country Club
Seyman Köyü, Altıntepe Mevkii, Silivri (W of Istanbul).
Tel (0212) 710 13 13.
W **klassisgolf.com.tr**

Sailing and Cruising Holidays

Alternative Travel Group
69–71 Banbury Road, Oxford OX2 6PE, UK.
Tel (44) 1865 315 678.
W **atg-oxford.co.uk**

Arya Yachting
Caferpaşa Cad 21/A, Bodrum. **Tel** (0252) 316 15 80. W **aryatours.com**

Gino Group
Netsel Marina, Marmaris.
Tel (0252) 412 06 76.
W **ginogroup.com**

Westminster Classic Tours
108 Monkleigh Road, Morden SM4 4EP, UK.
Tel (44) 20 8286 7842.
W **westminsterclassic tours.com**

Diving

Ayısığı Diving
Bağdat Cad, İçlaiye Apt 24/4, Kızıltoprak, Istanbul.
Tel (0216) 418 22 44.
W **ayisigidiving.com**

European Diving Centre
Fevzi Cakmak Cad 53, Fethiye. **Tel** (0252) 614 97 71. W **european diving centre.com**

Golf

Kemer Golf and Country Club
Göktürk Beldesi, Kemerburgaz, Istanbul.
Tel (0212) 239 70 10.
W **kg-cc.com**

Pamfilya Travel Agency
Isıklar Cad 57/B, Antalya.
Tel (0242) 243 15 00.
W **pamfilya.com**

Historical and Cultural Tours

Andante Travels Ltd
The Clock Tower, Southampton Road, Whaddon, Salisbury, SP5 3HT, UK.
Tel (44) 1722 713 800.
W **andantetravels.co.uk**

Gallipoli and Troy Tours
Kenan Çelik, Öğretmenler Sitesi 2 Utku Apt. D:2, Çanakkale. **Tel** (0532) 667 57 38. W **kcelik.com**

Martin Randall
Barley Mow Passage, Chiswick, London W4, UK.
Tel (44) 20 8742 3355.
W **martinrandall.com**

The Traveller
2 Bury Place, London WC1A 2JL, UK.
Tel (44) 20 7269 2770.
W **the-traveller.co.uk**

Wildlife Tours

Greentours
Gauledge Lane, Longnor, Buxton SK17 0PA, UK.
Tel (44) 1298 83563.
W **greentours.co.uk**

Religious Tours

Pacha Tours
295 Madison Avenue, New York, USA.
Tel (800) 722 4288 (US).
W **pachatours.com**

Food Tours

Cooking Alaturka
Akbıyık Cad 72, Sultanahmet. **Tel** (0212) 458 59 19. W **cooking alaturka.com**.

Istanbul Eats
W **istanbuleats.com**

Peter Sommer Travels
Chippenham House, 102 Monnow Street, Monmouth, NP25 3EQ.
Tel (01) 600 888 220
W **petersommer.com**

Other Specialist Holidays

Exclusive Escapes
Alexander House, 15 Princes Road, Richmond, TW10 6DQ, UK. **Tel** (44) 20 8605 3500. W **exclusive escapes.co.uk**

Fotografevi
Tütüncu Çikmazı 4, Galatasaray, Beyoğlu, Istanbul.
Tel (0212) 249 02 02.

Kaş Eflatun Art Camp
Çukurbag, Kaş, Antalya.
Tel (0242) 839 54 29.
W **kasartcamp.com**

Spas and Hot Springs

Turkey's geophysical matrix, which occasionally causes earthquakes and tremors, has an unexpected upside seen in the geothermal springs on which the country seems to be floating. Over 1,000 thermal hot springs (and some icy cold ones) bubble from deep seismic fissures at high temperatures and under great pressure. Roman armies soothed battle wounds in the rich, therapeutic mineral pools and Turkish families have taken the waters for decades. Tourists are increasingly travelling here for their rejuvenating properties.

Bathers in the rehabilitating calciferous pools at Pamukkale

Geothermal Spring Resorts

Turkey's most potent thermal springs have a high mineral content. There are springs all over the country but very few have accommodation facilities; these are among the best.

Reputed to have soothed the wounds of Agamemnon's Greek soldiers, **Balçova Thermal Hotel** was a pioneer in thermal tourism. The 70°C (158°F) geothermal springs have an exceptional mineral count.

Bursa is one of Turkey's most venerable spa cities. The **Yeni Kaplıca** complex is historic and hot, 85°C (185°F). The spa for men is a traditional 16th-century domed building. Mineral baths and treatments for families are also available.

Of the many geothermal areas north and west of Ankara, Kızılcahamam is best suited to accommodate visitors. Among these is the **Hotel Ab-ı Hayat**.

The mineral waters at **Yalova Thermal Hot Springs** bubble up at 65° C (149°F) from a deep volcanic source and are considered to be the most remedial in Turkey. The cascading calciferous pools at Pamukkale *(see p190)* are very popular. A short distance away at Karahitit, the waters contain iron and the source is much hotter. **Pam Thermal Hotel** is one of the most professional and well-run of the thermal hotels.

Five-Star Spas

Turkey's leading spa hotels are located in Istanbul, Ankara and near Bodrum. None has geothermal springs but all offer a sensual and invigorating experience.

The **Kempinski Hotel Barbaros Bay** is a renowned Six Senses Spa, the only in Turkey. Eastern traditions and remedies meet Aegean atmosphere at this fine spa.

One of the country's most spiritual spas is at **Hôtel Les Ottomans**, which adheres to Oriental feng shui concepts.

Ankara's impressive **Swissôtel Amrita Spa and Wellness Centre** is huge and combines heavenly, healthy and wholesome treatments.

At the **Ritz Carlton's Laveda Spa**, staff are superbly trained and the focus is on inner health and harmony. The healthy regime promotes relaxation and rejuvenation.

Hamams

The traditional Turkish bath, or *hamam (see p81)*, was an integral part of the Ottoman social structure, and scrubbing and massages were a ritual procedure. Top spa hotels all have *hamams*. Look for quality in the central stone – it should be transparent, smooth and highly polished. Bursa's **Çakır Hamam** is simple but friendly and dates from 1484. The historic Ottoman **Cağaloğlu Baths** in Istanbul are very popular. On the Aegean coast, **Bodrum Hamam** *(see p198)* has a hotel pick-up service. **Sefa Hamami** in Antalya is a restored 13th-century Seljuk bath, while the **Kelebek Hotel** is a cave hotel in Göreme with a splendid *hamam*.

Therapeutic Spas

Medical tourism is popular in Turkey and several spas concentrate on specific health problems. **Natur-Med Thermal Springs & Health Resort** offers treatments for, among others, chronic disease, weight loss and detoxification. Near Sivas *(see p299)* in the secluded hills are the **Kangal Fish Springs**, a healing centre for psoriasis. The hot springs contain selenium and support a type of fish that nibbles affected skin. Documented since Roman times, **Ayaş İçmece ve Kaplıcaları** is noted for cures and rehabilitation. There are two spas here sharing a thermal

The Turkish hamam at the luxury Hôtel Les Ottomans

Clients taking the healing waters of Natur-Med Thermal Springs

source. The waters are so hot and heavily mineralized that drinking and bathing are done under medical supervision.

Rural Spas

Ayder is a well-known Black Sea thermal centre, with hot springs ideal for physical therapy and rehabilitation. The facilities bask in pastoral high-altitude surroundings, with about 20 simple pensions.

A delightful spa village of small streams, gardens and rustic bridges forms the backdrop for the thermal waters of **Hamamayağı**. The healing spring contains radon in therapeutic quantities.

A remedial watering hole since the Phrygia era (800 BC), the **Hüdai** thermal waters relieve many of life's modern twinges.

Set in a tranquil, rural location on the banks of the Meander River, **Umut Thermal Resort and Spa** is ideal. Standards are high and the atmosphere is clinical but friendly.

Located on the Meander River embankment, **Yenice Ilıcası Kamara İşletmesi** offers 15 basic rooms; however, clientele return regularly for its uncomplicated charm.

Aqua Accessories

Beautiful spa and *hamam* products can be found in shops such as **Derviş Bath Accessories**, which has two outlets in Istanbul's Grand Bazaar, and **Abdullah Natural Products**.

Derviş Bath Accessories' products

TOURIST INFORMATION

Geothermal Spring resorts

Balçova Thermal Hotel
Vali Hüseyin Öğütcen Cad 2, Balçova, İzmir.
Tel (0232) 259 01 02.
W balcovatermal.com

Hotel Ab-ı Hayat
Kazım Karabekir Cad, Kızılcahamam, 06890.
Tel (0312) 736 56 20.

Pam Thermal Hotel
Beytur Turizm İşletmeleri A. Ş., Karahayıt, Pamukkale.
Tel (0258) 271 41 40.
W pamthermal.com

Yalova Thermal Hot Springs
Yalova Termal, 77400.
Tel (0226) 675 74 00.
W yalovatermal.com

Yeni Kaplıca
Kükürtlü Mah, Yenikaplıca Cad 6, Osmangazi, Bursa.
Tel (0224) 236 69 68.

Five-Star Spas

Hôtel Les Ottomans
Muallim Naci Cad 168, Kuruçeşme, Istanbul.
Tel (0212) 359 15 00.
W lesottomans.com

Kempinski Hotel Barbaros Bay
Kızılağaç Köyü, Gerenkuyu Mevkii, Yalıçiftlik, Bodrum,
Tel (0252) 311 03 03. **W kempinski-bodrum.com**

Ritz-Carlton
Süzer Plaza Elmadağ, 34367, Şişli, Istanbul.
Tel (0212) 334 44 44.
W ritzcarlton.com

Swissôtel Amrita Spa and Wellness Centre
Yıldızevler Mah, Jose Marti Cad 2, Çankaya, Ankara.
Tel (0312) 409 36 66.
W amritaspa.com

Hamams

Bodrum Hamam
Cevak Şakir Sok, Fabrika Sok 42, Bodrum.
Tel (0252) 313 41 29.
W bodrumhamami.com.tr

Cağaloğlu Baths
Cağaloğlu, Istanbul.
Tel (0212) 522 24 24.
W cagalogluhamami.com.tr

Çakır Hamamı
Atatürk Cad 101, Osmangazi, Bursa.
Tel (0224) 221 25 80.

Kelebek Hotel
Aydinli Mah, Yavuz Sok 1, Göreme.
Tel (0384) 271 25 31.

Sefa Hamamı
Kokatepe Sokak Barbaros Mahallesi 32, Antalya.
Tel (0242) 241 23 21.
W sefahamamı.com

Therapeutic Spas

Ayas İçmece ve Kaplıcaları
İçmeler Mevkii Ayaş, Beypazarı, Ankara.
Tel (0312) 718 31 01.
W ayasicmece.com.tr

Kangal Fish Springs
Kavak Köyü Mevkii, Kangal, Sivas.
Tel (0346) 469 11 51.
W baliklikaplica.biz

Natur-Med Health Resort
Davutlar, Kuşadası.
Tel (0256) 657 22 80.
W natur-med.com.tr

Rural Spas

Ayder Turizm A.Ş.
Çamlihemşin, Rize.
Tel (0464) 657 21 02.
W ayderkaplicalari.com

Hamamayağı Tesisleri
Between Havza and Ladık.
Tel (0362) 782 00 01/02.

Hüdai Yeni Thermal Hotel
Sandıklı, Afyon.
Tel (272) 535 73 27.
W hudai.sandikli.bel.tr

Umut Thermal Resort and Spa
Hasköy Tekke Köyü Yolu üzeri 9 km, Kokar Hamam Mevkii, Sarayköy, Denizli.
Tel (0258) 426 11 01.

Yenice Ilıcası Kamara İşletmesi
Yenicekent, Buldan, Denizli.
Tel (0258) 434 60 97.
W umutthermal.com

Aqua Accessories

Abdullah Natural Products
Alibaba Türbe Sok 25, Nurosmaniye, Istanbul.
Tel (0212) 526 30 70.
W abdulla.com

Derviş Bath Accessories
Kesiciler Cad 33–35, Kapalıçarşı, Istanbul.
Tel (0212) 514 45 25.
W dervis.com

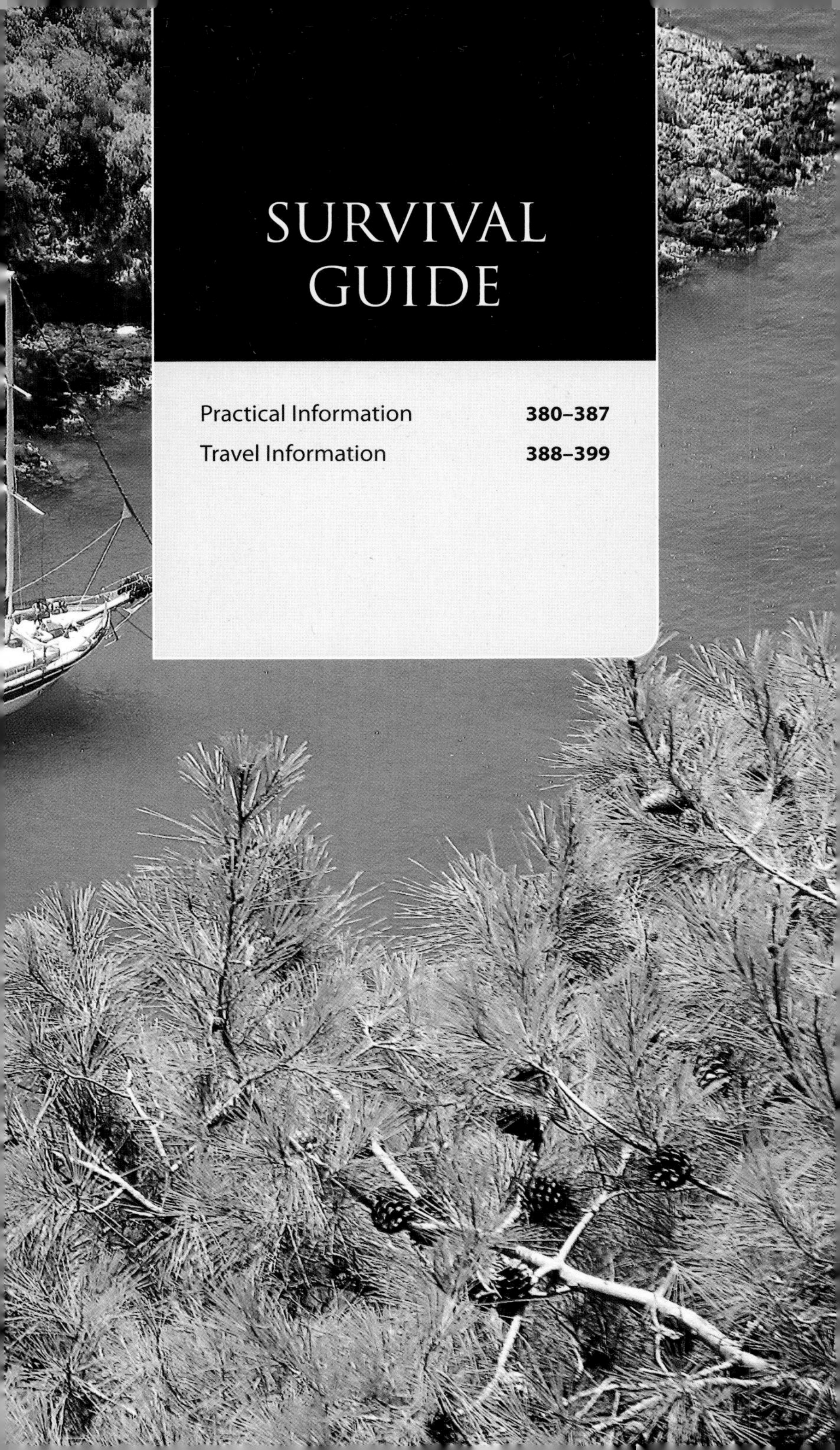

SURVIVAL GUIDE

Practical Information 380–387

Travel Information 388–399

PRACTICAL INFORMATION

Many first-time visitors to Turkey expect the country to be sedate and reserved, due to the influence of Islam, so the exuberant and lively character of Turkish life comes as a pleasant surprise. Observing a few local customs and learning some basic Turkish words or phrases will get you off to a good start. Always show respect for the laws of the country and for its religious differences, culture and class structure, even if you do not agree with the beliefs or politics. By and large, Turkish people are very friendly and all Turks will welcome any effort to appreciate their lifestyle and respect their traditions.

Visas and Passports

Visitors to Turkey must have a full passport with at least six months' validity. Unless citizens of a visa-exempt country, visitors to Turkey must obtain a visa. It is possible to apply for this online at www.evisa.gov.tr. Visitors will need to fill out a form and make a payment online. Printed visas need to be carried at the point of entry into Turkey. The fee for citizens of the USA, UK and Ireland is US$20. For citizens of Australia and Canada, the fee is US$60. Visas are multi-entry, and valid for 90 or 180 days. Requirements change, so for up-to-date information visit www.mfa.gov.tr or contact the Turkish consulate or embassy in your country.

Customs Information

Airports and main road entry points offer a full customs service, but customs hours at major ports are 8:30am–5:30pm on weekdays. Outside these hours, a fee must be paid for a customs official to carry out their inspections.

You can buy duty-free items at the airport upon entering the country. Visitors over 18 can bring in 1.5 kg (3 lb) of coffee, 120 ml (4 fl oz) of perfume, 1 litre or two 75 cl bottles (35 fl oz) of spirits and 200 cigarettes. There is no limit to how much currency you can bring in. The maximum when leaving is US$5,000 (or equivalent), but this is rarely enforced. You need a permit to export antiquities *(see p363)*.

Customs service emblem

Turkey is strict regarding drugs; sniffer dogs are used at some airports. Contact the Turkish consulate or embassy in your country for more customs information.

Tourist Information

The sign for a tourist information office is a white "i" on a green background in a white box. There are tourist offices in most Turkish cities and resorts. They are usually open 9am–5pm Monday to Saturday, but some stay open later in summer; the one at Atatürk Airport is open 24 hours a day. In provincial areas the staff may speak only basic English. The Turkish tourist board in your own country will also be a good source of information.

Admission Fees and Opening Hours

Entry fees to major attractions in Turkey's main tourist areas (Istanbul, Cappadocia, the Western Mediterranean and the Aegean) are comparable to those in Europe. Lesser-known establishments are cheaper, as are sights in less touristy areas. Most museums close one day a week, often Monday, though closing days vary in Istanbul. Exhibits in the major museums are usually labelled in both Turkish and English, while less visited venues may have information in Turkish only. Museums tend to open from 9am to 5:30pm, sometimes with a lunch break. Archaeological sites often operate from 9am to 7pm in summer and from 9am to 5pm in winter.

Most banks are open from 8:30am to 5pm Monday to Friday, and state banks close for lunch from noon to 1:30pm. Exchange offices *(döviz)* are usually open until 8pm or 9pm *(see p384)*.

Visitors on the steps leading up to Dolmabahçe Palace

Shops open from 9am to 7pm *(see p362)*. Some close on Sundays, although shopping malls, supermarkets and small grocers are usually open seven days a week from 10am to 10pm.

Etiquette

Turks tend to dress smartly. In eastern areas of the country, conservative cities such as Konya and Kayseri, and devout areas of Istanbul, such as Fatih, many women cover their heads, arms and legs in public. Visitors are not expected to follow suit, but be aware that some Turks may be offended by exposed limbs. Public drunkenness is frowned upon, and men should avoid walking around shirtless away from the beach, even in resorts.

Make sure you always show respect for Atatürk, whose image you will see often.

Istanbul has a lively gay scene. Homosexual visitors are unlikely to experience problems, but it is best to avoid overt displays of physical affection.

◀ Yacht in a picturesque bay, Aegean Sea

Smoking is prohibited in all enclosed spaces, including public transport, restaurants and bars, and even water-pipe *(nargile)* cafés.

Visiting Mosques

Large mosques are open all day, closing after last prayers in the evening, while smaller ones open only for the five daily prayer times *(namaz)*. Non-Muslims should not enter a mosque during prayers, the times of which are clearly displayed on a board outside or just inside the mosque. Prayer times are also signalled by the call to prayer *(ezan)* from a loudspeaker fixed to the minaret of the mosque.

Dress appropriately when visiting a mosque *(see pp36–7)*. Everybody should cover their shoulders, and women should cover their heads, too; do not wear shorts or miniskirts, and remove your shoes. Shawls to cover your head, arms and shoulders are provided by some mosques. Shoes are usually left on racks, either outside or just inside the main entrance. Mosques frequented by lots of tourists often provide plastic bags for visitors to carry around their footwear during the visit. Make as little noise as possible inside and show consideration for anyone who is praying there.

Language

Turks will appreciate any attempt to speak their difficult language, so try to learn a few words. Menus are printed in several languages in many restaurants and cafés, and in areas with lots of foreign visitors most shopkeepers can speak one other language.

Public Conveniences

Public toilets are thin on the ground in Turkish cities, but most mosques have facilities for both men and women. As with public toilets, there is usually an attendant and a small fee to pay on exit. Toilets are marked *Bay* for men and *Bayan* for women. The attendant may supply toilet paper, but it is a good idea to carry tissues with you.

If you are reluctant to use the squat toilets generally found in public and mosque facilities, you can ask to use the western-style toilets in most hotels, restaurants and cafés. Museums and major sights all have toilets, too, and outside the cities, motorway service areas have excellent, often free, washroom facilities.

Time

Turkey is 2 hours ahead of Greenwich Mean Time and British Summer Time. New York is 7 hours behind and Los Angeles is 10 hours behind.

Electricity

Turkey's electrical current is 220–240 volts AC. Plugs have two round pins, which fit most European two-pin plugs. Bring a universal adaptor for all other voltages.

Colourful display of fruit and vegetables at a market stall

Responsible Tourism

Environmental awareness is a fairly new concept in Turkey, though a few recycling bins grace the streets of Istanbul and other cities. Traditionally, recycling is carried out by the Roma community, who, pulling handcarts fitted with giant sacks, scavenge through the waste bins left out on the street for collection. Plastics, paper, metal and glass are sold to private operators for recycling. Some Turks help out by leaving recyclable materials next to, rather than in, the bins.

Electricity is expensive in Turkey, so many people use solar-energy systems for their hot-water needs. If you are serious about energy conservation, check that your proposed accommodation has such a system installed.

DIRECTORY

Consulates in Istanbul

Australia
Asker Ocaği Cad 15, Elmadağ. **Map** 1 C3.
Tel (0212) 243 13 33/36.

Canada
Buyukdere Cad 209, Tekfen Tower, 16th Floor, Levent 4.
Map 1 A4. **Tel** (0212) 385 97 00.

New Zealand
Inönü Cad 48/3, Taksim.
Map 1 C4. **Tel** (0212) 244 02 72.

United Kingdom
Meşrutiyet Cad 34, Tepebaşı.
Map 1 C4.
Tel (0212) 334 64 00.

United States
Kaplıcalar Mevkii 2 (to be renamed Üçşehitler Sok), İstinye.
Tel (0212) 335 90 00.

Customs Information

The main customs office in Ankara will answer queries in English. Their website details items that can be brought into Turkey.
Tel (0312) 306 80 00.
W gumruk.gov.tr

Tourist Information

Australia
428 George Street, Room 17, Level 3, Sydney NSW 2000.
Tel (61) 29 223 3055.

United Kingdom
29–30 St James's St, London SW1A 1HB.
Tel (44) 20 7839 7778.
W gototurkey.co.uk

United States
821 United Nations Plaza, New York, NY 10017.
Tel (212) 687 2194.
W tourismturkey.org

Personal Security and Health

For the sensible visitor, Turkey is probably safer to visit than many European countries. Unfortunately, however, high unemployment and the huge gap between rich and poor mean that petty theft and pickpocketing are on the rise in big cities. Health care is of a high standard, with a thriving private health sector alongside the state-run system, but it is essential to keep basic immunization up to date before you travel.

Police

There are a number of police forces in Turkey, from traffic wardens to rapid-response motorcycle units (Dolphin Police). The *Jandarma*, who are attached to the army, are responsible for policing rural areas. In towns, the *Emniyet Polisi* (Security Police) carry out law-enforcement duties. A special tourism police force *(Turizm Polisi)* operates in Istanbul and other tourist areas. The navy-blue-uniformed *Zabıta* is a municipal police force that patrols bazaars and other areas of commerce.

It is obligatory to carry some form of identification with you in Turkey, either the original or at least a photocopy. The police and *Jandarma* carry out spot checks on cars, buses and trucks. A passport or driving licence is usually sufficient.

Police officers are very helpful, but should you need help, the first place to contact is your embassy. Most countries have missions in Ankara, and some have consulates in Istanbul *(see p381)*, İzmir or Antalya.

Badge of the Dolphin rapid-response unit

What to be Aware of

Petty crime is on the rise in Turkey. Visitors to Istanbul should be particularly vigilant, especially on the crowded public transport system, as pickpocketing is a growing problem. Bag-snatching is less common, but be wary. Use a money belt, or wear your bag across your chest and walk on the inner part of the pavement. Do not leave valuables lying around in your hotel room. Whether you are male or female, avoid lonely areas, such as Istanbul's old city walls, especially at night.

It is also best to avoid urban protests of any kind, particularly in areas such as Istanbul's Taksim Square *(see p115)*, because they can quickly spiral out of control.

Security policeman

Traffic policeman

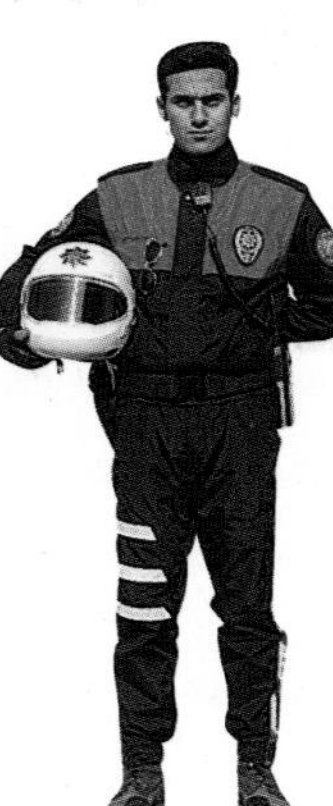

Dolphin policeman

If you are planning to visit remote areas, it is best to travel in a group. The ethnically Kurdish southeast has been unstable for many years, with protests and outbreaks of stone-throwing occurring from time to time. Visitors who wander into rural areas in this region may be viewed with suspicion by security forces.

The army, Atatürk and the Turkish flag are fundamental symbols of Turkish identity, and disrespect towards them is seen as an insult to the state. Always ask permission before taking photographs of any individuals, even in public places. Taking pictures of military installations is strictly forbidden. The political turmoil and conflict in Syria has increased security concerns in Turkey's southeast.

In an Emergency

If your condition is life-threatening, you should be treated automatically, but it is a good idea to have your insurance details on you at all times in case your ability to pay is questioned. In Istanbul, the state-run **Taksim Ilkyardım Hastanesi** (Taksim Emergency Hospital) has a good reputation; in provincial cities, it is best to use one of the many excellent private hospitals, several of which have an office staffed by at least one fluent English (and other languages) speaker.

Lost and Stolen Property

Turks will go to great lengths to return lost property. It is always worth returning to the last place your item was seen, or going to the tourism police. In Istanbul, property left on public transport can be reclaimed from the I.E.T.T. *(see p397)*.

If you have anything stolen in an area where there are tourism police, such as Istanbul, report the theft to them. Elsewhere, report it at a police station *(Emniyet Polis Merkezi)*, but bear in mind that most officers have either no, or only very basic, English language skills. To make an insurance claim, you will have to give (and sign) a statement. Contact your embassy or consulate for help *(see p381)*.

Fire engine

Security Police *(Emniyet Polisi)* car

State ambulance

Hospitals and Pharmacies

The Turkish health system has both public and private hospitals. Private hospitals are generally better equipped and staffed, and less bureaucratic, than state hospitals. They may run their own ambulance services, and they are also more likely to have staff speaking a foreign language. Go to http://turkey.usembassy.gov/medical_information.html for a list of state and private hospitals.

Most non-prescription medications are available at reasonable prices from a pharmacy (*eczane*), and many types of antibiotics are available over the counter. Visitors are allowed to bring into the country sufficient quantities of medications as are required for the duration of their trip. Turkish pharmacists are professional and well trained; most are also qualified to give injections (*iğne*). If you need advice outside normal business hours, the name of the duty pharmacist (*nobetci eczane*) for that day is usually posted in a pharmacy window.

Condoms *(prezervatif)* are available in most pharmacies, even if not on display.

Minor Hazards

Before travelling to Turkey, be sure that your basic inoculations (diphtheria, polio, typhoid and tetanus) are up to date. Check with your doctor about hepatitis A and hepatitis B too.

Some visitors experience digestive upsets due to the amount of oil used in Turkish cooking. Try to eat lightly for the first few days, and keep alcohol intake to a minimum. Should you suffer from stomach troubles, remedies available include Lomotil, Ge-Oral (oral rehydration salts) and Buscopan. If you have serious and/or persistent stomach problems, it might be food poisoning and it is advisable to seek medical assistance.

Bottled water is safer to drink than tap water. Grilled meat is sometimes served lightly cooked. Ask for it well done (*iyi pişmiş*), and avoid foods that may have been sitting in the sun.

Mosquitoes can be an annoying problem along the Aegean and Mediterranean coasts, and even in big cities like Istanbul, so bring mosquito repellent from home. There is a very remote risk of contracting malaria in the Tigris and Euphrates river basins between April and July and you should consult a travel clinic for the latest advice. At the seaside, watch out for sea urchins *(deniz kestanesi)* clinging to the rocks. If you step on one, seek medical attention at once. In rocky terrain, look out for scorpions and snakes.

Rabies is prevalent in Turkey, so don't approach stray animals. If bitten, consult a doctor immediately. If you are hiking in remote areas, you may come across fierce shepherd dogs – don't come between the dog and its flock. More serious is a potentially fatal tick-borne disease, Crimean haemorrhagic fever. If you are hiking or camping, do not expose any bare flesh.

Travel and Health Insurance

Take out travel and medical insurance before leaving, and make sure repatriation cover is included. Turkey's state health system has few agreements with other countries, and private hospital costs are high. You have to pay for treatment and claim the money back on your insurance. Both state and private medical facilities accept major credit cards.

DIRECTORY

Emergency Numbers

Ambulance
Tel 112.

Fire
Tel 110.

Jandarma
Tel 156.

Police (Emergency)
Tel 155.

Tourism Police
Yerebatan Cad 6, Sultanahmet, Istanbul.
Tel (0212) 527 45 03 or 528 53 69.

Hospitals

Ahu Hetman Hospital
Marmaris.
Tel (0252) 417 77 77.
W ahuhastanesi.com

Bayındır Medical Centre
Eskişehir Highway, 2 Söğütözü, Ankara. **Tel** (0312) 287 90 00.

International Hospital
Yeşilköy, Istanbul.
Tel (0212) 468 44 44.
W internationalhospital.com.tr

Medical Park
Antalya. **Tel** (0242) 314 34 34.
W medicalpark.com.tr

Alanya Yaşam Hastanesi
Alanya. **Tel** (0850) 777 07 77
W yasamhastahaneleri.com.

Özel Letoon Hospital
Fethiye. **Tel** (0252) 646 96 00.
W letoonhospital.com.tr

Taksim Ilkyardım Hastanesi
Taksim, Istanbul. **Map** 1 B4.
Tel (0212) 252 43 00.

Banking and Currency

There is no limit to the amount of foreign currency you can bring into the country. After decades of high inflation, the Turkish lira *(Türk Lirası)* has stabilized, with inflation of around 7.5 per cent in 2015. A sign of this new-found confidence was the introduction in 2012 of the ₺ symbol to denote the currency. Note that, although many goods and service prices are shown with the ₺ symbol or TRY, many places still use the "old" abbreviation for the *Türk Lirası*, TL. In large cities and the vast majority of coastal resorts, it is easy to pay for everything using credit or debit cards, and to withdraw money from ATMs.

Cash dispenser with instructions in a range of languages

A branch of the Turkish bank Garanti in Istanbul

Banks and Bureaux de Change

Most private banks, such as **Garanti** are open 9am–5pm; some bigger branches have limited opening hours on Saturdays. State banks, such as **Ziraat**, close noon–1:30pm for lunch. Service can be slow, but they give the best exchange rate.

Even the smallest Turkish town will have at least one bank, generally found on the main shopping street. A number of foreign banks, such as Citibank and HSBC, can also be found in most cities.

Most banks offer an automated queuing system. Take a numbered ticket from the dispenser (for currency exchange there's usually a button marked *döviz*), and wait for your number to flash up on screen. Existing customers have priority, so you may wait a long time.

The İş Bankası at Istanbul's Atatürk Airport is open 24 hours a day. Several other Turkish banks also have outlets at airports, offering a full range of banking services, and there are plenty of ATM machines.

An alternative to banks are the numerous exchange offices *(döviz)*. One such office is **Bamka Döviz** in Istanbul. *Döviz* are open for longer hours than banks, and usually on Saturdays too. Be aware that their exchange rate is sometimes lower than in banks, though few now charge commission.

ATMs

Automated Teller Machines (ATMs) accept most debit cards and some credit cards, such as MasterCard and Visa, allowing you to withdraw around £250 daily. There is an English-language screen prompt on every machine. It is worth remembering that using a debit or credit card at an ATM usually involves a fee.

Always exercise caution while using ATMs; be aware of anyone standing close to you and shield the numbered keypad when entering your PIN.

Travellers' Cheques and Credit Cards

Travellers' cheques are very difficult to cash, so visitors are advised not to bring them.

Credit cards such as **Visa**, **MasterCard** and **American Express** are accepted in most hotels, restaurants and shops. Many debit cards issued by international banks such as HSBC and Citibank are also accepted, but check that your card is valid internationally before you travel. Notify your bank before you leave, so they expect the card to be used in Turkey.

There is no fee for using credit cards, although many hotels offer discounts for cash payment. If you purchase an airline ticket from a travel agent, however, they will charge a commission of about 3 per cent of the fare.

If you need money in an emergency, try a money order *(havale)* service, such as Western Union, which works in conjunction with some banks and the Turkish Post Office (PTT, *see p387*), providing a safe, speedy – but expensive – way to transfer money.

Value-Added Tax

Value-added tax (*KDV* in Turkish) runs at 18 per cent and is included in all prices. If you need a receipt for purchases, ask for a *fiş*; if you need an invoice, ask for a *fatura*. For information on tax refunds, *see p362*.

DIRECTORY

Banks and Bureaux de Change

Bamka Döviz
Cumhuriyet Cad 23, Taksim, Istanbul. **Map** 1 C3.
Tel (0212) 253 70 00.

Garanti
Yeniçeriler Cad 25, Eminönü, Istanbul. **Map** 4 C4.
Tel (0212) 455 52 50.

Ziraat
Yeniçeriler Cad 55, Beyazıt, Istanbul. **Map** 4 C4. **Tel** (0212) 517 06 00.

Credit Cards

American Express
Tel (0212) 244 25 25.

MasterCard & Visa
Tel (0212) 225 00 80.

Currency

The currency in Turkey is known as the Turkish lira (or, more officially, as your credit card statement will show, TRY). A half-anchor symbol for the currency was introduced in 2012. The lira is divided into the kuruş, with 100 kuruş equalling ₺1. The lowest denomination note is ₺5, and the highest is ₺200. Be aware that some Turkish people, out of habit, still talk in old, hyper-inflated lira terms, asking, for example, *bir milyon* (one million) for a glass of tea. Visitors are allowed to take up to US$5,000 out of Turkey in cash.

Banknotes

Turkish banknotes come in six denominations – ₺200, ₺100, ₺50, ₺20, ₺10 and ₺5 – each with its own colour. All notes show the face of Atatürk on the front, with another leading figure from Turkish history on the reverse.

200 lira

100 lira

50 lira

20 lira

10 lira

5 lira

Coins

Coins are in denominations of 5 kuruş, 10 kuruş, 25 kuruş, 50 kuruş and ₺1 (100 kuruş). All coins feature Atatürk on one side.

1 lira

50 kuruş

25 kuruş

10 kuruş

5 kuruş

Communications and Media

Throughout the country, Türk Telekom monopolizes fixed-line telephone communications. Major Turkish cities enjoy easy access to high-speed broadband connections. Internet cafés abound, though their reign is being challenged by an ever-increasing number of places offering Wi-Fi and 3G technology.

Although slow, the postal service is pretty reliable. Post offices are clearly identified by the letters PTT. Many of them change foreign currency and offer a service for sending and receiving money *(see p384)*. Making phone calls from countertop metered phones within a PTT building is fairly economical, too.

There are dozens of Turkish papers vying for readers' attention, ranging from the pro-Islamic to the staunchly secular – and all persuasions in-between. Satellite TV has revolutionized the country's once-staid broadcasting, and many foreign-language channels are available.

Making a call from a public telephone box in Istanbul

International and Local Telephone Calls

Istanbul has two area codes: 0212 for the European side and 0216 for the Asian side. To call a 0212 number from the Asian side, you must use the prefix 0212, and vice versa. To call another city in Turkey, use the appropriate area code, for example, 0224 for Bursa.

To make an international call from Turkey, dial 00 followed by the relevant country code (Australia: 61; Canada and the US: 1; New Zealand: 64; Republic of Ireland: 353; UK: 44). For international operator services, dial 115; for intercity services, 131.

Mobile Phones

Mobile (cell) phones are popular and essential items in modern Turkey. The market is dominated by three players: **Türkcell**, **Vodafone** and **Avea**.

Most visitors with a roaming facility can use their existing mobile phone as they would in their home country, since Turkey uses the standard 900 or 1800 MHz frequencies. North American phones, however, are not compatible with the Turkish system and will not work there.

Calls made using a locally bought SIM are cheaper than using your roaming facility. It is possible to buy a SIM locally, from the stands of the operators at both Istanbul airports and in most Turkish towns and cities. The big drawback is that the phone will be locked after two weeks. If you are staying longer, you can get around the problem by registering your phone with one of the main operators and paying a one-off import tax. Alternatively, buy a cheap second-hand phone in Turkey.

Türk Telekom Kontörlü Kart, one of several phonecards in Turkey

Public Telephones

Telephone calls can be made from public phone boxes, post offices (PTT), Türk Telekom (TT) centres or street kiosks using phonecards. The Alocart, with its scratch-off code, allows you to make calls from any landline in Turkey. The chipped Türk Telekom Kontörlü Kart comes in units of ₺5, ₺10 and ₺25. Both cards can be purchased from PTT and TT centres and, for an additional charge, from street sellers and kiosks. Many public phones also take credit cards.

Using a laptop computer in a designated Wi-Fi area

Internet Access

Internet cafés can be found in every Turkish town and city, although many are largely devoted to teenagers playing online games. They charge a very modest fee by the hour, but you can usually negotiate a half-hour rate for minimal usage. Most also offer hot and cold drinks and snacks at reasonable prices. Keyboards here naturally incorporate Turkish characters, which can make them very frustrating to use. Be particularly wary of the dotless "i" (ı), which, if typed in by mistake, renders Internet searches useless. The @ symbol is generally found on the Q key.

Many cafés in big cities and tourist resorts offer free wireless Internet connection. Wi-Fi is also found in most hotels and pensions, where it is usually free, although upmarket business hotels

An Internet café in Istanbul

sometimes charge a fee. Most hotels also have fixed terminals where you can check your emails.

A cheap way to make phone calls is by using VoIP (Voice over Internet Protocol). This system lets you make phone calls anywhere in the world from your own computer. The most popular one is Skype.

Postal Services

There are **post offices** (PTT) in every city in Turkey and all major towns and resorts. Letters and postcards can be handed over the counter at a post office or mailed in letterboxes, which are yellow and labelled "PTT". A sign indicates which slot you should put your letter in: *Şehiriçi* (local), *Yurtiçi* (domestic) and *Yurtdışı* (international).

Surface post is slow, so it is best to use air mail *(uçak ile)* when sending items abroad. Letters to Europe take around a week; allow twice as long for mail to other continents. A recorded delivery service (called APS) is available from post offices, with delivery in three days within Turkey.

If you want to send a parcel by surface mail, use registered *(kayıtlı)* post. To meet customs regulations, the contents of a package must be inspected at the post office, so take tape to seal your parcel at the counter.

Local courier companies such as **Yurtiçi Kargo** and **Aras Kargo** will deliver letters and parcels inland in a day or so at a comparable price, and they are much more efficient than the PTT. Both have websites in English, but don't expect staff to speak it fluently. International players like **DHL** also have offices throughout Turkey, but they charge a little more for their services. Sending parcels abroad with courier companies is more expensive than using the PTT, but the service is more reliable and easier to track.

Newspapers and Magazines

Three daily English-language newspapers – *Today's Zaman* (www.todayszaman.com), *Daily Sabah* (www.dailysabah.com) and *Hürriyet Daily News* (www.hurriyetdailynews.com) – give a roundup of Turkish and foreign news. They are available in cities with large expat communities, such as Istanbul and Ankara, and in resort towns, but harder to find in provincial towns and cities. *Today's Zaman* is liberal Islamic in its outlook, *Daily Sabah* is the mouthpiece of the AKP – the leading political party in government, while *Hürriyet Daily News* is nationalist and secular. All papers can be read online.

A range of foreign newspapers and magazines can be found in major tourist resorts and cities. For listings in Istanbul, try *Time Out Istanbul* or *The Guide Istanbul*.

Newspaper stand outside the Topkapı Palace

TV and Radio

Satellite TV has blossomed in Turkey, with dozens of Turkish and foreign channels competing for viewers. Widely available foreign news channels include BBC World News, Al Jazeera and CNN, with English-language entertainment provided by the likes of CNBCE, E2, BBC Entertainment and MTV. For foreign sports, look out for Eurosport, Lig TV and SporMax. Most hotels receive global satellite television, but check in advance of booking if you particularly want foreign channels in your room. Large flat-screen TVs are to be found in many restaurants and bars, usually screening either local pop music or Turkish football.

The state-owned TRT (Türk Radyo ve Televizyon) runs six television channels and three radio stations. TRT2 television has news bulletins in English, French and German at 7pm and 10pm. TRT3 radio (FM 88.2) broadcasts news in English, French and German throughout the day (at 9am, noon, 5pm, 7pm and 9pm).

DIRECTORY

Mobile Phones

Avea
Tel 444 15 00.
W avea.com.tr

Türkcell
Tel 444 05 32.
W turkcell.com.tr

Vodafone
Tel (0542) 444 05 42.
W vodafone.com.tr

Postal Services

Aras Kargo
Tel 444 25 52.
W araskargo.com.tr

DHL
Tel 440 00 40.
W dhl.com.tr

Post Office (PTT)
W ptt.gov.tr

Yurtiçi Kargo
Tel 444 99 99.
W yurticikargo.com

TRAVEL INFORMATION

The easiest way to get to Turkey is by air. Turkish Airlines (THY) offers regular direct flights from many airports in Europe, North America and Asia. Several major European carriers, such as Lufthansa and KLM, also fly direct to Istanbul. Atatürk Airport, on the European side of the city, is still the most used Istanbul airport, but many airlines, especially the budget ones, use Sabiha Gökçen, on the Asian side of the city. There are also budget and charter flights from many European cities to resort destinations in the Aegean and Mediterranean. In addition, it is possible to reach Turkey overland, by coach or train, or by ferry.

The country's network of domestic flights is far-reaching, with Turkish Airlines and several private operators linking Istanbul and Ankara with many other Turkish destinations. Alternative internal travel options include a comprehensive intercity coach network and a rapidly improving rail network.

Green Travel

Although domestic flights are tempting in terms of the time saved reaching far-flung regions, Turkey's wonderful intercity bus network is a greener and cheaper alternative – as is the rail network with its fast-growing number of high-speed services.

In most large Turkish cities the main points of interest are often clustered together in the historic centre, so try to reach them on foot. In Istanbul, even the more remote sights can usually be reached easily enough by public transport. In Istanbul and many other conurbations, buses use natural gas, as do most taxis.

The weather in Turkey means it is very pleasant to spend time in the great outdoors, so environmentally aware visitors may wish to consider a walking, trekking or cycling holiday.

Arriving by Air

Many visitors arrive at either Istanbul's Atatürk Airport, on the European side of the city, or at Sabiha Gökçen, on the Asian side. For onward travel within Turkey, you can change to a domestic **Turkish Airlines** (THY) flight or use one of the several low-cost domestic carriers *(see Directory)*.

Most major European carriers, including Lufthansa, KLM, Austrian Airlines and British Airways, have at least one daily flight to Istanbul. American Airlines, Qantas and other international carriers also serve the city, although not always with a direct flight.

In terms of budget airlines, easyJet and **Anadolujet**, a subsidiary of Turkish Airlines, connect the UK with Sabiha Gökçen Airport; the Turkish carrier **Pegasus Airlines** flies into both Istanbul airports from the UK and several European cities; while the German/Turkish carrier **Sunexpress** serves Sabiha Gökçen from many northern European countries. Aegean and Mediterranean resorts, notably Antalya, Bodrum, and Dalaman, are served by UK charter airlines, such as Thomas Cook and Thomson, as well as budget Turkish carriers, such as the Sunexpress and **Atlas Jet**.

May to October is peak season, but flights also fill up during school and religious holidays, including the annual Muslim pilgrimage to Mecca, the date of which varies with the lunar calendar.

Airports

Istanbul's **Atatürk Airport** (Atatürk Hava Limanı) lies 25 km (16 miles) west of the city centre, in Yeşilköy. Its huge international terminal *(Dış Hatları)* is a 15-minute walk from the domestic terminal *(İç Hatları)*, linked by moving walkways and corridors. The international terminal has all the facilities you would expect, including 24-hour banking, car-hire outlets, a tourist information office and a hotel-reservation desk. Allow at least 2 hours to check in for departures from busy Atatürk Airport.

Many domestic carriers, as well as international budget airlines, use **Sabiha Gökçen Airport**. Set in the suburbs on the Asian side of Istanbul, 32 km (20 miles)

Planes parked at Istanbul's Atatürk Airport

southeast of the city centre, it is less conveniently located but smaller and easier to navigate than Atatürk Airport, with all the usual facilities on offer.

Visitors flying to Ankara land at **Esenboğa Airport**, which is located 28 km (17 miles) from the city centre.

Buses operated by **Havataş** shuttle passengers from both Istanbul airports to the city centre, while the same service is provided by **Havaş** in Ankara and provincial cities *(see p397)*.

Domestic Air Travel

Turkey is a vast country, and flying is the most convenient (if not the greenest) way to travel from Istanbul to eastern cities such as Erzurum, Trabzon and Van. Several carriers compete on the same routes, so prices are reasonable (from ₺100) if booked early – between six and four weeks prior to departure. Tickets are available online or from high-street travel agencies at a slight premium.

It is possible to fly to several Turkish cities direct from both Istanbul airports, as well as from Ankara, İzmir and Antalya. Flights between other cities sometimes involve extended connection times in the hub airports of Istanbul or Ankara. Anadolujet and Sunexpress fly from Istanbul's Sabiha Gökçen. **Atlas Jet** and **Onur Air** use Atatürk Airport, while Pegaus Airlines and Turkish Airlines use both. Snacks and drinks are extras on all carriers except Turkish Airlines, and the baggage weight limit for budget airlines is usually 15 kg (33 lb).

Arriving by Rail

The Orient Express *(see p80)* no longer travels to Istanbul. The best overland route, which takes a couple of days, is from Munich via Vienna, Budapest and Bucharest. Information on train travel can be obtained from **The Man in Seat 61**, and bookings made through **European Rail Ltd**.

Istanbul's two historic railway stations, Sirkeci Station, at the European side of the Bosphorus, and Haydarpaşa, on the Asian side, have been sidelined by the Marmaray transport project. Trains arriving from Europe arrive at Halkalı, and trains heading into Anatolia depart from Pendik.

Arriving by Coach

Two leading Turkish coach companies, **Ulusoy** and **Varan**, operate direct services from several European cities to Istanbul, with tickets available online. Departure points for Ulusoy coaches include Munich and Frankfurt; Varan coaches depart from Budapest, Salzburg and Vienna.

Coaches arrive at Esenler coach station *(see p391)*, 10 km (6 miles) northwest of Istanbul city centre. Esenler is also the main terminal for domestic connections. Coach companies usually operate a courtesy minibus from the terminal to the city centre.

A network of ferries links Turkey to Greece and Northern Cyprus

Arriving by Sea

Ferries run from various Greek islands to Turkey. Routes include Samos to Kuşadası, Rhodes to Bodrum, Fethiye and Marmaris, Kos to Bodrum, and Lesbos to Ayvalık, though services are not always reliable. Ferries and high-speed catamarans (sea buses) also link Northern Cyprus to Turkey's southern Mediterranean coast.

The main cruise-ship docks in the country are at the Karaköy terminal, in central Istanbul, and at the Aegean resort of Kuşadası, gateway to the ancient city of Ephesus.

The **Feribot** website offers a wealth of useful information on sea travel.

DIRECTORY

Airports

Atatürk Airport
Tel (0212) 463 30 00.
W ataturkairport.com

Esenboğa Airport
Tel (0312) 590 40 00.
W esenbogaairport.com

Havaş
Tel (0212) 465 47 00 or 56 56.
W havas.com.tr

Havataş
Tel 444 26 56. **W havatas.com**

Sabiha Gökçen Airport
Tel (0216) 585 50 00.
W sgairport.com

Airlines

Anadolujet
Tel 444 25 38.
W anadolujet.com

Atlas Jet
Tel 444 33 87.
W atlasjet.com

Onur Air
Tel 444 66 87.
W onurair.com.tr

Pegasus Airlines
Tel 444 07 37.
W flypgs.com

Sunexpress
Tel 444 07 97.
W sunexpress.com

Turkish Airlines (THY)
Tel 444 08 49.
W turkishairlines.com

Arriving by Rail

European Rail Ltd
W raileurope.com

The Man in Seat 61
W seat61.com

Arriving by Coach

Ulusoy
Tel 444 18 88. **W ulusoy.com.tr**

Varan
Tel 444 89 99. **W varan.com.tr**

Arriving by Sea

Feribot
W feribot.net

Travelling by Bus and Dolmuş

Despite the proliferation of low-cost domestic flights in recent years, Turkey's intercity bus service remains arguably the best way to see the country. Travelling to a great number of destinations, buses are comfortable and often luxurious. In addition, bus travel is both cheaper and greener than air travel. There are also fewer hidden costs (for example, many provincial airports are way out of town, requiring a taxi into the city centre), and a bus ticket purchased near the departure date will likely be far cheaper than a last-minute flight. For a more informal travelling experience, and over shorter distances, a *dolmuş* (minibus) is the most cheerful, versatile and economical way to get around.

A modern, luxurious Kâmil Koç bus

Bus Travel

The profusion of coach and long-distance bus companies gives the impression that bus travel in Turkey is a highly competitive business. In fact, the entire industry operates on a franchise system: bus companies maintain relatively uniform fares based on petrol (gas) prices and the inflation rate. This system ensures that bus operators share revenue.

The leading intercity coach firms are **Kâmil Koç**, **Varan**, **Metro Turizm** and **Ulusoy**. They all run regular schedules with teams of well-trained drivers, comfortable vehicles and a steward who comes around at regular intervals to serve free hot or cold drinks and cakes or biscuits. Free water is available on request from the steward, who also supplies refreshing cologne. Some coaches are just three seats across, and all have on-board entertainment, such as films or television, with the more expensive companies offering personal screens and headsets. Many companies also offer free Wi-Fi on board. Most buses stop for 30 or 40 minutes every 4 hours or so, with a shorter facilities stop in between. Everything from a glass of tea to a full Turkish meal is available at most stops, and the quality of the food is surprisingly good, though prices are usually a little higher than the average high-street restaurant.

Journeys of more than 10 hours tend to be made overnight. As you move eastwards in Turkey, the intercity bus network becomes a little sparser, but these buses are often just as comfortable.

Although vehicles have tinted windows and air conditioning, it is best to sit on the side of the bus facing away from the sun in the hot summer months.

It is convention for passengers travelling alone to be seated next to someone of the same sex, though this custom is often ignored in western Turkey. Consumption of alcohol and smoking are forbidden on board *(see p381)*. It is also worth noting that intercity buses do not have on-board toilets, hence the frequent rest stops.

Bus Tickets and Fares

When travelling by bus, it is advisable to book your tickets well in advance, particularly on weekends and during any school or religious holidays (*see p41*), though on busy routes with several departures a day, you can usually just turn up at the bus station and find a seat. Bear in mind that certain bus operators have "hustlers" stationed at popular bus stations whose job is to take you to the ticket office of the company they work for. However, the bus company might not necessarily operate the most convenient departure times for you, so don't be persuaded to buy a ticket until you've seen what is available. Larger towns and cities often have several travel offices where you can purchase tickets and, usually, get a free shuttle to the bus station. Several firms have facilities for online booking and payment, with user-friendly websites in Turkish and English.

Despite fuel costs in Turkey being among the highest in the world, bus travel here remains very good value compared to most European countries. As a rule, a ticket from a standard bus company will cost about two-thirds of the price of an early-booking budget-airline ticket for the same route.

Travel offices in Marmaris selling long-distance bus tickets

Bus Stations

In most Turkish cities, the *otogar* (bus station) is located well away from the city centre. Typically, bus companies provide a free shuttle service from several central pick-up points to the *otogar*, and from there to the city centre at journey's end. In Istanbul, coach companies ferry passengers to and from their own terminals (close to the motorway) on the Asian and European sides of the city. In some cities, you will need to take a public minibus or, in the case of Antalya and Konya, the tram.

Istanbul's main intercity *otogar*, **Esenler**, is 10 km (6 miles) northwest of the city. It's a massive but rather drab affair, with more than 150 companies vying for business. There is also a bus terminal in **Harem**, on the Asian side. Some buses departing from Esenler stop at Harem before heading into Anatolia, but if that's where you're heading, boarding in Harem could save you tedious time stuck in Istanbul's notoriously congested traffic.

All major and most minor bus stations in Turkey have toilet facilities, which charge a small fee, shops selling everything from *lokum* (Turkish delight) and bottled water to newspapers, and amenities such as shoeshines, restaurants, cafés and even hairdressers. Turkish bus stations are generally safe places to be, even at night, although you should take precautions against pickpockets.

Dolmuş and Minibus Travel

In Turkey, a *dolmuş* means two things: a shared taxi that follows a fixed route and departs when full (*see p396*), and a minibus, often cream-coloured (although in Istanbul they are sometimes blue), that follows fixed routes according to a schedule and is generally packed with passengers.

A *dolmuş* a typical Turkish mode of transport

In most cities, *dolmuş* stops are indicated by a rectangular blue sign bearing a large "D" on a white or red panel. Destinations are shown on the front side of the vehicle, but be aware that these relate to districts rather than streets.

The best thing about travelling by *dolmuş* is that you can usually alight anywhere you like. Simply say *Müsait bir yer'de* ("at the next convenient point") or *İnecek var* ("somebody wants to get off"). The increased volume of traffic in some cities means that *dolmuşes* are no longer allowed to pull in wherever they like, though many still do.

Getting used to a city's *dolmuş* system is not easy. In practice, this mode of transport is most useful in tourist resorts, where the drivers know where visitors want to go and locals speak enough English to offer their help.

DOLMUS STOP

Sign for a *dolmuş* stop

Minibuses, also confusingly referred to as *dolmuş* by many locals, serve smaller towns and villages, usually departing from, and returning to, a garage or depot in a larger provincial settlement. Unfortunately, many minibuses serving small towns in rural areas tend to cater to the needs of the villagers, departing the town/village early in the morning and returning in the late afternoon, which is usually not convenient to visitors planning a day trip in the country.

Dolmuş and Minibus Fares

Payment on *dolmuşes* and minibuses is by Turkish lira in cash. Tickets and electronic smart tickets are not accepted. Note that if you sit in the front, you will be responsible for passing fares and change to and fro between the passengers and the driver. Fares are low, so be sure to carry small change, as drivers get irate if presented with a ₺50 note for a ₺2 journey.

Fares on minibuses are cheaper pro-rata than intercity bus fares, but the vehicles are often cramped and crowded, especially with villagers taking town-bought goods home.

DIRECTORY

Bus Travel

Kâmil Koç
Tel 444 05 62.
W kamilkoc.com.tr

Metro Turizm
Tel 444 34 55.
W metroturizm.com.tr

Ulusoy
Tel 444 18 88.
W ulusoy.com.tr

Varan
Tel 444 89 99.
W varan.com.tr

Bus Stations

Esenler
Bayrampasa, Istanbul.
Tel (0212) 658 05 05.
Open 5am–midnight daily.

Harem Station
Istanbul. **Tel** (0216) 333 37 63.
Open 5am–midnight daily.

Travelling by Train and Ferry

Turkey's once notoriously slow rail network is undergoing a major overhaul. A high-speed line now links Ankara with Konya and another links the capital to Istanbul, thus linking Turkey's two major cities. More high-speed links are under construction. In the meantime, the old rail network provides a cheap and leisurely way to see the country. Most of Turkey's boat traffic is centred on Istanbul's busy waterways, and a number of ferries and high-speed catamarans cross the Sea of Marmara.

The busy Ankara train station, connecting major cities in Turkey

Train Travel

Turkey's national railway system is run by **Turkish State Railways** (Türkiye Cumhuriyeti Devlet Demiryolları, or TCDD). The standard train network is slow, but it is good value for money and relatively comfortable. The high speed trains(YHT) provide a viable alternative to flying between Istanbul and the capital, Ankara. They also link Ankara with the southwest Anatolian city of Konya.

Rail trips can be booked via the TCDD website. However, since it is quite tricky to use the site successfully, it may be better to use one of the many travel agencies endorsed to sell train tickets. If you want to purchase a sleeper ticket, you must do it from the station of departure, but note that you cannot book further ahead than two weeks. Credit cards are accepted at most intercity train stations.

Rail Routes

To explore Anatolia by rail, the most logical way to begin is to take the high-speed train from Istanbul to Ankara, and then connect with the old Anatolian rail network.

The most interesting routes for visitors are Ankara–Kars, on the Armenian frontier, which is a journey of almost 40 hours; and Ankara–Lake Van, which takes 36 hours. Because of the formidable barrier created by the Taurus Mountains, which separate Anatolia from the Mediterranean, there is no rail line along the southern Aegean and Mediterranean coasts. There are rail networks, however, to the southern Mediterranean city of Adana from the Anatolian cities of Ankara, Kayseri and Konya. Another interesting route is to take the train from Bandirma (linked to Istanbul by high speed ferry) and travel to İzmir on the Central Aegean coast. Blue Trains *(Mavi Trenler)* are faster than the standard Express trains *(Ekspresler)*.

Sleepers, Seats and Service

Most trains offer comfortable two-berth sleeping cars *(yataklı vagon)*. These have air conditioning and a basin; soap, a towel and bedlinen are provided. There are squat toilets at either end of each sleeping car, and an attendant who will expect a small tip. There are also four- or six-berth couchettes, which are a little cheaper but less private since you will share the compartment with other

A TCDD train travelling through the scenic Turkish countryside near Polatlı in Western Anatolia

passengers. On some routes bedlinen is provided, while on others you will be expected to bring your own. Beds fold away in the daytime. The reclining Pullman seats are cheaper still, but for rock-bottom prices you can try an ordinary first- or second-class seat. Unless you are travelling as part of a group, however, a *yataklı vagon* makes the most sense, since it is the safest option – sleeping passengers make easy targets for thieves.

Many trains have a restaurant car *(büfe)* on board serving decent food and drinks. In remote areas, few stations have much in the way of facilities, so for long journeys it is wise to stock up before boarding.

A high-speed catamaran sailing on the Bosphorus

Rail Tours

Making your own rail-travel bookings in Turkey can seem intimidating. However, there are several websites that take the language barrier out of the equation. One such site is www.neredennereye.com, which is useful for general travel and booking information.

A rail package tour through the Anatolian interior combines visits to the major tourist sights with bus and air travel to save time where necessary. The most popular route is Ankara to Kars. For more details on specialized rail tours, see pp374–5.

If you are planning a longer trip to Turkey, consider a TCDD pass, which allows 30 days of unlimited rail travel. There are several different options, but the best one is probably the sleeping-car pass (₺550). A good option for those on a budget is the Express Train Tour Card, which allows 30 days of unlimited travel on all standard trains (except high-speed trains) for ₺210, though the reservation fee for travel in sleeping cars is not included. Cards can be purchased from most stations, but note that pass holders will still need to reserve their compartment in advance.

Ferries

High-speed catamaran (sea bus) and ferry services are mostly limited to Istanbul and the Sea of Marmara. Operated by the **Istanbul Seabus Company (IDO)**, ferries link the European and Asian sides of the city, and run up and down the Bosphorus. Sea buses also travel to the Princes' and Marmara Islands, and across the Sea of Marmara to Güzelyalı (for Bursa), Yalova (for İznik), Bandirma (for Çanakkale and rail services to İzmir and the Aegean coast) and Mudanya. Services are more frequent in the summer (mid-June to early September) and at weekends. For schedules, routes and fares, visit the IDO website.

Car ferries make the short hop across the Dardanelles, the strait joining the Sea of Marmara and the Aegean, useful if you are driving to Troy from Istanbul.

There are also ferries and sea buses to Girne, in Northern Cyprus, from Taşucu, Alanya and Mersin, and a thrice-weekly service linking Mersin and Famagusta.

DIRECTORY

Train Travel

Turkish State Railways (TCDD)
Talat Paşa Bulvarı,
06330 Gar, Ankara.
Tel (0312) 309 05 15 or 444 82 33.
W tcdd.gov.tr
Online booking and information on rail routes, timetables, services, fares, authorized ticket agents, discounts and contact details.

Rail Tours

W neredennereye.com
Rail and ferry timetables and booking information. Also covers bus and air travel. Five languages.

Ferries

Akgunler Denizcilik
Galeria Iş Merkezi Z/12,
Taşucu.
Tel (0324) 741 40 33.
W akgunler.com.tr
Ferries and sea buses between Taşucu and Northern Cyprus.

Fergün Denizcilik
Girne Yeni Liman Yolu,
Fergün Apt 1, Girne,
Northern Cyprus.
Tel (0392) 815 18 70.
W fergun.net
Sea buses between Alanya and Northern Cyprus.

Istanbul Seabus Company (IDO)
Kennedy Cad, Yenikapı
Hızlı Feribot İskelesi,
Fatih, Istanbul.
Tel 444 44 36.
W ido.com.tr
Online booking and information on schedules and fares (English menu).

Travelling by Car and Bicycle

Most areas of Turkey can be reached quickly and efficiently by road, with motorways and/or six-lane highways linking most major centres. The drawbacks are the high cost of petrol and the alarmingly high accident rate. In addition, Turkey is a large country, and places that may appear close on a map can take much longer than expected to reach, especially if you venture off the beaten track. The major international car-rental firms are widely represented in Turkey, and there are also many local (usually cheaper) companies. Alternatively, you can bring your own vehicle or caravan.

The rugged terrain and long distances make cycling a strenuous way to see the country. However, cyclists are certain to encounter helpful, friendly people during their journey.

The forecourt of a petrol station selling different types of fuel

The Bosphorus Bridge, one of two major road bridges in Istanbul

Car Rental

To rent a car, you need to present an international driving licence and your passport. To avoid having to pay a large deposit, use a credit card. Drivers must be over 18 years of age.

Be sure to read the small print on the rental contract; insurance cover usually excludes windscreen and tyre damage, or even theft. Keep your vehicle's documents *(rhusat)* with you at all times and do not leave them unattended in the car. Most international companies hire out vehicles with full tanks; many local firms with empty tanks. You return them the same way.

The easiest place to hire a car is at your arrival airport, but all major cities and most resorts will have several car-hire outlets. Most hotels can also arrange car rental for you.

Bringing your own Vehicle

If you drive your own vehicle into Turkey, you will need a valid driving licence and a Green Card to denote international insurance coverage. Documents such as proof of purchase or chassis number are not needed but can be useful. Cars can be brought into Turkey for a six-month period. The car's details will be entered in your passport so you cannot leave without it.

Fuel

Petrol (gas) is sold in leaded octanes of normal and super, and as unleaded *(kurşunsuz)*. Many local vehicles run on *otogaz* (liquid petroleum gas), which is cheaper than regular petrol, but few hire cars have been converted to this form of fuel. Diesel *(dizel)* is becoming more common in hire cars, since it is much cheaper than petrol. Pay the extra for a diesel vehicle if you plan to drive a lot. Credit cards are accepted without commission *(see p384)*.

Rules of the Road

When in Turkey, you must drive on the right, give way at junctions to traffic from the right, and wear a seatbelt. Distances are shown in kilometres, and road signs conform to the international standard. The police often stop cars to check identification; showing a passport or driving licence will usually suffice.

Look out for pedestrians, animals, tractors and vehicles without lights. Don't assume that you have the right of way. Drivers making a left turn may veer to the right and wait for traffic to pass. Turkish drivers often reverse on the motorway's hard shoulder if they have overshot their exit. On all major motorways and the Bosphorus Bridge, you will pay a fee, usually taking a ticket at the entry point and paying as you exit. Many toll motorways only accept pre-paid KGS (Kreditli Geçiş Systemi) smart cards – the larger hire car outlets should have them available and they are mandatory if you hire a vehicle at one of the two Istanbul airports.

Parking is a major problem in the cities. Street parking is possible, but in central areas there will be a charge. In open car parks, it is customary to leave your keys with the attendants so they can move your car if needed. Towaway zones are indicated by a sign showing a breakdown van.

Emergencies

If you have an accident, call the police. Note that moving your vehicle is a crime and may negate your insurance. Heavy city traffic can slow the progress of ambulances, which tend to arrive less quickly than the police. Blood-group details are displayed on Turks' driving licences; in case of a serious accident, this is a sensible precaution.

On secondary roads, local people are usually very helpful if you break down or have a flat tyre. On the motorway around Istanbul, emergency telephones every few kilometres connect you to the police. A firm called **Tur Assist** handles recovery services. The **Touring and Automobile Association of Turkey (TTOK)**, known simply as Turing, can provide detailed advice on driving in Turkey, transit documents and assistance with breakdowns, accidents and insurance. Your consulate or embassy *(see p381)* can also be helpful in the event of a minor emergency.

Repairs

Most towns have a designated *sanayi area* (industrial zone) or a specialized *oto sanayi* (automotive repair zone) to handle repairs. For punctures, look out for *otolastikci* (tyre repairer) signs at roadside establishments that are often little more than huts. If you bring your own vehicle, check whether spares for your model are available in Turkey.

Motorcyling and Cycling

Motorcycle enthusiasts usually ride overland through Europe to Turkey, or take a ferry from Greece *(see p389)*. Outside major conurbations, Turkey's big, open spaces and relatively traffic-free roads are major attractions for bikers.

The same regulations that apply to bringing a car into the country *(see opposite)* are valid for motorbikes. The risks associated with car travel in Turkey are magnified for motorcyclists, so ride carefully. Most resorts in Turkey have several outlets for motorcycle and scooter hire.

Cycling is a fun and eco-friendly way to travel around Turkey

You can bring your own bicycle into Turkey without any customs formalities. It is wise to bring extra inner tubes and any spares that may be necessary, particularly for a long-distance cycle tour, though most major towns have bike repair shops. It is also possible to rent bicycles, especially in coastal resorts and in Cappadocia *(see Directory)*.

Getting Around

Road maps of Turkey are often inadequate, making it difficult to find your way on country roads or to out-of-the-way places. Route signage is also poor, so it is wise to purchase a good map in your home country prior to travelling. Rural roads make for great adventures, but the potholes can be a hazard. In addition, Turkish drivers may show very little consideration for cyclists. Villagers are generally very helpful, but the language barrier may prove insurmountable.

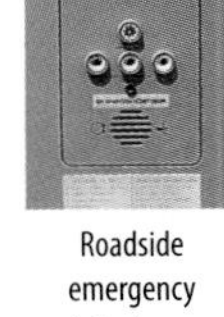

Roadside emergency telephone

Mediterranean and Aegean coastal areas are the best for cycling, with exhilarating opportunities for freewheeling. Cappadocia is less well known for cycling, but it has accessible off-road trails and tracks, and the terrain is flatter than on coastal areas. Finding your way on unmarked routes will likely be your greatest challenge here.

Travel agents and tour operators can arrange cycling tours. The adventure company Bougainville *(see p375)* offers mountain-biking tours, both on the Western Mediterranean coast and in Cappadocia, Middle Earth Travel *(see p375)* is also a good option in Cappadocia.

DIRECTORY

Car Rental

Avis
Central reservations
Tel 444 28 47 or (0216) 587 99 99.
W avis.com.tr
Atatürk Airport
Tel (0212) 465 34 55.
Sabiha Gökçen Airport
Tel (0216) 585 51 54.

Europcar
Central reservations
Tel (0216) 427 04 27.
W europcar.com.tr
Atatürk Airport
Tel (0212) 465 62 84.
Topcu Cad 1, Taksim
Tel (0212) 254 77 10.

Hertz
Central reservations
Tel (0216) 349 30 40.
Atatürk Airport
Tel (0212) 465 59 99.
Sabiha Gökçen Airport
Tel (0216) 588 01 41.
W hertz.com.tr

Emergencies

Touring and Automobile Association of Turkey (TTOK)
I Oto Sanayi Sitesi Yanı, IV Levent, Istanbul.
Tel (0212) 282 81 40.
W turing.org.tr

Tur Assist
W turassist.com

Cycle Hire

Argeus Travel
İstiklal Cad 47, Ürgüp.
Tel (0384) 341 46 88.
W argeus.com.tr

Mithra Travel
Hesapçi Sokak, Kaleiçi, Antalya.
Tel (0242) 248 77 47.
W mithratravel.com

Getting Around Istanbul

The central areas of the city are well served by Metro and tram lines. Buses and *dolmuşes* provide city-wide transport, but roads and vehicles are very crowded at rush hour. Ferries and water taxis ply the Bosphorus and, to a lesser extent, the Golden Horn. The ambitious Marmaray Project has overhauled the transport infrastructure of Istanbul. The underwater tunnel has created more than 70 km (43 miles) of suburban rail line under the Bosphorus and links the European and Asian sides of the city. Trains arriving from Europe arrive at Halkalı, and trains heading into Anatolia depart from Pendik. Both of these Istanbul suburbs will be linked to the city centre by metro.

Visitors strolling in front of the Blue Mosque *(see pp82–3)*

Walking

The creation of semi-pedestrianized areas, such as İstiklâl Caddesi and central Sultanahmet, and walking/jogging paths along sections of the Sea of Marmara and the Bosphorus, has made it possible to walk with ease around some parts of Istanbul. Quieter backwaters, like Eyüp *(see p124)* and parts of Fatih *(see p119)*, Fener and Balat, have relatively little traffic, making them attractive destinations for a stroll.

Wherever you walk, bear in mind that traffic only stops at pedestrian crossings controlled by lights. On main roads, always use pedestrian overpasses and underpasses.

Istanbul, like any large city, has some unsavoury areas that are best avoided. The Tarlabaşı neighbourhood of Beyoğlu has a bad reputation, as do the parts around the Theodosian Walls. If you plan to walk in places off the beaten track, seek local advice, take extra care and avoid walking in unfamiliar areas after dark.

Taxis

Taxis are ubiquitous in Istanbul. Operating day and night, they can be hailed in the street or found at taxi ranks. Hotel and restaurant staff can also phone for a taxi. Fares are cheap in comparison to other major European cities.

Cabs are bright yellow, with the word *taksi* on a sign on the roof. They take up to four passengers, and the fare is charged according to a meter. If you cross the Bosphorus Bridge, the toll will be added to the fare. Unless they have helped with your luggage, drivers will not expect a tip; simply round up the fare to the nearest convenient figure.

Most taxi drivers speak little or no English. They may not be familiar with routes to lesser-known sights either, so carry a map and have the name of your destination written down.

A bright-yellow taxi on the streets of Istanbul

Dolmuşes

In Istanbul, *dolmuşes (see p391)* run throughout the day until mid-evening, and later on busy routes. Points of origin and final destinations are displayed in the front windows. Fares generally range between ₺3 and ₺6.

The most useful *dolmuş* routes to the average visitor to Istanbul are on the Asian side of the Bosphorus. From Taksim, destinations include Aksaray, Beşiktaş, Kadıköy, Topkapı and Yedikule (for the Theodosian Walls). Vehicles depart from the Taksim end of Tarlabaşı Bulvarı and where İsmet Inönü Caddesi exits Taksim.

A *dolmuş* at a stop in Istanbul

Guided Tours

Several operators run special-interest tours of Istanbul, as well as general guided tours of the city and further afield. **Big Bus** offers two open-top bus tours of the city, starting from the square in front of the Haghia Sophia in Sultanahmet. The City Tour red route includes the major old city sights, crosses the Golden Horn to Taksim, then heads across to Asia. The Golden Horn blue route concentrates on the old city sights. Reliable companies that organize city tours, including walking tours, are **Backpackers**

Travel, **Fest Travel** and **Turista Travel**. For more companies providing trips outside Istanbul, *see pp372–5*.

If you are approached by individuals offering their services as tour guides, ask to see their photo ID first, then tell them clearly what you want to see and agree a fee. If you do not wish to travel by public transport, you can negotiate a private tour with a taxi driver. This is best arranged through your hotel.

Travel Pass

Although you may see locals using a metal token mounted in a plastic holder, these have now been phased out and replaced by a credit-card style travel pass known as an Istanbulkart. The card is valid on the tram and metro systems, funiculars, suburban railway, all ferries and most city buses. Available outside Sabiha Gökçen Airport, at the Havalimani (airport) stop on the light railway linking Atatürk Airport with the centre, and at many public transport offices across the city, the card costs a refundable ₺10, which includes ₺4 of credit. Load it up at the point of purchase at a machine or kiosk and keep it topped up using the automatic machines outside major transport stops. Swipe the card across the screen at the turnstile machines at the entrance to the platforms for the tram, metro, suburban railway, funiculars and ferries, or next to the driver on buses.

Travel Tokens

If you are not planning to use public transport very frequently you can purchase tokens *(jeton)* valid for most forms of Istanbul transport from *Jetonmatik* automatic vending machines near many tranpsort stops. However, you pay around a third more for each journey than if you use the Istanbulkart.

Useful Bus Routes

12 Kadıköy – Üsküdar
22 Kabataş – Istinye
25/A Levent Metro – Rumeli Kavağı
28 Edirenekapı – Beşiktaş
28/T Topkapı – Beşiktaş
36/E Eminönü – Edirnekapı
40 Taksim – Sariyer
80T Taksim – Yedikule
830 Otogar – Taksim

Airport shuttle bus bearing the Havaş logo

Buses

Innercity buses are run by two companies. **I.E.T.T.** (Istanbul Omnibus Company) operates buses and environmentally friendly green ones *(yeşil motor)*, while **Özel Halk** (a subsidiary of I.E.T.T.) has mainly green and light-blue-and-green buses. Both accept the Istanbulkart and *jeton*, but cash payment is not permitted. If you cross either of the Bosphorus bridges, expect to pay double fare.

You queue and enter at the front of the bus and exit by the middle or rear doors. Push the button above the door or attached to the support poles to alert the driver that you wish to alight at the next stop. A list of stops is displayed on a board on the side of the bus or on a video screen. Bus shelters also have details of routes and stops. Most buses run from 6am until 10 or 11pm.

Metrobuses run in dedicated lanes, but the routes are of little interest to the vast majority of visitors.

Airport Transfers

A **Havataş** shuttle bus runs between Atatürk Airport and Taksim via Aksaray (for Sultan-ahmet) from 4am to 1am daily. The trip takes 30–40 minutes and costs ₺10. There is also a Havataş bus from Sabiha Gökçen to Taksim, from 3:30am to 1am, which takes about an hour and costs ₺14. Taxis charge about ₺40 to Taksim from Atatürk Airport and about ₺95 from Sabiha Gökçen.

For travellers on a budget, the cheapest option from Atatürk Airport is to take the light railway to Zeytinburnu, then change to the tram for Sultanahmet. For Taksim, continue to Kabataş, from where you can ride the funicular up to Taksim. From Sabiha Gökçen, take the E10 bus to Kadıköy, then a Turyol ferry *(see p399)* across the Bosphorus to Eminönü.

DIRECTORY

Guided Tours

Backpackers Travel
Yeni Akbıyık Caddesi 22, Sultanahmet, Istanbul.
Map 5 D4.
Tel (0212) 638 63 43.
W backpackerstravel.net

Big Bus City Istanbul
Aya Sofya Karşısı.
Tel (0212) 283 13 96.
W bigbustours.com

Fest Travel
Barbaros Bulvarı 44/20, Beşiktaş, Istanbul.
Map 2 C3.
Tel (0212) 216 10 36.
W festtravel.com.tr

Turista Travel
Divanyolu Cad 16, Sultanahmet, Istanbul. **Map** 5 D4.
Tel (0212) 518 65 70.
W turistatravel.com

Buses

I.E.T.T.
Tel (0800) 211 60 68 or (0212) 245 07 20.
W iett.gov.tr

Özel Halk
Tel 444 18 71.
W iett.gov.tr

Airport Transfers

Havataş
Tel (0212) 465 56 56.
W havatas.com

A tram on Istanbul's modern tramway system

Tramway

Istanbul's tramway system is modern and efficient, if very crowded at peak times. Most useful for visitors is the T1 line, which runs from Zeytinburnu, where it connects with the M1 metro coming in from Atatürk Airport, through Aksaray and Sultanahmet. It then crosses the Galata Bridge to Kabataş.

Trams travel on the right-hand side of the street, so be sure to stand on the correct platform. To board a tram, buy a flat-fare token *(jeton)* from the machine *(jetonmatik)* near the platform. Tokens cost ₺4. The Istanbulkart is also accepted on the tramway. To access the platform swipe the Istanbulkart or push the token into a slot. Trams are frequent, running every 5 minutes from 6am to 11:50pm.

The Nostalgic Tram *(Nostaljik Tramvay)* trundles along İstiklâl Caddesi from Tünel to Taksim Square. The trams are the original early 20th-century vehicles, taken out of service in 1966 but revived in 1989.

Metro

Istanbul has several metro lines that are useful for visitors. To get to the old city centre (Sultanahmet and around) from Atatürk Airport, take the M1 metro to Zeytinburnu, then change to the T1 tram. Alternatively, continue on the M1 metro to Yenikapı then take a taxi. For Galata, Beyoğlu and Taksim, take the M1 metro to Yenikapı, then the M2 metro across the Golden Horn to the Şişhane or Taksim stops. To cross to Asia from the old city or Sultanahmet, use the Marmaray metro line, which runs through a tunnel under the Bosphorus. To use the metro, either purchase tokens *(jeton)* for ₺4 from *jetonmatik* machines near the stations, or use the Istanbulkart travel pass *(see p397)*.

Cable Cars and Funiculars

A cable car running from 8am to 10pm daily connects the shores of the Golden Horn in Eyüp with the Eyüp cemetery and tea gardens. There is also a cable car in Maçka Park, open from 8am to 8pm daily. Inaugurated in 1875, the Tünel is an underground railway climbing steeply from Karaköy

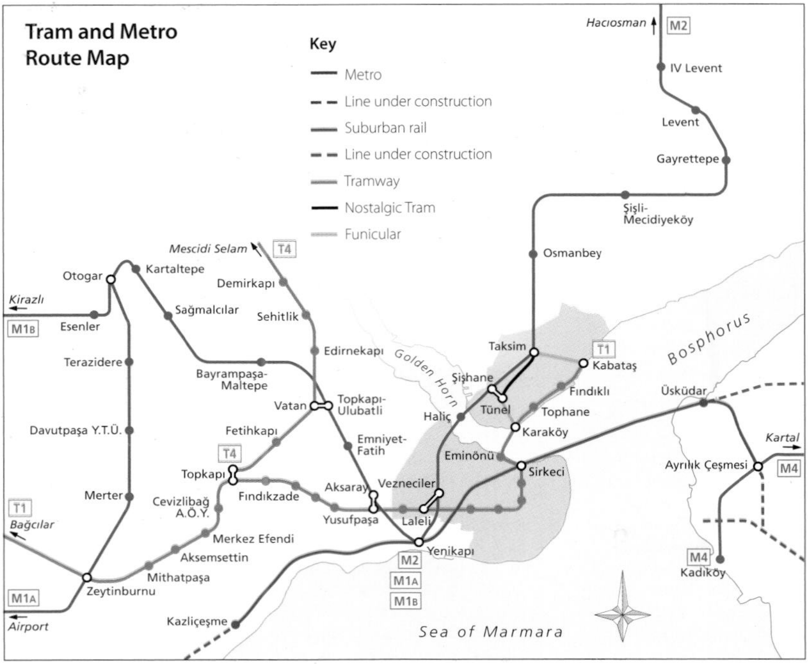

Tram and Metro Route Map

Key
Metro
Line under construction
Suburban rail
Line under construction
Tramway
Nostalgic Tram
Funicular

Hacıosman M2
IV Levent
Levent
Gayrettepe
Şişli-Mecidiyeköy
Osmanbey
Mescidi Selam T4
Demirkapı
Sehitlik
Edirnekapı
Otogar
Kartaltepe
Kirazlı
M1B
Esenler
Sağmalcılar
Terazidere
Bayrampaşa-Maltepe
Vatan
Topkapı-Ulubatli
Davutpaşa Y.T.Ü.
Fetihkapı
T4
Topkapı
Emniyet-Fatih
Merter
Cevizlibağ A.Ö.Y.
Fındıkzade
Aksaray
Vezneciler
Yusufpaşa
Laleli
T1
Bağcılar
Merkez Efendi
Aksemsettin
Mithatpaşa
Zeytinburnu
M1A
Airport
Kazliçeşme
Yenikapı
M2
M1A
M1B
Golden Horn
Haliç
Şişhane
Tünel
Taksim
T1
Kabataş
Fındıklı
Tophane
Karaköy
Eminönü
Sirkeci
Bosphorus
Üsküdar
Kartal
Ayrılık Çeşmesi
M4
M4
Kadıköy
Sea of Marmara

station, which is set back from the road just off the Galata Bridge, to Tünel Square in Beyoğlu. Here, it connects with the Nostalgic Tram on İstiklâl Caddesi. A token for the Tünel costs ₺4. The Tünel closes at 10pm.

A modern funicular, open from 6am to midnight, links Taksim Square with the ferry terminal at Kabataş (₺4).

Ferries, Sea Buses, Private Boats and Water Taxis

A great number of ferries *(vapur)* cross the Bosphorus and the Golden Horn. They are run by **Sehir Hatları (City Lines)**. The main ferry terminus on the European side is at Eminönü. Destinations include Haydarpaşa, Kadıköy and Üsküdar on the Asian shore. On the west side of the Galata Bridge is the pier for ferries sailing up the Golden Horn.

Another main terminus is Karaköy, situated opposite Eminönü; and from here ferries run to Haydarpaşa and Kadıköy. The international dock, where cruise liners berth, is also located here.

There are ferries every 15 minutes or so from Eminönü to Kadıköy between 7am and 9pm, and from Eminönü to Üsküdar from 6am to 11:30pm. Comprehensive timetables are available online or from ticket booths at each ferry terminal.

A number of craft run by private companies such as **Dentur** and **Turyol** cross the Bosphorus and Golden Horn at various points and run up the Bosphorus. These routes are also served by City Lines ferries, but private motorboats are more frequent, though slightly more expensive. Note that all motorboats accept only the Istanbulkart or tokens.

The modern, Swedish-built catamarans known as sea buses *(deniz otobüsleri)* are run by the **Istanbul Sea Bus Company** (İDO). Their interiors resemble aircraft cabins, with long rows of reclining seats, piped music and air conditioning. Sea buses are considerably faster and more comfortable than ferries, but they cost about three times as much. The most useful route is the one to the Princes' Islands (6–12 crossings daily).

There are 27 designated docks for water taxis across the city. To get a water taxi, either call a company such as **Deniz Taksi** or book online.

Buying Boat Tickets

For ferries and sea buses, buy a flat-fare token *(jeton)* from the booth at the pier. A ferry ticket costs ₺4, while the sea bus to the Princes' Islands is ₺9. You can use *jetons* for all local trips. Better still, use the Istanbulkart *(see p397)*, which works out cheaper and makes boarding quicker. You cannot use the Istanbulkart for the Bosphorus trip; tickets cost ₺20.

Sign for the Metro

To enter the pier, put the *jeton* into the slot beside the turnstile, and then wait in the boarding hall for a boat.

The Bosphorus Cruise

Istanbul Şehir Hatları runs daily excursions up the Bosphorus. They are very popular in the summer, especially at weekends, so arrive early to ensure that you get a deck seat with a view. The long Bosphorus Cruise costs ₺25 and is a 7-hour round trip. Light refreshments are served, with a lunch stop at the fishing village of Anadolu Kavağı. There is also a 2-hour version, going as far as the second Bosphorus bridge, costing ₺10, but there are no stops.

Alternatives to the official Bosphorus trip include the small private boats that also depart from Eminönü, just west of the Galata Bridge. They offer the equivalent of Şehir Hatları's short cruise and are slightly more expensive, but the departures are much more frequent. These only go halfway up the strait and do not stop on the way. You can also book a private cruise with a company such as **Hatsail Tourism**. For more on the Bosphorus cruise, *see pp130–31*.

The Marmaray Project

The biggest change to Istanbul's transport infrastructure in recent years was the opening of the Bosphorus tunnel in late 2013, linking the European and Asian sides of the city by metro. When the project is completed in 2018, the European and the Asian rail will be directly joined for the first time in history. In the meantime, thousands of commuters in Istanbul will be spared the 20 minutes travel by ferry across the Bosphorus Strait.

DIRECTORY

Tramway

Istanbul Transportation Co
Tel (0212) 568 99 70 or 444 00 88.
W **istanbul-ulasim.com.tr**

Ferries, Sea Buses, Private Boats and Water Taxis

Dentur
Tel (0212) 258 93 14 or (0216) 444 63 36.
W **denturavrasya.com**

Istanbul Sea Bus Company
Tel (0212) 444 44 36.
W **ido.com.tr**

Şehir Hatları (City Lines)
Tel 444 18 51.
W **sehirhatlari.com.tr**

Turyol
Tel (0212) 251 44 21.
W **turyol.com**

The Bosphorus Cruise

Hatsail Tourism
Tel (0212) 241 62 50/51.
W **hatsail.com**

General Index

Page numbers in **bold** type refer to main entries.

A

Abana 269
Abas I, King of Armenia 319
Abbasid Caliph 78
Abdalonymos, King of Sidon 76
Abdül Aziz, Sultan 75, 125
bedroom (Dolmabahçe Palace, Istanbul) 127
Beylerbeyi Palace (Istanbul) 132
Sile lighthouse 163
tomb of 95
Abdül Hamit I, Sultan 32
Abdül Hamit II, Sultan 61, 129
Beylerbeyi Palace (Istanbul) 132
tomb of 95
Yıldız Palace (Istanbul) 125
Abdül Mecid I, Sultan 72, 88
Ablutions fountains *see* Fountains
Abraham 37, 40, 305, 312
Accidents, road 395
Accommodation 326–39
Adana 212, **234–5**
hotels 335
map 235
restaurants 353
Adıyaman 308
Admission fees 380
see also Tickets
Adrassan, hotels 335
Adventure holidays **372–3**, 375
Aegean region **174–207**, 378–9
climate 42
getting around 177
hotels 333–4
itineraries 10, 13
map 176–7
restaurants 350–53
sights at a glance 176
A Week on the Aegean Coast 13
Aezani (Çavdarhisar) 261
Afyon 242, **260**
hotels 336
restaurants 356
Agora (İzmir) 183
Ağrı, Mount (Ararat) 153, 305, **319**
Ahmet I, Sultan
Blue Mosque (Istanbul) 83, 84, 92
tomb of 84
Ahmet III, Sultan 60
fountain (Istanbul) 35, 71, **78**
library (Topkapı Palace, Istanbul) 73
Air travel 388–9
Airlines 388, 389
Airport transfers 389, **397**
Airports **388**, 389
Akdamar Island (Lake Van) 304, 307, **318**
Aksaray (Archelais) 296–7
Alacahöyük (Hittite site) 48, 281, 282, **298**
Aladağlar Mountains 293
Alaeddin I Keykubad 29, 230, 254
Alanya 57, **230**
hotels 335
restaurants 353
Alanya International Triathlon 369
Alexander the Great **50–51**, 52
Alexander Sarcophagus 51, 76
Bodrum 198, 199
Gordion 251
İskenderun 237
Kaunos 214
Kütahya 262
Milas 197
Phaselis 221
Priene 194
Temple of Apollo (Didyma) 195
Termessos 224
Alexander Sarcophagus 51, 76
Alexius I Comnenus, Emperor 164
Alibey Peninsula 179
Alp Arslan, Sultan 56
Altar of Zeus (Bergama) 181
Altınkum 196
Altıntepe (Urartian site) 323
Amasra (Sesamus) 265, 266, **268**
restaurants 358
Amasya 281, 282, **302–3**
hotels 338
map 303
restaurants 359
Ambulances 383
Anadolu Kavağı 66, 131
Anamur 230
Anatolia
history 20, 28, **45–57**, 61
itineraries 11, 15
Museum of Anatolian Civilizations (Ankara) 241, 246–7
see also Ankara and Western Anatolia; Cappadocia and Central Anatolia; Eastern Anatolia
Anatolian lynx 26, 224
Anemurium 230
Ani 320–21
Anitta, King 48
Ankara 241, 242, **244–51**
events 369
history 61, 62
hotels 336–7
map 244–5
restaurants 356
Ankara and Western Anatolia **240–63**
Ankara 241, 242, **244–51**
climate 42
Ankara and Western Anatolia (cont.)
getting around 243
hotels 336–7
map 242–3
restaurants 356–8
sights at a glance 242
Antakya (Antioch) 56, 209, 213, **238–9**
Crusades 231, 238
hotels 335
maps 238
restaurants 354
siege of 231
Antalya (Attaleia) 15, 56, 209, 211, **222–3**
film festival 40, 368, 369
hotels 335
map 223
restaurants 354
Antioch *see* Antakya
Antiocheia-in-Pisidia (Eğirdir) 15, 52, **258**
Antiochus I Epiphanes, King 310
Antiques, shopping for 108–9, 248, **363**
Antonius Pius, Emperor 53
ANZAC Day 38
Aphrodisias 20, 175, **192–3**
Apple Mountain (Ankara) 250
Apricot Bazaar (Malatya) 308, 309
Aqueducts
Aqueduct of Valens (Istanbul) 55
Aspendos 225
Side 229
Aquila, Gaius Julius 186
Arabesque designs (ceramics) 32, 165
Arabesque music 371
Ararat, Mount 153, 305, **319**
Arcadius, Emperor 53
Arch of Domitian (Hierapolis) 190
Archaeology museums *see* Museums and galleries
Architecture
Byzantine 54, 83, 86–7
Ottoman 28–9, **34–5**, 79, 254
Seljuk 241, 293, 299
Aristotle 179
Armenian community 21
Artemision 184
Artvin 279
events 39
restaurants 358
Asansör (İzmir) 183
Askerlik (military service) 31
Aslankaya 261
Aslantaş 261
Aslantaş Dam 236
Aslantepe (Malatya) 308
Aspendos 15, **225**
events 39, 368, 369
Association of Small Hotels 327, 329

Assos (Behram Kale) 13, **179**
hotels 333
restaurants 350, 351
Assyrians 20, **47**, 49, 295, 300
Atakule (Ankara) 249
Atatürk 21, 22, 61, **62–3**, 268
bedroom (Dolmabahçe Palace, Istanbul) 127
commemoration events 38, 40, 41
death of 40, 63, 127
mausoleum (Ankara) 22, 240, 241, **248**, 249
museum (Alanya) 230
museum (Samsun) 269
Presidential Palace (Ankara) 249
statue (İskenderun) 237
villa (Diyarbakır) 315
villa (Trabzon) 275
Atatürk Airport (Istanbul) 388, 389, 397
Atatürk Boulevard (Ankara) 249
Atatürk Dam (Kâhta) 25, **308**
Atatürk Farm and Zoo (Ankara) 249
Atatürk Villa (Diyarbakır) 315
Atatürk's Villa (Trabzon) 275
ATMs 384
Attaleia *see* Antalya
Attalus II, King of Pergamum 222
Attalus III, King of Pergamum 52, 180
Augustus, Emperor 52, 244
"Auspicious Event" 61
Autumn in Turkey 40
Avanos (Venessa) 15, 287, 364
events 39
Ayasoluk Hill (Selçuk) 184
Ayder Plateau, hotels 337, 377
Aydın (Caesarea) 185
events 41
Ayvalık 174, **179**
hotels 333
restaurants 351

B

Bafa, Lake 13, 196
Baghdad Pavilion (Topkapı Palace, Istanbul) 73
Bagratid kings of Armenia 320
Balkan Wars 61
Balyan, Karabet 126
Balyan, Nikoğos 126, 132
Banks 384
opening hours 380
Bar Street (Marmaris) 204
Barbarossa, Frederick (Holy Roman Emperor) 231, 232
Barbarossa, Hayreddin (Admiral) 59, 60
Bargaining **134**, 328, 362, 367
Basil the Great, St 294
Basil I, Emperor 56, 96, 97
Basil II, Emperor 56, 89
Basilica Cistern (Istanbul) 12, 85, **90**
Baths *see* Turkish baths
Bayburt 277
Bayram throne (Topkapı Palace, Istanbul) 75
Bazaar Quarter (Istanbul) **98–109**
hotels 331
maps 99, 100–101
restaurants 346–7
sights at a glance 99
Bazaars *see* Markets and bazaars
Beaches **373**
Altınkum 196
Anatalya 222
Ölu Deniz 208, **216–17**
Princes' Islands 162
Turtle Beach (Dalyan) 215
Behram Kale (Assos) 13, **179**
hotels 333
restaurants 350, 351
Belediye (town hall, Bursa) 169
Belek
golf 228
hotels 335
Belisırma, restaurants 360
Belly dancing 137, 368, 371
Bençik 207
Bergama (Pergamum) 13, 50, 175, 176, **180–81**
hotels 333
map 180–81
restaurants 351
Bey Han (Bursa) 168
Beyazıt I, Sultan 133, 299
Yıldırım Beyazıt Mosque (Bursa) 166
Beyazıt II, Sultan 74, 158, 303
Beyazıt II Mosque (Edirne) 158
Çeşme 184
Koza Han (Bursa) 169
Beyazıt Square (Istanbul) 106
Beyazıt Tower (Istanbul) 106
Beykoz 131
Beyoğlu (Istanbul) **110–15**
hotels 331
maps 111, 112–13
restaurants 347–8
sights at a glance 111
Beyşehir 258
restaurants 356
Birds
of Anatolia 27
Bird Paradise National Park 156, **163**
Bosphorus 133
Eğirdir 258
Göksu Delta 232, 374
Lake Köyceğiz 214
Soğanlı 292
Sultansazlığı Bird Sanctuary 293
Black Sea region **264–79**
climate 43
getting around 267
hotels 337–8
map 266–7
restaurants 358–9
sights at a glance 266
Blue Mosque (Istanbul) 12, 21, 67, 82–3, 84, **92–3**
Blue Seminary (Amasya) 283, **303**
"Blue Voyage" *gulet* cruises 210, 373
Boats *see* Ferries; Yachts
Bodrum (Halicarnassus) 10, 13, 175, 177, **198–201**
events 40
hotels 333
map 199
restaurants 351
Bodrum Hamam **198**, 376, 377
Bodrum Peninsula tour 202–3
Boğazkale (Hittite site) 48, 281, 282, **300–301**
restaurants 359
Bolu 250
hotels 337
Bookshops 107, 135
Bor 293
Boris III, King of Bulgaria 80
Bosphorus Bridge (Istanbul) 132
Bosphorus Trip **130–31**, 399
Bossert, H.T. 236
Brassware 31, 135, 363
Breakdowns, vehicle 395
British War Cemetery (Istanbul) 129
Bronze Age 46, 47, 246, 247
Kültepe 47, **295**
shipwrecks (Castle of St Peter, Bodrum) 201
Bünyan 292
Bureaux de change 384
Burgaz Harbour (Princes' Islands) 155
Burgazada (Princes' Islands) 162
Bursa 157, **166–71**
hotels 332
map 167, 168–9
Market Area 168–9
restaurants 349–50
spas 376
Bürüciye Medresesi (Sivas) 299
Bus travel 390–91, 397
Butterfly Valley 210, **217**
Büyük Taş Hanı (Istanbul) 106
Büyük Yenı Han (Istanbul) 107
Büyükada (Princes' Islands) 162
Byzantine Architecture 54, 83, 86–7
Byzantine Empire 20, 44, **54–7**
Byzantine Great Palace (Istanbul) 84, 91, 94, **96–7**

Byzantine mosaics and frescoes 67, **122–3**
see also Frescoes; Mosaics

C

Caferağa Courtyard (Istanbul) 70, **79**
Calchas of Argos 224
Calligraphy 32–3, 79, 115, 133, 166, 184
Camekan (entrance hall, Turkish baths) 80, 81
Camel caravans 28
Camel tours 288
Camel wrestling 41, 185, 368
Çamlıhemşin 278
restaurants 358
Çamlık 184
Çamlık National Park 298
Camping 329
Çanakkale 13, **178**
events 38, 39
hotels 333
restaurants 350
Canakkale Destanı Tanıtım Merkezi (Gallipoli Peninsula) 172
Çankaya area (Ankara) 249
Canyoning 372, 375
Cappadocia and Central Anatolia 15, 19, 153, **280–303**
climate 43
getting around 283
hotels 338–9
map 282–3
restaurants 359–60
sights at a glance 282
Cappadocia Grape Harvest Festival (Ürgüp) 40
Car hire **394**, 395
Caravanning 329
Caria, Kingdom of 175, 197, 198
Carpets and kilims 31, **366–7**
Bazaar Quarter (Istanbul) 107, 109
Bünyan 292
Carpet Museum (Istanbul) 90–91
Malatya 309
Milas 197
shopping for 134, 135, 363, 366
Çarşi Hamamı (Adana) 235
Cartography, Ottoman 59
Castles and fortifications
Ayasoluk Hill (Selçuk) 184
Bayburt Castle 277
Castle of St Peter (Bodrum) 152, 177, **200–201**
Castle of St Peter (Çeşme) 184
Citadel (Amasya) 302
Citadel (Ani) 320
Citadel (Ankara) 248
Citadel (Boğazkale) 301
Citadel (Erzurum) 322
Citadel (Kayseri) 294
Castles and fortifications (cont.)
Fortress (Kütahya) 262
Fortress of Asia (Istanbul) 131, **132–3**
Fortress of Europe (Istanbul) 130, **133**
Fortress of Seven Towers (Istanbul) 120
Genoese Castle (Anadolu Kavağı) 66, 131
Genoese Fort (Kuşadası) 185
Genoese Fortress (Foça) 179
Genoese fortresses (Amasra) 268
Hemşin Valley 278
Infidel's Castle (near Haymana) 251
Karatepe 236
Kastamonu 268
Kızkalesi 212, **232–3**
Mamaris Castle 150–51, 204, **205**
Mamure Castle 230, 231
Red Tower (Alanya) **230**
Şanlıurfa Citadel 306, 312
Tophane Citadel (Bursa) 170
Trabzon Castle 265, **274**
Velvet Castle (İzmir) 183
see also City walls; Palaces
Çatalhöyük 46, 242, **258**
Cathedral, Ani 321
Catherine the Great, Empress of Russia 61
Çavdarhisar (Aezani) 261
Cave, Damlataş (Alanya) 230
Çavuştepe (Urartian site) 318
Çayeli, restaurants 358
Çekirge (Bursa) 171
Çelebi, Evliya 158
Çelik Palas Hotel (Bursa) 171
Cemeteries, War 129, 155, 156, 172
Ceramics
Amphora Exhibit (Castle of St Peter, Bodrum) 200
Avanos 287
Çanakkale 135, 178
Kütahya 135, 262
shopping for 134–5, 364
Topkapı Palace 74
see also İznik ceramics and tiles
Çeşme 184
hotels 333
restaurants 351–2
Çeşme (public fountains) *see* Fountains
Children 21
attractions for 137, 249, 369
in hotels 328
National Sovereignty and Children's Day 38, 41
Christianity 53, 97, 186, 195, 209, 286
Nicene Creed 164
Christie, Agatha 80, 112, 114
Churches
Ani Cathedral 321
Armenian (Yusufeli) 279
Barbara Church (Göreme Open-Air Museum) 289
Basilica of St John (Selçuk) 184
Byzantine church architecture 54
Constantine and Helen (Mustafapaşa) 292
Elmalı Church (Göreme Open-Air Museum) 289
Eski Gümüş Monastery Church (Niğde) 293
Fish Church (Zelve) 286
Georgian (Yusufeli) 279
Grape Church (Zelve) 286
Greek Orthodox Patriarchate (Istanbul) 118–19
Haghia Eirene (Istanbul) 71, **78**
Haghia Sophia (Istanbul) 21, 55, 67, 83, 85, **86–9**
Haghia Sophia (İznik) 164
Haghia Sophia (Trabzon) 153, 265, 267, **274**
Holy Cross (Akdamar Island, Lake Van) 304, **318**
Karanlık Church (Göreme Open-Air Museum) 289
Pammakaristos (Istanbul) 118
Panaghia (Istanbul) 113
Redeemer (Ani) 321
rock-cut churches 15, 281, 288, 296
St Anne's Church (Trabzon) 274
St Eugenius Church (Trabzon) 275
St George, Greek Orthodox Patriarchate (Istanbul) 119
St Gregory of Abugramentz (Ani) 320
St John of Studius (Istanbul) 54, **120**
St Mary Draperis (Istanbul) 112
St Peter's Grotto (Antakya) 238
St Polycarp Church (İzmir) 182
St Saviour in Chora (Istanbul) 12, 67, 117, **122–3**
SS Sergius and Bacchus (Istanbul) 54, **96–7**
St Stephen of the Bulgars (Istanbul) 118
Tokalı Church (Göreme Open-Air Museum) 288
Yılanlı Church (Göreme Open-Air Museum) 289
see also Monasteries
Çiçek Pasajı (Istanbul) 113
Cide 269
Cinci Hamamı (Safranbolu) 272
Cinci Hanı (Safranbolu) 29, 272
Cinema 23, 38, 40, 137, 368, 369
Çingene (gypsy music) 371
Çıralı 14, 221
Circumcision ritual (*sünnet*) 30

Cirit games (Erzurum) 40
Cistern of 1,001 Columns (Istanbul) 94–5
City walls
  Alanya 230
  Amasra 268
  Ani 321
  Antalya 222
  Bergama 180
  Bodrum 198, 199
  Boğazkale 301
  Diyarbakır 315
  İznik (Nicaea) 164
  Kaunos 214
  Side 229
  Theodosian Walls (Istanbul) 12, 55, 117, **120–21**
  Tophane 170
Cleopatra 181
Climate 42–3
Climbing 293, 372, 375
Coach travel 389, 390–91
Çobanisa 258
Columns and obelisks
  Burnt Column (Istanbul) 95
  Cistern of 1,001 Columns (Istanbul) 94–5
  Column of Constantine Porphyrogenitus (Istanbul) 94
  Column of Julian (Ankara) 244
  Constantine's Column (Istanbul) 95
  Egyptian Obelisk (Istanbul) 94, 95
  Serpentine Column (Istanbul) 94, 95
Committee for Unity and Progress ("Young Turks") 61
Communications and media 386–7
Complex of Valide Sultan Mihrişah (Istanbul) 124
Conquest of Istanbul 38, 58, 60, 121
Constantine I, Emperor 53
  Byzantine Great Palace (Istanbul) 96
  Constantine's Column (Istanbul) 95
  Council of Nicaea 164
  Hippodrome (Istanbul) 94
Constantine IX Monomachus, Emperor 44, 55, 87
Constantinople 53, 54–5
  fall of 38, 58, 60, 121
  see also Istanbul
Consulates 112, 381
Conu, Helmut 129
Copper Age 46
Copperware 31, 135, 363, 364
Çorlulu Ali Paşa Courtyard (Istanbul) 107
Coronation Square (Haghia Sophia, Istanbul) 87, 88
Çoruh Valley 279
Çorum (Niconia) 298–9
  Hittite festival 39
Crafts **31**
  Dumlupınar Fair 263
  Grand Bazaar (Istanbul) 109
  Istanbul Crafts Centre 85, **90**
  İzmir 182
  Kastamonu 268
  shopping for 134, 135, 363, **364–5**
  see also Markets and bazaars
Credit cards and debit cards 384
  in hotels 328
  in restaurants 341
  in shops 362
Crimean Memorial Cemetery (Istanbul) 129
Crimean War 61, 129
Croesus, King 49
Cruises, Bosphorus **130–31**, 399
Crusades 54, **56–7**, 164, 184, **231**, 238
Çubuk Dam 250
Cumalıkızık 163
Cunda Island
  hotels 334
  restaurants 352
Currency 362, **380**, **385**
Customs regulations 380, 381
Customs and traditions 380–81
Cycling 395
Cyprus 63, 233, 237

D

Dalyan 14, **214–15**
  hotels 335
  restaurants 354
Damlataş Cave (Alanya) 230
Dance 136–7, 368, **370–71**
  ballet 39, 225, 368, 369
  belly dancing 137, 368, 371
  folk dancing 23, 31, 136–7, 369
  Whirling Dervishes 41, 66, 112, 114, 252–3, **259**
Darius I 194
Darius III 50–51, 237
Datça 207
  hotels 334
Datça Peninsula Tour 206–7
Davraz Ski Centre 258, 372
Davut Ağa 107
Deësis Mosaics
  Haghia Sophia (Istanbul) 89
  St Saviour in Chora (Istanbul) 123
Demre (Myra) 219, **220**
  events 41
Denizli 193
  restaurants 352
Derinkuyu 15, 285, **286**
Dervishes *see* Whirling Dervishes
Deyr-az-Zaferan (Mardin) 313
Dialling codes 386
Didyma (Didim) 13, **195**
  restaurants 352
Dilek Peninsula National Park 185
Dionysius 198
Discos 368
Diving 201, 216, 218, **373**, 375
Divriği 323
Diyarbakır 305, **314–15**
  events 40
  hotels 339
  map 315
  restaurants 360
Doğubayazıt 153, 305, 306, **319**
  hotels 339
Dolmabahçe Palace (Istanbul) 60, 67, 116, 117, **126–7**, 130
Dolmuş (minibus) travel 391, 396
Domes
  Atik Valide Mosque (Istanbul) 128
  Blue Mosque (Istanbul) 93
  Haghia Sophia (Istanbul) 87, 89, 160
  İlyas Bey Mosque (Miletus) 195
  Prince's Mosque (Istanbul) 103
  Sabancı Central Mosque (Adana) 234
  Selimiye Mosque (Edirne) 160–61
  St Saviour in Chora (Istanbul) 122
  Süleymaniye Mosque (Istanbul) 105
Domestic flights 389
Don John of Austria 59
Döner Gazino (Kütahya) 262
Dorylaeum *see* Eskişehir
Dress
  etiquette 380, 381
  traditional 30, **31**, 63, 74, 371
Drinks *see* Food and drink
Driving 394–5
Dumlupınar, Battle of 39, 260, 262
Dumlupınar Fair 263

E

Earthquakes 24, **25**, 190, 215, 320, 323
Eastern Anatolia **304–23**
  climate 43
  getting around 307
  hotels 339
  map 306–7
  restaurants 360–61
  sights at a glance 306
Eastern Mediterranean coast *see* Mediterranean Turkey
Eceabat, restaurants 350
Ecevit, Bülent 63
Economic reforms 23, 63
Edessa (Şanlıurfa) 56, 231, 305, 306, **312**
  hotels 339
  restaurants 361
Edirne 154, **158–61**
  events 39, 155, 368
  hotels 332

Edirne (cont.)
map 159
restaurants 350
Edremit, restaurants 352
Eğirdir 258
restaurants 356
Eğirdir, Lake 15, 242, **258**
Egyptian Bazaar (Istanbul) 98, 99, **102**
map 100–101
Ehmedek 230
Elaiussa Sebaste 233
Electricity 381
Embassies 381
Emergencies
emergency numbers 383
personal security and health 382–3
on the road 395
Emigration 23
Eminönü (Istanbul) 101
English (Lion) Tower (Bodrum) 201
Entertainment 136–7, 368–71
Ephesus 13, 20, 175, **186–7**
Erciyes, Mount 282, 285, **292**
Erzincan 323
Erzurum 56, 305, **322–3**
Cirit games 40
hotels 339
map 322
restaurants 361
Esenboğa Airport (Ankara) 389
Esenler coach/bus station 389, 391
Eski Malatya 309
Eskişehir (Dorylaeum) 261
events 38
hotels 337
restaurants 356–7
Ethnography museums *see* Museums and galleries
Etiquette 380–81
Eumenes I, King of Pergamum 180
Eumenes II, King of Pergamum 180, 190
Euphrates, River 25, 45, 305, 323
Euromos 13, **196**
European Union 23, 63
Events, calendar of 38–41

F

Fabrics, shopping for 134, 135, 168, 230, 363, 365
"Fairy chimneys" rock formations (Cappadocia) 281, **284**, 286
Fasıl music 136, 369, 371
Fatih Büfe (Istanbul) 70
Fellows, Charles 214, 218, 220
Ferries 157, 177, 233, 389, **393**
Bosphorus Trip **130–31**, 399
Eminönü terminal (Istanbul) 101
Istanbul 393, 399
Fertile Crescent 45
Festivals and holidays **38–41**, 136, 368, 369
Fethiye 14, **216**
hotels 335
restaurants 354
Fidan Han (Bursa) 169
Films 23, 38, 40, 137, 368, 369
Finike 14, 221
Flora and fauna 26–7
Foça (Phocaea) 179
restaurants 352
Food and drink 340–61
Flavours of Turkey 342–3
local delicacies 365
mezes (appetizers) 340, 341, 344
shopping for 135
tours 374, 375
Turkish tea 278, 345
Watermelons 40, 314
What to Drink in Turkey **345**
see also Restaurants
Football 368
Fortresses *see* Castles and fortifications
Forum of Theodosius (Istanbul) 106
Fountains 34, **35**, 36, 37
Ahmet III (Istanbul) 35, 71, **78**
Beykoz Fountain 131
Blue Mosque, Istanbul 93
Executioner's Fountain (Topkapı Palace, Istanbul) 71
Great Mosque, Bursa 168
Haghia Sophia, Istanbul 87
Haymana Fountain 251
Kaiser Wilhelm II (Istanbul) 94
Marble Fountain (Grand Bazaar, Istanbul) 108
Mevlâna Museum, Konya 256
Nymphaeum and Vespasian (Side) 229
Selimiye Mosque, Edirne 160
Swan Fountain (Dolmabahçe Palace, Istanbul) 126
Zoodochus Pege (Istanbul) 121
France, colonisation 209, 234, 238, 239
French War Cemetery (Gallipoli) 156, 172
Frescoes
Barbara Church (Göreme Open-Air Museum) 289
Elmalı Church (Göreme Open-Air Museum) 289
Eski Gümüş Monastery Church (Niğde) 293
Haghia Sophia (Trebzon) 274
Holy Cross (Akdamar Island, Lake Van) 318
Karanlık Church (Göreme Open-Air Museum) 289
St Saviour in Chora (Istanbul) 122–3
Sumela Monastery 276
Tokalı Church (Göreme Open-Air Museum) 288
Friedrich I, Holy Roman Emperor (Frederick Barbarossa) 231, 232
Fuel 394
Funicular (Istanbul) 124, 398–9

G

Gagik I, King of Armenia 320
Galata Bridge (Istanbul) 8–9, **103**, 324–5
Galata Tower (Istanbul) 12, 111, **114**
Galen (physician) 180
Gallipoli Campaign 62, **173**
ANZAC Day 38
war memorials 38, 129, 152, 155, **172–3**, 374
Gallipoli National Historic Park 172–3
Gallipoli Peninsula 13, 155, 156, **172–3**
GAP (Southeast Anatolian Project) **25**, 305, 308
Gardens *see* Parks and gardens
Gas, natural 221
Gate of Hercules (Ephesus) 187
Gay and lesbian travellers 380
Gaziantep 305, **311**
hotels 339
restaurants 361
Gedik Ahmet Paşa 107
Gedik Paşa Hamamı 107
Gelibolu, restaurants 350
Geology 24–5
rock formations (Cappadocia) 281, 284–5
Geothermal springs *see* Spas and hot springs
Glassware
Castle of St Peter (Bodrum) 200
shopping for 135, 365
Topkapı Palace (Istanbul) 74
Göbeklı Tepe 312
Göcek 215
hotels 335–6
restaurants 354
Gods, Roman 52–3
Gökalp, Ziya 162, 314
Göksu Delta 232, 374
Göl Türkbükü 203
Gölbaşi Lake 250
restaurants 357
Golden Horn (Istanbul) 12, 103
Golden Orange Film Festival (Antalya) 40, 368, 369
Golf 228, **373**, 375
Gordian Knot 51, 251
Gordion 251
Göreme 15, **287**, 290–91
hotels 338
restaurants 360
Göreme Open Air Museum 15, **288–9**
Grand Bazaar (Istanbul) 12, 95, 99, **108–9**
map 108–9

Grease-wrestling Championship (Edirne) 39, 155, **158**, 368, 369
Great Lord's Seminary (Amasya) 302
Great Palace (Istanbul) 84, 91, 94, 96–7
Greece, exchange of ethnic population with 62, 216, 292
"Greek Fire" 55
Greek Orthodox community 21
Greek Orthodox Patriarchate (Istanbul) 118–19
Greek Orthodox School of Theology (Heybeliada) 162
Green Tomb (Bursa) 166
Green travel 381, 388
Gregory, St 88
Guided tours (Istanbul) 396–7
Gülets *see* Yachts
Güllük 197
Güllük Dağ National Park 224
Gümüşhane 277
Gümüşlük (Myndos) 202
Güpgüpoğlu Stately Home (Kayseri) 294
Güzelyurt 280, **296**
 restaurants 360

H

Hacı Bektaş 34, 261, **297**
 Commemorative Ceremony (Avanos) 39
 museum 297
 tomb of 297
Hacılar 46
Hadrian, Emperor 53, 158, 221
 Hadrian's Gate (Antalya) 223
 Temple of Hadrian (Ephesus) 187
Haghia Sophia (Istanbul) 21, 67, 83, 85, **86–9**
 floorplan 88
 historical plan 86
 mosaics 55
Haghia Sophia (Trabzon) 153, 265, 267, **274**
Haj (pilgrimage to Mecca) 37, 237
Halicarnassus *see* Bodrum
Halikarnas Club (Bodrum) 198
Hall of the Campaign Pages (Topkapı Palace, Istanbul) 74
Hamamayaği 377
Hamams see Turkish baths
Handicrafts *see* Crafts
Hans and *kervansarays* 28–9, 57
 Ankara 245
 Bursa 168–9
 Büyük Taş Hanı (Istanbul) 106
 Büyük Yenı Han (Istanbul) 107
 Cinci Hanı (Safranbolu) 29, 272
 Kızlarağaşi Han (İzmir) 29, 182
 Mylasa 29
 Sarıhan 287
 Süleymaniye Mosque (Istanbul) 104
 Sultanhanı (Askaray) 29
Hans and *kervansarays* (cont.)
 Tire 185
 Valide Han (Istanbul) 107
 Zincirli Han (Istanbul) 109
Hararet (intermediate room, Turkish baths) 80, 81
Harbiye 239
Harem (Topkapı Palace, Istanbul) 68, 72, **75**
Harpagus, General 214
Harpy Tomb (Xanthos) 51
Harran 312
Hasan, Mount 285, 296–7
Hasan Paşa Hanı (Diyarbakır) 314
Hatay Province 209, 238
Hattuşaş *see* Boğazkale
Hattuşaş National Park 283, **300–301**
Hattushili III, King 48
Havuzlu Lokanta (Istanbul) 108
Havza thermal springs 269
Haydarpaşa Station (Istanbul) **129**, 389
Haymana Hot Springs 250–51
Hazeranlar Mansion (Amasya) 302
Health 382–3
 Health Museum (Edirne) 158
 insurance 383
 therapeutic spas 376–7
Heavenly Seminary (Sivas) 299
Helen of Troy 47
Hellenistic Age 20, **50–51**
Hemşin Valley 278–9
Herakleia 196
Herbs, shopping for 135, 362, 363, 365
Herodotus 198
Heroon (Bergama) 181
Heybeliada (Princes' Islands) 162
Hıdırlık Tower (Antalya) 223
Hierapolis (Aegean region) 13, 175, **190–91**
Hierapolis (Castabala) 237
Hieroglyphics 236
Hippodamus of Miletus 194
Hippodrome (Istanbul) 12, 83, 84, **94**, 95
Hisarlık (site of ancient Troy) 178
Historic buildings
 Basilica Cistern (Istanbul) 12, 85, **90**
 Beyazıt Tower (Istanbul) 106
 Cistern of 1,001 Columns (Istanbul) 94–5
 Galata Tower (Istanbul) 12, 111, **114**
 Greek Revival Houses (Marmaris) 204
 Güpgüpoğlu Stately Home (Kayseri) 294
 Haydarpaşa Station (Istanbul) **129**
 Hazeranlar Mansion (Amasya) 302
 Hıdırlık Tower (Antalya) 223
Historic buildings (cont.)
 House of Mary (Meryemana) 186
 Hüsnü Züber House (Bursa) 170
 Kütahya Manor Houses 263
 Latifoğlu House (Tokat) 299
 Leander's Tower (Istanbul) 128
 Madımağin Celal'ın House (Tokat) 299
 Mevlevi Lodge (Istanbul) 112, **114**
 Ottoman houses (Konya) 254
 Pera Palace Hotel (Istanbul) 80, 112, **114**
 Pierre Loti Café (Istanbul) 124
 Selimiye Barracks (Istanbul) 129
 Sirkeci Station (Istanbul) 80
 Sublime Porte (Istanbul) 70, **79**
 Zağnos Tower (Trabzon) 274
 see also Castles and fortifications; Churches; Memorials and monuments; Museums and galleries; Palaces
Historical and cultural tours 374, 375
History 44–63
Hitler, Adolf 248
Hittite civilization 20, **48–9**, 241, **300**
 Adana Museum 234
 Alacahöyük 298
 Aslantepe 308
 Boğazkale 300–301
 Dündartepe 269
 İkiztepe 269
 Kalehöyük 297
 Karatepe 236
 Kemerhisar 293
 Mount Erciyes 285
 Sphinx Relief (Ankara) 247
 Treaty of Kadesh 77
 Yazılıkaya 298, 300, 301
Hittite Festival (Çorum) 39
Holiday villages 326
Homer 47, 178
Honorius, Emperor 53
Hopa 279
 restaurants 358
Horse racing 137, 368–9
Horse riding 373, 375
Hospitals 383
Hostel World 328, 329
Hostels 328
Hot springs *see* Spas and hot springs
Hotels **326–39**
 Aegean 333–4
 Ankara and Western Anatolia 336–7
 Black Sea 337–8
 booking 328
 budget hotels 327
 Cappadocia and Central Anatolia 338–9
 checking out and paying 328
 children in 328

Hotels (cont.)
Eastern Anatolia 339
holiday villages 326
hotel-based sports 373
Istanbul 330–32
luxury hotels 326
Mediterranean Turkey 335–6
prices and discounts 328
spa hotels 376, 377
Special Class hotels 326
Thrace and the Sea of Marmara 332
House of Mary (Meryemana) 186
Houses, Ottoman 35, **79**, 254, 272–3, 299
Hüdai 377
Hüsnü Züber House (Bursa) 170
Huzziya, King 48

I

Iasus 197
İbrahim Müteferrika 107
İbrahim Paşa 90, 91, 103
İç Bedestan (Grand Bazaar, Istanbul) 109
İçel *see* Mersin
İçmeler 205
Ihlara Valley 15, 296
İkiztepe 296
Ilgaz Mountain National Park 269
Ilıca mud baths 215
Imperial Porcelain Factory (Istanbul) 125
İnebolu 269
Inoculations 383
İnönü, İsmet 248, 308
Insects 383
Insurance 383
International Bodrum Cup Regatta 40
International Film Festival (Istanbul) 38
International İzmir Festival 39
International Opera and Ballet Festival (Aspendos) 39
Internet access 327, 386–7
Ionian League 179, 194
Ionian Renaissance 49
Irene, Empress 89, 119
İshak Paşa Sarayı (near Doğubeyazıt) 319
İskenderun 237
Islam 21
beliefs and practices 30, 37
Exploring mosques 36–7
Muslim holidays 40
Ramazan (Ramadan) 18, 37, 40
Islamic art 32–3
Isparta
hotels 337
restaurants 357
Issus, Battle of **50–51**, 237
Istanbul 19, **64–149**
airports 388, 389, 397
Bazaar Quarter 98–109
Istanbul (cont.)
Beyoğlu (Istanbul) 110–15
climate 42
entertainment **136–7**, 368, 369
events 38, 39, 40, 41, 368, 369
Further Afield 116–33
getting around 396–9
history 60–61
hotels 330–32
map 66–7
restaurants 346–9
Seraglio Point 68–80
shopping 134–5
Street Finder maps 138–49
Sultanahmet 82–97
transport map *see* Back endpaper
Two Days in Istanbul 12
see also Constantinople
Istanbul Biennial (festival) 40, 368, 369
Istanbul Crafts Centre 85, **90**
Istanbul International Music Festival 39, 368, 369
Istanbul Jazz Festival 39, 136
Istanbul Şehir Hatları 130, 399
İstiklâl Caddesi (Istanbul) 18, 112–13
tram 110, **398**, 399
İzmir (Smyrna) 62, 175, **182–3**
events 39, 41
hotels 334
map 182–3
restaurants 352
İzmit earthquake (1999) 24
İznik ceramics and tiles 74, 155, 164, **165**
Atik Valide Mosque (Istanbul) 128
Blue Mosque (Istanbul) 12, 84, 92, 165
Cezri Kasım Paşa Mosque (Eyüp) 121
Fatih Mosque (Istanbul) 119
Gazi Ahmet Paşa Mosque (Istanbul) 121
Green Mosque (Bursa) 166–7
Green Mosque (İznik) 33, 164
Mausoleum of Selim II (Istanbul) 87
Mosque of Selim I (Istanbul) 119
Muradiye Mosque (Bursa) 170
Muradiye Mosque (Edirne) 159
New Mosque (Istanbul) 102
Palace of the Porphyrogenitus (Istanbul) 121 121
Prince's Mosque (Istanbul) 103
Rüstem Paşa Mosque (Istanbul) 100, **102**
shopping for 135
Sokollu Mehmet Paşa Mosque (Istanbul) 96
Topkapı Palace (Istanbul) 74
İznik (Nicaea) 56, **164**
hotels 332
restaurants 350

J

Jandarma 382, 383
Janissaries 59, **60**, 61, 94, 133
Mehter Band 124, 126, **371**
Jansen, Hermann 241
Jazz 39, 136, 137, 368
Jewellery
shopping for 109, 134, 135, 363, 364
Spoonmaker's diamond (Topkapı Palace, Istanbul) 75
Jews 118, 237
John the Baptist, St 75
John the Evangelist, St 184, 186
John II Comnenus, Emperor 89
Julian, Emperor 244
Justin II, Emperor 162
Justinian, Emperor 54–5
Basilica of St John (Selçuk) 184
Byzantine Great Palace (Istanbul) 96
Haghia Sophia (Istanbul) 86
SS Sergius and Bacchus (Istanbul) 96–7
Justinianopolis (Sivrihisar) 260

K

Kaaba (Mecca) 37, 58, 75, 96
Kaçkar Mountains National Park 278
Kadesh, Treaty of 77
Kadıkalesi 202
Kafkasör Culture and Arts Festival (Artvin) 39, 279
Kahramanmaraş **309**
restaurants 361
Kâhta 308
hotels 339
Kale (Simena) 14, 220
Kalehöyük 297
Kalkan 14, **218**
hotels 336
restaurants 354–5
Kalkanı Mountains 277
Kalpakçılar Başı Caddesi (Istanbul) 109
Kanlıdivane 233
Karaalioğlu Park (Antalya) 223
Karacasu, restaurants 352
Karagöl-Sahara National Park 279
Karagöz shadow puppet theatre **30**, 155, 166, 167, 168
Karatepe 236
Karlowitz, Treaty of 60
Kars 305, 306, **319**
hotels 339
restaurants 361
Kartalkaya 250
Kaş 14, **218**
hotels 336
restaurants 355
Kaş-Lycia Culture and Art Festival (Kaş) 39, 218
Kasaba 269

Kastamonu 268–9
restaurants 358
Kaunos 14, **214**
Kavaklinddere area (Ankara) 249
Kayaköy 14, **216**
restaurants 355
Kaymaklı 286, **287**
Kayseri 281, 282, **294–5**
hotels 338
map 295
restaurants 360
KDV *see* Value-added tax (VAT)
Kebab houses 340
Keçibükü 207
Kekova Island 14, 220
Kemaliye (Eğin) 323
Kemer, hotels 336
Kemerhisar 293
Kervansarays see Hans and *kervansarays*
Kılıç Arslan II, Sultan 56, 254
Kılıç Kalkan (spoon dance) 371
Kilims *see* Carpets and kilims
Kınalıada (Princes' Islands) 162
King's Gate (Boğazkale) 283, **301**
Kırkpınar Festival (Edirne) 39, 155, **158**, 368, 369
Kırşehir 297
restaurants 360
Kızılcahamam **250**, 376
Kızkalesi 212, **232–3**
Kızlarağaşi Han (İzmir) 29, 182
Knidos 206
Knights of St John 152, 175, 184, 199, 200, 231
Knights Templar 231
Koca Sinan Paşa's tomb 107
Konak Clock Tower (İzmir) 182
Konaks (mansion houses) 35, 272–3, 281, 303
Konya 15, 56, 57, 241, **254–7**
events 41
fairground 254
hotels 337
map 254–5
restaurants 357
Köprülü Cayı National Park 224
Koran, the 32, 36, 37, 259
Korean War 63, 248
Kösedağ 57
Köyceğiz 214
Koza Han (Bursa) 169
Küçükkuyu Adatepe Köyü, restaurants 353
Külliye (mosque complex) 36, 195
Kültepe 47, **295**
Kümbet 261
Kurban Bayramı (Feast of the Sacrifice) 40
Kurds 62–3, 233, 305
Kürsü (throne in mosque) 37
Kurukahveci Mehmet Efendi (Istanbul) 100
Kuş Gölü lake 163
Kuşadası 13, 175, **185**
hotels 334
restaurants 353
Kütahya 241, **262–3**
hotels 337
map 263
restaurants 357–8
tiles and cermics 262

L

Labarna Hattushili I, King 48
Labour and Solidarity Day (national holiday) 41
Labranda 196–7
Lagina 197
Lake District 258
Lakes *see* by name
Landscape 24–5
Languages
Hittite 48, 236
Turkish 21, 62, 381
Latifoğlu House (Tokat) 299
Latmos, Mount 196
Lausanne, Treaty of 62
Leander's Tower (Istanbul) 128
Leather goods, shopping for 134, 135, 365
Lelegians 202, 203
Leo VI (the Wise), Emperor 88
Lepanto, Battle of 59
Letoön 216, 218
Libraries
Ahmet III (Topkapı Palace, Istanbul) 73
Celsus (Ephesus) 20, **186**
Library Ruins (Bergama) 181
Mahmut I (Haghia Sophia, Istanbul) 88
Lighthouses 97, 128, 163, 223
Listings magazines 136, 368, 387
Loge *(hünkar mahfili)* 37
Blue Mosque (Istanbul) 92
Green Mosque (Bursa) 166
Sultan's Loge (Selimiye Mosque, Edirne) 161
Loggerhead turtles 214, **215**
Lost property 382
Louis II, King of Hungary 59
Lucius Verus, Emperor 53
Luke, St 238, 276
Lycia 20, 49, 52, 209, 217
Sarcophagus (Xanthos) 51
tombs 51, 209, 216, 218, **219**, 226–7
Lycian League 218, 221
Lycian Way (walking route) 210, 217, **220**, 372
Lydians 49
Lysimachus 164, 186

M

Maçahel, hotels 337
Maçka, restaurants 358
Macunlar Mansion (Safranbolu) 273
Madımağin Celal'ın House (Tokat) 299
Magazines 136, 368, 387
Mahmut I, Sultan 80, 88, 115
Mahmut II, Sultan 61, 74, 115, 129
tomb of 95
Malatya 308–9
restaurants 361
Malik Şah, Sultan 57, 314
Malls, shopping 134, 135, 362, 380
Ma'mun globe (Istanbul) 78
Mamure Castle 230, 231
Manavgat River 229
Manuel VII Palaeologus, Emperor 274
Manuscripts
Mevlâna Museum (Konya) 256
Süleymaniye Mosque (Istanbul) 104
Sumela Monastery 276
Manzikert, Battle of 56
Maps
Adana 235
Aegean region 176–7
Amasya 303
Ani 320–21
Ankara 244–5
Ankara and Western Anatolia 242–3
Antakya 238
Antalya 223
Bergama (Pergamum) 180–81
Black Sea region 266–7
Bodrum 199
Bodrum Peninsula tour 202–3
Boğazkale 300–301
Bosphorus Trip 130–31
Bursa 167
Byzantine Empire 54–5
Cappadocia and Central Anatolia 282–3
Climate of Turkey 42–3
Datça Peninsula Tour 206–7
Diyarbakır 315
Eastern Anatolia 306–7
Eastern Mediterranean coast 212–13
Edirne 159
Ephesus 186–7
Erzurum 322
Europe 17
Gallipoli Peninsula 172–3
Hierapolis 190–91
Istanbul: At a glance 66–7
Istanbul: Bazaar Quarter 99
Istanbul: Beyoğlu 111
Istanbul: Egyptian Bazaar 100–101
Istanbul: First Courtyard of Topkapı 70–71
Istanbul: Further Afield 117
Istanbul: Grand Bazaar 108–9
Istanbul: Haghia Sophia 86
Istanbul: İstiklâl Caddesi 112–13

Maps (cont.)
Istanbul: Seraglio Point 69
Istanbul: Street Finder 138–49
Istanbul: Sultanahmet 83
Istanbul: Sultanahmet Square 84–5
Istanbul: tram and metro routes 398
Istanbul: transport map *see* Back Endpaper
İzmir 182–3
Kayseri 295
Konya 254–5
Kütahya 263
Marmaris 205
Safranbolu 272–3
Side 229
Thrace and the Sea of Marmara 156–7
Trabzon 275
Turkey 10–11, 16–17, 152–3
Western Mediterranean coast 210–11
Marcus Aurelius, Emperor 53, 183, 221
Mardin 313
hotels 339
restaurants 361
Mark Anthony 181
Market Street (Safronbolu) 273
Markets and bazaars 134–5, 362
Adana Covered Bazaar 235
Ankara 245
Antakya Bazaar 239
Apricot Bazaar (Malatya) 308, 309
Bazaar Quarter (Istanbul) 98–102, 107–9
Beyazıt Square (Istanbul) 106
Book Bazaar (Istanbul) 107
Bursa Market Area 168–9
Cavalry Bazaar (Istanbul) 85
Copper Bazaar (Malatya) 308, 309
Covered Bazaar (Bursa) 168
Egyptian Bazaar (Istanbul) 98, 99, 100–101, **102**
Flower Market (Bursa) 169
Galatasaray Fish Market (Istanbul) 113
Gaziantep 311
Grand Bazaar (Istanbul) 12, 66, 95, 99, **108–9**
Kapalı Çarşı (Şanlıurfa) 312
Kütahya Bazaar 263
Marmaris Bazaar 205
Safranbolu 272
Semiz Ali Paşa Bazaar (Edirne) 159
Three Bazaars (Kayseri) 294
Tire 185
Tulip Mosque (Istanbul) 106
what to buy 364–5
Marmaris 150–51, 175, **204–5**
events 38, 40
hotels 334
map 205
Marmaris International Yachting Festival 38
Martyrium of St Philip (Hierapolis) 191
Mary, Virgin 186, 374
Mausoleums 36
Atatürk (Ankara) 22, 240, 241, **248**, 249
Gümüşkesen Mausoleum (Milas) 197
Gümüşkesen (Milas) 197
Halicarnassus (Bodrum) 175, 198, **199**
Mehmet III (Haghia Sophia, Istanbul) 87
Murat II (Bursa) 170
Murat III (Haghia Sophia, Istanbul) 87
Selim II (Haghia Sophia, Istanbul) 33, 87
see also Memorials and monuments; Tombs
Mausolus, King of Caria 175, **198**, 199, 202, 214
Mavi boncuk (blue bead) 30
Measurements 363
Mecca 37, 58, 75, 96
Mecidiye Mosque (Ortaköy) 132
Media 387
Medical tourism 376–7
Medical treatment 383
Mediterranean Turkey **208–39**
climate 43
Eastern Mediterranean coast 212–13, 232–9
flora and fauna 26
getting around 210, 213
hotels 335–6
itineraries 11, 15
maps 210–11, 212–13
restaurants 353–6
sights at a glance 211, 213
A Week in Mediterranean and Anatolian turkey 15
Western Mediterranean coast 210–11, 214–30
Medreses (colleges) 36
Mehmet, Şehzade 103
Mehmet I, Sultan
Covered Bazaar (Bursa) 168
Green Mosque (Bursa) 166
Green Tomb (Bursa) 166
Old Mosque (Edirne) 158
Mehmet II (the Conqueror), Sultan 38, 58, 60, 158
Çanakkale fortress 178
Eyüp Sultan Mosque 124
Fortress of Europe (Istanbul) 130, **133**
Fortress of Seven Towers (Istanbul) 120
Grand Bazaar (Istanbul) 108
Mehmet II (the Conqueror) (cont.)
Great Mosque (Kütahya) 263
Theodosian Walls (Istanbul) 121
Tire evacuation 185
tomb of 119
Topkapı Palace (Istanbul) 72, 74
Mehmet III, Sultan 87
Mehmet V, Sultan 61
Mehmet Ağa 92
Mehmet Tahir Ağa
Fatih Mosque (Istanbul) 119
Tulip Mosque (Istanbul) 106
Mehmetçik Memorial (Gallipoli Peninsula) 173
Mehter Band 124, 126, **371**
Mellaart, James 258
Memorials and monuments
Atatürk Mausoleum (Ankara) 22, 240, 241, **248**, 249
Atatürk Memorial Statue (İskenderun) 237
Constantine's Column (Istanbul) 95
Dumlupınar Monument (Kütahya) 262
Gallipoli Peninsula 172–3
Hippodrome (Istanbul) 94
Mehmetçik Memorial (Gallipoli Peninsula) 173
Mount Nemrut **310**, 316–17
Vespasian Monument (Side) 211, **229**
see also Columns and obelisks; Mausoleums; Tombs
Menderes River Valley 176, **185**
Menteşe clans 214
Mersin (İçel) 233
restaurants 355
Meryemana Kultur Parkı 186
Mesnevi (Sufi poems) 259
Mesopotamia 45, 47
Metochites, Theodore 122, 123
Metro systems 245, 398
Mevlâna (Celaleddin Rumi) 15, 41, 114, 256, **259**
tomb of 257
Mevlâna Festival (Konya) 41, 368
Mevlevi Lodge (Istanbul) 41, 66, 112, **114**, 136
Mevlevi Order (Whirling Dervishes) 41, 66, 112, 114, 252–3, **259**
Mezes (appetizers) 340, 341, 344
Midas Tomb (Gordion) 251
Midas Tomb (Midasşehir) 261
Midyat 30
hotels 339
Mihrab (niche in mosque wall) 36
Alaeddin Mosque (Konya) 255
Atik Valide Mosque (Istanbul) 128
Eşrefoğlu Mosque (Beyşehir) 258
Green Mosque (Bursa) 167

Mihrab (cont.)
Green Tomb (Bursa) 166
Haghia Sophia (Istanbul) 88
Karaman Mihrab (Archaeological Museum, Istanbul) 76
Muradiye Mosque (Bursa) 171
Selimiye Mosque (Edirne) 161
Mikasonmiya Memorial Garden (Kirşehir) 297
Milas (Mylasa) 29, **197**
Miletus 13, **194–5**
Milvian Bridge, Battle of 53
Minarets 37
Blue Mosque (Istanbul) 82, 84, 92–3
Dört Ayaklı Minare (Diyarbakır) 314
Eğri (Leaning) Minaret (Aksaray) 296, 297
Fluted Minaret (Antalya) 222
Great Mosque (Adana) 235
Green Mosque (İznik) 33, 164
Mosque of the Three Balconies (Edirne) 158
Sabancı Central Mosque (Adana) 234
Selimiye Mosque (Edirne) 160
Seminary of the Slender Minaret (Konya) 254
Truncated Minaret (Antalya) 223
Twin Minaret Seminary (Erzurum) 322–3
Twin Minaret Seminary (Sivas) 299
Minbar (pulpit in mosque) 36
Atik Valide Mosque (Istanbul) 128
Blue Mosque (Istanbul) 92
Haghia Sophia (Istanbul) 88
Selimiye Mosque (Edirne) 161
Miniatures, Ottoman 33
Miniatürk 137, 369
Minibus travel 391
Minicity Antalya 222, 369
Mithridates VI of Pontus 52, 192, 214, 302
Mobile phones **386**, 387
Mohacs, Battle of 59
Mohammed, Prophet 37, 75, 257
Monasteries
Deyr-az-Zaferan (Mardin) 313
Kızlar Monastery (Göreme Open-Air Museum) 288
Mevlevi Lodge (Istanbul) 41, 66, 112, **114**, 136
Monastery of St George (Büyükada) 162
Sumela Monastery 265, 267, **276**
Money 384–5
Mongol invasion 57
Monuments *see* Columns and obelisks; Memorials and monuments
Mosaics
Antakya Archaeological Museum 239

Mosaics (cont.)
Gaziantep Zeugma Mosaic Museum 311
Haghia Sophia (Istanbul) 87, 88–9
Haghia Sophia (Trabzon) 274
Icon of the Presentation (Archaeological Museum, Istanbul) 77
Mosaic Museum (Istanbul) 84, **91**
Pammakaristos (Istanbul) 118
St Saviour in Chora (Istanbul) 122–3
Mosques **34–7**
Alaeddin Mosque (Bursa) 170
Alaeddin Mosque (Konya) 243, 254, 255
Alaeddin Mosque (Niğde) 15, 293
Atik Valide Mosque (Istanbul) 128–9
Behram Paşa Mosque (Diyarbakır) 314
Beyazıt Mosque (Istanbul) 106
Beyazıt II Mosque (Edirne) 158
Blue Mosque (Istanbul) 12, 21, 67, 82–3, 84, **92–3**
Cezri Kasım Paşa Mosque (Eyüp) 121
Eşrefoğlu Mosque (Beyşehir) 258
Eyüp Sultan Mosque (Istanbul) 124
Fatih Mosque (Amasra) 268
Fatih Mosque (Istanbul) 119
Gazi Ahmet Paşa Mosque (Istanbul) 121
Great Mosque (Adana) 235
Great Mosque (Afyon) 260
Great Mosque (Bursa) 168
Great Mosque (Denizli) 193
Great Mosque (Diyarbakır) 314
Great Mosque (Eski Malatya) 309
Great Mosque (Kütahya) 262–3
Great Mosque (Niğde) 293
Great Mosque (Sivrihisar) 260
Green Mosque (Bursa) 166–7
Green Mosque (İznik) 33, 164
Gülbahar Mosque (Trabzon) 274
Hacı Bayram Veli mosque and tomb (Ankara) 244
Hunat Hatun Mosque (Kayseri) 294–5
İlyas Bey Mosque (Miletus) 194, 195
İmaret (Süleymaniye Mosque, Istanbul) 104
İsa Bey Mosque (Selçuk) 184
İskele Mosque (Amasra) 268
İskele Mosque (Istanbul) 128
Junior Hacı Özbek Mosque (İznik) 34
Kalenderhane Mosque (Istanbul) 77, **103**

Mosques (cont.)
Kasım Padişah Mosque (Diyarbakır) 314
Kazdağlioğlu Mosque (Safranbolu) 272
Kızıl Minare Mosque (Aksaray) 297
Kocatepe Mosque (Ankara) 243, **249**
Konak Mosque (İzmir) 182
Köprülü Mehmet Paşa Mosque (Safranbolu) 272–3
Kurşunlu Mosque (Nevşehir) 286
Lala Mustafa Paşa Mosque (Erzurum) 322
Mahmut Bey Mosque (Kasaba) 269
Mecidiye Mosque (Ortaköy) 132
Mosque of Selim I (Istanbul) 119
Mosque of the Three Balconies (Edirne) 158
Mosque of Victory 115
Muradiye Mosque (Bursa) 170–71
Muradiye Mosque (Edirne) 159
New Mosque (Istanbul) 64–5, 101, **102**
Nusretiye Mosque (Istanbul) 115
Old Mosque (Edirne) 158
Orhan Gazi Mosque (Bursa) 168, **169**
Prince's Mosque (Istanbul) 34, **103**
Rüstem Paşa Mosque (Istanbul) 100, 102, **102**
Sabancı Central Mosque (Adana) 153, **234**
Selimiye Mosque (Edirne) 154, 158, **160–61**
Selimiye Mosque (Istanbul) 129
Selimiye Mosque (Konya) 34, 152
Şemsi Paşa Mosque (Istanbul) 128
Sokollu Mehmet Paşa Mosque (Istanbul) 32–3, **96**
Süleymaniye Mosque (Istanbul) 36, 66, **104–5**, 130
Sultan Beyazıt Mosque and Theological College (Amasya) 303
Tulip Mosque (Istanbul) 106
Ulu Cami (Great Mosque, Divriği) 323
visiting 381
Yavuz Sultan Mosque 119
Yıldırım Beyazıt Mosque (Bursa) 166
Zeynep Sultan Mosque (Istanbul) 70
Zeyrek Mosque (Istanbul) 119

Mosquitoes 383
Motor racing 368
Motorcycling 395
Motorways 394
Mountaineering **372**, 375
Mountains
flora and fauna 27
see also mountains by name
Mud baths (Ilıca) 215
Müezzin mahfili (platform in mosque) 36
Selimiye Mosque (Edirne) 160
Muradiye district (Bursa) 170
Murat I, Sultan 158, 171, 179
Murat II, Sultan 159, 168, 170
Murat III, Sultan 75, 87, 88, 95, 118
Murat IV, Sultan 73, 88, 132
Murat V, Sultan 125
Müren, Zeki 198
Museums and galleries
Alacahöyük Museum 298
Alanya Museum 230
Archaeological and Ethnographic Museum (Kahramanmaraş) 309
Archaeological and Ethnographic Museum (Samsun) 269
Archaeological Museum (Adana) 234
Archaeological Museum (Afyon) 260
Archaeological Museum (Antakya) 213, **239**
Archaeological Museum (Antalya) 15, **222**
Archaeological Museum (Bursa) 171
Archaeological Museum (Çanakkale) 178
Archaeological Museum (Erzurum) 322
Archaeological Museum (Gaziantep) 311
Archaeological Museum (Istanbul) 12, 71, **76–7**
Archaeological Museum (İznik) 164
Archaeological Museum (Kars) 319
Archaeological Museum (Malatya) 308
Archaeological Museum (Tokat) 299
Archaeology and Ethnography Museum (Amasya) 303
Archaeology Museum (İzmir) 182
Archaeology Museum (Kastamonu) 268
Archaeology Museum (Kayseri) 295
Archaeology Museum (Kırşehir) 297
Museums and galleries (cont.)
Archaeology Museum (Kütahya) 263
Arms and armour exhibition (Topkapı Palace, Istanbul) 72–3, **74**
Atatürk Ethnography Museum (Denizli) 193
Atatürk Museum (Samsun) 269
Aydın Museum 185
Baksi Museum 277
Bursa City Museum 167
Bursa Museum of Anatolian Carriages 171
Canakkale Destanı Tanıtım Merkezi (Gallipoli Peninsula) 172
Carpet Museum (Istanbul) 90–91
Çatalhöyük Museum 258
Çengelhan Rahmi M. Koç Museum (Ankara) 245
Çeşme Museum 184
Çinili Pavilion (Istanbul) 76
City Museum (Istanbul) 125
Clock exhibition (Topkapı Palace, Istanbul) 75
Çorum Museum 299
Divan (Topkapı Palace, Istanbul) 72, **75**
Emine Göğöş Culinary Museum (Gaziantep) 311
Ephesus Museum (Selçuk) 184
Ethnographic Museum (İzmir) 182
Ethnographic Museum (Kastamonu) 268
Ethnography Museum (Adana) 234
Ethnography Museum (Ankara) 245
Ethnography Museum (Sivas) 299
Fethiye Museum 216
Florence Nightingale Museum (Istanbul) 129
Gazi Museum (Samsun) 269
Gaziantep Zeugma Mosaic Museum 311
Gevher Nesibe Medical History Museum (Kayseri) 294
Glass Shipwreck Hall (Castle of St Peter, Bodrum) 200
Gordion Museum 251
Göreme Open-Air Museum 15, **288–9**
Hacı Bektaş Museum 297
Haleplibahçe Museum (Şanlıurfa) 312
Hasan Süzer Ethnography Museum (Gaziantep) 311
Health Museum (Edirne) 158
İftariye Pavilion (Topkapı Palace, Istanbul) 73
Museums and galleries (cont.)
Museum of the History of Science and Technology in Islam 78
Istanbul Museum of Modern Art 115
Kaleiçi Museum (Antalya) 223
Karatay Museum (Konya) 15, 241, **255**
Kossuth House Museum (Kütahya) 262
Mardin Museum 313
Marmara University Museum of the Republic 94
Marmaris Museum 205
Meerschaum Museum (Eskişehir) 261
Mersin Museum 233
Mevlâna Museum (Konya) 15, 152, 241, **256–7**
Military Museum (Istanbul) 124–5
Mosaic Museum (Istanbul) 84, **91**
Museum of Anatolian Civilizations (Ankara) 241, **246–7**
Museum of Innocence (Istanbul) 115
Museum of Islamic Artefacts (Erzurum) 322
Museum of the Ancient Orient (Istanbul) 76
Museum of the War of Independence (Ankara) 244–5
Museum of Turkish and Islamic Arts (Bursa) 167
Museum of Turkish and Islamic Arts (Edirne) 159
Museum of Turkish and Islamic Arts (Istanbul) 84, **91**
Museum of Wood and Stone Carving (Konya) 254
Naval Museum (Istanbul) 125
Open-Air Steam Train Exhibition (Çamlık) 184
opening hours 380
Ottoman Bank Museum (Istanbul) 115
Panorama 1453 Museum 121
Pera Museum (Istanbul) 113, **114**
Rahmi Koc Industrial Museum (Istanbul) 124
Republic Museum (Ankara) 245
Rize Museum 278
Roman Bathhouse (Side) 229
Sadberk Hanım Museum (Istanbul) 130
Sakip Sabancı City Museum (Mardin) 313
Science Museum (Istanbul) 78
Silifke Museum 232
Taksim Art Gallery (Istanbul) 115
Technology Museum (Istanbul) 78
Tile Museum (Kütahya) 262

Museums and galleries (cont.)
Trabzon Museum 275
Turkish Railways Open-Air Steam Locomotive Museum (Ankara) 248
Ürgüp Museum 287
Victory Museum (Afyon) 260
Village Life Museum (Okakköyü) 323
Yıldız Palace Museum (Istanbul) 125
Yozgat Ethnographic Museum 298
Zeki Müren Museum (Bodrum) 198
Zinciriye Medresesi (Aksaray) 297
Ziya Gökalp Museum (Diyarbakır) 314
Music **370–71**
Arabesque and pop 371
Çingene (gypsy) 371
classical 136, 137
fasıl 136, 369, 371
Mehter Band 124, 126, **371**
music festivals 136, 368, 369
rock and jazz 136, 137
Sufi music and chanting 371
traditional 136–7, 369, **370–71**
Musical instruments
Mevlâna Museum (Konya) 257
traditional 370–71
Muslims 21
beliefs and practices 30, 37
Exploring mosques 36–7
Muslim holidays 40
Ramazan (Ramadan) 18, 37, 40
Mustafa III, Sultan 75, 95
Mustafa Kemal *see* Atatürk
Mustafa Paşa Tower (Ortakent) 203
Mustafapaşa 292
hotels 338
restaurants 360
Müteferrika, İbrahim 107
Muvakkithane Gateway (Süleymaniye Mosque, Istanbul) 104
Mylasa (Milas) 29, **197**
Myndos Gate (Bodrum) 199
Myndos (Gümüşlük) 202
Myra 219, **220**
Myriocephalon, Battle of 56

N

Nahita (Niğde) 293
Nakkaşhane imperial design studio (Topkapı Palace, Istanbul) 32, 165
Nargile (water pipe), smoking 107, 364
National holidays 41
National parks
Bird Paradise 156, **163**
Çamlık 298
Dilek Peninsula 185
National parks (cont.)
Gallipoli 172–3
Göksu Delta 232
Güllük Dağ 224
Hattuşaş 283, **300–301**
Ilgaz Mountain 269
Kaçkar Mountains 278
Karagöl-Sahara 279
Koprulu Cayı 224
Nemrut Dağı 310
Soğuksu 250
Uludağ 163
National service 31
National Sovereignty and Children's Day 38
National Youth and Sports Day 38
NATO 22, 63, 182
Naval High School (Heybeliada) 162
Navy Day 39, 41
Necropolis (Hierapolis) 191
Nemrut Dağı National Park 310
Nemrut, Mount (Nemrut Dağı) 305, 306, **310**, 316–17
Neolithic period 45, 192, 246, 308
Nerva, Emperor 53
Netsel Marina (Marmaris) 204
Nevşehir (Nyssa) 286–7
hotels 338
"New Army" 129
New Spa (Bursa) 171
New Year 41
Newspapers 387
Nicaea *see* İznik
Nicene Creed 164
Nicholas, St 41, **220**, 222
Niğde (Nahita) 293
Nightclubs 137, 198, 368
Nightingale, Florence 129
Nika Revolt 94, 96
Noah's Ark 95, 153, 305, 319
North Anatolian Fault 24
Nymphaeum (Side) 229
Nysa 185
Nyssa *see* Nevşehir

O

Ocakköyü 323
Öcalan, Abdullah 63
Odeon (Ephesus) 187
Old Dockyard and Arsenal Point (Bodrum) 198
Old Harbour (Antalya) 222
Old Spa (Bursa) 171
Ölü Deniz 14, 208, **216–17**
hotels 336
restaurants 355
Olympos 221
Open-Air Steam Train Exhibition (Çamlık) 184
Opening hours 380
banks 380, 384
restaurants 341
shops 134, 362, 380
Orhan Gazi 58, 164, 170
Orhan Gazi Mosque (Bursa) 168, **169**
Orhaniye 207
Orient Express 80
Oriental Kiosk (Grand Bazaar, Istanbul) 109
Ortahisar, hotels 338
Ortakent 203
Ortaköy 132
Osman I, Sultan **57**, 58, 124, 163, 170
Osman II, Sultan 120
Osman Hamdi Bey 76
Otağ Music Shop (Istanbul) 70
Ottoman architecture 28–9, **34–5**, 79, 254
Ottoman Empire 20, **58–61**
Ottoman houses 35, **79**, 254, 272–3, 299
Outdoor activities 372–7
Özal, Turgut 63, 308

P

Painting, Ottoman miniatures 33
Palaces
Beylerbeyi Palace (Istanbul) 132
Bucoleon Palace (Istanbul) 97
Byzantine Great Palace (Istanbul) 84, 91, 94, **96–7**
Dolmabahçe Palace (Istanbul) 60, 67, 116, 117, **126–7**, 130
İshak Paşa Sarayı (near Doğubeyazıt) 319
Palace of the Porphyrogenitus (Istanbul) 121
Presidential Palace (Ankara) 249
Topkapı Palace (Istanbul) 12, 67, 68, 69, **70–75**
Yıldız Palace (Istanbul) 125
Palamut Bükü 206
Palandöken ski centre 250, **323**, 372
Paleolithic period 45
Pamphylian Plain 15
Pamukkale 13, 177, 188–9, **190**, 376
hotels 334
restaurants 353
Paragliding 372–3, 375
Parks and gardens
Alaeddin Park (Konya) 254
Gülhane Park (Istanbul) 70, **79**
Karaalioğlu Park (Antalya) 223
Konya Fairground 254
Koza Park (Bursa) 168
Mikasonmiya Memorial Garden (Kirşehir) 297
Yıldız Park (Istanbul) 117, **125**
Youth Park (Ankara) 248
Passports 380
Pastırma (cured beef) 100, 102, 294, 295
Patara 14, 41, 52, 218
Paul, St 20, 53, 179, 232, 233, 258
see also St Paul Trail
Pavilion of the Holy Mantle (Topkapı Palace, Istanbul) 75
Pedasa 203
Pedestrians 396

Peloponnesian War 178
Pension hotels (*pansiyon*) 326, 327
Pera Palace Hotel (Istanbul) 80, 112, **114**
Peré, Raymond 182
Pergamum *see* Bergama
Perge 15, 50, **224**
Personal security 382
Pessinus 260
Peter, St 238
Petrol 394
Pharmacies 383
Phaselis 14, 221
Philip II of Macedon 50
Philip, St 191
Phocaea (Foça) 179
Phonecards 386
Photography 382
Phrygians 20, 49, 51, 244, 260, 261
  Gordion Museum 251
  Serving Table 246
Pierre Loti Café (Istanbul) 124
Pınara 218
Pipes, water (smoking) 107, 364
Piri Reis 59, 60
Polatlı 251
  restaurants 358
Police 382, 383
Polonezköy 156, **162**
Pontus, Kingdom of 302
Pony trekking 373, 375
Pool of Abraham (Şanlıurfa) 312
Pop music 371
Porphyry Sarcophagi (Archaeological Museum, Istanbul) 77
Post offices (PTT) 387
Postal services 387
Pottery *see* Ceramics
Prayer times 21, 37, 381
Prehistoric Turkey 45, 258
Presidential Palace (Ankara) 249
Priam, King 178
Priene 13, **194**
Princes' Islands 12, 155, **162**
Public conveniences 381
Public telephones 386
Puppets
  Karagöz shadow puppet theatre **30**, 155, 166, 167, 168
Pylamenes, King of Galatia 244

R

Race Week (Marmaris) 40
Racing
  horse 137, 368–9
  motor 368
Radio 387
Rail travel 389, **392–3**
  Haydarpaşa Station (Istanbul) **129**, 389
  Metro (Ankara) 245
  metro (Istanbul) 398
  Open-Air Steam Train Exhibition (Çamlık) 184
  Orient Express 80
Rail travel (cont.)
  rail routes 392–3
  rail tours 393
  Sirkeci Station (Istanbul) **80**, 389
  sleepers and seats 392–3
  Turkish Railways Open-Air Steam Locomotive Museum (Ankara) 248
Ramazan (Ramadan, Muslim holiday) 18, 37, 40
Recycling 381
Red Tower (Alanya) **230**
Religion 20–21, 37
  Hittite 48
  religious tours 374, 375
  Roman 52–3
  see also Christianity; Islam
Religious services *see* Churches; Mosques; Synagogues
Repairs, vehicle 395
Republic Day 40
Responsible tourism 381
Restaurants **340–61**
  Aegean region 350–53
  Ankara and Western Anatolia 356–8
  Black Sea 358–9
  Cappadocia and Central Anatolia 359–60
  Döner Gazino (Kütahya) 262
  Eastern Anatolia 360–61
  Flavours of Turkey 342–3
  Istanbul 346–9
  Mediterranean Turkey 353–6
  mezes (appetizers) 340, 341, 344
  opening hours 341
  Şark Kahvesi (Istanbul) 108
  service and paying 341
  Thrace and the Sea of Marmara 349–50
  types of restaurant 340–41
  What to Drink in Turkey 345
  what to expect 341
Rhodes, capture of 204, 231
Riter, Otto 129
Rize 278
  hotels 337
  restaurants 358–9
Rize bezi fabric 278
Road travel 394–5
Rock formations (Cappadocia) 281, 284–5
Rock music 137
Rock of Van (Lake Van) 318
Rock tombs 214, 215, 218, **219**
  Amasya 302
  Fethiye 216, 226–7
Rock-cut churches and monasteries 15, 288–9, 296
Rococo style, Turkish 71, 78, 79, 87
Roma Community 381
Roman Baths (Ankara) 244
Roman Empire 52–3
Roman Stone Bridge (Adana) 235
Romanus IV Diogenes, Emperor 56
Roxelana 90
  Baths of (Istanbul) 85, **91**
  tomb of 104
Royal Pavilion (Istanbul) 101
Rugs *see* Carpets and kilims
Rules of the Road 394
Rumi, Celaleddin (Mevlâna) 15, 41, 114, 256, **259**
  tomb of 257
Rüstem Paşa Caravanserai (Edirne) 159
Rüstem Paşa's tomb 103

S

Sabiha Gökçen Airport (Istanbul) **388–9**, 397
Şadırvan *see* Fountains
Safety 382–3
Safranbolu 29, 265, 266, **270–73**
  hotels 337
  map 272–3
  restaurants 359
Sagalassos 52
Sailing and cruising holidays **373**, 375
St Nicholas Symposium and Festival (Demre) 41
St Paul Trail 258, 372
Saklıkent Gorge 11, 14, 24, 210, **217**
  restaurants 355
Samandağ 239
Samsun 38, 269
  hotels 337
  restaurants 359
Sandal Bedesteni (Grand Bazaar, Istanbul) 109
Şanlıurfa (Edessa) 56, 231, 305, 306, **312**
  hotels 339
  restaurants 361
Santa Claus 220
Sarcophagus of the Mourning Women (Archaeological Museum, Istanbul) 76
Sardis 52
Sarıhan 287
Sarımsaklı 179
Şavşat 279
Schliemann, Heinrich 178
Sea buses 389, 393, 399
Sebastopolis 299
Sebil (provision of water outside mosque) 35, 78, 107, 124
Şeker Bayramı (Sugar Festival, Muslim holiday) 40
Selale Waterfall (Tarsus) 233
Selçuk 13, **184**
  events 41
  hotels 334–5
  restaurants 353
Seleucas I, King of Syria 197
Seleucid Empire 52, 238
Seleukos III, King of Syria 51
Self-catering accommodation 329
Selge 224

Selim I ("the Grim"), Sultan 74, 75, 119, 262, 274
Selim II ("the Sot"), Sultan 60, 171, 237
  Mausoleum (Haghia Sophia, Istanbul) 33, 87
  Selimiye Mosque (Edirne) 160
Selim III, Sultan 124, 129
Selimiye Barracks (Istanbul) 129
Selimiye Mosque (Edirne) 154, 158, **160–61**
Selimiye Mosque (Istanbul) 129
Seljuk Rum Sultanate 56–7
Seljuk Turks 20, 28, 54, 56–7, 164
Sema ritual (Whirling Dervishes) 41, 66, 112, 114, 252–3, 259
Semahane (Ceremonial Hall, Mevlâna Museum, Konya) 257
Seminary of the Slender Minaret (Konya) 254
Semiz Ali Paşa Bazaar (Edirne) 159
Şemsi Ahmet Paşa's tomb (Istanbul) 128
Şengül Hamamı Turkish Baths (Bursa) 168
Septimus Severus, Emperor 94
Seraglio Point (Istanbul) **68–80**
  First Courtyard of Topkapı (Istanbul) 70–71
  hotels 330
  map 69
  restaurants 346
  sights at a glance 69
Sester, Karl 310
Sèvres, Treaty of 63
Seyhan River 234, 235, 236
Seyit Vehbi Efendi 78
Şeyitgazi Valley 261
Shiite Muslims 36
Shipwrecks 200–201
Shoemakers' Street (Safranbolu) 273
Shopping **362–7**
  antiques 108–9, 248, 363
  aqua accessories 377
  bargaining 134
  in Istanbul 134–5
  opening hours 134, 362, 380
  paying 362
  rugs 367
  sending purchases home 363
  shopping malls 134, 135, 362, 380
  sizes and measurements 363
  VAT exemption **362**, 363
  what to buy 364–5
  see also Markets and bazaars
Shrine of Apollo Delphinius (Miletus) 195
Shrine of Zoodochus Pege (Istanbul) 121
Side 11, 15, 209, 211, **228–9**
  hotels 336
  map 229
  restaurants 355
Şile 156, **162–3**
Şile bezi (cotton cloth) 163
Silifke 232
Silk Route 28, 74, 234, 274, 287
Silverware (Topkapı Palace, Istanbul) 74
Simena (Kale) 14, 220
Sinan, Koca Mimar 79, **105**
  Atik Valide Mosque (Istanbul) 128
  Baths of Roxelana (Istanbul) 85, 91
  Çemberlitaş Baths (Istanbul) 95
  Gazi Ahmet Paşa Mosque (Istanbul) 121
  İskele Mosque (Istanbul) 128
  Mausoleum of Selim II (Haghia Sophia, Istanbul) 87
  Prince's Mosque (Istanbul) 34, 103
  Rüstem Paşa Caravanserai (Edirne) 159
  Rüstem Paşa Mosque (Istanbul) 102
  Selimiye Mosque (Edirne) 160
  Şemsi Paşa Mosque (Istanbul) 128
  Sokollu Mehmet Paşa Mosque (Istanbul) 32, 96
  Süleymaniye Mosque (Istanbul) 66, 104
  tomb of 104
Sinop 56–7, 265
  hotels 338
Şirince 184
Sirkeci Station (Istanbul) 80, **80**, 389
Sivas 56, **299**
Sivas Congress 299
Sivrihisar (Justinianopolis) 260
Sizes of clothing and shoes 363
Ski centres
  Apple Mountain 250
  Davraz Ski Centre 258, 372
  Kartalkaya 250
  Mount Erciyes **292**
  Palandöken ski centre **323**, 372
  Uludağ 163
  Zigana 277
Skiing **372**, 375
Smbat II, King of Armenia 321
Smoking 327, 381
Smyrna *see* İzmir
Snakes 383
Society 21–2
Soğanlı 292–3
Soğukçeşme Sokagi (Istanbul) 70, **79**
Soğukluk (hot room, Turkish baths) 80, 81
Soğuksu National Park 250
Sokollu Mehmet Paşa 96, **237**
Southeast Anatolian Project (GAP) **25**, 305, 308
Spas and hot springs **376–7**
  Havza thermal springs 269
  Haymana Hot Springs 250–51
  Kızılcahamam **250**, 376
  Mud baths (Ilıca) 215
  see also Turkish baths
Specialist holidays 372–7
Sphinx Gate (Alacahöyük) 48, **298**
Sphinx Gate (Boğazkale) 301
Spice Bazaar *see* Egyptian Bazaar
Spices. shopping for 135, 362, 363, 365
Sports 137, 368–9, **372–3**, 375
Spring in Turkey 38
Stadium (Aphrodisias) 192
Steppe flora and fauna 27
Stolen property 382
Stone heads (Mount Nemrut) 306, **310**, 316–17
Strabo 224, 228, 230
Stratonikeia 197
Students
  discounts 137
  hostels 328
Sublime Porte (Istanbul) 70, **79**
Sufis 36, 114, 252–3, 259, 371
Süleyman the Magnificent, Sultan **60**, 90
  Erzurum 322
  Marmaris 204, 205
  Prince's Mosque (Istanbul) 103
  Süleymaniye Mosque (Istanbul) 104
  tomb of 105
Süleyman the Magnificent, Sultan 59
Süleymaniye Mosque (Istanbul) 36, 66, **104–5**, 130
Sultan Beyazıt Mosque and Theological College (Amasya) 303
Sultanahmet (Istanbul) 19, **82–97**
  hotels 330–31
  maps 83, 84–5
  restaurants 346
  sights at a glance 83
Sultanahmet Square (Istanbul) 84–5
Sultanhanı Caravanserai (Aksaray) 29
Sultansazlığı Bird Sanctuary 293
Sumela Monastery 265, 267, **276**
Summer in Turkey 39
Sünnet (circumcision ritual) 30
Sunni Islam 21, 36, 58
Suvla Bay (Gallipoli Peninsula) 172, 173
Synagogues
  Ahrida Synagogue (Istanbul) 118
Synthronon (Haghia Eirene, Istanbul) 78

T

Tahtakale Hamamı Çarşısı (Istanbul) 100
Taksim quarter (Istanbul) 115
Tango Festival (Marmaris) 40
Tanzimat Reforms 61
Tarsus 233
  restaurants 356
Taş Küle (Foça) 179
Taxes
  on alcohol 341, 345
  Value-added tax (VAT) 328, 341, **362**, **384**

Taxis 391, **396**
Tea, Turkish 278
Teaching Hospital (Amasya) 302
Telephone services 386
Television 387
Telmessus 216
Temples
  Aphrodite (Aphrodisias) 192–3
  Apollo and Athena (Side) 11, **228**
  Apollo (Didyma) 195
  Athena (Behram Kale) 179
  Athena (Herakleia) 196
  Athena (Priene) 194
  Augustus and Rome (Ankara) 244
  Euromos 196
  Great Temple (Boğazkale) 301
  Hadrian (Ephesus) 187
  Trajan (Bergama) 176, 180
  Zeus (Aezani) 261
  Zeus Olbios (Uzuncaburç) 232
  Zeus (Silifke) 212
Termessos 15, **224**
Teşılova Mound (İzmir) 182
Tetrapylon (Aphrodisias) 193
Teutonic Knights 231
Texier, Charles 216
Textiles 31
  Bursa 168
  Denizli 193
  Rize bezi fabric 278
  shopping for 134, 135, 168, 230, 363, 365
  şile bezi 163
  Tokat 299
  Topkapı Palace (Istanbul) 74
Thales (mathematician) 194
Theatre 137, 368, 369
Theatres, ancient
  Aphrodisias 192
  Aspendos 225
  Bergama 181
  Bodrum 199
  Ephesus 187
  Hierapolis 191
  Miletus 194, 195
  Priene 194
  Side 228–9
  Termessos 224
Theme parks 369
Theodora, Empress 55, 96
Theodosian Walls (Istanbul) 12, 55, 117, **120–21**
Theodosius I, Emperor 53, 120
Theodosius II, Emperor 55, 121
Theodosius III, Emperor 53
Thrace and the Sea of Marmara **154–73**
  climate 42
  getting around 157
  hotels 332
  map 156–7
  restaurants 349–50
Three Tombs (Erzurum) 323
Tickets 380
  boats and ferries 399
  buses and minibuses 390, 391
Tickets (cont.)
  for entertainments 136
  rail travel 392
Tigris, River 25, 45, 305, 314, 315
Tilework **32–3**
  Cuerda seca technique 119, 166
  Green Mosque (İznik) 33, 164
  Sokollu Mehmet Paşa Mosque (Istanbul) 32–3, 96
  Tile Museum (Kütahya) 262
  see also İznik ceramics and tiles
Time zone 381
Timur (Tamerlane) 195
Tios 14
Tire 185
  restaurants 353
Titus, Emperor 239
Titus Tunnel 239
Toilets, public 381
Tokat 31, **299**
Tombs
  Abdül Aziz (Istanbul) 95
  Abdül Hamit II (Istanbul) 95
  Ahmet I (Istanbul) 84
  Alexander Sarcophagus (Istanbul) 51, 76
  Cafer Paşa 198
  Erzurum 307
  Green Tomb (Bursa) 166
  Gülbahar (Trabzon) 274
  Hacı Bayram Veli mosque and tomb (Ankara) 244
  Hacı Bektaş 297
  Harpy Tomb (Xanthos) 51
  İbrahim Paşa (Istanbul) 103
  İlyas Bey (Miletus) 194
  İsmet İnönü 248
  Koca Sinan Paşa (Istanbul) 107
  Lycian 51, 209, 216, 218, **219**, 226–7
  Mahmut II (Istanbul) 95
  Mehmet I (Bursa) 166
  Mehmet II (Istanbul) 119
  Mevlâna (Konya) 257
  Midas (Gordion) 251
  Midas (Midasşehir) 261
  Necropolis (Hierapolis) 191
  Octagonal Tomb (Kayseri) 295
  Osman and Orhan Gazi (Bursa) 170
  Porphyry Sarcophagi (Istanbul) 77
  Rock tombs 219 *see also* Rock tombs (main heading)
  Roxelana (Istanbul) 104
  Rüstem Paşa (Istanbul) 103
  St John the Baptist 184
  Şemsi Ahmet Paşa (Üsküdar) 128
  Şeyyid Battal Gazi 261
  Sinan (Istanbul) 104
  Süleyman the Magnificent (Istanbul) 105
  Taş Küle (Foça) 179
  Three Tombs (Erzurum) 323
  see also Mausoleums
Tophane (Bursa) 170
Topkapı Palace (Istanbul) 12, 67, 68, 69, **70–75**
  collections 74–5
  maps 70–71, 72–3
  old stables 78
Tour operators, specialist holidays 374, 375
Tourism industry 22, 63, 222, 281
Tourism police 382, 383
Tourist information 380, 381
Tours by car
  Bodrum Peninsula 202–3
  Daçta Peninsula 206–7
Tower of the Seven Brothers (Diyarbakır) 315
Trabzon 264, 265, 267, **274–5**
  hotels 338
  map 275
  restaurants 359
Traditional dress 30, **31**, 63, 74, 371
Traditional music and dance 23, 31, 136, 369
Traditions *see* Customs and traditions
Trains *see* Rail travel
Trajan, Emperor 53
Tramways 110, **398**, 399
Travel **388–99**
  Aegean region 177
  air travel 388–9
  Ankara and Western Anatolia 243
  Black Sea region 267
  bus and *dolmuş* (minibus) 390–91, 396, 397
  cable cars (Istanbul) 398–9
  Cappadocia and Central Anatolia 283
  car 394–5
  coach 389
  cycling 395
  Eastern Anatolia 307
  ferries 157, 177, 233, 389, 393, 399
  funicular (Istanbul) 124, 398–9
  insurance 383
  Istanbul 396–9
  late-night transport (Istanbul) 137
  Mediterranean Turkey 210, 213
  metro (Ankara) 245
  metro (Istanbul) 398
  motorcycling 395
  Naval Museum (Istanbul) 125
  Nostalgic Tram (Istanbul) 110, 398
  Rahmi Koc Industrial Museum (Istanbul) 124
  rail travel 389, **392–3**
  sea buses 389, 393, 399
  Thrace and the Sea of Marmara 157
  tramways 110, **398**, 399
  water taxis (Istanbul) 399
Travellers' cheques 384
Treasure, diving for 201
Treasury (Topkapı Palace, Istanbul) 73, **74–5**
Trotsky, Leon 162

Troy 13, 20, 47, 155, **178**
restaurants 353
Troy Festival (Çanakkale) 39
Tudhaliyas IV, King 300
Tuff formations 284–5
Tuğra (personal monogram) 32
Tuğrul Bey, Sultan 56
Tulip Festival (Emirgan) 38
Tünel underground railway (Istanbul) 399
Turgut Reis 202
Turkish baths *(hamams)* 28, 81, 376
Baths of Faustina (Miletus) 194
Baths of Roxelana (Istanbul) 85, **91**
Bodrum Hamam **198**, 376, 377
Cağaloğlu Baths (Istanbul) **80**, 81, 376, 377
Çarşi Hamamı (Adana) 235
Çemberlitaş Baths (Istanbul) 12, 81, **95**
Cinci Hanı (Safranbolu) 272
Gedik Paşa Hamamı 107
New Spa (Bursa) 171
Old Spa (Bursa) 171
Şengül Hamamı (Bursa) 168
Umur Bey Hamamı (Bursa) 168
see also Spas and hot springs
Turkish Grand National Assembly (Ankara) 245
Turkish Republic, foundation of 22, 40, **62**
Turkish Rococo style 71, 78, 79, 87
Turkish State Railways (TCDD) 392, 393
Turkish Touring & Automobile Club (TTOK) 395
Turks, origins of 56–7
Turquoise Coast, A Week on the 10, 14
Turtle Beach (Dalyan) 215
Turtle Statue (Dalyan) 214
Twin Minaret Seminary (Erzurum) 322–3
Twin Minaret Seminary (Sivas) 299
Twin-turreted Theology Complex (Kayseri) 294

U

Üçağiz 14, **220**
Uçhisar 15, 282
hotels 338–9
restaurants 360
Uludağ National Park 163
Umur Bey Hamamı (Bursa) 168
Underground cities 153, 277, **285**, 286–7
UNESCO World Heritage Sites
Boğazkale 300–301
Çatalhöyük 258
Cumalıkızık 163
Divriği 323
Göreme Valley 288
Kayaköy 216
Letoön 218
Safranbolu 265, **270–73**
Xanthos 218
Upper Agora (Bergama) 181
Urartians 20, 49, 318, 323
Lion Statuette 246
Ürgüp 15, **286–7**
events 40
hotels 339
restaurants 360
Uzuncaburç 232
Uzungöl 264, **278**
restaurants 359

V

Vaccinations 383
Valide Han (Istanbul) 107
Value-added tax (VAT) 328, 341, **362**, **384**
Van, Lake 25, 305, 307, **318**
hotels 339
restaurants 361
Velvet Castle (İzmir) 183
Venessa *see* Avanos
Vespasian, Emperor 214, 239
Vespasian Monument and Arch (Side) 211, **229**
Victory Day 39
Villa of Sultan Kılıç Arslan 254
Visas 380
Viziers 60, 72, 74
Volcanoes 285

W

Walking and trekking **372**, 375
around Istanbul 396
Carian Trail 176, 206, 372
Lycian Way 210, 217, **220**, 372
St Paul Trail 258, 372
Walls *see* City walls
War memorials (Gallipoli Peninsula) 38, 129, 152, 155, **172–3**, 374
War of Independence 62, 260
Dumlupınar Monument (Kütahya) 262
museum (Ankara) 244–5
Water, drinking 383
Water taxis (Istanbul) 399
Watermelons 40, 314
Weaving 31, 366
Weddings 30
Western Anatolia *see* Ankara and Western Anatolia
Western Mediterranean coast *see* Mediterranean Turkey
Wetlands 26
Whirling Dervishes 41, 66, 112, 114, 252–3, **259**
Whitewater rafting 279, **372**, 375
WiFi 327, 386–7
Wildlife **26–7**
Anatolian lynx 26, 224
Atatürk Farm and Zoo (Ankara) 249
Butterfly Valley 210, **217**
Wildlife (cont.)
loggerhead turtles 214, **215**
tours **374**, 375
see also Birds; National parks
Wilhelm II, Kaiser 129
fountain (Istanbul) 94
Winter in Turkey 41
Women
etiquette 380, 381
segregation of 21, 30, 36, 80, 341
Wood, inlaid 364
Woodlands 24, **26**, 276
Woodworking 31
World War I 38, 61, 62, 63, 172–3, 305
cemeteries and memorials 38, 129, 152, 156, **172–3**, 374
World War II 63, 129, 248

X

Xanthos (Kınık) 51, **218**, 219

Y

Yachts 210, 373, 375
Bodrum 198
Bodrum Cup Regatta 40
Datça 207
Göcek 215
gülets 373
Marmaris 38, 204
Marmaris Race Week 40
Yakacık 237
Yakutiye Seminary (Erzurum) 322
Yalıkavak 202
Yalıs (waterfront villas) 35
Yatağan 197
Yazıköy 206
Yazılıkaya (Hittite site) 298, 300, 301
Yedikule Fortress (Istanbul) 120
Yeni Mevlanakapı Gate (Theodosian Walls, Istanbul) 121
Yenifoça 179
Yeniköy 131
Yeşilırmak River 281, 282, 302
Yıldız Palace (Istanbul) 125
Yıldız Park (Istanbul) 117, **125**
Young Turks 61
Youth hostels 328
Youth Park (Ankara) 248
Yozgat 298
Yunus Emre Culture and Art Week (Eskişehir) 38
Yusufeli 279
restaurants 359

Z

Zağnos Bridge and Tower (Trabzon) 274
Zelve 15, **286**
Zeugma 311
Zigana 277
Zinciriye Medresesi (Aksaray) 297
Zincirli Han (Istanbul) 109

Acknowledgments

Dorling Kindersley would like to thank the following people whose contributions and assistance have made the preparation of this book possible:

Main Contributor

Suzanne Swan graduated from Queen's University in Kingston, Ontario, Canada, and has lived in Turkey since 1990. She was contributing editor of *Antalya, the Guide* for two years and contributed to many articles and books on Turkey, including *Globetrotter Travel Guide to Turkey* and *Insight Guide to the Turkish Coast*. She is the Turkish correspondent for a trade publisher.

Contributors and Consultants

Dominic Whiting, a freelance writer-photographer, lived in Turkey for four years. He wrote *Footprints Turkey Handbook*, was a co-author of Time Out's *Istanbul City Guide*, and updated the *DK Eyewitness Guide to Istanbul*.
Dr Caroline Finkel is an Ottoman historian and academic researcher.

Dr Bianka Ralle has an MA in German Studies and worked in journalism as well as teaching and training programmes for developing countries. She was a consultant on Turkey for the Organization for Economic Cooperation and Development (OECD). Her doctoral thesis was on migration and modernization in Turkey.
Kate Clow was educated in the UK, but completed her MBA at Istanbul University in 1991 and stayed in Turkey. She has contributed to the *Rough Guide to Turkey*, *Top Treks of the World* and *Cornucopia Magazine*, and is the originator of the Lycian Way and St Paul Trail walks.
Terrance Duggan walked from Greece to Egypt in 1988–89, in the footsteps of Alexander the Great. A scholar and painter, he has written widely on Islamic and Turkish culture and art. His paintings of Seljuk and Ottoman designs have been exhibited in London, Istanbul and Italy.
Terry Richardson studied classics at Sheffield University, England. He has contributed to *Rough Guide to Turkey* and *Footprints Guide* and photographed for *Cornucopia Magazine* and *The Lycian Way*.
Nilüfer Tünay has a degree in Communication Technology, worked in the Turkish media sector and represented *Sea Trades Magazine* in Turkey. She is now retired.
Molly McNailly-Burke was Turkish correspondent for the *Irish Times* and a contributor to the *Insight* and *Columbus Guides*. She now lives in Hertfordshire, England.
Ronnie Askey-Doran edited a satirical broadsheet in Istanbul and now lives in her native Australia.
Christopher Gardner is a botanist and horticulturist who lives in England.
Rosie Ayliffe lived in Turkey for three years while working as a freelance writer in Istanbul. She was one of the authors of *Rough Guide to Turkey*, and contributed to the *Rough Guide to France*, *Time Out*'s London guides and the *DK Eyewitness Guide to Istanbul*.
Rose Baring is a travel writer who has spent many months exploring Istanbul. She was co-author of *Essential Istanbul* (AA) and *DK Eyewitness Guide to Istanbul*.
Barnaby Rogerson has travelled and lectured extensively in the eastern Mediterranean. With Rose Baring he co-wrote *Essential Istanbul* (AA) and contributed to other AA and Cadogan guides, as well as *DK Eyewitness Guide to Istanbul*.
Canan Silay was a journalist on the Turkish daily, *Hürriyet*, and then editor of *Istanbul, The Guide* for many years. She has contributed to several books on Turkey, including the Insight guides to Istanbul, Turkey and the Turkish coast.

Additional Contributors

Sean Fraser, Lisa Greenstein, Alfred LeMaitre.

Additional Photography

DK Studio/Steve Gorton, Nigel Hicks, Izzet Keriber, Dave King, Fatih Mehmet Akdan, Ian O'Leary, Clive Streeter.

Additional Cartography

Globetrotter Travel Maps; Haluk Inci, İki Nokta.

Revisions Team

Rudolf Abraham, Ashwin Adimari, Asad Ali, Emma Anacootee, Lale Aran, Jasneet Arora, Claire Baranowski, Kate Berens, Tarryn Berry, Marta Bescos, Sonal Bhatt, Hilary Bird, Nadia Bonomally, Leizel Brown, Jo Cowen, Lellyn Creamer, Dipika Dasgupta, Neha Dhingra, Claudia Dos Santos, Emer FitzGerald, Karen Fitzpatrick, Anna Freiberger, Rhiannon Furbear, Camilla Gersh, Emily Hatchwell, Jennifer Hattam, Barbara Isenberg, Shobhna Iyer, Jacky Jackson, Nazlı Koca, Priya Kukadia, Rahul Kumar, Simon Lewis, Irene Lyford, Alison McGill, Ian Midson, Jason Mitchell, Claire Naylor, George Nimmo, Catherine Palmi, Reetu Pandey, Susie Peachey, Helen Peters, Nicole Pope, Pure Content, Marisa Renzullo, Terry Richardson, Ellen Root, Sands Publishing Solutions, Rituraj Singh, Nikky Twyman, Gerhardt van Rooyen, Reinette van Rooyen, Conrad van Dyk, Ed Wright, Sophie Wright.

Proofreader and Indexer Pat Barton.
Publishing Manager Kate Poole
Managing Editor Helen Townsend
DTP Designer Jason Little

Cartographer

Casper Morris

Special Assistance

Dorling Kindersley would like to thank staff at museums, mosques, churches, government departments, shops, hotels, restaurants, transport services and other organizations in Turkey for their help.

Particular thanks are due to: Dr Oğuz Alpözen, Bodrum Museum; Ibrahim Baştutan; Emine Bilirgen, Topkapı Palace, Istanbul; Erol Çakir, İzmir Archaeology Museum; Süleyman Çakır; Sühelya Demirci, Sivas Museum; Hikmet Denizli; The Museum of Anatolian Civilisations, Ankara; Ercihan Düzgünoğlu, TÜRSAB, Istanbul; Veysel Ediz, Çorum Museum; Dr Donald Frey, Institute of Nautical Archaeology, Bodrum; Iclal and Muzaffer Guler; Ali Harmankaya, Side Museum; Kaili Kidner and Lars-Eric Möre, Göreme; Joanna March and Hülya Soylu, Turkish Tourist Office, London; Güney Paksoy, Yedikule and Rumeli Hisar Museums;

Feyza Sürücü, Ministry of Tourism, Ankara; Ertan Tezgör, Turkish Grand National Assembly, Ankara; Feridun Ülker, Presidential Palace, Ankara; Ürcel Üzerin, Bursa Archaeological Museum; Varan Turizm; Üsküdar Folklore and Tourism Society (ÜFTUD), Kırklareli region; Neco Yoksulabakan.

The following staff of provincial tourist offices were very helpful: Reşit Akgüneş, Diyarbakır; Nebahat Alkaya, Bodrum; Bülent Aslan, Amasya; Ayten Aydın, Dalyan; Mustafa Aydın, Kaş; Nurten Celikkaptan, İzmir; Polat Cengis, Çeşme; Ali Fuat Er, Amasya; Fadime Hanim, Sivas; Yaşar Gül, Kastamonu; Yücel Güneş, Nevşehir; Mehmet Hacıağaoğlu, Side; Hüsnü Küçükaslan, Tokat; Murat Keleş, Amasya; Mustafa Kurt, Amasya; Ferhat Malcan, Kaş; Halis Öğüt, Konya; Şentürk Özdemiş, Erzurum; Sare Özdemir, Safranbolu; Safiye Portal, Safranbolu; Kadir Savçı, Çanakkale; Cennet Tazegül, Kars; Ahmet Tazegül, Erzurum; Yüksel Unal, Samsun; Mevlut Uyumaz, Afyon; Erdal Uzun, Kütahya; Zübeyir Yılmaz, Antakya; İbrahim Yakup, Çorum; Garip Yıl, Osmaniye; Zeki Bey, Işak Paşa Saray, Doğubeyazıt.

Other associations and individuals whose assistance was invaluable: Faik Akın, Turkish Airlines, Istanbul; Çetin Akant, Pedasa/Bodrum; Baki Akpınar, Göreme; Ali Baba Rent a Car, Kaş; Dr Şakir Aktaş, Kaş; Ali Baysan, Foto Ali, Kaş; Ahmet Burcu, Istanbul; Ahmet Büyük Yilmaz, Director, Turkish State Mint; Hasan Dağlı, Kaş; Fatih Demirhan, Istanbul Ulaşim A.Ş.; Zafer Emeksiz, Payas/Yakacık Municipality; Ali and Nazife Gülşen, Kaş; Cengiz Güzelmeriç, Kaş; Prof. Dr Wilhelm Gernot, Würzburg University; Hülya Gürkan, Minitcity Antalya; Kamil Koç Otobüs İşletmeleri A.Ş., Bursa; Ahmet Karaşahin, Adana; Lars-Eric Möre, Kapadokya Balloons, Göreme; Kerim Mat, Alanya; Abdullah Muslu, Kaş; Myriam Hanim, St Polycarp Church, İzmir; Dr Munise Ozan, Kaş; Muhammed Özcan, Kaş; Aydın Özmen, Turkish Central Bank, Ankara; Cihat Şahin, Fethiye; Diler Şaşmaz, DHL, Antalya; Mustafa and Sultan Soylu, Kaş; Tahsin Bey Konak Hotel, Safranbolu; İsmail Tezer, Kayseri Governor's Office; Ömer Tosun, Ottoman House, Göreme; Tuğrul Bilen Unal, Turkish State Mint, Istanbul; Osman Uvuç, Kayseri Esnaf; Veysel Bey, İznik Municipality; Bayram Yıldırım, Bodrum; Özkan Yaşar, Kaş; Yenişehir Palas Hotel, Istanbul; Sevilay Yilmaz, İzmir Kültür ve Turizm Müdürlüğü; Hüsnü Züber, Bursa.

Photography Permissions

Dorling Kindersley would like to thank the following for their kind permission to photograph at their establishments: General Directorate of Monuments and Museums; Ministry of Culture; Ministry for Religious Affairs; İstanbul Valiliği İl Kültür Müdürlüğü; İstanbul Valiliği İl Müftülüğü; Milli Saraylar Daire Başkanlığı and Edirne Valiliği İl Müftülüğü.

Picture Credits

a - above; b - below/bottom; c - centre; f - far; l - left; r - right; t - top.

The publisher would like to thank the following individuals, companies, and picture libraries for their kind permission to reproduce their photographs:

123RF.com: Sadık Güleç 239c; **360 Entertainment Group:** Sashah Anton Khan 329tr; **4Corners Images:** SIME/ Schmid Reinhard 12tr. **A Turizm Yayinlari:** Topkapı Palace 74cr, 88tr; Archaeological Museum 76bl, 77tr. **Advertising Archives:** 112tr; **Aisa Archivo Icongrafico, S.A., Barcelona:** 73bl, 75tl, 123tc; **Akdeniz Hatay Sofrasi:** 348tl; **AKG Photo:** 62crb; Erich Lessing 1c, 51tl/bl; Haghia Sophia, Istanbul *Emperor Constantine IX Monomachus*, mosaic detail from south gallery 44; Musée du Louvre *The Abduction of Helena* by Guido Reni 47cr; National Museum of Archaeology, Naples *Battle of Alexander*, Roman mosaic from Pompeii 50–51; Bibliothèque Nationale, Paris from the *Djamil el Tawarik* 57crb; British Library, from the *Westminster Abbey Psalter* 57bl; Bibliothèque Nationale, Paris from *Avis directif pour faire la passage d'Outremer* by Jean Mielot (1455) 58bl; Topkapı Palace Museum *Map of the World* (detail) by Piri Reis (c.1513) 59tr; Erich Lessing/Künsthistorisches Museum, Vienna *Portrait of Süleyman the Magnificent* (c.1530), circle of Titian 59cr; Museo Civic Correr, Venice *The Battle of Lepanto*, Venetian 59br; **Alamy Images:** The Art Archive 8–9; Art Directors & TRIP/Brian Gibbs 387tl; David Crossland 344br; Luis Dafos 312tr; Peter Forsberg 390cl; Robert Harding World Imagery 304; Ali Kabas 343c; Justin Kase zsixz 383cla, 387bc; David Kilpatrick 394tr; Marshall Ikonography 116; Steven May 396cra; Hercules Milas 280; John Stark 342cla, 343tl; Peter Titmuss 395tc; **Ancient Art and Architecture Collection Ltd:** 55cr. **Ankara tourist attractions:** 248tr; **Aquila Photographics:** Hanne and Jens Eriksen 163tr; D. Robinson 25bl; Juan Martín Simón 293c. **Paul Artus** 21t; **Atlas Geographic:** Zafer Kizilkaya 32cl, 202bl, 206bl, 207tl/cr; **Tahsin Aydoğmus:** 55bl, 85cr, 86tr, 89bl, 92tr, 100tr, 123c/cr, 284cl, 285bl.

Baylo Suites: 326bl; **Ralf Bergmann:** 421cl; **Bridgeman Art Library, London:** British Library, detail from the *Catalan Atlas* (1375) 28cl; Yale Center for British Art, Paul Mellon Collection *Caravan at Mylasa* (1845) by Richard Dadd 29tr; Topkapı Palace Museum *Aristotle Teaching*, from *The Better Sentences and Most Precious Dictions* 56tr; Stapleton Collection *Osman I* by John Young 58cl; Topkapı Palace Museum *Süleyman the Magnificent at the Battle of Mohacs in 1526* (1588), by Lokman 58–9; Victoria and Albert Museum, London: 165cbl/cbr; © **The Trustees of the British Museum:** 165cla; **Reg Butler:** 21t; **Buzz Grill & Beach Bar:** 355tc.

Çalikoğlu Reklam Turİzm Ve Tİcaret Ltd.: 137tc; **Çanakkale Destanı Tanıtım Merkezi:** 172cl; **Cercis Murat Konagi:** 361tc; **Christel Clear Picture Library:** © Detlef Jens 40tl; **Cicek Lokantasi:** 357tr; **Manuel Çitak:** 113cr, 135tr; **Ciya Kebap:** 349bc; **Corbis:** Dave Bartruff 187t; Gardel Bertrand/Hemis 324-5; Marc Dozier/Hemis 316-7; Neil Farrin/JAI 150-1; Gavin Hellier/Robert Harding World Imagery 208; Sierpinski Jacques/Hemis 82; Robert Landau 394cl; Ron Watts 226-7; Xinhua Press / Mustafa Kaya 392cla; **Sylvia Cordaiy Photo Library:** © Anthony Bloomfield 31cl; © James de Bounevialle 24tr; ğ Gable 23c, 219cr; p.s. L infoot 38bl; © Jonathan Smith 17c, 31tc, 38ca, 62bc, 217tr, 369tr; © Chris Taylor 23bl, 219cl; Julian Worker 24cl; **Cosandere Tesisleri:** 359br.

Dervis: 377cra; **Divan Çukurhan:** 337br; **C.M. Dixon Photo Resources:** 76tr; **Dreamstime.com:** Annminina 64-5; Cobalt88; Richard Connors 98; Dbdella 312c; Sinan Durdu 154; Esen 361bc; Lukasz Frackowiak 15bc; Gecce33 264; Nadiia Gerbish 110; Pavel Losevsky 313bl; Maxfx 174; Nastya22 378-9; Rangpl 11tl; Rvc5pogod 10br, 14tl; Sailorr 12bl; Softdreams 380cra; Ali Riza Yildiz 240; Alexander Zotov 323cl.

Abbie Enock: 21br; **Mary Evans Picture Library:** 49t, 49c, 50cl, 52c, 52bl, 53c, 53bc, 53br, 55br, 56c, 58br, 59tl, 60tc, 60bc, 61tc, 61bl, 61br, 62tr, 173b, 178bc, 231cl/cr/bl/cb/br.

Ferahi Evler Butik Otel: 328tl; **ffotograff:** © Nick Tapsell 152tr; **First Army Hq, Istanbul:** 129bl; **Fondragonpearl Restaurant:** Grayling 352bc; **Dr Donald Frey:** 201bc.

Chris Gardner: 24tl/cr/clb/br, 25tl/cr; **Gaziantep Archaelogical Museum:** 311tr; **Getty Images:** AFP 18; Eyes-WideOpen: 396br; John and Tina Reid 290-21; Stone/ Travelpix Ltd 14bc; Lucas Vallecillos 68; **Ara Güler:** Mosaics Museum 91c; Topkapı Palace Museum 75cr, 95tr, 165bl; 367tr; **Şems/ Güner:** 127tr.

Halikarnas Disco: 198bc; **Sonia Halliday Photographs:** Bibliothèque Nationale, Madrid 55tr; engraved by Thomas Allom, painted by Laura Lushington 75br; Topkapı Palace Museum 90br; **Robert Harding Picture Library:** J.H.C; Adam Woolfitt 23tr, 25cl, 37cl, 105tr, 155b; **Hilton Worldwide:** Adana Hilton SA Hotel 335tc, Hilton Bursa Convention Centre & Spa 328bl, 332tl, 350bl; **Hotel Les Ottomans:** 376br; **Hulton Getty Images:** 26br, 27tl, 63tc; **The Hutchison Library:** © Robert Francis 31bl; © Jeremy Horner 30bl; © Joan Klatchko 190b, 237b; © Tony Souter 32b, 33bl, 138.

Idakoy Ciftlik Evi: 352tl; **iDO:** 389c, 393ca; **Istanbul Foundation for Culture and Arts:** Istanbul Music Festival/Bennu Gerede 368bl; **Istanbul Library:** 80b; **Istanbul Metropolitan Municipality:** 383tl; **Istanbul Museum of Modern Art:** Murat Germen 115tr.

Michael Jenner Photography: 187cr.

Ali Kabbas: 5c, 30tr, 33tc, 34b, 41b, 125tl; Museum of Turkish and Islamic Arts, Istanbul, from *Hadiqat al-Su'ada* (17th century), Baghdad 33br; **Kaplan Dağ Restaurant:** 353tr; **Gürol Kara:** 108cl; **Karakol:** 346bc; **İzzet Keribar:** 4–5, 20b, 21tr/c, 22cl, 24bl, 29b, 30cr/br, 32ba, 32–3, 35tr/bl, 48cl, 66bl/br; 78tr, 126tr, 132br, 137t, 153tl, 171c, 186tr, 197br, 209b, 210bl, 222tr, 232bl, 259crb, 267t/b, 276cra/bc, 281b, 285cr, 298tr, 314–15, 340bl, 374c; **Key Hotel:** 334; **Kinacizade Konagi:** 356bc; **Kippa Nature Photo Agency:** H. Glader 25bra; J. van Holten; 25bc; E. Pott 25br; **Koru Restaurant:** 358tc; **Kybele Hotel:** 329bc.

Lokanta Maya: 348bc; **José Luczyc-Wyhowska:** 366cr, 367cl/cr/bl/blc/brc/br.

Magnum: Topkapı Palace Museum/Ara Güler 67c; **Mimoza:** 351tc; **Alberto Modiano:** 23br, 30cl, 161b; with approval of ÜFTUD (Üsküdar Folklore and Tourism Society, Kırklareli region) 31bcr; **Museum of Anatolian Civilizations, Ankara:** 45bl, 45cb, 46tc, 46cr, 46bl, 46br, 47tc, 47bl, 47br, 48bl, 48bc, 49bc, 49br, 51ca, 52tl, 52br, 53tc, 246tr/bc, 247tl/cr/c, 300tr; **Museum Hotel:** 327tl.

Nar Lokanta: 347tl; **Natural History Museum, London:** 217crb.

Natur-Med thermal Springs and health resort: 377tl; **Network Photo-graphers:** Gerard Sioen/Rapho 5tr, 219c, 319tr.

Old Greek House: 360bl; **Dick Osseman:** 311cla, 311b; **Güngör Özsoy:** 4br, 161tl/tr, 305b.

Pera Museum: 113cb; **Photo Access Photographic Library:** Harvey Lloyd 26–7; **Photobank:** Adrian Baker 60bl; Jeanetta Baker 20t, 38cb, 194t, 195tr, 195b, 202cl, 374bl; Peter Baker 31tr, 178tl, 180tr, 181br, 186cl/bl, 196bl, 341br; **Pictures Colour Library Ltd.:** 28bl, 177cra, 228bl, 366cl;

Rixos Hotels: Rixos Sungate 336tc.

Safranbolu Tourism office: 300bl; **Sahil Balik:** 359tc; **Neil Setchfield:**152bl, 198cl, 274bl, 362cla; **George Simpson:** 41cr; **Jeroen Snijders:** 19b, 120tr, 362br; **Jeff Spiby:** 215bc; **Stella's Manzara:** 354bl; 354bl; **Superstock:** J.D. Dallet/age fotostock 252-3; Funkystock/age fotostock 2-3; Photononstop 270-1.

Golkhan Tan: 26tl/cl/c/cr/r/bl/bc, 200clb, 201crb; **TAV Investment Holding Co:** 388br; **TCDD - Turkish State Railways:** 392b; **Travel Ink:** Marc Dubin 27b, 191b, 196tr; Ken Gibson 175b; Simon Reddy 41t; **Trip Photographic Library:** 157tr; **Turkey Garantibank:** 384cla; **Turk Telekom:** 386tr.

Ürgüp Esbelli Ev: 339bc.

El Vino: 333bc, 351br.

Andrew Wheeler: 35cl, 363tl; **Peter Wilson:** 74c, 89cl, 89tr, 93tl, 122cl.

Yelken Cafe: 350tl.

Zorlu Grand Hotel: 326cra; 338tr.

Front Endpaper

Alamy Images: Robert Harding World Imagery Rbr; Hercules Milas main, Rbc; **Corbis:** Gavin Hellier/Robert Harding World Imagery Rbl; Sierpinski Jacques/Hemis Lbl; **Dreamstime.com:** Richard Connors Lbr; Sinan Durdu Ltl; Gece33 Rtl; Nadiia Gerbish Lfbr; Maxfx Ltc; Ali Riza Yildiz Ltr; **Getty Images:** Lucas Vallecillos Lfbl.

Jacket

Front: **Alamy Images:** Hercules Milas Main; **DK Images:** Courtesy of Durham University Oriental Museum/Gary Ombler bl.
Spine: **Alamy Images:** Hercules Milas.

All other images © Dorling Kindersley. For further information see www.DKimages.com.

Special Editions of DK Travel Guides

DK Travel Guides can be purchased in bulk quantities at discounted prices for use in promotions or as premiums. We are also able to offer special editions and personalized jackets, corporate imprints, and excerpts from all of our books, tailored specifically to meet your own needs.

To find out more, please contact:
in the US **specialsales@dk.com**
in the UK **travelguides@uk.dk.com**
in Canada **specialmarkets@dk.com**
in Australia **penguincorporatesales@penguinrandomhouse.com.au**